KU-020-908

THE
WORLD'S
GREATEST
HORRORS
& CRIMES

THE WORLD'S

GREATEST

HORRORS & CRIMES

B Bounty
Books

This collection first published in 2014 by Bounty Books,
a division of Octopus Publishing Group Ltd,
Endeavour House, 189 Shaftesbury Avenue,
London WC2H 8JY
www.octopusbooks.co.uk

An Hachette UK company
www.hachette.co.uk

Copyright © Octopus Publishing Group Ltd, 2014

All rights reserved. No part of this work may be reproduced or
utilized in any form or by any means, electronic or mechanical,
including photocopying, recording or by any information
storage and retrieval system, without the prior written
permission of the publisher.

The material in this book originally appeared in three separate
titles:
The World's Greatest Unsolved Crimes by Roger Boar & Nigel Blundell
The World's Most Infamous Murders by Roger Boar & Nigel Blundell
The World's Greatest Crimes of Passion by Tim Healey

ISBN: 978-0-753727-79-9

Printed and bound by CPI Group (UK) Ltd, Croydon, CR0 4YY

THE WORLD'S

GREATEST

HORRORS & CRIMES

THE WORLD'S
GREATEST
UNSOLVED
CRIMES

Contents

Acknowledgements

The editors would like to acknowledge the contributions of the writers and researchers whose work made this book possible. They are: Gerry Brown, Robin Corry, Rob Robbins, Brian McConnell, David Williams, Mike Parker, Marian Davison, Jack Pleasant, Frederick Rolph, Bernard Connor, Frank Garvan, Don Farmer, George Todd, Rodney Hallworth, Mark Williams, Ted Hynds, Paul Vallely and Iain Walker.

The publishers wish to thank the following organizations for their kind permission to reproduce the pictures in this book:

Mary Evans Picture Library 26, 29, 91, 117, 153, 177; Popperfoto 188; Topham Picture Library 2 left and right, 12, 31, 34–35, 34 below, 45, 49, 60, 78, 87, 88, 108, 123, 125, 137, 141, 149, 151, 157 above and below, 167, 170, 174.

Introduction

Mayhem, murder and mystery! They are the ingredients of the most intriguing crime stories of all – the crimes that go unsolved.

In most major criminal cases, there is a neat ending. The misdeed is detected, the suspect arrested and the culprit punished. The file can then be closed.

But not always. Often the massive manhunt and the painstaking investigation lead nowhere. A thief, a cheat or a homicidal monster may go free. A cunning criminal may live to strike again. Or, even when apprehended, a villain may leave an agonizing question mark over his or her foul deed.

Such cases are the very essence of whodunnits. But this book is devoted not to fiction but to fact. It reveals the astonishing, known facts about real acts of villainy ... and it probes the fascinating, missing facts that confound the law and keep a crime in the file marked 'UNSOLVED'.

Chapter
One

Crimes
Without Call

Who was R. M. Qualtrough?

William Herbert Wallace was a drab, colourless, boring man who lived a drab, colourless, boring life. He was thrifty and hard-working, mild mannered and a little snobbish, soberly dressed and utterly, utterly respectable. His idea of a night out with the boys was his regular fortnightly visit to a local café to take part in chess tournaments. A swinging party at home with his mousy wife, Julia, usually consisted of the couple playing duets on violin and piano.

Herbert's meek and unassuming manner was greatly appreciated by his employer, a solid dependable insurance company who employed him as a collector and agent. In 15 years in their employment he had proved to be utterly trustworthy. He was diligent and he never pushed for promotion.

His admirable personal qualities and those of his shy little wife made them ideal neighbours in their neat terraced house in Wolverton Street, Anfield, Liverpool. He was never known to show outbursts of exuberance or bad temper.

In fact, the jury at his trial decided, Herbert Wallace had all the characteristics of a sadistic brutal murderer.

His wife had been battered to death so violently that her brains had spilled out on to the floor. She had died at the hands of a man who deliberately laid a meticulous trail of false clues to throw the police off his scent.

There was no real evidence to connect her husband with Julia Wallace's death. In fact he had a near-perfect alibi. But then Herbert Wallace was a man who ordered his life with pedantic attention to detail.

He was too good to be true. The jury's verdict seemed to be that Wallace was so absolutely ordinary that he had to be capable of great evil ...

In spite of flimsy police theories which hardly stood up to defence cross-examination, in spite of a complete lack of motive on the part of the accused man, in spite of a summing-up by the trial judge who virtually begged the jury to acquit him, Wallace was found guilty of his wife's murder.

He sat impassively in the dock when the verdict was returned. It was this same lack of emotion which had led him there in the first place. 'I am not guilty. I cannot say anything else,' he whispered plaintively to the court as the judge prepared to pass sentence.

The judge, Mr Justice Robert Alderson Wright, showed more distress than the convicted man. But he had no option under law. Shaken by the jury's verdict, he donned his black cap and passed the only sentence open to him: to be hanged by the neck until dead.

And the mystery man who actually bludgeoned Julia Wallace to death heaved a deep sigh of relief. He had got away with the perfect murder.

The first sign that Herbert Wallace's humdrum life was about to be shattered came with a telephone call from a complete stranger to the City Cafe in North John Street, Liverpool, at 19.15 on Monday 19 January 1931. Herbert Wallace was due at the cafe that night to exercise his rather mundane skill as a chess player. He was taking part in a tournament aptly named 'The Second Class Championship'.

But the 52-year-old insurance agent was not there to take the telephone call. A waitress answered the phone and passed it to Samuel Beattie, Captain of the chess club, who explained that Wallace had not yet arrived. Did the caller want to phone back later?

The voice on the other end of the line asked to leave a message for Wallace. The caller identified himself as 'R. M. Qualtrough' and requested that Wallace should call on him at his home at 25 Menlove Gardens East, Mossley Hill, the following night to discuss some insurance business. Beattie wrote the message on the back of an envelope.

About the same time Herbert Wallace was setting off from his home at 29 Wolverton Street to catch a tram to the City Cafe for the chess club meeting.

The Wallaces had been married for 18 years, after a two-year engagement in their home town of Harrogate, Yorkshire. Herbert had a worthy, but lowly paid, job as political agent for the local branch of the Liberal Party. When the meagre party funds could no longer support his salary, he moved to the quiet suburb of Anfield in Liverpool.

Julia, five years younger than her husband, set about making their new home in Wolverton Street neat and tidy, just like their lives. In her earlier years she had spent some time in the genteel studies of music and painting, and a small upright piano took pride of place in the parlour of their trim terraced house. As Herbert settled in to his new job as a collector for the Prudential Insurance Company, the childless couple could afford little luxuries like the £80 which Mr Wallace had spent on a microscope.

He prided himself on being a diligent amateur scientist. He even lectured part-time in chemistry at Liverpool Technical College and often he and Julia would spend the evening in the little laboratory he had built just off his bathroom, examining slides on the microscope. At the age of 50, Herbert had even started to learn the violin and accompanied Julia on the piano.

His job paid him an annual salary of £250 and the thrifty couple lived quietly within their means. Herbert had a bank savings account of £152 and Julia had her own modest savings of £90.

The Wallaces' home

As Herbert Wallace wrote in his diary: 'We seem to have pulled well together and I think we both get as much pleasure and contentment out of life as most people.'

The only times he left Julia alone were his visits to the chess club and his lectures at the technical college. But when he stepped out that night to catch his tram to the café, there was a nagging worry in his mind. There had been a spate of burglaries in Anfield in the past few weeks and Wallace often kept large sums of his insurance company's money at home. 'Don't open the door to any strangers while I'm gone, dear,' he reminded Julia as he left.

Samuel Beattie never actually saw Wallace arrive at the City Cafe but shortly after the phone call he saw him seated, taking part in a game, and he passed on Qualtrough's message.

Wallace seemed puzzled by the telephone call. He did not know any Mr Qualtrough. The address was on the other side of the sprawling Liverpool suburbs, quite outside his normal insurance sales territory. On the way home from the club that night, he quizzed other members about the location of Menlove Gardens East. Which tram should he take to get there? How long would the journey take?

The following day Wallace set out, regular as clockwork, on his appointed rounds in Anfield, collecting a premium of a few pence here, paying out a claim of a few pounds there. He returned home punctually for lunch at 14.00, went back to work for the afternoon and finished in the evening at 18.00. While Julia prepared tea, Wallace went upstairs, washed and changed and filled his jacket pocket with insurance quotation and proposal forms.

At 18.30, their meal over, Julia Wallace answered a knock at the door. It was the milk boy, 14-year-old Alan Close. He handed Mrs Wallace a pint container of milk and she took it into the kitchen to empty the contents into her own jug, returning to the front door to give the boy the dairy's can. That was the last time she was seen alive.

About 15 minutes later Herbert Wallace left the house. He walked a few hundred yards and boarded a tram in Belmont Road for the first leg of his journey to meet the mysterious Mr Qualtrough. At 19.06, after travelling a mile and a half, he switched to a second tram in Lodge Lane. His behaviour was unusual for the normally reserved Herbert Wallace. He chatted amiably to the tram conductor Tom Phillips about his high hopes of selling a big insurance policy at his destination. At 19.15 he arrived at Penny Lane and switched to a third tram to complete his five mile journey. He asked conductor Arthur Thompson to let him off at the stop nearest Menlove Gardens East.

'Don't know it,' Thompson admitted. 'But we stop in Menlove Avenue. Just ask around, it's bound to be near there.'

For the next half hour Wallace tramped busily around the streets of Mossley Hill. He found Menlove Gardens North. He found Menlove Gardens West and Menlove Gardens South. But no Menlove Gardens East. He knocked on the door of Mrs Katie Mather at No 25 Menlove Gardens West and she told him there was no Menlove Gardens East. He remembered his Prudential Insurance supervisor, Joseph Crewe, lived nearby and found his home and knocked on the door. He got no reply.

He met Police Constable James Sargent on his beat in nearby Allerton Road and was advised to go to the local post office to check a street directory for Mr Qualtrough's address. Wallace agreed. Then he remarked on the late hour.

'Yes, almost eight o'clock', the policeman agreed. There was no directory available at the post office and Wallace found a newsagent's shop. He pestered the owner, Mrs Lily Pinches, into checking the names of customers on the shop's newspaper delivery round, explaining his errand to her in great detail. No, she confirmed, there is no Menlove Gardens East.

Wallace gave up and went home.

He arrived back at Wolverton Street shortly before 21.00 and his neighbours, John Johnston and his wife Florence, saw him struggling with the handle of his back door. Finally he managed to get the door open and went inside. The Johnstons were still watching as Wallace emerged a few moments later and calmly invited them in. 'It's Julia,' he explained flatly. 'Come and see, she has been killed.'

Within minutes the police were summoned. Julia Wallace was dead. Her skull had been battered by ten separate blows, any single one of which would have been fatal. There was blood everywhere. A total of £4 was missing from the little cash box in the kitchen cabinet. She had been killed, the forensic experts decided later, between 18.30 and 20.00 that night.

Herbert Wallace appeared to be almost unmoved by the sight of his dead wife. Later that night he left the murder house and moved in with his brother's family a few miles away. The detectives, meanwhile, moved in to 29 Wolverton Street. And the tongues wagged furiously.

Why had Herbert Wallace talked of his business so freely to tram conductors and total strangers in his quest to find Menlove Gardens East? Had he deliberately drawn the patrolling policeman's attention to the time? And who was R. M. Qualtrough, whose call the night before had lured him away from home? If the address in Mossley Hill never existed, did R. M. Qualtrough exist?

On 2 February 1931, a week after the body of Julia Wallace was buried in Anfield Cemetery, Herbert Wallace was charged with her murder. Cautioned by the police, he said simply and sadly: 'What can I say in answer to a charge of which I am absolutely innocent?' The press headlines had become so sensational and strident that when the trial opened at St George's Hall seven weeks later, even the prosecution made little objection to a defence request that no residents of the city of Liverpool should sit on the jury.

The prosecution made much of a key piece of evidence. They had traced the source of the call from 'R. M. Qualtrough'. By sheer chance, the call to the City Cafe the night before Julia Wallace's murder had to be routed through a telephone supervisor because the coin mechanism in the public phone box had been faulty. The call and the defect were duly logged. The call had come from Anfield 1627, a kiosk in Rochester Road, only 400 yards from Wallace's home.

Of course Wallace was not at the café to receive the call from 'Qualtrough', prosecuting counsel Edward Hemmerde, explained triumphantly. For the same reason, 'Qualtrough' couldn't phone back later to speak to Wallace after he arrived at the chess club, because Herbert Wallace was 'R. M. Qualtrough'.

Wallace, Hemmerde claimed, had made the telephone call himself then sprinted for a tram and arrived at the café to receive the message he had phoned through as 'Qualtrough'.

His pestering inquiries of tram conductors, the policeman and the residents of Mossley Hill the following night were all part of the plan to establish his alibi, the prosecutor insisted. And Wallace's unflurried demeanour when he returned home and found his wife's body was the action of a man who already knew murder had been committed.

Herbert Wallace's defence counsel, Roland Oliver, outlined his case simply. His client had not committed the murder and it was not for the defence to prove who had wielded the murder weapon. Wallace was not 'Qualtrough' and the defence did not need to establish the identity of the mystery man. Wallace made a fuss of finding Menlove Gardens East, he explained, because it was a break from his usual routine, a chance to earn the unexpected bonus of a sale. He was displaying an emotion that was rare for him: excitement. He had only reverted to character when he found his wife's body. He became placid and introspective. Wallace had no motive for killing his own wife.

By all the rules of criminal law, Roland Oliver was absolutely right. The police had no evidence, only suspicions. Herbert Wallace had to be presumed innocent. But on the fourth and final day of the trial, the jury took only an hour to reach their verdict: Guilty.

It is almost routine for a judge to express his agreement with a jury's verdict in a complex, tasking case. Mr Justice Wright, however, did not even offer them a word of thanks for their efforts. He pronounced the mandatory sentence of death by hanging.

The defence lodged an immediate appeal and a week after he should have been hanged Wallace was taken from the condemned cell to London, to appear at the Royal Courts of Justice in the Strand. Far from the hysteria and prejudice of Liverpool, three judges sifted through the hard evidence against Wallace. After a two-day hearing they retired for 45 minutes and pronounced their verdict: Appeal allowed, conviction quashed.

Wallace left the courtroom free – but spiritually broken.

Two days later when he returned home, Liverpool police pointedly announced they would not be re-opening their investigation into Julia Wallace's murder. The cruel implication was not lost on Wallace's hostile neighbours and his workmates. The insurance company gave him a desk job to try to shield him and a year later he retired on a pension.

In February 1933, just over two years after the death of his wife, Herbert Wallace became ill with a recurring kidney disease and died in a local hospital. Five days later he was buried in Anfield Cemetery beside his beloved Julia.

So who murdered Julia Wallace? Who was R. M. Qualtrough? There were only 14 people in the whole of Liverpool with the name Qualtrough and the police interviewed and cleared them all. In the atmosphere of outrage which followed the murder, Liverpool police reached the single-minded conclusion that Wallace was guilty. Squads of detectives armed with stop-watches and timetables spent days riding on trams and walking briskly around Anfield trying to demolish his timing of events.

Herbert Wallace had his own suspicions. In the long nights of lonely agony after his wife's murder, he wondered which of his small circle of acquaintances knew he was due at the City Cafe that fateful night and left the tantalising telephone message for him. Julia, he knew, would only have opened the door to a familiar face. Even facing the hangman's noose, shy Herbert Wallace could not bring himself to scream in righteous anger and point a forceful finger of accusation.

He apologetically mentioned the names of two men to the Liverpool detectives investigating the case. Both men were in their early twenties and both were former employees of the insurance company. At different times, they had both parted company from the insurance firm after cash shortages were found in their accounts. On separate occasions, they had filled in for Wallace on his rounds when he was ill. They knew all about his social routine, about his chess club meetings. And they knew that on some Tuesday nights, as on the night Julia was murdered, the cash box in the kitchen could hold as much as £50. Indeed when they stood in for him they had been inside his home and had handled the cash box. Julia would have readily opened the door to them, knowing they were former colleagues of her husband.

Police records show that detectives only interviewed one of these men – and even then accepted without question his assurance that he had an alibi for the night of the murder.

The police concentrated all their energies on the man they wanted ... the mousey little insurance agent whom everyone so desperately wanted to believe was a murdering monster.

Advertisement of Death

The voice on the telephone was smooth, fluent and persuasive ... and instantly Josephine Backshall was cocooned in a web of friendly familiarity. She knew the caller's voice well and had been longing for him to ring. After all, he was helping her to earn £100, a big enough sum of 'pin-money' to make a world of difference to the family budget.

There was nothing in the least shady about the job as a part-time model that Josephine was beginning to enjoy. In fact, the thought that the small advertisement she had placed in the local paper could be misconstrued in anything like an unseemly light had never crossed the mind of the house-proud, 39-year-old mother-of-three, who sang for the local church choir and was a leader of the town's Brownies troupe. And the idea that there could be anything sinister about the man who answered her advertisement and, in a 'trial session', had photographed her on the front lawn of the family's tidy, middle-class semi-detached home in Maldon, Essex, would have seemed too outrageous to contemplate.

The man, she told her husband Mike, seemed like a 'good sort'. And, as she spoke to him again on the 'phone, she realized that what he was offering her would be her biggest job so far: £100 for a day's work – probably, she thought, modelling for something no more glamorous than a cheap cosmetic firm.

The caller talked on, cool, collected, giving the impression of a very pleasant personality. A meeting was arranged for that evening and, after kissing her husband goodbye, she walked through the front door of their spruce home for the last time.

Three days later, at about 12.00 on Friday, 1 November 1974, she was found strangled to death.

Her body had been dumped in a shallow pond by the side of a lonely lovers' lane. Her hands were bound in front of her with a length of cord strapped tightly to her wrists. An identical cord was lashed to her neck.

Josephine Backshall, the church-going good neighbour who enjoyed an innocent life of simple pleasures, was killed because she put her faith in a confidence trickster. She trusted a mystery man whose identity the police have spent more than 100,000 man-hours trying to discover, with not a single clue to put them on the trail of a quarry whose disappearance has made the Josephine Backshall case one of Britain's most perplexing unsolved crimes.

No fewer than 40 detectives were assigned to the case in the first year of one of the biggest, yet most baffling, investigations of its kind. More than 19,000 members of the public were interviewed. All of them had either the Christian name of Pete or Dave, or the surname of Thomson or Johnson. It was a combination of those names that fitted the clues that Josephine had given her family and friends. It was to them that she had spoken of the man with the camera who was setting her up not, as she believed as a part-time model, but as a victim of brutal murder, even the motive for which has never been established.

Thousands of car registration plates were later painstakingly checked and rechecked by police trying to find the killer's car – possibly a blue Ford which was seen pulling away from the Fountain public house in Good Easter, Essex, on the night Josephine kept her fateful rendezvous with her killer.

Detectives established that Josephine and the man she so easily trusted did stop for a drink – one half-pint of beer each – at the Fountain about an hour after she had left her home. He was presumed to have picked her up nearby and taken her there after a 'business dinner' at a Chinese restaurant – an assumption based on the fact that forensic experts discovered the remains of Chinese food in her stomach.

Publican's wife Joan Jones became the last witness to the rendezvous of a killer and his victim when she saw the couple in the Fountain's saloon bar. 'I caught only a fleeting glance of him,' she says. 'He was a tall man. His head touched a line of beer mugs hanging over the bar. He never actually seemed to face me and, on reflection, it seemed almost as though he was trying to not let anyone get too close a look at him'.

Mrs Jones identified Josephine from a cine film containing family holiday shots which detectives showed her. 'I remembered her at once,' she says. 'She was an attractive woman. She had sat in the corner of the bar with the man and had seemed totally at her ease.'

For months, police kept details of the Fountain meeting secret in the hope that the killer would retrace his steps. It was a forlorn hope.

The only other potential lead detectives had to go on was a 'French connection'. A keen-eyed policewoman found a cosmetics sample in Josephine's bedroom which was one of a very limited batch which had been imported from France prior to a sales drive. Could the killer, detectives pondered, have been using Josephine to model this new range?

Inquiries again, however, came to nought – as did a scrupulous check on every photographic studio in both England and France from which a killer might have been tempted by Josephine's original advertisement, which read:

'Lady, late 30s, seeks part-time employment. Own transport. Anything considered. Previous experience: banking. Able to type.' Underneath was her home telephone number.

Josephine Backshall

It was the sort of advertisement often used to skirt the law as a method of offering sex-for-sale. A senior officer on the case later described it as 'positively naive'. He added:

'We all know what the phrase "anything considered" is taken to mean. The great irony and tragedy of this case is that any innuendo couldn't have been further from the truth. Mrs Backshall was a God-fearing woman – and that sort of interpretation of her advert simply wouldn't have occurred to her. It seems more than likely that her own innocence – a rare attribute in this day and age – may have, tragically, led her to set herself up as a victim of murder.'

Other senior officers have described the Josephine Backshall case as the 'most frustrating' they have ever worked on. But, as far as has been possible, they have managed to piece together this diary of death:

A few days after Josephine placed her ad, a male caller telephoned to offer her work 'modelling for cosmetics'. An appointment was made for a week later, 15 miles from Josephine's home, at Witham, Essex. The man never showed up. He 'phoned the following day, rearranged the appointment, and again failed to appear. Two weeks later, the 'phone rang once more – and Josephine happily arranged yet another meeting.

This time, the couple did meet. The 'photographer' took a series of pictures of Josephine on the front lawn of her home during the day. By that stage, Josephine's husband had begun to believe her part-time job would come to nothing and, ironically, expressed mild doubt as to the authenticity of the cameraman who was promising his wife tidy sums for what seemed simple work. Josephine allayed those fears, saying that the man seemed perfectly genuine and, indeed, a 'good sort'.

The telephone rang again on Tuesday, 29 October 1974 and the last, fateful meeting was arranged. Josephine left the family home in Norfolk Close, Maldon at about 18.00, driving to Witham in her red Ford Cortina, registration number BVW 374L.

Detectives have established that she was seen at Witham's Colingwood Road car park between 18.30 and 19.00. A passer-by told them her car may have broken down, because he saw her looking into the engine with the bonnet raised close to the car park entrance. Some time before 19.00, however, she must have met her killer.

There is a time gap between then and three days later, when a telephone line worker made the gruesome discovery of her body in the ditch at Bury Green on the Essex and Hertfordshire border.

The killer had left no clue behind. Chief Superintendent Jack Moulder, who still keeps the Josephine Backshall case file open, can only say: 'Someone, somewhere must know him.'

The Green Bicycle Murder

The tragic death of pretty Bella Wright would have been written off as a fatal road accident if it had not been for the shrewd curiosity of a young country constable.

For when 21-year-old Bella was found dead on a quiet road near the village of Stretton in Leicestershire, with her bicycle lying on the grass verge, it added a terrible weight to the complaints of the locals who cursed the reckless and speeding drivers in their peaceful little communities.

The dead girl's face was deeply gouged and matted with blood. Gravel from the roadway was embedded in her face where she had pitched forward from her bicycle and struck the ground. She had obviously been run off the road by some ruthless motorist, the villagers insisted. It was July 1919 and clattering motor cars were not yet a commonplace sight in the quiet countryside. Their drivers, according to popular rural opinion, terrified the farm animals and were a mortal danger to peaceful cyclists and rambling pedestrians.

A cursory examination of Bella's body by a local doctor seemed to confirm that opinion. He concluded that something had caused Bella to lose control of her bicycle, throwing her into the road where she died of loss of blood and head injuries.

The local constable, however, had some nagging doubts. He went to search the scene of the road accident for any further clues to showing exactly how Bella had met her death.

As he poked around the grass verges on either side of the narrow road, the constable found the blood-spattered body of a dead carrion crow. But there were no tyre marks near the bird. He turned its body over with the tip of his boot and continued his search. A few feet away, where Bella's bicycle had lain, he found another object which caught his attention. It was a spent bullet, pushed down into the soft earth by the imprint of a horse's hoof.

A fresh examination of Bella's body showed the grim truth about her death. In the swollen blood-stained tissue below her left eye was a bullet hole. Hidden in the tangled mass of her hair was an exit wound. Bella had been shot clean through the head.

The police search switched from the pursuit of a hit and run driver to the hunt for a cold-blooded murderer.

The night before Bella died she had been on one of her frequent cycling jaunts, riding to the village postbox to send a letter to her sweetheart, a young sailor aboard a warship which was stationed 240 km (150 miles) away in Portsmouth. The pretty brunette who lived with her parents had made male admirers, but she only flirted with them. Her deepest affections were reserved for the sailor she hoped would soon ask her to marry him.

Bella had finished a long tiring night shift as a mill hand in a factory in nearby Leicester when she returned home on Saturday 5 July and slept until late afternoon.

After a quick meal when she woke she cycled off briskly to post her letter, telling her parents she might pay a visit to her uncle, a roadworker, who lived not very far away.

When Bella arrived at her uncle's cottage two hours later, she was not alone. As she went inside the cottage a sallow-faced man waited outside for her, seated astride his green bicycle.

Bella's uncle, George Measures, teased her about her strange companion. She smiled: 'Oh him, I don't really know him at all. He has been riding alongside me for a few miles but he isn't bothering me at all. He's just chatting about the weather.'

When Bella was ready to leave for home an hour later, her uncle glanced through the window and saw the man with the green bicycle was still waiting outside. 'Oh, I do hope he doesn't get boring,' Bella laughed coyly. 'I'll soon cycle fast enough to give him the slip.'

The man with the green bicycle grinned happily at Bella when she left the cottage and pedalled his bicycle to join her as they rode off together in the warm summer evening's air.

An hour later a farmer driving his cattle along the peaceful Burton-Overy road, found Bella's body. An inquest on the dead girl returned a verdict of 'murder by person or persons unknown'. The vital witness, the man with the green bicycle could not be traced.

But his bicycle was found, seven months later, when a barge skipper on a canal outside Leicester found that a line trailing from his boat had snagged on a piece of junk on the canal bed. The junk brought to the surface was the frame of a green bicycle. Policemen who probed the muddy canal bottom soon uncovered a gun holster and a dozen revolver cartridges.

One of the serial numbers on the bicycle frame had been hastily filed off. But another identifying number inside the saddle support led police to the local dealer for the bicycle maker and then to the identity of the man who had bought it ten years before.

The owner of the bicycle was railway draughtsman Ronald Light, a moody shell-shocked veteran of World War 1 with a fascination for guns. He had been invalided out of the Army and had lived in Leicester until six months after Bella's murder.

When police traced 34-year-old Light he had left his home in Leicester he shared with his widowed mother and taken a job about 100 km (60 miles away) as a school teacher in Cheltenham. He was arrested and brought back to Leicester to be charged with the murder of Bella Wright.

His trial began at Leicester Assizes in June 1920 and from the opening speech of the prosecution the circumstantial evidence was stacked mercilessly against Ronald Light. Witness after witness identified him as the man with the green bicycle and a young maidservant from Light's own home told how he kept firearms and ammunition in the attic.

The prosecution amply proved that Ronald Light had been the mystery man who cycled off with Bella just before her death. Light himself admitted filing the serial number off his bicycle and throwing it, with the holster and cartridges, into the canal a few weeks after the murder.

The only arguably weak point in the prosecution's case was the lack of motive. Bella had not been sexually assaulted or robbed. Even though Light denied killing her, claiming that they parted company at the village crossroads, the irrefutable testimony seemed certain to lead him to the gallows.

One other piece of evidence seemed to cloud the case, almost irrelevantly. The bullet found by the village constable had several marks on it. The marks were caused by it passing through the dead girl's skull and the crushing effect of the steel-shod horse's hoof which had ground it into the earth. There was even one mark which might have been caused by a ricochet.

When Ronald Light gave evidence in his own defence, he seemed at first to be damning himself. He admitted trailing around after Bella on his bicycle on the night of her death, pestering her for the use of a spanner and a pump because his own cycle had developed a loose wheel and a flat tyre.

He told the jury of his own sad and tortured mental history: how he cracked up after three years of savage war in the frontline trenches, and how he was classified as a shell-shock victim and sent back to England in the closing stages of the war for psychiatric treatment.

But the effect of his testimony on the jury was electric. In a firm clear voice, without a trace of hesitation or emotion, Light told the court: 'I was an artillery gunner in the trenches from 1915 to 1918 when I was sent home a broken man. I kept my holster and ammunition because they were wrapped in a bag attached to my stretcher when they took me from the front. The Army kept my service revolver.

'When Bella Wright was murdered I knew from newspaper reports the next day that she was the girl I had been with just before she died. I knew the police wanted to question me.'

Staring blankly and coldly into space, Light admitted: 'I became a coward again. I never told a living soul what I knew. I got rid of everything which could have connected me with her. I was afraid.'

The jury looked at the gaunt face of the anguished war veteran before they retired to consider their verdict. They returned three hours later and pronounced him 'not guilty'.

As Light walked from the court a free man, the sharp-eyed constable who had turned her death into a murder investigation, blamed himself for one flaw in his inspired detective work...

The body of the dead carrion crow in the field. He had kicked it aside with hardly a second glance.

Had the bloodied crow also been blasted by a bullet from the same gun which killed Bella Wright? Had the same bullet ripped through the crow in flight and found a second, innocent human target? Could the bullet have ricochetted from a tree and ended Bella's young life?

Without the evidence of the crow and perhaps of further bullets and footprints at the scene, no one would ever know. But it was not beyond the bounds of possibility that an amateur marksman had been taking potshots at the sinister black shapes of the carrion crows in the field beside the country road.

Was there somewhere a thoughtless gunman who knew his wild shooting had killed an unsuspecting girl and who had fled from the scene to keep his terrified secret? A gunman infinitely more cowardly than the shell-shocked, broken ex-soldier Ronald Light.

The Enigma of Nuremberg

The teenage boy who appeared from nowhere, staggering through the streets of Nuremberg, Germany, on Whit Monday 1828, acted as if he was injured or drunk.

He walked unsteadily up to a complete stranger, a local cobbler, and gave him a letter addressed to the Captain of the 6th Cavalry Regiment, then stationed in the city, and mumbled repeatedly: 'I want to be a soldier like my father was.'

The cobbler helped the boy to walk with difficulty to the police station where the lad waited until the cavalry officer was summoned. At the police station the letter was opened and the senior police officer and the cavalryman read the poignant and bitter message.

The letter explained: 'I send you a boy who is anxious to serve his king in the Army. He was left at my house on 7 October 1812, and I am only a poor labourer. I have ten children of my own to bring up. I have not let him outside since 1812.'

With cruel indifference, the letter added: 'If you do not want to keep him, kill him or hang him up a chimney.'

The letter was unsigned and the police and the army officer sadly assumed that the 16-year-old boy, abandoned as a baby, was still unwanted. The scrawled message seemed to explain his peculiar behaviour, unable to walk properly on feet as soft as a baby's and with an infant vocabulary of only a few words. But the lad could write his own name in a firm, legible hand – Caspar Hauser.

The jailer in Nuremberg was fascinated by the boy and kept him in a room in his own quarters where he could watch him through a secret opening. It took him only a few days of careful observation before he decided that Caspar was neither a born idiot nor a young madman. With loving patience, the jailer, using sign language, taught Caspar to talk, noting how quickly and eagerly the boy began to learn new skills.

Within six weeks the burgomaster of Nuremberg had been summoned to the jail to hear the first halting details from Caspar of his wretched life.

All Caspar could remember was being kept in a small cell, about 1.8 m (6 ft) long, 1.2 m (4 ft) wide and 1.5 m (5 ft) high. The shutters on the window of the cell were kept permanently closed and he slept in threadbare clothes on a bed of straw. He saw nobody and heard virtually nothing all the years he was there, living on a diet of bread and water he found in the cell when he awoke each day. Sometimes, he revealed, the water tasted bitter and made him fall asleep. Every time this happened, he woke up to find his hair had been cut and his nails trimmed.

After years of isolation, Caspar recalled, a hand reached into his cell from behind and gave him a sheet of paper and a pen. The hand guided him each day until he could write his name and repeat the phrase: 'I want to be a soldier ...'

One morning his cell was unlocked and he was taken out into the street, into daylight and the company of other people for the first time in his life. It was the first time, too, that he wore shoes.

In the confusion of unfamiliar sights and sounds, Caspar remembered nothing until he found himself in Nuremberg with the letter in his hand.

The boy's story touched the burgomaster and the people of Nuremberg and soon young Caspar was 'adopted' by a Professor Daumer who began the task of educating the teenager into the ways of the world around him.

In a few months Caspar was transformed from a stumbling retarded child to a bright intelligent young man. With his mysterious background creating a

Caspar Hauser

buzz of excitement in his new home town, he became a much sought after guest in the homes of curious philosophers and wealthy intellectuals. And Nuremberg society soon began to remark on Caspar's startling physical resemblance to the members of the families of the grand dukes of Baden, the rulers of the province. Rumours abounded, the most popular being that Caspar was of noble birth and that his childhood isolation had been heartlessly planned to prevent him succeeding to power as a Baden prince.

At the time of Caspar's birth, two of the princes of the Baden family in direct line of succession had died in mysterious circumstances. The people of Nuremberg were convinced that Caspar Hauser was an unwanted son of the royal family, born to the Grand Duke Karl and his wife the Grand Duchess Stephanie.

Grand Duchess Stephanie had indeed given birth to a child sixteen years earlier, but she never saw the baby. Scheming palace doctors had told her that her baby had died soon after birth of cerebral meningitis, a diagnosis confirmed by a post-mortem examination.

And when Grand Duke Karl became seriously ill in 1829, he had no son and heir to succeed him.

Caspar, by that time, had been in Nuremberg for a year, living with Professor Daumer and growing in reputation as a personable, intelligent young man of distinct ability and culture.

As the Grand Duke's health failed, in October 1829, Caspar's already bitterly unhappy young life was almost ended. He was attacked and stabbed by a masked assailant in the basement of Professor Daumer's house, but he survived his wounds.

The following year the Grand Duke died and the royal succession passed to another line of the family, the sons of the Countess of Hochberg.

A few months later an eccentric English nobleman, said by many to be a friend of the Hochberg family, appeared in Nuremberg to petition the courts to become Caspar's guardian in place of Professor Daumer. Philip, the 4th Earl of Stanhope, won his court plea in spite of local opposition. And so, out of public sight, another period of isolation began for the wretched Caspar. He was taken away from his new found friends in Nuremberg on Lord Stanhope's orders and lodged with a surly Protestant pastor in the town of Ansbach, 20 miles away.

With Caspar safely out of the way, Lord Stanhope lost interest in his new foster son, leaving him to his miserable existence with Pastor Meyer.

On 11 December 1833 Caspar, then 21 years old and working as an apprentice bookbinder, was returning to his dismal lodgings through a park when he was stopped by a stranger. The man asked his name and when Caspar replied, he stabbed him repeatedly. Badly wounded, Caspar staggered back to Pastor Meyer's home. But the preacher never informed the police, cruelly taunting Caspar that he had inflicted the wounds himself to get attention. Three days later Caspar Hauser died in agony.

Hearing of his death, the Grand Duchess Stephanie was reported to have broken down and wept, sobbing that she believed the young man had really been the son she was told had died in infancy.

But none of his friends or the German courts could ever prove the background of the boy with no history and no future. They could never solve the riddle of who had locked him away for the first 16 years of his hopeless life, or who the mysterious assassins were who finally succeeded in killing him.

The boy who came from nowhere was buried in the churchyard at Ansbach. On his tombstone was the simple epitaph: 'Here lies Caspar Hauser, enigma.'

Sherlock Holmes' Real Case

It was a murder case worthy of the cold, calculating detective powers of Sherlock Holmes. An elderly widow had been battered to death by a brutal murderer who had rifled through her files of personal papers and who had, inexplicably, stolen just one cheap brooch from her valuable collection of diamonds and other gems.

A tall, dark-haired man of about 30 had been seen by witnesses walking calmly away from the murder house in Glasgow. It had not taken long for Scottish policemen, acting under the pressure of public outrage, to arrest a suspect who was tried for the murder and sentenced to hang.

Twenty-four hours before the convicted man, gems dealer Oscar Slater, was due to meet the executioner, his sentence was commuted to life imprisonment. Although his life was spared, he still faced a grim existence of hard labour in prison until his dying day. Yet there were some lingering doubts about the case ... fears that Oscar Slater was no more than an innocent scapegoat.

But who could prove his innocence? Who could sift through the evidence with enough authority and thoroughness to overturn the verdict of a powerful

Sir Arthur Conan Doyle

court backed by the full might of the Scottish legal system? Sherlock Holmes, that's who – in the form of the creator of the fictional detective, author Sir Arthur Conan Doyle.

Conan Doyle was disturbed by the case of Oscar Slater when he read of the murder investigation and conviction in the scholarly legal work *Notable Scottish Trials*. The book outlined how, on little more than suspicion and circumstantial evidence, Slater had been found guilty of murdering 82-year-old Miss Marion Gilchrist at her home in Queen's Terrace, West Princes Street, Glasgow, on 21 December 1908.

Miss Gilchrist had lived the life of a virtual recluse in her home, attended only by a young maidservant, 21-year-old Helen Lambie, and seeing only rare visitors, mainly relatives. The spinster's only pleasure in life seemed to come from the loving care of her collection of diamonds, valued at £3,000.

On the night her mistress died, Helen Lambie had followed her usual practice of leaving the house around 19.00 to buy the evening newspaper. Miss Gilchrist remained inside, secure behind the double-locked doors of her home. The outer door, leading to the street, was held only by a latch which could be opened by a cord from inside the apartment if Miss Gilchrist recognized a visitor at the street door.

A few minutes after Helen left, downstairs neighbour Arthur Adams heard the noise of a heavy fall from the apartment above and went to investigate. The outer door was open but the double-locked apartment door was still secure. As he stood there puzzled, Helen returned with the evening paper and the couple unlocked the door and went in. Just as they entered the apartment, a tall, well-dressed man walked calmly past them and into the street. Inside, Marion Gilchrist was dead in the dining-room, her skull crushed.

While Adams went to raise the alarm, Helen Lambie ran the short distance to the home of Marion Gilchrist's niece, Mrs Margaret Birrell, and told her she had recognized the man who had walked from the apartment. But the niece, in a burst of outrage, told Helen Lambie she must be mistaken and she must not 'smear the man's reputation' in any statement to the police.

The police took only five days to produce some results to still the public outcry which followed the murder. They learned that gem dealer Oscar Slater, who lived not far from the murdered woman, had pawned a brooch of about the same value as the missing one. They also discovered that he and his young French mistress had fled from Scotland aboard the liner *Lusitania* using assumed names.

Police pursued the couple to New York where Slater was arrested and, protesting his innocence, agreed to waive extradition formalities and return to Glasgow.

Oscar Slater's trial

At his trial the witnesses, with some hesitation, identified him as the mystery man. Slater, a German Jew, claimed: 'I know nothing about this affair, absolutely nothing.' But the jury found him guilty by a majority verdict. Slater suffered three weeks in the condemned cell before his reprieve.

The few doubts about Slater's innocence were carefully noted in the book which Conan Doyle read and it was enough to arouse his interest. He began to examine the case with the same fresh uncluttered mind that he had devoted to his fictional super-sleuth, Sherlock Holmes of Baker Street.

Three years after the trial, after careful study of the transcripts of the court proceedings and correspondence with witnesses, Conan Doyle caused an uproar with his book, *The Case of Oscar Slater*. In the same calm style as Holmes, he punched gaping holes in the prosecution case.

The brooch which had first drawn suspicion on Slater had been pawned three weeks before the murder. Slater, Conan Doyle pointed out, had fled with his mistress under assumed names because he wanted to give the slip to his domineering, grasping wife. Slater's own lifestyle, as a gambler and womanizer, had probably prejudiced the puritanical Scottish jury against him.

Conan Doyle demolished the conflicting evidence of witnesses, some of whom claimed that the mystery murderer had been clean-shaven, others who said he was bearded. And, drawing on his own forensic expertise, he pointed out that when Slater's entire wardrobe of clothes was seized in his luggage aboard the *Lusitania*, not a single trace of blood was found on any of them.

The 'Sherlock Holmes' investigation produced immediate demands for a re-trial or public inquiry. But the wheels of justice grind slowly. It took 18 years before Oscar Slater was released by the newly appointed Scottish Court of Criminal Appeal on the technicality that the judge at his trial had misdirected the jury. Slater was awarded £6,000 in compensation.

But Arthur Conan Doyle never published the final chapter of his important murder investigation. 'Sherlock Holmes' had proved Slater's innocence. But had he ever uncovered the real identity of the killer of Marion Gilchrist?

Shortly before he died in 1930, Conan Doyle revealed to a friend:

'I knew I had a difficult enough job in getting Oscar Slater freed. That was the most important objective I had to achieve. If I had tried at the same to lay the blame for the murder on the real guilty man, it might have prejudiced Slater's chances of release.

But I believe I know the identity of the real murderer, a man who was protected by the police because he was a prominent citizen who desperately wanted something from the private papers of Marion Gilchrist. He has gone unpunished. But it is more important to me that an innocent man is free. I am satisfied.'

Dead Men Cannot Talk

The liner *Georges Phillipar* was one of the best designed cruise ships afloat when she was launched by her French builders from the slipway at St Nazaire in 1930.

It took almost two years to fit out the 17,300 tonne (17,000 ton) ship to carry up to 1,000 passengers in sumptuous luxury in richly panelled cabins with comfortable, efficient air conditioning. And no expense was spared to guarantee their safety, with an automatic sprinkler system and the latest fire-fighting appliances.

Yet the fire which broke out on D Deck on the liner's maiden voyage, a round trip to China, spread with devastating speed, killing 53 passengers and sending the pride of the French liner fleet to the bottom of the Red Sea.

The commission of inquiry in Paris which later investigated the sinking of the *Georges Phillipar* could find no firm evidence that faulty electrical design had caused the blaze, or that the fire had been accidental. They left only a tantalizing, inconclusive hint ... that powerful international assassins had turned the liner into a floating fire-bomb just to kill one VIP passenger, a crusading French journalist.

Freelance writer Albert Londres had joined the *Georges Phillipar* in April 1932 in Shanghai for the return leg of its maiden voyage. He had spent almost a year in Indo-China on a gruelling and dangerous assignment and his carefully guarded notebook was crammed with information which would have caused public outrage against the profiteering industrialists of London, Paris and Berlin..

Millions of readers throughout Europe were waiting and wondering what scandalous subject the best-selling author would choose for his next devastating report. In his first book, *The Road to Buenos Aires*, published only three years before, he had exposed the vile white slave trade of young women from the brothels of Marseilles and Hamburg to South America. It earned him the undying hatred of the French and German vice kings.

Undeterred, Londres went on to expose a similar traffic in young European girls to the houses of pleasure in Shanghai, and followed this up with an investigation of the terrorist group who had assassinated the King of Yugoslavia on French soil.

Now he had completed his damning examination of the deadly arms trade in the Far East, where the Japanese Imperial armies were gearing themselves for an expansive war of aggression and the bandit Chinese war lords were slaughtering their own countrymen in their bloody battles to gain control of vast areas of China and Manchuria.

Word quickly spread among enthusiastic European publishers that Albert Londres was on his way home with a manuscript that would light a fuse underneath the European millionaire arms suppliers, the Merchants of Death.

Londres was safely installed in his cabin, working on the notes for his new book when the liner docked briefly at Saigon, the capital of French Indo-China, and took aboard more travellers, mainly French colonial officials and their families. With a complement of 800 passengers, the liner called at Singapore, Penang and Ceylon, en route for the Red Sea, the Suez Canal and the French Mediterranean port of Marseilles.

On the night of 15 May as Londres worked alone in his cabin, the other passengers gathered on deck for a dinner dance in the sultry evening air, admiring the twinkling lights of the Arabian coast and waving to the crew of the Russian tanker *Sovietskya Neft* which passed less than a mile astern.

Around midnight the master of the *Georges Phillipar*, Captain Anton Vicq,

Above: The liner *Georges Phillipar* on her maiden voyage,
a round trip to China. No expense had been spared in the design of this
luxurious ship.
Left: The *Georges Phillipar*, almost burnt out by the
mysterious fire in which 53 passengers died.

retired to his cabin, bidding goodnight to the last of the dinner-dance revellers who stayed on the starlit deck, sipping chilled champagne.

Two hours later he was roused by the officer of the watch who warned him that a passenger cabin on D Deck was ablaze. When he made an examination in portside Number 5 cabin, Captain Vicq noted that 'It was not a local accident, but a fire appearing to become general and widespread.'

As he retreated along the deck corridor to the sound of the alarm, Captain Vicq was confronted by Nurse Yvonne Valentin who screamed that her cabin, Number 7, was also engulfed in flames. Between the two, in cabin Number 6 on D deck, writer Albert Londres was unaware of the drama.

Trying vainly to contain the blaze, Captain Vicq ordered all portholes to be closed and stopped the liner's engines. Within minutes the flames had spread to the bridge and the captain gave the order to abandon ship.

As the lifeboats were lowered the radio operator broadcast a frantic series of SOS messages. But his transmission was cut suddenly short when his radio failed and power from the generator ceased. Following his well rehearsed emergency procedure, the radio operator reached for the sealed locker which held an ample supply of spare batteries – the batteries were missing.

As passengers wrapped wet towels round their faces to fight their way through the blinding acrid smoke, Captain Vicq and his crew calmly organized the evacuation of the ship. All floating furniture which could be used as liferafts was heaved overboard and terrified passengers were helped over the stern of the liner into the warm still waters of the sea.

The brief burst of pleading on the ship's radio had been enough to summon a rescue flotilla to its aid, including the Soviet tanker, two British steamers, a Japanese cargo ship and two other ocean liners.

The task of saving the souls in the lifeboats and clinging to the rafts was carried out speedily and most of them were soon aboard the mercy vessels. The stricken liner burned for three days in a column of flame which could be seen for 60 km (40 miles). When the *Georges Phillipar* finally heeled over, she sank within two minutes.

But no trace was ever found of the body of Albert Londres who had been trapped in his cabin between the two sources of the sudden, unexplained fire.

Survivors reported that they had last seen him crawling through his cabin porthole, his precious manuscript held tightly under his arm. The man who knew too much was officially logged in the disaster list as drowned.

His notebooks and manuscripts drifted away in the ebb and flow of the Red Sea's tides. And seven years later, the wealthy and ruthless arms dealers, unhampered by the spotlight of Albert Londres's unfinished investigation, saw their staggering investment in munitions bear fruit when all of Europe was plunged into war.

Disappearing Dorothy

Judge Jules Forstein telephoned his wife one October evening in 1950 to let her know he'd be delayed at a political banquet. 'I don't expect to be too late,' he said. 'Is everything all right?'

There was a reason for the question. The judge seldom left his wife and children alone because of an incident at the house five years earlier. But on this occasion Dorothy was cheerful and she assured her husband that everything was fine. 'Be sure to miss me,' she said.

Mrs Forstein had lived in a state of panic for five years, dating from the evening of 25 January 1945. That day, after leaving her two children with neighbours she had shopped briefly in a supermarket and then walked home alone to the three-storey house in a Philadelphia suburb. As she entered the house, someone leaped out of the small alcove under the front stairs and attacked her in the darkness. She had time to scream only once.

The police crashed through the front door of the Forstein home to find her lying in a pool of blood. She had a broken jaw, a broken nose, a fractured shoulder and concussion.

There was money and jewellery in the house, but nothing had been taken. The motive was murder, said police. The attacker had entered the house without leaving fingerprints or disturbing the locks on doors and windows. And there was no clue as to how he had left the house, either.

Judge Forstein had an unimpeachable alibi for the time of the attack. And Mrs Forstein had no known enemies. The intruder could have been an enemy of her husband's but months of investigation turned up no suspect.

Though there was a slow physical recovery, Dorothy Forstein never recovered emotionally from the beating. She made a frequent ritual of checking and rechecking the extra locks that had been put on doors and windows. She constantly sought the companionship of relatives and neighbours sometimes during parties she would retreat into deep silence.

But she was getting better, Judge Forstein reassured himself when he returned late from the banquet that evening five years after the attack.

Inside the dimly lit house, the first thing he heard were the screams of his two small children, Edward and Marcy. He found them huddled together in a bedroom, crying convulsively. 'It's mamma,' they told him. 'Something was here and took mamma away.'

Sick with fright, Forstein searched every room of the house. There were her purse, money and keys, but Dorothy Forstein was gone.

Through bursts of tears, Marcy told him what had happened. She had been awakened by terrifying sounds in the night and had run to her mother's bedroom. Through a crack in the door, she saw her mother lying face down on the rug with a shadowy figure crouching over her. 'She looked sick,' the little girl wept.

The intruder had then picked up her mother and thrown her over his shoulder with her head hanging down his back. He saw the child watching and said, 'Go back to sleep. Your mother has been sick, but she'll be all right now.' He went down the stairway carrying Dorothy Forstein, who was dressed only in red silk pyjamas.

When the police arrived, they confessed themselves baffled. There were no fingerprints anywhere, and it seemed incredible to them that any man balancing a woman on his shoulder could have left the house without grasping something for support. Why had no one tried to stop him when he walked down a busy street carrying an unconscious woman in pyjamas? And how did he get into the Forstein home through the multiple locks on the doors and windows?

The police checked every hospital in Philadelphia, as well as rooming houses, rest homes, hotels and the morgue. The search yielded no information about Dorothy.

Whoever had abducted the judge's wife had taken her away for ever. Dorothy Forstein left behind her only the haunting memory of her last words: 'Be sure to miss me.'

Mystery at Wolf's Neck

It was a bitterly cold evening in January 1931 when bus driver Cecil Johnstone saw a fire on a desolate moor at Wolf's Neck between Newcastle upon Tyne and Otterburn in Northumberland. He stopped to investigate. What he saw was almost unbelievable. On fire was the car owned by his boss's daughter, Evelyn Foster. Beside it lay Evelyn, badly burned but still alive.

Johnstone drove her to her home at Otterburn, where she told her parents and the police that she had been attacked by a man who had set fire to her car. She died the following day and left behind her one of the strangest crime stories of the decade. If indeed it was a crime at all ...

Evelyn Foster was 28 and the daughter of Mr J. J. Foster, who owned a garage at Otterburn. She had her own car, which she ran as a one-cab taxi business.

At 19.00 on 6 January 1931, she arrived home and told her mother that a man who had got out of a car at nearby Elishaw wanted her to drive him to Ponteland, near Newcastle, to catch the bus home. She said the man had looked respectable and gentlemanly when she picked him up at the Percy Arms Hotel.

The next time her mother saw her was when she was brought home dying of burns later that night by her father's bus driver, Johnson. And this is the story she told her mother and a doctor, nurse and policeman who had been called to the house ...

After she had driven through the village of Belsay, about 8 km (5 miles) from Ponteland, her passenger suddenly asked her to turn back. She had turned round and was driving back when the man hit her in the eye and took over the wheel. He stopped the car at the top of the hill at Wolf's Neck and started 'knocking her about'. He then put her into the back of the car and raped her.

The man then took a bottle or tin out of his pocket and threw something over her. She just 'went up in a blaze'. She then felt a bump as the car was going over rough ground. Evelyn told her mother: 'I was all alight. I do not know how I got out of the car. I lay on the ground and sucked the grass. I was thirsty.'

Her last words were said to have been: 'I have been murdered.' And it really looked as though she had been murdered – until doubts began to surface at the inquest.

To begin with, nobody other than Evelyn saw a stranger in the village that evening. Her father admitted that he had not seen the man. And the owners of the Percy Arms pub, where Evelyn was said to have picked him up, said that no stranger had been in the bar and they had heard no talk about a taxi to Ponteland.

The pathologist who conducted the post mortem on Evelyn, Professor Stuart McDonald, said there were no external injuries on the body apart from the burns. There was no trace or evidence of bruising of the face to suggest that she had been knocked about and there was 'no sign at all' that she had been raped.

Doubts were also cast on Evelyn's suggestion that she and the car had been set on fire before it was driven off the road on to the moor. There were signs of burned heather where the car was found just off the road – but no sign of burned heather by the side of the road itself.

In his summing up the coroner, Mr P. M. Dobbs, told the jury they could rule out suicide. The only two points they had to consider were: Was Evelyn Foster murdered? Or did she set fire to the car to obtain insurance money and set light to herself accidentally?

It took two hours for the jury to reach a verdict. It was: wilful murder on the part of some person or persons unknown.

Later, the police took the unprecedented step of declaring that, in their view, the 'murderer' did not exist. The Chief Constable of Northumberland, Captain Fullarton James, declared in a newspaper interview that the verdict of the inquest was against the weight of evidence and Evelyn Foster had not been murdered.

Gradually, the mystery of Wolf's Neck dropped out of the news – until just over three years later. At the beginning of 1934, a Yorkshire groom, Ernest Brown, was sentenced to death at Leeds Assizes for the murder of his lover's husband. In a 'confession' on the scaffold he is reported to have said either 'ought to burn' or 'Otterburn'. But he died seconds later.

Did Brown murder Evelyn Foster? Or did he know something about her death? The answer is unlikely ever to be known.

Spring-heeled Jack, the Demon of London

There was but one topic on the lips of the people of London in 1838 ... the identity of the mysterious fiend who pounced on young women at night and whose appearance left most of them too terrified even to give a cogent description of their attacker.

At first, tales of this devil-like figure had been treated as hysterical nonsense. But reports, mainly from people crossing Barnes Common in south-west London, continued – and in January 1838 this strange creature received official recognition.

At London's Mansion House the Lord Mayor, Sir John Cowan, read out a letter from a terrified citizen of Peckham describing a demonic figure. Other complaints flooded in from people who until then had been too afraid of ridicule to report their encounters with the creature who had become known as Spring-heeled Jack.

South London barmaid Polly Adams had been savagely attacked while walking across Blackheath. Servant girl Mary Stevens was terrorized on Barnes Common. And an unnamed woman was assaulted in Clapham churchyard. Eighteen-year-old Lucy Scales, a butcher's daughter was attacked in Limehouse. Jane Alsop was almost strangled by the cloaked creature in her own home before her family were able to beat off the attacker.

The description the Alsops gave of the mysterious fiend made him sound inhuman. Jane said: 'His face was hideous, his eyes were like balls of fire, and his hands had icy claws ...'

Her description was to be echoed repeatedly by other terrified and presumably hysterical victims. But police and public did not dismiss them. Even the Duke of Wellington, although nearly 70, armed himself and went out on horseback to hunt down the monster.

Reports of attacks persisted for several years, not only in London now, but from all parts of the country.

In February 1855 the inhabitants of five south Devon towns awoke to find that there had been a heavy snowfall in which mysterious footprints had appeared overnight. The footsteps ran along the tops of walls, over rooftops, and across enclosed countryside. The hoof-like footprints were attributed by many to Spring-heeled Jack.

In 1870 the army organized a plan to trap him after sentries had been terrorized at their posts by a horrific figure who sprang from the shadows to land on the roofs of their sentry boxes or to slap their faces with icy hands. Their plan failed.

Spring-heeled Jack was last seen in 1804 in Liverpool, leaping up and down the streets from the pavements to the rooftops, only to disappear into the darkness, this time for good.

The World's Last Airship

It was a monster of the skies, a wonder of technology and engineering. The giant airship *Hindenburg* was more than 245 m (800 ft) long and stabilized by a tailfin as high as a ten-storey building. Its four powerful diesel engines gave it the power to cruise effortlessly above the clouds at 36 metres per second (80 mph.). The airship could carry 100 passengers through the atmosphere for a week in a style as opulent as any ocean liner.

When all the 16 bags inside its 22.8 m (75 ft) diameter frame were filled with hydrogen, the airship would wrench itself away from the ground with a lifting force of 239 tonnes (235 tons), enough to raise a modern jumbo jet. Admittedly the properties of hydrogen gas, lighter than the surrounding air, which gave the *Hindenburg* the lift to soar into the sky, brought the risks and dangers of explosion. But with more than a quarter of a century of hard-won experience, the Zeppelin Company was confident that no mishap would endanger their new flagship. They knew that the hydrogen in the gas bags, more than 230,000 cubic metres (7,200,000 cubic feet) of highly inflammable gas, would erupt in a devastating explosion if it was ever ignited. But the design, they said, was flawless. Only an act of God, or deliberate sabotage by a madman, could damage the *Hindenburg*.

And when the *Hindenburg* was consumed in a fire-ball over New Jersey on 6 May 1937, killing 13 of its passengers, 22 of its crew and 1 ground control worker, both the American Goverment and Hitler's Nazi regime conspired to cover up any clues to what may have been the biggest crime in aviation history.

While the fledgling airliners of the 1920s and 1930s were plagued by bad weather and mechanical breakdowns trying to operate services between towns only a few hundred miles apart, the monster airships of Germany appeared regularly over the skyline of Rio de Janeiro and New York.

They had become known simply as Zeppelins, after their brilliant but eccentric designer, the Graf Ferdinand von Zeppelin. Born into a noble Prussian family in 1838, he was an adventurous 23-year-old when he obtained an introduction to US President Abraham Lincoln during the American Civil War and joined the Union Army as a 'guest' cavalry officer.

But the young soldier soon became bored by the slow pace of the war and joined a civilian expedition to explore the sources of the Mississippi River. On a scouting mission at St Paul, Minnesota, he took his first ride in a tethered balloon to survey miles of countryside in one brief flight.

If only balloons could be powered and steered, he enthused, what a perfect gun platform and bombing weapon they would make, soaring safely over the slogging infantry and cavalrymen on the field. His vision of giant balloons or dirigibles as weapons of war never left him but he stayed an earthbound cavalry officer until the end of his military career at the age of 52.

Within a few years of retiring, he had applied for a patent for an airship and began experimenting with the designer, Dr Hugo Eckener, an experienced sailor and meteorologist, at their little workshop near Lake Constance in southern Germany.

By 1909 Zeppelin had formed the world's first airship passenger service, Deutsche Luftschiffahrts Aktien Gesellschaft – DELAG. Operating flights between Berlin, Frankfurt, Hamburg and Dresden, his airships carried 32,750 passengers on 1,600 flights in 5 years without a single accident.

Then came 1914 and the Zeppelins went to war.

The Zeppelin raids over England caused little material damage but they raised panic among the population of London. The sight of the dreaded airships caught in the searchlights, cascading their bombs on to the capital, brought Londoners out into the streets, screaming and shaking their fists impotently in the air.

But within two years the British air aces in their tiny biplane fighters were more than a match for the Zeppelin monsters. In their hydrogen bags the Zeppelins carried the seeds of their own destruction. It took only one hit from the newly developed ZPT tracer bullets coated in burning phosphorus, to turn the airships into flying holocausts.

Graf von Zeppelin died in 1917, just as it was proved that his airships were too vulnerable to gunfire to be machines of war.

But Dr Hugo Eckener struggled through the post-war economic ruin of Germany as chairman of the Zeppelin Company, dreaming of a peaceful future for the airships as transatlantic transports.

In July 1928, the world's most advanced passenger airship, the *Graf Zeppelin*, made its maiden flight on the 90th anniversary of the old Count's birth. Three months later, with 20 passengers aboard, it made its first transatlantic voyage to New York where Eckener and the crew were treated to a ticker-tape welcome. In the next five years of operation on regular services to North and South America, the *Graf Zeppelin* established an unrivalled airship mastery of the skies.

The prestige of this achievement was not lost on the new Nazi masters of Germany. Eckener was not popular with the new regime. Before their rise to power he had made radio broadcasts in Germany condemning their brutality. But with the Nazis controlling the purse strings of German industry, including the Zeppelin Company, he was powerless to stop the traditional black, white and red livery colours of the Zeppelins being repainted with the swastika, the symbol of Hitler and his Nazis.

Eckener, a stubborn 68-year-old, was defiant when he was summoned before Dr Joseph Goebbels; the Propaganda Minister, in 1936 when his newest airship, the biggest, fastest and most powerful, was unveiled.

The airship must be called 'Adolf Hitler', he was told by the Nazi minister. 'No,' Eckener replied. 'I warn you the sight of the swastika on our airships is already provoking hostility when we dock in the United States. If the new airship is called "Adolf Hitler" it will be the target for hatred and sabotage.'

Eckener won the day, but Goebbels decreed that in the German press and on radio the new airship would not be referred to by its Zeppelin Company name, *Hindenburg*. In the Nazi press it was referred to by its works design title – LZ 129.

When the *Hindenburg* began its regular services from Frankfurt to the Lakeheath Naval Air Base in New Jersey it received a rapturous welcome. But as the trickle of persecuted refugees from the Nazis reached a flood-tide on America's shores, Eckener's fears of flaunting the swastika proved to be well founded. In August 1936 more than 100 American demonstrators, posing as celebrating visitors, boarded the German liner *Bremen* as she lay at a pier in New York and sparked off a riotous protest against Hitler's involvement in the Spanish Civil War.

Security was stepped up at the liner berths and at the *Hindenburg*'s hanger across the river at Lakeheath. The American government was concerned by reports that the *Hindenburg* had even been the target of riflemen who had fired potshots at the Zeppelin from atop the Manhattan skyscrapers and from the open fields of New Jersey.

The German ambassador in Washington had received hundreds of threatening phone calls and letters from opponents of the Nazis who were determined to destroy the *Hindenburg* and keep the swastika out of American skies.

Aware of the serious blow to their regime's prestige if the *Hindenburg* was sabotaged, the Sicherheitsddinst, the security élite of Hitler's SS, began to conduct searches of the *Hindenburg*'s hangar in Frankfurt, and the airship itself, before each flight.

On Monday 3 May 1937, Colonel Fritz Erdmann, the new chief of Special Intelligence for the Luftwaffe, was ordered to SS headquarters in Berlin for a briefing on the *Hindenburg* flight due to leave that day.

Erdmann and the two junior officers who were to accompany him in civilian clothes on the flight to America were startled by the briefing given to them by SS Sturmbannführer Major Kurt Hufschmidt. He told them: 'We have reliable information that an attempt will be made to destroy your flight.

The *Hindenburg* in flames

The sabotage will come by bomb, probably after the *Hindenburg* has arrived over American soil. This attack is designed to make the Fatherland look vulnerable in the eyes of our enemies, disloyal Germans, Jews and troublemakers in the United States.'

The ss man also revealed that in March 1935 a bomb had been discovered in the main dining saloon of the *Graf Zeppelin*, hidden underneath a table by one of the passengers. The bomb had been defused safely.

He also told of a Gestapo search of a Frankfurt hotel room for a mysterious passenger who had just arrived from America on a *Hindenburg* flight. The man had travelled on a forged Swedish passport and although he eluded the Gestapo, they searched his room and found detailed technical drawings of both the *Graf Zeppelin* and the *Hindenburg*.

Erdmann was given a rundown on suspect passengers who were making the flight with him. They included: a German couple, both journalists, who were known to have a Jewish writer as a friend, a young photographer from Bonn whose cut-price fare had been arranged by a senior Zeppelin executive since sacked for having Jewish ancestry, a 36-year-old American advertising executive who was known to be a spy for us intelligence, and Joseph Spah, a 35-year-old music hall entertainer from Douglaston, Long Island.

Spah was a comedian and acrobat who travelled on a French passport and had an American wife. But to the humourless ss man he was a suspect because his music hall act, popular in parts of Berlin, was known to contain jokes against people in authority.

At the departure hanger in Frankfurt, all passengers and their luggage were thoroughly searched. Security men confiscated all the young photographer's flashbulbs, fearing they could be used to start a deliberate fire. They also X-rayed a small Dresden china souvenir doll brought on board by Spah.

But the Luftwaffe intelligence officer accepted the assurance of the *Hindenburg* captain, Ernst Lehmann, that the two married journalists were both personal friends who were writing his biography. And Captain Lehmann insisted that the American spy working for the advertising agency had been under close surveillance and posed no threat. The intelligence officer accepted his explanation.

Joseph Spah, according to the captain, was no more than a nuisance. He had brought along a frisky young German shepherd dog which was travelling with him in order to become part of his new act at Radio City Music Hall in New York. The dog travelled in the freight compartment at the rear of the airship and twice Spah had been found unsupervised in the area, away from the authorized passenger lounges. But they accepted his explanation that he must personally feed the nervous young dog during the two-and-a-half-day journey.

Colonel Erdmann reassured the captain: 'Any of our passengers sabotaging the *Hindenburg* on this voyage would be committing suicide. I think the attempt will come after we have moored at Lakeheath. Then it will be the responsibility of the ground staff to ensure the safety of the airship.'

But according to many investigators and historians, a bomb was already on board. An incendiary device, wired to a darkroom photographic timer powered by two small batteries was hidden inside the explosive hydrogen atmosphere of Gas Cell Four, near the tail of the *Hindenburg*.

The *Hindenburg* was due to moor at Lakeheath at 06.00 on 6 May. But the night before it ran into strong headwinds over Newfoundland and the airship radioed it would not arrive until 18.00. The *Hindenburg*'s docking was always made precisely at 06.00 or 18.00 to allow definite working times for the ground crew.

A small reception committee waiting at Lakeheath for the *Hindenburg*'s arrival took advantage of the postponement to go off for dinner in the nearby town of Toms River. They included broadcaster Herbert Morrison, who was preparing to record a commentary on the airship's mooring for the listeners of station WLS in Chicago.

By mid-afternoon on 6 May the *Hindenburg* had passed Long Island sound and the sight of the giant airship with its glittering swastikas brought traffic to a halt in Manhattan. As it crossed the baseball stadium at Ebbet's Field in Brooklyn, the game between the Brooklyn Dodgers and the Pittsburgh Pirates was suspended while players and spectators alike gaped in admiration at the pride of Hitler's Germany.

Just before 16.00 the airship arrived over Lakeheath, but Captain Lehmann set a southerly cruising course to ride out the stormy winds for two hours until the ground crew mustered for his appointed time of arrival.

At 17.22, the *Hindenburg* was being advised by ground control to keep circling ahead of an approaching storm front. And it was then, it is believed, that a timer on the detonator of the fire-bomb hidden in Gas Cell Four was set – for two hours hence.

An hour later Lakeheath radioed: 'Advise landing now' and the airship headed for the airfield. At 19.05 the *Hindenburg* crossed the south fence of the airfield. As 92 US Navy men and 139 civilian workers prepared to reach for the mooring lines which would be dropped from the *Hindenburg* to secure the airship, radio reporter Herbert Morrison could see cheerful passengers at the open promenade deck windows waving at him.

At 19.22 the *Hindenburg* lowered the mooring lines and gave one last burst of her engines to line the airship up with the 61 m (200 ft) mooring tower.

If the airship had been on schedule, all the passengers would have disembarked and it would have been floating at the mooring mast with only a skeleton crew... But the timer on the bomb had been set to the original schedule.

At 19.22 there was a puff of flame and a fire-ball 122 m (400 ft) across erupted from the linen-covered framework of the *Hindenburg*.

Herbert Morrison had been describing the scene as the airship docked:

> What a sight it is ... a thrilling one ... a marvellous sight. The sun is striking the window of the observation deck on the westward side and sparkling like glittering jewels on the background of dark velvet. Oh, oh, oh ... it's burst into flames. Get out of the way please. Oh my, this terrible – it's burning, bursting into flames, it's falling. Oh, this is one of the worst, oh, all the humanity ...

His voice trailed off in tears.

When the film from the newsreel cameras which recorded the fire-ball were processed, it showed that it took only 34 seconds from the first explosion of flame until the glowing framework of the *Hindenburg* hit the ground. The millions of cubic feet of hydrogen had flamed off in less than a minute, although the blaze of engines, fuel oil and framework lasted for hours.

The crew men on the ground, holding the mooring lines underneath the burning giant, scattered and ran for their lives.

One of them, Allen Hagaman, tripped over the rails surrounding the mooring tower and the glowing framework of the airship crashed down on him. He was identified the next day by the scorched remains of his wedding ring.

But in the few seconds as the *Hindenburg* fell from the sky, there were miraculous escapes as passengers and crew leaped from the crashing airship, or simply stayed inside the burning wreckage until it settled on the ground and ran to safety through the white-hot hoops of the *Hindenburg* framework. Joe Spah was one of those who survived. He jumped more than 9 m (30 ft) from the burning airship and, with his acrobat's training, landed apparently unhurt. Luftwaffe intelligence colonel Fritz Erdmann, who had predicted an attack would come after the *Hindenburg* had landed, perished in the flames. Of the 36 passengers, 13 died. Of the 61 crew members, 22 died.

In the commission of inquiry that followed, German experts were invited to join the investigation as 'observers'. Most of the commission's discussions were 'off-the-record' talks between American government officials and high ranking German diplomats.

Documents now filed in the National Archives in Washington show that the American and German technical experts agreed not to consider sabotage as a cause of the disaster – at least in public.

The archives show that senior officers of the American Departments of Commerce and the Interior warned the commission solicitor Mr Trimble Jr that 'a finding of sabotage might be a cause for an international incident, especially on these shores'. The commission ignored a written report by Detective George McCartney of the New York Police Department bomb squad, who analysed the wreckage and reconstructed technical details of a firebomb which he believed had been placed in Gas Cell Four. And the chief of the Luftwaffe, Hermann Goering, ordered the German technical advisers to the commission not to cooperate with any avenue of investigation that hinted at sabotage by any member of the crew.

After a month-long hearing, the commission reached a conclusion backed by both the Americans and Germans. The hydrogen fire-ball had been sparked off, they claimed, by a freak spark of static electricity, an unfortunate phenomenon not seen before and not seen since. Hermann Goering concurred: 'It was an act of God. No one could have prevented it.'

But behind the scenes in Germany, the Gestapo were ruthlessly interrogating the families and friends of every one of the *Hindenburg* crew and passengers. Their suspicions eventually focussed on 25-year-old Eric Spehl. As a rigger on the *Hindenburg* he was one of the crew responsible for checking the gas bags for leaks.

Spehl had been a devout Catholic, never a fervent supporter of the Nazi regime. And he had one great weakness, a passionate love for a divorced woman ten years older than himself who had become his mistress.

Gestapo agents, who checked the gossip with Spehl's neighbours in Frankfurt, found that the young man had gone through a traumatic meeting with his mistress's ex-husband just before the *Hindenburg*'s last voyage. The man had come to Spehl's flat. He was an artist, he was haggard and half crazed with fear. He was on the run from the Gestapo and needed money to escape.

Spehl gave him all the money he had ... and then tipped off the Gestapo. The Nazi torturers arrested the artist and crushed his fingers one by one in a vice until the bones showed through his knuckles. Spehl was reported to be infuriated by the sight and still seething with anger when he boarded the fatal *Hindenburg* flight.

The Gestapo searchers in Frankfurt ripped Spehl's apartment to pieces. They could find no sign of his mistress, who had fled the city. And they could find no trace of Eric's beloved new gadget for his photographic darkroom, his two-hour timer.

Neither could they interrogate Eric Spehl. He died, horribly burned, in the emergency field hospital set up at Lakeheath, beside the glowing embers of the world's last great airship.

Chapter
Two

Crimes
of Our Time

The Computer as Crook

The unsolved crime is usually hailed as the perfect crime. It is a misnomer. More often than not, a crime remains unsolved thanks to a combination of poor planning, coupled with good luck on the criminal's part and sometimes helped by a faulty police investigation. The really perfect crime is never reported. It remains unsolved because it is unrecognized and undetected as a piece of villainy.

And in the criminal's quest for illegal perfection, many have found a willing new accomplice who never gets nervous about being caught and punished, who has no criminal record, leaves no fingerprints and never demands a share of the loot... The computer, an electronic brain without scruples or morals, is the perfect partner in crime.

At the beginning of the 1980s it was estimated that there were 300,000 large computers at work in businesses in the United States, Europe and Japan, juggling enormous amounts of cash and commodities every week. Unlike human clerks and bank tellers, with all their frailties and temptations, computers never get their sums wrong and do not possess sticky fingers to dip into the till.

The decision of the almighty computer is final, whether it is sending a demand for payment to a customer who is vainly disputing the bill or releasing vast amounts of hard cash on invoices it has cleared for payment. The computer is above suspicion.

Small wonder then that it has not taken long for criminals to realize the potential of getting the computer on their side. For the computer's infallibility is a double-edged sword. If crooked information is fed in at the start of the process, impeccably crooked instructions are produced at the other end and no one doubts the orders the machine gives them.

That is what electronic whizz-kid Jerry Schneider discovered when he became a millionaire by defrauding the master computer of the Pacific Bell Telephone Company in Los Angeles in 1972. Schneider's crime is still unsolved, only he knows exactly how he fooled the electronic brain. The computer records reveal nothing.

The 21-year-old high school graduate was struggling to form his own telephone equipment supply business when he discovered secret codes which allowed him to tap into the computer controlling the stocks in the warehouse of Pacific Bell in California. Using his own modified computer terminal at home, Schneider persuaded the electronic stock controller he was a legitimate installation contractor for the phone company and he began to order costly wiring and exchange equipment from the warehouse.

The computer accepted his instructions and despatched its expensive goods to locations all over Los Angeles, often to the pavements beside manhole covers where the delivery drivers dumped the bulky crates of electronics, assuming another crew would arrive later to install the equipment. They did not wait to see this operation.

Schneider, with his own truck painted to resemble the phone company vehicles, would hijack the equipment, then return home to tap into the computer once more and give it orders to wipe the whole transaction from its electronic memory.

With his giant rival supplying all his equipment free, Schneider's business boomed until he foolishly refused a pay rise to one of his employees, who then tipped off the police. Even after his arrest officials of the phone company refused to believe that Schneider had milked their warehouse of $1 million worth of equipment in less than a year. If their computer insisted there was nothing missing, they were not prepared to argue with it. Only after police investigators physically went round the warehouse, totalling up the stocks with old-fashioned pen and paper, did the phone company admit their losses.

But Schneider spent only a few weeks in prison. The phone company dropped charges against him after he gave them a secret briefing on the electronic loopholes in their system.

On his release from prison Schneider set himself up in a new business, as one of America's highest paid computer security consultants, revealing the secrets of his unsolved crime for fat fees and searching the electronic brains of his clients' machines for similar loopholes which can let crooked computer operators steal by remote control.

As Jerry Schneider said:

> 'Many of my clients had already been robbed blind without realising it. They had lost millions of dollars through computer manipulation and the culprits can never be traced because the electronic evidence of their crimes has been wiped out.
>
> Who needs to take the risk of leaping over a bank counter with a sawn-off shotgun when they can sit in the comfort of their own home and rob the bank of even more money just by using a telephone and a computer terminal?'

In the United States, FBI officials estimate the average haul in armed bank robberies amounts to $10,000 a time. But the average electronic bank fraud is enriching crooks by $500,000 a time with only a tiny percentage of the microchip embezzlements uncovered and solved.

In 1980 it was estimated that unsolved computer crime in the US and

Common Market countries was producing a haul of £200 million a year and growing fast.

New York police are still searching for the amiable young man who pulled off a childishly simple computer fraud when he signed a loan agreement with a local bank for $20,000 to buy himself a new car. The bank's computer paid the car dealer and the vehicle ownership papers were safely stored in the bank's filing cabinet as security for the loan. A few days later the proud new driver received his loan repayment book, with 12 monthly coupons to be processed by the computer as he coughed up the instalments over the next year.

The young man ignored the first 11 coupons and posted the twelfth with a money order to the computer when his first instalment was due. Then he waited.

There is nothing as blind as an infallible machine. The computer recognized only the magnetic ink code on the coupon as the twelfth and final instalment. With unfailing efficiency it sent the car driver a glowing letter thanking him for paying off the loan. It also posted him the ownership documents to the car and a printed assurance that he now had an outstanding credit rating at the bank.

More than a month later a puzzled bank official went to visit the new customer's address in search of an overdue instalment. His apartment was empty and the gleaming Cadillac had already been sold to a local car dealer who had happily, and legally, accepted the computer's decision that the car was paid for and owned by the young driver who wanted a cash sale to pay for a 'heart operation' for his ailing father. The mysterious driver was never traced despite strenuous efforts to do so.

Another stunningly easy fraud netted $350,000 in one week for the pretty blonde 'divorcée' who opened her own account with $200 when she arrived at a bank in Miami, Florida. She was planning to buy herself a luxury home near the beach, she explained, just as soon as her divorce settlement came through from her husband. The bank happily issued her with a chequebook and a book of paying-in slips with her own personalized account number printed in one corner in magnetic ink characters.

They never noticed her stop at the counter as she left, when she scooped up a handful of blank paying-in slips in a tray for the convenience of customers who had forgotten to bring their own personalized books.

Somehow (and no one has ever publicly explained the mystery) the young blonde printed her own account number in magnetic ink at the bottom left hand corner of all the blank slips. A few days later she reappeared at the bank and slipped her own specially doctored paying-in slips to the tray at the counter.

For the next five days, busy customers who had forgotten to bring their pre-printed paying-in slips reached for the apparently blank forms on the tray and paid their earnings and savings into the bank. The computer was programmed to direct the pen-and-ink slips into a storage basket for manual sorting. But it instantly recognized the magnetic ink numbers and faithfully credited all the money to the divorcée's account. When she returned a few days later she found her 'dream home' and she was accompanied by a burly male friend with a security attaché case.

She cleaned out all but a few hundred dollars from the account, scooping up a kitty of £150,060 which had been built up for her by unsuspecting customers who kicked up hell at the end of the month when their statements showed their hard-earned cash had not been credited to their accounts. The blonde and her friend were never seen again.

A more ambitious crook used his innocent girl friend as his unwitting accomplice when he robbed the computer of a bank in Washington, DC, in 1981.

The dapper middle-aged businessman boasted that he was a furniture manufacturer from San Francisco and would soon be bringing new jobs to Washington when he had found a suitable site for his new factory. The bank welcomed him as a potentially valuable customer when he opened his account and told them to expect a very large deposit to follow from his company account in San Francisco.

True to his word, a few days later the San Francisco bank made an electronic transfer of $2 million to Washington. The furniture manufacturer promptly presented himself at the bank, collected the money in a cashier's draft and set off 'looking for development land'. When he failed to reappear, and when the hard cash never arrived from San Francisco, bank investigators started to track down the source of the computer transfer of money.

After months of searching they finally traced the electronic message to one computer terminal at the bank in San Francisco, operated by a group of three female employees who all denied any knowledge of the transfer. But they did tell the investigators that a fourth woman had left her job at the bank only a few weeks before, broken-hearted after an unhappy love affair.

The woman was traced and told in tears how her middle-aged boyfriend had promised to marry her after returning home briefly to Washington to assure his friends and family that he had made his fortune in California. The boyfriend was a great fun-loving practical joker, she explained. He had even persuaded her to send a telex to a bank in Washington crediting him with $2 million as a prank to impress his friends and relations.

The telex message was the only souvenir the bank has left of the fraudster. Their computer had paid out without the need to see the cash or count laboriously through piles of crisp banknotes as a bored, under-paid human teller would have to do. To the computer a burst of electronic bleeps over a telephone line was as good as money in the bank.

But the prize for the most sought after computer conman of the new electronic age must surely go to the New York genius who was able tap his way into a municipal computer which controlled no cash, no valuable stocks, no sensitive information.

The AM Tote 300 computer at Belmont racetrack is just an adding machine which is supposed to total up the amount of money bet on each day's racing to an accuracy within a single cent.

Since revenue from the Tote betting tax contributes to the income of the City of New York, that figure is a matter of record. Each day New York newspapers publish the figure. It is simply a statistic which varies each day according to the amount of business done at the racetrack.

The final sum from the impartial computing machine is taken for granted as accurate even by the down-to-earth businessmen of the Mafia. And that daily betting total is the heart of the Mafia's illegal bookmaking enterprise, the numbers racket. The Mafia's persuasive street salesmen offer a daily lottery ticket where a gambler can choose any three digits which he or she thinks will form the vital last three numbers of that day's betting total at Belmont.

The chances of getting the numbers right are 999 to 1. But the organizers pay out odds of only 500 to 1, making a profit on half the $3 million New Yorkers bet on the racket each week.

On 30 September 1980, a crowd of 20,000 gamblers spent a day at the races and bet a total of $3,339,916. The following day the Mafia bookies paid out $250,000 to lucky holders who had chosen the winning number as number 916.

A few days later the auditors handling the racetrack's accounts announced that the computer had mistotalled the amount by $3 and altered the last three figures to 919. The Mafia bookies who had already paid out on the earlier figure, made the splendidly warm-hearted gesture of paying out again on the new total to enhance their reputation as nice honest guys to do business with.

Then the auditors completed an overhaul of the Tote 300 computer and checked its totals against actual cash deposits paid into the bank. In six months the Tote 300 had given the wrong betting total 80 times. Its simple adding machine memory had been accepting any last three numbers fed into it by a crooked computer operator who clicked its electronic register to any numbers he chose.

The Mafia had been conned out of $20 million.

CRIMES OF OUR TIME

A Sadistic Revenge

'Only a few evil sadists will carry with them to their graves the knowledge of whether her body was alive or dead when they set her on fire.'

The words come from the man known as the White Rat of Uganda: self-styled 'Major' Bob Astles, the British acolyte of one of the most barbarous tyrants the world has ever seen, Idi Amin. They refer to a gentle old woman with dual Israeli-British citizenship who unwittingly became caught up in the now legendary Israeli commando rescue of a hijacked aeroplane and its hostages at Uganda's Entebbe Airport in 1976.

Dora Bloch, aged 73, was one of 105 hostages freed by the bullet in one of the most daring, audacious military swoops of its kind in modern, peacetime history. Freed, tragically, only for an instant ... because she was hurt during the armed sortie and was left behind to recuperate in a Ugandan hospital.

The Ugandan capitulation afer the Entebbe raid was absolute. So, it soon became clear, was Amin's lust for revenge. And the pathetically frail object of that revenge appears to have been Mrs Dora Bloch.

It was only later that clues began to emerge about what really happened to this grandmother, whose only wish when she boarded the 747 Jumbo jet was to see again her relatives in Tel Aviv.

In 1980 a British journalist smuggled a message into Uganda's grim Luzira Prison, where Amin's British aide Astles was being held, following the flight of the tyrant and the country's liberation by troops sent in by neighbouring Tanzania.

In a letter smuggled out to the newsman, Mike Parker, Astles told how he had tracked down Mrs Bloch's grave at a time when Amin was denying to the world that his secret police had slain her.

Rumours in the country had been rife that Mrs Bloch had been tortured to death in the notorious State Research Bureau outside Kampala, along with thousands of others – enemies real and imagined – who had simply vanished after being abducted there.

Astles, however, told Parker in his smuggled letter that he confronted Amin after discovering Mrs Bloch's jungle grave. He wrote:

'Then, all hell let loose, I was summoned to see Amin – and he was in one of his most horrendous rages. His eyes glared with terrible anger.

I knew I was going to be in trouble for asking questions, but I wasn't going to back down. I said to Amin. "Bring me the body of Dora Bloch."

And then I was brought down to earth. It was flung at me, by Amin, that I had had a part in her killing. How could I have done? At the time, I was on leave in London.

I came back to Uganda because it was the only life I knew. And I vowed to Mrs Bloch's niece, Mrs Ruth Hammond, in a meeting at her London home, that I would discover what had happened to her aunt.

The truth is that I was working with Israeli Intelligence – but nobody knew at the time.'

'The truth' as propounded by Astles may be anything but fact. Nevertheless, documents recovered since Amin's overthrow – some of them from the so-called State Research Bureau – reveal that Mrs Bloch was dragged screaming from Mulago Hospital, Kampala, after being admitted there as a patient only hours after the successful commando raid on Entebbe Airport.

It was later claimed that she had been taken there for treatment after being unknowingly left behind by the Israeli troops. But subsequent statements from witnesses suggest that she was far too weak to travel and, for the sake of the safety of the rest of the liberated hostages, she was left behind in the hope that Amin would allow her to be treated and then released on her recovery.

It was not to be. Astles said:

'She was a suffering, pathetic old woman. But the State Research police were incensed by the Israeli attack. They wanted immediate retribution.

I have been told many stories about her death. But I was informed by a member of State Research that she was kicked and pummelled to the ground after being dragged from her hospital bed.

Her body, I was told, was finally set ablaze. And only a few evil sadists know whether she was alive or dead when they set her on fire.'

Astles added, chillingly:

'Animals from the State Research Bureau were openly bragging about the white woman they had killed. They were boasting of how she had been buried after being beaten and burned and it was an easy job to find her unmarked grave – at a place called Nakapinyi.

I arranged to go there with a friend, but somehow our secret got out. My friend was thrown into jail. And I, too, would have been imprisoned by Amin if I'd made any attempt to get to the body.

Despite my demands, Amin refused to acknowledge that Mrs

Idi Amin

Bob Astles

Bloch had been killed on Ugandan soil. He kept telling the outside world that the 'missing' Mrs Bloch was being searched for. But all along he knew the truth.

I think, in all honesty, that he was ashamed that his State Research Bureau had killed her. He would never admit that she died the horrible death that she did on his orders. And, despite my demands, he adamantly refused to let anyone else try to appease her mourning family by finding her body.'

Mrs Bloch's grave was, in fact, finally unearthed by Ugandan police in May, 1979. Her bones were identified by top Israeli pathologist Dr Maurice Rogoff and flown to her homeland for burial. A grave had been prepared for her in Jerusalem by one of her sons, Bertram, and at last she was laid to rest.

Bob Astles told reporter Mike Parker: 'The sorry way in which Dora Bloch died will serve forever as an indictment of Idi Amin. Her killing was needless – a sordid act of revenge by people against whom this fragile person was totally defenceless.'

Piracy 20th Century Style

There is nothing romantic about pirates. In the days of sail they were bloodthirsty killers. In the present day they are just as deadly, just as ruthless, just as merciless. The main difference is that in the days of Blackbeard and Captain Kidd, pirates usually ended their careers on the gallows or in Davy Jones's locker. In the 20th century, however, they get away. Their crimes almost always remain unsolved.

Piracy has become a renewed menace around the world, the most blighted regions being the Caribbean, the West African coast and the Far East. Many ships leaving Singapore for the open seas now frequently take on armed guards to protect them from attack by pirates, who mainly operate from nearby islands with high-speed boats.

In the Philippines, the British captain of a container ship dropped anchor to ride out a storm, and thought he and his crew were safe from danger. But under cover of darkness pirates drew alongside in a fishing boat, threw up grappling hooks and hauled themselves on board the container ship as it lay in Manila Bay. The bandits forced their way to the captain's cabin, pointed a gun at his neck and demanded money. Captain Arthur Dyason refused, and moved as if to parry the gun. The pirates opened fire and the captain died.

A horrifying massacre was carried out by pirates in the Tawitawi Islands, about 500 miles north of Manila. The passenger craft *Nuria* had dropped anchor in a calm bay when two crewmen and two stowaways jumped the crew and passengers. Wielding weapons taken from the armoury, they herded everyone to one side of the ship and stripped them of their valuables. Then they opened fire. In a hail of shots 11 people were killed – then callously thrown overboard. Panic ensued and 20 others dived into the sea and were drowned.

Meanwhile the four pirates transferred to two fishing vessels manned by accomplices. Twenty people survived the ordeal, and the pirates, thought to be natives of the region, were never caught.

In 1981 the International Maritime Bureau was established at Barking, Essex, to deal with and collate evidence of crimes committed at sea. Many of the cases the bureau deals with involve insurance fraud. But increasingly, cases of piracy are reported to the investigators. In one of its first reports, the bureau stated with alarm that fierce tribesmen armed with knives and poison-tipped arrows were hired to protect ships from pirates off West Africa.

But it is the Caribbean that is, as ever, the world centre of piracy. In five years, between 1977 and 1982, it was estimated that 1,500 people had been killed by pirates.

The yacht *Belle Esprit* limped into Nassau in the Bahamas with 50 bullet holes in the hull. The captain, Austin Evans, had beaten off an attack from five speed-boats and was eventually rescued by a police spotter plane. Within weeks, pirates raided three sailing boats heading for the Bahamas. They threatened the lives of those on board and robbed them of cash and supplies.

William and Pat Kamemer of Fort Myers, Florida, were murdered when they stumbled across an ocean drug transfer in the Exumas Islands. Walter Falconer and a companion vanished without trace along with their yacht, *Polyner III*, in the 76-mile stretch between Bimini and the Florida coast. After relatives offered a reward word filtered back that both men had been killed and the yacht hijacked to South America.

Peter Beamborough and Michael Collesta fought off four attacking boats near the Williams Islands. They reported afterwards that they sailed their 12-m (40-ft) yawl *Snowbound* to safety in a hail of gunfire. British businessman Michael Crocker died aboard his 9-m (30-ft) yacht *Nyn*, strangled by an armed intruder.

The reason for most of these attacks is the booming and seemingly unstoppable drugs trade. Whereas the currency of the pirates was once gold, it is now marijuana, cocaine and heroin. The route is from South America, through the Caribbean islands to the Florida coast. Mother ships carrying up to 62,000 tonnes (60,000 tons) of marijuana have been seen anchored outside territorial waters, waiting for darkness and the arrival of dozens of small vessels to transfer the cargo to hidden inlets and covers. Some victims have unexpectedly witnessed drug transfers at sea. Others have been attacked and killed, so that their vessels can be used as drug carriers.

In the Cayman Islands the police chief advertised six aircraft for sale – all confiscated from smugglers. He said: 'It doesn't stop the trade. It simply means that more yachts and planes will be stolen to replace them.'

The Colombian drug network is held responsible for most of the sea attacks, but many of the islanders are joining in the pirate operation.

Grafton Iffel, head of the Bahamas CID said: 'There are 700 small islands spread over 100,000 square miles. With limited resources it is an area impossible to control.'

American yachting magazines now openly warn readers: 'Take weapons with you – the bigger the better. Display them when other boats come near. Link up with fellow yachtsmen in harbours and buy the best radio equipment you can afford.'

Captain Mike Green who sailed off the Florida coast for more than 20 years, said:

'Fear is replacing leisure here. Nobody listens to fabulous fishing stories any more. The talk is of bullets across the bow and high-speed runs for safety.

The message to yachtsmen who want to fulfil a life's ambition by sailing these waters is simply – don't. It is no longer safe. These seas belong to the smugglers and the pirates.'

Double Dealing at the Dogs

The most spectacular swindle in the history of greyhound racing was pulled off at London's White City track on 8 December 1945. The perpetrators, who were never caught, got away with more than £100,000, a fortune at the time.

The swindle became apparent to the race fans as they watched the last event of the day. The second favourite, Fly Bessie, led at the first bend, closely followed by Jimmy's Chicken. Then, to the amazement of the 16,000 crowd, the dogs began to swerve drunkenly and lose ground. One by one, they started stumbling ... all except the rank outsider, a white hound called Bald Truth. He streaked home 15 lengths ahead of the second dog, with the favourite, Victory Speech, trailing in fourth.

No one was more amazed than Bald Truth's owner, Colonel B. C. 'Jock' Hartley, wartime director of the Army Sports Board. The dog had only been brought in as a late substitute and his £2 bet on it was prompted more by his heart than his head. He sat speechless as fans shouted and growled and track officials delayed making the official announcements. But there was nothing they could do. Number 4 went up in lights; Bald Truth the winner. Bets would be paid.

As far as Scotland Yard was concerned, however, the affair was far from over. Chief Inspector Robert Fabian was called in to investigate the coup, which had followed a series of minor frauds at tracks around the country. Slowly the pieces of the puzzle were fitted into place. The swindlers had used a dope called cholecretone, untraceable in pre-race examinations, but which had an alcoholic effect as the dogs heated up during a race.

Investigators decided that the culprit had crept into a disused kennel used to store straw and timber. Then, when all eyes were on the track during the penultimate race, he had crawled out, fed drugged pieces of fish to all the dogs except Bald Truth – the only white dog in the field – and returned to his kennel until the coast was clear. Meanwhile the rest of the gang were placing bets with bookies all over the country and on the course, bringing the price down from 33-1 to 11-2 by the start.

But that was all renowned sleuth Fabian of the Yard could discover. Despite the Greyhound Racing Association's offer of a £1,000 reward, the culprits were never caught.

A Fatal Flight

Two planes carrying 116 passengers mysteriously vanished in the Andes – and investigators believe both craft may have been hijacked.

Saeta Airlines Flight 11, with 59 passengers on board, left Quito, Ecuador, on 15 August 1976 on its 45-minute flight to the mountain city of Cuenca. It vanished without trace.

Two years later Saeta Flight 11 left with 57 people bound once again for

Cuenca. It passed over the same relay station as its 1976 namesake then vanished. Intensive searches found no signs of the aircraft or their passengers. But at a special hearing in Quito, five farmers and a teacher gave sworn statements that they saw the second flight suddenly veer from its normal southerly course and head north-east.

Major Carlos Serrano, president of Saeta, one of Ecuador's three domestic airlines, supported the theory that the two Vickers Viscount planes had been hijacked. He said drug smugglers may have been involved. 'They are the perfect planes for them,' he said 'They fly long distances, land on short runways and with the seats removed hold up to 12,000 pounds of cargo.'

Searches for the two planes involved the Ecuadorean Air Force and army patrols, a United States Air Force C-130 search plane and a helicopter with sophisticated laser reconnoitring devices. None of the searches were successful. And Commander Reinaldo Lazo, the United States Military Liaison Chief, said the C-130 crew had reached no conclusions after either of the week-long searches.

James Kuykendall, the Ecuador representative of the United States Drug Enforcement Administration, said his agency had found names of people with narcotics trafficking records on the passenger lists of the missing aircraft. He said his agency had no idea what had happened to the flights.

Saeta's Major Serrano, however, is more certain. He believes the passengers were pressed into service harvesting marijuana. The missing included 74 men, 36 women and 6 children – ranging from farm workers to doctors and lawyers.

Guillermo Jaramillo, a Quito lawyer whose 39-year-old son Ivan disappeared on the second flight, organized a committee of the grieving families to probe the mystery. Together with Saeta, they offered a $325,000 reward for information – without success.

Chapter
Three

Crimes
of Avarice

Conviction Without the Corpse

Life as the wife of a high-powered newspaper executive gave Muriel McKay all the trappings of suburban luxury – elegance a million miles removed from the street-wise world of the popular press in which her husband had made it to the top. Her world revolved around a genteel neighbourhood where every home had been built with the wealthy in mind and through whose letter-boxes you would hardly expect to find the daily diet of sin, sex and sensation which was the trademark of husband Alick's down-market journals of mass-appeal. But on the evening of Monday 29 December 1969, the McKays' world was turned, ruthlessly and without warning, upside down ...

Alick McKay, number two to newspaper tycoon Rupert Murdoch and deputy chairman of the huge-circulation *News of the World*, returned home shortly before 20.00. From the outside, everything looked normal at St Mary House in Arthur Road, Wimbledon, south-west London. It was only after he had rung the doorbell a second time and discovered that the front door was unlocked – alarming in itself since the couple had agreed to take special care following a burglary a few months previously – that he began to realize that something was seriously wrong.

His worst suspicions were confirmed as he stepped into the hallway. Muriel's black handbag was lying open with its contents strewn half-way up the flight of stairs; the telephone had been hurled to the floor; on the hall table was an opened tin of plasters, a bale of thick twine and a rusty, wooden-handled meat-cleaver. Instinctively, Alick picked up the cleaver and raced upstairs, yelling his wife's name, fearing the intruder or intruders were still in the house.

But Muriel McKay, and whoever else had invaded the family home, had gone. Within minutes, Alick, trying to remain calm, discovered that several items of jewellery, including an eternity ring, a gold and pearl pendant, three bracelets and an emerald brooch, and a small amount of money were missing from Muriel's handbag. His mind racing, Alick ran to a neighbour's to see if anyone had heard or seen what had happened. No one had, and from the house next door he phoned the police.

In similar cases the police approach is generally low-key at the outset. Every possibility has to be examined and, in most cases, the most tangible one

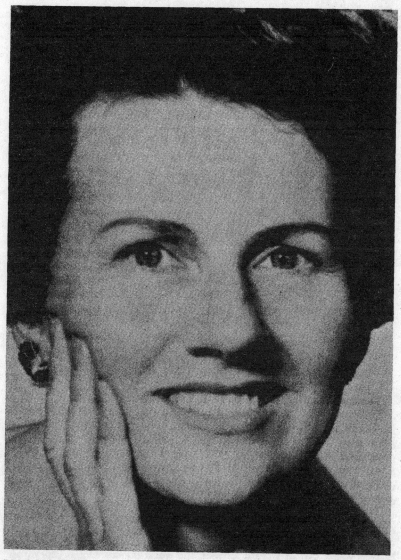

Muriel McKay

is that the person missing has put himself or herself on the missing persons list voluntarily – by simply walking out. And, in an overwhelming number of cases, if there is a culprit to be found, then it is more often than not the spouse who is 'left behind'.

But any thoughts that this was such a case were soon dispelled when, at 01.15 on Tuesday 30 December, the telephone rang at St Mary House. A detective who answered the call beckoned Alick to take the phone as he hurriedly picked up an extension. This was the chilling conversation that followed ...

Caller: This is Mafia Group 3. We are from America. Mafia M3. We have your wife.

McKay: You have my wife?

Caller: You will need a million pounds by Wednesday.

McKay: What are you talking about? I don't understand.

Caller: Mafia. Do you understand?

McKay: Yes, I have heard of them.

Caller: We have your wife. It will cost you one million pounds.

McKay: That is ridiculous. I haven't got anything like a million.

Caller: You had better get it. You have friends. Get it from them. We tried to get Rupert Murdoch's wife. We couldn't get her, so we took yours instead.

McKay: Rupert Murdoch?

Caller: You have a million by Wednesday night or we will kill her. Understand?

McKay: What do I do?

Caller: All you have to do is wait for the contact. That is for the money. You will get instructions. Have the money or you won't have a wife. We will contact you again.

The line went dead as the caller rang off.

Further evidence arrived with the morning post, in a letter sent 12 hours previously from Tottenham, north London. Inside, in faltering handwriting on a piece of blue, lined paper, was a pathetic message. Alick McKay recognized at once the writing of his wife: 'Please do something to get me home. I am blindfolded and cold. Please cooperate for I cannot keep going. I think of you constantly and the family and friends. What have I done to deserve this treatment? Love, Muriel.'

The Muriel McKay case had begun to escalate into a major investigation. And with it came the attendant media 'circus'. As the McKay family closed ranks in the house at Arthur Road, one story upon which the press pack thrived was a call to Gerard Croiset, the world-famous Dutch clairvoyant who counted among his more spectacular successes the accurate pinpointing of the graves of murdered schoolchildren in Britain's notorious Moors Murders case. Croiset's unique powers enabled him to point to an area on a map which was, although largely ignored by police at the time, to prove of great significance: the border of Essex and Hertfordshire, some 40 miles outside London.

By the time a full week had elapsed, however, the police, who by then had a 30-strong team of detectives working full-time on the investigation, were still perplexed. Not one positive lead had emerged, despite the usual combing of underworld contacts and a check of hundreds of jewellers to discover whether Mrs McKay's missing possessions had been 'fenced'. The newspapers were running headline stories such as 'The Case That Does Not Add Up', and the crank callers and con-men, one of whom was later fined for trying to extort money from Alick McKay, were hampering what few inquiries could reasonably be made.

By 6 January every Metropolitan Police officer had been issued with a full description of Muriel McKay, her photograph had been posted on 'Wanted and Missing' boards at police stations throughout the country, Interpol had been alerted and a special watch was being kept on all entry points to Australia, the McKays' country of origin.

The breakthrough came a fortnight later. A large envelope posted from Wood Green, north London, contained another letter from Muriel, which read:

> 'I am deteriorating in health and spirit. Please cooperate. Excuse writing, I'm blindfolded and cold. Please keep the police out of this and cooperate with the gang giving Code M3 when telephoning you. The earlier you get the money the quicker I may come home or you will not see me again. Darling can you act quickly. Please, please keep the police out of this if you want to see me. Muriel.'

Also in the envelope was the ransom demand for one million pounds.

Three more telephone calls from the so-called M3 group came the following day. As the kidnap gang issued a series of demands, rendezvous points and instructions, Alick McKay desperately pleaded for some form of proof that his wife was still alive.

The gang responded with a further letter, accompanied by three pieces of material – one from the green woollen two-piece outfit Mrs McKay had been wearing, another from her black top coat and a snip of leather cut from one of her shoes. From the fourpenny stamp on the envelope, police scientific experts were able to remove a thumb-print. It did not belong to Mrs McKay. Much later it was matched to the thumb of a man called Arthur Hosein.

Police began to plot the ransom handover. It was to be made in two stages – apparently of £500,000 a time. But only £300 of the money, borrowed for the operation from Alick McKay, was to be genuine. The rest would be duds.

A series of attempted drops of the 'ransom money' followed over the next few days, resulting in some farcical mix-ups. The tolerance of the kidnap gang was wearing thin. And to the police, the gang's indecisive, amateurish handling of the actual ransom forced them to consider the possibility that the kidnappers were 'first-timers'.

The crucial day was Friday 5 February. A final call came from the gang: 'If you do not drop the money, she will be dead. You must trust M3. We deal with high-powered telescopic rifles. Anyone trying to interfere with the cases – we will let them have it.'

An elaborate plan was agreed whereby, after a supposedly monitored journey by tube-train and taxi, the money was to be dropped off by a hedge close to a garage on the Bishop's Stortford road in Hertfordshire. This time the plan went like clockwork, with police 'staking out' the drop, ready to swoop on whoever collected the ransom.

It transpired that no one did. But the police, mercifully, had their first stroke of luck. A Volvo 144 car – registration number XGO 994G – was spotted twice circling the drop-off point. It was the same vehicle that had turned up on an earlier, abortive delivery run. It belonged to Arthur Hosein.

Hosein, a Trinidad-born immigrant tailor, had, he believed, finally found his niche in English society when, in 1967, he purchased for the modest price of £14,000 Rooks Farm in Stocking Pelham, Hertfordshire. Two years after he moved in with his German-born wife Else, his younger brother Nizamodeen joined them. They were, from the start, a bizarre family, constantly at odds with their rural neighbours.

Villagers remember how quickly Arthur became known as 'King Hosein', because of his incredible arrogance and boasts that it was his intention to become 'an English gentleman and a millionaire'. It was patently clear, even then, that he exerted an eerie, Svengali-like influence over his younger, easily-dominated brother. Arthur would talk expansively of his 'estate' – and if Nizamodeen ever dared remind him of the more mundane reality of failing, neglected Rooks Farm, he would be severely castigated.

Despite his Walter Mitty existence, however, Arthur did realize that his dreams of vast wealth were unlikely to be fulfilled were he simply to rely on his ailing smallholding. Then, two months before Christmas 1969, an idea for actually making that million took root in the brothers' minds.

They were watching television when they saw what they believed to be the answer to all their problems: the affluence of Rupert Murdoch. The press tycoon was a guest on the popular David Frost show, talking of his newspapers' involvement in the exposé of the notorious Christine Keeler sex-and-politics scandal. References were made to Murdoch's beautiful blonde

Arthur and Nizamodeen Hosein

wife Anna, as well as the sort of enormous sums his newspaper, the *News of the World*, was willing to part with in exchange for exclusive stories.

A crude, but seemingly foolproof plan was hatched to abduct Anna Murdoch and hold her to ransom for one million pounds. The plan was put into operation just after the Christmas break. Only it was Muriel McKay, the wife of Murdoch's second-in-command, who became the target, purely by accident when the bungling brothers got the addresses of the two executives mixed-up; they followed Rupert Murdoch's Rolls-Royce which was being used by the McKays while Murdoch was away.

At 08.00 on the misty morning of 6 February, a squad of 20 detectives, armed with a search warrant obtained by Chief Superintendent Smith of Wimbledon police in west London, walked up the short driveway to the house at Rooks Farm in Stocking Pelham. They told Arthur Hosein's wife Else, who answered the door, that they were making inquiries about a cache of jewellery which had been stolen in London 39 days previously.

At first, Arthur Hosein remained cool enough to cast doubt in the searchers' minds as to whether he might, indeed, be their man. His wife, who seemed understandably irritated at having so many men trample around her home, also showed no signs of stress. And Arthur himself, when questioned about the missing jewellery, calmly replied: 'I know nothing. I earn over £150 a week. I do not deal in stolen property. You can look where you like.'

Look the detectives did. Methodically, painstakingly they began their search of Rooks Farm. It was only a matter of minutes before a vital shred of evidence – the first of many – came to light. From an upstairs bedroom, a young detective constable emerged with some blue and yellow slips of paper, cut into the shape of flowers for the Hosein children, which were identical to scraps found at one of the earlier ransom drop-offs.

A writing pad, on which could be made out the indentations of words that had been written on a previous page, was taken away. Experts later matched the indentations to one of the pathetic letters Muriel McKay had been forced to write by her captors. More sinisterly, a shotgun, the double-barrels of which had been sawn down in the fashion now favoured by criminals, was discovered. Moreover, it had recently been fired. Later, a key witness was to say he had heard a single shot ring out from the direction of Rooks Farm several days earlier.

The mounting evidence then took a nightmarish turn – one which was to lead to the most grisly of theories and seal forever the mystery which surrounds the Muriel McKay case. Police discovered a billhook, recently used to slaughter animals, in the farmhouse. At the time of this sinister discovery, Arthur Hosein casually commented: 'I borrowed it from a farmer friend. I wanted to chop up a calf. It was Nizam [Arthur's pet name for his brother] who did the chopping. We fed it to the dogs and put the bones and head with the rubbish.'

The information was not, perhaps, sinister in itself. But allied to the fact that the Hosein brothers had recently sold a number of pigs at market, and that traces of bone were found in the fire at their house, police began to ponder the dreadful theory that Muriel McKay may have been murdered ... and then fed to the pigs.

Had they ever been able to trace the livestock the brothers sold, they might have found the traces of cortisone – a drug Mrs McKay had been prescribed by the family doctor – which would have proved the unthinkable. But the body of Muriel McKay never was discovered. Exactly how she died, where she died and when she died remains unsolved. The considerable efforts of the police to elicit a full confession from the Hosein brothers proved – and still prove – futile.

The brothers were found guilty of the murder of Muriel McKay, even in the absence of her body. The massive weight of circumstantial evidence which the police collected against them was compounded by the matching of Arthur Hosein's fingerprints to those not only on the letters from the 'M3 gang' to the McKay family, but also on a copy of the *Sunday People* newspaper which, ironically, the brothers had dropped in the drive of the McKays' house when they staged the kidnap.

During three days of intensive interrogation at Kingston Police Station in Surrey, the true characters of the Hosein brothers emerged. Weak, easily-dominated Nizamodeen cracked quickly, and twice tried to take his own life. At one stage, when asked where he was on the night of 29 December 1969, he replied in a state of panic: 'Oh, my! What has Arthur done to me? Where did Arthur say I was? I was with my brother Arthur.' Later, he threw his arms around a detective's shoulders and sobbed: 'Kill me. What have I done? Arthur always gets me into trouble. Kill me now.' Nizamodeen's defence lawyers even found it difficult to communicate with him. In deep shock, he completely refused for six weeks even to discuss the murder case with them, until finally they persuaded him to study statements made by the prosecution witnesses.

In contrast, Arthur, while never confessing to the murder of Mrs McKay, put on a show of bravado. Described by one senior officer as 'an aggressive psychopath', he would sit in the interview room dictating statements at a ferocious pace. At one stage he boasted to his interrogator that he intended to write a book about the McKay case and turn it into a film, starring Richard Burton as the policeman in command and Sammy Davis Junior as himself. Arthur's bombast and apparent unconcern at the charge of murder he was facing astonished detectives.

Even during their trial at the Old Bailey eight months after their arrest, the brothers played out their completely contrasting roles. Nizamodeen, pale and trembling, could barely be heard giving evidence in the witness-box, even with a microphone strapped around his neck. Arthur, on the other hand, was full of himself as ever. Having convinced himself he would be acquitted – a belief he confided to cellmates and police alike – he launched into an astonishing diatribe when convicted by the jury, yelling at the judge, Mr Justice Sebag Shaw: 'Injustice has not only been done, it has also been seen and heard by the gallery to have been done. They have seen the provocation of your lordship and they have seen your immense partiality.' Unmoved, the judge passed life sentences on both brothers, with further 25-year and 15-year sentences of imprisonment on Arthur and Nizamodeen respectively for the other charges relating to Mrs McKay's abduction.

During the months between the Hoseins' arrest and their trial, the police continued their desperate, fruitless search for the body of Muriel McKay. One inmate who shared a cell with Arthur while on remand claimed that he had told him that the body was disposed of in a reservoir. Police drained the huge site Arthur had named but, again, to no avail. The story was dismissed as having been either another instance of Arthur's many fantasies or an attempt by his fellow prisoner to swap phoney evidence for some sort of remission deal.

Eventually the police were forced to abandon their search – leaving forever three vital, unanswered questions. They are still unsolved: how was she murdered, when was she murdered and where was she murdered? Was she, it is still suggested, the victim of an indescribable fate and fed to the pigs of Rooks Farm? Only two men know the answers: Arthur and Nizamodeen Hosein.

In a final, heart-rending postscript to one of Britain's most perplexing, unsolved cases, the *Sun* newspaper published a statement from Alick McKay the morning after the trial of the Hoseins ended. It said:

'One can accept death in the ordinary way. It is something which has to be faced and one has to adjust one's life to take account of it.

But in these circumstances, one is unable to accept the explanation of death without finding a body, although I am convinced Muriel is never coming home again. I must face this situation of course and face my life as best I can.

I suppose I do not want to know the brutal facts really, and yet I must always ask, how did she die, what happened to her, where is her body?

However much I try to escape the tragedy and hurt of it, I suppose I really would like to know the answers ...'

Doctor Death

An 84-year-old retired doctor died in July 1983 in the genteel Sussex seaside resort of Eastbourne. His passing might have warranted no more than a paragraph in the local paper, but for one thing ... The doctor, John Bodkin Adams, was believed by many to be a man who literally got away with mass murder. And it was only upon his death that newspapers could safely produce their dossiers on the astonishing case, in which Adams was tried at the Old Bailey for the murder of one of his patients, Edith Morrell, a 72-year-old widow. If he had been convicted he would have been charged with further murders. Two other charges had been prepared and the Crown believed it had sufficient evidence to prosecute three other cases.

Early in the investigation one of the policemen involved, Scotland Yard Detective Chief Superintendent Charles Hewitt, believed Adams killed nine of his elderly patients. He later increased his estimate to 25, believing that Adams had probably 'eased' many others out of this world after influencing them to change their wills in his favour.

But none of this came to light at the Old Bailey. Adams was acquitted after a classic courtroom duel between the then Attorney-General, Sir Reginald Manningham-Buller QC, and a brilliant defence lawyer, Geoffrey Lawrence.

Lawrence disliked his client intensely but he fought tigerishly, turning the Attorney-General's over-confidence against him in a brilliant tactical coup which is still recalled and admired by lawyers. Manningham-Buller was certain he would destroy Adams once he had him in the witness-box. Lawrence simply told Adams to exercise his right to remain silent – and thus avoid cross-examination. It was that, the police and prosecution believed, that saved him from the rope. For with the linchpin of the Crown's case snatched away, the jury took just 45 minutes to find him not guilty.

The trial was such a disaster that the Director of Public Prosecutions lost confidence that a conviction on any other charge could be procured. So he announced there would be no further action.

What the jury never knew – and could not in law be told – was that the police had investigated the deaths of a further 400 of his patients. They had also exhumed the bodies of two of the women who had not been cremated. They had prepared cases on the deaths of nine patients and had evidence pointing to the murder of many others.

The police knew that over his 35 years of practice in Eastbourne, Adams had been the beneficiary of 132 wills, amassing £45,000 in cash – worth ten

77

Dr John Bodkin Adams

times that today – antique silver, jewellery, furniture and cars, including two Rolls-Royces, from the bequests of dead patients.

So was John Bodkin Adams merely a plausible rogue or was he the most cunning mass murderer of the century?

He was certainly the most fashionable doctor in Eastbourne, a town where the elderly could spend their last days peacefully in genteel retirement. He had arrived there virtually straight from medical school in his native Northern Ireland and built up a good practice with the cream of the town as his patients.

He was an ugly man, only 1.7 m (5 ft 5 in) tall and weighing almost 114 kg (18 stone), with a pink fleshy face, small eyes and thin lips and a rolling chin that sagged over the celluloid collars he wore. But to his elderly women patients he was charming. He caressed their hands and combed their hair.

However, the picture painted by the year-long investigation by Mr Hewitt, then a sergeant, and his 'governor' Detective Chief Superintendent Bert Hannam of the Yard's Murder Squad, was this:

Adams made his victims dependent on his drugs. They craved his morphine and heroin and became addicts. He influenced them to change their wills in his favour. Then they died.

His method, the police claimed, was not startling, shocking or gory. He eased them gently out of life with an overdose of drugs.

Scotland Yard's investigations showed that of all the patients for whom Adams signed death certificates, he explained an improbable 68 per cent as being due to either cerebral haemorrhage or cerebral thrombosis.

Even before the war there was gossip that Adams did his rounds with a bottle of morphia in one pocket and a blank form in the other. In 1936 he had been the beneficiary in the will of Mrs Alice Whitton, to the extent of £3,000 – a substantial amount then. Her niece contested the will in the High Court but Adams won and kept the money.

The tongues continued to wag into the mid-1950s. But it was not until 1956 that police investigations actually began and the evidence started to build, much of it circumstantial.

There was the case of William Mawhood, a wealthy steel merchant, who was such a long-standing friend of Adams that he lent him £3,000 to buy his first house. As Mawhood lay dying, Adams asked his wife Edith to leave the bedside for a moment. She heard Adams say: 'Leave your estate to me and I'll look after your wife.'

Mrs Mawhood rushed back into the bedroom. She said later:

'I grabbed my gold-headed walking stick and struck out at the doctor and chased him around the bed. He ran out of the room and as he dashed down the stairs I threw my stick at him. Unfortunately it missed, and broke a flower vase. I shouted to him to get out of the house. It was the last I wanted to see of him. I certainly would not tolerate the idea of Adams trying to get into my husband's will.'

There was the case of Emily Mortimer, whose family had a strict tradition, designed to keep its fortune intact. Whenever a Mortimer died, the bulk of the estate was divided among the surviving members of the family.

Adams persuaded Emily to break the tradition. In the year she died, she added a codicil to her will, transferring £3,000 worth of shares from the family to the doctor. Shortly before her death, she changed the will again so that Adams received £5,000 and members of the family were cut out. Adams signed the death certificate – the cause of death 'Cerebral thrombosis'.

Police discovered the case of the two old women who were persuaded by Adams to let him sell their house and move into a flat for the good of their health. He then refused to hand over the money from the house sale until forced to do so by a writ two years later.

Statements from local solicitors and bank managers on the doctor's insistent concern with the wills of his patients revealed a host of questionable activities. Visits to banks with patients to change details of wills already made; telephone calls to solicitors insisting on their immediate attendance to change or draw up a new will; a comatose patient who signed his altered will only with an X; wills changed on several occasions so that the deceased were cremated instead of buried as originally stipulated; and 32 cheques for the doctor amounting to £18,000 drawn on one old lady's account in the last few days of her life – and with highly suspect signatures.

Odious as such unprofessional behaviour was, it was not evidence of intent to murder. There was, however, plenty of other evidence ...

Clara Neil-Miller was an elderly spinster who had lived in genteel retirement with her sister Hilda for 13 years. When Hilda died she left everything to Clara. When Clara died, 13 months later, she bequeathed the bulk of her estate – £5,000 – to Adams.

Three years later the police exhumed both bodies and the post-mortem showed that Clara had died of pneumonia, not coronary thrombosis as Adams had put on the death certificate. Then one of the other guests in the rest home for the elderly where she died told the police:

'Dr Adams was called to Miss Clara the night before she died. She was suffering from influenza. He remained in her bedroom for nearly 45 minutes before leaving. I later became worried as I heard nothing from the room. I opened the door and was horrified by what I saw.

This was a bitterly cold winter's night. The bedclothes on her bed had been pulled back and thrown over the bedrail at the base. Her nightdress had been folded back across her body to her neck. All the bedroom windows had been flung open. A cold gush of wind was sweeping through the room. That is how the doctor had left her.'

Police found that, in addition to the £5,000 bequest, Clara had, in the weeks before her death, made out cheques for £300 and £500 to the doctor. The purpose was not clear. It could not be for medical treatment as, apart from the flu, she was not ill. Nor did she receive much in the way of medicines.

Adams had a financial interest in the rest home and sent many patients there. A potential key witness was the woman who ran it, Mrs Elizabeth Sharp. Ex Detective Chief Superintendent Hewitt recalled:

'Mrs Sharp was on the point of talking when we left Eastbourne for a week's conferences with the Attorney-General in London. She was the witness we needed. She knew much of what went on between Adams and his patients. She knew where the bodies were buried and she was scared and frightened. When we left, she was about to crack.

One more visit was all we needed, but when we were in London she died. When we got back to Eastbourne and heard the news, she had already been cremated on the doctor's instructions.

I always had a feeling, but no positive clue, that Adams speeded her on the way. It was too much of a coincidence when she died.'

Then there was the case of Julia Bradnum, a strong and healthy 82-year-old until one morning when she woke up with stomach pains. The doctor was called and remained in the room with her for five minutes. Ten minutes later she was dead.

Her body was also exhumed but it was too decomposed to show much more than that she had not died of the cerebral haemorrhage Adams' certificate claimed.

Only a few weeks before she died Adams had brought her a new will. He said something about her other will not being legal, she later told a friend, Miss Mary Hine. 'She asked me if I would witness the new one,' Miss Hine said. 'Dr Adams pointed to a spot on the paper where I was to sign. I turned over the paper to see what I was witnessing, but Dr Adams put his hand on the writing and turned it back.'

Another of the doctor's patients was Harriet Maud Hughes, aged 66, whom Adams had started to treat only three months before her death of 'cerebral thrombosis'. She spoke of changing her will in his favour. A few weeks before her death, she became ill but then recovered sufficiently to go to her bank with the doctor, who asked the bank manager in her presence to make him the executor of her will. Afterwards, she told her domestic help:

'You should have seen the bank manager's face. He was most surprised at my choice of executor.'

After her death it was discovered that she had added two codicils to her will. The first that she should be cremated. The second, added a month later, left £1,000 each to a Mr and Mrs Thurston, acquaintances of Dr Adams. After the death, the police discovered Adams received 90 per cent of the bequests – giving the Thurstons 10 per cent for the use of their name.

Then there was the case of James Priestly Downs, a wealthy retired bank manager and widower who in his last days tried nine times to sign his will while in a drugged state. On the tenth occasion he signed it with an X. Adams guided his hand. The will left the doctor £1,000. All Mr Downs was being treated for was a fractured ankle. After a fortnight of the treatment, however, he was in a coma. A month later he died.

Annabelle Kilgour was a widow who had been ill for several weeks and was being looked after by a State Registered Nurse, Miss Osgood. One night Adams arrived and said he would give an injection to help her get a good night's sleep.

The nurse was astounded as she watched the doctor give what she regarded as being greatly in excess of the normal dose. 'This will keep her quiet,' he said, and left.

It did. She immediately fell into a coma and died the next morning. When Adams arrived, the nurse told him: 'Mrs Kilgour is dead. You realize, doctor, that you have killed her?'

The nurse later told the Yard men: 'I have never seen a man look so frightened in all my life.'

Once again Adams gave the cause of death as cerebral haemorrhage. In her will, Mrs Kilgour left the doctor a sum of money and an antique clock.

Margaret Pilling, a member of one of Lancashire's richest cotton families, was suffering from nothing more serious than flu when Adams was called to her. Within a fortnight she was practically in a coma. But her family insisted she should go to stay with them.

Her daughter, Mrs Irene Richardson, said later:

'At first we thought she was dying of cancer and that the doctor was being kind by not telling us. But we held a family conference and decided we were not satisfied with the treatment. Whatever her illness, she was definitely being drugged. Her condition was deteriorating rapidly.'

We took a house for her at Ascot, near one of her relatives. Within a fortnight she was on her feet and at the races. Had I not taken her away, I am quite satisfied she would have died.

But the case that really clinched the matter, as far as the police were concerned, was when Bobbie Hullett, a friend of the Chief Constable Richard Walker, died. Mrs Hullett, a vivacious woman of 49 widowed four months earlier, was not even really ill.

Late in 1955 her husband Jack, a retired Lloyds underwriter, became ill. 'Thank God I have a good doctor,' he told one of his nurses. When he was stricken by a heart condition one night in March the next year, the 'good doctor' sat on his bed and injected a dose of morphia. Seven hours later Jack Hullett died. In his will he left Adams £500. The residue went to Bobbie, who was shocked and grief-stricken. Friends rallied round – none more so than Adams, who prescribed drugs to help her sleep. In four months she was dead.

Perhaps in the beginning the sleeping drugs were a wise practice. But as the weeks passed the dosage was not cut down. The domestic staff said later: 'She staggered downstairs most mornings as though she was drunk.'

One of her closest friends was comedian Leslie Henson. He said: 'Her death shocked me greatly. My wife and I saw her turning into a drug addict. We invited her to our home to get away from everything, but she rushed back after 24 hours to get to her pills again. We saw her disintegrating mentally through them.'

After her death another of her friends, Chief Constable Walker, began to make a few discreet phone calls. It was established that two days before Bobbie fell into the coma from which she never recovered, she gave Adams a cheque for £1,000. He immediately drove to the bank and asked for a special clearance. Within hours the amount was credited to his account. At the time, Dr Adams' bank accounts had £35,000 in them. With his investment holdings amounting to a further £125,000, he was not exactly in urgent need of money.

At the inquest, Adams was severely criticized by the coroner for his diagnosis and treatment. A number of penetrating questions were asked. Why had he not told his co-doctor, called in as a second opinion, of his patient's depressive medical history? Why had he failed to get proper daytime medical attention for her or had her put in a nursing home? Why, after 34 years as a doctor, did he take the advice of a young house surgeon in administering a new drug? Why had he failed to call in a psychiatric consultant? And why had he persisted in his diagnosis of a cerebral catastrophe after a pathologist had suggested it might be poisoning?

The doctor replied: 'I honestly did what I thought was best for her.'

The coroner was unimpressed. 'There has been an extraordinary degree of careless treatment,' he said.

And that was the moment that Chief Constable Walker called in Scotland Yard.

So what went wrong? Why, in the face of all this evidence, was John

Bodkin Adams not charged with other offences? Why did the prosecution choose to concentrate on the case of Edith Morrell, the 72-year-old widow of a wealthy Liverpool shipping merchant?

One prosecution lawyer said afterwards: 'We chose it because it was such a clear and obvious case of murder that I should have thought no jury could have regarded it in any other way.'

But Mr Hewitt says:

'Adams was allowed to escape because the law made an ass of itself. I will never forget that conference we had with Manningham-Buller in the Attorney-General's office at the House of Commons. Bert Hannam and I felt sick with disbelief when he announced he was going for Mrs Morrell. It was madness when we had so many better cases, with more specific evidence – and, what's more important, with bodies.

Mrs Morrell had been cremated. This meant we could not use evidence of the best forensic scientist of the day, Dr Francis Camps. But Manningham-Buller was so arrogant he would not listen to his junior counsel, Melford Stevenson and Malcolm Morris, or Mr Leck of the Director of Public Prosecutions' office.

He knew the doctor was a worried man and he would destroy him in the witness-box. But it never happened because Manningham-Buller never considered for a moment that Adams might not be called to give evidence.'

Adams came to trial on 25 April 1957 – six years after Mrs Morrell's death. Prosecution witnesses testified that over a period of six weeks, Adams had prescribed a massive dose of more than 4,000 grains of barbiturate and heroin for Mrs Morrell.

The British Pharmaceutical Association's recommended maximum daily dosage was a quarter morphia grain. But in the last day of her life Adams injected into his barely conscious patient 18 grains of the drug, they said.

But Geoffrey Lawrence managed to discover the nurses' daily record books which gave a more accurate account of the medicine Adams prescribed than the memories of the nurses themselves. Then came his master stroke of not putting Adams into the box.

Three months after his acquittal Adams appeared at Lewes Assizes and pleaded guilty to 14 charges, including the forgery of National Health Service prescriptions and failing to keep a record of dangerous drugs. He was fined £2,400 and ordered to pay costs. In November that year he was struck off by the General Medical Council.

On 22 November 1961, at the age of 62, he was readmitted to the medical register, an event which went largely unnoticed. Only the Home Office retained some doubts: his licence to dispense dangerous drugs was never returned.

His practice in Eastbourne picked up again, although never to its previous size. In 1965, a grateful patient left £2,000 to Adams in her will.

Shortly before his death Adams was interviewed at his Eastbourne home. He refused to talk about his personal life. 'I don't want any more publicity,' he said. 'I have had too much of it. God knows, I have.'

The Nazis' Gold

War is the ideal cover for crime. World war provides an even more effective diversion. While the Nazi war machine fanned across Europe in World War 2, a criminal operation was carried out on the most colossal scale ...

Quite simply, Adolf Hitler and his generals set about systematically stealing the untold wealth of conquered countries in an orgy of blatant crime-for-profit. Like 20th-century pirates, they planned to make themselves rich in plunder at the expense of their victims. They stole not only the few miserable possessions of the millions of Jews they sent to the death camps. They literally stripped sovereign nations of their entire wealth – billions and billions of pounds in gold and diamonds and works of art. From the treasure houses of the former Czars, deep inside Russia, to the art galleries of Paris and the bank vaults of Rome, the Nazis stole and stole and stole.

Even decades after the end of the war, many governments still refuse to admit the extent of the fortunes stolen from them by the Nazis. Intelligence experts on both sides on the Iron Curtain estimate that as much as £50 billion worth of gold is still unaccounted for and that hundreds of Nazi crooks and their families are leading lives of luxury on the proceeds of the biggest robbery in history.

Much of the missing billions is still probably hidden inside Germany, sunk out of reach at the bottom of lakes or in the depths of collapsed mine shafts. Fortunes in gold were certainly channelled through Swiss bank accounts into the coffers of South American governments who charged £5 million a head to give sanctuary to fleeing Nazi criminals at the end of the war. But stunned and sickened by the debris of the war, grimly completing the task of counting the toll in death and destruction, the Allied forces gave a low priority to tracking down stolen cash and bullion. By the time they started trying to recover the astronomical sums of wealth stolen by the Nazis, the fortune had vanished into the creaking remains of the international banking system. Stolen Nazi gold is undoubtedly the basis for many of the multi-national businesses which flourish today.

In their panic-stricken flight, however, many Nazis found the sheer bulk of their loot impossible to move and they literally dumped billions by the roadsides of Europe. Even now those caches of casually hidden treasure are being uncovered. In June 1983 workmen renovating the well of an abandoned monastery in northern Italy, near the Austrian border, found the shaft blocked by heavy metal chests. They finally raised them, and counted 60 tons of gold, worth more than £540 million at 1983 prices.

An embarrassed Italian government then admitted publicly for the first time that the Nazis, their wartime Allies, had emptied the Central Bank of Rome in 1944 and had made off with 120 tons of gold. The scramble to prove ownership of the gold brought a counter-claim from neighbouring Yugoslavia that the bullion was just part of the reserves from their own national bank in Zagreb, looted by Nazi occupying forces and loaded into a convoy of trucks to be driven back to the Fatherland.

Throughout the history of warfare, victorious soldiers have plundered and looted their vanquished opponents. The looters have ranged from humble infantrymen who 'liberated' enemy wine cellars to high-ranking officers who commandeered whole castles for their private estates. Their motto: To the victor belong the spoils.

For Adolf Hitler's Third Reich, however, there was to be no petty thieving. With Teutonic thoroughness, the thefts were to be carried out on a grand scale, meticulously planned and on the direct orders of the Führer himself. Organized bank robbery was as much a declared war policy of the Nazis as the conquest of Europe and the mass murder of the Jews. The formation of an official looting department in the Nazi government was born out of Hitler's smouldering resentment of his fellows.

As a brooding teenager, Adolf Hitler moved to the Austrian town of Linz in 1903, after the death of his father in their home town of Braunau, some 20 miles away. He struggled through school, ignored by teachers and disliked by his fellow pupils, nursing only an ambition to become an artist. When his mother died in 1908, Hitler, then 19 years old, felt free to leave Linz and take his meagre talents to the glittering Austrian capital of Vienna. He marvelled at the city's splendid galleries and museums and his first call was on the Academy of Fine Arts where he applied for enrolment as a student. The

Priceless treasure is unearthed at Hermann Goering's castle

Academy examiners were unimpressed with his barely competent portfolio of drawings and recommended he try for training elsewhere, perhaps in the less demanding profession of apprentice draughtsman.

For the next few years, until he left for Munich in 1913, Hitler seethed with anger as he scraped a miserable living in doss-houses, selling his poorly painted watercolours to bar-room patrons who pitied him because he looked so ragged and pathetic. The experience left him with a sense of humiliation which remained with him for more than 20 years, until he became the all-powerful Führer and annexed Austria into the Greater Germany. That is when Hitler became master of Vienna – and had his revenge on the city he despised.

As he planned to launch war on the rest of Europe, so Hitler also planned his artistic revenge on the cultured city of Vienna. In March 1938, while

Recaptured treasure is inspected at New York's United Nations Galleries

basking in a rapturous welcome from the citizens of the drab town of Linz, his adopted home, he summoned the director of the town's provincial museum, Dr Karl Kerschner. 'I will make Linz the art capital of the world,' he promised him. 'It will have the finest treasures all of Europe can provide. I will make those ungrateful peasants of Vienna feel they are living in a slum.'

Then Hitler, the failed artist, began to sketch out his amateur architectural plans for rebuilding the city, centred around his dream of a Führermuseum which would be crammed with paintings and sculpture, tapestries and rare books, and all the golden treasures he could loot from the four corners of Europe. He sent for his squat, bloodthirsty deputy, Martin Bormann, and instructed him: 'Wherever German tanks roll, I want them to bring back to Linz all the treasures they can carry.'

And so was formed Sonderauftrag Linz – the Linz Special Mission – history's only example of a select gang of gold bullion robbers, diamond, jewel and art thieves, armed with bombers, tanks, high explosives and carte blanche to murder on behalf of their Government. But before the looting gangs bothered to turn their attentions to the treasure houses beyond Germany's boundaries, they first set out ruthlessly stripping the fortunes of their own tortured Jewish population.

While Hitler ordered vaults to be built inside the air-raid shelters of Munich as temporary store-rooms for the Linz collection, his special squad began to 'confiscate' the belongings of Jewish families. Their first target was Baron Louis von Rothschild, the richest man in Austria. Rothschild was arrested by the Gestapo and interrogated by Hitler's roving art and bullion assessor, Dr Hans Posse of the Dresden Art Museum.

Baron Louis was stripped of all his possessions, as a colossal ransom to allow him and his family to leave the country and escape from Nazi persecution. His priceless collection of gold coins was seized, together with all his valuable works of art including paintings by Van Dyck, Holbein, Tintoretto and Gainsborough.

Fortunes fell into Nazi hands even before their armies began to cross the borders into the Netherlands, Belgium and France. As fear and panic spread through the wealthy and well-to-do classes of Europe, Jews and non-Jews alike, homes and possessions were sold at give-away prices and the dwindling assets of great merchant families began pouring into the banks of neutral Switzerland.

Martin Bormann was one of the Nazi hierarchy given the task of trying to harass and bully the Swiss bankers into handing over the accounts of clients whose funds had been earmarked for seizure by the German government. Scornfully oblivious to the wrath of the Nazis, the bank managers of Geneva and Basle stood firm. They would not even discuss the identities of their clients. Ironically, a few years later, that lesson was not to be lost on the Nazi leaders who had cursed the tight-lipped Swiss money men.

As Hitler's war machine rumbled through Europe, with the Führer's hand-picked vultures following in their tracks, the section leaders of Sonderauftrag Linz were swamped. They could no longer cope with the tidal wave of treasure which began piling up in the Munich air-raid shelters. They were furiously building new offices to house the records of their glittering hoard when the most glittering prize of all fell into their hands – Paris.

Enough gold and works of art had already been allocated to the Linz project to transform the town many times over. And now the untold wealth of the Louvre, the Palace of Versailles and the vaults of the Bank of France were at their mercy. Even veteran looter Hans Posse was overwhelmed. So another unit was established specially to supervise the pillage of Paris. Art expert Alfred Rosenberg was given his own top priority organization to strip France of its national heritage and to transport the country's wealth back to Germany.

Rosenberg, son of an Estonian shoemaker, set about his task with gusto, hampered only by the overwhelming greed of the obese Luftwaffe chief Hermann Goering. The air marshal could not resist setting out to build up his own personal fortune, diverting train loads of looted art works and gold to his own private estate, Karinhall, near Berlin.

For four years the Nazi leaders stole everything they could lay their hands on. From Russia came the treasure of the palaces of Emperor Alexander and Empress Catherine. While German infantrymen died of starvation and exposure trying to capture the cities of Stalingrad and Leningrad, the looting sections plundered a total of 427 museums and banks, transporting their booty back to Berlin in fifty special trains each month.

The bank vaults of Poland and Czechoslovakia were stripped and two thirds of the national wealth of Belgium and Holland were stolen. By 1944 it was estimated that the Nazis had plundered a staggering total of £15 billion from occupied countries, worth about twenty times that amount at present-day prices. Goering's own personal fortune was built on his share of 21,903 objects of art shipped back from France.

Then the tide of war turned against the Nazis.

Hitler's dream of his Imperial Museum at Linz began to crumble as Allied bombers hit deeper and deeper into the heart of Germany. With defeat staring them in the face, the Nazis scrambled to dispose of their loot. The salt mines of the remote Austrian village of Alt Ausee were crammed with art treasures and gold, the Hohenfurth monastery, just inside the Czech border, was filled with diamonds and the castle of Schloss Neuschwanstein, near Fussen, Bavaria, packed with bullion. For the demented Führer there was no

Hermann Goering

hiding place where he could scuttle for safety. But those of his accomplices who thought they could save their own skins met in Berlin to form the secret organization Odessa, devoted to financing the escape of the most wanted men in Europe. At their disposal were billions of pounds. War criminals like Bormann, death camp doctor Joseph Mengele and extermination leaders Adolf Eichmann and Walter Rauff began to bless the secrecy of Swiss banks. Using the same well-oiled banking system which had helped to protect some of their victims a few years earlier, the Odessa men funnelled gold through secret accounts to buy themselves new identities and safety in South America. Vast ranches and villas throughout Argentina, Bolivia, Paraguay and Chile were established on the stolen wealth of the men who were never caught, whose crimes are still unpunished. Odessa spent recklessly to finance its fugitives, but it is certain that pockets of Nazi gold still lie undiscovered throughout Europe.

In 1982 Danish naval divers trying to locate sunken Nazi gold in Lake Ornso, in central Jutland, came under sniper fire. The theory police came up with at the time was that it was from a former Gestapo informer who feared the hoard might reveal details of his collaboration in looting Danish banks.

During the final collapse of Germany in May 1945, the most bizarre bank robbery in history took place as American and Russian troops raced each other into the heart of Berlin. The Americans were ordered by General Eisenhower to storm the Reichsbank in Berlin, blow the vaults and transport the contents by jeep and truck back behind American lines for safekeeping. The troops responded enthusiastically, but some £200 million in gold and negotiable Swiss securities went missing on the journey back to American headquarters. Three and a half decades later, in April 1979, three men in Ontario, Canada, were jailed for trading in some of those missing war-time securities. It is also estimated that American soldiers and stragglers from the German Army helped themselves to £90 million in gold bullion, foreign exchange and jewels from the bank. Not a penny was ever recovered and not a single soldier charged with robbery.

But South America was not the only final resting place for missing Nazi gold. In the United States and Europe the fortunes of respectable business empires thrive today on the proceeds of the Nazi looting during World War 2. Yet the wartime Allies have decided that the scandalous details of history's most massive unsolved robberies will never be published. At the headquarters of the British secret service and the World War 2 Records Division of the National Archives in Washington, the files holding the names of the worst criminals and the details of their crimes will remain Most Secret until at least the 21st century – and probably well beyond.

The Unpaid Debt

They called him Mr Big – the playboy gambler who could fix anything from a roulette wheel or stud poker game to the World Series baseball tournament. He lived a life of luxury and thought nothing of betting $4,000 on odd or even car number plates passing his hotel-room window. He won and lost fortunes on horses and cards; he bought and sold cops, politicians and financiers and was rarely seen without a beautiful showgirl on his arm.

Even on the day he was gunned down – 4 November 1928 – he was trying to talk his way out of an $80,000 gambling debt. But that debt, the one thing Arnold Rothstein could not fix, led to his shooting outside Park Central Hotel, New York.

Police were certain Rothstein knew his killer. Only half an hour before the shooting he took a telephone call in a Broadway restaurant. As he left, he told the head waiter: 'George McManus wants me.' Yet Rothstein died in hospital two days later, from a bullet wound in the stomach, without naming his killer. The only thing he did on his deathbed was to make a will – providing generously for his wife Carolyn, for Ziegfeld Follies showgirl Inez Norton (she got more than $100,000) and for friends.

Perhaps the oddest aspect was that the police had plenty of clues – an overcoat, four glasses and a revolver – yet they failed completely to get a conviction. The owner of the overcoat was another gambler, George McManus. The glasses and revolver were covered in fingerprints, some of them almost certainly those of known hoodlums. Only McManus was charged with the murder. He pleaded not guilty and was acquitted because of insufficient evidence. That was the end of the police investigation. Nobody else was charged and the case went on the 'unsolved' files.

There was talk at the time that McManus and his henchmen had 'nobbled' the cops. The then police commissioner was soon swept out of office. It is also possible that the police may have taken the view that since Rothstein was part of the underworld, his killer had done society a service ...

In his 46 years Rothstein had become the 'King of the Gamblers'. He hobnobbed with gangsters such as Al Capone, Dion O'Bannion and Big Jim Colosimo and wagered around $10,000,000 on games of chance. He once backed Jack Dempsey to beat Jess Willard in a world heavyweight fight and won $200,000. He picked up $300,000 when he backed Gene Tunney against Dempsey. And in what he described as the 'biggest gamble of my life' he won almost $300,000 when a horse called Sidereal won at the Aqueduct track, Long Island, on Independence Day, 1921, at odds of 30-1.

Poker was another of his passions – and it was this that was to cost him his life. He sat in on a stud poker game with George McManus and other gamblers including 'Titanic' Thompson, so-called because of his reputation for 'sinking' opponents. At the end of two days and nights Rothstein owed $150,000. His biggest creditor, Nathan Raymond, to whom he owed $80,000, was in no mood to wait for his money. Rothstein had never welshed on a bet in his life. But this poker debt was to prove the exception. One underworld theory was that Rothstein had suspected he had been cheated, though he never made any accusation. It would certainly explain his reluctance to settle up – for he had assets to cover the debt many times over.

Over the next few weeks the gangster-gamblers put the squeeze on. But still Rothstein refused to pay up. Then on that fateful Sunday night in November, Rothstein went to Room 439 at Park Central Hotel to make his excuses to McManus.

The theory is that there was a lot of whiskey drunk and a lot of shouting – then McManus or one of his henchmen pulled a gun. Rothstein tried to wrest the gun from his killer, but in the struggle it went off and Rothstein fell to the floor. McManus and his gang fled, throwing the gun out of the window. Somehow Rothstein then staggered down two flights of stairs to the street. Police believe that Rothstein was murdered in the heat of the moment. Only one shot was fired – and gangsters intent on murder, they reasoned, usually pumped their victims full of lead.

But they are just theories. And George McManus, the one man who could have proved or disproved them, died in New Jersey in 1940 of natural causes.

The Black Widow

For a woman who did very little farming, widow Belle Gunness ate very well. While her neighbours in La Porte, Indiana, raised crops, Belle planted bodies and produced a bumper yield of dollars.

Once she had been Mads Sorenson's wife – but thanks to a stein of beer she gave him in their home on Lake Michigan, their marriage did not last long. The beer was generously laced with strychnine, and the self-made widow had Mads cremated before the insurance investigators knew what was happening. The company objected, but the policy brought her $8,500.

She had no trouble finding a new husband. At 31, Belle was still an attractive woman. It was an attraction that was to prove fatal for real estate promoter Peter Gunness of La Porte. Belle married Gunness and had three children – two girls and a boy –and a domestic life with which she was satisfied till the day the money ran out.

One day in December 1902, Gunness told Belle he was down to his final asset: a $10,000 insurance policy that would have to be cashed. He had invested everything in real estate options near a railroad that had never been built. Belle helped him find the policy and went with him to the door. As he turned to kiss her goodbye, she raised a meat cleaver and smashed it into his skull.

Gullible police accepted her story that Gunness had slipped on the icy pathway and had split his own skull against the doorstep. But the insurance underwriters were more suspicious and there was an investigation that lasted for months before Belle could cash her second husband's cheque.

Belle then began to publish advertisements in the lonely hearts columns of a Minneapolis newspaper. The bait was her sumptuous 12-room house on a 75-acre farm 'adjoining a boulevard'. And even more tempting to greedy or lonely men were her personal charms. She picked through the replies with care. She wanted men without relatives – but with plenty of cash.

George Berry of Tusca, Illinois, came first, in July 1905. He had obediently brought his life savings, $1,500 in cash. But he was puzzled by the sight of Belle, who had now become fat, walked with a waddle and had a growth of hair on her lip. She decoyed him from the station to her farmhouse with assurances that she was only the beautiful widow's maid. And while he waited patiently for the beauty to appear, she approached him through a side door with a well-honed axe in hand.

In the next year the farm had three other visitors all with their nest-eggs in hand. None were to leave.

In 1908 the black widow's pit claimed two more bodies. One was Andrew Helgelien, who wrote to Belle from Aberdeen, South Dakota – but chose to conceal the fact that he had an older brother named Asle.

When Asle heard nothing from his brother for two weeks, he sent a pointed letter of inquiry to Mrs Gunness. The widow replied that her Andy had mysteriously disappeared and begged Asle to come to La Porte and join her in the quest, bringing with him all the money he could raise. But the man who arrived was not Asle at all, it was the sheriff of La Porte county, tipped off by the suspicious brother. The widow pleaded for time. She had just heard from Andy, she told the sheriff, and would be able to produce the missing man if he came again the following day.

But the sheriff had to return to the murder farm before the end of the day. He was greeted by a curtain of red flame against the sky. It was the Guinness farmhouse, its old timbers reduced to charcoal in a matter of minutes. Under freshly turned earth at the back of the barn, the sheriff found six corpses. The first was that of Andrew Helgelien. In the ashes of the house were four more bodies – three of them small, one large. Belle and her children?

The authorities wanted to believe so, but there was macabre evidence which meant they could never close the file on Belle Gunness. A witness said that an hour before the fire he had seen the widow drive past his farm with a wagon and a team of horses. And in one of the local cemeteries next day, there were reports of mysterious vandalism – the gravestones of an adult and three children had been dislodged.

Unrelenting to the end of his life, Asle Helgelien went on looking for the widow. He never found her.

The Wreck of the Chantiloupe

When winter storms lash the sea to boiling and great waves pound across the bay, villagers snug in their cottages shudder at the memory of a hideous crime that taints them still. There are those who swear that, above the roar of the wind and breakers crashing on the shore, they have heard the screams of men and women who perished in a shipwreck more than 200 years ago.

But not all those who died were victims of the cruel elements. At least one, a wealthy woman passenger, was killed for her jewellery by heartless looters. Their names have remained a shameful secret ever since.

In summer, Thurlestone Sands, in south Devon, ring with the happy laughter of romping children, and the sunbathers soak up the warmth. But in winter, long after the last holidaymaker has gone home, as the gales howl in from the Atlantic, it is easy to picture the last moments of the Plymouth-bound brig *Chantiloupe* in 1772.

It had been a smooth voyage from the West Indies but, as she neared port, a south-westerly gale blew up so suddenly that there was no time to turn into it. The captain's only choice was to run before it, past Plymouth and up the Channel. Soon, with massive cliffs looming ahead, he was forced to strike sail and drop all anchors. But nothing could hold the *Chantiloupe* against the raging wind and sea, and the captain decided on a desperate gamble to save his passengers and crew.

Ordering full sail, he altered course by a few degrees and headed directly for the smooth, golden carpet of Thurlestone Sands. He told passengers and crew that he aimed to run his ship high up the beach, so they could all jump to safety.

The passengers hurried to their cabins to collect what valuables they could. One of them, Mrs James Burke, whose nephew was the famous Whig politician Edmund Burke, came on deck in her finest gown wearing all her jewellery.

The small ship raced for the shore as though on wings, carried on the shoulders of mighty waves, and it seemed the captain's daring bid would succeed. But one wave, higher than the rest, suddenly hoisted the stern. The keel beneath the bows struck bottom and the *Chantiloupe* swung broadside, almost capsizing under the next wave.

All on board were hurled into the raging sea, and most died within minutes. But Mrs Burke struck out for the shore and, miraculously, reached it alive. Gratefully she let strong hands grasp her and pull her from the water.

But these three men were not rescuers ... they were thieves and killers. Barely had her last scream been carried away by the wind before they were fighting over her jewels.

They ripped off her earrings and, finding her rings too tight to remove, hacked off her fingers. Then they buried her in the sand, and soon the raging sea had washed away any traces of the killing.

Perhaps it would never have come to light, if a man had not happened to walk his dog past the burial spot two weeks later. He was Daniel Whiddon, later to be immortalized in the folk song 'Uncle Tom Cobleigh'. His dog began scrabbling in the sand and unearthed Mrs Burke's body.

The secret was out, and the local paper reported the crime in these words:

'The savage people from the adjacent villages, who were anxiously waiting for the wreck, seized and stript her of her clothes, even cutting off some of her fingers and mangling her ears in their impatience to secure the jewels and left her miserable to perish.'

There was an autopsy, which showed that Mrs Burke was alive when she reached the shore. An inquest, before the jury of local men, returned the verdict: 'Murder by person or persons unknown.'

There can be no doubt that some people in the nearby villages of Thurlestone Sands, Galmpton, Hope and Bolberry, knew the identity of the killers. But lips were sealed. Edmund Burke himself visited the area to seek the truth, and learned nothing.

More than 100 years later, the Rev Frank Coope, Rector of Thurlestone from 1897 to 1921, probed the mystery. He wrote: 'It was well known in the neighbourhood who did it, and their surnames are remembered to this day. The three men who were "in it" all came, it is said, to a bad end within the year. One hanged himself in an outhouse, another went mad, ran into the sea and was drowned, and the third was killed in an accident.'

Was this the truth – or a tale to put the rector off the scent?

Today the neatly thatched villages around Thurlestone Sands are picturesque and welcoming. But behind the whitewashed walls and stout oak doors, there may still be families who know the names of those long-ago killers.

Chapter
Four

Vanishing
Tricks

The Disappearing Parachutist

The skyjacker who commandeered the Northwest Airlines Boeing 727 flight from Portland, Oregon, to Seattle, Washington, was cold, calculating and ruthless. He terrified the cabin staff when he opened the canvas bag he was carrying in his lap and showed them a home-made bomb – tightly wrapped sticks of dynamite packed round a detonator.

As the jet cruised at 6,000 m (20,000 ft) above the Cascade Mountains, he threatened to blow apart the aircraft, killing himself and the 35 other passengers on board.

But the man who cruelly bargained with the lives of the passengers and the crew pulled off such a daring and lucrative coup that he is now fondly remembered as a folk hero, a swashbuckling pirate of the jet age. Songs have been written in his honour, fan clubs have been formed to cherish his memory and thousands of his admirers wear T-shirts emblazoned with his name. The souvenir industry and the posters in praise of D. B. Cooper would undoubtedly carry his photograph and glowing testimonials about his personal history – if anyone knew what he looked like or who he really was.

But the true identity of the man who literally vanished into thin air with his $200,000 booty still remains a mystery. No-one knows who he was, where he came from or where he went.

D. B. Cooper may be a frozen corpse, a broken body lying in a mouldering heap of banknotes in an impenetrable forest in the mountains of the northwestern United States. Or he may be sunning himself on a beach in Mexico and gloating over his perfect crime.

The last confirmed sighting of D. B. Cooper came from the pilot of the Boeing air liner from which the skyjacker leaped clutching a white cloth bag containing ten thousand $20 bank notes. Cooper vanished into thin air at 2,000 m (7,000 ft) as the air whistled past in a 90 metre per second (200 m.p.h) slipstream at a temperature of $-23°C$ ($-10°F$).

That was the last time 'D. B. Cooper' was seen. The first time was in the departure lounge at Portland Airport, Oregon, when he bought his one-way ticket for the 400-mile journey to Seattle, Washington. It was 24 November 1971 – Thanksgiving Day – and the other travellers were all anxious to get home to their families for the annual holiday celebration.

The quiet middle-aged man with the canvas carrier bag and dark, tinted glasses paid cash for his ticket and gave his name as 'D. B. Cooper'. After a 45-minute wait in the lounge, where no one looked at him twice, he filed aboard when the flight was called and the jet roared off into the darkening skies.

Halfway through the one-hour flight, Cooper pushed the button in the overhead panel to summon one of the cabin crew to his seat. Stewardess Tina Mucklow approached with a tray, ready to take his order for a drink.

Cooper simply thrust a crumpled note into her hand and then reached under his seat to pull his canvas bag on to his lap. He waited a few seconds for the stewardess to read the note. It warned: 'I have a bomb with me. If I don't get $200,000 I will blow us all to bits.'

As the terrified stewardess tried to control her panic, Cooper calmly opened the bag to let her glimpse the dynamite and detonator inside. While the girl walked slowly up to the flight deck, Cooper settled back in his seat and peered out at the storm clouds below.

Within seconds a special transmitter on the flight deck of the Boeing was 'squawking' its coded electronic message over the radio frequencies ... 'Hijack ... Hijack ... Hijack ...'

At Seattle Airport a team of FBI agents, local police sharpshooters, hostage negotiation experts and airline officials were hastily gathered as the plane prepared to land. The passengers were still unaware of the drama when the jet came in for a perfect touchdown and rolled gently to a halt at the end of the runway.

There was a groan of annoyance from the impatient travellers when the captain made the terse announcement: 'Ladies and gentlemen, there will be a slight delay in disembarking. Please remain in your seats until we are ready to taxi to the terminal building.'

Only one passenger ignored the announcement. Cooper unbuckled his seat belt and, clutching his bag, walked swiftly up to the flight deck and positioned himself behind the crew. 'Now gentlemen,' he said softly, 'don't bother to look round.'

In 20 minutes of unyielding demands over the ground control radio from the flight deck of the airliner, Cooper stuck to his original threat and no one dared to call his bluff.

As the passengers began to grow more and more restless, there was a hiss of pneumatic power and the forward door of the Boeing slid open. The flight engineers in overalls – undercover armed FBI men – came aboard with a trolley of 'catering equipment'. They clearly saw the figure of the man with the canvas bag watching them from the flight deck door, then, under instructions by two-way radio from their superiors, they withdrew and the door slid closed and locked again.

The trolley was wheeled up to the flight deck by a stewardess and Cooper studied its contents. It contained a tough white sack with $200,000 and two backpack and two chestpack parachutes.

Cooper complained that he wanted the money in a rucksack which he could have strapped on to his body. But he quickly relented and told the pilot: 'You can let the passengers go now.'

Loudly complaining, the unsuspecting travellers filed off the aircraft to a waiting bus and Seattle ground control breathed a sigh of relief. But they were still left with the problem of Cooper in charge of the aircraft and its three-man crew as the jet was refuelled to maximum capacity by two giant tankers.

Minutes before the Boeing took off again, three military pursuit fighters and a small fleet of helicopters were scrambled from Seattle Airport and a nearby US Air Force base with orders to try to keep the jet in sight.

'We are heading for Mexico now,' Cooper told the pilot, Captain W. Bill Scott. But 10 minutes after take-off he issued new instructions.

As the aircraft climbed away from Seattle and headed south, Cooper insisted with calm precision: 'Fly with the flaps lowered 15 per cent and the landing gear down, keep the speed below 90 metres per second (2000 m.p.h), don't climb above 2,000 m (7,000 ft) and open the rear door.'

'We'll burn up too much fuel,' Captain Scott protested. 'We'll have to put down for some more fuel if we fly like that.'

'OK,' Cooper snapped. 'Stop for refuelling in Reno, Nevada. I'll give you further orders there. Now just fly south and keep the door locked behind you.'

The hijacker paused only briefly on the flight deck to retrieve his ransom note from the captain's tunic pocket. He was determined not to leave any clues behind, not even a sample of his handwriting.

The whole aircraft filled with a deafening roar as the pilot throttled back and lowered the rear door ramp into the slipstream.

When the flight recorder 'black box' was checked later, the sensitive instrument measured a tiny change in the aircraft's altitude, equivalent to the loss of a weight of 73 kg (160 lb) in the tail section. The time was 20.13 hours, 32 minutes after leaving Seattle. That's when D. B. Cooper leaped out.

Four hours later, as the Boeing lost height and glided gently towards the twinkling lights of the airport at Reno in the Nevada Desert, the co-pilot unlocked the flight deck door to warn Cooper that the tail ramp would have to be closed for landing.

The cabin was deserted. Cooper and the money had gone.

Two parachutes had been left behind. A backpack chute was intact but a chestpack was ripped to shreds. Cooper had probably torn it apart to make a harness to strap his sack of money to his body.

The danger of mid-air death and destruction had passed. And the hunt to find D. B. Cooper was on. FBI and Federal Aviation Agency officials who plotted the flight path of the hijacked Boeing quickly realized that Cooper had bailed out over some of the most densely wooded, inhospitable mountains in the American West, where the chances of survival for an inexperienced woodsman were pretty slim. He had plummeted to earth clad only in a lightweight lounge suit, a raincoat and with a pair of flimsy moccasin shoes on his feet. In the thin atmosphere of the high altitude, the parachute would only have slowed him to a bone-crushing 18 metres per second (40 m.p.h.) before he hit the mountain peaks which tower up to the same height as the Boeing had flown.

Only a super-fit expert could have hoped to escape alive. Police began detailed and intensive scrutiny of the only group of men who would have the nerve or experience to attempt that kind of death-defying descent – the 'smoke jumpers' of the Forestry Service fire-fighting teams. But they drew a blank. Cooper was not a 'smoke jumper' and the professional experts who are trained to parachute into the high forests with full radio communication and ground support facilities agreed to a man that Cooper's leap from a speeding jet in a rain storm was suicidal.

Aerial searches covering thousands of square miles of the states of Oregon, Washington and Nevada failed to show any trace of a parachute canopy.

Then, three weeks after the hijack, came the first enigmatic clue. A typewritten note, posted in Seattle and signed by D. B. Cooper, arrived at a Los Angeles newspaper. The writer revealed:

'I am no modern-day Robin Hood, unfortunately I have only 14 months to live. The hijacking was the fastest and most profitable way to gain a few last grains of peace of mind. I didn't rob Northwest because I thought it would be romantic or heroic or any of the other euphemisms that seem to attach themselves to situations of high risk.

I don't blame people for hating me for what I've done nor do I blame anybody for wanting me caught or punished – though this can never happen. I knew from the start I would not be caught. I've come and gone on several airline flights since and I'm not holed up in some obscure backwoods town. Neither am I a psychopath, I've never even received a speeding ticket.'

The note sparked off a new hunt for Cooper and as the list of potential suspects dwindled, hundreds of troops from the Fort Lewis Army base in Portland, Oregon, were ordered to comb the mountains searching for clues. They were backed up by spotter planes and even satellite surveillance photographs from orbiting spacecraft.

There was still no sign of Cooper.

But FBI agents were confident that if Cooper had survived the jump, he would be nailed as soon as he tried to spend a penny of the ransom money. The serial numbers of every one of the bank notes in his haul had been noted and all US banks and major money clearing houses abroad had been alerted to raise the alarm as soon as they began to trickle into circulation.

In the meantime the airlines took the costly precaution of ensuring that no one would imitate Cooper's hijack and high level parachute escape ever again. All Boeing 727s were recalled to the manufacturers and their tail door ramps sealed so they could never be opened in flight.

And as the widely publicised FBI manhunt began to lose steam, the mystery hijacker began to gather a cult following from a fascinated public. Graffiti slogans appeared on public buildings and airline advertising hoardings over the Pacific north west – 'D. B. Cooper, where are you?' Disc jockeys dedicated records to Cooper.

A year after the hijack, when FBI officals adopted the official attitude that D. B. Cooper must have died in the parachute fall, they had to admit that there was no sign of the hijack money and that the $200,000 was probably still hidden with his body in the wooded mountains. Then the first groups of enthusiastic amateur explorers, calling themselves the 'Ransom Rangers', began scouring the woods in Oregon and Washington, searching for the ransom treasure.

Finally on 24 November 1976, the FBI officially closed the file on D. B. Cooper. Five years had elapsed since the crime, so under the Statute of Limitations if D. B. Cooper was alive, he was now a free man.

And not a single dollar of the ransom money had ever turned up. If Cooper was a corpse in the mountains, the money was there with him, just waiting to be found.

Most of the population of Portland and Seattle seemed to catch 'Cooper fever' and the hills were alive with the sound of marching feet. But they scoured the mountains in vain.

The fever subsided until 1979 when a solitary deer hunter in the dense forest above the village of Kelso, Washington, stumbled across a man-made intrusion in the virgin forest. It was a thick plastic warning sign from the tail door hatch of a Boeing 727. Its futile message read: 'This hatch must remain firmly locked in flight.'

Overnight the village became a boom town as thousands of amateur sleuths stormed the peaks trying to find Cooper's treasure one step ahead of the FBI teams who descended by helicopter. Astrologers, mapmakers and local tourist guides made almost as much money as Cooper's missing loot from the hopeful punters.

'The mountains were almost trampled flat by the crowds,' admitted State Police Inspector Walter Wagner. 'But none of us found a thing.'

Had Cooper got clean away with all the cash?

That riddle was partially solved seven and a half years after the hijacking.

Industrial painter Harold Ingram and his son Brian, eight, were wading along the sandy shore of the Columbia River just outside the Washington state border when they stirred up a bundle of weathered banknotes from the river bank.

The money amounted to about $3,000 of Cooper's cash, according to one of the 30 FBI men who cordoned off the Ingrams' family picnic site and fought off the new wave of treasure seekers.

Scientific tests on the bank notes and the mud caked around them showed that the money had probably been washed downstream six years before from an area 80 km (50 miles) upstream – on any one of hundreds of tributaries higher up the mountain range.

The hunters vanished over the rocky skyline, sawing and digging their way through the forests once more.

'That's the closest we ever came to him,' Special Agent John Pringle of the FBI reported. 'But we are still looking for an invisible needle in a mountain range of haystacks.'

If D. B. Cooper is still alive, he can freely identify himself to the FBI now. The legal time limit on his crime means he will never face a criminal prosecution for the Thanksgiving Day hijacking. But there is probably one big obstacle which could prevent the world's only successful skyjacker from coming forward ...

The FBI may have given up, but at the offices of the Internal Revenue in the nation's capital in Washington DC the file on D. B. Cooper remains open forever.

The skyjacker faces a bill for $300,000 – more than his ransom haul – and a 10-year jail sentence for failing to file income tax returns.

The taxman explained:

'We tax illegal money just as we tax legal money; it's all income as far as we are concerned.

D. B. Cooper became $200,000 dollars richer after the hijack and he never paid his tax on that money. Now he owes us interest on that sum and penalty payments. We have assessed his tax liability as a bachelor with no dependants and no additional source of income. If he wants to arrange an appointment with our auditors to claim some allowances and expenses we will be happy to meet him.

Until then we are still looking for Mr D. B. Cooper, and his assets. There is no Statute of Limitations for tax dodgers.'

The Canine Sherlock Holmes

It stands, just over 0.3 m (1 ft) high, as the ultimate, golden goal of some of the world's greatest sporting stars. Whether held high in triumph or simply coveted from afar, the Jules Rimet Trophy is the prize of prizes in the field of professional soccer.

It has embraced the dreams of hundreds of nations, of legendary players such as the great Pele and of literally millions of waving, cheering fanatics from all corners of the globe.

It is more commonly known as the World Cup – a once-in-a-lifetime reward every four years to one country and its eleven most gifted, idolized footballers.

Such is the occasion of its presentation that it is passed into the hands of the football players only from those of kings and queens, presidents and prime ministers.

When it was brought to England a few weeks before the start of the 1966 World Cup tournament it was promptly stolen. The cup over which rival countries had, through the years, fought so bitterly – even off the playing field and in the political arena – was pilfered from a stamp exhibition at London's Central Hall, Westminster, where it had been on display. It was considered an international scandal.

Scotland Yard was summoned immediately. Questions were asked in parliaments around the world. Huge rewards from all sorts of organizations were offered for the cup's safe return. Outside England the mood was hostile and angry, especially in those nations where soccer seems almost to vie with religion for the hearts and souls of the people. No cost or effort was to be spared to restore not only a football trophy, but also national pride, to its rightful place.

The police who had been ordered in hot pursuit of the World Cup thief or thieves found themselves on a cold trail. The trophy had, apparently, vanished into thin air and the hunt for clues or suspects was a bitterly frustrating one. It was unlikely that anyone would have stolen the cup simply to melt it down. The actual gold content was then worth only about £2,000 despite the fact that it was insured for £30,000. The real value, however, was priceless.

Private collectors, undaunted by dealing on the black market to procure their secret hoards of treasure, would have paid a fortune to have the legendary cup in a hidden vault. That was the only theory on which the beleaguered police could pin any hope.

For a fortnight in early March 1966, the world held its breath as the desperate search for the stolen cup continued in vain. It was a tragedy of enormous proportions to dedicated followers of football. But, more than that, it was an almighty embarrassment to England, which was playing host to the prestigious tournament for the first time in its sporting history.

It was vital that the cup was found immediately.

Screaming newspaper headlines posed all sorts of questions, some of them unthinkable to the hierarchy of FIFA, soccer's world governing body ... Was it in the hands of an unscrupulous millionaire? Was it stolen and then simply thrown away to be lost forever when the thief realized the enormity of his crime? Was it being held by a syndicate of villains, waiting to sell it off to the highest bidder?

Had it, been melted down or destroyed? The possibilities were endless.

The answer came, in the most unexpected – and rather unglamorous – way on the night of 19 March.

David Corbett, a 26-year-old Thames lighterman, was taking a family dog, Pickles, for a walk near his home in Beulah Hill, Norwood, South London, when, out of the corner of his eye, he spotted a glint, a reflection that lasted for just a split second.

It had come from what had appeared to be a bundle of dirty old newspapers under a laurel bush that Pickles, a cross-bred collie, had been sniffing and pawing at with great interest. Mr Corbett called to his dog. But Pickles would not come.

As David Corbett recalled later:

'I bent under the bush, lifted the top layer of newspapers, and there it was. I knew what it was at once. It was the World Cup.

I think that the first thing I actually saw was an inscription on the cup. The words 'Brazil 1962' were written near the base. I'm a keen football fan and I had been following all the reports in the newspapers. You can imagine how absolutely taken aback I was.

I took it back to our flat to show my wife Jeannie and then we phoned the police, who were as astounded as we were. Yet the truth is that I would not have given the old bundle of newspapers it was wrapped in a sideways glance or a second thought if it hadn't been for Pickles. He was the real hero of the hour.'

Indeed he was. Animal lovers from all over the world began to shower gifts on the canine sleuth. England's National Canine Defence League bestowed

Pickles and his owner at the *Café Royal* with Henry Cooper

on him its highest honour: a silver medal inscribed with the words 'To Pickles, for his part in the recovery of the World Cup, 1966.' At the ceremony at which it was presented, the league's secretary enthused: 'Pickles, by his action, has given prominence to the canine world and so helped us in our task.'

At the same ceremony – and there were many others for the 'furry Sherlock Holmes' as he was dubbed – a hotel pageboy stepped up with a silver salver of further gifts. There was a rubber bone, £53, collected among the hotel's staff – and the best steak for him to eat.

Pickles, oblivious to the importance of the occasion, simply lay down and yawned.

But the still unanswered question was: who actually stole the World Cup? It was a question, despite a number of suspicions, that the police were never to answer.

Yet, as in all unsolved crimes, when the finger of suspicion is pointed, however wrongly, there are people who are bound to suffer. That, amazingly, was the sad plight of none other than Pickles' owner, Mr Corbett. Less than two months after his alertness helped recover the prized trophy, Mr Corbett told a newspaper:

'I wish I'd never seen the damn thing. I was quite excited about it at the time but I seem to have had nothing but trouble since.

When I gave it to the police, they appeared at first not to believe my story about Pickles finding it under a laurel bush. They grilled me. They asked me where I was on the day the cup was stolen, whether I collected stamps, if I had ever been to Central Hall, Westminster, and so on.

Eventually, they believed me. But the trouble didn't end with the police. Ordinary people have been suspecting me of having had something to do with the theft of the cup. My wife and I were in Trafalgar Square and a group of boys saw us. They shouted at me: "He's the one who stole it. Let's drown the dog in the fountain." It was terrible.'

In the end, of course, Mr Corbett was completely vindicated – and received rewards totalling more than £6,000. He did not watch the World Cup itself, but he did join in the spirit of Pickles's success when he allowed the dog to be taken to meet each member of the West German final team – all of whom touched him for luck, hoping they would find the cup theirs at the end of the football match.

But it was not to be. England took the trophy and, thanks to Pickles, who sadly died only four years later, erased memories of the most embarrassing episode in soccer history.

The Missing Murderers

It is more than half a century since Adolf Hitler brought the Nazis to power in Germany. Just 12 years later they were vanquished, leaving behind the evidence of what has been called the greatest crime in history: the annihilation of Europe's Jews.

The Nazis also left behind a maze of mysteries – a criminal enigma of as great a magnitude as the crime itself. For the full story of the massacre of millions of Jews can never be told until all the missing culprits are brought to account. Only then will the question marks that still hang over history's most shameful act ever be removed.

Many of the mysteries surrounding Hitler's attempted genocide were answered when his death-camp supremo, Adolf Eichmann, was captured by the world's chief Nazi hunter Simon Wiesenthal. But Eichmann's trial and execution did nothing to stop the heated debate that continues to this day about how many of those in German government, judiciary, armed forces and civil service knew and condoned the dreadful pogrom.

In 1983 a few more pieces were fitted into the jigsaw after Klaus Barbie, the wartime Gestapo chief in Lyons, was extradited from Bolivia to face trial in France. It was the excuse for Dr Wiesenthal to update his list of the most wanted Nazis still at large.

Asked why, at the age of 76, he still pursued them from his Jewish Documentation Centre in Vienna, Wiesenthal said:

'When history looks back on this century I want people to know that the Nazis were not able to kill 11 million people and get away with it. Mine is the last organization in the world still hunting the Nazis. If I stopped, the Nazis and history would say, "The Jews gave up."'

Wiesenthal's list at that time named the ten most wanted Nazis, whom he placed in order of responsibility for crime as well as actual criminal activity. He said: 'I have a compact with the dead. If I could get all ten it would be an achievement. Sometimes I think if I could just get Josef Mengele my soul would finally be at peace.'

At that time, Wiesenthal believed he had located Dr Mengele, No. 3 on his list and known as the 'Angel of Death' of Auschwitz. But Mengele, said to be living in a remote Mennonite religious community on the border of Bolivia and Paraguay, was thought to be impossible to extradite. He was reported to be a registered refugee and a Paraguayan citizen.

The escaped Nazi leaders have now grown old, however, and despite Dr Wiesenthal's patient efforts, death rather than justice is more likely to catch up with these ten killers in hiding ...

1. Heinrich Mueller: Chief of the Gestapo.

Mueller was known as the killer with the fountain pen. He would never kill anyone himself. He only wrote out the orders. He very seldom visited a concentration camp or a gas chamber or an execution.

A World War 1 Army officer, he joined the Bavarian police and only in 1939 the Nazi party – out of necessity rather than belief. Hard-working, he always sheltered under the orders of others, beginning his instructions 'the Reichsführer has ordered' this or that. His industrious, low-profile, comradely but never friendly character led to his appointment as Gestapo general.

Although he himself never killed anybody, he was responsible for the deaths of millions of Jews, prisoners and hostages. He knew every detail about the concentration camps, could quote statistics about inmates and even the death rate at notorious camps like Auschwitz. The bureaucratic killer vanished at the end of World War 2, was thought to have died in the Berlin street fighting. But when his grave was opened three skulls were found. Not one of them was Mueller's.

Since then, the Nazi hunters have followed leads that he went over to the Russians, then moved on to Albania. Others tracked him to Spain, then Suez and in 1963 he was confidently identified as a resident in Cairo, safe from the Israelis. Israeli agents were arrested in Frau Mueller's home in Munich but they found no lead to his whereabouts.

His aliases include Jan Belinski, Pole; Amin Abdel Megid and Alfred Mardes, Arab. Officially, his fate and whereabouts are unknown.

2. Richard Gluecks: Inspector-general of all concentration camps.

Less is known about Gluecks than about most Nazi war criminals, except that he was a Gruppenführer, head of the administration bureau of the RHSA, the Reich Security Head Office in overall control of concentration camps.

In 1938, 20,000 Jews were sent to 'protective custody' in these camps. By 1939 six major camps had been established, including the notorious Dachau, Buchenwald and Ravensbrück. Eight others were to follow in the next three years including the most notorious, Auschwitz, where more than a million people died. Gluecks, who ordered deportations and managed the network of camps, vanished without trace. His fate and whereabouts are unknown.

3. Dr Josef Mengele: Chief Medical Officer, Auschwitz concentration camp.

Mengele was accused of being directly responsible for the deaths of 400,000 people. A medical graduate of both Frankfurt and Munich universities – both of which have cancelled his academic qualifications – he was known as 'The Angel of Death' to Auschwitz concentration camp.

As the prisoners filed through the main gate, beneath the sign 'Work Makes Men Free', Mengele would prod them with his stick and order them to be worked to death, to undergo hideous experiments or to be taken directly to the gas chambers. All the time, a band played on.

One of his experiments, aimed at proving Hitler's theory that Germans were a super-race, was to alter the hair and eyes of victims by genetic manipulation. Many who did not die were blinded.

He escaped from West Germany after the war, travelled to Italy and then Argentina, before settling in Paraguay where he became a naturalized citizen in 1973. He took out citizenship papers largely because West Germany, and the Nazi hunters, had located him and were offering vast sums of money in reward for his return.

Mengele had to remain constantly on the move, unable to sleep in the same bed for more than two weeks at a time.

At the end of 1978 and early 1979 his fellow Nazis put about the story that Mengele was dead in order to protect the strong war criminal colony in Paraguay. They even circulated pictures of Mengele on the mortuary slab showing the scar on his right arm where his tattooed ss number had been removed. It was, in fact, the body of ss Captain Eduardo Roschmann who sent 80,000 Jews to their deaths at the concentration camp at Riga, Latvia.

As a Paraguayan citizen, Mengele continued to live in that country under goverment protection.

4. Walter Rauff: Commander of a unit which provided gas trucks for concentration camps.

Rauff is accused of being responsible, directly and indirectly, for the deaths of 250,000 people – despite the fact that there is little evidence of direct contact between Rauff and his victims.

He was 'the ambulance chief'. His transports looked like ordinary Red Cross ambulances into which Jews and others regarded as racially undesirable were herded. But they were not taken to hospital, as their guards promised. Once inside the 'ambulances', the doors were locked and the guards opened the valves on cylinders attached to the vehicles. The passengers were gassed to death.

According to Weisenthal in 1983, Rauff is alive and well in Chile where he openly ran a meat freezing factory. He was even known to answer letters addressed to him in Punta Arenas, but goverment protection ensured he was not molested.

At one time Dr Wiesenthal pleaded with Dr Henry Kissinger, then American's roving ambassador, to help secure Rauff's extradition. Dr Kissinger, himself a Jew and of German origin, declined because he could not interfere without compromising himself and his country diplomatically.

Rauff, like Mengele, has been used in a number of works of fiction including Frederick Forsyth's famous novel, *The Odessa File*. But his real post-war existence in South America has been stranger than fiction. Both Mengele and Rauff have been suspected of drug racketeering. The Chileans have had to deny a number of stories about Rauff, notably that the Chilean government was employing him as an anti-Communist agent.

The government at one time denied that Rauff was living in Chile ... but the former ss colonel's own letters were ample proof to the contary.

5. Anton Burger: Field officer and assistant to Adolf Eichmann, head of the Gestapo's Department of Jewish Affairs.

Burger was deputy commander of Theresienstadt concentration camp, on the Czech-German border. The 'model' camp was used to dispel stories of Nazi atrocities. It was even opened to neutral visitors to show that stories about the concentration camps were simply Allied propaganda. But behind the scenes, the inmates of Theresienstadt were subject to 'experiments'. Some were to be poisoned. Women were forced to undergo abortions to prevent the increase of the Jewish race. Others were sterilized.

In the hunt for Nazi war criminals Anton Burger was often mistaken for Wilhelm Burger, chief administrator at Auschwitz.

In 1948 Anton Burger escaped from the prison where he was awaiting trial. In the search which ensued the authorities eventually arrested Wilhelm Burger, accused for his part in ordering lorry loads of gas with which to murder Jews at Auschwitz.

Wilhelm was jailed for eight years – but because he had spent eight years in a Polish prison he was freed. Anton vanished and his whereabouts are unknown.

6. Rolf Guenther: Deputy to Adolf Eichmann.

Rolf and his brother, Hans, were both ss majors but it was Rolf, the quiet one, who was entrusted with carrying out Hitler's programme for exterminating the Jews.

When Eichmann was kidnapped in Argentina and returned to Israel to be tried, he accused Guenther of taking a personal initiative in the death camps and of carrying out some orders behind his back. He insisted that Guenther must have had and acted on special orders direct from Mueller, by-passing Eichmann.

The truth was that Guenther had been chosen as Eichmann's second in command because he would willingly carry out the 'final solution' to the Jewish problem. He was sent to remove all Jews from Denmark. He visited Greece, Hungary and other countries as an expert on 'the Jewish problem'.

Ample documentation proves that Guenther had a confidential instruction to arrange sterilization, medical experiments and the gassing of inmates.

Guenther disappeared at the end of the war. His whereabouts are unknown.

7. Alois Brunner: Another of Eichmann's assistants.

According to Wiesenthal's files, Brunner is specially responsible for the deaths of thousands of Jews in Czechoslovakia and Greece.

Like Guenther, he worked for Eichmann in the 'Jewish Museum', a propaganda section at the head office of the Nazi Party. He then moved to the Jewish section of the Gestapo and early in the war was appointed field officer in France.

There he arranged the deportation of, at first, stateless Jews, then foreign Jews and finally French Jews. They were taken to local concentration camps and then mostly to Auschwitz.

As in the case of Guenther, Eichmann tried to maintain that once Brunner had left him to visit some other country he was out of Eichmann's jurisdiction. But Eichmann, who was not believed, and was hanged for his war crimes, left behind considerable evidence, which helps condemn Brunner.

Yet, according to Wiesenthal, in 1983 Brunner was living under Arab protection in Damascus, Syria, under the name of Dr Fisher.

8. Josef Schwamberger: Another of Eichmann's assistants, former commander of the Jewish ghetto at Przemysl, Poland.

Before the war about 500,000 Jews lived in Galicia, Poland. Then the Germans came and herded them into ghettos. Schwamberger is thought to have been responsible for the deaths of 15,000 of them. The Warsaw ghetto, where there was bloody revolt, uprising and suppression, was the most infamous. But there were many others.

After the war, Schwamberger, a member of the so-called Odessa escape group, fled to Italy and then to Argentina, where Nazis still received asylum. Despite denials as to his presence, Argentinian police arrested him in 1973 after requests by West Germany that he be extradited.

The powerful group of Nazis resident there intervened. The request was refused – and he was released.

9. Dr Aribert Heim: Director of the concentration camp at Mauthausen, Austria.

In February 1941, the Germans made their first mass arrests in Holland by rounding up 400 Jews in Amsterdam and sending them first to Buchenwald and then to Mauthausen. The Red Cross revealed that only one survived.

The camp's 'death book', found by the Allies, revealed 35,318 deaths, a total which compared with camps like Dachau and Buchenwald.

The inmates had a saying that if you reached Mauthausen, Dr Heim would 'look after you'. The grim truth was that many were taken from the notorious Auschwitz on a death march to Mauthausen. Some survived that march –

only to be sent on another to Zeltenlager.

One witness who survived both marches said they were so hungry that when the Allies bombed the area he 'saw people eating human flesh, the flesh of victims of the air raid'.

After the war Dr Heim vanished. His whereabouts are unknown.

10. Friedrich Wartzog: Commander of the Lemberg-Janowska concentration camp, Russia, formerly Poland.

Wartzog is accused of ordering the killing of 40,000 people. Some of the worst evidence against him was given on oath by Eichmann at his trial, when he talked of 'a spring of blood gushing from the earth' where executed Jews had been buried at Lemberg-Janowska.

Prisoners were kept without food for three days, existed on grass and then if found unfit were shot. One hobby of the guards was shooting at the prisoners as they went to work – at their ears, noses, fingers. If they were badly injured an executioner would finish them off.

Wartzog, who presided, escaped. His whereabouts are unknown.

France's Uncrowned King

Before the revolutions of peasants and elected parliaments began to sweep through Europe in the 18th and 19th centuries, the royal dynasties of kings and princes jealously guarded their awesome power with strict codes of bloodline and heritage and succession.

The rulers who claimed a God-given right to govern millions of subjects, built their fabulous fortunes on elaborate rules of royal lineage. Loyal courtiers were always on hand to advise on the interpretation of the laws of succession in the tangled web of regal inter-marriage, first-born sons, feuding cousins and charlatan pretenders to great thrones and titles.

Often when powerful monarchs passed from the gilded stage and their relatives fell to squabbling among themselves, the line of succession could pass the mantle of power to tiny babies, first-born crown princes not old enough to walk or talk.

Jealous royal power brokers would often cast an envious eye on the cradle of some child-king, knowing that in many cases a quirk of fate, like a bout of fatal chicken pox, could swing an empire into the hands of a rival relative.

Sometimes they were not slow to realize the advantages of giving fate a helping hand. Snatching a kingdom from a child, taking the royal candy from a baby, was fair game, even if the infant was a close blood relative.

When little Charles Louis was born into the royal family of Bourbon in 1785, he seemed set for a life of luxury. He was the younger of two royal children, but as the male heir, the Dauphin, he took priority over his older sister Marie Thérèse. His destiny was to rule France as the inheritor of its palaces and grand estates. But the overburdened French peasants had other ideas. Louis was only four years old when the Revolution burst on to the streets of Paris and the mobs began to howl for an end to monarchy.

The little Dauphin's parents, Louis XVI and Marie Antoinette, whose free spending lifestyle had so outraged their poverty stricken subjects, were soon prisoners of the Revolution. For two years Louis and Marie and their children were kept under house arrest as French democracy went through its own turbulent infancy, ruling the country in a confusion of committees and assemblies.

Luck ran out for King Louis and his Queen in 1793 during the session of the newly appointed Convention which unleashed the infamous Reign of Terror. Louis and Marie became just two of the stream of doomed French nobility whose lives were ended by the guillotine.

While the members of the Convention transferred the little Dauphin and his sister to the Temple Prison in Paris, the exiled royalists who had fled abroad immediately proclaimed the seven-year-old boy their new King, Louis XVII.

There is little doubt that many of the fiery members of the new Republic's National Assembly would happily have guillotined the boy king and his sister. But they could not overlook his potential as a pawn in the bargaining game they had to play with their hostile neighbours of Austria, Prussia and Spain, where the ruling royal families, fought frequent invasion skirmishes with the French to try to restore the monarchy. As long as the Dauphin and his sister remained prisoners in the Temple, their continued safe-keeping had some value if the National Assembly used them as hostages to buy off the pressure from threatening outsiders.

In the meantime, the royalists in exile and their sympathizers inside Paris, began a whole series of plots to free the bewildered little Dauphin by bribery or subterfuge.

Even some National Assembly members, worried that the Revolution might be short-lived, considered smuggling the Dauphin to their own secret hideaways to bargain for their own lives if the royalists ever regained the upper hand. Soon all Paris was abuzz with rumours that the Dauphin had been spirited out of the temple to become a youthful figurehead for a Royalist revival.

Louis XVII

To quell the speculation, the National Assembly appointed a team of guardians and commissoners to make regular visits to the Temple to check the well-being of the Dauphin and his sister, and to report back to them.

A puzzling report was recorded after a visit on 19 December 1794, when National Assembly member Harmand inspected the nine-year-old boy in his cell at the Temple. He noted he met a child in poor health, suffering from a disabling swelling on his arms and legs. The most bizarre aspect was the boy's responses to Harmand's inquiries about his treatment. The boy showed no signs of hearing his questions and never uttered a sound in reply. He was totally deaf and dumb. Harmond's report was quickly hushed up.

In May 1795, the boy in the Temple became seriously ill and doctors were ordered to attend him. The health of the boy, apparently still a deaf mute, deteriorated still further until the night of 8 June when he died.

Four doctors authorized by the Committee of Public Safety carried out a quick autopsy on the dead boy, removing his heart and dissecting his head. They diagnosed the cause of death as scrofula, tuberculosis of the glands of the neck.

But they never carried out an formal identification of him by his sister, Marie Thérèse, who had been kept prisoner for two years in another cell on the other side of the Temple. The body, the head swathed in bandages, was placed in a coffin and hustled off for burial in a common grave in the churchyard of Sainte Marguérite.

The next day, amid continuing rumours that another child had been switched for the Dauphin in the Temple, the Convention announced his death without making any further comment.

And so the royal house of Bourbon seemed doomed to wither as the French Republic embarked on a new era of its history under the leadership of a dynamic young Army officer from Corsica, Napoleon Bonaparte.

Napoleon took less than a decade of glorious military conquest before he tried to found his own royal dynasty, crowning himself Emperor and handing out royal titles to his own children, brothers and friends.

But after his defeat at Waterloo in 1815, the victorious allies decided it was time for real royalty to regain the throne of France. Their choice was the brother of the guillotined Louis XVI, the uncle of the Dauphin. The new monarch, next in line after the boy-king who had never ruled, became Louis XVIII. It was the sign for resurrected Dauphins to pop up all over Europe.

Dozens of 'dauphins', all about the right age of 30 and all well versed in the folklore of the alleged switch in the Temple, put forward their claims and where exposed as blatant frauds.

The most curious claim came 15 years later from a Prussian watchmaker living in London. In 1830, when another Revolution, less bloody and violent, had swept the royal family of Bourbon off the French throne of France yet again watchmaker Karl Wilhelm Naundorff came forward. He insisted he did not want to try to rule France, only to prove himself to be the missing Dauphin and to try to benefit from what little privilege was still attached to the title.

Naundorff gave a long, detailed account of how he recalled 35 years earlier being carried out of the Temple on 8 June, 1795, after being drugged with opium, and spending the next 14 years being passed from 'safe house' to 'safe house' in France, England and Germany. In 1800, he claimed, the King of Prussia had organized false identity papers for him in the name of Karl Naundorff. He then married and settled down, after serving a short prison term for counterfeiting coins.

In 1833 in France, Naundorff organized a meeting with Madame Rambaud, the dead Dauphin's former nanny, and Vicomte de la Rochefoucauld, an emissary from the Dauphin's sister, then Duchess of Angoulême. The nanny was convinced about his identity and the Vicomte reported that he was very impressed with Naundorff's claims and the watchmaker's striking physical resemblance to his 'father', the dead King Louis XVI.

But the Duchess, the Dauphin's sister, took no notice until 1836 when Naundorff tried to force her into a civil court case to prove his claim. He was arrested by French authorities and deported back to England. At home in London he set about pressing his claim, in an exhaustively researched book published later that year.

All copies of the book sent to France were seized by French customs officials at Calais. Naundorff continued to bombard the French authorities and the Duchess with petitions, undeterred by an attempt on his life at his home in Clarence Place, London. He was shot, literally with his pants down, in the outdoor toilet in his garden. He survived the wound and a Frenchman was later arrested and charged with the attack.

Two other attempts were made on his life in 1841 as Naundorff struggled to earn a living as an inventor of artillery weapons. He was badly burned in a deliberate explosion in his workshop and another arson attack on his home later that year.

With his business burned out, Karl Naundorff was bankrupt and spent four years in the grim Newgate debtor's prison in London.

Released in 1845, he travelled to Holland to try to interest the Dutch government in his designs for a new field gun. Before negotiations were complete, Naundorff died on 10 August.

The official Dutch death certificate identified him as Charles Louis de Bourbon, Duke of Normandy, Louis XVII, aged 60, son of Louis XVI and Marie Antoinette. The Dutch doctor who performed the routine autopsy noted his body bore certain marks – a mole on the thigh, triangular vaccination marks on his arm and a scar on his upper lip. The marks correspond exactly to the descriptions given by Madame Rambaud, the governess to the Dauphin Louis from his birth until 1792, the year before he was locked away in the Temple.

If Karl Naundorff was indeed the young Dauphin, the leaders of the French Revolution who locked him away as a child, without trial or charge, denied him his heritage and his chance to change the course of history.

But if his story was true, which cruel and heartless conspirators, royalists or double-crossing revolutionaries, snatched him from the Temple and left a terrified deaf mute boy to die of disease and maltreatment in solitary confinement in his place?

The Sinking of the *Salem*

The 96,000 ton supertanker *Salem* was a floating time bomb, in danger of erupting into a massive fire-ball at any moment. But her captain, officers and 18 crewmen were calm, apparently refusing to panic, waiting quietly on deck and scanning the horizon for passing ships.

On 17 January 1979, the Greek captain of the *Salem* noted in his log that the ship had been rocked by a series of explosions which had left it floating helpless and without engines in the Atlantic Ocean 160 km (100 miles) off the African coast of Senegal.

The ship's log also noted with relief that the mysterious explosions and small fires had failed to ignite any of the brimming cargo of 200,000 tons of volatile Kuwaiti crude oil which packed the tanker's holds.

The *Salem* remained afloat for another 30 hours. Almost inevitably in the busy shipping lanes, she was spotted by the tanker *British Trident*, outward bound from England and headed for the same Persian Gulf terminal the *Salem* had left more than a month before. Twenty minutes after the *British Trident* first sighted the *Salem*, the British ship recorded the first and only distress radio call from the stricken ship.

As *British Trident* turned to answer the SOS call a bright cloud of orange smoke billowed up from the *Salem*. But there was no need for the rescuers to approach too close. Within 30 minutes the *Salem*'s powerful lifeboats had met them halfway. The British sailors could only marvel at the *Salem*'s crew, unhurried and magnificently composed in the face of awesome danger, as they filed aboard the *British Trident* in an orderly queue, with their suitcases neatly packed.

The ship had survived a day and a night still afloat although listing slightly. With reasonable luck it could be presumed that the *Salem* might survive a lot longer, even long enough to put a damage repair and salvage crew aboard.

But within ten minutes of her crew being rescued, the *Salem*'s bows dipped below the swell and she sank out of sight.

The crew of the *British Trident* were relieved when the potential fire-bomb slipped below the waves. Now they put their own tanker's engines full ahead to get well clear of the catastrophic fountain of oil which would gush to the surface from the *Salem*'s hold. They knew that the *Salem*'s massive cargo, valued at £25 million, was likely to produce one of the worst oil slicks the world had ever known.

Almost as a warning of the impending pollution disaster, one gigantic oil bubble broke the surface of the ocean. And then it stopped.

The *Salem* slipped further and further downward into the Atlantic, in water too deep for any diver to reach her. She was gone and lost for good, of that there was no doubt.

The following day the crew of the *Salem* were put ashore in Dakar, the capital of Senegal. The captain dismissed his grateful crew and prepared himself for questioning at a routine inquiry into the loss of his ship. He notified the owners of the *Salem*, a newly formed shipping company sharing the same accommodation address in Monrovia, Liberia, as 200 other shipping owners, that their vessel had foundered. He informed the owners of the oil, Shell International Trading in London, that their valuable cargo had been lost and compensation would have to come from the insurers.

The skipper carefully filed his own insurance claim, £12 million for the cost of the *Salem*, less than half the value of its cargo. Then, as soon as the Senegal authorities agreed to release him, he flew home to Athens.

As insurance investigators began to unravel some of the unexplained causes of the sinking of the *Salem*, one of the tanker's crew added a new twist to the riddle.

The crewman, a Tunisian, turned up in Paris, spending money like water. He claimed that the money he flung so recklessly around the nightclubs came from a bonus of thousands of Swiss francs paid by the owners of the *Salem*.

And that bonus, he claimed, was paid to all the crewmen who entered into a conspiracy of silence a few days after the *Salem* left the Kuwaiti oil loading terminal at Mena Al Ahmdi and cleared the Persian Gulf. The high living crewman boasted that the shadowy businessmen who owned the *Salem* had bluffed their way into a fortune by offering their services to carry the cargo of oil from Kuwait to England.

The Kuwaiti oil would have been worth double its value to one group of customers 3,220 km (2,000 miles) away, the industries of South Africa. Most Arab oil exporters maintain a united anti-apartheid policy against the South African regime and refuse to sell them any of their output. South Africa buys its oil wherever and whenever it can – and pays top price.

The crewman insisted that this ship made a secret rendezvous with a South African tanker off the Cape of Good Hope, transferred its precious cargo and then partially flooded its tanks to prevent it riding suspiciously high in the water. Then it continued its journey as part of an elaborate charade. It sank conveniently off Senegal, its nearest point to land after leaving South African waters.

In Athens the skipper of the *Salem* dismissed his crewman's uncorroborated allegations as a sailor's yarn, meant to add spice and intrigue to a sad but perfectly plausible explanation for the loss of the tanker. The South African government maintained a discreet silence.

But insurance investigators were already suspicious that the *Salem* had taken more than a month to reach the Senegal coast after leaving Kuwait. It should have made that part of its journey in only three weeks. The time gap, many of them claim, can only be explained by an unscheduled detour somewhere along the route.

It is unlikely that anyone will ever be able to solve the riddle of the ship which seemed to sink on cue. The wreck of the *Salem* lies deep beneath the stormy waters of the Atlantic Ocean. Are its cargo tanks filled with £25 million worth of oil, seeping away quietly and unnoticed? Or are they filled with nothing more than sea water?

A Peer's Great Gamble

When Veronica, Lady Lucan, ran hysterical and bloodstained from her home in Lower Belgrave Street, Belgravia, London, on the night of 7 November 1974, her frantic cries for help sparked off one of the most baffling unsolved murder mysteries of the age.

Lying behind her in the elegant town house, just a stone's throw from Buckingham Palace, was the body of her children's nanny Sandra Rivett, aged 29, brutally battered to death, her body thrust into a canvas sack.

Lady Lucan reached the door of the crowded saloon bar of the nearby pub, The Plumbers Arms, and sobbed: 'Help me. Help me, I've just escaped from a murderer.'

Sandra Rivett

And the tale she told from her hospital bed to detectives a few hours later set them on the fruitless search to find her husband, John Bingham, the 7th Earl of Lucan. With bruising on her face and severe lacerations to her scalp, Lady Lucan, 26, told how she had tackled a tall, powerful maniac bent on murder.

She recalled how she had been spending a quiet evening at home with her two children – with the unexpected company of nanny Sandra who had originally been given the evening off to spend with her boyfriend. Sandra, who doted on Lady Lucan's children, had decided instead to stay in the house, in her own quarters.

Around 21.00 Sandra had popped her head round the door of Lady Lucan's lounge and offered to make a cup of tea for the family. Half an hour later when the nanny had not re-appeared, Lady Lucan walked down two floors to the kitchen, puzzled by the delay.

There she saw the shadowy figure of a man, crouched over the dead body of the nanny, bundling her lifeless form into a canvas sack.

As soon as Lady Lucan screamed, the man attacked her, beating her badly. She could not recognize the figure in the darkness, but as she struggled free and ran upstairs, she heard what she said was the unmistakable voice of her estranged husband call out after her.

Moments later, as she lay trembling on her bed, her husband was at her side, trying to comfort her. And when Lady Lucan ran from the house for help, her husband slipped away into the night.

A massive hunt immediately began for Lord Lucan. Police first checked his rented flat only a few streets away, where he had moved the previous year when he had separated from Lady Lucan and started divorce proceedings. But by that time, barely two hours after the murder, Lord Lucan had already turned up at a friend's house 72 km (45 miles) from the scene of the crime, driving a borrowed car.

There the socialite peer, a man-about-town and professional gambler, told one of his closest family friends his own version of the horror of the nanny's murder. He claimed he had been walking past his wife's home on his way to his own flat to change for dinner at one of his fashionable gambling clubs and saw through the venetian blinds of the basement kitchen what looked like a man attacking Lady Lucan.

'I let myself in with my own key and rushed down to protect her,' Lucan told his friend. 'I slipped on a pool of blood and the attacker ran off. My wife was hysterical and accusing me of being her attacker.'

Despite his denial, Lord Lucan never stayed around to confirm his version of events to the police – or to anyone else. The day after the murder, his car, which carried a portion of the same lead pipe which had been used to kill

Lord and Lady Lucan

Sandra Rivett, was found abandoned at Newhaven, Sussex, a port with a regular ferry service to France.

Police began a thorough check of Lucan's aristocratic friends in England, suspecting that wealthy socialites might be shielding him. But all lines of inquiry petered out.

A year later the coroner's inquest into the death of the nanny weighed up all the evidence and took the unusual step of officially recording her death as murder – and naming Lord Lucan as the man who had committed the murder. English law was changed shortly after that judgement to ensure that never again could anyone be named as a murderer until they were found, charged, tried and found guilty under normal criminal procedure.

Seven years after the murder, when Lucan had vanished without touching any of his bank accounts, without surrendering himself, and still undiscovered by any of the police searches which spread from Africa to America, the fugitive peer was declared legally dead.

The two policemen who led the search have both retired from Scotland Yard, still arguing about the unsolved crime. Superintendent Roy Ransom, who studied every single statement and grilled scores of witnesses, maintained: 'He killed the nanny by mistake, thinking he could dispose of his wife and get the custody of the children he loved. When he realized the error, he killed himself in some remote spot, like a lord and a gentleman.'

But Superintendent Dave Gerring, who supervised the same murder hunt, concluded: 'Lucan is still in hiding somewhere and he is the only man who knows the full story. He is a lord and a gentleman, but he is still a gambler. And he is still gambling on the odds that no one will ever find him.'

Suspect Deceased

The finger of suspicion pointed unwaveringly at Graham Sturley. He was the classic murder suspect. The 37-year-old former private detective had certainly studied case histories of people who had vanished and never been seen alive again. And when Linda, his own wife, went missing, Sturley had the know-how, the motive and the opportunity to have murdered her.

METROPOLITAN POLICE
Appeal for Assistance

MISSING

Mrs Linda Jacqueline STURLEY, 5'4" tall with shoulder length, fair hair and aged 29, left her home in Main Road, Biggin Hill, Kent, between 9pm on Friday 17 July and Saturday 18 July, 1981.

She was 6 months pregnant. She was last seen wearing a blue maternity dress.

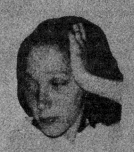

DO YOU KNOW HER?
HAVE YOU SEEN HER RECENTLY?
DO YOU HAVE ANY OTHER INFORMATION?

**Please contact the Police at
CATFORD POLICE STATION
Tel:01-697 9502**

All information treated as strictly confidential

The detectives who first called at his home in Biggin Hill, Kent, were quickly convinced that Sturley, earning a living as a property developer, had killed his petite, unfaithful 29-year-old wife. He openly admitted to them his hatred for her flaunted love affairs with other men.

But the police began their investigation with one great disadvantage. Linda Sturley had been missing for 12 months by the time her worried mother, Mrs Ada Webb, walked into her local police station and reported her daughter's disappearance. She had been stalled long enough by assurances from son-in-law Sturley that, although Linda had left home, she had been in touch with him by telephone.

When the police arrived on the doorstep of Sturley's neat suburban bungalow he told them frankly: 'Yes, she's gone and I don't expect to see her again. I don't know where she is and I'm glad to get rid of her.'

Then the detectives began to piece together the facts.

Linda Sturley had last been seen at her home in July 1981, when her sister visited her. Tearfully Linda, who was six months pregnant, confessed that her husband had beaten her and punched her in the stomach during a violent argument the night before, when he raged that one of her lovers was the father of the child she was expecting.

The next day Linda, a pretty and vivacious sales representative for the Avon cosmetics company, vanished.

The Sturleys' home

Graham Sturley

With an air of finality, Sturley had told his two children, a six-year-old girl and a four-year-old boy, that their mother would never be returning. Neighbours noticed that Sturley had a garden bonfire, burning a complete wardrobe of his wife's clothes. And for the next year, until July 1982, Sturley lived as if Linda had simply gone away.

He even telephoned his wife's family to reassure them that Linda was still well, at the same time as someone with a detailed knowledge of the missing woman's bank passbooks had forged her signature to take everything out of her savings accounts and cash cheques for her maternity benefit payments.

Linda Sturley's family doctor revealed that the missing woman would need to give birth to her baby by Caesarian operation. Government health officials checked the records of every maternity hospital and clinic in Britain and no patient answering her description had been admitted.

And the police discovered that her jealous husband had even used the techniques of his former detective agency to tap his own telephone and record conversations between Linda and her lovers.

'We know your wife had a string of lovers and she was a bad wife,' one policeman told Sturley sympathetically. 'And we understand that sometimes pressure like that can drive a man to murder.'

But Sturley, who had a history of poor health and heart ailments, never faltered once during long sessions of police interrogation. 'You think I have buried her in the garden,' he accused bitterly. 'Well I wouldn't have been so silly, that would have poisoned the flowers.'

It was only a matter of time, police thought, before they found Linda Sturley's body and broke through her husband's brooding, angry defiance to gain a confession.

Sturley, unshakeably refusing to admit any part in his wife's disappearance, told them: 'She had walked out on me so many times in the past I didn't bother to report her as a missing person. I'm glad she's gone, I never want to see her again.'

When intense publicity in national newspapers and on TV and radio failed to bring any response from the missing woman, the search began in earnest for Linda Sturley's body.

The floorboards were ripped up in the living room of Sturley's house and the brickwork of walls probed for hidden cavities. Infra-red and heat-seeking detection equipment was used to scan the gardens around the house and tracker teams with dogs combed the surrounding woodland and parks. Police divers plunged into lakes, streams and ponds and forensic experts were sent to examine the bones of a woman's body unearthed in a forest 48 km (30 miles) away. But there was still no sign of Linda Sturley, dead or alive.

In a series of thorough interrogations Graham Sturley taunted the police, mocking their failure at every attempt to discover the fate of his wife. Detectives, aware of his history of heart trouble, handled him with kid gloves, probing and questioning as toughly as they dared.

After three months of intensive investigation, the head of the murder inquiry squad, Detective Chief Inspector George Cressy, examined all the circumstantial evidence and decided he had enough to recommend arresting Graham Sturley and charging him with the murder of his wife.

As police legal experts began preparing the case for his arrest, confident of their prosecution and eventual conviction, Graham Sturley died of a heart attack. The murder inquiry on Linda Sturley was closed, the case file marked 'Suspect deceased'.

Graham Sturley's lawyer revealed later: 'A will was left by Mr Sturley disposing of his assests, but there was nothing dramatic in it one way or another, no confessions, no admissions.'

The Kent detectives saw no useful purpose to be served by their presence a week later at Sturley's cremation after a ceremony in the quiet chapel in Honor Oak, London.

They never saw the strange final tribute that was laid on his coffin – a wreath with the message: 'Well you got that out of the way, Sturley. All my love...'

The Disappearance of Goodtime Joe

With a leggy showgirl on his arm, Judge Joseph Crater stepped out of a plush nightclub on New York's 45th Street and hailed a taxi. He gave his companion an affectionate squeeze and a kiss on the cheek. 'See you tomorrow, Ruby,' said the judge, whose unorthodox social life had earned him the nickname Goodtime Joe. But he didn't. A little later, he was seen buying a theatre ticket for the Broadway hit, *Dancing Partners*.

From that moment, on 6 August 1930, Judge Joseph Crater vanished, and it happened so mysteriously and in such politically-scandalous circumstances that in America 'pulling a Crater' is still used to describe a baffling disappearance. In New York, he is still officially listed as missing, although he would now be 93 years old, and the police department still checks regular reports of sightings.

Judge Crater was a sentimental family man – and a womanizer on a grand scale. He was a pillar of society, yet he enjoyed the company of rogues. He believed fervently in the sanctity of the law but became part of the most corrupt administration in New York's history. He had been a brilliant professor of law at New York University, but he wanted to be rich. As a lawyer with an obvious interest in making money, he was welcomed by the city's then-shady administration. In the summer of 1929 he acted as a receiver when the bankrupt Libby Hotel was sold to a finance company for $75,000. Six weeks later, the hotel was resold to the city of New York to be demolished in a road widening scheme. The price: $2,800,000. Many members of the administration, including Crater, made a lot of money from the deal.

By 1930, he had the life-style of a very rich man. More good fortune came his way when Franklin D. Roosevelt, then Governor of New York State, made him a justice of the city's Supreme Court. Crater had finally made it. He was rich and powerful. Then, on the evening of 2 August, something happened to threaten his cosy world.

He was on holiday with his wife at their summer cottage in Maine when he received a mysterious phone call. It was enough to send the judge hurrying back to New York. 'I've got to straighten some fellows out,' was all he told his wife, promising to return for her birthday a week later. She never saw him again.

In New York on 6 August he wrote two cheques for a total of $4,100 and sent his assistant, Joe Mara, to the bank to cash them. When Mara returned, Crater had stuffed papers from his office files into four large portfolios and two briefcases. He told Mara he was going 'up Westchester way for a few days'.

That evening, however, he turned up at his favourite nightclub on 45th Street, but after a few drinks with showgirl Ruby Ritz he left, saying he was going to the theatre.

Amazingly, it was four weeks and a day before the disappearance of one of the city's top judges finally leaked out. Friends and enemies alike, terrified at the idea of a scandal which might implicate them, were desperate to hush up the affair. Manhattan District Attorney, Thomas Crain, was anxious to question Mrs Crater. She refused to talk and the judge's politically-powerful friends kept Crain at bay.

Soon, reports of alleged sightings were coming in from around the world.

In 1955 a photograph of Crater was shown to the Dutch clairvoyant Gerard Croiset. He claimed that the judge had been murdered on the first floor of a farmhouse near the Bronx, New York, and his body buried in the garden.

Remarkably, there was just such a house in the area, which in Crater's day had been used by city officials for secret meetings with their girlfriends. Investigators discovered that the late owner, Henry Krauss, had once claimed that on the morning of 10 August 1930, he had found the kitchen covered with blood ... But of a body there was no sign.

Death at the Opera House

Snow swirled silently through the deserted streets and only the footprints of an occasional policeman or passer-by marred its crisp whiteness. It was Christmas in Toronto. But while most people were surrounded by joy, and laughter and goodwill, one woman remained alone, surrounded by silence and suspicion. Three weeks before Christmas Day 1919, Theresa Small's husband had mysteriously disappeared – and there were rumours of murder.

In a few years Ambrose Small, ruthless and mean, had made a fortune out of property. His most important possession was Toronto Grand Opera House. He had started there as an usher. Then he became treasurer. In the end he owned it. He was a millionaire before he was 40 and owned theatres throughout Canada.

At 56 he decided to sell his theatrical empire. A deal was fixed with a financier from Montreal and on 2 December 1919, Small and his wife met him at his lawyers in Toronto. The financier gave Small a cheque for $1,000,000 as down-payment and Small gave the cheque to his wife, who deposited it in his account. The Smalls then went to lunch with their solicitor.

Afterwards Mrs Small went home alone in her chauffeur-driven car while her husband went back to the opera house. He had arranged to meet his solicitor there at 16.00. He was seen entering the theatre. But nobody saw him leave.

His solicitor said later that he had stayed with Small and his secretary, John Doughty, for an hour and a half. Small, he said, was still at the opera house when he left at 17.30.

Doughty left the theatre to have supper with his sister. Later he said he had to go to Montreal and was driven to the station by his sister's husband. On the way they stopped at the opera house, where Doughty collected a small brown paper parcel. He gave this to a second sister in the car and asked her to look after it. Doughty caught the Montreal train – and it was to be two years before he would be back in Toronto.

Small failed to come home that night, so Theresa assumed he had gone to Montreal with Doughty. She waited and waited. But there was no sign of her husband.

It was the opera house manager, however, who raised the alarm. Police issued Small's description – and at once there was a sensational development. Found pinned to the door of a Toronto church was a card which read: 'Prayers for the soul of Ambrose Small.'

The search for a missing man had now become a hunt for a possible murderer. Suspicion fell first on Theresa Small. She was of German extraction, and Germans were far from popular just after World War 1.

Doughty, too, fell under suspicion. But where was he? The police announced rewards of $50,000 for the discovery of Small dead or alive and $15,000 for Doughty.

In the summer of 1920 police obtained a court order to open the strongbox at Small's bank. From their inquiries they expected to find a fortune inside. But bonds worth $105,000 were missing – and the last recorded visitor to Small's safety vaults had been John Doughty. Police investigations intensified. A boilerman at the opera house said that there had been a fight between Small and Doughty on the night Small was last seen alive. Officers raked out the boilers at the opera house looking for human remains.

Then a year later Doughty was discovered working in a lumber camp in Oregon. He was taken back to Toronto and the missing bonds were found in the attic of his sister's house. The police, convinced that they had a murder charge on their hands, confronted Doughty with the alleged fight in the opera house. He vehemently denied it and he was eventually charged with theft.

Doughty said he had taken the bonds from the bank on 2 December to use as a lever against Small who had promised him a share in the theatre deal. But he said he had panicked and fled across the border when he heard of Small's disappearance. Doughty was found guilty of theft and jailed for five years in March 1921.

Yet still there was no sign of Small. Police dug up the floors of his wife's house, but found nothing. Rumours persisted that he had been murdered by racketeers but again widespread searches revealed nothing.

Small was officially declared dead in 1924. Twenty years later the opera house was demolished and detectives made one last effort to solve the case. Again nothing.

To this day what happened to Ambrose Small remains as much a mystery as it was when he vanished off the face of the earth in 1919.

The Impossible *is* Possible

Neither the woman nor her 13-year-old daughter heard the alarm clock ring at 04.00 in the adjoining bedroom. Nor did they hear the soft 'phut' of the silenced gun. If they had, one of America's most baffling murder mysteries might have yielded a clue, however tiny.

Respectable family man Roy Orsini was dead, face-down in his pyjamas, shot in the back of the head by a .38 bullet fired at close range.

On the morning of 12 March 1981, veteran homicide detective Sergeant Tom Farley realized he had the 'impossible' crime on his hands. Orsini had been shot in his bedroom, with the door and windows locked from the inside. He could not possibly have committed suicide.

Orsini, a 38-year-old heating engineer, was a model husband and father. He lived with his wife, Lee, and schoolgirl daughter, Tiffany, in a pleasant suburb at North Little Rock, Arkansas. As far as anyone knew, he hadn't an enemy in the world.

Orsini went to bed early on 11 March to prepare for an early appointment with a client 96 km (60 miles) out of town. He set the alarm for 04.00 to beat the morning traffic jams.

Orsini always slept alone on such nights so that his early rising would not wake the household. The family would sleep in Tiffany's room, next to his own. Soon after 21.00 he kissed them both goodnight and went upstairs to the main bedroom. It was the last time they saw him alive.

Next morning Mrs Orsini rose at 07.00. She and Tiffany had breakfast and walked to the daughter's school nearby. Back home, she began her housework. When her downstairs work finished, she went upstairs to do the bedrooms, starting with her husband's. It was closed, not like Roy at all, she thought. Normally, when he was making an early start, he left the door wide open, and left the room in a bit of a mess.

She tried the handle. The door was locked from the inside. That door had never been locked since they moved in before Tiffany was born 13 years ago. Had he somehow slept in? Had he been taken ill? Again and again, she twisted the handle of the door, knocked and called: 'Roy, Roy, are you all right?'

There was no reply. Lee Orsini, by this time thoroughly alarmed, dashed out of the house and frantically called on next door neighbour Mrs Glenda

Bell. Together the two women managed to prise open the bedroom door. Lee Orsini uttered a piercing scream. Her husband still in his striped pyjamas, lay on the bed.

Sergeant Farley and his squad were on the scene within minutes of receiving Mrs Bell's telephone call. They quickly established that, like many Americans, Roy Orsini had a gun. But it was in a closed drawer several feet from the bed and, although it was a .38, the same calibre as the weapon which had been used to kill him, it was a Smith and Wesson. The fatal bullet had been fired from a Colt. It would anyway have been impossible for Orsini to shoot himself in the back of the head, replace the gun in the drawer and then go back to the bed.

Then there was the problem of the door and windows, all of which had been securely locked from the inside. The alarm clock had been set for 04.00 and had run down. Had the death shot been fired before or after this? There was no means of knowing.

Neither Mrs Orsini nor Tiffany had heard the shot, so the .38 must have been fitted with a silencer.

Farley ordered detailed inquiries into every known relative or business contact of Orsini. A similar discreet check was made on his wife. Both had led totally blameless lives and had been devoted to each other and their daughter. There was nobody who could have had a motive for murder.

Farley said: 'I've been involved with many homicides, but never anything like this. Any way you look at it, it belongs in a book, not in real life.'

A Riddle in Life and a Riddle in Death

One sweltering lunchtime in July, Jimmy Hoffa kissed his wife Josephine, promised to be home by four, and drove away in a bullet-proof limousine.

He was on his way to a lunch date. But how far he got towards keeping his appointment no one knows. For after leaving his luxury home on the outskirts of Detroit at 12.30 on 30 July 1975, Jimmy Hoffa, America's most notorious union boss, was never seen again.

A few hours later an anonymous gravel-voiced phone caller told the police where they could find Hoffa's abandoned car. It sounded more like an

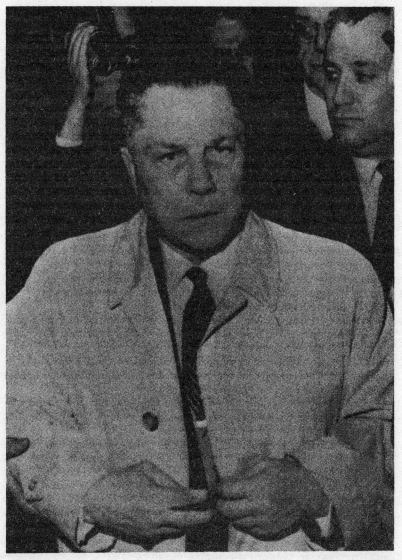

Frank Hoffa

epitaph than a tip-off. They found it shining in the sun, with no sign of a struggle and no body. Just a pair of white gloves neatly folded on the back seat.

There were three main theories about the disappearance of James – middle name Riddle – Hoffa, former president of the Teamsters Union.

The first suggestion was that he was eliminated by the Mafia who feared he would expose illegal 'loans' made by the Teamsters to underworld figures. The second theory was that he died because of a battle for power within the union. The third – and most intriguing – theory was that, knowing there was a contract on his life, he chose to disappear of his own free will. Just two days earlier he had withdrawn more than a million dollars from union funds. Like Hoffa, the money never came back to its rightful home.

His distraught family offered a $200,000 reward for information which might lead to the finding of his body, dead or alive. But there were no takers.

If there were violent and sinister overtones to the disappearance, no one should have been surprised. For this had been the pattern of Hoffa's life almost from the very beginning. As a teenager, he got a job loading trucks and, at 17, he organized his first strike. As a union leader, he favoured lieutenants who had criminal records. Many were chosen for their expertise in terror and extortion. Nevertheless, Hoffa became a hero to many of the Teamsters who had seen their wages virtually doubled in the space of a decade. He also poured millions of dollars into his own pockets and then bought a Miami bank to look after his wealth.

When the crusading Robert Kennedy was made chairman of the Senate Rackets Committee, Hoffa became his prime and very personal target. He described Hoffa's leadership of the Teamsters as a 'conspiracy of evil'. As a result of this probe initiated by Kennedy, Hoffa was eventually jailed in 1967, sentenced to serve 13 years for jury tampering and defrauding the union's pension fund to the tune of almost two million dollars.

Hoffa decreed that Frank Fitzsimmons, a long-time ally, should take his place as president on the strict understanding that he was simply holding down the job until Hoffa regained his freedom.

In 1971, Hoffa was pardoned by President Nixon on condition that he should hold no union office until 1980. But he still had a taste for power, and so began a campaign to persuade the appeal court to lift Nixon's ban.

Fitzsimmons, however, had no intention of relinquishing the reins. Detroit became a battleground as the Fitzsimmons and Hoffa factions fought for supremacy.

This, then, was the background against which Jimmy Hoffa disappeared. It seems probable that the lunch meeting never actually took place. A Hoffa aide received a phone call, supposedly from Hoffa, saying that his companions had not turned up.

But had someone set up the lunch with the intention of luring Hoffa into a trap and then abducting him at gunpoint? This was the theory the FBI favoured.

The FBI also investigated the story of Charles Allen, a former crook turned informer, who became friendly with Hoffa when they were in prison together. Allen claimed that Hoffa was beaten to death by a contract killer known as 'Monster Man' who was 2 m (6 ft 4 in) and weighed 108 kg (17 stone). The body, said Allen, was then taken to New Jersey, cut into small pieces, hidden in two oildrums, and flown to Florida.

The police, unable to verify the story, replaced the Hoffa file in the 'unsolved' category. James Riddle Hoffa was well named.

The Mysterious Mummy

A 'wax' mummy hung in an old amusement park funhouse for 50 years until a strange event revealed its horrible secret – that underneath the ghastly bandages was the embalmed body of an outlaw killed in a turn-of-the-century shootout.

The grim reality surfaced in December 1976, when a television production crew visited the old house to shoot an episode of the TV series *The Six-Million Dollar Man*. Filming was under way when one of the crew gave out a shrill scream ... One of the mummy's stick-like arms had snapped off and fallen. Where it had shattered were leathery shreds of skin and horrible clumps of human tissue clinging to the human bone.

The mummy was rushed to an autopsy room in the Los Angeles county morgue and history's strangest manhunt began. Under the many layers of wax, Los Angeles coroner Dr Thomas Noguchi found the withered body of a man. He had died long ago in his early 30s from a gunshot wound. The corpse had then been carefully embalmed with such heavy concentrations of arsenic that it had turned into a virtual mummy.

The thing had been on display in the Long Beach, California, funhouse since the 1920s, when it was brought from a bankrupt carnival operator. The time lapse meant that the police had little chance of solving the mystery. They feared that the mummy was the victim of a crime. But the only theory that anyone could come up with was stranger even than that. For it was suggested the mummy might have been a criminal himself!

The incredible story put forward by a former employee of the funhouse was that underneath the wax coating was the corpse of an Oklahoma outlaw named Elmer McCurdy.

Oklahoma authorities confirmed that there had been an Elmer McCurdy operating in the wild Oklahoma Territory in the early 1900s. He specialized in robbing trains and banks. After a Jesse James-type robbery in October 1911, McCurdy escaped to an outlaw hangout on the Big Caney River. When a posse from Pawhuska tracked him down, he died in the shootout.

But who would pick up the bill for embalming a footloose outlaw? The undertaker saw only one way to get his money: An embalmed Elmer stood in the corner of the funeral parlour where visitors could gape at him for a nickel apiece. He then fell into the hands of the travelling carnival man who sold him to the amusement park.

Fact or fiction? No one can be sure. The only question worrying Los Angeles county was what to do with the body. The answer was supplied by the Oklahoma Territorial Museum in Guthrie. The outlaw was returned to Oklahoma on 14 April 1977, and in an elegant old hearse pulled by a team of horses, Elmer was buried in the town's Boot Hill cemetery.

The Prairie's Murder Inn

One of the most notorious women in frontier America, bloody Kate Bender, operated a 'murder inn' on the Kansas prairie. Travellers who stopped there for a night were never seen again. For the few dollars in their carpetbags, Kate hid behind a curtain and split the lodger's skulls with a hatchet while they were enjoying one of her home-cooked meals.

Suspicious authorities finally raided the inn, but by that time Kate herself had grown wary. Officials found no trace of the woman, though evidence of her handiwork was plentiful. Digging behind the inn, they unearthed a human boneyard. Few of her victims were identified and the number of dead remains unknown. Even more grisly was the suspicion that Kate had fed some of her victims the flesh of earlier ones.

The riddle of Kate Bender's eerie disappearance intrigued mystery-lovers everywhere. In the hectic little mining camp of Silver City, Idaho, old-timers in the mercantile store pondered it as they sat around the pot-bellied stove.

Kate Bender's home

When Joe Monahan came in for his weekly supplies, they tested their theories on him. Not much of a talker, the young man was always a good listener. When they suggested Kate might have entered a convent or might even be running another murder inn, he simply nodded and went on his way.

To the rest of Silver City, Joe himself was a riddle. A frail little man, he shunned the camp's roaring saloons and girls of the line. Joe's home was a dugout cut into a cliff on Succor Creek near Silver City. To raise the few dollars he spent in the store he kept chickens, pigs and six scrawny cows.

In December 1903, Joe drove his cattle to winter pasture on the Boise River. But the hardships of the trail were too much. Soon after his return to Succor Creek he fell ill and died. When his body was prepared for burial, the barber-mortician ran out of the back room, stunned and sick . . .

Unbelievably, little Joe Monahan had been a woman.

The dugout was ransacked for any clues to her identity. All they found was a yellowed clipping from the *Kansas City Star* about the unsuccessful hunt for Kate Bender. Inevitably, the camp drew its own conclusions: in spite of 'Little Joe's' mild personality, had she been the ruthless killer?

To the day of the funeral there were rumours that a group of 'public minded citizens' meant to dig up the body and send it to Kansas for identification. The minister had heard the rumours too. On that windswept afternoon, he murmured a brief prayer for the unknown woman, then raised his eyes to the graveyard which was jammed with miners. 'I don't believe that this poor woman was a killer,' the minister said. 'Whatever her secret may have been, she died trying to protect it – and, in simple mercy, I ask that you let it die with her.'

The miners drifted away. There was a public subscription that evening in Silver City saloons to cover the burial costs. No one disturbed the unmarked grave. So the mystery lived on.

Who Did She Bury?

In the little coal mining town of McVey, Washington State, Nels Stenstrom and his wife Anna were among the most industrious merchants. Working side by side, they spent twelve hours of almost every day of the week in the McVey Mercantile Store – 'Where Everybody Finds Everything'.

Then a mysterious tragedy entered their lives. On 5 June 1895, Nels Stenstrom vanished without a trace. There were those who said the big man had a roving eye and might possibly have left with a woman. But no one wanted to carry that rumour to the steely-eyed Anna, who was devoted to her husband.

But Anna kept on running the store as if Nels were at her side, and it expanded and grew more prosperous.

In the summer of 1902, Stenstrom was declared legally dead. And that same day Anna made the strange announcement that was to reach newspapers throughout the US: Although he might only be legally dead, she said, he would have a proper grave.

With or without a body, she wanted a casket, a burial plot and fitting church services for her husband.

It was an idea so unusual that crowds of reporters and curious spectators poured into the little town. There was standing room only in the church when the funeral began at 14.30 on 1 July 1902. Nels had been a war veteran, and the vacant coffin was prominently displayed under a US flag. After a few words from the minister, old friends appeared at the lectern to eulogize the departed.

Anna was the last to speak. But she had scarcely started when there was sudden confusion in the crowd. A grizzled derelict in shreds of clothing staggered into an aisle whimpering and clutching his breast. Some said he looked imploringly into Anna's face before he collapsed, unconsious, to the floor.

She was the first to reach him and grope for a pulse. The tears were running down her cheeks when she raised her eyes. All she could say was 'It's Nels.'

The town's one doctor signed the death certificate, marvelling that this alcoholic wreck could be the once powerful Nels. Hundreds watched as the remains of the vagrant were borne to the Stenstrom burial plot.

But the story had an incredible sequel.

While the nearby towns of Roslyn and Cle Elum prospered, the veins of coal ran thin in McVey. It became a shabby ghost town. After Anna died and was buried with her husband, a contractor bought the store for its old lumber.

When he was bulldozing the building down, shallow graves were found beneath the floorboards. Two skeletons lay side by side. Between them was the axe that had split their skulls.

One was the skeleton of a woman destined to remain as nameless as the vagrant buried with Anna. The man's body was equally unidentifiable ... Could it have been the body of the real Nels Stenstrom?

Acrobats of Death

U go Pavesi stepped out onto the third-storey balcony of his home. An extortionist and general hoodlum, he liked to spend his evenings there while he plotted further criminal enterprises.

Usually, he would have been accompanied by his girlfriend but on this occasion 17-year-old Lorna Perricone was in hospital. As a disciplinary measure, he had put her there himself with a dozen savage blows to the face and stomach.

In the street below Pavesi's home, there were three witnesses who later reported seeing an impossible sight. They claimed to have seen a black giant 5.4 m (18 ft) tall emerge from the shadows and make his way towards the man on the balcony. The giant lifted him casually from the deck chair and let his squat body plunge to the pavement. Pavesi's severed head fell beside it, wrung from the body in an incredible display of strength.

In the deep, soft soil of the shrubbery surrounding Pavesi's home, police found the footprints of the killer. Displacement of the soil indicated that he had weighed no less than 410 kg (900 lb). But he had vanished completely in the confusion that followed the murder at Van Nuys, California, on the night of 13 November 1941, and no one knew where he would strike again.

A shrewd policeman who had been only a few blocks from the area was put on the case. Sergeant Lou Grandin toured the run-down area. One of his calls was on a psychic who called herself Madame Olga.

His visit was interrupted by the entrance of the old lady's three boarders, the powerful Perricone brothers Mario, Tony and Giorgio. Big, balding men with no-nonsense eyes, their timing and precision as an acrobatic team had won them high praise.

Mario, the spokesman, told Grandin that in 50 years of theatrical experience he had never known a giant like the alleged Van Nuys killer. Then he shocked the policeman by telling him: 'The girl Pavesi put in hospital was our sister, sergeant. And I'm using the past tense because she died a few minutes ago.'

'I'm sorry,' Grandin said humbly. 'I ask only that you stay in San Francisco until we get this thing cleaned up.'

But it was a warning that went unheeded. The date was 7 December, 1941 and something was to happen that day that changed the history of the world. The Perricone brothers were among the first to enlist after Pearl Harbor. So, too, was Sergeant Lou Grandin.

The case of the vanishing giant preyed on Grandin's mind throughout the war. On his return to the United States, he decided to pay one last visit to Madame Olga. The aged psychic was still alive but frail.

She told the ex-cop that the Perricone brothers had all died in the war – which was why she felt free to suggest a possible explanation for the death of Ugo Pavesi.

She drew out a yellowed vaudeville poster. There were the three Perricone brothers in the centre of the stage, Mario with Tony standing proudly on his shoulders. And on Tony's shoulders stood Giorgio, ripping a thick telephone directory to shreds in his big hands. The three would have made an impressive giant: Mario the planner, Tony the middleman, and Giorgio – with the huge, powerful hands.

The Oldest Kidnap Victim?

Excited scientists named him Peking Man. He was a collection of bones about 500,000 years old, unearthed near Peking in the 1920s and a vital missing link in man's knowledge of evolution. Then, in 1941, with the Japanese advancing on the city it was decided to ship the bones to America – they still have not arrived.

Dr Harry L Shapiro, former Professor of Anthropology at Columbia University, has been searching for them ever since. His theory is that they were purloined by a Marine officer who took Peking man back to America.

The story was given credence when a Chicago businessman offered $5,000 to anybody with information. A mysterious woman met the businessman on the 102nd floor of the Empire State Building in New York. She said that her husband had returned from China with fossils of some prehistoric man. She produced a photograph of the remains but before a deal could be made the woman disappeared without trace.

The FBI have followed reports of GIs returning home from Asia with strange-looking skulls, as souvenirs – without success.

A Sydney businessman maintained he had acquired the bones and buried them in a forest in Tasmania. He would reveal the spot at a price.

It is possible that Peking Man is now in both America and Australia or even in Britain. The mystery of this strange kidnap remains unsolved.

Chapter Five

Murder
Most Foul

House of Horror

When Timothy Evans walked into the police station at Merthyr Tydfil, South Wales, he was distressed and confused. He told the desk sergeant: 'I want to give myself up. I have disposed of the body of my wife.'

Evans went on to explain that he was spending a lonely self-imposed exile in Wales with relatives and that the body of his dead wife would be found in a drain at their home in London, at 10 Rillington Place, Notting Hill, where Evans rented the top floor flat.

The first police search on 30 November 1949, produced nothing. But Evans, a 24-year-old semi-literate van driver insisted that his wife was dead, the result of an attempted abortion carried out by their downstairs neighbour John Reginald Halliday Christie.

A fresh search by police produced evidence of a grisly double murder. In a small back-yard wash-house they found the body of Beryl Evans. And they found a dead baby, Evan's daughter Geraldine.

Evans seemed shattered by his daughter's death but quietly and morosely, confessed to both murders. At his trial a few months later, he retracted his admissions and blamed Christie for their murders. His accusations against his respectable neighbour hardly carried any weight in court.

Christie, aged 55, was a diligent Post Office Savings Bank clerk who had done his duty as a reserve Metropolitan policeman a few years earlier during World War 2.

Evans tried to claim in court that Christie, who often pretended to have some medical knowledge, had bungled an abortion on Beryl and she had died. Confused and hesitant, Evans insisted that Christie had promised that he would dispose of Beryl's body down the drain and arrange for baby Geraldine to be cared for by a young couple who lived nearby. Evans had given up his job and left the baby behind for 'adoption', going off to live in Wales until he could bear his guilty secret no longer. Under cross-examination he floundered deeper and deeper into hopeless excuses about why he had confessed to the murders and then turned his story round to implicate his neighbour.

Reginald Christie, who had lived quietly at Rillington Place for a dozen years with his wife Ethel, gave his evidence with calm assurance and heard the prosecution describe him as 'this perfectly innocent man'.

That was enough for the jury. They found Timothy Evans guilty of the

10 Rillington Place

murder of baby Geraldine and had no need to proceed on the charge of the murder of Beryl.

Evans was hanged and the murders dismissed as a squalid tragic case of a rather stupid young man who had cracked under the pressure of living in the London slums, earning a pittance and trying to support his family. That, it appeared at the time, was all there was to it.

What the jury and the police did not know was that 10 Rillington Place was not just the temporary crypt of Beryl and Geraldine Evans. The nondescript terrace house was a veritable graveyard. And Reginald Christie was far from the pompous, respectable minor civil servant he pretended to be.

When the police began their first search for the body of Beryl Evans, they had literally been standing on top of the bodies of the previous victims of Christie's bizarre sexual killings.

As the detectives had surveyed Christie's barren patch of back garden, discussing the possibility of digging there, Christie's little mongrel dog began scratching the soil and pawing at the skull of one of the two women he had already murdered, Muriel Eady. Christie shooed the dog away and casually kicked the earth back into place.

The police decided to have another pry around the drains and outbuildings. When they found bodies in the wash-house they were satisfied. Christie, close to panic, unearthed the skull that night and hurried off across Notting Hill with it tucked under his raincoat. He threw it into the remains of a gutted building where it was found next day by two schoolboys. And Muriel Eady was duly logged by police as an unidentified and previously undiscovered victim of the wartime bombing blitz.

Christie had a close call when the police came to investigate the deaths of Beryl and Geraldine Evans. But as the nervous shock subsided, his lust to kill again overcame his fear.

Christie's wife Ethel had no reason to suspect that two murder victims were already buried in the garden. But she may have thought that her husband was more involved in the deaths of Beryl and Geraldine than he admitted to her. She was silenced anyway by Christie, strangled and her body hidden beneath the boards of the sitting-room floor. In quick succession Christie lured three more women to his flat, all prostitutes, and killed them. It was said he could only gain sexual satisfaction from dead women.

With the remains of six dead bodies buried in the garden, dumped into a crudely papered-over kitchen cupboard and hunched underneath the floorboards, Christie left Rillington Place and moved to other lodgings.

On 24 March 1953, a prospective new tenant looking over the flat detected a foul smell from the sealed kitchen cupboard. He picked away at the wallpaper until he could glance inside – and then went straight to the police.

They arrested Reginald Christie and then began the long re-investigation into the guilt or innocence of Timothy Evans who had been hanged three years earlier.

The wave of public outrage over the murders and the execution of Evans provoked a stormy debate in Parliament and led to the suspension of capital punishment for a period of five years. But not before Reginald Christie was convicted, sentenced and hanged for murder.

Christie had hoped to cheat the noose by confessing gleefully to mass murder and having the jury judge him insane. 'The more the merrier', he confessed.

He outlined his bizarre method of killing his victims – first getting them drunk, then forcing them to inhale coal gas from the mains supply until they were unconscious. He then strangled and raped them.

Christie confessed to murdering Beryl Evans, although strangely, he denied killing baby Geraldine – a murder that Timothy Evans had already confessed to after admitting to the murder of his wife.

John Reginald Halliday Christie

Was it possible that two men, both strangers and both unaware of each other's murderous characters, had lived together under the same roof? Such a coincidence seemed unbelievable.

In 1966 a judicial review of the case under Mr Justice Brabin concluded it more probable that Evans murdered his own wife but not his baby daughter.

No one knows for sure who killed Beryl Evans. Her husband Timothy and Reginald Christie both took their terrible secrets to the gallows with them. Only one of the two men knew the complete certainty whether or not the other one was lying.

Poetry, Passion and Prison

Adelaide Bartlett was boyishly attractive, with bobbed hair, full lips and flashing eyes. She had few friends outside her husband's immediate family, and even they were often at loggerheads with the wilful young foreigner who had come into their midst.

Adelaide was born in Orléans, France, in 1856 to an English father and a wealthy, but unmarried, French mother. At the age of 17 she came to England to complete her education, staying in London at the home of her guardian. A regular visitor to the house was her guardian's brother, Edwin Bartlett, who speedily wooed, won and wed her.

Edwin, who at 29 was 10 years older than Adelaide, was a hard working and prosperous family grocer, a kindly man – but one whose life-style was not to his young bride's taste.

Adelaide fell out with Edwin's family – all except his younger brother, Frederick, with whom she had an affair. While Edwin devoted himself ever more diligently to his business, the bored wife remained at home sewing and organizing the household chores – and waiting for Frederick's illicit visits.

She made so little secret of her attraction to Frederick that the brothers' father intervened. After one acrimonious row, during which Adelaide learned that the older Mr Bartlett was planning to move in to the family home at her husband's invitation, she stormed from the house and was not seen again for some days. Since Frederick was also absent for this period, tongues began to wag ... so much so that when Adelaide's anger cooled and she returned home, she forced her father-in-law to write a letter of apology to her.

In 1885 the Bartletts moved to a grander home in Pimlico. There they were visited regularly by a young Wesleyan minister with a penchant for poetry, the Rev. George Dyson.

Edwin considered Dyson to be an improving influence on his wife and encouraged their friendship. What he may not have realized was that the minister's flowery poetry was often directed at Adelaide. He wrote to her:

Who is it that hath burst the door,
Unclosed the heart that shut before
And set her queen-like on its throne
And made its homage all her own?
My Birdie!

The Rev. Dyson did not confine his expressions of love to the written word. And his love affair with Adelaide was aided by her husband's strange reaction to the couple's growing closeness. Bartlett not only condoned his wife's friendship, he actively encouraged it. He even made a will leaving everything to his wife and naming Dyson as the executor.

Then, in December 1885, Edwin Bartlett fell ill. He had always prided himself on being particularly fit but this illness, diagnosed by the family

The trial of Adelaide Bartlett

doctor as acute gastritis, took its toll on him and he sank fast. Edwin died on New Year's Day 1886.

The doctor was sufficiently suspicious to press for a post-mortem examination, which revealed large quantities of liquid chloroform in his stomach. Everything pointed to poisoning. Yet there was one inexplicable fact ... there were no traces of the burning chloroform in Edwin's mouth or throat.

Both lovers were charged with murder, although the case against Dyson was later dropped for lack of evidence despite his admission that he had bought quantities of chloroform at various chemists' shops.

At her trial, the attractive Adelaide played brilliantly on the emotions and Victorian prejudices of the jury. She admitted dosing her husband with chloroform. But she claimed pathetically that she had first used the drug to curb his sexual demands, then later to help Edwin sleep during his illness.

The jury were sympathetic. They were also baffled by the means by which the chloroform was administered without causing burning of the throat. They acquitted Adelaide Bartlett, who disappeared without trace after her trial. It was reported that she had emigrated to America.

A famous surgeon, Sir James Paget of London's St Bartholomew's Hospital, commented: 'Now that it is all over, she should tell us in the interests of science how she did it.'

The Vicar and the Choirmistress

Even today the headlines would cause a sensation ... 'Vicar And Choirmistress Murdered In Lovers' Lane'. The congregation were scandalized to learn of the a love affair between their clergyman and a married woman and horrified by the killing. Yet no one was ever convicted of the double murder, and the mystery remains to this day.

A courting couple discovered the bodies of the Rev. Edward Wheeler Hall and Mrs Eleanor Mills, choir leader at his church, on 16 September 1922. The spot, by an abandoned farm near New Brunswick, New Jersey, was a favourite with lovers seeking solitude.

Hall, minister of St John the Evangelist Church, in New Brunswick, and his mistress had both been shot through the head. But more sinister ... the choir leader's vocal cords had been cut in an act of savage hate. The pair's passionate letters to each other were strewn contemptuously around the bodies.

Hall's wife Frances was questioned, as was Mrs Mills' husband James, but no charges were brought. Mrs Hall was a popular figure among the church-going community. There were stories of detectives ignoring clues, of vital evidence going missing, and of a prosecutor unwilling to take action. There was neither a post-mortem nor an inquest.

There the case might have been conveniently closed, but for a news-hungry editor convinced there had been a cover-up.

Philip Payne of the *New York Mirror*, sent his own sleuths to the scene to piece together the evidence. They managed to get hold of Hall's calling card, which police had found propped against his body, and Payne claimed it carried the fingerprints of Mrs Hall's brother Willie.

Faced with this and other evidence, police brought murder charges against Mrs Hall, her cousin Henry Carpender, a brother Henry Stevens and Willie.

Willie, the strangest defendant, was an eccentric who liked to dress up in fireman's uniform and put out fires in his own backyard.

They were finally brought to trial four years after the killings, in November 1926. After so long, memories were failing. The wealthy Mrs Hall's high-powered lawyers made mincemeat of the prosecution witnesses' shaky testimony.

Soon it became clear that the prosecution's case rested on one alleged eye-witness – Jane Gibson, a pig farmer. Dying of cancer, she was wheeled into court in a hospital bed and whispered her vital evidence.

Four years earlier, then a fit and vigorous countrywoman, she said she had been exercising her mule Jennie on the night of the murders. She identified the four defendants and said she had seen them in the lane where the bodies were later found.

With them were the Rev. Hall and Mrs Mills. Voices were raised in anger, she said and there was mention of love letters. Mrs Gibson rode away, wanting no part of a family quarrel.

Her testimony, delivered firmly despite her pain, obviously impressed the jury. But then a relative gave evidence denying that Mrs Gibson had been out of the house that night.

Moments later the courtroom was rocked by the news that a prisoner in jail in New York had confessed to the killings. But he was exposed as a sensation-seeker who was nowhere near New Brunswick when the murders were comitted.

Witnesses gave the Stevens brothers and cousin Henry watertight alibis, and the defence then suggested that Mrs Gibson had shot the couple, thinking they were thieves after her corn.

But the most telling witness of all was the incredibly calm Mrs Hall. She had loved her husband dearly, she said, and had never suspected an infidelity. Least of all with Eleanor Mills, whom she had always regarded as her dearest friend.

Mrs Hall said she could not account for Jane Gibson's testimony, but would forgive her because of her suffering. The jury believed the wronged wife, and all four defendants were acquitted.

It was a subdued crowd who left the courtroom, knowing that somewhere in their midst a killer was still at large.

And some strange events followed.

Mrs Hall sued the *New York Mirror* for two million dollars.

Philip Payne, desperate to rebuild his reputation, set out to make a record transatlantic flight to Rome. His plane vanished.

Officials who had been accused of concealing evidence lived under a cloud. And those involved in the prosecution were eased from office.

Witnesses for both sides were struck by a succession of tragedies. Soon after Mrs Gibson's death, Mrs Hall also died of cancer. And so, one by one, did the other defendants.

The case remains unsolved.

Death in Happy Valley

When 57-year-old Sir Henry 'Jock' Delves Broughton married a young blonde with a passion for clothes and jewels in 1940, he told her: 'If you ever fall in love with someone else and want a divorce, I won't stand in your way.'

The old Etonian baronet also promised his beautiful bride Diana, 30 years his junior, an income of £5,000 a year for 7 years should she ever leave him for another man.

Just three months after the marriage, Diana did exactly that. She fell in love with another Old Etonian, Josslyn Hay, the 39-year-old Earl of Erroll.

The brevity of the marriage would seem extraordinary even in more modern, permissive times. But in the strange, close circle in which Hay and

Above: Josslyn Hay's car
Right: Josslyn Hay

the Broughtons lived, it was not too unorthodox. Their home was an area of colonial Kenya known as Happy Valley, where wild drinking, cocaine-snorting and wife-swapping were prevalent in 1940.

Josslyn Hay himself was a dedicated philanderer whose favourite saying was 'to hell with husbands'. But his amoral attitude appeared not to worry Sir Henry, the cuckolded husband. At a dinner party he threw at the local country club, he toasted his wife and her lover: 'I wish them every happiness and may their union be blessed with an heir. To Diana and Joss.'

Broughton returned home visibly drunk, leaving Erroll and Diana to dance. Erroll then drove off alone, remarking as he left: 'The old boy's so nice, it smells bad.'

Two hours later Erroll was found on the floor of his Buick, a bullet through his head. But the murder weapon was not to be seen.

Though Broughton seemed the obvious suspect, such was the cuckolded baronet's calm and masterful conduct in the witness box that he was found 'not guilty'.

After the acquittal Broughton and Diana soon split up. He committed suicide the following year, still protesting his innocence.

Lizzie and the Axe

Crime historians still work to clear the name of Lizzie Borden, long portrayed as the fiendish axe-murderer who 'gave her mother 40 whacks ... and her father 41.'

Although Hollywood labelled poor Lizzie a killer and gossips insisted she was a cruel murderess, the 32-year-old spinster was actually acquitted by a jury and lived to a ripe old age, a gentle woman and a benefactor to animals. But until her death in 1937, she was taunted by one of the most cruel jingles in history:

Lizzie Borden took an axe
And gave her mother 40 whacks
When she saw what she had done
She gave her father 41.

In a popular television movie actress Elizabeth Montgomery portrayed Lizzie as a vicious killer who hacked her parents to death in the nude to avoid getting bloodstains on her dress. But many people believe that Lizzie was really the victim of bungling officials who let the real killer slip through their fingers.

Her ordeal began on the morning of 4 August 1892. In the living room of a bleak old house in Fall River, Massachusetts, Lizzie found her father, banker Andrew Borden with his head beaten to 'an unrecognizable pulp'. He lay on a blood-soaked sofa, where he had apparently been napping when the murderer struck. And in the horror of that discovery it would be an hour before Lizzie knew that there were other horrors ahead.

The young woman's stepmother, Abby Borden, had supposedly been called from the house to the sickbed of a friend. But she had not gone after all. She was on the floor of an upstairs guest room, her skull a mass of blood and splintered bone.

Inescapably, the net began to tighten around Lizzie Borden. She told police she had been in the barn looking for fish-line sinkers when the killings took place.

Bridget Sullivan, the Borden's hired girl had been upstairs dozing through the heat of the day. Emma Borden, Lizzie's older sister had been out of town. And John V. Morse, a visiting uncle, had been out making business calls. Excluding Bridget – whom Lizzie 'vouched for' – that left Lizzie herself.

Lizzie Borden was brought to trial in June 1893 and the evidence at first began to stack against her. There had been no love lost between the Borden daughters and their shrewish stepmother, who reputedly nagged at her husband to cut them off without a penny. Nor had there been any show of affection for their father, whose stinginess and domestic tyranny were bywords in Fall River.

It was suggested that Lizzie had butchered her parents in an epileptic seizure and had no memories of the crime. But police had unearthed no murder weapon, no witnesses, no shreds of bloody clothing, and the circumstantial evidence was just too flimsy.

Acquitted to a chorus of rousing cheers, Lizzie went back to the bleak old house. She was to share with her sister until 1923, when they parted company.

There were suspicions about three people who had testified against Lizzie but, for reasons never explained, the police failed to reopen the case.

As the years passed, the old jingle haunted Lizzie Borden's life and wax museums continued to cast her as an axe-wielding fiend. Friends deserted her. In her last days, there were no visitors in the Fall River house. She died leaving a fortune to charity, including a $30,000 bequest to the Society for the Prevention of Cruelty to Animals. Gentle in life and forgiving in death, she said nothing about the agonies she had once suffered.

The Harry Oakes Affair

The sub-tropical paradise of the Bahamas boasts 700 islands and rocky islets or cays, most of them uninhabited, surrounded by the sparkling blue-green waters of the Gulf Stream. Only 80 km (50 miles) away across the horizon is the millionaire's paradise of Miami and all the brash excitement of Florida, Land of the Stars and Stripes.

The Union Jack flies in Nassau, capital of the Bahamas, testimony to its position as an outpost of British civilization and administration, a veneer of respectability over its fabled history as a haven for buccaneers and rum runners, adventures and soldiers of fortune.

But to Edward Albert Patrick David, Duke of Windsor, former monarch of the British Empire, life in the Bahamas had held all the appeal of exile in an Arctic waste. His appointment as Governor General in August 1940 was seen as a deliberate punishment by the wartime cabinet of Winston Churchill.

For four years, since his abdication as King Edward VIII, the headstrong and impetuous duke had been a grave embarassment to his government and loyal subjects. He had provoked a constitutional crisis and world-wide scandal when he abdicated his throne to marry the woman he loved, American divorcee Wallis Simpson. A year after their marriage the duke and his restless American duchess had even visited Nazi Chancellor Adolf Hitler in Germany while he was arming his nation for war against Britain. The duke quickly became a propaganda pawn for the Nazis.

The duke had only set foot on English soil once since his marriage before being caught up in the roaring tide of war as the Germans invaded France and sped towards the Windsors' new adopted home in Paris.

The former king and his wife fled south to neutral Spain and sought safety in Madrid. Fearful that the duke might be the victim of a kidnap and used as a hostage, Churchill asked him to return home by flying boat to Britain.

But the Duke of Windsor, resentful that his wife would not be accorded any privilege or status as a member of the royal family, refused. He chose the only alternative Churchill gave him, the post of Governor General of the Bahamas, thousands of miles across the Atlantic where he could be safely isolated from the intrigues of wartime Europe.

Lonely and ostracized, the Windsors arrived in Nassau to be greeted by the Bahamas' most prominent citizen, Sir Harry Oakes. Sir Harry's title was no genteel hereditary honour from a long line of ennobled forefathers. He was reputedly one of the richest men in the Empire, a newly created baronet, a self-made multi-millionaire. He was a ruthless businessman who had battled and bullied his way to the top from a hell-raising existence as a Yukon and Alaskan gold prospector. This hardened man of the world swiftly became the Duke of Windsor's close friend.

Their social and personal lives became entwined and Oakes even turned over his palatial home in Nassau to the Windsors while the Governor General's mansion was refurbished. The two men were constant drinking and dining companions on their frequent trips to the American mainland where Oakes introduced the duke to his social and business acquaintances.

The duke's lifetime of royal grooming as a man born to handle the gravest of personal and national crises helped him maintain his composure on the morning of 8 July 1943 when his equerry roused him from sleep and told him that Oakes was dead. He had been savagely beaten and stabbed, his skull had been fractured and an attempt had been made to burn his bloodstained body beyond recognition.

The former king quickly invoked his authority under the Emergency War Powers Act, using his powers of censorship to insist that news of Sir Harry's murder should be hushed up. A few hours later he belatedly put the wheels of legal investigation into motion – by calling in a personal contact in the Miami police.

The duke made the baffling request to Miami Police Department: 'I think one of our leading citizens has committed suicide. Can you come and confirm this?' In fact Sir Harry Oakes's 'suicide' had all the hallmarks of a Mafia gangland contract killing.

Harry Oakes had not been born a British subject. The son of a schoolteacher in Sangerville, Maine, he was a daydreamer who spent his college days boasting of the great fortune he planned to amass. After two years as a student doctor at Syracuse he gave up college. Harry told his fellow students, all dedicated young medical men: 'You can make a good living, but you'll never get filthy rich as a doctor. I want to be filthy rich.'

Harry put his medical training to use as a hospital orderly in the prospecting camps of the Canadian north, treating frostbite and gangrene and malnutrition, while he gleaned every scrap of information he could from experienced old panhandlers.

For 14 years he followed the restless waves of prospectors chasing every elusive strike from California to Yukon, Australia and the Congo. His dogged persistence paid off in 1910 when, with a partner, he finally struck gold at Kirkland Lake in northern Ontario. It was the second largest gold find in North America and over the next 12 years he connived and wheedled and spent part of his growing fortune to buy out his partner's interests and gain sole control.

Oakes was a crude and ruthless tycoon by 1923 when, at the age of 48, he married Australian bank typist Eunice MacIntyre who he met on a cruise liner. To strengthen his links with the country which provided his massive wealth, Oakes renounced his American citizenship and became a naturalized Canadian.

But Harry Oakes became disenchanted with his adopted country as his tax bill climbed higher and higher and he found himself paying 85 per cent of his income to the taxman.

On holiday with his wife and five children at one of his homes in Palm Beach, he met real estate promoter Harold Christie who boasted of the tax advantages of the Bahamas, where the British administration charged no income tax or death duties. It did not take Oakes long to decide to protect his fortune by moving to Nassau and he became a grateful benefactor. He poured millions of pounds into the islands, buying hotels and landscaping golf courses, funding charities to provide milk for children and hospitals for the poor.

His generosity soon spilled over into Britain itself where he bestowed £250,000 on one hospital. A grateful King George VI, the Duke of Windsor's younger brother who had succeeded to the throne after the Abdication, conferred a baronetcy on him in 1939.

The colourful and brash businessman who greeted the Windsors on their arrival set about making himself the power behind the Duke of Windsor's new 'throne'. All major legislation required the consent of the Governor General – the duke – and Sir Harry had him eating out of his hand.

This was the cosy relationship that real estate developer Harold Christie had to explain to his business associate when they met in Palm Beach, Florida, to discuss the prospect of opening a casino in the Bahamas.

He had already ingratiated himself with the duke and had his tacit endorsement. But Sir Harry was blowing hot and cold about the plan. Harold Christie may have wanted to apply some more gentle persuasion to the cantankerous old tycoon when he met him on the night of 7 July 1943 at Sir Harry's palatial home 'Westbourne' in Nassau.

Sir Harry was due to leave in two days time to join his family at yet another holiday home, in Maine, and Christie could not afford to miss the opportunity for some business talk. Sir Harry had guests to a small dinner party that night but they left at 23.00.

Then, according to Harold Christie, he went to bed and Christie retired to another bedroom further down the corridor. Neither man left the house again that night, Christie claimed, and although wakened during the night by the thunder of a tropical storm, he heard no sound from Sir Harry's bedroom.

When he rose for breakfast at 07.00 he strolled along the balcony to the screen door leading to the master bedroom and called out for Sir Harry. There was no reply, so he waited a few seconds and stepped inside.

Christie chilled at the sight that greeted him. The room was filled with smoke, but there was no fire. Sir Harry Oakes lay on his back on the bed, his face caked with blood, his skull fractured with four puncture marks, his flimsy pyjamas burned off and sticking to the open blisters on his charred skin.

Christie's calls of alarm alerted a housekeeper and within minutes he made the first of his frantic telephone calls to the Island Police Commissioner and to the Governor General, the Duke of Windsor.

The Bahamas police were no experts in matters of sudden, violent death and it was not entirely without relief that the commissioner received the news that the duke had asked for help from the Miami Police Department to confirm Sir Harry's 'suicide'.

The duke had spoken to Captain Edward Melchen, chief of the homicide bureau, a policeman who was also a personal friend, having acted as a bodyguard for the duke on his frequent visits to Miami. Within hours, Melchen arrived in Nassau accompanied by another trusted detective, Captain James Barker. The two men made one cursory inspection of the blistered body on the smoke-blackened bed.

'Face up to it,' Melchen told the Duke. 'This is no suicide.'

Throughout the following day, while the two Americans set up a temporary headquarters at 'Westbourne' interviewing members of the staff and the dead baronet's family, Christie and the Duke of Windsor kept in constant touch with each other by telephone. That afternoon the duke visited the murder house himself to see the scene of the gruesome crime and he spent some twenty minutes alone with Captain James Barker.

Two hours later, a suspect for the murder of Sir Harry Oakes was arrested.

Alfred de Marigny was a lean, lanky 36-year-old with a dark complexion, a native of the Indian Ocean island of Mauritius. He was also Sir Harry Oakes's son-in-law.

De Marigny had been married and divorced twice before he began his courtship of 17-year-old Nancy, Sir Harry's eldest daughter. He had been living in the Bahamas squandering the divorce settlement from his wealthy second wife when he set his sights on Nancy, and the locals all agreed he was a shiftless gigolo.

His relationship with his mercurial father-in-law had been stormy ever since de Marigny's marriage to Nancy in New York two days after her 18th birthday ... two days after becoming old enough to marry without her parents' consent.

At the time of her father's death, Nancy de Marigny had been in Florida for medical treatment and Alfred had thrown a dinner party with his houseguest and 'hanger-on', fellow Mauritian playboy George de Videlou.

Alfred left the house at 01.00 to drive two of his guests home. His route could have taken him past 'Westbourne' in the middle of the night, the prosecution insisted at his trial.

And there was evidence to link him with the murder, prosecuting attorney Eric Hallinan claimed. Whoever killed Sir Harry tried to spread flames around the room to burn evidence of the crime. And when de Marigny was examined by police, it was found the hairs on his right arm had been singed and burned.

More importantly, according to the prosecution de Marigny's fingerprints was found on an ornamental Chinese screen in the murder bedroom.

The importance of the singed hairs on de Marigny's arms was quickly squashed by defence counsel Godfrey Higgs who extracted testimony from a witness, one of de Marigny's dinner guests, that Sir Harry's son-in-law had scorched his arm trying to light a candle inside a lantern on the dinner table.

The evidence of the fingerprint became the crucial turning point in the case and highlighted some inexplicably inept investigation. Miami cop Captain James Barker testified that he had 'lifted' a fingerprint of Alfred de Marigny from the Chinese screen. He had used a gummed strip of rubber to obtain the imprint of the moist fingermark – at the same time destroying any permanent evidence that the print had been on the surface of the screen.

The space where de Marigny's print was alleged to have been was blank. Captain Barker, whose evidence became more hesitant, admitted he had not brought his own camera with him from Miami to photograph fingerprint evidence 'in situ'. He told the court, quite reasonably: 'I thought I was coming to confirm a suicide. The fingerprint camera didn't seem important.'

Barker's credibility was finally demolished by the defence's own expert, Maurice O'Neil of the New Orleans Police Department, a past president of the International Association of Identification. He examined a photograph of the sharp contours of de Marigny's fingerprint and declared it could not have been lifted off the screen without being superimposed on the pattern of intricate etchings which also covered the screen.

De Marigny's fingerprint, he deduced, had been lifted from a smooth surface, possibly from a tumbler or a cigarette packet the accused man had handled in Sir Harry's bedroom long after the murder when he was invited to the house by the American detectives.

Defence attorney Higgs never made any suggestion why he thought Captain Barker should give such blatantly phoney evidence. And there was little explanation for another crucial piece of cross examination ...

Harold Christie, the property developer who slept in the murder house, swore on oath that neither he nor Sir Harry had left 'Westbourne' after 23.00

that night. Then Higgs called to the witness stand Captain Edward Sears, a reliable Bahamian policeman, assistant superintendent in charge of traffic.

Sears, who had know Christie since their schooldays together, confidently testified that he had seen him in George Street, Nassau, at 01.00 on the night of the murder. Christie had been a passenger in a station wagon speeding away from the direction of Nassau harbour. Sears could not identify the other man in the car, the driver. He only knew he was a white man, a stranger to the islands.

The jury retired for two hours to consider their verdict. They found Alfred de Marigny not guilty of the murder of his father-in-law.

No one else was ever charged with the murder of Sir Harry Oakes.

One blood-spattered clue to the identity of the man who may have murdered Sir Harry was uncovered nearly ten years later in Miami, on 26 December 1952, when Captain James Barker was killed by a .38 bullet from his own revolver.

The trigger was pulled by his son who tearfully told Dade County Court that Captain Barker had become a violent drug addict, corrupt and depraved. The policeman's slaying at the hands of his son was ruled 'justifiable homicide'.

It came as no surprise to his colleagues who had known for years that Barker was on the payroll of Meyer Lansky, the tough and ruthless gangster who ran the Mafia crime syndicate in Florida and Cuba.

At the time of Sir Harry's death, Lansky desperately wanted official approval to open a lucrative gambling casino in Nassau. He pulled every trick he knew and used the services of any influential people in the Bahamas he thought could be won over to his cause.

Lansky told his henchmen that one obstinate man was standing in his path and would have to be taught a lesson.

To this day people in the Bahamas still talk about the powerful motor cruisers which used to slip in and out of Nassau harbour any time they pleased, without bothering with customs and immigration formalities. They were the ships of Lansky's fleet, crewed by gun-toting skippers who knew the waters between Miami and Nassau from the days of Prohibition, when they ran illicit booze from the liquor warehouses of the British Bahamas to the speakeasies of Florida.

If Harold Christie was seen sitting as a terrified passenger in a car speeding from the docks the night Sir Harry Oakes was murdered, had he been to a meeting aboard one of those boats? Had Sir Harry been with him?

Was Sir Harry's bleeding body hunched in the back of the station wagon, fatally beaten after telling Lansky's emissaries that nobody pushed Harry Oakes around, not even the Mob?

The unidentified white man seen by police Superintendent Sears ... was the man Meyer Lansky sent to Nassau to teach Sir Harry Oakes a lesson?

Did Captain James Barker, the Miami policeman on Lansky's payroll, have orders to find a scapegoat? Did he try to frame the hapless de Marigny to shift suspicion from a contract killer?

As soon as decently possible after the end of World War 2 the Duke of Windsor left the Bahamas, hurrying back to a civilized European exile in Paris. He never discussed the Oakes murder.

Harold Christie was later knighted for his services to the Government of the Bahamas. He died in September 1973 while travelling in Germany.

Killings in the Congo

Assassination is the murder which touches the lives of millions and changes the course of history. The life of a national hero is ended by a bullet from a telescopic rifle, or a tyrant and his entourage are swept away in one blast from a hidden bomb.

The motives of a single assassin can be complex, from a madman harbouring a murderous grudge for some imagined injustice, to a lone patriot willing to sacrifice his own life to end the rule of a dictator. Often assassination is murder by committee, by a political group who want to wrest power from their opponents by destroying their figurehead.

Almost always assassination is an open outrage. The murder of a public figure usually has to be carried out in a public place, a factor dictated by the need to catch the victim when he is most exposed and vulnerable – and often a grisly ploy by the assassins to demonstrate their power and determination before a stunned audience. Assassins plot murder in secret and kill in public. And they are not slow to accept the responsibility for their crime. The lone madman is rewarded with the public platform he seeks, the political committee want to announce their success widely and clearly.

But the deaths of two prominent political figures within nine months of each other in 1961 may have provided rare case histories of assassinations unadmitted and undeclared.

Both deaths are linked together in the turbulent world of African politics. One was explained away as an unplanned, unfortunate killing. The other was

Patrice Lumumba shows his wrist which was injured during imprisonment

neatly catalogued as a fatal flying accident, the understandable failure of man and machine on a tricky night flight. Doubts still linger about the real causes of the deaths of firebrand African revolutionary Patrice Lumumba and international statesman Dag Hammarskjoeld, the peace-making Secretary General of the United Nations.

Patrice Emergy Lumumba was a fiery, erratic orator, a 35-year-old inexperienced politician with a driving, ruthless ambition. His lust for power and his ability to whip up an emotional crowd made him a force to be reckoned with in 1960 when the colonial rulers of the vast tract of the Belgian Congo felt the wind of change sweeping through Africa.

Foreseeing the explosive force of rising African nationalism, the Belgians had no great wish to pay the heavy price for hanging on to their African colony. But neither could they see any prospect for a smooth transition to independence as they began to hand over power to the people of the Congo in the elections of 1960. They were dismayed by the growing support for rebel leader Moise Tshombe who was leading the movement to wrench his own rich Katanga Province from the new independent Congo into a separate nation. But they watched most closely two political rivals who both swore to force Katanga to stay within the new Congo and who would hold the balance of power between them.

The Belgians were quietly satisfied when the election returned the quiet, educated civil servant Joseph Kasavubu to the post of President. They saw danger signs in the wave of popular support which swept Patrice Lumumba, a rebellious postmaster, into power as Prime Minister. Lumumba, they knew, had courted the promise of military backing from the Soviet Union to help him win office.

The new Prime Minister, expelled from a Roman Catholic mission school as a teenager for sexual promiscuity and later jailed for two years for embezzlement, confirmed their worst fears. Within weeks the enthusiastic and naive Lumumba found he had unleashed forces he could not control. The political theorists and policy managers of Moscow supervized his every move as the Congolese began to feel they were being freed from one foreign colonial ruler just in time to inherit another. Lumumba's reaction was to begin a bloody purge against dissident tribesmen using the resources of the teams of Russian technicians and military advisers pouring into the country.

Lumumba personally directed his troops to carry out the massacre of 3,000 Baluba tribesmen, flying his army to the scene in 19 Ilyushin jet transports provided by the Russians.

Some international observers condoned his ruthlessness as the brute force needed to weld the newly born country together. Others saw him provoking an increasingly bitter civil war.

Under pressure from the Belgians, President Kasavubu had Lumumba arrested and removed from office. There followed a cat and mouse game in which Lumumba escaped from house arrest and, according to his supporters, was greeted by cheering crowds in every village he visited.

The departing Belgians, who wanted to have a stable ally in the new Congo Republic to protect their commercial interests, were angered by Lumumba's freedom, although they seemed to regard him more as a nuisance than a serious menace, a naive troublemaker who would soon outlive his usefulness to his political controllers.

Lumumba was re-arrested in January 1961 and sent to an area where he could not expect any cheering crowds of villagers, the rebellious province of Katanga. Within a week he was dead, together with his two trusted followers Joseph Okito and Mauruce Mpolo.

But that was not the way the story was told ... Initially, Patrice Lumumba was reported to have escaped from custody yet again. A poker-faced Katanga Minister of the Interior Paul Munungo held a brief press conference to show newsmen the hole in the wall where he claimed Lumumba and his accomplices had tunnelled their way to freedom from their villa in Elisabethville, under the noses of their guards. 'We are offering a reward for their capture,' he explained.

His next press conference, three days later, was equally brief and subdued. Lumumba, according to the minister, had escaped from Elisabethville by car, travelling more than 321 km (200 miles) through unfriendly country, and stopped at a remote settlement in the bush outside the town of Kolwezi. There the villagers, anxious to claim the £3,000 reward, had promptly hacked him and his companions to death. A Katangese official had visited the site and confirmed the three men were buried in an unmarked grave.

All pressure from the journalists for further details was brushed aside.

'We forgot to specify on the reward posters that we wanted Lumumba captured alive', the Minister apologized. 'So the villagers are not to blame for his death. Besides he was a criminal so there's no harm done.'

And the location of the un-named village? It had to be kept secret, was the reply, to prevent any potentially ill-advized pilgrimages by Lumumba supporters. Lumumba's untimely death was doubtless a relief to the harassed Belgians. But the Russians who had been seen to be powerless to protect their protégé, were furious.

'Assassination' they cried and grandly set about planning a university for African revolutionaries in Moscow, to be named as a memorial to Patrice Lumumba. In the meantime they demanded the resignation of the Secretary General of the United Nations, the international body which was overseeing the Congo's transition to independence.

The wreckage of Dag Hammerskjoeld's aircraft

Being the target of scathing abuse and demands that he quit his job were nothing new for Dag Hammarskjoeld. The Scandinavian elder statesman suffered the violent criticism of Western leaders who claimed he was not making enough use of the multinational UN armed forces at his command to speed up the creation of the new Congo state. Eastern leaders complained bitterly that he interfered too much.

When Gurkha troops provided by India for the UN peace-keeping operation beat and killed hundreds of Katangan rebels, Hammarskjoeld shouldered the responsibility, burdened by the sharp condemnation of world leaders who were appalled by his mishandling of the delicate situation. Russian premier Nikita Krushchev branded the UN official: 'A bloody handed lackey of the colonial powers'.

Hammarskjoeld simply went about his job as he saw it, impartially trying to be a peaceful midwife in the bloody and painful birth of the new Congo.

He seems not to have hesitated when he received the invitation from the Katangan rebel leader, Moise Tshombe, to meet him for talks on a possible peace initiative in the battle between the breakaway province and the rest of the Congo. The talks were to be held in neutral territory, in Ndola in Rhodesia, the neighbouring country to Katanga.

From the outset, the flight was surrounded in furtive secrecy and disastrous planning. Hammarskjoeld planned to fly from Leopoldville in a DC4 Skymaster plane, specially prepared at the airport for him. At the last minute, to avoid the waiting packs of journalists, he switched to another aircraft, a DC6 airliner.

The DC6 was certainly better equipped. It was the personal plane of General Sean McKeown, commander of the UN forces in the Congo. With its four powerful engines it had a comfortable cruising range of more than 4,000 km (2,500 miles).

But 24 hours before, the DC6 had come under attack as Congolese soldiers had blasted one of its engines with anti-aircraft fire. The DC6 had been hastily repaired and left unguarded in a dispersal bay at Leopoldville Airport.

The pilot, Per-Erik Hallonquist, added to the confusion, designed to throw journalists off the track, by filing a flight plan for a journey to a small airport in Kisai Province, about halfway along his secret route to the Rhodesian border town of Ndola.

He took off in mid-afternoon, with 15 other people on board, including a radio operator with no flying experience. Only minutes before becoming airborne did he realize that the page of maps and instructions giving details of his approach to Ndola, was missing from his flight briefing book.

The flight, however, seems to have begun uneventfully. After four hours flying, around his expected time of arrival, Hallonquist contacted Ndola air traffic control, asking about weather and runway conditions and reporting his intention to descend from high altitude to 9,700 km (6,000 ft), obviously preparing to begin his approach to the airport.

The control tower responded and waited. And waited and waited . . .

Two and a half hours later, the controllers were startled to see the DC6 approach the airfield from the south-west, flying from deep inside Rhodesian territory as if it had overshot its destination by 160 km (100 miles) and was re-tracing its route. There had been consternation over the non-arrival of the DC6 but no panic. The aircraft still had enough fuel to stay aloft for another seven hours.

Hallonquist radioed again, with matter-of-fact calmness. 'I have your runway lights in sight . . . Overhead Ndola . . . . Now descending.' Without the benefit of radar coverage, the air traffic control staff peered into the night, beyond the runway, waiting for a glimpse of the DC6. They saw only a sudden brilliant flash of flame. Then darkness. The DC6, turning on its final approach, had struck a tree with its wingtip and plunged burning into a forest close to the airport.

In the confusion, darkness and thick jungle, it took almost two hours for the first rescue team to locate the aircraft. They found bodies scattered all round the strewn wreckage. And they found the macabre clues which seemed to show that the final fatal plunge of the DC6 might not have been a simple misjudgement by its pilot.

The fuselage, near the flight deck, was peppered with bullet holes. The body of Dag Hammarskjoeld lay sprawled in the aisle between the twisted seats. A few feet away was a revolver. And tucked into the lapel of his jacket was a playing card, the Ace of Spades.

Only one man was found alive that night, security officer Harry Jullian, an American. He was unconscious, suffering broken limbs and burns to 50 per cent of his body.

The next day the investigators began to piece together the evidence. Hammarskjoeld had not died instantly of his injuries and he had not been shot. But the long delay in reaching the crash site meant that he died without being able to tell anything about the final few minutes of the flight.

Smashed bottles of whisky and brandy had been found in the wreckage, adding weight to reports that many of the flight crew and and security escort had boarded the plane weary and staggering after an all-night binge in a Leopoldville drinking club.

Technical experts found that the plane's altimeter had an inexplicable mechanical error of 37 m (1,200 ft), giving the pilot a deceptively safe reading of his height above the ground.

And one witness had reported hearing the whistle of jets above the airport only minutes before the DC6 crashed. The only jets within flying distance were the fighter aircraft of the rebel Katangese, 160 km (100 miles) away in Elisabethville.

Later that day Sergeant Jullian recovered consciousness. The investigators sat by his bedside.

'Where had you been during the missing two hours?' they asked. 'Why didn't you arrive when you were expected?''

'Mr Hammarskjoeld told us to turn back, he didn't say why,' was all the injured man could reply. He died two days later without speaking again.

A Rhodesian inquiry firmly blamed the crash on pilot error. Later a five-man UN Commission sifted through the evidence, considering sabotage and gunfire, and concluded that the cause of the crash still remained unexplained.

The Katangese, who had bitter memories of their treatment at the hands of the UN's Gurkha troops, refused to take part in any investigation.

If Dag Hammarskjoeld's plane was brought down by a time delay bomb or a gunfight in the cabin or an attack by jet fighters, no one gloated openly or took the blame for killing him.

But who put the mark of death, the Ace of Spades, across the chest of the dying statesman? Could it have been someone who shared that last flight with him?

Streets of Fear

He struck terror into the heart of London's East End. Fear and panic stalked the streets, and the mention of his name would silence a noisy pub.

Jack the Ripper was what they called him ... this twisted and mysterious killer who preyed on women forced by poverty to sell their bodies for a few pennies in the alleys and backstreets.

Jack the Ripper's reign of terror was mercifully short. Three months after he first struck, on a warm summer night a century ago, he claimed his last victim.

He is known to have murdered at least five women, and some criminologists believe the true tally is eleven. But his identity has remained a mystery. Scotland Yard files on the case will be made public in 1992 but they are expected to cast little new light on the mysterious attacker.

One of Jack the Ripper's victims was found behind this shop

All that is known for certain is that the Ripper had some medical knowledge and was left-handed – as police surgeons examining the remains of his victims noticed. He is believed to have been a tall, slim, pale man with a black moustache. Several people, including a policeman, saw such a man hurrying away from the vicinity of the crimes. In each case he was said to be wearing a cap and a long coat, and to walk with the vigorous stride of a young man.

The terror began shortly after 05.00 on the morning of 7 August 1888, when a man found the mutilated body of a woman on the landing of a Whitechapel tenement block.

She was identified as Martha Turner, a prostitute. She had been stabbed several times.

The murder of East End prostitutes was no rare thing in those days. London's docks were always filled with ships from around the world, and foreign seamen packed the pubs and sleazy drinking dens near the waterfront.

But the mutilation was unusual. And when a second, similar murder happened 24 days later, fear brought a chill to the warm late summer evenings.

The body of 42-year-old Mary Ann Nicholls – known as Pretty Polly – was found in the early hours of 31 August. Mary had been trying to earn fourpence, the price of a dosshouse bed, with perhaps a few coppers more for a couple of tots of gin. When last seen she was approached by a tall, pale man, and disappeared into the shadows with him. She was found with her throat cut, and her body savagely mutilated.

A detective said, 'Only a madman could have done this.' And a police surgeon added: 'I have never seen so horrible a case.'

A week later the Ripper struck again, killing 'Dark Annie' Chapman, who was 47 and dying of tuberculosis. Her disembowelled body was found by a porter from Spitalfields market, her few possessions neatly laid out alongside.

On 25 September, 18 days after Annie's death, a letter arrived at the Central News Agency in Fleet Street. It read:

'Dear Boss, I keep on hearing that the police have caught me. But they won't fix me yet ... I am down on certain types of woman and I won't stop ripping them until I get buckled.

Grand job, that last job was. I gave the lady no time to squeal. I love my work and want to start again. You will soon hear from me, with my funny little game.

I saved some of the proper red stuff in a ginger beer bottle after my last job to write with, but it went thick like glue and I can't use it. Red ink is fit enough, I hope. Ha, ha!

Next time I shall clip the ears off and send them to the police just for jolly.'

The letter was signed 'Jack the Ripper'. It was the first time the name had ever been used. And it immortalized this twisted and mysterious killer of the London backstreets.

The next victim was Elizabeth 'Long Liz' Stride, whose body was found behind a factory gate by a policeman on the morning of Sunday 30 September. She had not been mutilated, and police suspected the Ripper had been disturbed in his grisly task.

But he soon found another victim, and left the only clear clue to his identity. The bloody remains of 40-year-old Catherine Eddowes were found about 1.5 km from where Liz's body had been discovered. She was the most terribly mutilated victim so far. Her ears had been cut off. And a trail of blood from the corpse led to a chalked message on a wall: 'The Jewes are not men to be blamed for nothing.'

But this one clue was not examined properly. Sir Charles Warren, head of the Metropolitan Police, fearing it might provoke an outbreak of violent anti-semitism, had it erased and kept secret.

Rumours swept through the streets.

Some said the Ripper carried his instruments of death in a little black bag, and any innocent passer-by carrying such a bag risked being set upon by fear-crazed locals.

He was a foreign seaman ... a Jewish butcher ... a mad doctor ... a Russian sent by the Czar to try to cause unrest in London ... a puritan intent on ridding the streets of vice ... a mad midwife who hated prostitutes.

Some said the Ripper must be a policeman, which was why he could prowl the streets at night without arousing suspicion. An even wilder theory held that he was Queen Victoria's eldest grandson, Prince Albert Victor, the Duke of Clarence.

The Ripper claimed his last victim, Mary Kelly, a 25-year-old blonde, on 9 November. Unlike the others she was young and attractive. One of the last people to see her alive was a George Hutchinson, when she approached him and asked him for money to pay her rent. He said he could not help, and noticed her approach a slim, well-dressed man with a trim moustache and a deerstalker hat.

When rent collector Henry Bowers called on Mary next morning he could get no reply. Seeing the window to her room open, he reached in and pushed aside the sacking curtain. He took one horrified look at the sickening sight inside and ran for the landlord. He said later: 'I shall be haunted by it for the rest of my life.'

With Mary's death, the Ripper's reign of horrific crimes ended as suddenly as it had begun.

Two convicted murderers claimed to be the Ripper. One, who poisoned his mistress, said when arrested: 'You've got Jack the Ripper at last.' But there was no evidence to support his claim.

Another killer, sentenced to death, cried out as the gallows trapdoor opened: 'I am Jack the ...' But he had been in America when the Ripper's murders were committed.

Some policemen believed they knew the Ripper's identity. The Assistant Commissioner of the Metropolitan Police said in 1908: 'In saying that he was a Polish Jew I am merely stating a definitely established fact.'

Inspector Robert Sagar, who had been on the case and died in 1924, wrote

A *Punch* satire on the police's inability to catch the murderer

in his memoirs: 'We had good reason to suspect a man who lived in Butcher's Row, Aldgate. We watched him carefully. There was no doubt that this man was insane and, after a time, his friends thought it advisable to have him moved to a private asylum. After he was removed, there were no more Ripper atrocities.'

Author and broadcaster Daniel Farson, who for several years ran a riverside East End pub, has offered another solution. He said recently that he suspects Montagu John Druitt, a failed barrister with medical connections and family history of mental instability.

Farson based his belief on the notes of Sir Melville Macnaghten, who became head of the CID in 1903. Mcnaghten named three main suspects – a Polish tradesman, probably Jewish, who hated women, a Russian doctor and Druitt.

A few weeks after the death of Mary Kelly, Druitt's body was found floating in the Thames.

After that Jack the Ripper claimed no more victims. But there is a postscript to the affair . . .

Two victims of Jack the Ripper have returned to haunt the scenes of his heinous crimes, according to witnesses. The ghost of Mary Ann Nicholls, the 42-year-old prostitute who was the second of the grisly butcher's six victims, has been seen dozens of times – glowing mysteriously in the gutters of Durward Street, Whitechapel, close to where the Ripper left her lying after cutting her throat and stomach. Piercing screams heard nearby, in Hansbury Street, Spitalfields, are said to be those of another of his victims – 47-year-old Annie Chapman.

Jack the Stripper

A mass murderer called Jack the Stripper roamed the streets of west London for 12 savage months. The killer, like the Ripper before him, preyed on prostitutes. And like the Ripper, he was never caught.

He left his victims naked, with one or more of their front teeth removed. And perhaps, if one or two of their men customers had come forward, some of them would still be alive today.

The Stripper's reign of terror began when the body of pretty, 30-year-old

Hannah Tailford was found on the Thames foreshore near Hammersmith Bridge, in west London, on 2 February 1964. All her clothes were missing except her stockings, which were rolled down to her ankles, and her pants, which had been stuffed in her mouth probably to stifle her screams.

Hannah, small and slim, had come to London from Heddon-on-the-Wall, Northumberland. She had a wild background and specialized in group sex sessions. Police found cameras and lighting equipment at her flat, and she had apparently taken compromising photographs at her orgies.

There was a theory that she might have been killed by someone she was blackmailing.

Enquiries revealed only that she had last been seen nine days before her death. And the pathologist reported that she had been pregnant.

The Stripper's second victim, 25-year-old Irene Lockwood, was discovered on 8 April on the Thames foreshore at Duke's Meadow, Chiswick, about 274 m (300 yd) upstream from where Hannah's body had been found.

Again, police at first suspected blackmail as a motive. Then a man stepped forward and confessed he was the killer. He was able to describe Irene accurately, and he was charged.

But Jack the Stripper struck again during the trial. The man was acquitted and returned to obscurity.

The third victim, 22-year-old Helen Barthelemy, was a petite Scots girl who had worked as a circus trapeze artist and as a stripper on Blackpool's Golden Mile. Her body was found on 24 March, at Brentford, and gave police some useful leads.

Unlike the others, the body was found on dry land, in an alley. Her clothes had clearly been removed after death. Four of her front teeth were missing, and traces of spray paint were found on her body.

Police began a systematic examination of workshops and garages in the area where spray paint was used, and appealed to the public for help. The publicity seemed to scare off the killer. There were no more killings for three months.

The Stripper's fourth victim, 30-year-old Mary Fleming, was found on 14 July, propped up against the garage door of a private house in Chiswick. She too, was naked, and her body also showed small traces of spray paint.

The discovery was made at 05.00 by a chauffeur who lived directly opposite. Painters working overnight at business premises nearby reported hearing the doors of a vehicle being slammed as it reversed. A few minutes later it drove off at speed but the men could not read the number plate because they were behind frosted glass.

Scotland Yard scientists established that the paint found on the victims was of a type and colour range in use by some car manufacturers. It seemed fairly certain that the bodies had been kept in or near premises used for car body repairs.

By now terror was stalking the streets of west London. Most women refused to go out alone after dark, and the area's prostitutes walked the streets in twos and threes.

The fifth victim was discovered under a pile of rubbish in a car park at Hornton Street, Kensington, on 25 November. She had last been seen alive on 23 October, and had been dead for about a month. The girl, 20-year-old Glasgow-born Margaret McGowan, had been involved in the Profumo scandal of the previous year, and had given evidence at the trial of Stephen Ward. Using the name Frances Brown, she had told how Ward had sketched her at his flat.

Everyone connected with the Profumo scandal was traced and questioned, and all were eliminated.

Margaret had been with another prostitute, Kim Taylor, for 24 hours before she disappeared. She had drunk about 19 whiskies before the two of them went out soliciting together in Portobello Road.

They were picked up by two men in separate cars, and it was arranged that all four should meet at Chiswick Green. But Kim and her customer lost the other car in Bayswater Road, and Margaret was not seen alive again.

It was nearly a year after Hannah Tailford, the Stripper's first victim, disappeared, that he claimed his last.

She was 28-year-old Bridget 'Bridie' O'Hara, who vanished from her home and usual haunts on 11 January 1965. That evening she visited the Shepherd's Bush Hotel, a pub, and was recognized by several male acquaintances, who spoke to her. The pub closed at 23.00 and she probably died soon after that.

Her body was found on 16 February behind a small workshop alongside a busy railway line. She had been strangled and the body had clearly been stored somewhere and dumped shortly before its discovery.

As with the other victims, there were traces of paint, plus specks of oil, suggesting she had been kept near some kind of machinery.

Chief Superintendent John du Rose, who was leading the murder hunt, marked off a wide sector of west London and sent out hundreds of detectives to visit every possible garage, workshop and factory that might have held the body. Police began taking the numbers of kerb-crawling cars, and the drivers were brought in for questioning.

As a psychological ploy, du Rose increased the publicity being given to the case, and dropped hints that he was getting close to being able to identify the Stripper.

Police discovered a building housing a transformer where the bodies of

Helen and Bridie had been stored. It was close to a paint-spray shop, at the rear of a factory on the Heron Trading Estate in Acton.

Now du Rose concentrated his hunt on the immediate area. But still the killer eluded the teams of detectives. At first they thought they had scared him off. But soon it became clear that the killings had stopped altogether.

On a hunch, du Rose began a search through all the suicides, accidental deaths and jailings in London since Bridie's murder. He came up with a prime suspect – a 45-year-old man who had lived in south London and had worked for a security firm in west London. He had a van and the paint-spray shop was one of the buildings he patrolled. Shortly after the discovery of Bridie's body he had committed suicide, leaving a note saying he was 'unable to stand the strain any longer'.

To save the feelings of his wife and children, who were quite baffled by his death, police did not name the man.

Was he really Jack the Stripper? Probably no one will ever know.

Death in the Churchyard

Nurse Olive Bennett was leading a double life ... and it was to bring her a violent death. For most of her adult life, 45-year-old Olive had lived in the prim, starchy style expected of a midwife and spinster. But since joining the staff of a maternity home at Tiddington, Warwickshire, she had begun to kick over the traces.

She had taken up smoking, and was making large withdrawals from her Post Office savings account. On her evenings off she would spend an hour or two dressing and making-up, and usually take the bus to nearby Stratford-on-Avon.

She became a familiar figure in the town's old-world pubs, chain-smoking and drinking large sherries. She would often arrive back at the nurses' home by taxi in the early hours of the morning. Once she told a colleague she had been with her boyfriend.

So nothing seemed amiss when she was still not back by midnight on 23 April 1954.

It was Shakespeare's 390th birthday, and all Stratford was celebrating. The Memorial Theatre was staging *A Midsummer Night's Dream* and restaurants and pubs were packed.

That night Olive caught the 20.15 bus to Stratford. Her first call was probably the Red Horse Hotel, where she was seen drinking until 21.00. She was seen later in other pubs. In one she said to a man: 'I've had five schooners of sherry already. Aren't I a naughty girl?' The night porter at the Red Horse Hotel recalled seeing her again at 23.45 standing outside the hotel. He was the last man to see Olive alive.

Next morning the gardener at Holy Trinity Church beside the river noticed a headstone was missing. Nearby were a pair of spectacles a woman's brown shoe and a set of lower dentures.

Within hours police had found Olive's body in the river, weighted down with the missing headstone. She had been strangled.

Her diary contained the names of several men friends. All were questioned and eliminated from police enquiries. Every soldier at the nearby Long Marston camp was interviewed.

Scotland Yard was called in, and the legendary Detective Superintendent Jack Capstick – famed for his motto 'Softly, softly, catchee monkey' – arrived to head the case. Hundreds more people were questioned, but still the police drew a blank. Reluctantly, Capstick returned to the Yard leaving the case wide open.

Not until eight years later did two sisters come forward with a story that could be linked with the murder. The girls, both bus conductresses, from Leamington Spa, said they had been in Stratford on the night of the murder and had been picked up by two soldiers. At 23.00 the four of them had gone for a walk in Holy Trinity churchyard.

The older girl said: 'We were standing by some graves when my soldier began getting fresh. I told him to stop it.' The soldier said, apparently as a joke, that he would push her in the river, with a headstone to weigh her down.

The girls had kept quiet at the time because one was married, and the other did not want her mother to know. Perhaps if they had spoken up at the time Olive's murderer would have been found and brought to justice. The time lapse made that impossible.

Painstakingly the police traced and re-interviewed soldiers who had been at Long Marston camp at the time of the murder. Again, they drew a blank, and today it seems unlikely that the mystery of **who** killed Olive Bennett will ever be solved.

The Arm in the Shark Case

The story hit the headlines on Anzac Day – 25 April 1935. It was labelled in shrieking type across the front pages as 'The Arm In The Shark Case'. To incredulous newspaper readers that day, to police and forensic experts, it was one of the most bizarre mysteries ever.

The mystery began in the Sydney seaside suburb of Coogee. Fisherman Bert Hodson had set out in his small boat to examine lines he had baited with mackerel about 1.5 km off shore. He was after shark. Hodson was in luck: he found not one but two of the dread killers. One small shark was already firmly hooked to one of his lines. Another, a 4.2 m (14 ft) tiger shark, was in the process of devouring the smaller one. The fisherman hauled in the line and found the tiger shark was now firmly ensnared. Turning his boat for the shore, he headed home with the creature in tow.

Hodson would normally have killed the shark and hung it on the boathouse scales. But the fisherman's brother, Charles, ran an aquarium at Coogee and Bert knew that the prize tiger shark would provide an excellent attraction for the paying customers who crowded down from the city.

And so it proved. The shark circled menacingly round the aquarium to the delight of the trippers for a few days. Then, on 25 April the fascination on the faces of the visitors turned to horror as they witnessed the most astonishing spectacle. The tiger shark went into convulsions. It surged around the water, disgorging the contents of its stomach: rats, birds, parts of the smaller shark – and a human arm.

Charles Hodson acted swiftly. He fished out the arm and telephoned the police. They found the grisly specimen to be the left arm of a man, with a tattoo of two boxers slugging it out. Attached was a length of rope.

At first, police put the case down as a shark attack on a lone swimmer or yachtsman until, over the days, their suspicions became aroused. No one had been reported missing off a Sydney beach. And a police surgeon who examined the arm claimed that it had not be bitten off by a shark but cleanly amputated with a sharp knife.

Fingerprints were taken of the hand and, although they were blurred, experts were able to match the prints of the thumb and ring finger with those of a man in police files. They belonged to James Smith, who ran a billiard room grandly titled the Rozelle Sports Club, and who had once been arrested for illegal bookmaking. Smith had been missing from his home for 28 days. His brother, Edward, positively identified the arm but was unable to give any

183

hint as to Smith's movements. And all that the victim's wife, Gladys, knew was that her husband had left home saying that he was taking a party on a paid fishing trip.

The police sought out Smith's friends. One of them John Brady, was not easy to find for he was wanted by Tasmanian police on a forgery charge. But he was eventually run to ground on 17 May, living with his wife in a small flat in north Sydney. Under interrogation, Brady admitted having stayed with Smith in a cottage at Cronulla, on the same stretch of coastline as the shark had been caught, but denied knowing anything about the crime.

Over the next few months, divers and chartered aircraft searched the waters of Cunnamatta Bay, near Cronulla, hoping to find further clues.

The police had a theory, however. They believed that Smith went to stay with Brady at Cronulla to plan their next fraud, but that the two men fell out over the sharing of the loot. Brady, they believed, killed his accomplice and hacked up the body. He placed the remains in a metal trunk – but could not fit in the arm. So he roped it to the outside of the trunk and dumped the terrible evidence into the sea. A small shark, attracted by the blood, attacked the trunk, severing the rope with its razor-sharp teeth. As the arm floated free, the shark swallowed it whole.

The shark's next meal was the mackerel on Bert Hodson's line. And that was when the shark became a meal for the larger tiger shark.

The police theory sounded far-fetched. But the 'Arm In The Shark Case' was soon to prove that fact can be even stranger than fiction.

The crime that detectives believed Smith and Brady had been plotting was an insurance fraud over a yacht that had apparently disappeared. Police interviewed the yacht's former owner, whom they regarded as a key witness. But the day before an inquest was due to be held into Smith's death, the witness was found shot dead in his car beneath the approaches to Sydney's famous Harbour Bridge.

The following day, detectives received another blow. The coroner who was to have held the inquest ruled that he could not do so without a complete body. Nevertheless, Brady was charged with murder and sent for trial.

The trial lasted only two days. The judge refused to admit as evidence signed statements that had been taken from the witness before he was found shot dead. Without this evidence, the jury was directed to acquit Brady. Two men were charged with murdering the witness, but they too were acquitted.

Brady continued his career of crime. In all, he spent more than 20 years of his life in jail. During all that time, the only person who knew the full facts of the 'Arm In The Shark Case' never once hinted at what the truth might be.

And the full story never will be known. John Brady suffered a heart attack at the age of 71 in a prison repatriation hostel. His secret died with him.

The Motorway Monster

The brutal killing of an attractive woman hitchhiker led to Britain's biggest-ever motorway murder hunt. In all, 1,500 police officers quizzed more than 125,000 people and took nearly 50,000 statements in their fruitless bid to track down the killer of schoolteacher Barbara Mayo.

Tall, dark-haired Barbara set off from her flat in Hammersmith, London, in October 1970 to hitchhike to Catterick, Yorkshire, to pick up her boyfriend's car which had broken down there. Her own car had been giving her trouble and she did not want to risk a breakdown in it. Two days after she had left London, her boyfriend physics graduate David Pollard, reported her missing.

Four days later a miner rambling with his family in a wood just off the M1 at Ault Hucknall, near Chesterfield, Derbyshire, stumbled on her partly clothed body under a pile of leaves. Barbara, aged 24, had been raped and strangled.

Police knew it would be a tough case to crack. For the most baffling murder cases are those in which an element of association between victim and killer is missing. In the case of Barbara Mayo, there were no locals with helpful information; she was found 321 km (200 miles) from home and there was nothing to connect her murderer with her or the area where she was found. The killer could have been a commercial traveller, a commuter or a driver looking for casual sex with hitchhikers.

The police investigators – headed by Detective Chief Superintendent Charles Palmer of Scotland Yard – followed up every lead. They spent months checking thousands of Morris 1000 Travellers after a witness said he had seen Barbara, or a girl fitting her description, in a white Morris Traveller at Kimberley, Nottinghamshire. At that time more than 100,000 of this type of car were still on the road. Each owner had to be traced and eliminated.

The murder hunt also revealed something of the murky world of the motorway hitchhiker. In tests along the M1, police discovered that a man might have to wait between 30 minutes and two hours for a lift. But an attractive girl would be picked up in minutes. It seemed to indicate that there were men who drove on motorways simply to pick up girl hikers – and one of them might have picked up Barbara.

But the most worrying aspect was that girls, knowing the dangers they faced, still hitchhiked alone – often wearing provocative clothing to catch the eye of the drivers.

Police set up checkpoints along 320 km (200 miles) of the M1 between London and Leeds and asked motorists: 'Were you on this motorway 14 days ago? Did you see this girl?'

Each driver was shown a picture of Barbara with this description: 'Barbara Janet Mayo, aged 24 years, 1.7 m (5 ft 9 in), slim build, high cheekbones, brown eyes, light tanned complexion, good teeth ... wearing navy-blue coat with eight silver buttons, gold and tan brocade slacks, hipster style, lilac jersey, blue socks, corduroy lace-up shoes.' But nothing led the police any closer to 'The Monster of the Motorway', as the newspapers dubbed the ruthless killer.

Next, police plastered posters with Barbara's picture and a detailed description all over Britain. Chief Superintendent Palmer said: 'I let it be known that if any motorist who had given a girl a lift on the M1 on 12 October came forward, I would meet him anywhere – and his wife would not be told.' But nobody came forward.

A London policewoman impersonating Barbara went from Barbara's flat by tube to Hendon, where the M1 then began. She stood at the roadside, thumbing lifts.

A butcher at Kimberley, Nottinghamshire, who saw the reconstruction on television told police: 'I'm sure she came into my shop and asked for two freshly cooked faggots.' She had then crossed the road and walked down a hill towards the main road.

Was it Barbara Mayo? Or just another girl who looked like her? The question remains unanswered.

Charles Palmer said:

'I still hope that somebody, somewhere will come forward with vital information. And though there are people who can live with murder on their conscience, I still don't rule out the possibility that the person or persons responsible for Barbara's death will confess.'

There is one person, however, who believed that the police were largely wasting their time in the nationwide hunt for Barbara's killer. That person is her mother, widow Mrs Marjorie Mayo. She said:

'I have never believed Barbara was hitchhiking. I believe her murder took place in London and was carried out by somebody in a bad crowd Barbara had got in with. Her body was probably taken in her own car and left by the M1 to put the police off the trail. She came to see me the day before she disappeared. She said: 'Mummy I'm so frightened.' But before she could explain, some people called at the house and the conversation was lost.

Barbara is never far from my thoughts – she is still very real to me. And I don't believe her murder will ever be solved.'

Death of the Black Dahlia

The corpse found on an undeveloped building site in a Los Angeles suburb on 15 January 1947 had been savagely mutilated. It was the body of a young woman, cut in half at the waist and with the initials 'B. D.' carved into her thigh.

It was the use of those initials that gave the case its notoriety. They stood for 'Black Dahlia', the nickname given to a pretty 22-year-old small-time movie actress, Elizabeth Short. She was known simply as Betty or Beth to her friends. But she also revelled in the nickname of Black Dahlia because of her liking for jet-black clothes. And, from fingerprints, the body was identified as being hers.

Elizabeth Short's brief life was not a happy one. She had been a juvenile delinquent but found love and a chance of a fresh start when she met a young serviceman. He proposed, they became engaged, then parted when he was posted overseas in World War 2.

He never came home – and his death sent Elizabeth on a downhill path. She turned to drink and tried her luck as a bit-part actress in Hollywood. But jobs were hard to come by and she began working as a waitress by day and haunting sleazy bars and pick-up joints by night. The inevitable happened. Elizabeth started to accept money for her favours. She soon became known for her black apparel – including her black silk underwear.

The Black Dahlia had one further chance of rescue when a second lover proposed to her. Cruelly, he too died ... and Elizabeth's fate was sealed.

When the discovery of the poor girl's butchered body was reported in the Los Angeles newspapers, a strange reaction set in. Perhaps it was the photographs of the beautiful young victim – before and after death – that incited an astonishing spate of false reports and confessions.

The first came from a waitress who said she had heard two killers discussing the crime at a table. She gave the police a description – and inquiries revealed that the 'killers' were a couple of detectives having an off-duty coffee. Another tip came from a blonde dancer who told police: 'I'm meeting a man at First and Temple Streets at nine o'clock and I have reason to believe he's the Black Dahlia killer.' Detectives arrested the pair and took them in for questioning. The man turned out to be an innocent executive who had once spent a night with the blonde, following which she had been trying to blackmail him, without success. The 'tip off' to the police was just her way of applying extra pressure.

A photo of Elizabeth Short from her family album

One piece of evidence the police took much more seriously was a package sent to a Los Angeles newspaper enclosing a message cut from press headlines. It said: 'Here are Dahlia's belongings. Letter to follow.' The package also contained Elizabeth's social security card, her birth certificate and an address book – with one page torn out. Police said they believed that these articles had been removed from the body – no clothing was found at the scene – and that the missing page in the address book would have revealed the name of the killer. Fingerprints were taken from the social security card but they matched none in police files.

Later, a small-time underworld figure gave himself up to police, saying 'I killed the Black Dahlia.' This time detectives thought they had solved the case, because in Elizabeth's address book had been the name of a firm the suspect had once worked for. But a lie-detector test showed he was just another crank.

Years later, a 29-year-old army corporal was held on suspicion after volunteering the information: 'When I get drunk I get rough with women.' He knew many details of the killing. But again, he was finally dismissed as being mentally unbalanced.

In all, around 50 men have claimed they committed the murder – but the case of the Black Dahlia remains unsolved.

The Torso in the Trunk

Barely glancing up, the left-luggage clerk handed the man a ticket and heaved his heavy trunk into a corner of the office. 6 June, 1934 – Derby Day – was a busy day at Brighton railway station, with racegoers bound for Epsom and early holidaymakers swelling the usual commuting crowd.

The trunk was the seventieth to be deposited in a few hours and stuffing ticket CT1945 in his pocket, the man vanished in the crowd. He probably caught the next train to London.

It was not until 17 June that a clerk at Brighton station, noticing an unpleasant smell, opened the trunk and recoiled in horror at the terrible sight that met his eyes. Inside was the torso of a woman, wrapped in brown paper and tied around with a venetian blind cord.

An immediate search of other railway left-luggage offices led to the discovery of a suitcase containing the murder victim's severed legs at London's King's Cross station. It had been deposited there on 7 June.

What had happened to the head and arms? No one can be sure. But on 10 June a couple walking on the beach found a female human head in a pool.

Incredibly, they left it there and reported it to no one. When police heard of their find a month later and questioned them, they said they assumed someone had committed suicide by jumping off a cliff, and that the police had swept the remains they did not need into the sea.

Pathologist Sir Bernard Spilsbury said the murder had taken place on about 30 or 31 May, and that the victim had been a healthy young woman aged 21 to 28. She was about 1.7 m (5 ft 2 in) tall, weighed 54 kg (8 st 7 lb) and was pregnant. And there was no other means of identification.

Police came to the conclusion that the killer was probably a married man of some social standing who had an affair with the woman. She became pregnant, and when her condition became noticeable she asked him for help. He refused, and she threatened to tell his wife about their affair. They had a row, which became violent, and in the heat of the moment she was killed by a blow to the head.

On one of the pieces of brown paper detectives found the final part of a word written in blue pencil. The syllable FORD was easily recognizable, and the previous letter could have been a D or an L.

A woman working in a London warehouse came forward to identify the writing as her own. She regularly returned defective consignments to a confectionery firm at Bedford.

Police identified the brown paper she used as the type wrapped around the woman's remains. And they established that when such sheets arrived at the Bedford factory, they were re-used to dispatch goods to all parts of the country.

They followed every possible lead, but the trail went cold.

Chief Inspector Robert Donaldson from Scotland Yard took charge of the case. In an attempt to identify the victim, he launched a massive round-up of missing girls. In all, 732 who had left home were traced. He had detectives check every hospital, nursing home and doctor's surgery for details of women who had sought pre-natal advice. One London hospital alone produced 5,000 names.

Other detectives checked makers and retailers of trunks, and made discreet inquiries into thousands of purchases. But again they drew a blank.

Of all the thousands of clues that led nowhere, one statement seems to point to the killer. Porter Todd, at London Bridge Station, recalled helping a man with a heavy trunk on the 15.00 train for Brighton on 6 June. He had bought his cheap-day third-class ticket at Dartford, and was noticed by a girl on the same train. Only five cheap-day tickets to Brighton had been sold at Dartford that day. Four of the travellers were traced by the police ... but the fifth was never found.

Katyn – 1940

Murder is horrific enough when it involves just one victim, one body. But in the annals of unsolved crime there is one outrage against humanity so monstrous that it defies comprehension. It is the Katyn Massacre, one of the most cold-blooded atrocities in history, in which 4,300 innocent people were put to death. It is also a crime without a culprit – for no nation will accept responsibility for it.

The story begins on 17 September 1939, the day that Hitler and Stalin divided conquered and battle-ravaged Poland between them. From their sector, the Russians transported 15,000 Polish officers and intellectuals to labour camps in the Soviet Union.

About 500 were saved from the brutality of camp life to be indoctrinated into the communist system. The remainder languished in the camps until April 1940 – and then every one of them vanished.

In June 1941 the Nazis broke their peace pact with Stalin and marched into Russia. Two years later, German troops dug up an area of woodland at Katyn, near the Soviet city of Smolensk. They unearthed at least 4,300 bodies, which, from the documents still on the corpses, were proved to be those of some of the missing Poles.

The Nazis immediately blamed their communist foes for the massacre. But, in the midst of war, there was no way of proving the guilt of one nation or another.

Then, in 1944, the tide of war changed and the Russians recaptured Katyn from the retreating Germans. The Soviets immediately counter-claimed that it was the Nazis, not them, who had been responsible for the massacre.

The balance of the evidence, however, weighs against the Russians. It is reported that Soviet soldiers were sent to Katyn in 1940 and ordered to dig a pit 30.5 m (100 ft) long and 15 m (50 ft) wide. A cattle train then arrived with a human cargo. About 4,300 Poles were ordered out and marched to the wooded site, out of the direct view of the villagers. The Poles were then lined up in rows. The Russians strode down the ranks, shooting each man in the back of the head and rolling the corpse into the pit. When ammunition seemed to be running low, some of the prisoners had sawdust stuffed into their mouths in order to suffocate them and were then buried alive beneath the next line of victims to be shot.

According to one report, some of the Soviet soldiers refused to carry out the executions. They committed suicide, throwing themselves into the pit. The soldiers who obeyed their orders were later dispersed to other units around Russia.

The Soviet Union has never faltered in its vehement denials that it bears any guilt for the massacre. But in recent years, the evidence of Poles who escaped Stalin's purge and fled to the West has been threaded together to provide apparent confirmation of the German story.

In London in 1976, a 6 m (20 ft) cenotaph was unveiled to the memory of the 14,500 missing Poles, including the 4,300 killed in Katyn. But the British government failed to send an official representative to the ceremony, adhering to the line that the story of a massacre had not been proven.

Polish ex-servicemen, wearing their cherished wartime uniforms and rows of medals, paraded their colours before the black stone cenotaph. They wept openly when the widow of one of the massacre victims drew aside the British and Polish flags which draped the memorial and revealed the simple inscription: 'Katyn 1940'.

Whether the Russians were responsible for the massacre or not remains in question. Also a mystery is what happened to the other 10,000 Poles who were transported to Russian labour camps? How many other Katyns are yet to be exposed?

The World's
MOST
INFAMOUS
MURDERS

Contents

Introduction

Life is very frail, death very final and murder often a simple crime to commit. Which is perhaps why that fearful crime so fascinates us all.

Most people at one time or another have thought or said: I'd like to murder him. Or her. They do not usually mean it, but the thought is there.

Most murders are not committed with premeditation. They are the product of one manic moment. Often they are the result of long pent-up emotions erupting in a fatal outburst when the mind can take no more and restraint suddenly snaps.

But there are other causes of murder; more sinister, less simple to understand, less easy to forgive.

The murders that horrify us most are those caused by greed or envy, or those which are the sadistic product of a twisted mind. Sometimes they seem to be caused by nothing but sheer bloodlust.

Assembled in this volume are the most infamous of those killings. They are collected together in no particular order . . . there is no league table of terror and the awfulness of the crimes defies analysis.

No-one, for instance, can hope to explain the savage slaughters of Jack the Ripper, the maniacal fervour of Charles Manson's band of assassins, the callous child slayings of the Moors Murderers.

The type of crime the reader will find in the following pages is that which Shakespeare described as:

'Murder most foul, as in the best it is;
But this most foul, strange and unnatural.'   *Hamlet*

The Son of Sam

DAVID BERKOWITZ

Son of Sam killer David Berkowitz cold-bloodedly murdered six people and wounded another seven during the year he terrorized New York. He shot five women and one man dead in a series of vicious killings which spread panic round the city during 1977. Son of Sam struck at courting couples and lone women. The killer also turned his gun on two dogs. When the spate of killings were linked, hysteria mounted. Discos and restaurants were deserted as the frightened population made sure they were home before dark.

It was in the last few months Berkowitz was at large that he became known as Son of Sam. Police found a letter lying in the road just a few yards from the dead bodies of two young lovers. The letter read: 'Dear Captain Joseph Borelli, I am deeply hurt by your calling me a woman hater. I am not. But I am a monster. I am the Son of Sam.' Berkowitz left the letter in the road after he fired at a couple as they embraced in a car.

He had already killed three people and wounded four, but after the chilling letter was published New York's Mayor Beame ordered police: 'Catch this man.' A special squad of 200 detectives was formed. Every rumour and tip-off was followed up but the identity of the killer remained a mystery. More than 100 police were put on nightly patrols in areas of the Bronx and Queens where it was thought he might strike again.

Police described the killer as 'neurotic, schizophrenic and paranoid'. They came up with the theory that he might believe himself the victim of demonic possession. Because of the uncanny way Berkowitz escaped detection, it was believed at one time that he might be a policeman using inside information to vanish undetected. Meanwhile the killings continued.

One night a high-school girl and her boyfriend were shot as they got into their car. Berkowitz fired through the windscreen, hitting the boy in the arm and the girl in the head, neck and shoulder. A month later he struck again. Two 20-year-olds on their first date together were shot as they kissed in a car. Bobby Violante was just telling Stacy Moskowitz how much he cared for her when the bullet which was to blind him smashed into his face. Stacy was also shot in the head, and she died 38 hours later on a hospital operating table.

Berkowitz was caught eventually because of a parking ticket. He watched from the shadows while police stuck a ticket on his car. When they had gone he

David Berkowitz with inset of 17-year-old
victim, Judy Placido

walked over and screwed up the ticket. But he was seen by a woman walking her dog. She thought he had a strange smile on his face and when he came close to her she saw he had a gun in his hand. She called the police the next day and told them about the parking ticket. They traced the car through their records. The next day police lay in wait for Berkowitz. He walked to his car with the .44 calibre gun in a paper bag. When challenged he told police in his soft voice: 'I'm Sam.' The officers remember that he had a peculiar, child-like smile on his face. At his trial he claimed bloodthirsty demons made him kill. He said that one of the dogs he shot had the spirit of a 6,000-year-old man who ordered him to kill.

Berkowitz, now 28, was sentenced to 30 years in jail after he pleaded guilty to the series of attacks and killings. Since his trial he has claimed that he was a member of a New York satanic cult and other men were involved in the murders. Now he passes his days writing letters to girlfriends, newspapers, congressmen and journalists.

Police still believe that Berkowitz acted alone. But other people take seriously his claims that more people were involved. Eyewitness descriptions of the killer varied markedly in height and appearance. And none of the four different police sketches of the murderer closely resembled Berkowitz. Nor does the handwriting on many of the messages sent to police and newspapers by Son of Sam match up with Berkowitz's. The most intriguing riddle involves Sam Carr, who owned the dog that Berkowitz claimed bewitched him. Carr's two sons, John and Michael, both died in suspicious circumstances after Berkowitz was arrested. John Carr was found shot to death in his girlfriend's apartment and Michael died when his car crashed for no apparent reason. These factors have led some lawyers to claim that Berkowitz was only a lookout for a group involved in the murder conspiracy.

People who knew Berkowitz before his arrest say he was a loner without any personal charms. He loved to gorge himself on junk food. His favourite meal

---

Mentally deranged sex-maniac, German-born Bruno Ludke, had committed no fewer than 85 murders before his arrest in 1943. From the age of 18 he raped, robbed, stabbed or strangled his prey for pleasure. When humans were not available he resorted to torturing animals. Finally, when Ludke was arrested for sexual assault, Himmler's SS sterilised him. When he confessed to all his crimes, his prosecutors realized that, in several cases, other people had been executed for Ludke's killings. The scandal was hushed up and Ludke was sent to hospital in Vienna, where he became the guinea pig for medical and psychiatric experiments. He died there in 1944.

was hamburgers followed by chocolate ice-cream. When he was arrested, police at first took him to be retarded. Two guns were pressed against his head and he was ordered to 'freeze', but his only response was to keep smiling. Arresting officer John Falotico remembers: 'He had that stupid smile on his face, like it was a kid's game.'

Nobody knows why Berkowitz started to kill. But after the first killing of Donna Lauria, the murders became an addiction. He drove around New York night after night looking for victims. He also liked to return to the scene of his murders. One night after shooting a courting couple, instead of fleeing the scene he drove on a few blocks to catch a glimpse of the apartment block where his first victim Donna had lived. He told police that after a murder he felt 'flushed with power'. After a killing he would go to a late night snack bar to eat his favourite chocolate desserts.

It was Berkowitz's ordinariness that helped him escape capture. At one place where he lodged, all that the family could remember of him was that he was a 'regular sort of guy who used to take his car out in the middle of the night'.

Since he has been in prison Berkowitz has gone some way to achieving his ambition of becoming a celebrity. He has unlimited letter writing privileges and conducts torrid pen-pal romances with women. Berkowitz has made more than $200,000 from various articles, a book and film rights to his life. A court battle by the relatives of his victims to prevent him getting any of the money failed.

The Glamorous Lovers

BONNIE PARKER AND CLYDE BARROW

Despite the popular image of Bonnie and Clyde as glamorous, rather hard-done-by bank robbers, the reality was very different; they were extremely vicious thieves and murderers.

Handsome Clyde Barrow was born on 24 March 1909 to a poor Texas farmer. Even as a young child he displayed sadistic tendencies, taking great delight in torturing farm animals.

Bonnie Parker born in 1911 came from a devout Baptist family. Her father died when she was four and the family then moved to Cement City, Texas. She was a pretty, petite girl with blue eyes and fair hair. Bonnie had married a Dallas tearaway named Roy Thornton when she was only 16 but the marriage had ended when he was sentenced to 99 years' jail for murder. Her mother was delighted when she met Clyde Barrow because she felt he would help Bonnie to get over her broken marriage. Bonnie was then nineteen-years-old and Clyde twenty-one.

Their relationship did not get off to a good start. The first night that Clyde visited Bonnie's house he was arrested on seven accounts of burglary and car theft. He was given a sentence of two years, but escaped when Bonnie smuggled a gun into the jail. He was recaptured after robbing a railway office at gunpoint, only a few days after his escape. Clyde Barrow was sentenced to prison for fourteen years.

Life in Texas prisons was brutal and extremely tough. Desperate to get out,

---

Charles Arthur Floyd, a strapping farm worker from Okalahoma, felt that he had suffered enough poverty in his life – so he took to robbing banks and machine-gunning guards. A madam of a whorehouse in Kansas City nicknamed him 'Pretty Boy' Floyd and the title stuck to him throughout his criminal career.

During one bank robbery getaway he killed a policeman and was sentenced to 15 years. But he escaped from the train taking him to jail and went on to commit numerous other robberies and at least two more murders. An FBI bullet finally struck him down in a field at East Liverpool, Ohio, in 1934.

Bonnie Parker and Clyde Barrow

Blackbeard was the monster of the Spanish Main whose overpowering 2 metre (6ft 4in) frame put the fear of God in both foes and allies. He had no hesitation in shooting his men – just to let others know who was in charge.

Despite his Latin looks, Blackbeard was born Edward Teach in Bristol, England. He fed his sexual appetite with a bevy of 14 wives and mistresses. And when he was in a flirtatious mood, he would adorn his twisted black beard with silk ribbon. When a price of £100 was put on the scoundrel's head, he met his match in Lieutenant Maynard, captain of a British boat. In 1718 Maynard cornered Blackbeard's boat and he and his men fired 25 shots into his body. Maynard celebrated his victory by flying the murderer's beard from the bowsprit.

Clyde persuaded another prisoner to cut off two of his toes with an axe. He was released on crutches and headed straight back to Bonnie.

To please Bonnie's mother he took a job in Massachusetts in an attempt to make an honest living. However, he could not bear being so far from home and was soon back in West Dallas. Bonnie left home just three days later, to embark on a life of robbery and murder. The couple were joined by a friend of Clyde's called Ray Hamilton, and two other men.

The first murder was committed in April 1932 for the paltry sum of $40 when they shot a jeweller named John W. Bucher in Hillsboro, Texas. Bonnie was in jail at the time on suspicion of having stolen a car, but she was released three months later without any charges having been made. During that time Clyde and his associates brutally gunned down a Sheriff and a Deputy-Sheriff outside a dancehall.

The gang's biggest ever haul was $3,500, stolen from a filling station at Grand Prairie. Bonnie and Clyde decided to celebrate with a motoring holiday around Missouri, Kansas and Michigan, staying at top hotels and eating at expensive restaurants.

Not surprisingly, the money did not last long. They reverted to petty crime, murdering for surprisingly small amounts of money. Bonnie coolly shot a Texas butcher three times in the stomach before robbing him, and William Jones, a 16-year-old member of the Barrow gang, shot dead the son of the owner of a car they were caught stealing. Shooting to kill was now an automatic reflex.

In March 1933 the gang was joined in Missouri by Clyde's brother, Buck, and Blanche, Buck's wife. They narrowly escaped arrest from the apartment they were all staying in and shot dead two policemen in their escape bid.

It was now no longer safe for the fugitives to stay anywhere and they fled from town to town, robbing and killing as they went. They were both very aware that they would not remain at liberty for much longer and, indeed, Bonnie predicted their deaths in her poem, *The Story of Bonnie and Clyde*. Their greatest fear seemed to be that they would not see their parents again, to whom they were both deeply attached.

Near Wellington, Texas, their car plunged to the bottom of a gorge. Clyde and Jones were thrown clear but Bonnie was trapped and seriously burned when it caught fire. She was rescued, with the help of a local farmer. The gang were sheltered for a few days by the farmer and his family who soon became suspicious and called the police. Once again, the fugitives escaped at gunpoint, and were rejoined by Buck and Blanche. Bonnie was still seriously ill.

In July the gang decided to rest at a tourist camp in Missouri. Again, the police surrounded them. Although they shot their way to freedom Buck had been hit through the temple and Blanche was blinded by glass. Desperately hungry, with the two women seriously ill and Buck dying, they stopped to buy food. Within minutes the police were upon them and Buck was shot in the hip, shoulders and back. The police had found him, after the shoot-out, with his wife crouched over him, sobbing. Buck died in hospital six days later and Blanche was given a 10-year prison sentence.

Bonnie and Clyde spent the following three months desperately running from the police, but their luck could not hold out. On 23 May 1934 their Ford V-8 sedan was ambushed by six police officers. Their car was pumped full with 87 bullets and they died immediately, their bodies bloody and broken. Clyde was 25 and Bonnie just 23.

Incredibly, the glamorous legend of the two ruthless lovers had already begun. Vast crowds flocked to their funeral in Dallas, snatching flowers from the coffins as souvenirs. Time has done nothing to erase their memory, and despite their callous, cruel deeds, they are remembered by many as folk heroes.

The Fall River Axe Murders

LIZZIE BORDEN

According to the immortal rhyme, Lizzie Borden took an axe and gave her mother forty whacks; when she saw what she had done she gave her father forty one. But according to American justice, the 32-year-old spinster was not responsible for the bloody slaughter of Andrew J. Borden and his wife Abby. She was acquitted after a ten-day trial, and the courtroom rang with applause at the verdict. Ever since, the world has wondered why.

The Borden household at 92 Second Street in the Massachusetts cotton spinning town of Fall River had never been a happy one. Andrew was a crusty, puritanical character whose one aim in life was making money, and holding on to it. He had amassed half a million dollars from shrewd business dealings, first as an undertaker, then as a property speculator and banker. His first wife, Sarah Morse Borden, died in 1862, two years after giving birth to his second daughter, christened Lizzie Andrew because Borden wanted a boy. Borden married again two years later, but it was no love match. Abby Durfee Gray was a plain, plump woman of 37, more of a housekeeper than a wife. And there was no love lost between her and Borden's two girls. The elder sister Emma called her Abby. Lizzie called her Mrs Borden, refused to eat at the same table as her, and spoke with her only when it was essential.

Despite Borden's wealth, the family lived in conditions worse than many of the town's humble millworkers. The unsanitary whitewood house had staircases at the front and back, which was as well, because the friction in the family meant that bedroom doors upstairs were kept locked at all times, the parents reaching their room via the rear stairs, the girls using the front ones.

Lizzie's resentment of her stepmother, and the way they lived, boiled over when her father, whom she loved dearly, put up the money for Abby's sister, Mrs Whitehead, to buy the house from which she faced eviction. Borden presented the title deeds to his wife, and when Lizzie found out, she regarded it as further proof that Mrs Borden was only after her father's riches. Shortly afterwards, Mr Borden arrived home from business to be told by Lizzie that his wife's bedroom had been ransacked by a burglar. He reported the incident to police, but soon cut short their inquiries when it became clear that Lizzie herself had done the damage during 'one of her funny turns'.

Lizzie was plain, introspective and repressed with genteel pretensions. The curly-haired redhead had a small circle of very close friends. Though she belonged to the Women's Christian Temperance Union, was treasurer and secretary of the local Christian Endeavour Society, and taught a Sunday School of Chinese men at the local Congregational church, she spent most of her time in more solitary pursuits – fishing, or merely brooding at her bedroom window. There was plenty for her to brood about.

In the summer of 1892 Fall River sweltered in a heatwave. In May the tedium of the Bordens' lifestyle was interrupted when intruders twice broke into outhouses at the bottom of their garden. Mr Borden's reaction was somewhat bizzare. Sure that the intruders were after Lizzie's pet pigeons, he took an axe to the birds and decapitated them.

By August the heat had become so bad that Emma left to stay with friends in the country at Fairhaven, 20 miles away. Lizzie stayed at home for a special meeting of the Christian Endeavour Society. The weather made no difference to Mr Borden's plans for running an economical household. The family sat down to a monstrous joint of mutton, cooked by their only servant, an Irish girl called Bridget, and served up in various guises at every meal. Everyone except Lizzie was violently ill.

Although 4 August dawned as the hottest day of the year, the family routine went on just the same. After breakfast Mr Borden set out to check on his businesses; John Morse, brother of his first wife, who was staying for a few days, left to visit other relatives; Mrs Borden began dusting the rooms, and Bridget, still queasy from food poisoning, washed the windows. Lizzie came down later than the rest, and was soon seen ironing some clothes in the kitchen.

Shortly after 09.30, Mrs Borden, on her knees dusting in the spare bedroom upstairs at the front of the house, was struck from behind with a hatchet. It was a

---

Mystery will always surround 44-year-old Gilles de Rais, branded one of history's most shocking sadists. Once a lieutenant of Joan of Arc and a Marshal of France, he turned a life of near obscurity to one of notoriety.

He derived pleasure from sexual attacks on children and occasionally heightened the excitement by torturing or decapitating them first.

More than 120 children came into his evil clutches – all were first kidnapped then brutally murdered. After each of his sadistic adventures he sank into a coma. Finally, in 1440 he was sentenced to be strangled and then burned.

The axe allegedly used by Lizzie Borden

crushing blow to the head, and killed her instantly. But 18 more blows were inflicted on her before she was left in a room awash with blood.

Just before 11.00, Mr Borden arrived home to find the front door locked and bolted. Bridget the maid, by now cleaning the windows inside the house, went to let him in, and expressed surprise that the door was double locked. She heard a laugh behind her, and turned to see Lizzie coming down the front staircase, smiling.

Mr Borden was nearly 70, and walking in the morning heat had clearly tired him. Lizzie fussed round him, told him his wife had gone out after receiving a note about a sick friend, and settled him on the living room settee where he began to doze, his head resting on a cushion. Lizzie went back to the kitchen, and chatted to Bridget about some cheap dress material on sale in town. But Bridget was still feeling unwell, and decided to retire to her attic bedroom for a while. She heard the clock strike 11.00 as she went up the back stairs.

Ten minutes later she dashed downstairs again. She heard Lizzie shouting: 'Come down quick. Father's dead. Someone came in and killed him.' Lizzie would not let the maid into the living room – she sent her across the road to fetch the local doctor, a man called Bowen. He was out on a call. Lizzie then sent Bridget to fetch Alice Russell, one of her closest friends. By this time, the maid's rushing about had attracted the attention of neighbours. Mrs Adelaide

Churchill, who lived next door, spotted Lizzie looking distressed, and asked what was wrong. She was told: 'Someone has killed father.'

Mr Borden had been hacked to death in exactly the same way as his wife, though his head had been shattered with only ten blows. The hatchet had landed from behind as he slept, a tricky task as the settee was against a wall. Blood had splashed everything – wall, settee, floral carpet. Dr Bowen arrived and examined the body. The blows seemed directed at the eyes, ears and nose. He was completely satisfied the first blow had killed the old man. He placed a sheet over the body.

Mrs Russell and Mrs Churchill did their best to comfort the bereaved Lizzie, fanning her, dabbing her face with cold cloths, rubbing her hands. But both noticed that she did not really need comforting. She was not crying or hysterical, and she assured them she did not feel faint. She was still strangely calm when the police arrived, declining their offer of delaying the necessary interview until she had had a chance to rest.

At first suspicion fell on John Morse, who behaved strangely when he returned to the house. Though a large and excited crowd had gathered in front of the building, he was seen to slow down as he approached. Then, instead of going inside, he wandered round to the back garden, picked some fruit off one of the trees, and started munching it. Inside the house, his alibi came so glibly, in the most minute detail, that it almost seemed too perfect. But when tested it was found to be true.

Attention then turned to Lizzie, whose behaviour had been equally strange, and whose statements were not only curious but contradictory. When Bridget had asked her where she was when her father was killed, she replied: 'I was out in the yard and heard a groan.' When Mrs Churchill asked the same question, she said: 'I went out to the barn to get a piece of iron.' She told the same story to the police, saying she had eaten three pears while searching in the attic of the barn. But a policeman who checked the attic found no cores, only undisturbed dust.

Mrs Churchill also recalled the extraordinary reply Lizzie had given when she first arrived, and asked where her mother was. Lizzie said: 'I'm sure I don't know, for she had a note from someone to go and see somebody who is sick. But I don't know perhaps that she isn't killed also, for I thought I heard her coming in.' It was some minutes before Mrs Churchill and Bridget began to search for Mrs Borden. They knew she was not in her own room, for the sheet that covered her husband came from there. So they started climbing the front staircase. Halfway up, Mrs Churchill glanced through the open door of the spare bedroom, and saw the body lying on the floor beyond the bed.

Why had Lizzie not seen it there when she came down the stairs to welcome her father home? Why had she been trying to buy prussic acid, a lethal poison, only the day before from shops in town? And why, the previous evening, had she visited her friend Mrs Russell, told her of the food poisoning episode, and complained about her father's brusque way with people, saying she was afraid one of his enemies would take revenge on him soon?

Those were the questions police asked themselves as they pieced together the clues, and studied Lizzie's statements. They were sure that the murders had been committed by someone in the household. Though neighbours had noticed a young man outside the Borden home at 09.30, looking agitated, they had not seen him go in. And police thought it unlikely that a killer could hide in the house for 90 minutes between the murders while Bridget and Lizzie were going about their chores.

Bridget was considered as a suspect and dismissed. Neighbours had seen her cleaning the windows. Some had even seen her vomitting because of the food poisoning. And she had no known reason for killing her employers. But Lizzie had motives in plenty. The tension in the family, the quarrels about money, the hatred of the stepmother, were all well known in the area. She was warned that she was under suspicion and told not to leave the house. She accepted the conditions, in the arrogant, off-hand way that she had dealt with all the police's questions.

The police obtained a warrant for her arrest, but did not serve it until after the inquest. Though they had found an axe-head that had recently been cleaned in the cellar of the Borden house, they had no proof that it was the murder weapon, or that Lizzie was the murderer. Once she was arrested, she could use her legal right to silence. It was important to hear her evidence at the inquest.

More than 4,000 people attended the funeral of Mr and Mrs Borden. The two heads were cut off before burial, and the battered skulls sent for forensic examination. A few days later, the inquest opened. It was held in secret, conducted by the public prosecutor, who gave Lizzie a tough time in cross-questioning. And once again she started contradicting herself.

She claimed now that she had not been on the stairs when her father arrived home shortly before 11.00, but was downstairs in the kitchen. Asked why she had changed her story, she explained: 'I thought I was on the stairs, but now I know I was in the kitchen.' She also denied saying she heard her stepmother returning to the house. The public prosecutor was certain she was guilty of the killings. So were the newspapers, which daily poured out torrents of emotional calumny on Lizzie, adding smears and lies to the known facts. But it was one thing to obtain a conviction in print, quite another to win one in a court of law. And the public prosecutor confided in a letter to the Attorney General that he was not confident.

His fears were well founded. The tide of anti-Lizzie propaganda in the press turned public feeling in her favour. How could such a God-fearing, quiet,

Lizzie Borden

Brush manufacturer Henry Wainwright tired of his mistress, slit her throat and shot her. Then he buried her in his shop. When he became bankrupt a year later he dug up her body and to his horror found she was still 'intact'. He had buried her in chloride of lime instead of quicklime. Wainwright then meticulously chopped up the body and put the pieces into parcels to await disposal. But when he went in search of a London cab, a workman picked up one of the parcels and a hand fell out. Wainwright was executed at Newgate in 1875.

---

respectable girl do such horrible and bloody deeds? Flowers and good luck messages began pouring into Fall River for her from all over the country. Suddenly the state was the villain of the piece for persecuting her.

Lizzie had something else on her side also. She hired the best lawyer in Massachusetts, George Robinson, a former governor of the state. One of the three trial judges was a man Robinson had elevated to the bench while governor. He owed the defence lawyer a favour – and he delivered. The judges refused to allow evidence of Lizzie's attempts to buy prussic acid, saying it was irrelevant to the case, and they ruled that transcripts of her questioning at the inquest were inadmissable.

Lizzie's friends also rallied round. Both Emma and Bridget gave favourable evidence, playing down Lizzie's enmity for her stepmother. Mrs Russell admitted that Lizzie had burnt one of her dresses the day after her parents' funeral, but insisted there were no blood stains on it. Lizzie, too, played her part perfectly in court. When she fainted halfway through the hearing, there was an outcry at the way she was being tortured. And as she stood in the dock, modest, refined, neatly dressed, it was easy for George Robinson to say to the jury: 'To find her guilty, you must believe she is a fiend. Gentlemen, does she look it?'

The jury agreed she did not. After a ten-day trial her ordeal was over, and she was whisked off for a lavish celebration party, laughing at newspaper clippings of the hearing that friends gave her. She was now very rich, able to inherit her murdered father's wealth, but surprisingly she chose to stay on in Fall River, buying a larger house in the better part of town. Bridget, whom many suspected of helping Lizzie to dispose of clues to the killings, returned to Ireland, allegedly with a lot of money from the Borden bank account. She later returned to America and died in Montana in 1947, aged 82.

For a while Emma shared the new home with Lizzie, but the sisters quarrelled, and Emma moved out. Lizzie became something of a recluse, living alone, unloved and whispered about, until she died in 1927, aged 67. Emma, nine years older, died a few days later. They were both buried in the family plot, alongside their real mother, their stepmother, their father and their sister Alice, who had died as a child.

Can Lizzie rest in peace beside the victims of that hot morning in August, 1892? No-one else was ever arrested for the murders. No-one else was even seriously suspected. The case has become one of the most intriguing unresolved mysteries in the annals of crime. Five stage plays, a ballet, and countless books have been written about it. Opinions range from those who say she was a cunning, calculating killer who twice stripped naked to ensure her butchery left no blood-stained clothes, to the Society of Friends of Lizzie Borden, which still exists today to persuade us she was innocent.

Perhaps, in a way, she was. In her book *A Private Disgrace*, American authoress Victoria Lincoln argues convincingly that Lizzie committed the murders while having attacks of temporal epilepsy, the 'funny turns' her family were accustomed to. Lizzie suffered attacks four times a year, usually during menstruation. Miss Lincoln says: 'During a seizure, there are periods of automatic action which the patient in some cases forgets completely and in other remembers only dimly.' That could explain Lizzie's confusing statements and her coolness when accused of the killings.

Miss Lincoln even suggests the trigger to Lizzie's attacks. A note was delivered to 92 Second Street on the morning of 4 August, but it was not from a sick friend. It was to do with the transfer of a property to Mrs Borden's name. The first such transaction had driven Lizzie to vandalism. Did the second drive her to murder?

The Moors Murders

IAN BRADY AND MYRA HINDLEY

I t was the Swinging Sixties and everyone was into wild fashion, weird cults and *The Beatles*. But it wasn't long before Britain was stunned by what were labelled the most cold-blooded killings of the century. Even 20 years later, the horror was still etched in peoples' minds. A country could not forget Myra Hindley and Ian Brady, perpetrators of the notorious Moors Murders.

The 27-year-old stock clerk and 22-year-old typist committed some of the most macabre crimes ever recounted before a British jury. Britain of the sixties was hypnotised by the couple's blood-lust, of how they enticed young children back to their home, sadistically tortured them, murdered them and then buried their bodies on the desolate Pennine moors.

The couple's terrible crimes were committed while capital punishment was still in force but they were found guilty after its abolition. A short year separated them from the gallows and sentenced them to a life behind bars.

Many years later, reformers, such as Lord Longford, were to argue for Hindley's release. The brassy blonde, once infatuated by her lover was said to have undergone a startling change. In her 20 years in Holloway Prison she had turned to religion and taken and passed an Open University degree in humanities. She had, said Longford and his supporters, reached the point where she was no longer a danger to the public.

In 1973, Hindley was given her first taste of freedom since her life sentence -- 'life' in Britain normally being 10 years with the possibility of release on licence at the Home Secretary's approval after a third had been served. Along with a prison officer, she was taken on early morning excursions to a London park, but her bouts of freedom raised a howl of protest from the public who could neither forgive or forget the killing of the innocents.

It was Myra Hindley's brother-in-law, David Smith, who eventually gave away the perverted couple's secrets. On 7 October, 1965 at 6.20 am, he contacted the police. The realization of what was going on at number 16, Wardle Brook Avenue on the Hattersley council estate, Manchester, was too strong for him to bear. Shaking, he walked to a public telephone kiosk and rang nearby Stalybridge police station. Within minutes, a young patrol car officer found Smith quaking beside the telephone box. He was so agitated that he could hardly wait to bundle himself into the officer's car.

Ian Brady

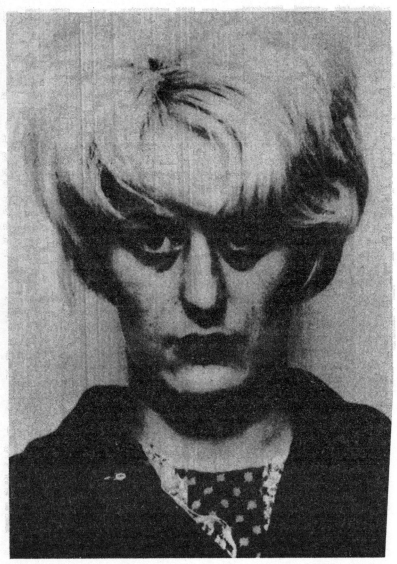

Myra Hindley

> **Alfred Stratton, 22, and his brother Albert, 20, were the first British murderers to be convicted by their fingerprints. It happened in May 1905, after the battered bodies of Thomas Farrow and his wife were found in the flat above their paint shop in south-east London. A right thumbprint was discovered on the forced cashbox, and after extensive inquiries the police found that it belonged to Alfred who, with his brother, was known to be a burglar.**
>
> **At the Old Bailey trial, the defence argued strongly that fingerprints were inadmissible evidence, but the judge ruled otherwise. The two brothers were hanged.**

As David Smith blurted out his tales of horror, one of the biggest searches ever seen in Britain was begun. Hundreds of police spent weeks scouring the desolate moors for the graves of 10-year-old Lesley Ann Downey and 12-year-old John Kilbride. John had vanished on 23 November, 1963 and Lesley had disappeared a year later, on Boxing Day, 1964.

But first the police had to gain entry to the house in Wardle Brook Avenue where the children had met their deaths. A police superintendent borrowed a white coat and basket from a bread roundsman and approached the house, which belonged to Hindley's grandmother. He knocked on the door which was opened by Hindley.

Brady was lying on a divan bed writing a letter. The note was to his employers saying he wouldn't be at work that day because he had injured his leg. At his trial, it was revealed he had planned to spend the day back on the moors – digging another grave.

With Brady and Hindley separated and safely behind bars, police concentrated all efforts on the moorland search. There they found the grave of 12-year-old John Kilbride. A few yards away, on the other side of a road which split the wild moorland in two, they found the remains of tiny Lesley Ann Downey. They were helped in their search by 'souvenir' photographs, taken by the couple, of Hindley standing over the two graves.

Then came the trial at Chester Assizes – and a courtroom and country shaken by tales of horror and torture. Brady and Hindley, it was revealed, kept vile photographs of their mutilated victims.

But nothing shocked the courtroom more than the playing of a tape. On it were the pleadings, the screams and last dying moments of Lesley Ann Downey.

It took the jury – all male – 18 days to listen to the most horrific evidence ever put before a British court. All seemed to lower their heads when prosecutor Sir Elwyn Jones, the Attorney General, played the tape of young Lesley Ann

---

Cicero's tongue finally got the better of him in AD 43. The Roman orator was assassinated after vexing Mark Anthony with his caustic speeches. As a result, he lost his head and hands, which were displayed in Rome.

Anthony's wife, Fulvia, took great glee in ripping Cicero's tongue out of his head and repeatedly stabbed it with a hairpin. She could never match his wit in life – but in death he could not answer back.

Downey's last moments. People in the court swayed with disgust and onlookers buried faces in their hands.

Brady, quizzed in the witness box, could only say that he was 'embarrassed' when he heard the tape. Hindley did not have her partner in crime's arrogance, but she still held her poise and confidence in the witness box. As her part in the killings became clear she kept uttering 'I was cruel. I was cruel'.

At precisely 2.40 pm on Friday, 6 May, the jury retired. For two hours and 20 minutes, they considered the verdict in 'the trial of the century'. Brady was given concurrent life-sentences for 'these calculated, cruel, cold-blooded murders'. Then came the final words that put Brady behind bars: 'Put him down'. Myra Hindley, for the first time, stood alone in the dock as the judge turned to her. She swayed, as if to faint as she too, was given life-sentences.

The Voyage of Terror

THOMAS BRAM

On the stormy night of 13 July, 1896, Lester Monks, a passenger on the sailing ship *Herbert Fuller*, unlocked his door and stepped warily into the captain's cabin with a loaded revolver in his hand. He had been roused from sleep by what sounded like the scream of wind through the halyards. But wider awake, he knew it was more than that – a woman had been screaming.

The captain's cot had been toppled to its side and the skipper, Captain Charles Nash, lay dying in a pool of blood. His wife, Laura was on her bunk. Like Nash she had literally been chopped to death, her skull smashed in front and back and both jaws broken.

Monks staggered up the forward companionway to find the first mate, Thomas Bram, pacing the deck. And from the moment that he heard the news, Bram's conduct was bizarre. He refused to alert the second mate, August Blomberg, because he thought the man was inciting the crew against him. And in the end, incredibly, he slumped to the deck and hugged the passenger's legs, begging for protection.

At dawn they roused steward Jonathon Spencer and the three went to Blomberg's cabin. There they found the door wide open and the second mate hacked to death in his bunk, two of his severed fingers on the floor.

Surprisingly, Bram, who had by now assumed command of the ship, was able to lead them to the murder weapon on deck – a new axe sticky with blood and flesh. Still more strangely, the big man gave a throaty shriek and hurled the weapon overboard.

At a meeting of crew and passengers, Bram urged that the three bodies be thrown into the sea – an idea vetoed by all. He tried to blame the killings on the

Billy the Kid, whose real name may have been William Bonney or Henry McCarty, was reputed to have carried out 21 murders. It is now believed, however, that he killed 'only' four people. New York-born Billy was shot dead by Sheriff Pat Garrett, of Lincoln City, New Mexico, in 1881.

dead Blomberg, insisting that the second mate must have died of his own wounds. And he wanted to take the murder ship to French Guiana in South America.

An air of terror filled the big square-rigger, which had left Boston on 3 July bound for Argentina with a cargo of timber. In the six days that it took to return to port, no one aboard slept easily in his berth.

Bram managed to convince the crew that one of their members, Charley Brown, was acting suspiciously. If anything, the silent Brown looked relieved when they manacled him in a cabin. There were reasons why. Just before the ship reached Halifax, Brown told other crewmen he had seen the captain slain. As he had stood at the helm on that bloody night, the scene in the chartroom had been visible to him through a small window in front of the wheel. And afterwards, Brown said, he had heard Laura Nash screaming.

But he had kept the knowledge to himself because he was afraid of the maniac with the axe – their commander, First Mate Bram.

Bram's trial began in Boston on 14 December, 1896. Former shipmates testified that he had often approached them with the idea of killing various ship's officers and selling the stolen cargo. Bram himself boasted of looting two other vessels.

Sentenced to the gallows, he won a new trial on technical grounds and was committed to the U.S. penitentiary in Atlanta. He would have stayed there except for one thing – the strange intervention of mystery writer Mary Roberts Rinehart, author of *The Bat*, *The Cat and The Canary*, and other thrillers.

Mrs Rinehart had managed to convince herself that Bram was an abused innocent who had been framed by his shipmates. She wove the notion into a sensational novel, *The After House*, and managed to convince President Woodrow Wilson that she was right.

Thomas Bram was pardoned in 1919.

Convicted by his Crooked Teeth

THEODORE BUNDY

Law student Theodore Bundy was tall, handsome, charming and well educated, but this gentle, polite young man, with the looks to make girls swoon and the old-fashioned courtesy to appeal to their parents, was consigned to Death Row. The all-American boy Bundy is believed to be one of the worst mass murderers in American history – responsible for the savage rape and killing of 36 young women. Authorities in four states are convinced that beneath his disarming appearance lurked a Jekyll and Hyde. His victims were raped, clubbed, strangled and beaten to death. Investigators found that in every case Bundy had been nearby.

Bundy collected three death sentences in different trials. He was sentenced for the murders of two students in a Tallahassee sorority house in 1978, for the kidnap and murder of a Salt Lake City police chief's 12-year-old daughter, and for the kidnapping and battering of an 18-year-old girl out shopping in Salt Lake City. Yet the college graduate, who has planned to become a lawyer, always maintained his innocence. 'I have never killed, never kidnapped, never desired to injure another human being', he told a court.

The bloody trail of murders which bogged Bundy's footsteps began in 1974, when six strikingly similar and attractive young women vanished in the Seattle area. In January the first girl vanished from her bedroom. The only hint of her fate was a bloodstain on her pillow. Then in March a 19-year-old chemistry student left her dormitory at Evergreen State College for a concert. She was never seen again. A month later the third girl left her college to go to the cinema. She too never returned. In May and June three more girls vanished. No traces have ever been found of them.

All the girls were shapely brunettes. The other common factor was that each had been approached on the beach during the summer by a young, handsome man. He called himself Ted. There were no other clues to the disappearances until some forestry students strolling in the countryside found a jawbone and other bones in a shallow grave.

The discovery of the bones sent shock waves through the community. Detectives made little progress. But they later linked the murders with the disappearance of two more girls. The girls went missing at a picnic park. Three months later their corpses were found 10 miles from the other grave. Again

Drunken gunslinger Jack Slade was notorious for his savage killing of Jules Bene, an old enemy who had once ambushed and shot him. Slade took a slow revenge when they met again. He fastened Bene to a post and, between swigs of whisky, shot at his limbs. Then he blasted off his head and cut off an ear as a key fob.

But it was not the murder of Jules Bene that finished Slade. It was his drunken gun-slinging antics around Virginia City, Montana, whose townsfolk hanged him from the main beam of the saloon in 1864.

His wife soaked the corpse in raw alcohol for the long trip to his native Illinois. But he never made it. Slade's decomposed body ended up in a Mormon cemetary in Salt Lake City.

witnesses talked of the mysterious and charming young man called Ted who had been seen before the girls vanished.

Theodore Bundy was never charged with these murders. But he was arrested for the attempted abduction of a 17-year-old girl. He was left alone in a courtroom during a recess and he escaped. He was recaptured but he escaped again. By this time Bundy was awaiting trial for the murders of a Michigan nurse and a policeman's 14-year-old daughter. His escape launched a nationwide hunt by police, who already suspected him of being a mass murderer. But no trace was found of him until seven months later when four students in a sorority house on Florida State University campus were bludgeoned with a broken tree branch. Two of the girls died. After a hunt, Bundy was arrested.

The trial which followed was one of the most sensational in American history. The entire nation followed the proceedings on television, which under Florida law was allowed into the courtroom. The bizarre twists in the case attracted newsmen from around the world.

Bundy was convicted after evidence about the one flaw in his perfect appearance. He had distinctly crooked teeth. And it was those teeth that gave him away.

Evidence from a dental expert proved that bite marks on the body of one of Bundy's victims matched his teeth. As one of the girls lay dying she had been brutally bitten on her breast and buttock. The other dead girl had been battered and strangled – so violently that a police witness said at first he thought she had been decapitated.

When the verdict was announced, Bundy's mother shrieked in anguish and screamed out that he was innocent. But Bundy, who was baptized as a Mormon just before the murder spree began, was described as the 'most vicious criminal in history' by a Utah police captain who investigated some of the murders.

The personality of Bundy remains a mystery. To those who watched him calmly facing the death penalty in courtrooms, it seemed incredible that he could be the same man who battered women to death in frenzied sprees of violence. He was born in a home for unmarried mothers. But after that his background was impecable. He was a Boy Scout and worked as an assistant programmes director at the Seattle Crime Commission, where he battled against white-collar crime. He even helped write a booklet for women on rape prevention.

One person still convinced of his innocence is Carole Boone who married Bundy in a hurried ceremony in a court in Florida just before he was handed his third death sentence. Carole, who has kissed her husband only once, would drive regularly the 150 miles from her home to Talahassee where Bundy waited in a Death Row cell. She knew him before he was arrested and said: 'Ted is not vicious or a savage mass murderer. The charges were the result of snowballing hysteria on the part of law enforcement people looking for a fall guy on whom they could pin all their unsolved crimes. From the beginning, I believed in his innocence. When I looked into the evidence, I was convinced of it'. But the jurors who decided Bundy should die for the murders he committed feared that if he remained alive he might break out of jail and 'do it all a second time'.

The 'Monster in Human Shape'

MARY ANN COTTON

Welfare worker Thomas Riley walked briskly through the early morning summer sunshine. It was 06.00 and he was on his way to another day's duties at the village workhouse in West Auckland. Times were hard for the people of County Durham, and Riley was kept busy trying to care for those who could not cope. As he turned into Front Street, he recalled the widow at No 13. She had come to him only six days earlier, asking if he had room in the workhouse for her seven-year-old stepson, Charles Edward. 'It is hard to keep him when he is not my own, and he is stopping me from taking in a respectable lodger,' she said. Riley joked about the identity of the lodger. Was it the excise officer village gossips said she wanted to marry? 'It may be so,' the woman had replied, 'but the boy is in the way.'

Now, as he walked to work, Riley noticed the widow in the doorway of her three-room stone cottage. She was clearly upset, and he crossed the road to ask why. He could not believe his ears at what she told him: 'My boy is dead.'

Riley went straight to the police and the local doctor. What he told them was the first step in an investigation that was to brand the widow, Mary Ann Cotton, the worst mass murderer Britain had ever seen.

Riley was suspicious about the death because the lad had seemed in perfect health when he saw him six days earlier. Dr Kilburn was also surprised to hear of the tragedy. He and his assistant Dr Chambers had seen the boy five times that week for what they thought were symptoms of gastro-enteritis, but they never thought the illness could be fatal. Dr Kilburn decided to withhold a death certificate and asked for permission to carry out a post-mortem examination. The coroner agreed to the request, and arranged an inquest for the following afternoon, Saturday, 13 July, 1872.

The pressures of their practice meant the two doctors could not start their post-mortem until an hour before the hearing. After a cursory examination, Dr Kilburn told the jury in the Rose and Crown Inn, next to Cotton's house: 'I have found nothing to suggest poisoning. Death could have been from natural causes, possibly gastro-enteritis.' The jury returned a verdict of natural death, and Charles Edward was buried in a pauper's grave.

But Dr Kilburn had taken the precaution of preserving the contents of the boy's stomach in a bottle. On the following Wednesday he at last had time to put them to proper chemical tests. He went straight back to the police with the results. There were distinct traces of arsenic. Next morning, widow Cotton was arrested and charged with murder. The boy's body was dug up and sent to Leeds School of Medicine, where Dr Thomas Scattergood, lecturer in forensic medicine and toxicology, discovered more arsenic, in the bowels, liver, lungs, heart and kidneys.

Meanwhile, Thomas Riley was pointing out to the authorities that the death of Charles Edward was not the first in the family. In fact, there had been four in the two years since Mary Ann Cotton, a former nurse, had arrived in West Auckland. Her fourth husband, coal miner Frederick Cotton, died from 'gastric fever' on 19 September, 1871, two days after their first wedding anniversary. He was 39. Then, between 10 March and 1 April, 1872 10-year-old Frederick, Cotton's son by a previous marriage, Robert, Mary Ann's 14-month-old son, and Mary Ann's former lover, Joseph Nattrass, who had moved in with her again, all died. Gastric fever was again the cause of death on their certificates, except for the baby, who died from 'teething convulsions.'

Those three bodies were exhumed while Mary Ann waited for her trial in Durham Jail, and Dr Scattergood found traces of arsenic in all of them. Newspapers began looking more closely at the life of the miner's daughter from the Durham pit village of Low Moorsley. They unearthed a horrifying dossier of an apparently kind, good-natured and devout Methodist who seemed to spread death wherever she went.

In 1852, aged 20, she had married a labourer called William Mowbray, and moved to Devon. She had five children there, but four died. The couple returned to the north-east, moving from house to house in the Sunderland area, while Mary Ann worked at the town's infirmary. They had three more children. All died. Then Mowbray died. Mary Ann married again. Her husband, an engineer called George Wood, died in October 1866, 14 months after the wedding.

A month later, Mary Ann moved in as housekeeper to widower James Robinson and his three children. She soon became pregnant and married Robinson. But within weeks of her arrival in the household, Robinson's 10-month-old son John was dead. On 21 April, 1867, Robinson's son James, six, went to his grave. Five days later, his sister Elizabeth, eight, followed him. And on 2 May, nine-year-old Isabella, the only survivor of Mary Ann's marriage to Mowbray, lost her life.

Mary Ann had two daughters by Robinson. The first died within days of birth. The second was given away to a friend when the marriage broke up. Robinson survived, possibly because he resisted his wife's pleas to take out insurance on his life. But others who knew Mary Ann were not so lucky. She went to visit her mother because she feared she 'might be about to die'. No-one

THE WORLD'S MOST INFAMOUS MURDERS

Morbid American cannibal Albert Fish enjoyed a variety of dishes. The quiet painter and decorator confessed to having slaughtered six children – although the true total may have been 15. Most of the tender little bodies he swooped on were carefully cut up and stewed with vegetables. In the electric chair at Sing Sing in 1936, Fish seemed quite excited about being roasted himself – and even helped the executioner fix the electrodes.

---

else was worried about the apparently sprightly 54-year-old, but within nine days she was dead. Mary Ann moved on, laden with clothes and bed linen.

She met and became friends with Margaret Cotton, and was introduced to her brother Frederick. Mary Ann quickly became pregnant, and married her new lover bigamously – her third husband, Robinson, was still alive. The wedding was slightly marred by the unexpected death of Margaret, whose £60 bank account went to the newly-weds. In all, 21 people close to Mary Ann lost their lives in less than 20 years. She had given birth to 11 children, yet only one survived – the girl she gave away. Small wonder, then, that on the morning of her trial, a local newspaper, unfettered by today's laws of libel and contempt, ran the headline: 'The Great Poisoning Case At West Auckland – Horrible Revelations'. But when she stepped into the courtroom at Durham Assizes shortly before 10.00 on 5 March, 1873, she was charged only with one killing, that of her stepson, Charles Edward.

The prosecution, led by Sir Charles Russell, later to become Lord Chief Justice, alleged the 40-year-old widow had poisoned the boy because there was a Prudential Insurance policy on his life worth £8, and because he was an impediment to her marraige to her excise officer lover, a man called Quick-Manning, by whom she was already pregnant. 'She was badly off and Charles Edward was a tie and burden to her,' said Sir Charles.

Mary Ann Dodds, a former neighbour of the accused, told the court she had bought a mixture of arsenic and soft soap from one of the village's chemist's shops in May 1872, two months before the boy's death. 'The mixture was needed to remove bugs from a bed in Mary Ann's home,' she said. 'I rubbed most of it into the joints of the bed and the iron crosspieces underneath.'

Chemist John Townend said the mixture would have contained about an ounce of arsenic – about 480 grains. Three grains were enough to kill an adult. He also thought it significant that his shop was not the closest chemist's to widow Cotton's home.

Thomas Riley gave his evidence about Mary Ann's eagerness to get the boy off her hands, and Dr Kilburn explained the medical steps he had taken. It was then that controversy entered the trial. The prosecution wanted to introduce evidence of earlier deaths in the family. Defence lawyer Thomas Campbell Foster, appointed only two days before the trial because Cotton could not afford her own legal representation, protested that his client was charged with only one death, which he maintained was an accident caused by arsenic impregnation of some green floral wallpaper. To discuss the earlier deaths would prejudice a fair trial, he said.

But Judge Sir Thomas Archibald ruled against him, citing legal precedent. From that moment on, the verdict was a foregone conclusion. The defence introduced no witnesses, and at 18.50 on the third day of the trial, the jury returned after only an hour's deliberations to pronounce Mary Ann Cotton guilty of murder.

The judge donned his black cap to sentence her to death, saying: 'You seem to have given way to that most awful of all delusions, which sometimes takes possession of persons wanting in proper moral and religious sense, that you could carry out your wicked designs without detection. But while murder by poison is the most detestable of all crimes, and one at which human nature shudders, it is one the nature of which, in the order of God's providence, always leaves behind it complete and incontestable traces of guilt. Poisoning, as it were, in the very act of crime writes an indelible record of guilt.'

They were fine words, but not strictly true. The state of medical knowledge in the 1870s was not as sophisticated as it is today. In an unsanitary age, gastric fever was a common killer, and overworked doctors could not examine every corpse without strong reasons. Though the final toll of deaths in Mary Ann's circle was high, she avoided suspicion by moving house frequently, and always calling in local doctors when her victims began complaining of stomach pains. The fact that she had once been a nurse, and was well known for caring for sick neighbours, also made people trust her.

No-one will ever know how many of the 21 unlucky people around her were poisoned either for insurance money, possessions, or because they stood in the way of a new marriage. Most people put the number of murders at 14 or 15. But despite the horror at what the *Newcastle Journal* newspaper described as 'a monster in human shape', many people had misgivings about her death sentence. There were doubts about hanging a woman, doubts about the way

---

Fugitive Leonard T. Fristoe was on the run from the law for 46 years. Jailed for life in 1920 for killing two deputy sheriffs, he served only three years of his sentence before escaping. His luck ran out when, at the ripe old age of 77, he was recaptured at Compton, California, after being turned in by his own son.

her defence in court had been organized, doubts about whether evidence of earlier deaths should have been allowed, doubts about the lack of any witnesses for the defence.

The *Newcastle Journal* admitted:

'Perhaps the most astounding thought of all is that a woman could act thus without becoming horrible and repulsive. Mary Ann Cotton, on the contrary, seems to have possessed the faculty of getting a new husband whenever she wanted one. To her other children and her lodger, even when she was deliberately poisoning them, she is said to have maintained a rather kindly manner.' The paper felt instinctively that the earth should be rid of her, but added: 'Pity cannot be withheld, though it must be mingled with horror.'

Mary Ann spent her last few days in jail trying to win support for a petition for a reprieve. She gave birth to Quick-Manning's daughter, Margaret, and arranged for her to go to a married couple who could not have children. Five days before her execution, the baby was forcibly taken from her. On 24 March, 1873, still maintaining her innocence, she went to the scaffold at Durham. It was three minutes before the convulsions of her body stopped.

Within eight days, a stage play, *The Life and Death of Mary Ann Cotton*, was being performed in theatres, labelled 'a great moral drama'. Mothers threatened recalcitrant children with the prospect of a visit from the West Auckland widow, and youngsters made up a skipping rhyme which began: 'Mary Ann Cotton, she's dead and rotten.' But she remains today one of the most enigmatic figures in the gallery of killers – a simple-minded mass murderer who evoked revulsion and sympathy in equal measures.

A Miscarriage of Justice?

JOHN CHRISTIE

John Reginald Halliday Christie was regarded by his neighbours as hard-working and respectable, although not particularly likeable. They often took his advice on medical matters, of which he affected a knowledge. It was also rumoured that he could help a girl terminate a pregnancy which may be why he apparently found it so easy to lure prostitutes to his home . . . and to their deaths.

For 14 years Christie lived in a run-down terraced house at 10 Rillington Place in London's decaying Notting Hill district. Christie and his wife Ethel had taken the ground-floor flat in 1938 at a time when he was trying to play down his five criminal convictions, one of which was for assaulting a woman. During the war he applied for a job as a reserve policeman and, because his record was never checked, he got it. After the war he worked briefly in a factory, then took a job as a post office clerk.

Christie's wife disappeared while the couple were living at number 10, and the solitary widower finally moved to another flat in 1952.

In March 1953 a prospective tenant was looking over the ground floor flat at 10 Rillington Place when he detected a foul smell which seemed to be emanating from a papered-over kitchen cupboard. Thinking that a rat had found its way inside and died, he ripped open the cupboard. What he found made him rush to the nearest telephone box and dial 999.

When the police arrived, they stripped the flat. In the kitchen cupboard they found the bodies of three prostitutes. Two more bodies were found buried in the back-yard. And beneath the sitting-room floor was the body of Ethel Christie.

Christie confessed to the six murders. In one of the most sensational and horrifying trials in history, it was said that he could gain sexual satisfaction only with dead women. Christie hoped to be found guilty but insane, and his life spared, but he was sentenced to death by hanging.

That, however, was far from being the end of the story. For as well as the six bodies found at 10 Rillington Place, Christie also confessed to murdering Beryl Evans, the wife of an ex-neighbour, Timothy Evans. The confession, however, came too late to help poor Timothy Evans, for in 1950 he had been sentenced to death by hanging – for murder.

To this day, no-one knows for sure which of the two men killed Beryl Evans.

Above left: 10 Rillington Place. Victims from left to right: Beryl Evans, Hectorina MacLennan, Muriel Amelia Eady, Kathleen Maloney, Rita Nelson, Ruth Fuerst
Above right: John and Ethel Christie

> Bible-loving Earle Leonard Nelson claimed he was 'a very
> religious man of high ideals'. But in less than two years, he raped
> and strangled at least 22 landladies across the United States and
> Canada in a trail of terror that began in San Francisco in
> February 1926, and ended in Winnipeg, Canada, in June 1927.
>
> He was finally captured after changing his clothes at a
> secondhand store, and leaving behind a fountain pen taken from
> the home of his last victim, Mrs Emily Paterson. At his trial in
> Winnipeg, accused of her murder, he pleaded insanity. However,
> the jury decided that a man who kept on the move, changing his
> clothes and name after each killing, was not insane. He was
> hanged on 13 January, 1928, aged 36.

What is certain is that no jury today could possibly convict Timothy Evans of the crime.

Evan's confession was made on the spur of the moment when he walked into a police station in Merthyr Tydfil, South Wales, on 30 November, 1949, and told the officer at the desk: 'I would like to give myself up. I have disposed of the body of my wife.'

Evans, a gullible, illiterate van driver who ws largely under the spell of the evil Christie, told detectives that they would find his wife's body in a drain at 10 Rillington Place, where the Evans family had occupied the top-floor flat.

Police searched the house but could not find the dead woman in the drains. A later search, however, revealed the body in a small wash-house at the back of Number 10. She had been strangled, the same means of death meted out by Christie to all his victims. But more horrifying still was the discovery of a second corpse in the wash-house. It was the body of Evans's baby daughter, Geraldine. Evans appeared to be shattered by the discovery of his daughter. He at first admitted both murders but at his trial he accused Christie of the crimes.

The unfortunate Evans said that his wife was pregnant for the second time and that Christie had offered to give her an abortion. Evans agreed and left the two together. Afterwards, Christie showed Evans the woman's body and said that she had died during the abortion. He advised Evans to get rid of all his wife's clothes and other possessions and to leave London for a while. Meanwhile, Christie would arrange for little Geraldine to be unofficially adopted by a couple he knew. But apparently he decided to get rid of her, too.

That was Evans's story but the jury did not believe him. In court Christie, the ex-policeman, was a much more convincing witness. His previous conviction for viciously assaulting a woman was not mentioned to the jury. The prosecution described Christie as 'this perfectly innocent man'.

A MISCARRIAGE OF JUSTICE?

The simple-minded Evans was convicted – technically for murder of his baby only – and hanged. Christie stayed free for another three years . . . free to commit another four murders. He murdered his wife and then three prostitutes in close succession. Their bodies were added to those of the two women whom Christie had murdered in 1943 and 1944 and buried in the back-yard.

Christie was brought to justice in June 1953. He was tried for the murder of his wife and hanged at Pentonville Prison on 15 July, 1953.

But that was not the end of the story. Public outcry grew over the years for an inquiry into what was seen as a ghastly miscarriage of justice over the execution of Timothy Evans. But it was not until 1966 that pressure for an official review of the case succeeded in prompting the government to authorize an inquiry under Mr Justice Brabin. He ruled: 'It is more probable than not that Evans killed Beryl Evans, and it is more probable than not that Evans did not kill Geraldine.'

The ruling fell short of the sort of verdict that the pro-Evans campaigners had fought for over the years. But it did mean that Evans, whose conviction was for killing his daughter, could receive a posthumous royal pardon. His body was exhumed from Pentonville Prison and reburied in consecrated ground.

What the ruling did not do was to answer some extremely pertinent questions about the efficiency of the police, who failed to turn up the evidence that would, right from the start, have pointed the finger clearly at scheming, glib, persuasive mass-strangler Christie.

Why, when investigating Evan's allegations, did they fail to take note of Christie's previous record, happily accepting his wartime police service as evidence of his good character? Why did they unquestioningly accept Christie's claim that he could not have helped dispose of Beryl Evans's body because his fibrositis prevented his lifting any heavy weight?

Why, on the first two occasions that police searched 10 Rillington Place for the body of Mrs Evans, did they not look in the wash-house? It was only on the third visit that they made their grisly discovery. And then only after standing with Christie in his back-yard and discussing with him the possibility of digging up his tiny garden to find out whether Beryl Evans was buried there.

If they had decided to dig up the yard, the detectives would have found the shallow grave of, not Mrs Evans, but the two other women who had been lured to the house, murdered and buried by Christie. As they chatted to Christie on that chill December morning in 1949, the detectives were standing on top of the two bodies. While the men spoke, Christie's small mongrel dog dug in the earth around their feet – and uncovered a woman's skull. Christie shooed the dog away and kicked earth over the evidence. The detectives noticed nothing.

If they had been more observant, four women might have been saved from murder, and Timothy Evans saved from the gallows.

The Strychnine Specialist
NEILL CREAM

Neill Cream had a surprise for the hangman when he mounted the scaffold on 15 November, 1892. He unexpectedly confessed that he was Jack the Ripper. But the authorities knew better. They realized it was just another attempt by the pathetic psychopath to glamourize his career as a killer. Cream described by one acquaintance as 'a degenerate with filthy desires and practices', certainly killed the same targets, in the same area, as the Ripper, but he did so in a style that was even more loathsome than that of London's most notorious murderer.

Cream was a pitiless sadist who revelled in drawing attention to his exploits. He committed the worst of his murders after being released from a life sentence in jail. Cream was born in Glasgow in 1850, but his parents emigrated to Canada when he was only four, and were prosperous enough to send him to Montreal's McGill College, where he qualified as a doctor in 1876.

But it was taking life, not saving it, that interested him most. He became an abortionist, a profitable though illegal trade in those days. Cream was doing well, until the father of Flora Brooks, a girl to whom he gave an abortion after making her pregnant, forced him at gun-point to marry her. The honeymoon lasted one day, before Cream left to continue his medical studies in London. The reluctant bridegroom returned after a year to find his wife dead of consumption. He again worked as an abortionist, adding blackmail as a sideline, but as his reputation grew more notorious, he moved south to the United States, to try his luck in Chicago. By 1880 he was known to the police. He was arrested for murder after Julia Faulkner, a girl whose pregnancy he aborted, died. He was, however, tried and cleared. Later two of his few legitimate patients died, the first a spinster who was going to Cream for medicine, the second an epileptic railway worker, Daniel Stott, whose wife collected pills for him, and enjoyed Cream's sexual favours, at the clinic.

The police were not suspicious about either death, until Cream went out of his way to attract their attention. He wrote to the coroner saying the chemist must have put too much strychnine in Stott's pills, and asking for the body to be exhumed. When it was, it soon became clear that the chemist was not responsible for doctoring the pills. Cream, who had eloped with Stott's widow, was arrested, and jailed for life for second degree murder.

Neill Cream

But in July 1891, after less than ten years, the governor of Illinois commuted the sentence, and Cream was released. His father had died, leaving him $16,000, and powerful friends of the family pulled strings to set him free to enjoy his new riches. Cream returned to Canada, but not for long. He soon sailed for England and the gas-lit streets of Lambeth where he had wandered as a student.

Cream had studied the career of Jack the Ripper, and was proud to walk where his hero had struck. He also had a penchant for prostitutes, boasting to acquaintances that he sometimes took on two at a time, or visited three in one night. But sex was not his only pleasure. He gave some girls pills which he said would cure the spots on their faces. In fact, they contained strychnine, the most agonizing of all poisons. And as the girls trustingly took them after he left, Cream got his kicks from imagining the excruciating pain of the victims as they writhed violenty before death.

Late in 1891, two young prostitutes, Elizabeth Masters and Elizabeth May, were watching for Cream from their window in Hercules Road, Lambeth. But as he walked towards their room, he was accosted by another lady of the night, Matilda Clover, aged 26, and followed her to her lodgings in Lambeth Road. Ten days later, on 20 October she died there in terrible pain, blurting that she had been poisoned by pills given to her by a man named Fred. But Matilda's doctor, who was treating her for alcoholism, wrote 'Natural Causes' on the death certificate.

Seven days earlier, on 13 October, Ellen Donworth, a 19-year-old prostitute, had been found in dreadful agony in Waterloo Road. Before she died on the way to hospital, she told of a tall man with cross-eyes and gold spectacles who had given her a bottle containing white fluid to drink. The man also wore a silk hat and had bushy whiskers. A post-mortem examination revealed that Ellen had been killed by strychnine.

Cream followed up his two murders with the curious correspondence that the British police only later realized was his trademark. He wrote in false names to Lord Russell and a Dr William Broadbent, accusing them both of killing Matilda. He demanded £2,500 from the doctor, under threat of exposing him. Broadbent went to the police, but the blackmailer never turned up as arranged. Cream also wrote to the coroner who was to hear the Ellen Donworth case, saying he had information about the murderer which he was prepared to sell for £300,000. Police consigned the letter, signed G. O'Brian, detective, to their idiot file.

What Cream's purpose was in writing the letters has never been discovered. Some experts in psychology say he wanted to keep his crimes in the public mind, inventing sensational sums of money merely to make the murders more newsworthy. Certainly he was never interested in collecting the sums he demanded. Others say he had a death wish, almost wanting to be arrested so he could bask in what he imagined to be the glory of public recognition. Perhaps also he remembered that Jack the Ripper had taunted his pursuers through the mail.

Cream sailed home to Canada in January 1892, after getting engaged to Laura Sabbatini, and whiled away the hours on board by bragging to fellow passengers about his sex life, the poisons he used to 'get women out of the family way' and the false whiskers he wore to make sure he was not recognized. Back in Canada, for no apparent reason, he had 500 posters printed. They read: 'Ellen Donworth's Death. To the guests of the Metropole Hotel: Ladies and Gentleman, I hereby notify you that the person who poisoned Ellen Donsworth on the 13th last October is today in the employ of the Metropole and that your lives are in danger as long as you remain in this hotel'. He signed the posters, 'Yours respectfully, W. H. Murray,' and datelined them 'London, April, 1892.' But why he picked on the Metropole Hotel was never explained. And, in fact, the posters were never distributed there.

Cream left New York for Liverpool on 23 March, and was back in Lambeth by 11 April, when he enjoyed a three-in-a-bed romp with 18-year-old Emma Shrivell and 21-year-old Alice Marsh. He left at 02.00, giving each girl three pills for her complexion. The two prostitutes died horribly that night, gasping to companions that the pills had come from a man called Fred.

The inquest verdict caused a sensation in a city still not certain that it had heard the last of Jack the Ripper. The two girls had been killed by strychnine. But again Cream could not leave well alone. And this time, it was to lead to the hangman's noose.

He wrote to a Dr Harper, accusing his son Walter, a medical student who lodged near Cream in Lambeth Palace Road, of causing the deaths of Alice and Emma. This time the price for suppressing the information was £1,500. Harper had nothing to fear, so he went to the police. They compared the handwriting with a letter Cream himself had given them. It was allegedly sent to Alice and Emma, warning them to beware of Dr Harper, who had killed Matilda and a certain Lou Harvey. The writing matched, and Cream was charged with attempted blackmail and false pretenses. Meanwhile, police exhumed Matilda Clover's body from her pauper's grave in Tooting. She too had died from strychnine, despite her doctor's diagnosis of natural causes.

Cream had made a fatal mistake – only Matilda's killer would have known that she had been murdered. By accusing another man, he had convicted himself. Elizabeth Masters and Elizabeth May were prepared to testify that they had seen Cream with her before her death. The police knew they had a cast iron case. Only one thing troubled them. Who was Lou Harvey? They arrested Cream on 3 June, charged him with murder, and set about finding out.

Lou Harvey, when discovered in Brighton, turned out to be the one girl who had cheated Cream's murderous plans. She had met him the previous October in London's Soho and spent the night with him at a hotel. Before he left next morning, he gave her some pills to clear up acne on her forehead, and arranged to meet her that evening near Charing Cross. Lou – short for Louisa – never took the pills. The man who lived on her earnings did not like the look of them, and forced her to throw them away. And when she kept the evening date, he was watching from a distance.

Cream bought the girl a drink and presented her with roses. He then gave her two more pills to take, but she managed to throw them away surreptitiously, and he seemed satisfied when he asked to see her hands, and they were empty. Cream left to enjoy his death agony fantasies – and seemed astonished, a month later, to see her alive and apparently well in Piccadilly.

Lou's story was added to the dossier against Cream, and on 17 October, 1892, the heartless poisoner went on trial at the Old Bailey. He had no credible evidence to offer against the accusations of Louisa and the two Elizabeths. A chemist testified that Cream had bought nux vomica, a vegetable product from which strychnine is extracted, and gelatin capsules. Police revealed that seven bottles of strychnine were found in Cream's lodgings. The jury took only 12 minutes to find him guilty. Nobody mourned when the rope put an end to his miserable life less than a month later.

Two curious claims kept Cream's name before the public for a while longer. In an extraordinary letter to *The Times*, his optician claimed that his moral degeneracy might have been avoided if his cross-eye defect had been corrected at an early age. And Sir Edward Marshall Hall, one of the most renowned advocates in British legal history, said he once successfully defended Cream against a charge of bigamy by claiming he was in prison in Sydney, Australia, at the time. The governor of the jail there confirmed that a man answering Cream's description had indeed been in his custody.

When Marshall Hall later learned that Cream had never been to Australia, he became convinced that the poisoner had a double in the underworld, and that the two look-alikes supplied alibis for each other when necessary. Some writers have even argued that the double may have been Jack the Ripper. But despite his claim on the scaffold, Cream could not have been the Ripper. For he had an unshakable alibi at the time of the Ripper's reign of terror in 1888 – he was serving a life sentence in Chicago's Joliet Prison.

Caught By A New Invention

DR CRIPPEN

No name in the annals of murder is more notorious than that of Dr Hawley Harvey Crippen. Yet Crippen killed only once and, but for three fatal errors, might have got away with it. He was a quiet, inoffensive little man, intelligent, courteous and kind with a touch of nobility about his actions. Perhaps that only served to enhance the horror of his ghastly crime.

Born in Coldwater, Michigan, in 1862, he studied long and hard for his medical degrees in Cleveland, Ohio, London and New York. He practised in several big American cities, and was already a widower when, at 31, he became assistant to a doctor in Brooklyn, New York. Among the patients there was a 17-year-old girl who called herself Cora Turner. Attractive and lively, she was the mistress of a stove manufacturer by whom she was pregnant. She miscarried.

Despite her circumstances, Crippen fell in love with her, and began trying to win her affections. He found that her real name was Kunigunde Mackamotzki, that her father was a Russian Pole and her mother a German, and that the girl wanted to be an opera singer. Crippen paid for singing lessons, though he must have known her dreams were bigger than her talent. They married in 1893.

In 1900, Crippen, now consultant physician to Munyon's, a company selling mail-order medicines, was transferred to England as manager of the head office in London. Later that year Cora joined him, and decided to switch her singing aspirations to music hall performances. She changed her name to Belle Elmore, and Crippen too took a new name. He dropped Hawley Harvey and called himself Peter.

Cora cultivated a large circle of Bohemian friends, dressing gaudily, bleaching her hair, and acquiring false blonde curls. She was extrovert and popular, particularly with men, and for a time her insignificant husband, small, slight and with an over-sized sandy moustache, was happy to observe her gay social whirl through his gold-rimmed spectacles, occasionally buying her furs or jewellery which he loved to present in front of her friends. The finery contrasted with the squalor of their home – neither had much inclination for household chores, and both were content to live in a dingy back kitchen, surrounded by dirty crockery, piles of clothes, and two cats that were never let out.

Any bliss that there had been in this marriage of apparent opposites vanished while Crippen was away on the company's business in Philadelphia. He returned after several months to be told by Cora that she had been seeing an American music hall singer called Bruce Miller, and that they were fond of each other.

In September, 1905, the Crippens moved to 39 Hilltop Crescent, off Camden Road, in north London. It was a leafy street of large Victorian houses, enjoying its heyday as a good address, and cost £52 50p (£52 10s) rent a year – a large slice out of Crippen's £3 a week salary. But the new home did nothing to heal the growing rift between husband and wife. Crippen was to recall: 'Although we apparently lived very happily together, there were very frequent occasions when she got into the most violent tempers and often threatened she would leave me, saying she had a man she would go to and she would end it all. She went in and out just as she liked and did as she liked. I was rather a lonely man and rather miserable.' Soon they were sleeping in separate rooms.

Cora threw herself into working for the Music Hall Ladies Guild, pretending to be a big star helping the less lucky members of her profession via the charity organization. She also took a succession of lovers, some of whom gave her gifts and money. Crippen found consolation too, in the form of Ethel Le Neve, a secretary at Munyon's offices in New Oxford Street. She could not have been less like Cora. Quiet, lady-like, she craved respectability, and the doctor had to use all his powers of persuasion before she at last agreed to accompany him to a discreet hotel room for the first time. Thoughts of her kept Crippen's spirits up as life at home became even worse. His wife began taking in 'paying guests', and when he returned from work, he was expected to clean their boots, bring in their coal, and help with cleaning.

By 1909, Crippen was also a paying partner in a dental clinic, and his expenses, with two women to support, were strained. That November, he lost his job as Munyon's manager, and was paid only a commission for sales. The following month, Cora gave their bank 12 months notice that she was withdrawing the £600 in their joint deposit account. She did not need her husband's consent for that. Cora had also learnt of Crippen's affair with Ethel, and told friends she would leave him if he did not give the girl up.

On 17 January, 1910, Crippen ordered five grains of hyoscine from a chemist's shop near his office. The drug, a powerful narcotic used as a depressant in cases of mental or physical suffering, was then virtually unknown in Britain, and the chemist had none in stock. He delivered it to the doctor two days later.

On 31 January, the Crippens entertained two retired music hall friends to dinner and whist. It was, according to one of the guests, Clara Martinetti, 'quite

Dr. Crippen's wife

a nice evening and Belle was very jolly.' Clara and her husband Paul left at 01.30. Then, according to Crippen's later statements, Cora exploded with fury, threatening to leave home next day because he, Crippen, had failed to accompany elderly Mr Martinetti to the upstairs lavatory.

Cora Crippen was never seen alive again. On 2 February her husband pawned some of her rings for £80 and had Ethel Le Neve deliver a letter to the Music Hall Ladies Guild, saying that Cora, by now treasurer, would miss their next few meetings. She had rushed to America because a relative was seriously ill. On 9 February Crippen pawned more of his wife's gems, receiving £115. And soon her friends noticed still more of her jewels and clothes – being worn by Ethel Le Neve. She even went to the Guild's benevolent ball with Crippen, and wore one of Cora's brooches.

Inquiring friends started to get increasingly bad news about Belle Elmore from her husband. First she was uncontactable, 'right up in the wilds of the mountains of California.' Then she was seriously ill with pneumonia. And on 24 March, Crippen sent Mrs Martinetti a telegram just before he and Ethel left for a five-day Easter trip to Dieppe. It read: 'Belle died yesterday at six o'clock.' Two days later, notice of the death appeared in *The Era* magazine. Her body, according to Crippen, had been cremated in America.

Meanwhile, Ethel Le Neve had moved into 39 Hilldrop Crescent as housekeeper, bringing a French maid with her. She told her own landlady that Crippen's wife had gone to America. Clearly she was not likely to come back – Ethel left half her wardrobe behind, expecting to use Cora's clothes.

Crippen had given his own landlord notice of quitting, but he grew more confident as the constant questions about Cora tailed off, and so extended his lease until September. Then, on 28 June, came the first of what would prove fatal blows. A couple called Nash arrived back from touring American theatres, and told Crippen they had heard nothing of Cora's death while in California. Unhappy with his answers, they spoke to a highly-placed friend of theirs in Scotland Yard.

In 1914 society beauty Henriette Caillaux, wife of the French finance minister, shot dead Gaston Calmette, editor of the newspaper *Le Figaro*. Henriette had become enraged over a campaign against her husband by Calmette, who in two months had written 130 vitriolic articles about the minister. The final straw came when *Le Figaro* printed a revealing love letter written to Henriette by Caillaux before their marriage. The trial jury obviously sympathized with her. Henriette, who claimed her gun had fired by mistake, was acquitted.

CAUGHT BY A NEW INVENTION

Brian Donald Hume, a 39-year-old racketeer and psychopath, knew that he could not be tried for murder twice. He had been arrested for chopping up his business partner, Stanley Setty, and throwing the bits from a plane over the English Channel. He was cleared of murder but admitted to being an accessory and collected a 12-year sentence.

In 1958 Hume sold his confession to a Sunday newspaper and went off to Switzerland where he began a new career as a bank robber. In Zurich he murdered a taxi driver and, while awaiting trial, penned a novel *The Dead Stay Dumb*. Sentenced to life imprisonment in 1976, Hume was sent back to Britain where he was declared insane and despatched to Broadmoor.

On Friday 8 July, Chief Inspector Walter Dew and a sergeant called at Crippen's office, and asked to know more about Cora. Did her husband have a death certificate? Crippen admitted that the story of her death was a lie, designed to protect her reputation. She had, in fact, run off to America to join another man, probably her old flame Bruce Miller. The doctor dictated a long statement over five hours, broken only for amicable lunch with the policemen at a nearby restaurant. He readily agreed to accompany the officers back to Hilldrop Crescent for a search of the house. Dew was mildly puzzled that Mrs Crippen had left behind all her finest dresses, but he left satisfied nothing was amiss.

Crippen did not know that, however. He panicked, and made what would prove to be his biggest mistake. Overnight, he persuaded Ethel to leave with him for a new life in America. Early next morning, he asked his dental assistant to clear up his business and domestic affairs, then sent him out to buy some boy's clothes. That afternoon Crippen and Ethel left for Europe.

On the following Monday, Chief Inspector Dew returned to ask Crippen to clarify a few minor points in the statement, and discovered what had happened. Alarmed, he instantly ordered a more thorough search of Crippen's house and garden. At the end of the second day, Dew himself discovered a loose stone in the floor of the coal-cellar. Under it he found rotting human flesh, skin and hair, but no bones.

A team of top pathologists from St Mary's hospital, Paddington, painstakingly examined the remains, and decided they were of a plump female who bleached her hair. Part of the skin came from the lower abdomen, and included an old surgical scar in a position where Mrs Crippen was known to have one. The remains also contained huge traces of hyoscine, which kills within 12 hours if taken in excess. On 16 July, warrants for the arrest of Crippen and Ethel were issued. They were wanted for murder and mutilation.

Crippen had made two errors. He had carved out the bones of the body, and presumably burned them in his kitchen stove. But he had treated the fleshy remains with wet quicklime, a corrosive substance only effective when dry. And he had wrapped them before burial in a pyjama jacket with the label 'Shirtmakers, Jones Brothers, Holloway.' All might still have been well but for his third error, fleeing.

The discovery of the body aroused horrified indignation in the British press, but the two runaways, staying in Rotterdam and Brussels, did not realize the storm had broken. On 20 July, they left Antwerp in the liner *SS Montrose*, bound for Quebec. Crippen had shaved off his moustache and discarded his glasses, and was posing as John Philo Robinson, while Ethel, dressed in the boy's clothes Crippen's assistant had bought, pretended to be his 16-year-old son, John. But if they thought they were safe, they were wrong.

The ship's commander, Captain Kendall, had read all about the gruesome findings at Hilldrop Crescent, and was aware that the *Daily Mail* had offered £100 for information about the couple the police were hunting. Kendall noticed an inordinate amount of hand-touching between Mr Robinson and his son. The boy's suit fitted badly, and he seemed almost lady-like when eating meals, when his father would crack nuts for him or offer him half his salad.

Kendall surreptitiously collected up all the English-language papers on board so as not to alarm the couple. He checked Crippen's lack of reaction when he called him Robinson, and invited the couple to dine at his table. After two days at sea, he sent a message to the ship's owners over the newly-installed wireless telegraph, reporting his suspicions. On 23 July, Chief Inspector Dew and his sergeant set sail from Liverpool in the *Laurentic*, a faster trans-atlantic liner, which would overtake the *Montrose* just before it reached Quebec.

Then followed eight bizarre days. Crippen sat on deck, admiring the 'wonderful invention' of the wireless telegraph, not realizing that he was the subject of the crackling messages. Kendall's daily reports were avidly printed by the *Daily Mail*, whose readers relished every word as the net closed in on the unsuspecting doctor.

It was 08.30 on 31 July when Dew, accompanied by a Canadian policeman, boarded the *Montrose* disguised as a pilot. The ship was in the St Lawrence, and only 16 hours from Quebec. After reporting to Captain Kendall, Dew walked down to the deck and approached his suspect. 'Good morning, Dr Crippen,' he said. 'I am Chief Inspector Dew,' Crippen said only: 'Good morning, Mr Dew.' Ethel, reading in her cabin, screamed, then fainted, when a similar introduction was made. Crippen said later: 'I am not sorry, the anxiety has been too much. It is only fair to say that she knows nothing about it. I never told her anything.' He described Ethel as 'my only comfort for these past three years.'

Dr. Hawley Harvey Crippen, with inset of Ethel,
dressed as a boy

55

> Ivan the Terrible claimed to have seduced 1,000 virgins, killed 1,000 of his own illegitimate offspring, poisoned three of his eight wives, together with their families, and speared to death his own son. Having done away with so many of his own children, he died of syphillis in 1584 leaving only one direct heir, an imbecile called Feodor.

Extradition formalities took less than three weeks, and on 20 August, Dew set sail for England with his celebrated prisoners aboard the liner *SS Megantic*. Dew, who was travelling as Mr Doyle, kept Crippen, now known as Mr Nield, apart from Ethel, though on one evening he did allow the two to gaze silently at each other from their cabin doors, after a request from Crippen. Huge, angry crowds greeted the two at every stage of their rail journey from Liverpool to London. And public feeling was still at fever pitch when their trials began. Crippen was charged with murder, Ethel with being an accessory, and wisely they elected to be tried separately.

The doctor refused to plead guilty, even though he knew he had no credible defence. Seven days before his hearing began, at the Old Bailey on 10 October, the remains found at Hilldrop Crescent were buried at Finchley as those of Cora Crippen. Yet her husband claimed in court that they could have been there when he bought the house in 1905. That argument fell when a buyer for Jones Brothers swore that the pyjama material in which the remains were wrapped was not available until 1908. Two suits in it had been delivered to Crippen in January, 1909.

Crippen had no answer to questions about why he had made no effort to search for his wife after she vanished on 1 February, why no-one had seen her leave the house, why he had then pawned her possessions or given them to Ethel. Bruce Miller, now married and an estate agent in Chicago, said he last saw Cora in 1904, and denied ever having an affair with her.

On the fifth day of the trial, the jury found Crippen guilty after a 27-minute retirement, and Lord Chief Justice Alverstone, who had been scrupulously fair throughout the proceedings, sentenced him to death. Crippen, who had stood up remarkably well to cross-examination, declared: 'I still protest my innocence.'

A curious story, that Crippen had rejected a suggested defence because it would compromise Ethel, began circulating. The line, allegedly suggested by eminent barrister Edward Marshall Hall, was that the doctor had given his nymphomaniac wife hyoscine to calm her demands on him, because he was also making love to Ethel, and that Cora had died through an accidental overdose. Crippen was wise to reject the story, if he did so. For if death was accidental, why go to so much trouble to chop up the body, remove the bones, and to hide the flesh?

All along, he had been anxious to clear Ethel Le Neve's name, and on 25 October the Old Bailey did so after a one-day trial dominated by a brilliant speech by her defence lawyer, F. E. Smith, later Lord Birkenhead. He asked the jury if they could really believe that Crippen would take such care to hide all the traces of the murder, then risk the 'aversion, revulsion and disgust' of a young, nervous woman by telling her: 'This is how I treated the woman who last shared my home, and I invite you to come and share it with me now.' Ethel was found not guilty and discharged.

But she did not desert her lover, and as he waited for execution, he thought only of her, continually proclaiming her innocence, kissing her photograph, and writing touching love letters to her. He also wrote in a statement: 'As I face enternity, I say that Ethel Le Neve has loved me as few women love men . . . surely such love as hers for me will be rewarded.'

The man whose name has become synonymous with murder was hanged in Pentonville Prison on 23 November, 1910, still protesting that he had murdered no-one. His last request was that Ethel's letters and photograph be buried with him. They were. A curious kind of sympathy had grown for the quiet, considerate little man, both among prison staff and those who came into contact with him. F. E. Smith called him 'a brave man and a true lover.' And there were many who agreed with Max Beerbohm Tree's verdict on the day of execution: 'Poor old Crippen.'

Ethel Le Neve slipped quickly into obscurity. Some say she emigrated to Australia, and died there in 1950, others that she went to Canada or America. Another report was that, for 45 years, she ran a tea-room near Bournemouth under an assumed name. And there have been rumours that she wrote her version of the Crippen affair, to be published after her death. But all the theories could be as wide of the mark as the wild legends that have turned her mild-mannered lover into the most monstrous murderer the world has even seen.

The Boston Strangler

ALBERT DESALVO

I t was a hot steamy night in June, 1962, when police were called to a run-down apartment building in the centre of Boston. In the bedroom, they found the body of a young woman. Partially clothed, with her limbs arranged in an obscene posture, the woman had been strangled with one of her own stockings.

Although, on that sticky, humid night, the killing seemed only to be a random sex murder, the discovery was the beginning of a reign of terror that was to grip the city and capture the morbid imagination of the nation for more than 18 months. For the murder was the first carried out by one of the most notorious mass murderers of the century . . . 'The Boston Strangler'.

For a year-and-a-half, police sought in vain to unmask the fiend who left his trademark on 11 of the 13 bodies: a single stocking tied tightly around the neck of his victim. Of the two other victims, one was stabbed to death, and another died of a heart attack, allegedly in the arms of the Strangler.

The man behind the mass murders was former US Army boxing champion, Albert DeSalvo. In a twist as bizarre as the killings themselves, DeSalvo was never tried for the Strangler murders, but for an assorted series of robberies and sex attacks on women whom he did not kill.

Although some still express doubt that DeSalvo was the Boston Strangler, the thick-set handyman, who always wore his black hair slicked back and had an obsession for dressing in neat, freshly laundered white shirts, did make a confession to the killings. Facts which only came to light after he was sentenced to life imprisonment seemed to confirm that DeSalvo was indeed the Strangler.

Albert DeSalvo had been in trouble with the law since his childhood, mostly for breaking into homes -- a skill that was to be put to terrifying use when he began his killing spree. As a young man he served with the US Army's occupation force in Germany, where he married a local girl, Irmgard. But after having two children, the couple were divorced. He became the Army's middleweight boxing champion, but left the service on his return to America and became a handyman.

DeSalvo had a sexual drive that some doctors described as 'uncontrollable'. Back in his army days, according to one psychiatrist who gave evidence at his trial, his wife constantly complained about his sexual demands. 'She refused

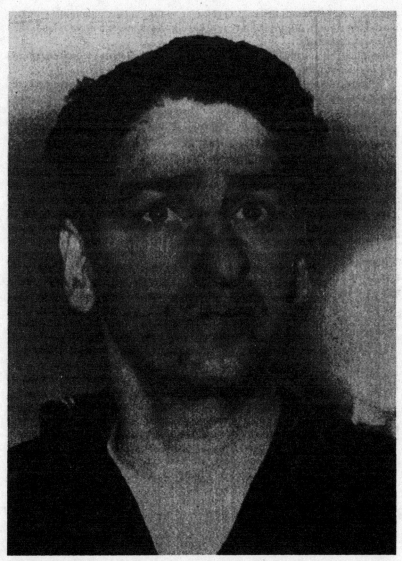

Albert DeSalvo, aged 35

him sex', said Dr James Brussel, 'because he made excessive demands on her. She did not want to submit to his type of kissing which was extensive as far as the body was concerned.'

He added that during his off-duty hours in the army, DeSalvo would engage in wild orgies with the wives of officers who were absent.

'DeSalvo was without doubt, the victim of one of the most crushing sexual drives that psychiatric science has ever encountered', said his lawyer, the famous defence attorney, F. Lee Bailey. 'He was without doubt schizophrenic.'

The wave of killings began in 1962 and, despite the setting up of a special 'Strangler Squad' by law enforcement officers, they continued unabated until 1964. In each case, the women who fell victim to the Strangler were killed in their own homes. DeSalvo gained access to their apartments by posing as a delivery man or by claiming he had been sent by the superintendent of the building to check a leaking waterpipe.

Many of the Strangler's victims were sexually molested, which was in keeping with DeSalvo's insatiable sex drive. They were nearly all undressed, and their bodies arranged in obscene poses.

As the murders continued unabated, so the fear and panic among the citizens of Boston increased. Few took to the streets by themselves at night. Husbands going away on business left their wives loaded guns at their bedsides. Police patrols reached an unprecedented level. But despite the rising death toll, and the almost daily arrest – and release – of possible suspects, Albert DeSalvo, then 32 was never once interviewed by police. He should have been a prime target for investigation . . . having only just been released from prison after serving six months for sex offences. He had posed as an agent for a top modelling agency, and persuaded young women to allow him to take their measurements. But it was just an excuse to molest them, and he was arrested for what became known as the 'Measuring Man' attacks.

Then in 1964 he was arrested for the 'Green Man' attacks. He was nicknamed the 'Green Man' because of his love for green trousers, which he always wore when he broke into the homes of single women. He would strip his victims at knife-point and kiss them all over, before making his escape. A description given by one of the victims, however, was matched by a detective, as being an exact description of the 'Measuring Man', and DeSalvo was brought in.

After his arrest, he was taken to the Bridgewater Mental Institute in Massachusetts, where the terrible truth was to come out.

At his trial for the 'Green Man' offences, psychiatrist Robert Mezer stunned the court when he revealed that DeSalvo had admitted to him in hospital that he was the Strangler. He said that during an interview at Bridgewater, DeSalvo had confessed he strangled 13 women. 'He went into details about some of them, telling me some of the intimate acts he had committed.'

But by Massachusetts' law no doctor who takes information from a suspect in a case can give it as evidence in a courtroom, so the full story never came out at DeSalvo's trial. However, there is little doubt in the minds of most experts that DeSalvo was the Boston Strangler. Probably the most telling revelations came from his defence lawyer, F. Lee Bailey, in his book, *The Defence Never Rests*. He explained that that DeSalvo had made another confession, this time to doctors and law enforcement officers, in a dramatic meeting in July 1965. But because of a special deal between the police and the defence, the evidence was never used.

> 'I wanted DeSalvo studied by experts, and the authorities wanted to be able to end their investigation. In both cases, DeSalvo's identification as the Boston Strangler had to be irrefutably established. That was only possible if the police interviewed him and matched his memory against the myriad of details of the 13 murders.'

After striking the bargain that the conversations with DeSalvo would not be used in court, the meeting took place at the Bridgewater Mental Institute. It was supposed to take only 15 minutes. Instead it took more than five hours, as more and more damning evidence that DeSalvo was the Strangler was to emerge. He revealed information about the victims that only the real murderer could possibly have known. He said there was a notebook under the bed of victim number eight, brunette Beverly Samans. He was also able to draw floor plans of the apartments of his victims, and could give clear descriptions of the furnishings and decoration.

These and other details added up to more than 50 hours of tapes made at subsequent interviews with DeSalvo and more than 2000 pages of transcript. All details were checked and all were correct.

But the dramatic details that could have convicted DeSalvo as the Boston Strangler were never fully revealed until after his trial for the other offences. And the only man who could know with certainty whether he had killed 13 women, Albert DeSalvo, is now silenced for ever. In 1973, six years after he was sent to Walpole State Prison, in Massachusetts, DeSalvo was stabbed to death by three other inmates, in a row over drugs.

The Lonely Hearts Killers
RAYMOND FERNANDEZ AND MARTHA BECK

Raymond Fernandez and Martha Beck were two social misfits whose crimes outraged the society that had scorned them. Both had at one stage led almost normal, useful lives, but fate had played cruel tricks on them. After they teamed up in 1947, it was they who played the cruel tricks. And they paid for them with their lives.

Fernandez, born in Hawaii of Spanish parents, moved to Spain in the 1930s and married a Spanish woman. After serving in Franco's forces during the Civil War, and gaining the reputation of a war hero, he worked with distinction for British intelligence in the Gibraltar docks. In 1945, he sailed for America, working his passage on an oil tanker. During the voyage, a hatch cover fell on his head. He recovered in hospital at Curaçao, but his personality had changed radically. He became a cunning, ruthless swindler, convinced that he had supernatural powers over women, and determined to use them to the utmost.

He began advertizing in lonely hearts magazines, and fleecing the gullible people who answered his pleas. By 1947 he had claimed more than 100 victims. He was just back from Spain, where his latest dupe had died mysteriously during their holiday, when he decided to follow up an intriguing letter from a woman in Florida with a personal visit.

Martha Beck's name had been forwarded to the lonely hearts club as a joke by one of her friends. Martha was an outsize woman of 280lb whose bulk and sexuality constantly made her a figure of fun to others. At 13 she had been raped by her own brother, who continued the incestuous relationship until she complained to her mother. For reasons which Martha never understood, she was blamed for the sordid affair, and forced to live a cloistered existence which deprived her of normal relationships as a teenager.

She became a nurse, moving to California and an army hospital. But the scandals of her nymphomaniac sex life forced her to return east, where she became superintendent of a home for crippled children at Pensacola, Florida. There she met Fernandez, who was using his business name, Charles Martin.

A torrid affair quickly began, Fernandez introducing Martha to new perversions which satisfied her sexually for the first time in her life. She gave up her job and left behind her two children, one illegitimate, the other the product

THE LONELY HEARTS KILLERS

Raymond Fernandez (second from left) and Martha Beck examined at court in Michigan

of a disastrous marriage, to follow Fernandez. When he explained his line of business, she agreed to become his accomplice, posing as his sister. But she loved him too much to allow him a free hand. He could woo and wed women – but she would not allow him to consummate the marriages.

Such jealousy hampered the romantic con-man. The first joint effort resulted in the victim claiming back her car and $500, and refusing to sign over her insurance policies. The ill-starred lovers moved on to Cook County, Illinois, and Fernandez married Myrtle Young in August 1948. But again there were violent rows when the bride expected to sleep alone with her husband, and Martha refused to allow it. Myrtle was given an overdose of barbiturates, and put on a bus to Little Rock, Arkansas. She collapsed and died there. Fernandez and Beck made $4,000 and gained a car.

In Albany, New York, that December, Fernandez charmed a naive widow, Janet Fay, 66, into signing over all her assets and her $6,000 insurance policy to him. Then she was strangled and battered to death with a hammer. The body was stuffed into a trunk, and the couple took it with them to New York City, where they rented a house in Queens, and buried the makeshift coffin under cement in the cellar.

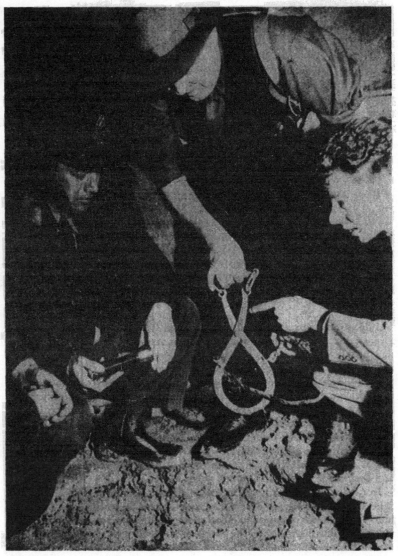

Bloodstained tongs discovered in the cellar where Mrs Downing and daughter were found

THE LONELY HEARTS KILLERS

The following year Fernandez and Beck were in Grand Rapids, Michigan, trying to fleece a 28-year-old widow called Delphine Downing. Once again, Martha reacted angrily when Fernandez started sleeping with her. Then Delphine saw her husband without his toupe, and threatened to leave him. Fernandez and Beck were out at the cinema, found the two bodies, and arrested Rainelle. Both bodies were cemented into the cellar floor, and curious neighbours were told that Delphine and her daughter were away on holiday.

But suspicious relatives called the police. They searched the house while Fernandez and beck were out at the cinema, found the two bodies, and arrested the couple on their return. A curious tug-of-war between two states now began. Michigan did not have the death penalty, but New York did. The murder of Janet Fay had been discovered, and New York asked for the couple to be sent there for trial. Public fury at the couple's evil exploits played some part in New York getting its way.

Fernandez and Beck were charged with three murders, and suspected of 17 more, including that of Myrtle Young. The trial began in July 1949, and lasted 44 days. Press coverage of the proceedings was unprecendented in its hatred and intolerance, and every intimate detail of the sordid sex life of the couple created sensational headlines. Crowds flocked to the courtroom to catch a glimpse of the 'monster' and his 'overweight ogress'.

The verdict was never in doubt. Fernandez and Beck were found guilty of first-degree murder, and sentenced to death on 29 August. Their appeals were dismissed and on 8 March, 1951, they went to the electric chair at Sing-Sing Prison.

Two hours before the execution, Fernandez sent Martha a message of love. She said: 'Now that I know Raymond loves me, I can go to my death bursting with joy.' But there was nothing joyful about the death. Newspapers gleefully reported the struggle to fit her huge bulk into the chair, and the prolonged writhing as the electric shocks struggled to have an impact through her flabby body. Such was public distaste for the Lonely Hearts Killers that more people laughed at that last ordeal than felt pity for its victim.

The Killer Clown

JOHN WAYNE GACY

When they christened him with the name of their favourite film star, John Wayne Gacy's parents had high hopes that their little boy would one day become famous. In a way they saw their dreams realized – although not quite as wished.

John Wayne Gacy today is a name that conjures up revulsion among millions of Americans. He is one of the country's most sadistic and prolific mass murderers, and known as the Killer Clown. When he was finally tracked down and tackled by the Chicago police in 1978, Gacy readily admitted to murdering no fewer than 33 young men and boys. Before strangling and stabbing them to death, he had brutally raped them.

Gacy was a fat, lonely homosexual with an insatiable sexual appetite. He longed to be loved by the neighbours who regarded him as 'a wierdo'. And he had aspirations of becoming somebody in local politics. To that end, he began a deliberate campaign to win over the local populace in the Chicago suburb of Norwood Park Township. A friend with connections in the Democratic Party showed him how: he would have to become a local benefactor with particular emphasis on the neighbourhood children.

Gacy set about this task with gusto. He designed three clown outfits himself, then set about creating a character. Very soon he was a local celebrity as Pogo the Clown, performing in the streets, at children's parties and other functions. He was so successful that President Carter's wife Rosalynn posed with him for a photograph, then sent him an autographed copy. He treasured that.

But while 38-year-old Gacy clowned for the kids and posed for posterity, the Chicago police were baffled by the mysterious disappearance of a number of local youths. On their files were also several missing persons from other states.

It took the police six years to nail Gacy. When they did, they met with a torrent of abuse from residents of Northwood Park for the appalling record of overlooked clues and bungled detective work. Had they been more efficient, people argued, at least some of the Killer Clown's victims might have lived. In fact, on four occasions between 1972 and 1978, Gacy's name had appeared on police files as a suspect in the missing persons cases. He had also been convicted twice for sex assaults on young men.

Interviewed at police headquarters, Gacy drew a detailed map of his

Above: Police search John Wayne Gacy's home for more bodies

Right: John Wayne Gacy, convicted of killing 33 men and boys

property, pinpointing the location of 28 of the bodies. After raping and killing his victims, he had methodically buried them in the extensive, landscaped garden of his neat and modern ranch house. The bodies of five other boys had been thrown into the Des Plaines river, near his home.

Gacy had been heavily influenced by his mother since childhood. His older sister also seemed to dominate him. He was a weak-willed man who carried his resentment towards women with him through later life. Nevertheless, he was determined to succeed in business. And that much he did. From humble beginnings, he built up a construction business that flourished.

Gacy took advantage of the rising unemployment in Chicago and offered jobs to young unskilled men who stood the least chance of finding employment. His local lads were all under 20 and receiving unemployment benefit. Others he picked up from the Greyhound Bus station in Chicago: these were often drifters heading for California hoping to find their pot of gold. Instead they found death.

'I wanted to give these young people a chance' he told police during questioning. 'Young people always get a raw deal. But if you give them responsibility they rise to the occasion. They're hard workers and proud of their work.'

Gacy's teenage workforce were well-paid and happy. As the contracts continued to pour in, he needed more labourers. At the end of a hard day – for he put in many hours himself – Gacy would get into his Oldsmobile and head for the Greyhound Station, looking for more employees among the itinerants. He always found somebody.

He had been married in 1967 and again five years after that. His first wife, who divorced him in 1969, bore him two children. She said of him. 'He was a likeable salesman who could charm anything right out of you.' Wife number two, Carole Hoff, said her husband 'started bringing home a lot of pictures of

---

Unrepentant sex assaulter, robber and murderer Carl Panzram could not wait to be hanged. He told his executioner at Fort Leavenworth, Texas, in 1930: 'While you're fooling around, I could hang a dozen men.' Panzram's life was one of insatiable hatred. 'I hate the whole darn race, including myself,' he said. And he had proved it by murdering more than 21 people and committing thousands of burglaries.

Sentenced to 25 years at Fort Leavenworth, he threatened to kill the first man who angered him. He carried out the threat shortly afterwards by murdering a prison laundry worker. When sentenced to be executed, he said he looked forward to it as 'a pleasure and a great relief'.

> John Wesley Hardin started out as a Texas Sunday school teacher
> and ended up a cold, calculating killer. From the age of 15, when
> he murdered a negro slave and shot two soldiers who tried to
> catch him, he continued his rampage of slaughter until his death
> in 1895 at the age of 42. He was reputed to have murdered
> between 24 and 40 people, most of them black.

naked men' just before they separated. They were divorced in 1976. Both his
wives described him as 'mysterious' and said he had been a normal husband for
the first few months of marriage, but then began staying out at night in his car.
He beat his wives.

Where did Gacy go? Later it emerged that he would frequent 'Bughouse
Square', a notorious corner of Chicago populated at night by legions of young
homosexuals and male prostitutes. He picked up young men and they, like the
itinerants and the local boys who worked for his building company, were
among the dead found later by police.

All this time, Gacy was winning friends and influencing people with his Pogo
The Clown antics. He made hefty contributions to the Democratic Party,
which he supported wholeheartedly. In the three years before his capture, Gacy
funded and organized an annual political summer fete with beer, hamburgers
and music and attended by five hundred local dignitaries and business bigwigs.
The proceeds went to President Carter's re-election fund, and for his efforts he
was lauded by the White House.

A pure coincidence led to his arrest. One of Gacy's political contacts during
this time had known one of the victims, and harried police into mounting an
extraordinarily intensive search for the missing youngster. Once again, as had
happened on several occasions years before, the trail seemed to lead to Gacy.
Police raided his luxury ranch house in December 1978. They placed Gacy
under arrest and a team of forensic experts moved in, combing the place for
clues.

As the horrified neighbours watched, police systematically dug up the
garden. By the third day, the remains of 28 different bodies had been
unearthed. Gacy had at first denied murdering anyone, but gradually admitted
the first few, then finally drew a detailed map of his garden for police. The five
remaining corpses were fished out of the Des Plaines river by police frogmen in a
massive dredging operation.

Details of Gacy's *modus operandi* emerged over the ensuing months. Since
boyhood, he had had a fixation for police matters. He loved to play policeman,
and owned guns and other paraphernalia, including handcuffs. When he got a

A German tailor was hanged for Britain's first murder on a train, mainly because he picked up the wrong hat at the scene of the crime. Bank clerk Thomas Briggs, 70, was found dead on the railway line between Hackney Wick and Bow, London, on 9 July, 1864. His gold watch and hat were among the items missing, and a silk hat found near the body was identified as belonging to Franz Muller, 25. Police discovered that Muller had set sail for America on the *SS Victoria*. They took a faster liner, and were waiting to arrest him at New York. Despite a personal plea to Queen Victoria from the Prussian king, Muller was hanged on 14 November, 1864.

young man back to his house he would show the unsuspecting fellow the 'handcuff trick', assuring him that he would be released after only a few seconds. Instead, of course, once the victim was in Gacy's power, he would become the subject of a wild homosexual rape. Instead of learning, as Gacy had promised, how to get free from the handcuffs, the victim would hear Gacy say: 'The way to get out of these handcuffs is to have the key. That's the real trick.'

The handcuff trick was quickly followed by the 'rope trick' and this always spelled the end for the victim. Gacy would throw a piece of cord around the victim's neck, and tie two knots in it. Then he would push a piece of wood through the loop and slowly turn. Within seconds the victim was unconscious: a few seconds more and he was dead.

At his trial in 1979, Chicago District Attorney William Kunkle described him as a sick man who methodically planned and executed his many murders. Kunkle asked for the death penalty; the State of Illinois was then debating whether to reintroduce execution for certain types of murder.

Defence attorney Sam Amirante pleaded that Cary was insane at the time he committed the murders. But there had been so many, and over such a long period of time that Gacy was convicted and given life imprisonment.

The Vampire Killer

JOHN HAIGH

Donald McSwann entered a den of death when he followed his friend John Haigh into his basement workshop. McSwann operated a pinball arcade in London where Haigh sometimes worked as a mechanic. Haigh boasted about his workshop and it was, indeed, a basement to be proud of. There was equipment for every kind of craftsman . . . for the carpenter, the welder, the sheet metal worker – and the murderer.

McSwann stared at the 40-gallon vat of sulphuric acid in one corner. His curiosity drove him to ask about the need for such a strange array of equipment. His questions were never answered. Crouching behind him, Haigh viciously swung a hammer in a deadly arc . . . and he had slaughtered his first victim.

According to Haigh, when he later confessed to the crime, he drank some of McSwann's blood. Then he spent the night methodically dismembering his body and feeding it into the vat. The sulphuric acid bubbled and smoked, occasionally forcing him to escape outdoors for a breath of fresh air. By the next afternoon, McSwann's remains had dissolved into a mass of sludge. Haigh disposed of it, bucket by bucket, sloshing the ghastly residue into a basement manhole connected to the sewer system.

It was September 1944 and no one thought anything of McSwann's disappearance. Haigh's murder-for-profit scheme was succeeding to perfection.

He assured McSwann's aging parents that their son was hiding out in Scotland until the end of the war. Haigh even went to Scotland once a week to post a letter to them signing McSwann's name.

In between the trips, he ran the pinball arcade business that had belonged to his victim. Wartime crowds poured into the arcade and Haigh was taking in money hand over fist. But it was still not enough to buy the lifestyle he wanted, and greed drove him to his next murder for profit.

His victims were to be McSwann's parents. He wrote to them, again forging their son's name, and begged them to meet him at the home of his dear friend, John Haigh.

On the night of 10 July, 1945, Haigh bludgeoned them to death in his workshop. Afterwards he dissolved their bodies in the vat of acid and poured the reeking sludge down the drain.

Using forged documents Haigh helped himself to the entire estate – five

71

The kidnapping of the 20-month-old son of world-famous aviator
Charles Lindbergh scandalized America on 1 March, 1932. The
boy was taken from his luxury New Jersey home, and the
anguished father was desperate enough to pay a $75,000 ransom,
but there was no child in return. On 12 May the boy's body was
found in a shallow grave near Lindbergh's home. But it was
September before the killer was found – he handed in a note from
the ransom money at a petrol station, and was traced through his
car registration number. Bruno Hauptmann, 36, a former
German soldier who had entered America illegally in 1923, went
to the electric chair at Trenton, New Jersey, on 3 April, 1936.

---

houses and a fortune in securities and later transferred it to his own name.

Because of his inveterate gambling, self-indulgence and a string of bad
investments, he was broke again by February 1948. He decided to invite a young
married couple, Rosalie and Dr Archie Henderson, to look at his new workshop
at Crawley, south of London. Both went into the acid bath.

Although the Henderson's estate had been profitably disposed of in 1949
Haigh found that he needed one more victim. Still convinced he was living a
charmed life, he chose this one with little caution.

She was Mrs Olive Durand-Deacon, a 69-year-old widow whose husband
had left her £40,000. She lived at the same London residential hotel as Haigh,
who had not paid his bills for months and who was desperate for money.

Mrs Durand-Deacon believed that, apart from having a private income,
Haigh had made money by patenting inventions. She put to him an idea for
false plastic fingernails. Haigh showed interest, invited her to visit his Crawley
workshop and in February 1949 drove her down there.

What happened next was described by Haigh in a statement he made to
police and which was read at his trial:

> She was inveigled by me into going to Crawley in view of her interest in
> artificial fingernails. Having taken her into the storeroom, I shot her
> through the back of the head while she was examining some materials.
>
> Then I went out to the car and fetched a drinking glass and made an
> incision – I think with a penknife – in the side of her throat. I collected
> a glass of blood, which I drank.
>
> I removed her coat and jewellery (rings, necklace, earrings and
> crucifix) and put her in a 45-gallon tank.
>
> Before I put her handbag in the tank, I took from it about 30
> shillings and a fountain pen. I then filled the tank with sulphuric acid,
> by means of a stirrup-pump. I then left it to react.

As an afterthought, Haid added: 'I should have said that, in between having her in the tank and pumping in the acid, I went round to the Ancient Prior's [a local teashop] for a cup of tea.'

It took some days and two further trips to Crawley to check on the acid tank before Mrs Durand-Deacon's body appeared to have been entirely dissolved. Meantime, the police had questioned her fellow guests at the hotel, including Haigh.

The killer's glib, over-helpful manner made one detective particularly suspicious and he checked on the 39-year-old suspects background. He unearthed a prison record for minor frauds and arrested Haigh. The murderer confessed, but claimed that he could never be proven guilty because police could never find any of his victims' remains.

He was wrong. Forensic scientists examined the foul sludge that had been emptied from the tank onto the ground in the yard of the Crawley workshop. They were able to identify a gallstone, part of a foot, remains of a handbag and an almost complete set of false teeth. These were shown to Mrs Durand-Deacon's dentist, who confirmed that they had belonged to the trusting widow.

In court Haigh's lawyers claimed that the killer was insane. They pointed to a strict and unhappy childhood – his parents belonged to the Plymouth Brethren – and to his claimed habit of drinking his victims' blood. But although the British press labelled him The Vampire Killer, the judge and jury failed to accept this bloody trait as evidence of insanity. After a trial of only two days, he was found guilty of murdering Mrs Durand-Deacon and sentenced to death. Asked if he had anything to say, Haigh replied airily: 'Nothing at all.'

On 6 August, 1949, he was hanged at Wandsworth Prison.

The A6 Lay-By Murder

JAMES HANRATTY

The A6 murder has led to more controversy than almost any other killing in Britain. An illiterate, feeble-minded petty criminal called James Hanratty was hanged for it after the longest murder trial in English legal history. Ever since, an extensive and distinguished lobby of authors has campaigned to persuade the public that British justice executed the wrong man.

At dusk on 22 August, 1961, two scientific workers at the Road Research Laboratory in Slough, Buckinghamshire, were cuddling in the front seat of a grey Morris Minor saloon in a cornfield at Dorney Reach, beside the river Thames between Windsor and Maidenhead. Michael Gregsten was 38, a married man with two children. Valerie Storie was an attractive, single 23-year-old who had been his mistress for three years.

They were interrupted by a tap on the driver's side window. Gregsten wound down the window, and the man standing there pointed a gun at him. The terrified couple thought it was a hold-up. They offered the man their money, watches, even the car. He sat in the back seat, warning them not to look at him, toying with the gun. He told them he was on the run, and that every policeman in Britain was on the look-out for him. But he seemed undecided about what he was going to do.

Finally, at about 23.30, he ordered Gregsten to start driving. There followed a bizarre 30-mile drive through the northern suburbs of London, Slough, Hayes and Stanmore, broken only by stops to buy petrol and cigarettes. Gregsten, nervous already, was put further on edge by the back-seat driving of his captor, issuing instructions about the route and urging care at blackspots. They turned on to the A5 towards St Albans, Gregsten occasionally flashing his reversing lights to try to attract attention, and keeping an eye out for policemen, so he could stage a crash. He saw none.

On the A6, between St Albans and Luton, the gunman ordered Gregsten to pull into a lay-by. He said he wanted 'a kip', and made an attempt to tie Miss Storie to a door handle. He asked Gregsten to hand him a duffle bag, but as the driver reached for it, he was shot twice in the head. 'He moved too quick, he frightened me,' the gunman said as the girl screamed: 'You bastard.'

As blood flowed from her lover's wounds, Miss Storie was forced into the back seat, ordered to remove some of her clothes, then raped. The man then made Miss Storie pull Gregsten's body from the car to the edge of the concrete lay-by. She sat beside the body, too stunned to cry, while the man continued to dither about what to do next.

Eventually, Miss Storie gave him a £1 note if he would leave quickly. He took it, and seemed to be going. But as he approached the car, he unexpectedly turned, and pumped five bullets at the girl. One pierced her neck, close to the spinal cord. She lay still, pretending to be dead, as he strode over to inspect his work. Convinced he had eliminated the only witness to his earlier killing, he drove off.

Passing drivers failed to hear Miss Storie's screams. She took off and waved her petticoat, but no-one saw it in the dark. At last she passed out, and was found at around 06.30 by a teenager arriving for a traffic census. She recovered consciousness in hospital, and began giving waiting police officers extremely detailed descriptions of all that had happened. Her wounds had paralyzed her, consigning her to life in a wheelchair, but her mind was unaffected.

Two identikit pictures were issued, based on her descriptions, and those of witnesses who saw Gregsten's car being driven before it was abandoned in Ilford, Essex. Police were following a confusing trail of clues. At first they suspected Peter Louis Alphon. Two .38 bullets were found in the hotel room at the Vienna Hotel, Maida Vale, where he spent the night after the murder. Ballistics experts matched them with those that had killed Gregsten. But when Alphon was put in an identity parade, Valerie Storie failed to pick him out. She selected one of the stooges who could not possibly have been the murderer. Alphon did not match the identikit descriptions, nor did James Hanratty. And the police did not suspect him because he was known to them only as a petty and none-too-successful villain. But then he seemed to go out of his way to attract attention.

Police were already puzzled by anonymous calls to the hospital where Valerie Storie was recovering, threatening her life. They moved her to a fresh

Twice-convicted murderer Walter Graham Rowland almost cheated the gallows before his luck finally ran out. Rowland strangled his two-year-old daughter and killed a 40-year-old prostitute, Olive Balchin, with a hammer. He was convicted of the child's murder, sentenced, then reprieved.

It seemed as if he would escape the gallows a second time when a prisoner in Walton Jail, Liverpool, confessed to the prostitute's murder. But the statement was found to be false and Rowland was hanged in 1947.

Bugsy Siegel was a cunning killer who mixed with the Hollywood stars and thought there was nothing more important than a touch of class. From the squalor of Brooklyn, he graduated to racketeering and bootlegging and became New York's top hit man. In 1945 he borrowed $3 million to build a hotel in Las Vegas. Siegel refused to repay the money and was murdered in his home by an unknown gunman in 1947.

bed every night, and reinforced the guard on her. Then Hanratty phoned Detective Superintendent Acott, the man in charge of the hunt, saying he was anxious about being suspected for the A6 murder, and denying his involvement. Since the call was completely unsolicited, Hanratty immediately became a prime suspect.

Police discovered that he had asked an associate, Charles France, whether the back seat of a London bus was a good place to hide a gun. Hanratty was known to have acquired a .38 Enfield revolver earlier in the year. A similar gun was found behind the rear seat on the top deck of a No 36 bus. Police also discovered that Hanratty had booked into the Vienna Hotel the night before Alphon, staying in the same room as J. Ryan. And Gregsten's widow named him as the likely killer of her husband, though many wondered how she could possibly know.

Hanratty was arrested in Blackpool on 9 October and put in an identity parade. Valerie Storie again failed to pick him out, though she had now mentioned piercing blue eyes in her description of the killer. Hanratty had such eyes. She then asked each of the line-up to say the words the murderer had used several times: 'Be quiet, will you, I am thinking.' Hanratty always pronounced the last work 'finking'. And it was then that Miss Storie indentified him.

The trail began on 22 January, 1962. The police were given a hard time by the defence, who accused them of concentrating on implicating Hanratty instead of hunting down the truth. Much was also made of Miss Storie's identity parade failures, and the changes in her description of the killer.

But the defence was not helped by Hanratty himself. Though he pleaded not guilty, he was cocky and insolent throughout. A fellow prisoner who had been in custody with Hanratty swore that he had confessed to the killing and gave details of it known only to police and Miss Storie. Hanratty claimed that at the time of the murder he was in Liverpool with friends. But he refused to name them, saying to do so would break their trust in him. Then, inexplicably, he changed his alibi, and said he was in Rhyl, North Wales. Again he could not prove it.

There were enough doubts about both the prosecution and defence cases to keep the jury out for nine-and-a-half hours on 11 February. Once they returned for guidance from the judge. Then they filed back to court to return a verdict of guilty. He said only: 'I an innocent.' Every appeal was rejected. Hanratty, aged 25, was hanged at Bedford Prison on 4 April, 1962.

But even today, there are those who say there was too much 'reasonable doubt' about the affair to condemn any man. Peter Alphon made a series of sensational confessions to newspapers, saying Hanratty's conviction was contrived. Later, however, he withdrew them all. Charles France, Hanratty's friend, who had given evidence about the gun against him in court, hanged himself, leaving a note about the case. But it was not read at the inquest on the grounds that it was not in the public interest. Witnesses then came forward to claim that they had seen Hanratty in Rhyl on the night of the murder.

Books by Louis Blom-Cooper, Paul Foot and Ludovic Kennedy all helped to make Hanratty the greatest *cause célèbre* since Timothy Evans, another none-too-bright man executed for murder. But whereas Evans was condemned by Christie's evil lies, and was posthumously pardoned, Hanratty had virtually condemned himself by changing his alibi in court. And for everyone who claimed he was unjustly hanged, there were others who agreed with Detective-Superintendent Acott that Hanratty was 'one of the worst types of killers in recent years.'

The Mass-Murderer of Hanover

FRITZ HAARMANN

Wild terror, more akin to the Middle Ages than the 20th century, swept the north German town of Hanover in the spring of 1924. In winding alleys beneath the gabled roofs of the old quarter, people whispered that a werewolf was at large, devouring anyone foolish enough to venture out after dark. Some said children were being butchered in cellars. Police doctors were inundated with strange-tasting meat brought in by housewives who feared it was human flesh. The authorities dismissed the alarm as 'mass hysteria'. And they blamed a prank by medical students when children found the first of many human skulls beside the river Leine on 17 May.

The authorities were as wrong as the panic-stricken public. But the truth, when it emerged later that year, was just as macabre as the people's wildest fears. It ended in execution for a 45-year-old mass murderer called Fritz Haarmann, the jailing of his 25-year-old partner in crime – and a national scandal.

Haarmann had been a wandering vagrant, hawker and pilferer for most of his life. He worshipped his mother – an invalid after his birth in Hanover on 25 October, 1879 – and hated his father, a morose, miserly locomotive stoker known to all as Sulky Olle. When Fritz's bitterness spilled into violence, his father tried to get him committed to an asylum. But doctors decided that, though the boy was incurably feeble-minded, there were no grounds to commit him.

He roamed the country, a popular figure with the underworld and the police of many cities. Fellow petty crooks regarded him as fat and stupid, but kind, always ready to offer help, money and advice to those worse off than himself. The police liked him because he always came quietly when arrested, laughing and joking with them. He was always a model prisoner, accepting and even enjoying jail discipline. He served time for picking pockets, petty thieving and indecent behaviour with small children.

In 1918, Haarmann emerged from a five-year sentence for theft and fraud to find post-war Germany in chaos. Law and order had broken down, and profiteers, swindlers and crooks reigned supreme in the anarchy. These were the people Harrmann understood. He returned to Hanover, spending most of his time among the con-men and dubious traders at the straggling markets outside the central railway station. He became obsessed with the people inside the station – refugees from all over Germany, human flotsam without jobs or money, homes or hopes, who cowered round stoves by day, and huddled on platform benches at night.

Haarmann knew he could make a living in this twilight world, but, as he grew more and more acustomed to it, he realized there were other opportunities for him. Among the down-and-outs were many teenage boys, some no more than 12 years old. They had run away from home, often unable to cope with life there once their stern fathers returned from the war after years away. Haarmann turned on his charm with them, listening to their grievances, offering them advice, winning their confidence. In a country where everyone was carefully documented, he had discovered a constant flow of people nobody could trace. They could disappear for ever, and their parents and the police would be none the wiser.

Haarmann took lodgings at 27, Cellarstrasse, and set up in business as a meat-hawker and seller of secondhand clothes. He could haggle with the best of the market traders, and his business soon prospered. Housewives quickly learned that his prices were lower than anyone else's, and that his stock was always plentiful and varied. But he still spent his evenings with the boys at the station, laughing and joking with them, handing round chocolates and cigarettes, greeting hungry, forlorn new arrivals with the cheery offer of a meal and a mattress for the night.

Within weeks, Haarmann was such a familiar face there that welfare workers considered him almost as one of them. And the police decided to use his services, too. They needed spies in the underworld to try to stem the growing crime and corruption, and rewarded their 'narks' by turning a blind eye to their activities, legal and otherwise. Haarmann was delighted to help. Using the intimate knowledge of crooks he had gained over the years, he quickly earned the nickname of 'Detective' by reporting crimes, hiding places and plots. In return, the police did not pry into his business. And they were loathe to inquire too closely in September, 1918, when the parents of 17-year-old Friedel Rothe reported him missing after he was seen with Haarmann in a billiards room. It took the threat of force to persuade the officers to visit Haarmann's rooms, and their search was merely cursory.

Six years later, Haarmann was to brag at his trial: 'When the police examined my room, the head of the boy Friedel was lying wrapped in newspaper behind the oven.' For the truth was that the 'Detective' was not the bluff, genial do-gooder he seemed. The wretched youngsters he befriended were taken to his home for a good meal, often sexually assaulted, then killed in the most savage fashion – a bite at the throat. The bodies were then dismembered, the meat being sold, the skull and bones being disposed of in the river Leine.

THE WORLD'S MOST INFAMOUS MURDERS

That narrow escape in 1918 did not make Haarmann more cautious. If anything he became bolder as the police relied more and more on his information. And in September 1919 he met the accomplice who was to incite him to more murders. Hans Grans was then 20, and himself a runaway from home. Slim, graceful, cynical and emotionless, the librarian's son soon established ascendancy over his social inferior, taunting him with insults and sarcasm. And he began to order the killing of selected victims, often merely because he coveted their clothing.

The two men moved to rooms in Neuestrasse, then into an alley called Rothe Reihe (Red Row), almost on the banks of the Leine. Neighbours noted that a constant stream of young boys went into the apartment, but that none ever seemed to come out. They overheard sounds of chopping and splashing. Occasionally police brought the grief-stricken parents of missing boys to the rooms. They had heard that their sons had last been seen with the 'Detective'. Somehow, they always left satisfied that Haarmann had nothing to do with the disappearances.

One morning, a neighbour met Harrmann on the stairs. As he stopped to gossip and joke with her, a paper covering the bucket he was carrying slipped slightly, and she saw that the bucket was full of blood. But she said nothing to the authorities. After all, Haarmann had to hack carcasses of meat as part of his trade. Another neighbour once heard him chopping in his room, and asked: 'Am I going to get a bit.' He chuckled: 'No, next time.' She also saw a young boy lying very still on Haarmann's bed, but was told: 'Don't wake him, he's asleep.' A customer took a piece of meat bought from Haarmann to the police doctor because she was suspicious of its taste. She was told it was pork.

By 1923, Haarmann had made himself indispensible to the police. Not only was he still informing on criminals, he had set up a detective agency in partnership with a highly-placed police official, and was also recruiting for the Black *Reichswehr*, a secret organization working against French occupation of the Ruhr. He was so sure of police protection that he was taking enormous risks, selling the clothes of victims only a day or two after murdering them. One woman bought a pair of socks from him for her son, and found two spots of blood on them. She threw them away. A man spotted Grans wearing a suit that, days earlier, had belonged to a boy at the railway station.

But pressure was building up on the police. Newspapers had noted that large numbers of youths from all over north Germany had arrived in Hanover, then vanished. One paper claimed that 600 had disappeared in just one year. Hanover was acquiring a sinister reputation. The published fears brought out into the open suspicions many had been prepared to keep to themselves. The discovery of the skull by the river Leine in May 1924 was the final straw.

Now the police had to deal not with the occasional distraught parent, but with outraged public opinion. Another skull was discovered by the river on 29 May – a small skull, about the size of a young boy. Two more were unearthed on 13 June. A police spokesman claimed they could have been swept down-river from Alfeld, where hurried burials were taking place due to a typhus outbreak. But the explanation was not accepted by the frightened public. They believed a monster was preying on their town – and many were convinced that he lived in Rothe Reihe. Faced with a mounting tide of witnesses pointing the finger at Haarmann, the chief of police decided to act.

Haarmann still had powerful friends, impressed by the help he was giving the authorities. So the police chief moved cautiously. He brought in two detectives from Berlin, instructing them to watch Haarmann's movements at the station. On the evening of 22 June, 1924, he approached a boy called Fromm who objected to his attentions. They began to quarrel, then fight, and the detectives moved in to arrest them both.

With Haarmann safe at headquarters, a police squad swooped on his rooms. The walls were splashed with blood, and there were heaps of clothing and personal possessions. Haarmann protested that since he was both a meat trader and a clothes salesman, such findings were not unexpected. Then the mother of a missing boy recognized his coat – being worn by the son of Haarmann's landlady.

The game was up, and Haarmann knew it. He broke down and confessed to several murders, accusing Grans of instigating and assisting in many of them. Grans was immediately arrested. Meanwhile, more and more human remains were being discovered beside the River Leine. Boys playing in a meadow found a sack packed with them on 24 July. When dredgers probed the black ooze of the riverbed, watched by thousands lining the banks, they brought to the surface 500 bones.

Haarmann and Grans were tried at Hanover Assizes on 4 December, accused of killing 27 boys aged between 12 and 18. Haarmann was allowed to interrupt the proceedings almost as he pleased, and his grisly attempts at humour only added to the horror as the full story of his butchery unfolded.

'You're doing fine,' he shouted when the prosecution finished their opening speech. When one witness took his time pondering a question, Haarmann yelled: 'Come on, old chap. You must tell us all you know. We are here to get the truth.' Impatient when a distressed mother broke down while giving evidence about her lost son, the killer asked the judges if he could smoke a cigar – and was granted permission. And one morning, he protested that there were too many women in court, saying: 'This is a case for men to discuss.'

The names of boys were read to him, and he was asked if he had killed them. 'Yes, that might well be,' he said of 13-year-old Ernest Ehrenberg. 'I'm not sure about that one,' he replied about Paul Bronischewski. And he turned angrily on the anguished father of Hermann Wolf when shown a photograph of the boy.

'I should never have looked twice at such an ugly youngster as, according to his photograph, your son must have been,' he sneered. 'You say your boy had not even a shirt to his name and that his socks were tied on to his feet with string. Deuce take it, you should have been ashamed to let him go about like that. There's plenty of rubbish like him around. Think what you're saying man. Such a fellow would have been far beneath my notice.'

Newspaper reporters in court could not disguise their disgust for the killer, or their sympathy for the relatives of his victims. One journalist wrote:

'Nearly 200 witnesses had to appear in the box, mostly parents of the unfortunate youths. There were scenes of painful intensity as a poor father or mother would recognize some fragment or other of the clothing or belongings of their murdered son. Here it was a handkerchief, there a pair of braces, and again a greasy coat, soiled almost beyond recognition, that was shown to the relatives and to Haarmann. And with the quivering nostrils of a hound snuffling his prey, as if he were scenting rather than seeing the things displayed, did he admit at once that he knew them.'

Twice a shudder ran through the court. 'How many victims did you kill altogether?' asked the prosecution. Haarmann replied: 'It might be 30, it might be 40. I really can't remember the exact number.' The prosecution asked: 'How did you kill your victims?' Haarmann replied coldly: 'I bit them through their throats.'

Only when Grans's part in the murders was in doubt did Haarmann lose his composure. 'Grans should tell you how shabbily he has treated me,' he shouted. 'I did the murders, for that work he is too young.' He claimed Grans incited him to kill some victims because he had taken a fancy to the boy's trousers or coat. Grans left him alone overnight to do the murder, returning in the morning for the clothes. Once, though, he was too impatient. Haarmann told the court: 'I had just cut up the body when there was a knock at the door. I shoved the body under the bed and opened the door. It was Grans. His first question was, "Where is the suit." I sat down on the bed and buried my face in my hands . . . Grans tried to console me, and said: "Don't let a little thing like a corpse upset you." '

The cold-hearted cynicism of Grans aroused more horror in court than the unsophisticated blundering of Haarmann. The younger man denied every accusation, but there was never any doubt that both would be convicted. Haarmann knew that, and his main concern throughout was that he was not found insane. Early in the trial he shouted: 'Behead me, don't send me to an asylum.' And after two psychiatrists declared him mentally sound, the court decided he should have his wish.

THE MASS-MURDERER OF HANOVER

Twelve armed policemen faced the public gallery on the day of judgment, 19 December, 1924, after anonymous threats that Haarmann would be shot in revenge for his monstrous crimes. The courtroom was packed as sentence of death was pronounced on him. Grans was jailed for life, later commuted to 12 years.

Haarmann remained to the end. On the last day he screamed:

'Do you think I enjoy killing people? I was ill for eight days after the first time. Condemn me to death. I only ask for justice. I am not mad. It is true I often get into a state when I do not know what I am doing, but that is not madness. Make it short, make it soon. Deliver me from this life, which is a torment. I will not petition for mercy, nor will I appeal. I want to pass just one more merry evening in my cell, with coffee, cheese and cigars, after which I will curse my father, and go to my execution as if it were a wedding.'

Next morning, Haarmann was beheaded, and the town of Hanover was at last free from the curse of the worst mass-murderer in modern history. No-one will ever know exactly how many teenage boys he and Grans massacred – but one police source guessed that, during their final 16 months, they were killing two every week.

The Sadistic Romeo

NEVILLE HEATH

Neville George Clevely Heath had the looks that boys' comic heroes are made of. His wide, blue eyes and fair, wavy hair set off a fresh-complexioned face which had women swooning. And his suave charm around the clubs and restaurants of London ensured that he was never short of a pretty companion when the evening ended. Girls fell for his impeccable manners, and his tales of derring-do in the war that had just finished. But Heath's handsome face hid a terrible secret. Possibly bored with the conventional sex that was so readily available to him, he began pandering to a sadistic streak. And in the summer of 1946, that perversion turned him into a ladykiller in every sense of the word.

Heath was then 29, and well known to both the police and the armed forces. He had served time in civilian jails for theft, fraud and false pretences. He had been court-martialled by the British RAF in 1937 (absent without leave, escaping while under arrest and stealing a car), the British Army in 1941 (issuing dishonoured cheques and going absent without leave) and the South African Air Force in 1945 (undisciplined conduct and wearing unauthorized decorations). In April 1946, he was fined £10 by magistrates at Wimbledon, London, for wearing medals and a uniform to which he was not entitled. By then, unknown to the authorities, he was also indulging in much more sinister fantasies.

A month earlier, the house detective at a hotel in London's Strand burst into a locked room after other guests reported hearing screams. He found Heath standing over a naked girl who was bound hand and foot, and being savagely whipped. Neither she nor the hotel wanted any publicity, and Heath was allowed to slink away. But in May he was at it again. This time he had a more willing victim, a 32-year-old masochist called Margery Gardner. She was a film extra, separated from her husband, and known as Ocelot Margie to doormen at the clubs where she turned up in an ocelot fur coat, looking for men prepared to satisfy her craving for bondage and flagellation. Heath was more than ready to oblige, but when he took her to the Pembridge Court Hotel in Notting Hill Gate the hotel detective again intervened after hearing the sound of flesh being thrashed.

Ocelot Margie did not learn from her escape. When Heath phoned her a few

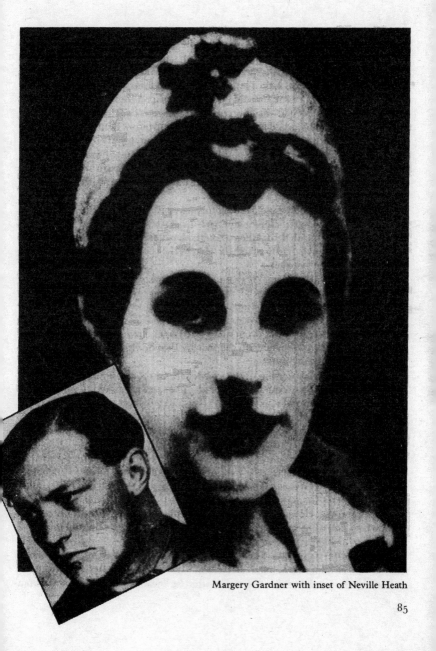

Margery Gardner with inset of Neville Heath

weeks later, she agreed to meet him on Thursday, 20 June. After drinks at one of Heath's favourite haunts, the Panama Club in South Kensington, they took a taxi back to the Pembridge Court, where Heath had booked in four days earlier with another girl who had since left. It was after midnight when they arrived. Guests in adjoining rooms heard nothing to disturb their slumbers that night.

At 14.00 next day, a chambermaid entered Room 4 on the first floor of the 19-bedroom hotel and recoiled with horror when she drew back the curtains. The two single beds were bloodied and disordered. And in one of them lay the lifeless body of Ocelot Margie. She was naked, her ankles bound tightly together with a handkerchief. Her face and chin were bruised, as if someone had used intense force to hold her mouth closed. There were 17 criss-cross slash marks on her face, front and back. Her breasts had been badly bitten. And she had been bleeding profusely from the vagina.

Police forensic experts quickly built up a grisly picture of the indignities inflicted on the woman before her death from suffocation. Her wrists also showed signs of being tied together, though the bond had been removed and was missing. The killer had washed the face of the corpse, but left dried blood in the nostrils and eyelashes.

On Saturday Heath was in Worthing, Sussex, wining and dining the girl with whom he had first occupied the room in Notting Hill. She was Yvonne Symonds, a 19-year-old who had met the chilling charmer at a dance in Chelsea seven days earlier, and only consented to spend the following night with him after accepting his whirlwind proposal of marriage. Now she was back at her parents' home. Heath booked into the nearby Ocean Hotel, and took her for dinner at a club at Angmering.

There he told her his version of the murder in the room they had shared. He said he met the victim on the evening of 20 June, and she asked to borrow his room to entertain another man, since they had nowhere else to go. Heath claimed he slept elsewhere, and was taken to the room by an Inspector Barratt next day and shown the body. It was, he told Yvonne, 'a very gruesome sight.' He added that the killer must be 'a sexual maniac.'

Both Yvonne and her parents were puzzled next morning to read in the Sunday papers that police were looking for Neville George Clevely Heath. Surely they had already seen him? Yvonne rang Heath at the Ocean Hotel, and he told her he was going back to London to clear up what must be a misunderstanding. He did indeed leave Worthing – but not for London. He went further down the south coast, to Bournemouth, where he booked in at the Tollard Royal Hotel as Group Captain Rupert Brooke.

Before he left Worthing, he posted a letter to Inspector Barratt at Scotland Yard. The two had never met, but Heath, who signed the letter with his real name, said he felt duty bound to report what he knew of the murder in his room.

He again said Margery Gardner asked for his keys, but said she was obliged to sleep with the other man for mainly financial reasons. She hinted that, if Heath arrived back at 02.00 she would spend the rest of the night with him. He arrived at the appointed time, found her 'in the condition of which you are aware', then panicked and fled because of his 'invidious position'.

Heath gave a fictitious description of the other man – a slim, dark-haired character called Jack – and curiously added: 'I have the instrument with which Mrs Gardner was beaten and am forwarding this to you today. You will find my fingerprints on it, but you should also find others as well.'

The instrument never arrived, though Inspector Barratt was not surprised by that. Yet despite his suspicions, increased by the letter, Scotland Yard did not issue a photograph of the wanted man. Heath was thus able to enjoy himself in Bournemouth for 13 days, drinking freely, going to shows, and chatting up holidaymaking girls at dances. On 3 July, he invited the friend of one of his dancing partners to tea, and they got on so well that a dinner date was fixed for that night at his hotel. Just after midnight, Heath left to walk her home along the promenade. He was asleep in his own bed at 04.30 when the night porter checked, not having seen him return.

Two days later, the manager of the nearby Norfolk Hotel reported one of his guests missing. Miss Doreen Marshall, a 21-year-old from Pinner, Middlesex, had last been seen leaving for dinner at the Tollard Royal. The manager there asked 'Group Captain Brooke' about his guest, and suggested he contact the police. Heath duly called at the station, identified the girl from photographs, and consoled her anguished father and sister.

But an alert detective constable thought the handsome six-footer fitted a description Scotland Yard had sent them. Heath was asked if he was the man wanted for questioning about a murder in London. He denied it, but was delayed long enough for other officers to take a good look at him. When he complained of feeling cold as the evening drew in, an inspector went to the Tollard Royal to collect Heath's jacket. And in the pockets was all the evidence the police needed.

As well as a single artificial pearl and the return half of a first class rail ticket from London to Bournemouth, there was a left-luggage ticket issued at Bournemouth West station on 23 June. It was for a suitcase which contained clothes labelled Heath, a bloodstained neckerchief, a scarf with human female hairs stuck to it, and a vicious-looking leather-bound riding crop, with a criss-cross weave. The end had worn away, and there was blood on the exposed wires.

Heath was taken to London and charged with the murder of Margery Gardner. On the same evening, 8 July, the body of his second victim was discovered. A woman walking her dog in a deep, wooded valley called

Branksome Chine, a mile west of the Tollard Royal, noticed swarms of flies around a rhododendron bush. She called the police, having read of the missing girl. And officers found a sickening sight.

Doreen Marshall was naked except for one shoe. Her battered body had been covered with her underwear, her inside-out black dress and yellow jacket. Her ripped stockings, broken pearl necklace and powder compact were discarded close by. Her wrists were tied and the inside of her hands ripped, as if she had been trying to avert the blade of a knife. One of her ribs was broken and sticking into her lung, as if someone had knelt on her. And her flesh had been mutilated – mercifully, as forensic experts later proved, after she had been killed with two deep cuts across the throat.

Heath told police that he left Doreen near Bournemouth pier, and watched her walk towards her hotel through some public gardens. He then returned to his own hotel at around 00.30; and because he knew the night porter would be waiting for him, decided to play a practical joke on him, climbing to his room via a builder's ladder left outside. He described it as 'a small deception'. The police dismissed the whole statement as a great deception. And on Thursday 24 September, Heath was charged at the Old Bailey, London, with the murder of Margery Gardner.

His guilt was easily proved. And because he had subsequently killed again, Heath was unable to use what might have been a plausible defence – that Ocelot Margie willingly submitted to whipping and beating, and died accidentally when things got out of hand. Heath knew the game was up, and wanted to plead guilty and accept his punishment coolly and calmly. But his defence counsel persuaded him, against his better judgement, to plead insanity. The attempts of a psychiatrist called on his behalf to try to prove that insanity provided the only memorable moments of the two-day trial.

Dr William Henry de Bargue Hubert, a former psychotherapist at Wormwood Scrubs jail, and one of the leading practising psychiatrists of the day, was utterly discredited by the prosecution cross-examination. A year later, he committed suicide.

Under close questioning from Mr Anthony Hawke for the prosecution, Dr Hubert claimed Heath knew what he was doing when he tied up and lashed Mrs Gardner, but did not consider or know it to be wrong. Did he then think it was right, Dr Hubert was asked. Yes came the reply. 'Are you saying, with your responsibility, that a person in that frame of mind is free from criminal responsibility if what he does causes grievous bodily harm or death?' asked the astounded Hawke. Hubert said he was, because sexual perverts often showed no regret or remorse.

Hawke then asked: 'Would it be your view that a person who finds it convenient at the moment to forge a cheque in order to free himself from financial responsibility is entitled to say that he thought it was right, and therefore he is free from the responsibility of what he does?' Hubert: 'He may think so, yes.'

Hawke: 'With great respect, I did not ask you what he thought. I asked whether you thought he was entitled to claim exemption from responsibility on the grounds of insanity.' Hubert: 'Yes, I do.'

Hawke: 'You are saying that a person who does a thing he wants to do, because it suits him at the moment to do it, is entitled, if that thing is a crime, to claim that he is insane and therefore free from responsibility?' Hubert: 'If the crime and the circumstances are so abnormal to the ordinary person, I do.'

It was an extraordinary thing to claim, and even Heath knew the doctor was harming, not helping, his case. He passed anguished notes to his own counsel, urging him to drop the insanity ploy.

In 1946 the dividing line between the noose and being confined in a mental hospital was the difference between psychopath and psychotic. Psychopaths were considered able to control their evil urges, psychotics were not. In Heath's case, two Home Office prison doctors said he was certainly abnormal, a sadistic sex pervert, but as a psychopath, he was not insane.

The jury of 11 men and one woman found him guilty after only an hour's consideration, and Heath was sentenced to death. He did not bother to appeal, expressed no remorse or sympathy for the families of his victims, and refused to discuss his life or beliefs with any of the experts sent to examine him. He spent most of his last days writing letters, one of which was to his parents: 'My only regret at leaving the world is that I have been damned unworthy of you both.'

He was hanged at Pentonville Prison in London on 26 october, 1946.

The Heartless Husband

JOHANN HOCH

Johann Otto Hoch had never believed in very long courtships or in long marriages. He had at least 24 wives in 15 years – and he brutally murdered all of them. The diabolical 'Bluebeard' even proposed to his sister-in-law over the deathbed of his wife, who was dying from a massive dose of arsenic. She accepted. 'Life is for the living.' Hoch told her. 'The dead are for the dead.'

Throughout Hoch's bizarre years of marriage and murder in the United States between 1892 and 1905, a tough Chicago cop named George Shippy stalked him relentlessly. Shippy knew Hoch was cutting a bloody trail of murder but was never able to prove it.

Born Johann Schmidt in 1862, Hoch had emigrated from Germany at 25 leaving his wife and three children behind. A big, jovial man with a sweeping handlebar moustache, he found work in the country as an itinerant bartender.

From 1887 to 1895 it was anybody's guess how many women he murdered. In April 1895 he found a woman in a saloon in Wheeling, West Virginia. Using the name Jacob Huff, he married her and then killed her three months later.

As with his other murders, the doctor thought the woman died of kidney disease for which there was no cure. But the lady's pastor knew better and Hoch fled from the town after converting his wife's estate to cash. Leaving his clothes and a suicide note behind, he walked naked into the River Ohio. A hundred yards up he had anchored a boat with new clothing in it. He clambered aboard and rowed to the Ohio side.

In 1898, using the name Martin Dotz, the murderer ran foul of Inspector George Shippy. The killer was arrested in Chicago on a minor swindling charge. But the Wheeling preacher saw a newspaper photo, recognized Jacob Huff and contacted Shippy.

Hoch breezed through a year in the Cook County jail while Shippy backtracked the man's elusive trail and investigated dozens of unsolved cases of murdered women. The determined cop went to Wheeling and had the body of Hoch's ex-wife exhumed, only to find that Hoch had removed many of the woman's vital organs.

After serving his sentence, Hoch married and murdered another 15 women between 1900 and 1905. His weapon was always arsenic, which was easily available in any drugstore. The victims were always lonely but wealthy women overwhelmed by Hoch's animal charm. And slipshod doctors were always too quick with the wrong diagnoses.

By now Hoch was acting like a man possessed. He slipped like a ghost from city to city, murdering in record time. Frequently he married and murdered in less than a week.

In 1904 he buried his last victim, Marie Walcker, and promptly married her sister. He fled with his new wife's savings account and the enraged woman contacted Shippy. Her sister's body was exhumed and this time the medical examiner found enough arsenic to kill a dozen women.

Shippy then made his long-awaited arrest.

Throughout the trial Hoch maintained an air of boyish innocence. Even after the guilty verdict, Hoch was confident he would never swing from the gallows.

As guards led him to the scaffold on 23 February, 1906, the killer joked and said: 'You see, boys, I don't look like a monster, now do I?' Nobody answered the question as Hoch's massive hulk fell through the trapdoor.

East End Terror

JACK THE RIPPER

On 25 September, 1888, a letter was delivered to the Central News Agency in London's Fleet Street. It read:

'Dear Boss, I keep on hearing that the police have caught me. But they won't fix me yet . . . I am down on certain types of women and I won't stop ripping them until I do get buckled.

Grand job, that last job was. I gave the lady no time to squeal. I love my work and want to start again. You will soon hear from me, with my funny little game.

I saved some of the proper red stuff in a ginger beer bottle after my last job to write with, but it went thick like glue and I can't use it. Red ink is fit enought, I hope. Ha, ha!

Next time I shall clip the ears off and send them to the police just for jolly.'

The letter was signed 'Jack the Ripper'. It was the first time the name had ever been used. And it immortalized this twisted and mysterious killer who lurked in London's backstreets.

Jack the Ripper's reign of terror was a short one. He first struck on a warm night in August 1888. On a chill, foggy night three months later he claimed his last victim. He is known to have slaughtered at least five women – and some criminologists have credited him with 11 murders.

All that is known for certain about Jack the Ripper is that he had some medical knowledge and that he was left-handed – a fact obvious to police surgeons who examined the grisly remains of his victims. He was probably a tall, slim, pale man with a black moustache. This was the description given by witnesses, including one policeman who saw someone hurrying away from the vicinity of one of the crimes. Each time, he wore a cap and a long coat, and he walked with the vigorous stride of a young man.

But it is unlikely that anyone will ever be able to identify him. Even in 1992, when the secret Scotland Yard files on the case are finally made public, they are expected to cast little new light on the case.

The story of London's most mysterious and ferocious mass-murderer began shortly after 05.00 on the morning of 7 August, 1888. A man hurried down the stairs of the Whitechapel hovel in which he had a room – to be confronted by a

The face of Jack the Ripper

by DANIEL FARSON

From the Evening News

bundle lying on the first floor landing. He tried to push the bundle out of his way, then recoiled with horror when he realized that what lay at his feet were the bloody remains of a woman. She was identified as Martha Turner, a prostitute. Her throat had been slit, she had been stabbed several times, and bestial mutilations had been carried out on her body.

As the murder of prostitutes was no rare thing in those days, the case was soon shelved. But when a second, similar murder was committed 24 days later, fear and panic began to sweep the mean streets of the East End. The mutilated body of 42-year-old Mary Ann Nicholls – or Pretty Polly as she was known – was found in the early hours of 31 August.

Mary had probably taken no heed of the grisly fate of Martha Turner. She was desperate for money. She needed fourpence for a doss-house bed, and when a tall, pale man approached her she looked forward to the chance of making a few coppers, with perhaps something left over for a couple of tots of gin.

The man drew her into the shadows. If she finally realized there was anything wrong, it was too late. The Ripper put a hand over her mouth and dexterously slit her throat. Then the crazed killer set about his savage butchery. A detective who examined the body said: 'Only a madman could have done this.' And a police surgeon said: 'I have never seen so horrible a case. She was ripped about in a manner that only a person skilled in the use of a knife could have achieved.'

93

Two extracts from *The Illustrated Police New*

THE WORLD'S MOST INFAMOUS MURDERS

It was just one week before the Ripper struck again. His prey was 'Dark Annie' Chapman, 47 years old and dying of tuberculosis when she was hacked down. When found in Hanbury Street by a porter from nearby Spitalfields Market, her few pitiful possessions had been neatly laid out beside her disembowelled corpse.

The next victim was Elizabeth 'Long Liz' Stride. On the evening of Sunday, 30 September, a police constable spotted a white-stockinged leg sticking out from a factory gate. Unlike earlier cases, Elizabeth Stride's body had not been mutilated – which led police to surmise that the Ripper had been disturbed in his grisly task. But, to satisfy his bloodlust, he soon found another victim. And it was during this killing that he left the only clue to his identity.

Just 15 minutes walk from the spot where Long Liz's body had been found was discovered the bloody remains of 40-year-old Catherine Eddowes. Her body was the most terribly mutilated so far – the Ripper had even cut off her ears. And from the corpse a trail of blood led to a message scrawled in chalk on a wall: 'The Jewes are not men to be blamed for nothing.' But this vital piece of evidence was never studied properly. Sir Charles Warren, head of the Metropolitan Police, perhaps fearing a violent backlash of hatred aimed at the Jews, ordered the slogan to be rubbed out and kept a secret.

Rumours now began to sweep like wildfire through the sleazy streets of London's East End. . . . . . The Ripper carried his instruments of death in a little black bag – and terror-crazed crowds chased any innocent passer-by carrying such a bag. He was a foreign seaman – and anyone with a foreign accent went in fear of opening his mouth for fear of being set upon. He was a Jewish butcher – and latent anti-Semitism already simmering because of the influx of Jewish immigrants fleeing the Russian and Polish pogroms began bubbling to the surface.

An even wilder theory, popular in the most squalid areas where there was no love lost between the inhabitants and the police, was that the killer was a policeman. How else would he be able to prowl the streets at night without creating suspicion?

The killer was in turn thought to be a mad doctor, a homicidal Russian sent by the Czar's secret police trying to cause unrest in London, a puritan obsessed with cleansing the East End of vice, and a crazed midwife with a hatred of prostitutes.

On 9 November, the Ripper struck again. Mary Kelly was unlike any of the other victims. She was younger – only 25 – blonde and she was attractive. The last person to see her alive was George Hutchinson whom she had asked for money to pay her rent. When he said he could not help she approached a slim, well-dressed man with a trim moustache and a deerstalker hat. She was never seen alive again.

Early next morning, Henry Bowers knocked impatiently at her door for his unpaid rent. Finally he went to the window of Mary's room and pushed aside the sacking curtain. The sickening sight within made him forget all about the rent and sent him running for the police. Later, he was to say: 'I shall be haunted by this for the rest of my life.'

With Mary Kelly's death, the Ripper's reign ended as suddenly and mysteriously as it began.

Two convicted murderers claimed to be the Ripper. One, who poisoned his mistress, said when arrested: 'You've got Jack the Ripper at last.' But there is little evidence to suggest that he was telling the truth. The second cried out as the trapdoor on the gallows opened 'I am Jack the . . .' But it was later proved that he was in America when the Ripper crimes were committed.

Some members of the police force were sure they knew who the Ripper was. In 1908, the assistant commissioner of police said flatly: 'In stating that he was a Polish Jew, I am merely stating a definitely established fact.'

But Inspector Robert Sagar, who played a leading part in the Ripper investigations and who died in 1924, said in his memoirs:

'We had good reason to suspect a man who lived in Butcher's Row, Aldgate. We watched him carefully. There was no doubt that this man was insane, and, after a time, his friends thought it advisable to have him removed to a private asylum. After he was removed, there were no more Ripper atrocities.'

Even Queen Victoria's eldest grandson has been named as a suspect. He was Prince Albert Victor, Duke of Clarence, who, if he had lived, would have become king when his father, Edward VII, died.

But perhaps the most likely solution is the one arrived at by author and broadcaster Daniel Farson. He pointed the finger of suspicion at Montagu John Druitt, a failed barrister who had both medical connections and a history of mental instability in his family.

Farson based his accusation on the notes of Sir Melville Macnaghten, who joined Scotland Yard in 1889 and became head of the Criminal Investigation Department in 1903. Macnaghten named three Ripper suspects – a Polish tradesman, who hated women and was probably Jewish, a homicidal Russian doctor, and Druitt.

The soundest basis for blaming Druitt for the murders is that a few weeks after the death of Mary Kelly, Druitt's body was found floating in the River Thames. After that, there were no further attacks by Jack the Ripper

The One Who Got Away

BELA KISS

I f the term 'kiss of death' had not already existed, headline writers would have invented it to describe Bela Kiss. For the well-to-do, middle-aged Hungarian murdered at least 23 people before 'dying' on a battlefield during World War One, and escaping to freedom in America. He is one of the few mass murderers to evade justice.

Kiss was 40 when he arrived in the Hungarian village of Czinkota in 1913 with his beautiful, 25 year-old bride Maria. He had bought a large house and taken on servants, and the locals soon warmed to the man who collected stamps, grew roses, and did a little writing, especially on astrology. From time to time he would drive to Budapest on business in his smart red car, and the village policeman, Adolph Trauber, readily agreed to keep an eye on the home of the man with whom he had struck up a close friendship.

War was clearly only months away, and Constable Trauber was not surprised when his friend started returning from Budapest with oil drums. Kiss explained they were full of petrol so that he could continue his business trips when fuel became scarce. Trauber decided to keep quiet about the fact that, while Kiss was away, his wife was entertaining a young artist called Paul Bihari. But the affair was common knowledge among villagers and servants at the house. And they sympathized when, after another trip to Budapest the distraught husband emerged from his empty home to show them a note, saying the couple had eloped together.

For several months, Kiss shut himself away, refusing to see anyone, even Trauber. But in the spring of 1914, the constable persuaded him to rejoin the world, and found him an elderly widow to act as housekeeper. Kiss resumed his journeys to the Hungarian capital, returning each time with more oil drums. He told Trauber that the petrol was in payment of a debt owed to him by a Budapest garage owner. But Kiss brought other things from Budapest – women, not young like Maria, but sometimes even older than himself. Several times his housekeeper stormed out when her kitchen was invaded, only to return when Kiss told her the offending female had left.

Kiss and Constable Trauber spent many evenings together in conversation, and during one of their chats, the policeman mentioned the disappearance of two widows in Budapest. They had vanished after answering a lonely hearts advertisement in a newspaper, placed by a man named Hofmann. Both had drawn heavily on their savings after meeting him. Kiss joked that he too had had some unsuccessful affairs with middle-aged widows, and both men laughed.

War broke out that August, but Kiss was not among the first to be called up. He continued his trips to Budapest, returning with more oil drums and more women. When he was eventually conscripted, he left the house and his petrol stockpile in Trauber's care. And the constable continued to look after them after May 1916, when news arrived that Bela Kiss had been killed in action.

Later that summer, soldiers arrived in Czinkota looking for petrol. Trauber remembered the oil drums, and led the way to where they were stood. But a horrific discovery awaited him. Instead of petrol, each of the seven drums in the house contained alcohol. And each contained the doubled-up body of a naked woman.

Detectives called in from Budapest combed the gardens, and dug up yet more drums, each containing a grisly secret. In all, there were 23 tin-can coffins. The victims, who included faithless Maria and her lover, had all been garotted. Letters found in the house made it clear that Kiss and lonely-heart Hofmann were the same person, and that he had taken money or possessions from each of his fatal conquests. But there was nothing police could do: Their quarry had died at the front. The file was closed.

Then, in 1919, a friend of one of the victims recognized Bela Kiss crossing Margaret Bridge in Budapest, and reported the sighting to police. Shocked detectives discovered that Kiss had exchanged identities with a fallen colleague during the war, but before they could find him, he vanished again.

In 1924, a deserter from the French Foreign Legion told French police of a colleague called Hofmann, who had boasted of garotting exploits. But by then Hofmann, too, had deserted. It was ten years before he was again recognized, in Times Square, New York. And in 1936, he was reportedly working as a janitor at a Sixth Avenue apartment block. Fellow Hungarians there described him as a small, plain, inoffensive man in his middle sixties, a man with a bleak future. Bela Kiss did not talk about his even bleaker past.

The Vampire of Düsseldorf

PETER KURTEN

He is the king of sexual delinquents . . . he unites nearly all perversions in one person . . . he killed men, women, children and animals, killed anything he found.' Those were the chilling words used to describe Peter Kurten, the Vampire of Düsseldorf, at his trial in 1930. They came not from the judge, nor the prosecution, but from defending counsel, pleading for a verdict of insanity. But Kurten, 47, did not escape the execution his reign of terror so richly deserved, because the court agreed with the verdict of one of the top psychiatrists called to examine the callous killer: brutal sadist Kurten 'was at the same time a clever man and quite a nice one.'

Psychopaths ran in the Kurten family, and young Peter, the fifth child in a family of 13, saw the exploits of one at first hand in his home at Cologne-Mulheim. His father would arrive home drunk, beat the children, and sexually violate his unwilling wife in front of them. He also committed incest with his 13-year-old daughter, and Kurten followed his father's example with her. From the age of nine, he also had another teacher. The local dog catcher initiated him to torturing animals. Kurten was an enthusiastic pupil, and progressed from dogs to sheep, pigs, goats, geese and swans. What excited and aroused him most was the sight of their blood. He frequently cut the heads off swans and drank the blood that spurted out.

Soon Kurten switched his attentions to human victims. As a boy he had drowned two playmates while all three swam around a raft in the Rhine. By the age of 16, he was living with a masochistic woman who enjoyed being beaten and half-strangled. She had a daughter of 16, and all three enjoyed a sordid co-existence, interrupted only when Kurten's attempts at theft and fraud landed him in prison. He was later to claim that the inhumanity and injustice of his treatment in jail led to his blood-soaked career as a killer. In fact prison provided him with another outlet for sadism. He deliberately broke prison rules to gain solitary confinement, where he indulged his erotic reveries.

'I thought of myself causing accidents affecting thousands of people,' he was to recall in court. 'I invented a number of crazy fantasies such as smashing bridges and boring through bridge piers. Then I spun a number of fantasies with regard to bacilli which I might be able to introduce into drinking water and so cause a great calamity. I imagined myself using schools and orphanages for the purpose, where I could carry out murders by giving away chocolate samples containing arsenic. I derived the sort of pleasure from these visions that other people would get from thinking about a naked woman.'

When he was freed from prison, Kurten began to turn his daydreams into nightmare reality. He became an arsonist – 'the sight of the flames delighted me, but above all it was the excitement of the attempts to extinguish the fire and the agitation of those who saw their property being destroyed.' And he began to attack defenceless women and children.

His first attempt at murder was unsuccessful. He admitted leaving a girl for dead after assaulting her during intercourse in Düsseldorf's Grafenburg Woods. But no body was ever found. It was assumed that the girl recovered enough to crawl away, to ashamed or scared to report the incident. Eight-year-old Christine Klein was not so lucky. She was found in bed, raped and with her throat cut. Her uncle was arrested and tried, and though aquitted for lack of evidence, the shame of the charge stuck to him until he died during World War One. Kurten must have enjoyed that. His own trial was shocked by the detailed, fussy, matter-of-fact way he related what had really happened, 17 years earlier.

'It was on 25 May, 1913,' he recalled in the clipped, precise tone that only made his deeds seem more ghastly. 'I had been stealing, specializing in public bars or inns where the owners lived on the floor above. In a room above an inn at Cologne-Mulheim, I discovered a child asleep. Her head was facing the window. I seized it with my left hand and strangled her for about a minute and a half. The child woke up and struggled but lost consciousness.

'I had a small but sharp pocketknife with me and I held the child's head and cut her throat. I heard the blood spurt and drip on the mat beside the bed. . . The whole thing lasted about three minutes, then I locked the door again and went home to Düsseldorf. Next day I went back to Mulheim. There is a cafe opposite the Klein's place and I sat there and drank a glass of beer, and read all about the murder in the papers. People were talking about it all around me. All this amount of horror and indignation did me good.'

Kurten was not prepared to use his sadism on the Kaiser's behalf when war broke out. He deserted a day after call-up, and spent the rest of the hostilities in jail, for that and other minor crimes. Released in 1921, he decided to marry, and chose a prostitute at Altenburg as his bride, overcoming her reluctance by threatening to kill her. He gave up petty crime and went to work in a factory as a moulder. He became an active trade unionist, and a respected pillar of society, quiet, charming, carefully dressed and meticulous about his appearance – even a little vain. Those who knew he was having affairs with other women did not tell his wife. And the women were not prepared to confide that Kurten was a rough lover, who enjoyed beating and half-choking them.

But once Kurten and his wife moved to Düsseldorf in 1925, blood lust again got the better of him. Though his relations with Frau Kurten remained normal, his assaults on his mistresses became more vicious. Soon he was attacking innocent strangers with scissors or knives, aroused by the sight of their blood. As he escaped detection, he stepped up the rate of attacks, varying his style to cover his tracks. By the summer of 1929, the town of Düsseldorf was in the grip of terror. Police had pinned 46 perverted crimes, including four killings, down to someone who seemed to have vampire tendencies. But they had not clues as to the monster's identity.

On the evening of 23 August, two sisters left the throng at the annual fair in the suburb of Flehe to walk home through nearby allotments. Louise Lenzen, 14, and five-year-old Gertrude stopped when a gentle voice sounded behind them. 'Oh dear, I've forgotten to buy cigarettes,' the man said to Louise. 'Look, would you be very kind and go to one of the booths and get some for me? I'll look after the little girl.' Louise took his money and ran back to the fair. Kurten quietly picked up her sister, carried her into the darkness behind a stand of beanpoles, and efficiently slaughtered her, strangling her and cutting her throat with a Bavarian clasp knife. When Louise returned, he pocketed the cigarettes, accepted his change – and did the same to her.

Twelve hours later, a servant girl called Gertrude Schulte was stopped by a man who offered to take her to a fair at nearby Neuss. As they strolled through woods, he attempted to rape her, but she fought him off. He produced a knife, and began stabbing her in a frenzy, piercing her neck, shoulder and back. When he threw her to the ground, the knife snapped, leaving the blade in her back.

Gertrude was lucky – her screams alerted a passer-by, and she was rushed to hospital. But Kurten had escaped again. The newspapers continued to report his exploits with mounting hysteria. In one half hour, the 'Vampire' attacked and wounded a girl of 18, a man of 30 and a woman of 37. Later he bludgeoned serving girls Ida Reuter and Elizabeth Dorrier to death. And on 27 November he slashed five-year-old Gertrude Albermann with a thin blade, inflicting 36 wounds on her tiny body.

Gertrude was the last victim to die, but the attempted murders and vicious attacks continued through the winter and early spring, attracting headlines across Germany. Maria Budlick, a 21-year-old maid, had read the stories while working in Cologne, 30 kilometres away, but when she lost her job, she boarded a train for Düsseldorf, her desperation for employment outweighing any fears about the vampire.

It was 14 May, 1930, when she stepped on to the platform at Düsseldorf, and

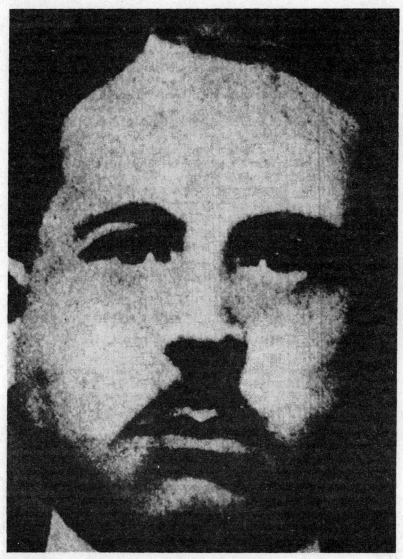

Peter Kurten

was soon approached by a man who offered to show her the way to a girls' hostel. She accompanied him happily through the streets, but when he turned into the trees of Volksgarten Park, she drew back. The man assured her she had nothing to fear, but she refused to be placated. As they argued, another man emerged from the shadows and asked: 'Is everything all right?' Maria's escort left, and she was left alone with her rescuer – Peter Kurten.

Convinced that he had saved her from a fate worse than death, or death itself, Maria agreed to go with him to his home for a meal. Kurten gave her a glass of milk and a ham sandwich, then offered to take her to the hostel. They boarded a tram – but for the second time in less than an hour, poor Maria was being misled. Her rescuer led her straight into Grafenburg Woods, on the northern edge of town, then lunged at her, gripping her throat and attempting to rape her against a tree. Maria struggled, but the man was too strong for her. Then, as she was about to pass out, he let go of her, and asked: 'Do you remember where I live, in case you ever need my help again?" Maria gasped: 'No.' Kurten escorted her out of the woods, and left her.

Maria had remembered where he lived, but surprisingly she did not go to the police. Instead, she wrote about her ordeal to a friend in Cologne. The letter was incorrectly addressed, and opened at the post office to be returned to the sender. An alert official realized the implications of its contents and contacted the authorities. Next day, plain clothes detectives took Maria back to the street she remembered, Mettmannerstrasse, and she identified Number 71 as the home of her assailant. She also saw Kurten, but he vanished before she could tip off her police escort.

Kurten had also seen Maria, and realized that the net was closing in on him. He went to the restaurant where his wife worked, and confessed everything to her. He had never felt guilt for his crimes, and even admitting them now did not affect his appetite. He ate not only his own meal, but the one his shocked wife could not touch. On the morning of 24 May, Frau Kurten went to the police, and told them she had arranged to meet her husband outside a certain church at 15.00. Armed officers surrounded the area, and when Kurten arrived four rushed at him, revolvers pointing at his chest. He smiled and offered no resistance, saying: 'There is no need to be afraid.'

In his 15-year career of law-breaking, Jesse James murdered about 10 people and stole about $200,000. He was also one of Quantrill's Raiders who massacred 150 inhabitants of Lawrence, Kansas. He was shot in the back by his cousin, Bob Ford, while fixing a picture on his cabin wall in St Joseph, Missouri, in 1882.

THE VAMPIRE OF DÜSSELDORF

> **Hungarian countess Elizabeth Bathory bathed in the blood of her victims because she believed it preserved her beauty. In the black depths of her castle dungeons at Csejthe, the countess stored well-fed girls ready to have their veins cut open and filtered into pipes that ran into a blood bath. When her blood craving reached a peak, she would nibble one of her victims to a premature death.**
>
> **Tried for 610 murders, the countess was sentenced to be walled up for life in a room from which all light and sound were excluded. In 1614, she expired after three years of this living death.**

The trial, when it opened in a converted drill-hall at Düsseldorf's police headquarters on 13 April, 1931, was almost a foregone conclusion. Thousands surrounded the building to try to catch a glimpse of the man who had admitted 68 crimes, apart from those for which he had already served time, while being questioned. He was charged with nine murders and seven attempted murders, and the prosecution hardly needed to produce any evidence to gain a conviction – Kurten admitted everything coldly, calmly, and in astonishing detail. Sleek and immaculate, he confessed to being a sex maniac, a rapist, a vampire, a sadist, an arsonist. He gave chapter and verse about his bestiality, his jail fantasies, and how he had strangled, stabbed and clubbed women and children to death. He admitted drinking blood from one woman's cut throat, from a wound on a man's forehead, from the hand of another victim. he described how he had enjoyed reading about Jack the Ripper, and how he had visited a waxworks Chamber of Horrors, and promised himself: 'I'll be here one day.'

A shoulder-high cage had been built round the accused man's stand to prevent him escaping. Behind him were the exhibits – the knives and scissors he had used to kill, the matches he had used to burn property, the spade he had used to bury one woman, the skulls of the innocent strangers he had butchered for the sake of an orgasm. The judge treated him gently, guiding him carefully through the catalogue of appalling crimes. There was no need to be tough, Kurten was as mild-mannered and courteous as his unsuspecting neighbours had always known him. But by the time it came to the prisoner's final speech, even the hardened judge was sickened.

Incredibly, Kurten, who had blamed his childhood and prison for turning him into a killer, now began preaching puritanically about the behaviour of others. He said:

'My actions as I see them today are so terrible and horrible that I do not even make an attempt to excuse them. But one bitter thing remains in my mind. When I think of the two Socialist doctors accused recently of abortions performed on working class mothers who sought their advice, when I think of the 500 murders they have committed, then I cannot help feeling bitter.

The real reason for my conviction is that there comes a time in the life of every criminal when he can go no further, and this spiritual collapse is what I experienced. But I do feel that I must make one statement: some of my victims made things very easy for me. Man-hunting on the part of women today has taken on such forms that . . .'

The judge could stand no more unctuous rhetoric, and angrily banged his desk for silence.

The jury took 90 minutes to find Kurten guilty on all accounts, and he was sentenced to death nine times. On 1 July, 1932, he chose veal, fried potatoes and white wine for the traditional last meal, and enjoyed it so much that he asked for second helpings. At 06.00 next morning he marched to the guillotine in Cologne's Koingelputz prison, and was beheaded after declining the attorney general's offer of a last wish.

But the twisted mind of Kurten had had one final wish. He asked the prison psychiatrist, minutes before he left his cell for that last walk, 'After my head has been chopped off, will I still be able to hear, at least for a moment, the sound of my own blood gushing from the stump of my neck?' As the appalled official sat stunned in silence, Kurten smiled and said: 'That would be the pleasure to end all pleasures.'

The Killer Who Kept Quiet

HENRI DESIRE LANDRU

Few murder trials in history have aroused so much controversy, as that of Henri Desire Landru at Paris in November 1921. He was accused of 11 murders, but the prosecution could produce no bodies, no proof of how he killed his victims, and no proof of how he disposed of them. The jury convicted him on circumstantial evidence, then petitioned for mercy. Eventually Landru went to the guillotine still protesting his innocence – and even today, there are those who believe him.

The court proceedings themselves degenerated into farce. France was demob-happy after World War One, and hungry for entertainment. The French government was happy to divert attention from the peace talks at Versailles which were going badly. A nation that still holds romancers in high esteem could not resist the small, thin, bald, strange-looking man with deep-set, flickering black eyes who was said to have made the acquaintance of 283 ladies in five years. In court, men roared and cheered as this curious Casanova baffled his frustrated accusers by resolutely refusing to discuss his amours. Women blew him kisses and made blatant gestures of sexual invitation. When one woman arrived late in the packed courtroom, Landru earned applause by gallantly getting to his feet, and offering her his seat in the dock.

The facts of the case, alas, were less romantic. Henri Desire Landru was a small-time thief and swindler well-known to the police since his first arrest in 1900. He had progressed from petty pilfering to conning widows and lonely spinsters out of their savings via lonely-heart matrimonial advertisements in the Paris newspapers. But he was not very good at it. As soon as his dupes realized he was only interested in their money, many went to the police. Landru was in and out of prison until 1914. His father, a respectable ironworker who had retired to the Dordogne, committed suicide in 1912 when he came to visit his son, only to find him in jail for fraud.

By July 1914, the French judicial system had had enough of Landru. He was convicted, in his absence, of a motor cycling business swindle, and sentenced to four years, with a recommendation that he be banished to the penal establishment in New Caledonia as a habitual criminal. Landru, who had a wife and four children, was on the run, knowing that one mistake would mean transportation and exile. Yet he needed money to live. His answer, according to the prosecution at his trial, was chillingly simple. He continued to seduce willing ladies for profit, but ensured that they would not complain to the authorities by murdering them.

Had the French police not been undermanned and fully stretched because of the war, Landru could never have survived for so long. He had a distinctive, disproportionately big red beard, which later earned him the inevitable nickname 'Bluebeard', and he continued to visit his old haunts around Paris, particularly the garages where he hoarded stolen goods. It was at one of them, in February 1914, that he had met Madame Jeanne Cuchet.

She was 39, a widow working in a Paris store, and was accompanying her son Andre, 18, who had applied to Landru for a job. She quickly became infatuated with the smooth-talking man who called himself M. Diard, said he was a well-to-do engineer, and wore an impressive violet ribbon, an 'Order' he had invented and bestowed upon himself. Madame Cuchet's married sister was suspicious of Diard, however, and went so far as to break into his villa at Chantilly, discovering letters from several women addressed to a variety of differently-named men. But Madame Cuchet was not to be deterred.

She agreed to her lover's suggestion of renting a villa called The Lodge at Vernouillet, on the outskirts of Paris, and happily paid six months rent. They moved in on 8 December, 1914, and the woman and her son were last seen alive in the garden the following 4 January. By that time Madame Cuchet's family had washed their hands of her, and though she was later reported missing, the inquiries into her whereabouts were almost non-existent.

Encouraged by this success, which netted him about 15,000 francs in jewels, furniture and securities, Landru embarked on another conquest. Madame Therese Laborde-Line was 47, a widow with little money and no relatives in France – she came from Buenos Aires, Argentina. Recklessly using the name Cuchet, Landru wooed her and won what she possessed. He took her to Vernouillet in June 1915, and she too vanished there.

This was convenient for Landru, for on 11 May, he had placed this advertisement in the Paris morning paper, *Le Journal*: 'Widower with two children, aged 43, with comfortable income, affectionate, serious and moving in good society, desires to meet widow with a view to matrimony.' Three of the women who answered the advertisement that May were to disappear before the year was out.

Madame Désiree Guillin was 51, a former governess with a legacy of 22,000 francs. She was delighted at the prospect of going to Australia as the wife of 'diplomat M. Petit', and happily went to The Lodge with him on 4 August. She was never seen again. Landru sold her furniture and forged her signature to get at her bank balance. The bank should have spotted that, but again the war was the excuse.

Henri Desire Landru

Landru decided to leave The Lodge for somewhere more secluded. He picked the Villa Ermitage, a large, sparsely-furnished house in a little-used side road near the village of Gambais in the department of the Seine. It was close to the forest of Rambouillet just outside Paris, with several lakes and ponds nearby. One of the few improvements Landru made was to install a small stove. Then he was ready to entertain guests.

The first was Madame Heon, a 55-year-old widow who replied to the May advertisement, and fell for 'M. Petit', now head traveller for a large South American company. She was last seen alive at Gambais in December, which left Landru free to pursue his wooing of the third likely candidate from his advertisement, Madame Anna Collomb.

She was 44 – though she discreetly put her age at 29 in her letter to him – and a widow. Landru had at first told her he was M. Cuchet, a war refugee from Rocroi who had a factory at Montmartre, and she fell for him, she told her mother, 'because he is a real gentleman and says such beautiful things to me.' The infatuated woman moved in with him at a flat in the Rue Chateaudun, and gave him her furniture to put in store. When she visited Gambais with him, she found he was known there as M. Fremyet. Landru explained to her suspicious mother that he used two names to secure a double war indemnity, a fact that confirmed her opinion of him as a crook. But Anna's love was unshakeable. On Christmas Eve, she invited her sister Madame Pelat to Gambais, and Landru spoke warmly of his plans to marry Anna and move to Nice. Madame Collomb was not seen again after 27 December.

Landru was 8,000 francs richer when he met his next lover, a 19-year-old serving girl, on the Paris Métro in January. Though she was penniless, Andree Babelay was pretty, and he dallied with her for nearly four months. She was last seen on 12 April at Gambais, after which Landru renewed his acquaintance with 44-year-old Madame Celestine Buisson, another widow who agreed to trust him with her furniture and securities. She disappeared on 17 August.

Three more ladies were to take a one-way trip to Gambais: Madame Louise Jaume, 38, a devout Catholic separated from her husband, who vanished only hours after she and Landru knelt in prayer at a church in November, 1917; Madame Anne-Marie Pascal, 33, a divorcée, who seemingly bequeathed Landru her false teeth and umbrella when she disappeared in April, 1918 – he sold them for 30 francs – and Madame Marie-Therese Marchadier, 37, a lodging house keeper with a lurid past who was seen no more after 13 January, 1919. Landru then cleared everything from her Paris apartment.

But by then the web of deceit Landru had woven was slowly being unravelled. Madame Pelat, sister of Anna Collomb, was puzzled when she received no replies to letters she sent to the Villa Ermitage. She wrote to the mayor of Gambais, asking if he knew the whereabouts of M. Cuchet-Fremyet.

Shortly before, the mayor had had another letter, from Mademoiselle Lacoste, the sister of Madame Buisson, inquiring about the man she had called on at the villa, M. Dupont. The mayor wrote to both women, suggesting that they contact each other. When they met, it did not take long to discover that Cuchet-Fremyet and Dupont were one and the same man.

The two women went to the police, and the name Cuchet rang a bell. Madame Cuchet and her son were still listed as missing after going away with a man named Diard. The coincidence seemed too strong to be ignored. And the description of the wanted man – small, bald, with a big red beard – also fitted an engineer named Guillet, suspected of fraud and theft. On 10 April, 1919, an arrest warrant was issued.

Just one day later, the search was over. Mlle Lacoste was walking in the Rue de Rivoli when she spotted the man she knew as Dupont strolling arm-in-arm with a smartly-dressed young woman. She followed them into a shop, and heard them order a white china dinner service. Mlle Lacoste lost the couple in the crowds, but went straight to the police, who discovered that the china had been ordered in the name of Lucien Guillet. Early next morning, they swooped on the address he had given, No 76 Rue de Rochechouart.

Landru at first protested that he was Guillet, born at Rocroi in 1874. But when he was searched, he tried to throw a small, loose-leaved black book out of the window. That book was to send him to the guillotine. For Landru had been insanely meticulous about keeping details of his affairs. He had listed each reply to his lonely hearts advertisements under seven headings – to be answered *poste restante*; without money; without furniture; no reply; to be answered to initials *poste restante*; possible fortune; to be investigated. He had noted every expense, even down to the two sous he put in the collection box when he went to church with Madame Jaume. More seriously, he had described the tickets bought for his trips to Gambais – a return one for himself, a single ticket for his ladies.

On the front cover of the book he had written in pencil: Cuchet, J. *idem*, Bresil, Crozatier, Havre, Buisson, A. Collomb, Babelay, Jaume, Pascal, Marchadier. The police knew only three names on the list at that stage, but they were enough for them to arrest Landru for murder. Painstaking investigations revealed that women answering to the names Babelay, Jaume, Pascal and Marchadier had also vanished, that Bresil denoted Madame Laborde-Line (Landru may have muddled Argentina and Brazil), that Madame Guillin lived in the Rue Crozatier, and that Madame Heon came from Havre.

Police searched the Villa Ermitage on 9 April but found nothing. After the arrest, they raided all Landru's properties, and discovered intimate papers and identity cards for all the missing women, plus clothes and personal trinkets belonging to them. They also found two wax cords, of the type sometimes used to strangle people. On 29 April, they returned for a thorough search of the villa at Gambais. Sifting through ashes beside the stove, they came across 295 fragments of bone, as well as fastenings from parts of buttons and other remains of women's clothing.

The French judicial system involves a preliminary interrogation by an examining magistrate, with wide-ranging powers to prepare the ground for a trial. An able inquisitor called Bonin was assigned to Landru. Aided by witnesses and the best advice from crime experts, he questioned the little man for two-and-a-half years, going over and over the evidence in the black book, warning him that forensic experts had identified the bone fragments as being from three human bodies, asking him about each missing woman in turn. Landru took refuge in his right, under the law, to remain silent.

To most questions, he replied: 'I have nothing to say.' Occasionally he would tell Bonin: 'I am a gallant man. I cannot allow you to ask me questions concerning the ladies. If they have disappeared, it is nothing to do with me. I know nothing of what became of them. Discover proofs, bring them to me, and then I will discuss them with you.' Another time, Bonin said: 'You are a murderer.' Landru replied: 'You say so. Prove it. Look, investigate, imagine, but prove it if you can.'

Asked about Madame Cuchet, he said: 'Her hiding place is a secret between herself and me. I am a man of honour, and though I understand the accusation you have brought, I will not reveal it. I have given my word.' When Bonin pointed out that she had broken off contact with her closest friends, Landru replied stonily: 'Madame Cuchet was heartbroken by the hypocrisy of the world, as I am.'

It was a remarkable feat of endurance by Landru, particularly as he was weakened by attacks of gastritis. The authorities had evidence that black, acrid smoke had been seen coming from the chimney at Gambais, and that a man answering Landru's description had been seen throwing a package into a lake near the Villa Ermitage. The bones of Madame Marchadier's two griffon dogs had been dug up in the grounds. But there was still no concrete proof of murder, and no bodies. Nonetheless, in France, unlike Britain, a man was guilty until proved innocent.

In September 1921, M. Bonin sent the result of his examinations – 7,000 documents – to the Department of Criminal Prosecution. The trial began at the Versailles Palais de Justice on 7 November. Landru was only 52, but his illness and prison pallor made him look like a weary old man. It took three hours for the clerk to read the indictment – an astonishing catalogue of seduction, swindling, forgery and multiple murder. Landru seemed indifferent, reacting only when the phrase 'exploitation of women' was read out.

On the second day of the trial, the court president questioned the prisoner, who disputed some facts in his statement, saying: 'The police are often inefficient.' When asked why he had not co-operated with M. Bonin, Landru said: 'It is not my business to guide the police. Have they not been accusing me for the past three years of deeds which the women who disappeared never for one moment reproached me with?' The president stifled a burst of laughter in court with the words: 'It is you who have made it impossible for these women to complain.'

Landru claimed the names in his book were all business clients. He bought their furniture, ready to sell it back to them once the Germans had left France. When the prosecution pointed out that, on one day, he had met six or seven women, Landru replied: 'That proves well that I was not concerned with any affairs.' He claimed the matrimonial advertisements were an innocent business ruse, 'to flatter their conceit'. But again he refused to discuss details of his dealings with the women, saying they were 'private matters'.

Landru parried some questions with black humour. Asked what had become of Madam Guillin, he said: 'It is not for me to say, it is for the police to find out. They took six years to find me. Perhaps they will end up finding Madame Guillin.' To the prosecutor, he said: 'I fully recognize, sir, that you are after my head. I regret that I have not more than one head to offer you.'

But on one occasion, a witness wiped the smile from his face. Madame Friedmann, sister of Jeanne Cuchet, shouted at Landru: 'My sister loved you so much that she would not have left you to be condemned if she had been living.' Then, in hushed tones, she told of a dream in which her sister had appeared before her, and told her that Landru had slit her throat while she slept. Madame Friedmann's sobbing, and the emotional response of the public galleries, forced the session to be adjourned. No court of law could accept dreams as proof of murder. Yet no jury could forget such a powerful moment.

Though no-one had proved that Landru burned any bodies, lengthy testimony from a medical jurist on the effects of burning human remains was allowed. It made grisly listening. 'A right foot disappears in 50 minutes,' the jury was told, 'half a skull with the brains taken out in 36 minutes, a whole skull in 1 hour and ten minutes.'

Civil lawyers representing relatives of the missing women were also allowed to make dramatic accusations against the prisoner, denouncing him as a murderer who chopped up bodies, without a shred of conclusive factual justification.

Faced with a mounting tide of circumstantial evidence against his client, defence attorney Moro-Giafferi one of the most distinguished lawyers in France, put up a brave fight. He produced the girl Landru was with when he was arrested, Fernande Segret, who made the most of her big moment in a sealskin coat and picture hat. She described herself as a 'lyric artist', and no singer could expect a more enthusiastic welcome than she got from the men in the court. When order was restored, she declared that Landru was a good lover, strongly passionate, and that he made her very happy. She said she had cooked for him on the stove at Gambais, where Landru was alleged to have burned the bodies, and had cleared the cinders afterwards without noticing any skulls or bones.

Moro-Giafferi then made an emotionally brilliant speech, saying that under civil law, none of the missing women would have been presumed dead for several years. Why assume they were now, when a man's life depended on it. He claimed that Landru was a white slave trader, who had dispatched the women to brothels in Brazil, and that that was the real reason for the word Brazil appearing in the little black book. But the jury were not prepared to believe that Brazilians had a penchant for middle-aged widows.

There was uproar in court when Landru was convicted. Photographic flashlights exploded, men cheered, women fainted. Moro-Giafferi was shattered. He was convinced his man was not guilty, and immediately drew up a petition for mercy, which the jury signed. Landru, under the sentence of death, found himself in the bizarre position of consoling his crestfallen counsel.

Moro-Giafferi was there on the morning of 25 February, 1922, when Landru went to the guillotine. The prisoner refused offers of Mass and confession, and waved aside a tot of rum and a cigarette. Asked if he had anything to say, he retorted: 'Sir, to ask such a question at such a time is an insult. I have nothing to say.' But he turned to Moro-Giafferi, shook his hand, and said: '*Maître*, I thank you. You have had a desperate and difficult task to conduct. It is not the first time that an innocent man has been condemned.'

Landru begged them not to cut off the bushy red beard of which he was so proud. They merely trimmed it. Followed by his lawyer and the rejected priest, he walked out into the cold dawn air, shivering slightly with the cold, and muttering: 'I will be brave.'

His death solved none of the still unanswered questions. Had he killed all the women? If so, how? And how had he disposed so expertly of them, the murder weapons, and any other tell-tale clues? If he killed for money, why did he kill a penniless serving girl and the impecunious Madame Pascal? Was it because they discovered papers relating to the other women? Those questions will probably never be answered, despite an alleged confession printed by newspapers in 1968. The reports claimed that a framed picture given to a defence lawyer had the words, 'I did it, I burned their bodies in my kitchen oven' scribbled on the back.

The intriguing Landru story has two other odd postscripts. On the night before his execution, he wrote a letter to the man who had prosecuted him, the Advocate General *Maître* Godefroy, which was said to have greatly distressed the man. It read:

'Why could you not meet my gaze when I was brought back to court to hear my sentence? Why did you so indignantly rebuke the crowd for its unseemly behaviour? Why today are you still seeking for the vanished women, if you are so certain that I killed them?

It was all over. Sentence had been pronounced. I was calm. You were upset. Is there a conscience that troubles uncertain judges as it ought to trouble criminals? Farewell, *Monsieur*. Our common history will doubtless die tommorow. I die with an innocent and quiet mind. I hope respectfully that you may do the same.

Nearly 50 years after the execution, a film called *Landru*, scripted by novelist Françoise Sagan, was released. To the film-makers' astonishment, Landru's last mistress, Fernande Segret, turned up and sued them for 200,000 francs damages. She got 10,000. Since nothing had been heard of her for years, she had been presumed dead. In fact, she had been working as a governess in the Lebanon. After winning her case, she retired to an old people's home in Normandy. But the money did not buy her peace. She drowned herself, because she was tired of being pointed out as 'the woman in the Landru case.'

The Monster of the Andes

PEDRO LOPEZ

The guards fingered their pistols and watched nervously as the steel door to cell 14 was unlocked. There, in Ambato Jail, high up in the Andes mountains in Ecuador, was the man who held the world's most horrible distinction.

Inside, cowering in a corner of his cell in the women's section of the prison, was Pedro Alonzo Lopez. He was petrified that he might be burned alive, or castrated, by the other inmates or the guards themselves. Lopez, known in South America as 'the Monster of the Andes' had admitted to murdering 300 young girls. Lopez has been credited with being the world's worst mass sex killer, with the highest ever tally of victims.

Like most mass killers, Lopez' motive was sex. Before the 300 were strangled, they were first raped. Lopez did away with girls in this fashion at the rate of two a week for the three years he was on the rampage.

In Ambato alone, nestling 3,000 metres up in the Andes, the killer took police to the secret graves of the bodies of the 53 girls all aged between 8 and 12. At 28 other sites he described to police, bodies could not be found because the graves had been robbed by prowling animals. Some of the girls' bodies were buried at construction sites, and police have had to assume that they are now encased in concrete, perhaps never to resurface. Others are under roads.

In his confessions, Lopez admitted to killing 110 girls in Ecuador, another 100 in neighbouring Colombia and 'many more than 100' in Peru. Retired Major of Police, Victor Hugo Lascano, director of Ambato prison, said: 'We may never know exactly how many young girls Lopez killed. I believe his estimate of 300 is very low, because in the beginning he co-operated and took us each day to three or four hidden corpses. But then he tired, changed his mind and stopped helping.'

Lopez was eventually charged with 53 of the murders but another charge listed 110 more bodies named in his confession. Major Lascano said: 'If someone confesses to 53 you find, and hundreds more that you don't, you tend to believe what he says. What can he possibly invent that will save him from the law?'

In his cell in the women's section of Ambato Prison, Lopez was kept out of immediate danger from enraged guards and male prisoners. The women prisoners were considered to be in no danger themselves 'because his sex drive was geared only to young children.'

This mass child-killer was born the seventh son in a family of 13 children. His mother was a prostitute in the small Colombian town of Tolima, who threw him out onto the streets when he was eight for sexually fondling one of his younger sisters. A stranger found the boy crying and hungry, took him in his arms and promised to be his new father and care for him. Instead, the stranger took young Pedro to a deserted building and raped him. For the rest of his life, Lopez would be afraid to sleep indoors.

'I slept on the stairs of market places and plazas', he told police. 'I would look up and if I could see a star, I knew I was under the protection of God.'

In Bogota, an American family fed and clothed the street urchin, and enrolled him in a Colombian day school for orphans. When he was 12 he stole money from the school and ran away with a middle-aged woman teacher who wanted to have sex with him.

At 18 he stole a car and drove across Colombia. He was caught and jailed. On his second day in prison he was raped in his cell by four male prisoners. Lopez made himself a crude knife. Within two weeks, according to the story he told police, he had murderered three of the men: the fourth stumbled across their bodies and ran screaming through the prison. Lopez was given an additional two-year sentence for the killings, which were deemed self-defence.

Released from jail, Lopez found himself excited by pornographic magazines and movies. But he was afraid of women and therefore unable to communicate with them. 'I lost my innocence at the age of eight', he told police, 'so I decided to do the same to as many young girls as I could.'

By 1978, Lopez had killed more than 100 Peruvian girls, many of them belonging to indian tribes.

His crimes first came to light when he was caught by Ayacucho indians in the northern sector of Peru as he carried off a nine-year-old girl. They stripped and tortured him, then put him in a deep hole . . . they were going to bury him alive.

An American woman missionary saved his life. She convinced the indians that they should not commit murder. She took Lopez in her jeep to the police outpost. Within days he had been deported; the police did not want to bother with dead indian girls at that time. Only later, when the full story emerged, was a proper investigation begun.

Across the border in Ecuador the real killing spree then began. 'I liked the girls in Ecuador' Lopez told police. 'They are more gentle and trusting, and more innocent. They are not as suspicious of strangers as Colombian girls.'

Lopez would walk through market squares seeking out his victims. He said he deliberately sought out young girls with 'a certain look of innocence'. In graphic detail he told police how he would first introduce the children to sex, then strangle them.

I would become very excited watching them die.' 'I would stare into their eyes until I saw the light in them go out. The girls never really struggled – they didn't have time. I would bury a girl, then go out immediately and look for another one. I never killed any of them at night, because I wanted to watch them die by daylight.'

Police in the three countries were by now collating information, but they still did not realize they were looking for a mass killer. Their main theory was that an organization had been kidnapping the girls and transporting them to work as maids and prostitutes in large cities.

In April 1980, a rain-swollen river overflowed its banks near Ambato and horrified townspeople discovered the remains of four missing girls. Police launched a manhunt, but it was unsuccessful.

Days later, Carlina Ramon Poveda, working in the Plaza Rosa market, discovered her 12-year-old daughter Maria was missing. Frantically, she ran through the plaza, calling for her. She saw her walking out of the market, holding a stranger's hand.

Carlina followed her daughter and the tall man to the edge of town and then called for help. A dozen local indians jumped on Lopez and pulled him to the ground. They held him until the police arrived.

In jail awaiting trial, Lopez was tricked by police into making a confession. A priest, Pastor Cordoba Gudino, masqueraded as a fellow prisoner. For a month he stayed locked in the same cell as Lopez, and developed a behind-bars friendship with him. From the information he gave Gudino, the Ecuadoran police were able to extract a full confession from Lopez. Subsequent liaison with the police forces of Colombia and Peru substantiated Lopez's story.

Convicted of the murders in Ecuador, Lopez received a life sentence, which, in that country, means a maximum of 16 years, with good behaviour he could be a free man by 1990. Had he been convicted in Colombia, Lopez would be dead. There, the penalty for murder is death by firing squad.

The Murderous 'Family'

CHARLES MANSON

Charles Manson preached bloody revolution and ruled a satanic cult who killed at his bidding. He was sentenced to die in the gas chamber, but with the death sentence now abolished in California he is serving nine life sentences for nine murders. On his orders, his followers slaughtered the actress Sharon Tate, the wife of film producer Roman Polanski, and three friends at her Hollywood home in August, 1969.

Two nights later he sent his followers into action again to butcher close neighbours of the Polanskis, supermarket owner Leno la Bianca and his wife Rosemary. He was also found guilty of beheading stuntman Donald Shea and of ordering the execution of musician Gary Hinman.

Manson, 48, is the illegitimate son of a prostitute. When he was young his mother and brother were jailed for beating and robbing men she picked up.

At 11, Manson fell foul of the law and was sent to reform school. He spent the next 21 years in penal institutions, emerging at 32 never having slept with a woman or drunk a glass of beer. Confused by freedom, he caught a long-distance bus chosen at random and alighted at San Francisco's Haight-Ashbury district, centre of the world hippie movement.

It was 1967, the height of the peace-and-love flower-power era. Manson grew his hair long, wore a beard and played the guitar. Soon he had a circle of admirers. Girls came to kneel at his feet. One said: 'The first time I heard him sing, it was like an angel. He was magnetic.' Another, Lynette 'Squeaky' Fromme, said: 'With Charlie, I was riding on the wind. Making love with Charlie was guiltless, like a baby.'

But Manson had little respect for women. At the commune he set up in the Hollywood hills, they outnumbered men four-to-one. One of the rules of his 'family' was that the dogs had to be fed before the women. Girls had to submit instantly to the men Manson named. He banned contraceptives, alcohol and the wearing of spectacles. Questions by the girls were forbidden and they could not use the word 'Why?' But they worshipped him as a god.

Women would travel miles to ask him to sleep with them. A film actress who begged for his favours was told to first climb a nearby mountain. Another woman brought along her 15-year-old daughter. Manson told the mother to go because she was too old, and to leave her daughter. She obeyed.

Charles Manson, in the chapel of Vacaville jail, California

THE MURDEROUS 'FAMILY'

Manson's incredible magnetism gave him an entry to the wilder fringe of the Hollywood party circuit. It is almost certain he and some of his followers had been entertained by the Polanskis before the night Sharon and her friends died.

The slaughter was the culmination of months of testing to which Manson had subjected his disciples. Bored with their simple adoration of him, he started to organize law-breaking exercises. He made them steal cars, commit petty thefts and prowl round people's homes in 'creepy-crawling' black clothes. Then he ordered them to Sharon Tate's house to terrorize a man whom he said had broken several promises to him.

Polanski was in Europe making a film, and he asked an old friend, Voytek Frykowski and his girlfriend Abigail Folger, to move in with Sharon to keep her company.

On the evening of 8 August, Jay Sebring, Sharon's ex-lover and now a friend, had dropped in too. They and an 18-year-old youth visiting Frykowski, were to die horribly that night at the hands of three girls and an ex-football star, trusted members of Manson's inner circle. Sharon, who was eight months pregnant, was stabbed 16 times. The word 'Pig' was written in her blood on the front door.

Today the man whose reign of bloody terror stunned the world is serving out his sentence as caretaker of the prison chapel at Vacaville, in southern California. He is unrepentant about the past, claiming to feel no guilt for the bestial crimes committed at his command. He told the British photographer Albert Foster: 'I am not ashamed or sorry. If it takes fear and violence to open the eyes of the dollar-conscious society, the name Charles Manson can be that fear.'

Inset: Sharon Tate with Roman Polanski at their wedding, 1968

Bad But Not Mad

PETER MANUEL

Sentencing Peter Thomas Anthony Manuel to death at Glasgow in May, 1958, the judge Lord Cameron said: 'A man may be very bad without being mad.' Manual, who callously killed at least nine people, certainly qualified as very bad. But does a sane man pick victims at random, murder for no apparent reason, attempt to extort money from a man he has made a widower, then eagerly offer the evidence that will lead him to the gallows?

Manuel was certainly no fool. Halfway through his trial, he dismissed his lawyers and conducted his own defence so well that Lord Cameron congratulated him on his peformance. He used legal knowledge studied during his frequent prison sentences for burglary, theft, indecent assault, rape and violence. But he forgot one vital fact: in Scotland, a multi-murderer is charged with every killing. In England, on the other hand, he would have been charged with only one of them, on the grounds that evidence of other crimes might prejudice a jury unfairly.

Manuel's astonishing record as a killer reads like that of a gangster in Chicago, and he would have been proud of the comparison. He was, in fact, born in America. His parents left Scotland for New York in the 1920s, and Peter was born there in 1927. But the Depression forced them back to Britain, and their misfit son was soon in trouble. By the time he was 16, a senior probation officer said he had the worst record he had ever known in a boy. In January 1956, Manuel added murder to that record.

Anne Kneilands was just 17 years old. She was waiting for her boyfriend in an East Kilbride street when Manuel met her. He had rugged, Teddy Boy good looks, and she agreed to go to a nearby cafe with him. But as he walked her home later, he suddenly dragged her into a wood, and smashed her to death, beating her skull with a piece of iron.

Police were baffled by the seemingly motiveless attack. They interviewed all the possible suspects on their books, including Manuel, but put the scratches on his face down to Hogmanay excesses. Manuel had had enough police interviews in his life to know exactly what to say.

During that summer Manuel, the rebel without a cause, decided he needed a gun. His criminal ego was growing. He had killed once and got away with it. He could do it again.

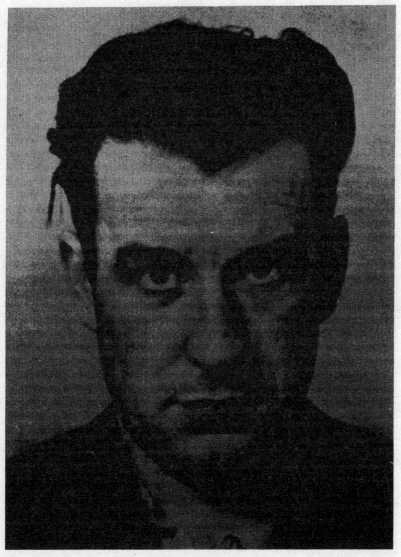

Peter Manuel

Isabelle Cooke, murdered in January, 1958

On 16 September, 1956, he and two other men and a woman went on a robbery expedition to the wealthy area of High Burnside, a few miles south of Glasgow. They plundered one empty house, and even started a drinking party there. Manuel pointed out another home nearby, but the others were reluctant to stage a second break-in. Manuel went alone.

Getting in on the ground floor, he went straight upstairs, and saw two women asleep in one room. He opened another bedroom door, and saw 16-year-old Vivienne Watt. She was awake, and sat up in fear when she spotted him. Manuel bounded across the room, knocked her out and tied her up. Then he returned to the other room. Mrs Marion Watt, a semi-invalid and Vivienne's mother, was still asleep. So was her sister, Mrs Margaret Brown. Manuel calmly drew his gun and shot them both at close range. Then he walked back to Vivienne, who had come round and was struggling with her bonds. Holding her roughly down on the bed, he shot her through the left eye.

Manuel interfered with the night-dresses of all three women but, again, did not touch them. Expert witnesses later declared that he got sexual satisfaction from killing without the need for contact. It was 03.00 when he rejoined his pals in the first house, and about 05.00 when they went back to Glasgow.

But Manuel's shot had not killed Vivienne instantly. Her body was still warm when the family's daily help arrived next morning. And if that gave Manuel added satisfaction, the next development delighted his twisted mind. Police arrested Mrs Watt's husband, William, and accused him of the three murders.

Mr Watt, a baker, had been staying at a hotel in Lochgilphead, Argyll, 80 miles away, on the night of the killings. Witnesses had seen him there at midnight and 08.00. But police proved it was possible for him to have driven to his home and back comfortably in those eight hours. And they had witnesses who swore they had seen Mr Watt in his car on the Renfrew Ferry at 03.00.

The unfortunate man spent two months in prison before he was set free. The police could find no reason why a prosperous, loving father would kill his happy family. But Mr Watt's ordeal was not over. For Peter Manuel, who had equally little reason for killing his loved ones, now tried to extort money from the bereaved man. First he told Watt's solicitor he could name the Burnside murderer for a price. Then he met Mr Watt, and offered to remove lingering suspicions by killing the Burnside murderer, and making it look like suicide. It would only cost £120. The baker declined.

Manuel was playing with fire, but amazingly he got away with it. And he was also continuing to kill. On 8 December, 1957, he took a train to Newcastle upon Tyne, south of the border. He then took a taxi and ordered Sidney Dunn, the driver, to a deserted moorland road near Edmondbyers, then shot and stabbed him. Just after Christmas, he met 17-year-old Isabelle Cooke on the outskirts of Glasgow, dragged her into a field, tore off most of her clothes, and strangled her.

He then buried the girl he had never seen before in a shallow grave.

While the rest of Scotland was sleeping off Hogmanay, Manuel broke into the Glasgow bungalow of Peter Smart on New Year's Day, 1958. He found £25 in a wallet, and could have left undetected because Mr Smart, his wife Doris and their son Michael had not heard a thing. Instead, Manuel went into their bedrooms and shot all three dead. Then he calmly fed two tins of salmon to the family cat.

But at last Manuel had made a mistake. Under routine surveillance as he was after every major crime, he was seen passing some new blue £5 notes – notes of the type Peter Smart had drawn from the bank before his death. The home Manuel shared with his parents was searched, and after discovering housebreaking equipment, the police arrested both Manuel and his father. Manuel then agreed to make a statement on condition his father was released.

What he told them was an emotionless, detailed story of his murders. The cold-blooded confession stunned hardened officers, who reported that, when he led them to Isabelle Cooke's grave, he said almost light-heartedly: 'This is the place. In fact, I think I'm standing on her now.'

Manuel craved the limelight, and longed to be feared as a big man. But neither the police, nor the court, were awed by his exploits. After listening to 250 witnesses and a three-hour closing speech from Manuel himself, the jury found him guilty of seven of the eight murders with which he was charged – the Newcastle killing was outside Scottish jurisdiction, and the killing of Anne Kneilands was not proven for lack of evidence.

Peter Manuel, a particularly vicious and wanton murderer, was hanged at Glasgow's Barlinnie Prison on 11 July, 1958.

The Prince of Poisoners

WILLIAM PALMER

William Palmer has gone down in history as the Prince of Poisoners, a murderer so notorious that the town where he practised his evil arts applied to the prime minister for permission to change its name. Palmer's trial has been hailed as the most sensational of the nineteenth century. What made it so was not that he was the first prisoner to use strychnine, but the incredible story of debauchery and lust that unfolded. For Palmer and his wretched relatives were leftovers from an earlier age. And an England trying to get used to the puritanism of Queen Victoria lapped up each lurid detail of Palmer's Regency lifestyle – sex, gambling, drinking, scandal . . . and murder.

Palmer was born in Rugeley, Staffordshire, in 1824, the second son of a sawyer who had swindled his employer, the Marquess of Anglesey, out of £70,000 by selling his timber, and a woman whose uncle had fathered an incestuous granddaughter by his own illegitimate daughter. Such a heritage need not have brought out the worst in young William – four of his brothers and sisters led perfectly normal lives. But his eldest sister, Mary Ann, turned to promiscuity, taking after her mother; his brother Walter became an alcoholic; and William himself turned to a life of wine, women and gambling – funded by theft and fraud.

His father died when he was 12, but any hopes William had of enjoying a life of leisure on his legacy were dashed when he received only a £7,000 share of the ill-gotten fortune. When Palmer left school, he was apprenticed to a Liverpool firm of chemists, Evans and Evans, but the demands of his heavy flutters on the horses, entertaining the ladies, and keeping up with the rich, idle circle of friends he formed soon exhausted his allowance. Palmer began stealing money sent with orders he collected for the firm from the Post Office. He was soon discovered and sacked.

His mother settled the bill for the missing cash and sent him to work for a surgeon, Edward Tylecote. Though outwardly industrious and ambitious, Palmer was more intent on profit and profligacy than medicine. He stole from his employer and took advantage of his position to seduce his patients. It is estimated that he fathered 14 illegitimate children during the five years he worked for Tylecote. Eventually the surgeon lost patience with his troublesome

127

assistant, and enrolled him as a 'walking pupil' at Stafford Infirmary. Palmer quickly found that this in no way lessened his opportunities for sex and stealing, and he also grabbed the chance to indulge a new passion – poisons. The hospital authorities were so alarmed by his activities that they barred him from the dispensary, but Palmer was not so easily rebuffed.

In 1846, an inquest was held at Stafford into the death of a man called Abley. He had been unwise enough to accept a challenge to a drinking bout from Palmer, who was having an affair with his wife. After only two tumblers of brandy, Abley was violently sick, and died within minutes. Though the authorities were suspicious, nothing could be proved against Palmer, who left shortly after the death to continue his studies at St Bartholomew's Hospital in London. In retrospect, most experts believe Abley was the poisoner's first victim in what may have been a toxicological experiment.

Palmer squandered more than £2,000 during a riotous year in London – an enormous sum in those days – and only just managed to qualify as a doctor. But in one subject he was top of his class. The only note he made in one of his textbooks was: 'Strychnine kills by causing tetanic fixing of the respiratory muscles.'

In August 1846, Palmer was back in Rugeley, setting up his practice in a large house opposite the Talbot Arms Inn. The lascivious reputation of both his widowed mother and himself made the locals far from eager to put their lives in his hands, and Palmer had few patients to keep him away from his first love, the race track. But already he was tumbling into debt, and was anxious to cut his expenditure in other directions. One day he asked to see the illegitimate daughter he had fathered by a maid he had known when working for Dr Tylecote. She died shortly after returning to her mother the same evening. Soon other illegitimate offspring unaccountably suffered fatal convulsions after licking the honey their fond father spread on his finger.

In 1847, Palmer took himself a wife. Ann Brookes was herself illegitimate. Her father, an Indian Army colonel, had committed suicide, and her mother, the colonel's former housekeeper, had taken refuge in drink. Both were well provided for, the widow inheriting property worth £12,000, the daughter living on the interest of £8,000 capital as a ward of court. One of her two guardians was a cousin of Palmer's former employer, Dr Tylecote, and was opposed to the marriage, but Palmer successfully asked the courts for permission to wed their charge. From all accounts, the two were very much in love, and their happiness was clouded only by the way their children kept dying. Four were killed by mysterious convulsions when only days or weeks old between 1851 and 1854. Only the eldest boy, Willy, survived.

Several of Palmer's relatives and racing companions were not so lucky. He called on his uncle, Joseph Bentley, a drunken degenerate, and suggested a trial

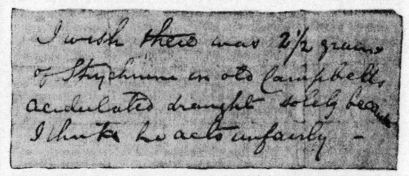

A note written by William Palmer to his council while in the dock at the Old Bailey

of drinking strength. Again, sharing brandy with Palmer proved a sickening experience. The uncle died three days later, leaving his nephew a few hundred pounds. In 1848, Palmer invited his mother-in-law to stay at Rugeley. Though an alcoholic, she still had enough of her wits about her to detest her daughter's husband. She confided to a friend before the journey to Rugeley: 'I know I shan't live a fortnight.' She died ten days after arriving.

That nobody found anything suspicious in the deaths of those around Palmer was due in large measures to his performance as an actor. To the community, he was a respected, church-going, unctious man, charming, pious, kind and generous. His wife believed he was doing his best to save her mother when he gave her medication and personally prepared her food.

Palmer also allayed suspicion by calling in a second opinion, a good-hearted, doddering local doctor named Bamford, who was over 80 and prepared to agree with his young friend's diagnoses. When Palmer told him death was due to apoplexy or English cholera, Bamford obligingly signed death certificates to that effect.

The death of Palmer's mother-in-law was not as profitable as he expected. Her property was tied up, and what little money accrued to the grieving newly-weds was only a drop in the ocean of the doctor's gambling debts. Already he owed thousands of pounds to a dubious Mayfair lawyer, Thomas Pratt, and lesser sums to Midlands' moneylenders called Padwick and Wright. His attempts to remove his own relatives continued, but when the wife of another uncle became ill while paying him a visit, she refused to take the pills he proferred, throwing them out of a window instead. Palmer managed to explain away the fact that chickens who pecked at the pills were dead next morning.

He turned his attentions to his racing companions. He owed a man called Leonard Bladen £800 after a run of back luck. He invited him to Rugeley, and after a convivial evening, the guest took to his bed with a stomach upset. Within a week he was dead. Bladen's wife, who heard about the illness from a third party, arrived just before the end, but was upset at not being allowed to see the body. She was also perturbed to be told that her husband had only £15 on him, and that Palmer expected £59 from the man's estate to settle a gambling debt. Her friends urged her to go to the police, but she refused, out of consideration for Mrs Palmer. Another gambler called Bly also learned how lethal it could be to win money from Palmer. Mrs Palmer was becoming upset at the string of deaths in the house. 'My mother died here last year, now these men,' she wailed. 'What will people say?'

Towards the end of 1853, Palmer's finances were in a more hopeless state than ever. He backed one of his own horses, Nettle, to win £10,000 in the Oaks. It lost. Twice he was declared a defaulter on bets, and barred from Tattersalls, the Mecca of the racing establishment. Pratt, Padwick and Wright were all becoming increasingly strident in their demands for payment – and interest on his gambling debts was now running into thousands of pounds. Palmer needed money desperately – desperately enough to kill the wife he loved.

In January 1854, the month he poisoned his fourth child, he took out three life insurance policies on Mrs Palmer, for a total of £13,000. They were arranged with the help of Pratt and a local attorney, Jeremiah Smith. Smith was having an affair with Palmer's mother, now aged over 60, but was not anxious for the news to be broadcast. Palmer knew of the liaison, and had used it to pressure Smith into helping him forge his mother's signature on guarantees for his own debts. Now Smith helped to fix up the three life policies – two, with Norwich Union and Sun Insurance, for £5,000 each, one, with the Prince of Wales company, for £3,000. The premium was a total of £760 a year, and apparently none of the companies bothered to ask how a country doctor with little income and a penchant for betting could afford to pay so much. In fact, Palmer borrowed the money from Pratt.

The Roman Emperor Tiberius was incredibly strong – he could poke his finger through an apple – but his weaknesses were even more dramatic. His lusts knew no bounds. He once broke the legs of two priests when they did not react favourably to his advances. And he would often have his lovers tortured and murdered when he no longer found them amusing.

Palmer managed to tide himself over during the summer, but a fresh cash crisis hit him in September. As luck would have it, his wife returned from visiting relatives in Liverpool with a chill. She took to her bed, and Palmer's devoted care soon turned a minor ailment into chronic antimony poisoning.

This time, he took the precaution of calling in not only Dr Bamford, but also his wife's former guardian, the once-suspicious Dr Knight. He too was now an octogenarian, and, like Bamford, was prepared to concur with Palmer's diagnosis. All three signed a death certificate citing English cholera. Palmer seemed distraught at the death, weeping and sobbing inconsolably. But he still managed to spend that night with his maid, Eliza Tharm, who gave birth to a child exactly nine months later.

At first the insurance companies were reluctant to settle the policies Palmer had taken out such a short time before. They were suspicious at such a sudden death in a seemingly healthy woman of 27. But faced with the verdicts of two doctors of good repute, they decided not to call for an inquest, and Palmer was given his money. He immediately gave £8,000 to Pratt and £5,000 to Wright. But Padwick stepped up his demands, and Pratt was soon insisting on further efforts to settle Palmer's account. Shrugging off the suspicions of the insurance companies, Palmer decided they were the best policy for saving him from ruin.

With Pratt's help, he devised a scheme to cover the life of his brother Walter, a bankrupt dipsomaniac, for an astonishing £82,000. The total was split between six companies, and Palmer persuaded Walter to co-operate by promising to lend him £400, and by offering to provide him with the drinks that Walter's wife was rationing.

The insurance companies, once bitten, were shy about dealing with the Palmer family again. Walter's doctor, a man called Waddell, signed one application form, declaring that his patient was 'healthy, robust and temperate'. But he added in a covering note: 'Most confidential. His life has been rejected in two offices. I am told he drinks. His brother insured his late wife's life for many thousands, and after the first payment she died. Be cautious.'

Palmer finally secured policies to a total of £13,000, invited his brother to Rugeley, and for five months plied him with gin. It has been estimated that Walter drank 19 gallons of the spirit before leaving for home in July, 1855. Palmer arranged to meet his brother at Wolverhampton races on 14 August, and prepared for the encounter by buying some prussic acid. Again Walter embarked on a gin binge, but this time the drinks were laced. Two days later he was dead of an apoplectic fit. By the time his widow learned of his demise, the body was already in its coffin.

Palmer instantly applied for the life insurance policies to be paid up, but the companies delayed settlement until they had investigated further. Palmer would have been wise to wait, but Pratt, who had been assigned the policy on

Walter as security for loans of £11,500, would not let him. In September, he demanded a £6,000 payment. Palmer desperately tried to take out new insurance policies on George Bate, whom he described as a 'gentleman farmer'. When the companies investigated, they found they were being asked to take a £25,000 risk on a penniless undergroom at Palmer's stables.

Palmer was told there would be no policy on Bate's life – and no payment on the insurance for Walter. If he went to court to claim his £13,000, they said, they would counter claim with a charge of murder. Palmer was now in desperate straits. Pratt was threatening to sue for his money by issuing writs against Palmer's mother, the unwitting guarantor. Palmer knew that the penalty for forging signatures was transportation. He also had a new problem to contend with. Some years earlier he had arranged an abortion for a Stafford girl, Jane Burgess, whom he had made pregnant. He unwisely sent her passionate love letters, described by one author who read them as 'too coarse to print'. Palmer had urged the girl to burn them, but she was not that foolish. Now she wrote to him, threatening blackmail.

On 13 November, 1855, Palmer went to Shrewsbury races with his pal John Parsons Cook, a 27-year-old rake who had squandered a £12,000 legacy from his father, but aimed to recoup some of it on his horse Polestar in the Shrewsbury Handicap. To the delight of both men, Polestar won. Cook collected £800 in cash from bets on the course, and unwisely showed Palmer a betting slip from Tattersalls for a further £1,200.

Cook, like Palmer, was generous in sharing his successes. He and a party of friends celebrated the victory with a slap-up champagne supper at the Raven Hotel in Shrewsbury. But after accepting a glass of brandy from Palmer, he was violently ill. He handed over his cash winnings to another man, saying: 'I believe that damned Palmer has dosed me.' Yet he agreed to Palmer's suggestion next morning that he come back to Rugeley for medical treatment.

Cook took rooms in the Talbot Arms, where Palmer, living just across the road, could keep a careful eye on him. On Friday, 16 November, Cook dined with Palmer and Jeremiah Smith. Next morning, he was again violently sick. Palmer kept popping in with medicines, and on the Sunday sent some broth across to the inn. A chambermaid who tasted it while heating it retched for the next five hours, but nobody blamed the broth, and Palmer was allowed to take a bowl up to his friend. Dr Bamford had already been called in for consultations, and by the Monday Cook was feeling a little better. This could have been because Palmer had gone up to London to cash Cook's betting slip at Tattersalls, and pay £450 of it to Pratt.

There could now be no turning back for Palmer. He returned to Rugeley at 22.00, and bought three grains of strychnine from the local surgeon's assistant on his way to the Talbot Arms. That night, Cook went through agony.

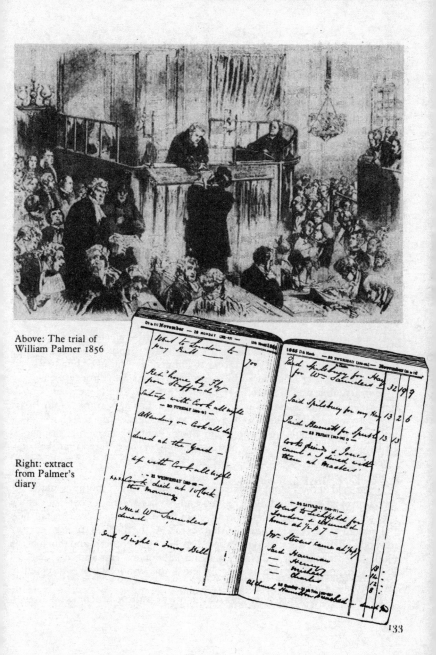

Above: The trial of William Palmer 1856

Right: extract from Palmer's diary

Chambermaid Elizabeth Mills was with him. She said later: 'He was sitting up beating the bedclothes with his hands. His body, his hands and his neck were moving then – a sort of jumping or jerking. Sometimes he would throw himself back on the pillow and then raise himself up again. He screamed three or four times and called out "Murder" '.

Next day, Cook refused to take any more medication. But Palmer had summoned Cook's own physician, Dr William Jones, from Lutterworth, and he, Bamford and Palmer persuaded the patient to take some pills made up by Dr Bamford. He agreed, not realizing that Bamford had given the pills to Palmer, who had bought more strychnine that morning, along with some prussic acid.

Cook's long ordeal was almost over. At midnight on Tuesday, the jangling bell in his room sent Elizabeth and her fellow chambermaid Lavinia Barnes hurrying upstairs. The patient was arched in excruciatingly painful contortions, resting only on his head and heels, as Dr Jones massaged his neck. Curiously, Cook was screaming for Palmer. One of the girls ran to the doctor's house, and found him fully dressed and ready. He forced two more pills through Cook's clenched teeth, and the poor man writhed in new agonies before slumping, lifeless, on the bed. The two chambermaids had watched the death scene in the errie candlelight with terrified awe. Now Elizabeth was amazed to see Palmer going through the dead man's pockets.

Desperation had forced the maniacal medic to throw all caution to the wind. he had already persuaded the Rugeley postmaster, Samuel Cheshire, to help him forge a cheque for £350 from Cook to Palmer. Now he asked him to witness a document saying Cook owed him another £4,000. Cheshire refused.

More trouble was in store for Palmer. On Friday, 23 November, Cook's stepfather, William Stevens, arrived in Rugeley. The appearance of the body, the haste with which it had been given to an undertaker, the search of Cook's pockets, and the claim for money from Cook's estate all made him suspicious. Unhappy with the stated cause of death, apoplexy, he ordered that the room where the body lay be locked, and left for London to see a solicitor, and demand a post-mortem.

It was held at the Talbot Arms on the following Monday morning, under the direction of a Dr Harland. Both Palmer and Bamford were present – one of the rare occasions a murderer has taken part in the search for clues to his murder. Palmer did all he could to obstruct that search. As the medical students cutting the body lifted out the stomach, Palmer brushed against them, and much of the vital contents spilled irretrievably back into abdomen. Harland reprimanded Palmer, assuming the doctor was playing a joke, and Palmer whispered to Bamford: 'They won't hang us yet.'

The stomach and intestines were sealed into a bottle, to be sent for analysis in

London. Then the bottle disappeared. Harland angrily demanded to know where it was, and Palmer produced it from behind his back. There were two cuts in the air-proof lid. Still Palmer would not admit defeat. He offered the post-boy £10 if he would upset the carriage taking Stevens and the bottle to Stafford to catch the London train. The boy refused.

Palmer waited impatiently for the results of the London autopsy. He learned them before anyone else. Postmaster Cheshire was in the habit of allowing his friend to read any mail that interested him, and Palmer was delighted to intercept the report from the analyst. No poison had been found, apart from slight traces of antimony.

Palmer now took leave of his senses. He wrote two letters to the coroner, saying he was confident of a 'death by natural causes' verdict at the inquest – and enclosing the gift of some game and a £5 note. The coroner handed both letters and gifts to the police and recorded a verdict of wilful murder. Palmer, already in the custody of the sherrif's officer because of his debts, was arrested and taken to Stafford jail.

The bodies of his wife Ann and brother Walter were exhumed for post-mortems, and soon all England was talking of the Rugeley poisoner, attributing him with even more grisly deeds than those that were suspected. A special Act of Parliament, still known as 'Palmer's Law', had to be passed to transfer the trial from Stafford to the Old Bailey in London. Local prejudice was the given reason – and according to one of Palmer's defence team, Edward Kenealy, it was the fear that a local jury would never convict him. Kenealy wrote in his memoirs: 'Palmer was such a general favourite and had so many personal friends and acquaintances that no verdict of guilty could have been obtained.'

The Crown had no such problems at the Old Bailey. The trial, which began on 14 May, 1856, attracted intense attention from high society. The courtroom was packed each day, and outside throngs of spectators blocked the pavements to watch the protagonists arrive and leave. Bound volumes of verbatim evidence sold in their thousands, even though much of it was conflicting technical jargon from medical men.

The prosecution, led by Attorney-General Sir Alexander Cockburn made problems for itself by specifying that Cook was murdered by strychnine. Though Palmer was known to have bought it, no traces were found in Cook's corpse. Both sides brought in batteries of experts to try to explain this. Palmer's attorney, Serjeant Shee, berated one doctor for cruelty to animals after he spoke of the effects of strychnine on rabbits. Another man said the state of Cook's stomach when it reached London would have made establishing cause of death virtually impossible, 'if I had not been informed that there was a considerable quantity of strychnine present.'

Medical science knew little about the relatively new poison, or how to detect it, and some experts were prepared to swear that Palmer had found ways of disguising it. If so, he was not about to share the secret. There was little doubt that Palmer was guilty of poisoning Cook, and the jury and three judges were happy to go along with the Attorney-General's convenient theory: that Cook had been softened up with other poisons, then finished off by strychnine in an almost imperceptible dose. On 27 May, having listened to a masterly closing oration from Sir Alexander Cockburn, and a strong recommendation to convict from Lord Chief Justic Campbell, the jury took one hour to find Palmer guilty of murder.

He accepted sentence of death philosophically, and was taken back to Stafford under strong escort. He showed little sign of conscience or depression in prison, except when news that the Home Secretary had rejected his appeal came through, and to the end refused to make any confession, beyond saying, ambiguously: 'I am innocent of poisoning Cook by strychnine.'

Nearly 30,000 people were outside Stafford Jail on the morning of 14 June, 1856. Packed trains arrived in the town from the early hours, and spectators paid up to a guinea to take their places on the 23 platforms erected to give them a better view. When Palmer arrived, apparently indifferent to and amused by his fate, police had trouble controlling the mob as it surged forward. The sensational details of his sordid life had enthralled the nation, but there was nothing exceptional about his death at the end of the rope.

Few murderers have rivalled William Palmer for cold-hearted, premeditated callousness and cruelty. Though convicted and hanged for only one killing, he was suspected of at least 15 more, many of the victims being innocent children he fathered through debauched lechery. But even his horrific story has two wry postscripts. The moneylenders who hounded him received nothing after his death, because his mother refused to honour forged guarantees. And when the town of Rugeley, shamed by the notoriety brought on it by its infamous son, applied to change its name, the prime minister is alleged to have replied: 'By all means, provided you name your town after me.' His name was Lord Palmerston.

The Murderous Musician
CHARLES PEACE

What kind of man could sit calmly in a court's public gallery and watch another condemned to die for a murder he had committed? Charles Peace could. And it was only after his arrest, two years later, for another murder, that he made a full confession to a chaplain and saved the innocent prisoner's life. For stony-hearted Peace lived his criminal life by the maxim, 'If I make up my mind to a thing, I am bound to have it.' And for 20 years, he had made up his mind to be one of England's most cunning crooks.

Peace was a small, wiry man who walked with a limp and used an artificial hook arm to conceal the loss of two fingers in a childhood accident. He played the violin well enough to be billed at local concerts as 'The Modern Paganini'. But at night, he turned into an expert cat-burglar, carrying his tools in a violin case and using his monkey-like agility and phenomenal strength to plunder from the rooftops. For many years he wandered from town to town, until 1872, when he returned to his native Sheffield with his wife Hannah and their son Willie, and set up shop as a picture framer and bric-a-brac dealer in Darnall.

He was then 40, an ugly man whose tongue seemed too big for his mis-shaped mouth. Yet he seems to have had a way with certain women. He began an illicit affair with Mrs Katherine Dyson, the buxom wife of one of his neighbours in Britannia Road, visiting pubs to satisfy her craving for drink, then going to the attic of a nearby empty house to satisfy his own cravings. Soon Peace grew less cautious, calling on the Dysons whenever the fancy took him, and eventually Katherine's husband Arthur, a giant of over 2 metres in height, banned him from the house.

But Peace could not stand rebuffs. Mrs Dyson recalled later: 'I can hardly describe all that he did to annoy us . . . he would come and stand outside the window at night and look in, leering all the while. He had a way of creeping and crawling about, and of coming on you suddenly unawares.' The Dysons went to the police after their persecutor made threats at gunpoint in July 1876, but he fled to Hull to escape the arrest warrant that was issued. The Dysons decided to move home, to Banner Cross Terrace, Ecclesall Road, but when they arrived at what they thought would be their haven, Peace walked out of the front door, declaring: 'I am here to annoy you and I will annoy you wherever you go.'

On the evening of 29 November, Mrs Dyson left the house to visit the outside

WC. Peace was waiting in the shadows, holding a gun. Her shriek brought her husband running from the parlour, and he chased Peace down the alleyway that ran behind the terraced houses. When they reached the street, two shots were heard in rapid succession, and Dyson fell dying, a bullet in his head. Peace fled, dropping as he went a bundle of notes Mrs Dyson had written him. And though a reward of £100 was put on his head by police, he evaded capture, burgling his way from town to town until he reached London, and set up home in Evelina Road, Peckham.

It was a strange household. His wife Hannah and their son lived in the basement, while Peace and his mistress masqueraded as Mr and Mrs Thompson on the floor above, throwing musical parties for new friends and neighbours, and attending church every Sunday. Eventually the 'Thompsons' had a baby boy.

Peace cultivated a respectable image quite deliberately, saying: 'The police never think of suspecting anyone who wears good clothes.' He dyed his grey hair black, shaved off his beard. By day he drove his cart round south London, ostensibly collecting other people's unwanted possession. At night he went out and stole the possessions they were not so keen to lose. Though his exploits made the newspapers, police had no idea who the daring raider was, and Peace made the most of their ignorance. He delighted in chatting to policemen he met on trains, and even shared lodgings with an officer while staying briefly in Bristol.

But on 10 October, 1878, his luck ran out. Police were waiting in force outside a house in Blackheath when Peace emerged at 02.00 carrying a silver flask, a letter case and a cheque book. The cornered villain threatened them with a gun, and fired four shots, but the officers ignored him. The fifth shot struck PC Edward Robinson in the arm, but he still managed to overpower the gunman with colleagues, inflicting quite a beating-up in the process.

Peace was tried under the false name he gave, John Ward, for attempted murder, and the Old Bailey jury took four minutes to find him guilty. Despite a whining personal plea for mercy from the 'most wretched, miserable man,' he was jailed for life. Then his mistress revealed his true identity so she could collect the £100 murder reward still on offer at Sheffield. Police brought Mrs Dyson from her native America, where she had gone after the death of her husband, and charged Peace.

On 22 January, 1879, two warders accompanied the handcuffed prisoner on to the 05.00 express from London to Sheffield. He proved troublesome throughout the journey, and when the train reached Yorkshire, he flung himself out of a window. The warders stopped the train and ran back a mile to find him unconscious in the snow, having landed on his head. Committal proceedings were held outside his cell in Sheffield, and Peace was sent for trial at Leeds.

The jury took 12 minutes to find Peace guilty, and he was condemned to

Engraved portrait of Charles Peace at his trial

An artist's impression of Charles Peace escaping from the train

death. He spent the days before the execution writing moralistic letters and praying. And he also revealed to the chaplain, the Rev J. H. Littlewood, that four months before the death of Dyson he had shot and killed a policeman who disturbed him during a robbery at Whalley Range, Manchester.

Even more chillingly, he confessed that he had sat in the gallery at Manchester Assizes when two Irish brothers were charged with the death, and had watched 18-year-old William Habron be sentenced to death on 28 November just 24 hours before he shot Dyson. 'What man would have done otherwise in my position?' he said when asked why he had remained silent at such a blatant miscarriage of justice.

Habron was pardoned and given £800 compensation, and at 08.00 on 25 February, 1879, aged 46, Charles Peace took his place on the scaffold at Armley Jail, Leeds, after complaining bitterly about the 'bloody rotten bacon' he was served for his last breakfast. Though he pretended contrition and trust in God in an odious final speech, he confessed to the chaplain: 'My great mistake, sir, has been this: in all my career I have used ball cartridge; I ought to have used blank.' His last words before Marwood the executioner pulled the trapdoor lever were: 'I should like a drink; have you a drink to give me?' And he left his own epitaph in his cell. He was executed, he wrote, 'for what I done but never intended.'

The Triangular Chamber of Death

DR MARCEL PETIOT

Few mass killers have cashed in on the chaos of war as profitably as Dr Marcel Petiot. When the guillotine sliced his scheming head from his body on the morning of 26 May, 1946, he had made more than a million pounds from murder. And but for foolish pride, the 49-year-old doctor, might have escaped to enjoy his ill-gotten gains.

The medical profession was a natural choice of career for a man who showed sadistic tendencies even as a boy in his native Auxerre, where he relished cruelty to animals and smaller children. He spent World War One in a casualty clearing station at Dijon, peddling stolen morphia to drug addicts, before entering an asylum, where he studied medicine. By 1921 he had qualified as a doctor, and set up a practice in Villeneuve-sur-Yonne.

Flouting the Hippocratic oath, Petiot quickly prescribed a life of luxury for himself. He overcharged the rich while treating the poor for free. And villagers soon realized that Petiot was the man to see if they wanted drugs or illegal abortions. The mysterious disappearance of his young and pretty housekeeper when she became pregnant, and strange cries of pain from the good doctor's house, caused no more than idle gossip, and Petiot was soon sufficiently well-regarded to be elected Mayor.

But by 1930 life at Villeneuve had become too hot for him. One of his patients, a local shopkeeper, was robbed and killed, and Petiot was suspected, though nothing could be proved. Another patient persisted in accusing the doctor while continuing to visit him for treatment for his rheumatism. When he died suddenly, Petiot wrote 'natural causes' on the death certificate, and headed for bigger things in Paris.

Again his readiness to supply addictive drugs and terminate unwanted pregnancies soon earned him plenty of loyal patients. Quickly his practice at 60 Rue Caumartin became one of the most lucrative in the city. Petiot kept up the pretence of the good citizen – model husband and father, attending church each Sunday. His outward respectability helped him survive a fine for drug offences and the disappearance of a woman who unwisely accused him of turning her daughter into a junkie. Then, in 1940, the Nazi army marched into Paris. And Petiot seized the chance to set up a sinister sideline that satisifed both his passion for profits and his sadistic perversions.

Dr Marcel Petiot, aged 49 in the Seine Assize Court

Gestapo activity had turned the French capital into a city of fear. Jews disappeared to concentration camp gas chambers, able-bodied Frenchmen were rounded up for labour camps, and those left behind soon learned that it did not pay to ask too many questions about friends who vanished. The situation was ideal for what Petiot had in mind.

He bought a disused mansion at 21 Rue Lesueur for half a million franc, then set about modifying it for his purposes. The house included a sound-proof triangular room with no windows and only one door. Petiot installed peepholes, telling the builders the room was for his mental patients. He installed a furnace in the cellar under the garage. Shortly before Christmas, 1941, everything was ready.

Petiot now spread the word that he was in touch with the French Resistance, and could smuggle people hunted by the Gestapo to safety in Spain or Cuba. The desperate refugees who contacted him were told that their escape would be costly, and that they would need innoculations before being allowed into their new lands. Such was their state of fear that they readily agreed, selling up all their possessions to meet the bills, or giving them to Petiot. One of the first customers, a Polish-born tailor, paid two million francs to get himself and his family out of France. One by one, they crept surreptitiously to Rue Lesueur, bared their arms for the necessary injections, and were ushered into the hidden triangular room. None of them left it alive.

When the doctor was satisfied, via his peepholes, that his deadly serum had done its work, he dragged the bodies to the cellar, where he treated them in quicklime – bought in bulk from his brother Maurice at Auxerre – before stuffing them into his grisly furnace. Then he scrupulously noted the details of each transaction – the money, jewellery, furs, gold and silver each victim had handed over.

As word spread, more and more customers queued at Petiot's door – Jews, people who had fallen foul of the Gestapo, rich families who were not prepared to wait until France was free of the Nazi terror. Petiot even dispatched a friend of his, Dr Paul Braumberger, a drug addict whose prostitute companion was appropriated by German troops, making it impossible for her earn the money to satisfy his cravings.

For 18 months, Petiot was able to combine curing patients at Rue Caumartin with killing them at Rue Lesueur. Though his wife noted how tired he was becoming, she never suspected the evil nature of his extra work.

But in the late spring of 1943, Petiot hit a snag. The Gestapo had been puzzled by the disappearance of several Jews they were seeking. When their investigations revealed that all had had links with Petiot they suspected he was what he pretended to be – a Resistance agent smuggling refugees to freedom. They sent a Gestapo man to Petiot, pleading to be sent abroad. Petiot had no reason to

Dr Marcel Petiot's execution

believe he was any different from his usual clients, and promptly killed him.

The Nazis arrested the doctor, and held him for several months before releasing him early in 1944. The suspicion was that Petiot had earned his freedom with one of the most bizarre defences ever – that he was only doing what the Germans were doing, killing Jews and anti-Nazis. However he had achieved it, he returned to his factory of death, and was soon busy burning bodies again.

Now, however, he had no way of treating them before throwing them into the flames. During his enforced absence, his brother Maurice had visited Paris, and called at the Rue Lesueur premises. Family loyalty and loathing for the Germans persuaded him to keep what he found there a grim secret, but he was no longer prepared to act as an accessory to disposing of human flesh, and cut off his supplies of quick lime.

Incinerating untreated remains made the smoke belching from Petiot's chimney even blacker and more acrid, and soon the doctor's neighbours, never happy about the pollution found it intolerable. On 11 March, 1944, the owner of 20 Rue Lesueur called both the police and fire brigade, saying the fumes were a fire danger. Petiot was not in, and a card on the door directed inquiries to his practice in Rue Caumartin. The gendarmes set off there while firemen broke in. They soon located the furnace, but what they found around it horrified them. Dismembered corpses littered the floor. Limbs, heads and torsos were scattered in grisly disarray. The firemen refused to do anything until the police returned.

Forensic experts later pieced together the bones and made a total of 27 human bodies. But when Petiot arrived, he blithely informed the gendarmes that all were Nazi collaborators who had betrayed the French maquis, and deserved the execution he had carried out. Amazingly, the police were prepared to give him at least some benefit of their doubt. Though still under the control of the Germans, they were Frenchmen who hoped the Allies would soon free them from Nazi oppression. They returned to HQ without Petiot.

The doctor was intelligent enough to know that the game was up. Once his story was checked, it would be obvious that he had lied. He fled Paris and for months laid low in the countryside. Meanwhile, senior police officers visited 21 Rue Lesueur, and discovered the cache of treasures, and Petiot's meticulous records. They showed that 63 people had entered the triangular room, never to leave it alive. And it was soon clear that none of them were traitors to France.

Far from being a patriot, Petiot was suspected of being a Gestapo agent. The front-page story of his horrific exploits stunned even a nation accustomed to Nazi atrocities. Yet the doctor declined to take his chance of disappearing in the confusion of the German retreat as the Allied armies reconquered France. He had talked his way out of so many awkward corners that he doubtless thought he could do it again. He wrote to the newspaper *Resistance*, claiming the Nazis had framed him by dumping bodies round the furnace while he was under arrest. Then he had the effrontery to enlist in the Free French forces under a false name.

As life returned to normal after the liberation, police began tidying up the loose ends of law and order. Petiot's case was a priority. Detectives guessed they had not seen the last of him, and they were right. When General de Gaulle led his army in a victory parade down the Champs Elysees, there was Petiot, marching proudly in rank with phoney medals on his chest. He had grown a beard, but he was wanted too badly to escape recognition.

Petiot insisted throughout his 18-month interrogation by a magistrate that he had killed only Germans and collaborators. But when he was brought to trial, the jury were not so gullible. They were shown 47 suitcases packed with more than 1,500 items of clothing, almost all without identity tags. They visited Petiot's triangular room, saw his cellar of death, and heard that he had plundered more than one million pounds from those he butchered.

When the verdict was announced, Petiot could not hear it above the excited babble of the court. He had to ask whether he had been found guilty or not. And when sentenced to death, he screamed: 'I will be avenged.' But he went to the guillotine quietly enough, leaving behind him an ironic epitaph to a blood-soaked life. He asked a companion on that final walk whether he could relieve himself. Permission was refused. Petiot was alleged to have joked: 'When one sets out on a voyage, one takes all one's luggage with one.' It was a luxury he did not allow any of his 63 victims.

The Teenage Monster

JESSE POMEROY

Horrified vacationers stumbled across the body of four-year-old Horace Millen on the beach at Dorchester Bay, near Boston, in April 1874. The child's throat has been cut and he had been stabbed no fewer than 15 times. Before he died, the boy had been savagely beaten. It was the work of a monster, and police immediately launched a full-scale hunt for the killer.

They were looking for a grown man, but some cross-referencing in the official files produced the name Jesse Harding Pomeroy: a lad of 14 who has been reprimanded and sent to a special reform school two years earlier for beating up young children. Fights among youngsters were commonplace, but the name of young Pomeroy, only just out of primary school, had been remembered by the authorities because of the extraordinary amount of unnecessary force he had used.

When police called on Jesse Pomeroy, his answers to questioning immediately aroused suspicion. He was arrested, brought to court and convicted. But Pomeroy's was one of the most remarkable murder cases ever. For, though sentenced to die, he was to live for another 58 years and the first 40 years – until he was 55 – were spent in solitary confinement.

The American public refused to take a chance on someone who had already displayed the most vicious cruelty. When arrested, he had been at liberty only 60 days after spending 18 months in the Westboro Reformatory. The magistrate who sent him there remarked on the savagery of the beatings he had handled out to children younger than himself and a short while after his trial for the Millen killing, it was established that just five weeks earlier he had killed nine-year-old Katie Curran. He had buried her body in the cellar of a shop.

At the Millen trial, Jesse Pomeroy pleaded innocence by way of insanity but it did him no good. He was convicted and sentenced to death. There were those who, because of his age, urged that his death sentence be commuted to life imprisonment but they were shouted down by the masses who demanded a swift execution. As it turned out, Pomeroy's life was spared only because of the legal complexities governing death sentences in the state of Massachusetts.

Although a judge had passed a sentence of death on him, the law required that the state governor of Massachusetts set the date of execution and sign the death warrant. Governor Gaston, in office at the time, refused possibly for political reasons to do anything at all: he would neither sign the death warrant nor commute young Pomeroy's sentence. He compromised with an order, signed and sealed, that Pomeroy must spend the rest of his natural days in solitary confinement. That order stood until long after Governor Gaston had passed away himself.

It was 1916, when Pomeroy was 54, before he was finally released from solitary and allowed to mix with other prisoners at Charlestown Prison. He had survived what must have been a superhuman ordeal by burying himself in studies. He read an immense number of books, and he wrote a lot himself.

If he had been mad at the time of the beatings, there was no longer any sign of it in his writings in these later years. One of the manuscripts he spawned was an autobiography which chronicled his early life, the crimes of which he had been convicted and an attempt he made to break out of jail.

Pomeroy died in the prison in which he had spent all his life, on 29 September, 1932. He was 73 and had spent more than 60 of those years behind bars.

The Suicide Murders

ROUSE, TETZNER, SAFFRAN AND KIPNIK

Over the years, many people have tried to evade their problems and responsibilities by disappearing, but three Europeans devized more fiendish means of vanishing. The men had never met, but within 12 months, each tried similar ways of escaping the mess they had made of their own lives – by taking the lives of complete strangers.

Alfred Arthur Rouse was known to his neighbours in Buxted Road, Finchley, London, as a cheery, chatty, charming chap. He and his wife Lily May had built a comfortable little home on the proceeds of his job as a commercial traveller for a Leicester company. Rouse loved his work. He was obsessed with cars, and had the gift of the gab when it came to selling.

Then, on 6 November, 1930, two plain clothes policemen called on Mrs Rouse. Her husband's Morris Minor car, registration number MU 1468, had been found burnt out in Hardingstone Lane, just off the London road near Northampton. A charred body had been found inside. Would she go with them to Northampton to try to identify some of the few personal effects left undamaged?

Mrs Rouse inspected some braces buckles and items of clothing, and thought they may have belonged to her husband. She was not allowed to see the corpse, which was virtually unidentifiable, but she was satisfied enough to start thinking of the £1,000 life insurance her husband had taken out on himself.

The police, however, were not so sure. Two young cousins, one of them the son of the village policeman at Hardingstone, had reported a strange encounter as they walked home from a 5 November Bonfire Night Party in Northampton. At 02.00, a car had flashed past them bound for London, and as they watched it, they saw a man scramble out of a roadside ditch. He was agitated and breathless, carrying an attache case and wearing a light raincoat, but no hat. As they wondered what he could be doing, they noticed a bright ball of flame 200 yards down Hardingstone Lane. The man said: 'It looks as if someone has had a bonfire.' But he went off in the opposite direction when the boys ran towards the blazing car.

That was enough to arouse police suspicions. What was a respectably-dressed man doing crawling about in a ditch at 02.00? Why did he not share the alarm

Alfred Rouse

Eight-year-old Fanny Adams was abducted while picking
blackberries at Alton, Hampshire in 1867. Her dismembered body
was found later that day. Her young killer was arrested and
subsequently hanged. Sadly for Fanny's memory, the Royal Navy
had just been issued with a new and unpalatable variety of canned
meat which the sailors jokingly referred to as 'sweet Fanny
Adams'. The phrase has since become part of the English
language.

of the youngsters, and try to see if he could help fight the fire? They issued a
nationwide alert for a man of between 30 and 35, about 2 metres (5ft 10in to 6ft)
tall, with a round face and black curly hair. And at 21.20 on 7 November, they
found him. Rouse was met by Scotland Yard detectives as he stepped from the
Cardiff to London coach. And slowly they pieced together an amazing story of
deception and callous cruelty.

Far from being a happily married suburban husband, Rouse was a bigamist.
He had discovered that his good looks and amiable chat worked wonders with
women, and he began to pick up waitresses and shop assistants on his travels.

In 1920, he made a 14-year-old Edinburgh girl pregnant. The child died
after only five weeks, but Rouse persisted in the relationship, posing as a single
man, and in 1924 went through a marriage ceremony with her at St Mary's
Church, Islington, North London. A second child was born, and Rouse
somehow persuaded her to let his real wife look after the boy from time to time
in Buxted Road. In 1925, Rouse met a 17-year-old maid servant from Hendon,
London, and was soon taking her with him on trips, and promising to marry her
when trade picked up. She had a child by him in 1928, and gave birth to a
second girl in October 1930 – seven days before he burnt his car. At the same
time, a girl in the Monmouthshire village of Gellgaer was lying ill in her parents
home. She too was pregnant by Rouse, and believed she was married to him.
Rouse had promised her parents he had bought and furnished a house for him
and his 'wife' at Kingston, and they would move there when the baby was born.

But the commercial traveller was earning only £10 a week. The new baby
and the imminent one only added to his problems, which also included an
illegitimate child in Paris and another in England. Rouse decided there was
only one thing to do. He had to disappear, and start a new life, unfettered by
responsibilities. A few days before the fateful 5 November, he met an
unemployed man outside a public house in Whetstone, London. The man told
him of his desperate hitch-hiking round the country in search of work, and
added: 'I have no relations.' A fiendish idea came to Rouse as he noted that the
man was about his own height and build.

On 5 November, Rouse visited the girl who had borne his daughter seven days earlier. She noticed that he seemed pre-occupied, constantly glancing at his watch. He left, muttering about bills he had to pay, and shortly after 20.00 met the unemployed man by arrangement in Whetstone High Road. He had promised to drive him to Leicester in search of a job.

Rouse was a teetotaller, but he brought along a bottle of whisky for his new friend, and the man drank from it liberally. Near St Albans, the inebriate switched off the car lights by mistake, and they were stopped by a policeman, but allowed to drive on after a warning. What happened next was told with chillingly clinical efficiency in a confession Rouse wrote just before his execution.

'He was the sort of man no-one would miss, and I thought he would suit the plan I had in mind,' he wrote. 'He drank the whisky neat from the bottle and was getting quite fuzzled. We talked a lot, but he did not tell me who he actually was. I did not care.

I turned into Hardingstone Lane because it was quiet and near a main road where I could get a lift from a lorry afterwards. I pulled the car up. The man was half-dozing – the effect of the whisky. I gripped him by the throat with my right hand. I pressed his head against the back of the seat. He slid down, his hat falling off. I saw he had a bald patch on the crown of his head.

He just gurgled. I pressed his throat hard. The man did not realize what was happening. I pushed his face back. After making a peculiar noise, the man was silent. I got out of the car, taking my attache case, a can of petrol and a mallet. I walked about eight metres (ten yards) in front of the car and opened the can, using the mallet to do so. I threw the mallet away and made a trail of petrol to the car. Also I poured petrol over the man and loosened the petrol union joint and took the top off the carburettor. I put the petrol can in the back of the car.

I ran to the beginning of the petrol trail and put a match to it. The flame rushed to the car, which caught fire at once. Petrol was leaking from the bottom of the car. That was the petrol I had poured over the man and the petrol that was dripping from the union joint and carburettor. The fire was very quick and the whole thing was a mass of flames in a few seconds. I ran away.'

In fact Rouse had planned the killing flawlessly. The left leg of the unconscious man was doubled up under the leaking union joint, so that the constant drip would send intense heat into the victim's face, making it unrecognizable. The man's right arm was stretched towards the can in the back seat, and soaked to produce another source of flames to the head and shoulders. And though he had tampered with the engine, the damage was consistent with what might be expected in an accidental blaze.

But the calculating killer had not reckoned on meeting two witnesses as he ran away. And it was that which proved his undoing. Knowing he had been seen, he panicked. Instead of escaping to a new life, he hitched a lift home to Finchley in a lorry, arriving at 06.20. He stayed only to change his clothes, then took a coach to Cardiff and Gellygaer. All the way, he unnecessarily told people his car had been stolen, but changed the details each time. To his amazement, the story of the burned-out car was on the front page of every newspaper. People who knew him in Gellygaer kept asking if it was his car. He denied it, and decided to return to London. Waiting for the coach in Cardiff, he again told conflicting tales about how his car had gone missing. He seemed almost relieved to be met at Hammersmith by the police.

But his horrific confession was still many months away. He first claimed that he had picked the man up as a hitch-hiker near St Albans, then lost his way. When the engine started to spit, he stopped to relieve himself, and told the passenger to fill the tank from his petrol can. The man asked for a cigarette. Next thing, Rouse claimed, he turned and saw a ball of flame. He ran back to the car, but could not get near it because of the heat. Then he had 'lost his head' after coming over 'all of a shake', and had fled, feeling vaguely responsible but not knowing what to do.

It was a plausible story, and though Rouse changed certain details in subsequent re-tellings of it, he still arrived at Northampton Assizes with a jaunty, self-assured air on 26 January, 1931. The prosecution, led by Norman Birkett, had a tricky task to prove murder, and Rouse knew it.

Unfortunately for him, his confidence was his undoing. Rouse had been invalided out of World War One with head wounds after a shell exploded close to where he was standing in the trenches at Givenchy, northern France. A medical report on him in September 1918 said: 'The man is easily excited and talkative.' That, as much as the chance meeting in the country lane, was to condemn him to the noose.

When Birkett suggested Rouse had thrown the man into the car carelessly, face down, Rouse was foolish enough to argue that he had more brains than to do that. Another witness, an expert on car fires, noticed that Rouse seemed unperturbed, even amused, while the court discussed whether the carburettor top might have melted or fallen off. Rouse was also too keen to offer technical explanations about what might have happened inside the blazing engine. He was too clever by half.

The most damning evidence was produced by the eminent pathologists Sir Bernard Spilsbury and Dr Eric Shaw. They testified that the victim had been unconscious but alive when the fire began, and that a tiny scrap of unburnt clothing from the crotch of his trousers was soaked in petrol. Other expert witnesses contended that the man could have spilled petrol over himself, but

The burned-out car containing Rouse's victim

they did not carry much weight with a jury who looked on appalled at an accused man who coldly discussed leaving his 'good wife' because she never made a fuss of him, inexplicably made no real effort to rescue the man in his car, and, worst of all, never showed the slightest compassion or concern for the unknown wretch who had died.

On 31 January, 1931, Mr Justice Talbot sentenced Alfred Arthur Rouse, one of the most ingenious yet most loathsome murderers in British criminal history, to death. His appeal against sentence was dismissed 23 days later, and on 10 March Rouse was hanged at Bedford.

A week later, Kurt Erich Tetzner, also a young commercial traveller, stepped into the dock at Ratisbon, Germany, accused of burning to death in his car an unknown man with intent to defraud insurance companies by passing the body off as his own.

Tetzner had been in custody for 14 months, having been arrested ten days after his burnt-out car was found on the outskirts of Etterhausen, Bavaria, on 25 November, 1929. The charred body at the wheel was buried in lavish style by a weeping Frau Tetzner, who had identified it as her husband, but police were alerted by insurance companies who stood to pay out nearly £7,500. They watched the widow take two telephone calls at a neighbour's house from a Herr Stranelli in Strasbourg, Alsace, and soon discovered that Stranelli and Tetzner were the same man.

Tetzner was worse than Rouse at explaining his crime. He admitted the insurance fraud, and at first confessed to murdering the passenger. But five months after his arrest, he changed his story, saying the man in the car was a pedestrian he had run over who had died as he took him to hospital.

The court found it inconceivable that anyone would confess to murder to try to cover up a case of manslaughter. And it doubted the second story after Tetzner made another admission. Once he had advertised for a travelling companion, but the man who answered dropped out. The second time, he had attacked his passenger, a motor mechanic called Alois Ortner, with a hammer and a pad of ether, after first giving him money to make himself look respectable by having a shave and buying a collar. But Ortner had proved too strong for him and escaped into a nearby forest. Ortner was called as a prosecution witness, and revealed that he had gone to police after the attack – but they refused to believe his 'fantastic' story.

Tetzner was condemned to death, and the sentence was carried out on 2 May, 1931. Shortly before, the young murderer at last confessed the truth. He had picked up an unknown young man in thin clothes who complained of being cold. Tetzner wrapped a rug around him, trapping his arms, then strangled him with rope. He then crashed the car into a tree, made a petrol trail and set fire to it.

The public prosecutor at Ratisbon referred to Rouse as 'just a pupil of Tetzner.' It is not known whether Rouse had heard of the German case before he hatched his own scheme. But the third man who tried to disappear by substituting another man's body for his own certainly had.

Fritz Saffran was young, good-looking and successful. He had made such a good job of running the Platz Furniture Store in Rastenburg, eastern Prussia, that the owner of the shop, whose daughter he married, felt able to retire early, and leave things to his 30-year-old son-in-law.

Then, on 15 September 1930, an explosion rocked the store, and flames quickly destroyed it. Thirty workers escaped, but one did not. Chief clerk Erich Kipnik claimed Saffran had dashed into the blazing building to try to save the ledgers. Sure enought, firemen sifting the debris found the charred body. It wore the remains of one of Saffran's suits, had two of his rings on its fingers, and his monogrammed watch in an inside pocket.

Saffran had been popular with all his staff and customers, but one employee in particular was inconsolable at his death. It was known that Ella Augustin had been in love with him for years, but that he had publicly refused to respond to her flirting. He was, after all, a happily married man.

Two days after the fire, Ella called at several garages in the town to try to hire a car to take her mother, who was seriously ill, to Konigsberg. The chauffeur who accepted the task was surprised to be asked to arrive at her house at 03.00. He was even more amazed when the ailing mother turned out to be Saffran.

The man drove to the village of Gerdauen; but refused to go further. He had worked for the Platz firm before, and was reluctant to go to the police. But he told a friend about the secret journey, and was arrested – though later cleared – for aiding Saffran's escape. The friend alerted the police, who quickly discovered that all was not what it seemed at the prosperous Platz store. Saffran had burdened the business with huge debts after hire purchase buyers defaulted on payments. He had also raised money fraudulently on fake hire purchase deals and falsified the ledgers. Ella Augustin had helped him do this, and was his secret lover.

Greedy Mongol Tamerlane the Great was feared as much by his own men as by his enemies. After one battle, he built pyramids out of layer upon layer of murdered prisoners' heads. And if anyone dared to tell a joke in his company, they would be instantly killed. He died after a month of gluttony in 1405.

> The seventeenth-century Tsar of Russia, Peter the Great, murdered his own son when he remonstrated with him about his cruel laws. Anyone who opposed this giant of over 2 metres in height suffered a chilling death. His mistress, a Scot named Mrs Hamilton, was unfaithful to him – so he pickled her head and placed it beside his bed.

She was arrested, and tried to smuggle a note out to Saffran. It told the police that he was staying with one of her relatives in Berlin. Saffran somehow learned that police in the German capital were looking for him. Seven weeks after his getaway he stole the relative's identity papers, took a local train to the suburb of Spandau, and boarded the 01.00 train to Hamburg, where he hoped to get a ship to Brazil. But a fluke thwarted his clever plans. The rail official at Spandau had lived in Rastenburg several years earlier, and recognized the fugitive. Police were waiting when the train pulled into Wittenburg, the next station down the line.

Dental records helped detectives identify the body in the Platz store as Friedrich Dahl, 25, a dairyman from Wermsdorf, near Konigsberg. And on 23 March, 1931, Saffran and Kipnik, arrested when he was implicated in the conspiracy, went on trial at Bartenstein charged with Dahl's murder, attempted murder, arson, forgery, bribery and insurance frauds. Ella Augustin was accused of incitement to murder and complicity in frauds.

It quickly became clear that all three were more than anxious to blame each other for the murder. And what emerged was a chilling story of cold, calculated killing. Ella claimed that Saffran started it, brandishing a newspaper and saying: 'Have you read the report about this man Tetzner? That is how I will do our job too.'

Saffran claimed he took out an insurance policy for £7,000 so his wife would be well provided for. It was his intention to commit suicide, but Ella argued him out of it. Kipnik then suggested securing a body and burning it. They considered digging up a corpse from a grave, but dismissed the idea as impractical for their purposes.

The court was hushed as Saffran continued: 'We established a murder camp in the Nikolai Forest. The girl stayed there while Kipnik and I, each in his own car, roved the countryside for miles around, looking for a likely victim, then reported to the camp at evening. After a while we all three began to go out on these manhunts together.'

Several countrymen had lucky escapes. Once, near the village of Sorquitten, a man accepted a lift. Saffran said he speeded up, then jammed on the brakes, and Kipnik was supposed to smash the victim's skull as it jolted back. But Ella lost her nerve, clutched Kipnik's arm, and the man got away.

Kipnik claimed that, on another occasion, they picked up a pedestrian and were about to kill him when he revealed that he had six children. Sometimes they hid in woods or behind hedges, waiting for a likely victim to come along. The search went on night after night. Finally, on 12 September, 1930, Kipnik and Saffran met a man near Luisenhof just about midnight. It was Dahl.

Both men accused the other of firing the fatal three shots into his head, and both made exaggerated claims of contrition when the victim's widow took the stand. The public prosecutor had to tell them sternly to stop play-acting. But both continued to speak in terms more suited to a playhouse than a courtroom. 'Gentlemen of the jury, think of my terrible position,' Saffran pleaded, arms outstretched. 'I was leading a double life. At home I had to appear cheerful and contented while my heart was breaking. At night I was forced to go out hunting for men to murder.' Later Kipnik shouted: 'Saffran has ruined my life. I place my fate in the hands of the court. I wish I could prove to them that I am really a decent man.'

The jury believed neither story, and both men were sentenced to death. Accomplice Ella was jailed for five years. But Saffran and Kipnik were luckier than Rouse and Tetzner. The Prussian government commuted their sentences to life imprisonment. Many Germans wondered why two such callous killers should be spared the fate they had so cold-bloodedly meted out to an innocent stranger.

The Rat Poisoner

LYDIA SHERMAN

Wherever Lydia Sherman went she found buildings infested with rats. Or at least that was the story she told the neighborhood druggists from whom she bought her poison.

The arsenic soon eliminated the rats and, as it turned out, some of the human beings she considered a nuisance, too. As many as 42 people are believed to have died by Lydia's hand.

Married to patrolman Edward Struck of the New York Police Department, the sturdy but attractive housewife kept a low profile until 1864. Then Struck was sacked by the police for a shabby display of cowardice and promptly turned into an unemployed drunk. Lydia put him to bed one evening with a lethal snack of oatmeal gruel and rat poison.

Puzzled as to the manner of his death, the doctor blamed it on 'consumption' but made up his mind to ask for an official investigation. But Lydia had ensured her husband had a quick burial and the authorities saw no reason to intrude on her 'grief'.

One by one Lydia's children died – Mary Ann, Edward, William, George, Ann Eliza, and finally the widow's namesake, tiny toddler Lydia. In every case she shrewdly called in a different doctor, all of whom obligingly took her word for the cause of death.

When the people of San José, California, heard the fate of local kidnap victim Brooke Hart, they decided to seek vengeance. In 1933, Brooke Hart, a 22-year-old heir to a hotel chain, was kidnapped by garage worker Thomas Thurmond and his old schoolfriend John Holmes. The pair attacked him with a brick, weighted him down and threw him into the sea. To their amazement Hart came to and began yelling, so they shot him.

Thurmond and Holmes demanded $40,000 from Hart's father for the 'safe return' of his son. But the police traced the kidnappers' phone calls and the evil couple were arrested. When Brooke Hart's body was discovered, a raging mob broke into Santa Clara Jail, put out one of Holmes' eyes and then hung him and Thurmond from nearby trees.

THE RAT POISONER

An ex-brother-in-law went to the authorities swearing Lydia was 'full of black evil' and demanding that the bodies be exhumed. But the bored bureaucrats refused to budge.

Lydia moved from one job to another. In 1868 she married an aging and rich widower named Dennis Hurlbut. With rat poison available at 10 cents a package, he was soon out of the way.

That left her free to marry Nelson Sherman, who took her with him to his Connecticut home. There she had problems, including a suspicious mother-in-law and the four Sherman children by a previous marriage.

Two of the children she disposed of at once. Mourning the death of his 14-year-old daughter, Addie, Nelson Sherman turned to alcohol and thus signed his own death warrant.

'I just wanted to cure him of the liquor habit,' Lydia said.

A Connecticut doctor was suspicious and insisted that his stomach and liver be analyzed. Toxicologists found enough arsenic to kill an army. The vital organs of the two children were also permeated with poison.

Pleading that she had murdered out of human compassion – 'all those people were sick, after all' – the fashionably dressed widow cut an impressive figure at her trial in New Haven, Connecticut. And in a way, her luck held. Amazingly gentle with the not so gentle murderess, Judge Park instructed the jury to consider only charges of second-degree murder.

Sentenced to life in Weathersfield Prison, she vowed she would never die in jail. But there her luck did end – she was still behind bars when she died in 1878.

The Yorkshire Ripper

PETER SUTCLIFFE

When the savagely-mutilated body of Wilma McCann, a 28-year-old prostitute, was found on 30 October, 1975, on playing fields in Leeds, no-one but the police took much notice. The newspapers dismissed her murder with a few paragraphs, and her neighbours, while shocked by the tragedy, explained that 'Hotpants' McCann was 'no better than she ought to have been'.

Only Wilma's four children and a handful of friends mourned her wretched end. The honest citizens of Leeds, long angered by the vice which flourished in the Chapeltown district where Wilma lived, quickly forgot about her death.

However, Dennis Hoban, the 48-year-old head of Leeds area CID could not forget the horrific injuries he had seen on McCann's body – the skull smashed in with a blunt instrument, the trunk punctured by 15 stab wounds. 'The attack was savage and frenzied,' Chief Superintendent Hoban told a press conference. 'It suggested the work of a psychopath and, with this kind of person, there is always the likelihood that he will strike again.' His words were grimly prophetic.

During the next five years the man who came to be known as 'the Yorkshire Ripper' struck many times, killing 12 more women and maiming seven – a terrifying, shadowy figure who brought near hysteria to the cobbled streets of West Yorkshire and who sparked off the biggest police hunt of the century.

His grim nickname, reminiscent of London's Jack the Ripper of 1888, did not hit the headlines until his second murder – that of part-time prostitute Mrs Emily Jackson, 42, in a Chapeltown alleyway on 20 January, 1976 – less than three months after the McCann killing.

Mrs Jackson's body, too, was dreadfully mutilated. Repeated blows from a blunt instrument had stove in the back of the skull and the bloodstained trunk was punctured by 50 cruciform-shaped stab wounds, caused by a sharpened Phillip's-type screwdriver.

Chief Superintendent Hoban appealed to the public: 'I can't stress strongly enough that it is vital we catch this brutal killer before he brings tragedy to another family.'

If the first murder had been virtually ignored, the second was given big play by the press. And it was George Hill, of the *Daily Express* who coined the soubriquet 'the Yorkshire Ripper'.

Wilma McCann

Emily Jackson

Joan Harrison

Irene Richardson

On 8 February, 1977, the Ripper killed again. His victim, another prostitute, was 28-year-old Irene Richardson, whose stabbed body was found in Roundhay Park, Leeds. Although Roundhay is a highly-respectable, middle-class suburb, it is little more than a mile from the edge of the Chapeltown district where McCann and Jackson had died.

Less than three months later the Ripper's grim 'score' rose to four and, once again, the victim was a prostitute, Tina Atkinson, aged 32, who was found battered to death on 24 April. She was on the bed of her flat in the Lumb Lane area of Bradford, a 'red light' district smaller than Leeds's Chapeltown, but with an equally bad reputation.

As in the three previous killings, the Ripper had left precious few clues for the police beyond his 'trademark' of hammerblows to the skull. Of the few clues, however, one was vital: the footprint made by a boot, which exactly matched a print found at the scene of Emily Jackson's murder.

It was a useful break for the weary and bewildered CID men, but they were still being hampered by lack of public concern. What they needed was something that would bring forward witnesses who, up to then, had refused to get involved on the grounds that the victims were 'only prostitutes'.

They got what they wanted on the morning of Sunday 26 June, 1977, but there was not a policeman in the West Yorkshire force who did not wish that it could have happened some other way.

Jayne MacDonald was found battered and stabbed to death in a children's playground in the heart of Chapeltown. But Jayne, just 16, blonde and with filmstar good looks, was no prostitute – just a happy teenager, ruthlessly cut down by the Ripper while walking home after a night out with a boyfriend. Now, at last, after almost two years of working against public apathy, the police had an 'innocent' victim on their hands.

From that moment there was no shortage of information. On the contrary, the Ripper Squad began slowly to founder under the weight of facts, theories and suppositions from the general public.

There is no doubt that the slaying of Jayne MacDonald led to the death of her father, railwayman Wilf MacDonald, two years later. Soon after Jayne's killing he told reporters how his daughter had bent to kiss him on the head before going out on that fateful night. 'She was so sweet and clean,' said Mr MacDonald. 'She was untouched and perfect, just like a flower.'

The next time he saw her was on a mortuary slab. He said: 'The pain of seeing her blonde hair, which had been so shiny and clean the night before, now caked in blood was so indescribable it haunts my every waking moment.'

From that moment Wilf MacDonald waited for death, praying for the moment when he would be released from the horror that the Ripper had visited upon him. When he died broken-hearted on 11 October, 1979, he was a Ripper

cia Atkinson

Jayne MacDonald

Jean Jordan

Yvonne Pearson

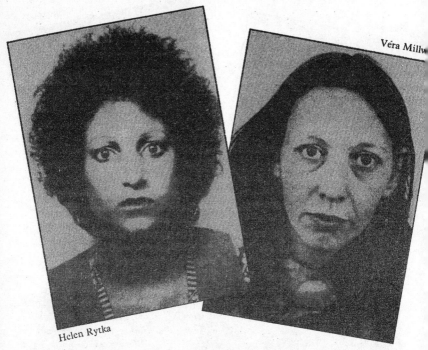

Vera Millw

Helen Rytka

victim just as surely as if he had been killed by a blow from a ball-pein hammer.

By then six more women had been murdered: Jean Jordan, aged 21, prostitute, murdered and hideously mutilated on allotments in Manchester, on 1 October, 1977. Yvonne Pearson, aged 22, prostitute, murdered on 21 January, 1978, on waste ground in Bradford. Her badly decomposed body was not found until 26 March. Helen Rytka, aged 18, prostitute, murdered beneath a railway viaduct in Huddersfield, West Yorkshire, on 31 January 1978. Vera Millward, aged 41, prostitute, murdered in the grounds of Manchester Royal Infirmary on 17 May, 1978. Josephine Whitaker, aged 19, a respectable building society clerk, bludgeoned to death near her home in Halifax, Yorkshire, while taking a short cut through Savile Park on the night of 4 April, 1979. Barbara Leach, aged 20, a respectable student at Bradford University, killed near Bradford city centre in the early hours of 2 September, 1979.

Three months before the slaying of 'Babs' Leach, a sensational twist to the Ripper inquiry had echoed all round the world, giving newspapers, television and radio one of the most bizarre crime stories ever to hit the headlines. It was in the form of a cassette tape, played at a press conference on 26 June by Assistant Chief Constable George Oldfield, head of West Yorkshire CID.

'I'm Jack,' said the voice on the tape in a chilling monotone. 'I see you are still having no luck catching me. I have the greatest respect for you, George, but, Lord, you are no nearer catching me than four years ago when I started. I reckon your boys are letting you down, George. you can't be much good, can ya? The only time they came near catching me was a few months back in Chapeltown when I was disturbed. Even then it was a uniform copper, not a detective.

I warned you in March that I'd strike again. Sorry it wasn't Bradford. I did promise you that, but I couldn't get there. I'm not quite sure when I will strike again, but it will be definitely some time this year, maybe September or October, even sooner if I get the chance. I am not sure where, maybe Manchester. I like it there, there's plenty of them knocking about. They never learn, do they, George. I bet you've warned them, but they never listen.

At the rate I'm going I should be in the book of records. I think it's up to eleven now, isn't it. Well, I'll keep on going for quite a while yet. I can't see myself being nicked just yet. Even if you do get near I'll probably top myself first.

'Well, it's been nice chatting to you, George. Yours, Jack the Ripper.

No good looking for fingerprints. You should know by now it's as clean as a whistle. See you soon. Bye. Hope you like the catchy tune at the end. Ha. Ha. Ha.'

The music that followed was the six-line reprise of 'Thank You For Being a Friend', a 1978 song by Californian musician Andrew Gold.

As the music faded, George Oldfield said: 'I believe that we have now got the break we have been waiting for.'

But that was where it all started to go wrong. The Ripper inquiry went off course at a tragic tangent. For the voice on the tape was identified by dialect experts as belonging to someone from the Castletown district of Sunderland. From that moment detectives manning the £4,000,000 hunt for the Ripper began looking for a man with a Geordie accent. . .

Peter William Sutcliffe did not have a Geordie accent. His voice, slightly high-pitched and hesitant, was flat with the broad vowels of his native town of Bingley, a few miles to the west of Bradford.

There, on the fringes of the Brontë country, Sutcliffe was born on 2 June, 1946, the first child of John and Kathleen Sutcliffe who lived in a one-up, one-down cottage in Heaton Row, close by the edge of the wild moors above Bingley.

Peter was a shy boy, prone to blushing in the company of girls, though his polite good manners were much admired by his parents' neighbours. He left

THE WORLD'S MOST INFAMOUS MURDERS

Cottingley Manor School, Bingley, at the end of spring term in 1961, aged 15, and for three years drifted through a variety of undistinguished jobs before starting work as a gravedigger in Bingley Cemetery in 1964. With the exception of a short break in 1965, he remained at the job until he was sacked for bad timekeeping in 1967 . . . and loved every minute of it.

Sutcliffe's gravedigging career is littered with revolting stories of desecration and grave-robbing that tell of the dark shadows that were already gathering in his mind. Often he outraged his workmates by interfering with corpses, sometimes to steal rings or gold teeth, but other times simply because he seemed to enjoy handling dead bodies.

Eventually he managed to get himself attached to the mortuary as an attendant and would regale his friends with descriptions of the cadavers he had seen cut open for post-mortem examination. Often, after a night in the pub, he would rattle the mortuary keys and ask if anyone wanted to see the latest body. There were never any takers.

Sutcliffe was married on 10 August, 1974, at Clayton Baptist Chapel, Bradford. It was a double celebration for that day was also the birthday of his bride, Sonia Szurma, an attractive 24-year-old teacher, daughter of eastern European refugees. A shy girl, Sonia looked even more demure than usual at her wedding. She could not have known that her groom had ended the previous evening's stag night celebrations by taking himself down to Bradford's red light district of Lumb Lane. But the darkly-handsome, sallow-faced Sutcliffe was a frequent visitor to Lumb Lane, and to Leeds's Chapeltown, and to Manchester's Moss Side.

Fourteen months after marrying Sonia, Sutcliffe killed Wilma McCann, and those infamous districts became a slaughterhouse where women lived in terror and police sought desperately for a murderer with a Geordie accent.

They had one gift of a clue – a brand new £5 note found in the handbag of the Ripper's first Manchester victim, Jean Jordan, murdered on 1 October, 1977. The serial number, AW51 121565, was traced to the Midland Bank at Shipley, a suburb of Bradford. The manager explained to detectives that the note had been issued only five days before it had been handed over to Jordan – probably in the pay-roll of a local firm.

Manchester police sent a team over to Shipley to join their West Yorkshire colleagues, and thousands of local men were interviewed. Among them was the entire workforce of T. and W. H. Clark, an engineering and haulage firm, based in Canal Road, Shipley.

One of the men interviewed was a lorry driver called Sutcliffe. In the cab of his lorry was pinned this handwritten notice: 'In this truck is a man whose latent genius, if unleashed, would rock the nation, whose dynamic energy would overpower those around him. Better let him sleep.'

Josephine Whitaker

Barbara Leach

...line Hill

Olivia Reivers and Denise Hall

If the detectives trying to trace the owner of the £5 note saw the notice they did not read any significance into it for Peter Sutcliffe was questioned and cleared.

He was to be interviewed another eight times throughout the remaining span of the Ripper enquiry . . . and each time he was cleared and released. His workmates at Clark's even joked about the number of times he was questioned and gave him the nickname 'the Ripper'.

By now, under the influence of the intelligent, well-educated Sonia, Sutcliffe was busy bettering himself. Always immaculately dressed in crisp, fresh overalls, he had a reputation as one of Clark's top drivers. And he and Sonia moved into the decidedly middle-class Heaton district of Bradford, buying a four-bedroomed detached house in Garden Lane.

But strange things happened behind the respectable lace curtains at Number 6. There was domestic friction with the tiny, frail Sonia often heard ranting and shouting at her embarrassed husband, ignoring his pleas to keep her voice down 'in case the neighbours hear'.

It is a bizarre concept – the monstrously evil killer as a henpecked husband, but in Sutcliffe's case it was true. More than one detective on the Ripper Squad has said: 'Every time he killed, he was really killing Sonia.'

The faithful and devoted husband, the loyal and hardworking employee, the polite and helpful friend, these were the faces that Peter Sutcliffe showed to the rest of the world. The face of the fiend was one he reserved for darkness – and his victims. At first they had been prostitutes and, in a perverted way, he could try to justify their deaths, as did the original Jack the Ripper, by claiming that he was ridding the streets of 'filth'.

But then had come the murder of Jayne MacDonald. She had been no whore. Nor had Jo Whitaker or Babs Leach, victims number ten and eleven. Nor had several of the women who had survived his attacks. So now there could be no pretence of being a crusading 'street-cleaner'.

Was he seeking to punish the domineering Sonia? Or was he seeking revenge on all womankind? For in 1972 Sutcliffe, his two sisters and two brothers, had been astounded and horrified to discover that their mother, Kathleen, the woman they called 'the Angel', had been having a secret affair. Highly religious, even prudish, Kathleen had slipped from the pedestal on which her doting children had placed her.

Perhaps it is significant that the twelfth victim was, like the late Mrs Sutcliffe (she died in November 1978), middle-aged and highly respectable. Margo Walls was 47, a former sergeant in the WRAC, an unmarried civil servant who lived alone in Pudsey, a small town between Leeds and Bradford.

After working late on 22 August, 1980, she set off to walk the half mile from her office to her home – and met Sutcliffe. He reared out of the dark shadows of a gateway and aimed a blow at her head. Although stunned, Miss Walls fought

Peter Sutcliff and Sonia on their wedding day

Peter Sutcliffe's fantasy woman, Theresa Douglas

back savagely, punching and clawing at her attacker. But the slightly built Sutcliffe was strong and managed to get a garotte around her neck. When Margo was dead, Sutcliffe stripped her body, dragged her up the driveway – that of a local magistrate – and buried her beneath a pile of grass cuttings.

Police investigating the murder decided that it was not the work of the Ripper. The garotte, they said, was not his style. But three months later, on Monday 17 November, 1980, the Ripper struck again and this time there was no doubt in the minds of the investigating detectives.

The victim was Jacqueline Hill, a 20-year-old student at Leeds University. At 21.23 that fateful Monday night she alighted from a bus outside the Arndale shopping centre in the residential district of Headingley, Leeds, and began walking the 200 metres up Alma Road towards her hall of residence.

Sutcliffe, who minutes before had been eating chicken and chips from a nearby Kentucky Fried Chicken shop, leapt out of his parked Rover and rained hammerblows on the back of her head. She went down without a sound, laying limply as her attacker dragged her across Alma Road into some bushes behind the Arndale Centre. There, with a sharpened screwdriver, he set about inflicting his terrible trademark on her body. The final wound was the worst of all – a stab through the retina of the eye 'because', Sutcliffe explained after his arrest, 'she seemed to be staring at me.'

The killing of yet another respectable victim, particularly in the straight-laced heart of middle-class Headingley, caused a more violent eruption of public fury and indignation than before. West Yorkshire's Chief Constable, Mr Ronald Gregory, was being pressed hard by the public and local politicians who demanded action fast.

On 25 November he announced the formation of a 'super squad' – a think-tank of senior officers drawn from other forces. Assistant Chief Constable George Oldfield was, effectively, taken off the case, although he remained head of West Yorkshire CID.

It must have been a bitter blow for Oldfield who had lived, day and night, with the case almost from the start. The hunt for the Ripper had become a personal crusade, especially since that tape recording had arrived to taunt him.

In his place, with the temporary acting rank of Assistant Chief Constable, Mr Gregory appointed Jim Hobson, head of Leeds area CID, successor to Chief Superintendent Dennis Hoban who had begun the inquiry and who had died suddenly at the age of 51 in March 1978.

Hobson and Oldfield did not see eye to eye. Their relationship was correct rather than cordial and Hobson lost no time in getting rid of the albatross of the 'Geordie accent' that had hung round the neck of the inquiry for so long. Oldfield, who had virtually staked his reputation on the tape, could only watch.

Then Hobson, in a statement that was almost clairvoyant, announced that if the Ripper was caught 'it will be by an ordinary uniformed copper, going about his normal duties'.

That is exactly what happened on the night of Friday, 2 January, 1981, as Peter Sutcliffe prepared to kill his fourteenth victim – a coloured Sheffield prostitute called Ava Reivers. The two of them were sitting in Sutcliffe's Rover V8 in the driveway of an office block in Melbourne Drive, Sheffield. Sutcliffe had handed over a £10 note for sex, but had failed to get an erection. On the back seat were a hammer, a garotte and a sharpened screwdriver.

The man who had called himself 'Dave' suddenly whispered to Ava: 'I'm scared – really scared.' But it was Ava who was scared; somehow she knew beyond doubt that this 'punter' intended her harm.

At that moment the police arrived, a sergeant and a PC in a panda car, making a routine check on the cars parked in the leafy lovers' lane. 'Dave' was reduced to near panic.

Ava, pleased for the first time in her life to see a policeman, was relieved to be taken to the police station for questioning about her 'lover's' identity and for him to be quizzed as to why the Rover was carrying false number plates.

It was during that interview that Sergeant Arthur Armitage, after studying the man who claimed to be 'Peter Williams', suddenly spoke up. In his broad South Yorkshire accent he said: 'Tha's t' Ripper, thee!'

The nightmare was over.

On Friday, 22 May, 1981, Peter William Sutcliffe stood in the dock at the Old Bailey's Number One court and listened impassively as the jury found him guilty of 13 murders and seven attempted murders.

Mr Justice Borcham sentenced him to life imprisonment on each count, adding: 'I shall recommend to the Home Secretary that the minimum period which should elapse before he orders your release shall be 30 years. That is a long period, an unusually long period in my judgement, but you, I believe, are an unusually dangerous man. I express the hope that, when I have said life imprisonment, it will mean precisely that.'

Sutcliffe is currently serving that sentence in the maximum security wing of Parkhurst Prison on the Isle of Wight.

The cruel hoaxer who threw the whole Ripper hunt awry with his mocking Geordie voice – and so helped kill three woman – remains free.

The Lethal Romeo

GEORGE SMITH

Many men have made a living by playing with the affections of plain, naive, lovelorn spinsters, then abandoning them once they have handed over their savings. The public often find the foolish victims of such romantic con-men comic rather than tragic figures, and found reasons for amusement even at the trial of Henri Landru, who was accused of killing ten such dupes. But nobody found anything remotely funny about the exploits of another wicked womaniser, George Joseph Smith.

Smith was born in London's Bethnal Green in 1872, and was soon the despair of his parents. His mother predicted he would 'die with his boots on', and she was hardly surprised when, at the age of only nine, he was sentenced to eight years in a Gravesend reformatory. But the sentence merely helped train him for a life of crime, and, apart from three years as a soldier in the Northamptonshire Regiment, he became a full-time thief, constantly in and out of prison.

Smith was cunning. He realized he was having little success stealing for himself, so he decided to get others to do it for him. Though his bony face was not really attractive, he had small, dark mesmerising eyes that seemed to have an extraordinarily magnetic power for some women. 'They were little eyes that seemed to rob you of your will,' one of his victims told police later.

Smith found it easy to persuade women to work with him, and not to implicate him if they were caught. Using the proceeds of one woman's raids, he opened a baker's shop in Russell Square, Leicester, in 1897, and a year later married an 18-year-old bootmaker's daughter, Caroline Beatrice Thornhill, despite her family's disapproval. He was then 26 and calling himself George Love.

They moved to London, and Smith found his wife employment as a servant with a succession of wealthy families in Brighton, Hove and Hastings. She had no trouble getting work. She had impeccable references from a past employer – Smith. But late in 1899 she was arrested trying to pawn the loot from one theft, some silver spoons, and was jailed for a year. Smith abandoned her, which increased her bitterness, and after her release, she spotted him by chance in London, and alerted the police. In January 1901, he was jailed for two years for receiving stolen goods. Revenge was in his mind, too, once the sentence ended. He travelled to Leicester, bent on killing his wife. But her family beat him up, and Caroline later emigrated to safety in Canada.

THE WORLD'S MOST INFAMOUS MURDERS

Smith had already discovered a new way of making women work for his living. In 1899 he had bigamously married a middle-aged boarding-house keeper, milking her of what money she had while living rent free at her lodgings. Now he began to tour the south coast, particularly seaside resorts, wooing, wedding and walking out on his brides, who were often too humiliated to reveal the truth to police or their friends and relations.

He did it all in the cheapest way possible – third-class rail travel, meagre lodgings, outings to places of free entertainment. In that way, he made the maximum of profit from each of them. In June 1908 he met Florence Wilson, a Worthing widow with £30 in her Post Office savings account. They married in London after a whirlwind three-week affair. On 3 July, he took her to the White City exhibition and left her there, claiming he was going out to buy a newspaper. In fact he dashed back to their rooms in Camden Town and sold all her belongings.

In October 1909, calling himself George Rose, Smith married Southampton spinster Sarah Freeman and they set up home in Clapham, South London. Smith played the charming gent, in smart frock coat and top hat, and his bride did not demur when he said he needed money to set up an antiques business. She withdrew her savings, and sold her Government stocks. On 5 November he took her to the National Gallery, excused himself to go to the lavatory, and scuttled back to their rooms, clearing out everything, and leaving his deserted bride destitute. In less than a month he had made £400, four times the average annual wage.

In between these two coups, Smith had taken another wife, Edith Mabel Pegler. Dark-haired, round-faced and plump, she was 28 when she answered his advertisement for a housekeeper in a local newspaper at Bristol, where he had opened a shop in Gloucester Road. But for once Smith, who used his own name this time, was not after money. What he took from others, he gave to Edith. And though he left her from time to time, claiming he was travelling in search of antiques, he always returned after his matrimonial adventures.

Those adventures now took a more sinister turn. In August 1910, he met 33-year-old spinster Beatrice Constance Anne Mundy while strolling in Clifton, a resort near Bristol. The ardent wooer could hardly believe his luck when she told him of the £2,500 in securities her father, a Wiltshire bank manager, had left her when he died. The legacy, managed by a trust of relatives, paid her £8 a month. Smith, now going under the name of Henry Williams, whisked her off to Weymouth, where they set up home in Rodwell Avenue. They married on 26 August and began to flood the relatives with reassuring letters.

But the relatives had more sense than bride Bessie. They did not like the look of Williams, suspecting that he was a fortune hunter, and it was December before they finally sent £134 owed in interest. Smith, despairing of collecting

George Smith and Beatrice Mundy

> Gangster, racketeer and murderer Al Capone did not die with a
> bullet in his back. He died an ungentlemanly death of
> neurosyphilis. The man whose Twenties crime empire brought in
> $5 million a year and left 1,000 bodies on the streets of Chicago
> died in Florida in 1947, an ex-jailbird with hardly a dime in his
> pocket.

the capital, abandoned Bessie on 13 December in an especially heartless way. He left her a letter claiming she had 'blighted all my bright hopes of a happy future' by infecting him with venereal disease, and accusing her of not being 'morally clean.' He was off to London to be cured, 'which will cost me a great deal of money.' So he took the £134, advising her to tell her relatives it was stolen while she was asleep on the beach.

Poor Bessie resumed her spinster life, telling friends, on Smith's advice, that her husband had gone to France. Smith went back to Edith Pegler, moving to Southend, then London, and back to Bristol again. The VD accusation had only been an excuse, though it must have upset a woman who was far from worldly-wise.

That she missed her adoring husband was only too clear when, 18 months later, they met again by sheer chance in Weston-super-Mare. Bessie, staying with a friend, popped out to buy daffodils one morning in March 1912, and spotted Smith on the seafront. The smooth-talking Casanova had an explanation for his note, his long absence, and the fact that he had spent all her money, and by mid-afternoon the besotted girl was ready to ignore her friend's pleas and leave with her husband, taking none of her belongings.

They travelled across country, and in May set up a modest home at 80 High Street, Herne Bay, Kent. Smith had been asking expert advice on how he could get at Bessie's £2,500 nest-egg, and in July a lawyer told him that it was only possible if she left it to him in her will. The wily bigamist wasted no time – and seemingly had no qualms about turning to murder to feather his nest. On 8 July the couple signed wills, leaving their wordly possessions to each other should they die. On 9 July, Smith bought a tapless zinc bath, haggling 12½p (half-a-crown) off the ironmonger's price of £2.

On 10 July, he took Bessie to a young, inexperienced doctor, claiming she had had a fit. Two days later the doctor called at their home after another fit was reported. He found Bessie in bed, flushed but seemingly well, and left a prescription for sedatives. That night, Bessie wrote to her uncle, telling him of her attacks, of how her husband was looking after her well, and of how they had both made their wills.

At 08.00 next morning, Saturday 13 July, the doctor received a note saying: 'Can you come at once? I am afraid my wife is dead.' He arrived to find Bessie submerged in the bath. She was naked and lying on her back, a bar of soap clasped in her right hand. Smith said his wife had filled the bath herself, making 20 trips downstairs to the kitchen to fetch water for it. He had gone out to buy some fish, and returned to find her dead. The police were called, but saw no reason to think the death was suspicious. Smith wept throughout the inquest on the following Monday, and was offered words of comfort by the coroner, who recorded a verdict of misadventure.

No-one asked why Bessie had drowned in a bath far shorter than her full height, or why Smith had left her lying under the water until the doctor arrived, instead of trying to resuscitate her. Nor was it found suspicious that she had just made a will, a point Smith was foolish enough to mention to the estate agent when he cancelled the letting of their home.

He had been careful to time the murder for a Saturday. Although he wired news of the death to Bessie's uncle, saying a letter would follow, there was no time for relatives to get to the inquest, or the economy-version funeral which followed just 24 hours later. Trustees of Bessie's legacy asked in vain for a post-mortem examination, and tried to stop Smith getting her money. But he had been too clever for them, and reluctantly they handed over £2,591 13s 6d.

Smith had one last piece of business to attend to. He took the bath back to the ironmonger to avoid having to pay for it. Then he left for Margate, and summoned Edith Pegler to join him. He told her he had made a nice profit selling antiques in Canada, but lost his temper when she revealed that she had been looking for him in Woolwich and Ramsgate. 'He said he did not believe in women knowing his business,' she was to recall. 'He remarked that if I interfered I should never have another happy day.'

Smith was one of the few big-time bigamists not to squander his earnings. He bought eight houses in Bristol with Bessie's money and opened a shop, and also invested in an annuity for himself. By October 1913, he was anxious for more cash, and there seemed no reason why a once-successful scheme should not work again.

Alice Burnham was short, plump and 25, a private nurse to an elderly invalid, when she met a tall, charming stranger at Southsea. Her father, a Buckinghamshire fruit-grower, took an instant dislike to the man, but that did

> **Dr Edward William Pritchard** was the last person to be publicly hanged in Scotland. He had murdered his wife and mother-in-law by poisoning them with antimony. No fewer than 100,000 people watched the doctor go to his death in 1865.

not stop her marrying him at Portsmouth on 4 November, one day after he took out a £500 insurance policy on her life. Nor did it stop Smith writing immediately to her father, demanding £104 he was holding for his daughter, and withdrawing £27 from his bride's savings account.

Then he decided to take his new wife on holiday. It was Wednesday, 10 December when they arrived in breezy Blackpool for their bracing, out-of-season break. They called first at a boarding house in Adelaide Street, but Smith rejected the offered rooms – there was no bath. Mrs Crossley at 16 Regent Road had one, however, and the couple booked in there for ten shillings a week. A local doctor was consulted about Mrs Smith's headaches, and the dutiful wife wrote to her father, saying she had 'the best husband in the world.'

On the Friday evening, the couple asked for a bath to be prepared for Mrs Smith while they went for a walk. At 20.15 the Crossleys were having a meal downstairs when they noticed water staining the ceiling. They were about to investigate when a dishevelled Smith appeared at the door carrying two eggs which he said he had just bought for next day's breakfast. Then he went upstairs, and shouted down: 'Fetch the doctor, my wife cannot speak to me.'

Alice had gone the same way as Bessie, and though Smith was asked at the inquest next day why he had not lifted her from the bath, or pulled the plug out of it, an accidental death verdict was recorded. Again Smith wept copiously throughout the hearing, but at least one person was not impressed by his tears. Mrs Crossley was so appalled at his seeming indifference to his wife's death that she refused to let him sleep in her house that Friday night. She also noted that, while waiting for the inquest on the Saturday afternoon, he played the piano in her front room and drank a bottle of whisky.

Even worse was to come. Smith refused to have an expensive coffin for the burial, which took place at noon on Monday. He said: 'When they are dead, they are done with.' He left by train for Southsea – to clear out and sell all Alice's belongings – immediately after the funeral, and Mrs Crossley shouted 'Crippen' at him as he left the house. She also wrote on the address card he gave her: 'Wife died in bath. We shall see him again.' She could not know how prophetic those words were.

Smith rejoined the faithful Edith Pegler at Bristol in time for Christmas and used the £500 insurance money to increase his annuity. By August they were in Bournemouth, via London Cheltenham and Torquay. Smith announced he was going up to London again, alone, for a few days. He had met and wooed a maid called Alice Reavil while listening to a band on the seafront. They married at Woolwich on 17 September, but Smith did not stay long. He was back in Bristol with the girl's £80 savings and some of her clothes – a gift for Edith – by late autumn.

The callous truth was that Alice was so poor she was not worth killing. Smith

Blood-shedding Mongol leader Genghis Khan never let up on his
bouts of mayhem and murder – even when he was in his coffin. He
left orders that if anyone looked at his coffin, his funeral guards
were to ensure that the next coffin would be theirs.

Genghis Khan once had 70 enemy chiefs stewed alive. He did not
believe in taking prisoners and tore open victims' bellies in case
they were hiding jewels. His prisoners' heads would be cut and
banked up in sickly pyramids.

Genghis Khan is reputed to have been the biggest mass killer in
history. He is believed to have been responsible for the deaths of
20 million people – one-tenth of the world's population at that
time. He died in 1227.

abandoned her in some public gardens after a long tram ride. But he already
had a third murder victim in mind. He had met Miss Margaret Lofty, a 38-
year-old clergyman's daughter, in Bath the previous June. She worked as a lady's
companion, living between jobs with her elderly widowed mother. And she was
ripe for exploitation – she had discovered earlier in the year that her 'fiance' was
a married man.

Smith was now calling himself John Lloyd and posing as an estate agent. He
took her out to tea on 15 December and two days later they were married in
secret. Smith had taken the precaution of persuading his beloved to insure her
life for £700 and had even generously paid the first premium. They moved to
London, taking rooms at 14 Bismarck Road, Highgate. Naturally they had a
bath. But Smith seemed to have grown over-confident after the success of his
two previous killings. This time he was amazingly impatient.

He took Margaret to see a local doctor on their evening of arrival, 17
December. Next morning, he took her to a solicitor to make her will – leaving
everything to him. Then she wrote to her mother, describing her husband as 'a
thorough Christian man.' By 20.00 on 18 December, she was having a bath.
Her landlady, ironing downstairs, later recalled a splashing sound, and a noise
'as of someone putting wet hands or arms on the side of the bath.' Then there
was a sigh, followed by the strains of the hymn Nearer My Go To Thee on the
harmonium in the front room. Ten minutes later the landlady answered the
doorbell and found 'Mr Lloyd' standing outside, saying he had forgotten his key
after popping out to buy tomatoes for his wife's supper. Sadly, Mrs Lloyd was
not alive to eat them.

Though Margaret was buried on the following Monday morning, the
inquest was held over until after Christmas. Smith hurried home to Bristol
again, and even had the cheek to tell Edith to beware of taking a bath, adding:

THE WORLD'S MOST INFAMOUS MURDERS

'It is known that women have often lost their lives through weak hearts and fainting in the bath.' That had been the coroner's verdict on Alice Burnham, and the Highgate coroner saw no reason to think differently when he considered the death of Margaret 'Lloyd' on 1 January, 1915.

But it was to be no happy new year for George Joseph Smith. His impatience to get rid of Margaret proved his undoing. The previous deaths had not attracted too much press attention. But this one had all the ingredients of a front page story. 'Found dead in bath,' said the headline in the *News Of The World*. A second headline read: 'Bride's Tragic Fate On Day After Wedding.'

Two readers, miles apart, noticed the story and thought it was too much of a coincidence. In Buckinghamshire, Alice Burnham's father contacted his solicitor, who went to the police. And in Blackpool, landlady Mrs Crossley also passed on her fears to the authorities. They began investigating possible connections between John Lloyd, estate agent, and George Smith, bachelor of independent means, and pieced together the incredible story of Smith's bigamous philanderings. On 1 February, a detective inspector and two sergeants arrested the deadly bridegroom as he left his solicitor's office, where he was making arrangements to collect the £700 insurance on his third victim.

Though the bodies of all three women were exhumed, and examined by famous pathologist Sir Bernard Spilsbury, there were no obvious signs of how they had drowned. And though Smith was charged with all three murders, he could only be tried, under English law, with one, that of Bessie Mundy. Smith denied strenuously that he had murdered anyone. He described the deaths of three brides in the same way as a 'phenomenal coincidence.' Any jury might have been prepared to accept that one such death was just an unfortunate accident. The prosecution therefore had to apply for permission to produce evidence about all three killings to show proof of a 'system.' Smith's attorney, Sir Edward Marshall Hall, protested, realizing that his only hope of a successful defence would be destroyed. But Mr Justice Scrutton agreed to consider all three deaths.

Marshall Hall, who believed privately that Smith used hypnotic powers to persuade all three wives to kill themselves, had another setback before the trial. Some newspapers had agreed to foot the defence bill in return for Smith's

In 1880, at the age of 26, Australian bushranger Ned Kelly was hanged at the end of a rope, watched by a huge crowd outside Melbourne jail. Kelly and his gang had killed at least four troopers in their flight from the law. Ned Kelly's last words on the scaffold were: 'Such is life!'

exclusive life story. But the Home Office vetoed the plan, and since all Smith's money was tied up in annuities, Marshall Hall received only a paltry fee under the Poor Persons Defence Act.

He received no help at all from his client. Smith repeatedly soured opinions, both at committals and at his trial, which began at the Old Bailey on 22 June, 1915, with bad-tempered outbursts at witnesses, his own lawyers and the judge. At one stage he screamed: 'It's a disgrace to a Christian country, this is. I'm not a murderer, though I may be a bit peculiar.'

The irony of the timing of the trial during World War One was not lost on Mr Justice Scrutton. A month before it, 1,198 lives were lost when a German submarine torpedoed the *Lusitania*. On the morning the trial began, *The Times* listed 3,100 men killed in the trenches. 'And yet,' said the judge in his summing-up, 'while this wholesale destruction of human life is going on, for some days all the apparatus of justice in England has been considering whether the prosecution are right in saying that one man should die.'

It took the jury only 22 minutes on 1 July to decide that he should. They had heard pathologist Spilsbury explain how Smith could have lifted his brides' legs with his left arm while pushing their heads under water with his right. And they had watched a dramatic reconstruction of such a possibility, carried out by a detective and a nurse in a bathing costume in an ante-room of the court. Even though the nurse knew what was about to happen, she still needed artificial respiration after her ordeal.

Smith was taken from Pentonville Jail to Maidstone Prison, still protesting his innocence. He remained unrepentant, though he turned to religion and was confirmed by the Bishop of Croydon, who was said to be impressed with his sincerity. On the eve of his execution, Smith wrote to Edith Pegler, who had wept for him outside the Old Bailey, saying: 'May an old age, serene and bright, and as lovely as a Lapland night, lead thee to thy grave. Now, my true love, goodbye until we meet again.'

Edith alone mourned on Friday, 13 August, when Smith was led to his execution. One day later, his first and only legal wife, Caroline Thornhill, took advantage of her widowhood to marry a Canadian soldier in Leicester.

Atlanta's Streets of Fear

WAYNE WILLIAMS

The 'Missing and Murdered Children' file in the Atlanta Police headquarters had 26 unsolved cases by late spring of 1981. Throughout the two previous years black children had been snatched from the streets or simply disappeared in this town in America's deep south and it was sometimes months before their bodies were discovered hidden in undergrowth or dumped in a river. Murder had reached epidemic proportions in Atlanta. The victims were always coloured and often too young to have had any chance to defend themselves. Death was usually due to strangulation. Forensic experts believed the children, one of whom was aged only seven, were being attacked from behind by a man who squeezed the life out of them by locking his arm around their necks.

A shroud of fear fell over the town while the homicidal maniac stalked the streets. At night the roads and the pavements were deserted. Parents too scared to let their children out of their sight for more than a few seconds were locking their doors to keep them inside. Vigilante parent patrols were formed. Fathers often armed themselves with baseball bats.. And over everything hung suspicion. Was a white man carrying out his own macabre mission against blacks or was a crazy cult killer on the loose?

The two-year search for the killer had broken the health of many senior police officers, stretched the resources of the whole town and even caused the State Justice Department to set up a special unit to join in the hunt. Every time another child went missing the efforts were intensified. But despite millions of dollars spent, the murders continued.

FBI officers had to be drafted in to Atlanta to help police chief Lee Brown who was under universal attack from the townspeople. And hordes of cranks arrived in town eager to pick up the $100,000 reward for information leading to the arrest of the killer. It was a frightening and macabre mystery – made the worse by the fact that the police believed the killer was taunting them.

After November 1980, when the eleventh killing occurred, children were being murdered at intervals of about three and a half weeks. The bodies, instead of being hidden, were left conspicuously in parks. And despite all precautions the parents were taking, the killer was still finding victims.

As he stepped up his campaign of death, a grisly pattern was beginning to

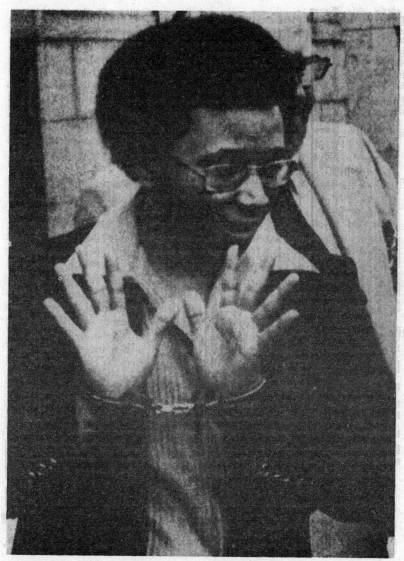

Wayne Williams leaving Fulton County Court, August 1981

emerge. All the children had been aged between 7 and 14 years and all but two were boys. Yet despite fears of a crazed pervert being on the loose, there was no evidence that any of the children had been sexually assaulted. Worse, the police were worried that if just one person was responsible for all the deaths then other psychopaths may be encouraged by the apparent ease and lack of detection. The desperate hunt for the killer was one of the biggest police operations ever launched in the United States. Twenty-thousand citizens were interviewed by officers, another 150,000 were questioned over the telephone. Tens of thousands of children were spoken to because the police believed that at sometime the killer could have tried to abduct a child unsuccessfully. Thirty-five FBI agents were permanently stationed in Atlanta and had been told they would stay there until the investigation was over.

Then one night in May 1981 there was a dramatic breakthrough. Two police officers and two FBI agents were huddled in a corner under the arches of the four-lane South Drive Bridge. They were one of dozens of teams which undertook around-the-clock vigils in the city. Ironically they were not watching the river on that misty night. They were merely covering the bridge because it formed one of the main routes to and from the town and they could quickly be on the road to join in any chase or stop any suspect leaving Atlanta. But as they chatted in whispers they were startled by something splashing into the water only a metre or so away. Two of the men went into the water to try to help whoever had gone in, and two sprinted up to the road and were there within a few seconds. They radioed ahead and a patrol car arrived almost instantly at the end of the bridge and stopped the traffice coming off it. Drivers were questioned briefly and then allowed to go on their ways.

Two days later police frogmen fished out of the river the body of Nathaniel Cater a 27-year-old negro. Strangulation was given as the cause of death.

If the same killer had struck again, then he had broken his pattern. The victim was black and had died from strangulation . . . but he was an adult. There

---

John Lee was the man they could not hang. Lee, a 19-year-old servant with a previous conviction for theft, was controversially found guilty of murdering his employer, Miss Emma Keyse, who had her throat cut and skull crushed in November 1884. Three times, he took his place on the scaffold, but each time the trapdoor refused to open, though it worked perfectly when tested with weights in between. Lee, who said: 'It was the Lord's hand which would not let the law take away my life,' was given a prison sentence instead, and released in 1907 after serving 22 years. He then married, emigrated to America, and died there in 1933.

> **Anna Maria Zwanziger took a terrible revenge on the legal profession after her husband, an alcoholic lawyer, died leaving her only debts. She took housekeeping jobs in the homes of judges, then proceeded to poison her employers and their families.**
>
> **She is known to have murdered one judge who refused to marry her, the wives of two more, and the child of one of them. Altogether, she poisoned an estimated 80 people, though most escaped with violent illness. After her arrest, police noticed that she trembled with pleasure when confronted with arsenic powder. She was executed by the sword in Bavaria in 1811.**

were enough similarities for the police to suspect that Cater was number 27 in the chain of killings. The 'Missing and Murdered Children' file was renamed 'Missing and Murdered People'.

A few days later the body of a second victim, 21-year-old Ray Payne, also a negro, was recovered from the river. He had been thrown in at the same time as Cater and had also died from strangulation. Knowing that four of the child victims had previously been recovered from the river, the investigation team went back to the drivers they had stopped on the night the surveillance team had been under the bridge.

One of the men they questioned was Wayne Bertram Williams a 23-year-old black who lived quietly with his parents, both retired school-teachers, in a modest single-storey house in north-west Atlanta. He was taken to the city police headquarters and held overnight but was released despite the police discovery that he lived a bizarre lifestyle and considered himself a genius. Williams was a self-described 'media groupie'. He used to sit around in his car with a short-wave radio and tune in to police and fire services listening out for crimes or fires. Then, equipped with a camera, he would rush to the scene, usually arriving ahead of reporters and television crews and sell his exclusive pictures to the highest bidder. At the age of 14 he had started broadcasting on his own small pirate radio station in Atlanta. An only and lonely child, he had been convicted at 18 of impersonating a police officer. All his friends were shocked and surprised when they learnt that he was a police suspect.

On 3 June he was again taken in for questioning by police and given a 12-hour grilling. The next day, he rang newspapers and TV stations and held a press conference. Professing his innocence, he claimed the police had told him he was the prime suspect in some of the slayings. He said: 'One cop told me "You killed Nathaniel Cater. It's just a matter of time before we get you." I never killed anybody and I never threw anything from the bridge.'

For the next two and a half weeks Williams was under constant surveillance.

THE WORLD'S MOST INFAMOUS MURDERS

Charles Whitman went to pieces after his parents split up in March 1966. The 25-year-old student complained of headaches, showed violent temper tantrums, and became convinced he had a growth in his brain which was making him mentally ill. In the early hours of 1 August, he stabbed and shot his mother, then stabbed his wife. Taking several pistols, a radio and sandwiches, he climbed a 100 metres high observation tower at the University of Texas in Austin, clubbing a receptionist to death and barricading the stairway.

Two people climbing to the tower were shot, and at 11.40, Whitman, an expert shot after Marine service, began shooting indiscriminately at students. He killed 16 and wounded 30 in the next 90 minutes, defying attempts by police and low-flying aircraft to dislodge him. Finally police stormed the barricade he had built, and shot him to pieces. They later found a note from him saying: 'Life is not worth living.'

And then the results of tests on fibres taken from his car came from the laboratory. The fibres matched those on clothing of murder victims Cater and Payne. Williams was arrested and indicted on the charge of murdering Cater. The Payne charge was added later.

The police then faced up to the real problem of trying to get Williams convicted. Their evidence was not good. They had no witnesses either to the killings or the dumping of the bodies. All their hopes were pinned on the wizardry of the forensic scientists.

Their fears were justified as the nine-week trial got under way. Firstly, there was no motive, though prosecution lawyers suggested that Williams was 'a frustrated man driven by a desire to purify the black race by murdering poor young blacks'. Defending the accused man was Alvin Binder a well-known Mississippi trial lawyer, who was clearly scoring points as he tore the prosecution's evidence into shreds. Then the trial took a remarkable turn when the judge made a surprise ruling after a plea from the prosecution. With their case literally hanging by threads, the lawyers persuaded him to allow them to introduce evidence linking Williams to the deaths of ten other victims. The assistant District Attorney, Joseph Drolet, said: 'He has not been formally charged with the killings but the cases will reveal a pattern and bent of mind.'

The evidence brought to life a case that had slipped into a repetition of complicated forensic evidence. A boy aged 15 said he had been fondled by Williams who he later saw with 14-year-old Lubie Geter whose decomposed body was found clad only in underpants. Other witnesses said they had spotted him with more of the victims. One music business contact of Williams' said the accused man had once passed him a note which said: 'I could be a mayor – I could even be a killer.'

When Williams took the stand he denied everything. No, he had not stopped his car on the bridge, nor even slowed down. No, he had not thrown Cater's body over nor did he believe he would have had the strength to lift it. No, he was not a homosexual. Yes, all the witnesses and even the police had lied. He told the jury: 'I never met any of the victims. I feel just as sorry for them as anybody else in the world. I am 23 years old and I could have been one of the people killed out there.'

Later, under persistent cross-examination, he accused the prosecutor of being a fool and he described two FBI men who had interviewed him as 'goons'.

Finally the jury of eight blacks and four whites retired. They deliberated for 12 hours before returning a verdict of 'Guilty'.

As he was being led away to start two consecutive life terms Williams turned with tears streaming down his face, and protested his innocence 'from my heart'. His father, Homer Williams, cried out: 'It's impossible to find a young man like this guilty.' But guilty he was found and he went to jail knowing that it would be 14 years before he could be eligible for parole.

His lawyers immediately made plans to appeal – a process which many expected to take years.

The Case of the Lethal 'Cuppa'

GRAHAM YOUNG

He was the most charming and efficient tea boy. His coffee was good, too. But a price had to be paid for it. It cost two people their lives. In April 1971, 23-year-old Londoner Graham Young, who was on a government training course at Slough, Berkshire, answered a 'help wanted' advertisment in a local paper. It said that John Hadland, manufacturers of specialist, highspeed optical and photographic instruments, needed a storeman at their small factory in the Hertfordshire village of Bovingdon.

Young said on his application form that he had 'previously studied chemistry, organic and inorganic, pharmacology and toxicology over the past 10 years' and had 'some knowledge of chemicals'.

He told the managing director, Mr Godfrey Foster, that before going to the training centre he had a nervous breakdown after his mother's death and had had mental treatment. Mr Foster was sent the report of a psychiatrist who had treated Young. It said that Young had made 'an extremely full recovery' from a 'deep-going personality disorder' and would 'do extremely well training as a storekeeper'. It also said Young was of above-average intelligence and 'would fit in well and not draw any attention to himself in any community'.

The report was hopelessly wrong on all counts – as Young's workmates were to find out. They did their best to make him feel at home, and he was befriended in particular by the head storeman, Bob Egle, 59, Frederick Biggs, 61, head of the works-in-progress department, and storeman-driver Ronald Hewitt, 41. Rob and Frederick would often lend him cigarettes and money, and Young offered to get tea and coffee for everybody who was kind to him.

Then a strange illness which was nicknamed the 'Bovingdon Bug' began to hit the staff at Hadland's. About 70 members of the staff went down with the illness. Symptoms included diarrhoea, stomach pains, loss of hair and numbness in the legs. Some said their tea tasted bitter, and a medical team was called in to find out if the chemicals used at the factory were responsible. The 'bug' killed two members of the staff – the kindly Bob Egle and Frederick Biggs. Bob died first. He became ill less than a month after Young joined the firm. His condition deteriorated rapidly and he was admitted to hospital. His heart

THE CASE OF THE LETHAL 'CUPPA'

Above: Broadmore where Young was sent as a 14-year-old schoolboy

Left: Graham Young, aged 24

stopped twice while he was in intensive care unit and he died, paralyzed, on 7 July. Young appeared to be very concerned at Egle's death and attended the funeral. Then, in September 1972, Frederick was taken ill with stomach pains and vomiting. He died three weeks later in a London hospital.

When he heard about it Young is reported to have said: 'Poor old Fred. I wonder what went wrong? He shouldn't have died. I was very fond of old Fred.'

With Biggs' death, panic set in at the factory and several employees threatened to resign. Iain Anderson, the firm's medical officer, became suspicious when Young boasted about his knowledge of medicine and poisons. Detective Chief Inspector John Kirkland, of Hemel Hempstead police, was called in and asked Scotland Yard to check Young's background. When the answer came back, Young was arrested on suspicion of murder.

Police found that his bedsitter was full of bottles containing various chemicals and poisons, and the walls plastered with photographs of his heroes – Hitler and other Nazi leaders. A bottle of thallium, a deadly poison, tasteless and odourless, was found on Young when he was arrested.

Young went on trial at St Albans in July 1972. It took the jury less than an hour to find him guilty of two murders, two attempted murders and two charges of administering poison.

He was jailed for life and placed in a top security hospital. But it was only there that his background came to light. The hospital in which he had been treated for his breakdown turned out to be Broadmoor. In 1962 he had pleaded guilty at the Old Bailey to poisoning his father, his sister and a friend. Young was, in fact, a compulsive poisoner before he was 15.

Mr Justice Melford Stevenson had committed Young to Broadmoor with a recommendation that he should not be released for 15 years. He was discharged nine years later as having made 'an extremely full recovery', and the result was that two kindly innocent men died.

The World's
GREATEST
CRIMES OF
PASSION

Contents

Acknowledgements

A book of this nature must inevitably draw on existing published material. The author wishes to acknowledge his particular debt to:

Crimes of Passion, Treasure Press, 1983; *Strange Crimes of Passion*, Leonard Gribble, John Long, 1970; *A Crime of Passion*, Stanley Loomis, Hodder and Stoughton, 1968; *Crime of Passion*, Derrick Goodman, Elek Books, 1958 *The Chalkpit Murder*, Edgar Lustgarten, Hart-Davis, 1974; *'Orrible Murder*, Leonard De Vries, Macdonald and Jane's, 1974; *Vintage Murder of the Twenties*, Gerald Sparrow, Arthur Barker, 1972; *Crime and Detection*, Julian Symons, Studio Vista, 1966; *Forty Years of Murder*, Professor Keith Simpson, Harrap, 1978; *Murder: 'Whatdunit'*, J.H.H. Gaute and Robin Odell, Harrap, 1982; *Tragedy in Three Voices*, Sir Michael Havers, Peter Shankland and Anthony Barrett, Kimber, 1980; *The Minister and the Choir Singer*, William M. Kunstler, Gollancz, 1964; *Society Sensations!* Horace Wyndham, Robert Hale, 1938; *The Trial of Ley and Smith*, Ed. C.E. Bechhofer, Roberts, Jarrolds, 1947; *The Trial of Rattenbury and Stoner*, Ed. F. Tennyson Jesse, William Hodge, 1935; *The Lives of the Gallant Ladies*, Abbé de Brantôme, (trs. Alec Brown), Elek Books, 1961; *A Pictorial History of the Wild West*, James D. Horan and Paul Sann, Spring Books, 1954; *Murder and its Motives*, F. Tennyson Jesse, Harrap, 1952; *A Book of Trials*, Sir Travers Humphreys, Heinemann, 1953; *Lord Darling's Famous Cases*, Dudley Barker, Hutchinson, 1936; *The Sex War and Others*, Rayner Heppenstall, Peter Owen, 1973; *Young Thomas Hardy*, Robert Gittings, Heinemann, 1975; *Royal Murder*, Marc Alexander, Muller, 1978; *English Treason Trials*, C.G.L. Du Cann, Muller, 1964; *Crimes and Cases of 1933*, Roland Wild, Rich & Cowan, 1934; *The Trial of Bywaters and Thompson*, Ed. Filson Young, William Hodge, 1923; *The Burning of Evelyn Foster*, Jonathan Goodman, David and Charles, 1977; *Encyclopaedia of Modern Murder*, Colin Wilson and Donald Seaman, Arthur Barker, 1983; *Detection Stranger than Fiction*, Leo Grex, Robert Hale, 1977; *Mrs Harris*, Diana Trilling, Hamish Hamilton, 1982; *White Mischief*, James Fox, Jonathan Cape, 1982; *The Trials of Mr Justice Avory*, Bernard O'Donnell, Rich and Cowan, 1935; *Ten Real Murder Mysteries*, Sidney Sutherland, Putnam, 1929; *Doctors on Trial*, Michael Hardwick, Herbert Jenkins, 1961; *Doctors of Murder*, Simon Dewes, John Long, 1962; *Ruth Ellis, A Case of Diminished Responsibility?* Laurence Marks and Tony Van Den Bergh, Macdonald and Jane's, 1977; *Crime Within the Square Mile*, Ernest Nicholls, John Long, 1935; *Twelve Against the Law*, Edward D. Radin, Heinemann, 1950.

The publishers wish to thank the following for their kind permission to reproduce the pictures used in this book:
Topham Picture Library 15, 16, 18, 35, 38, 41, 47, 48, 51, 59, 71, 76, 105, 108, 112/3, 113, 115, 117, 135, 138, 143, 146, 166, 175, 179; Mary Evans Picture Library 21, 64, 81; National Portrait Gallery 62; BBC Hulton Picture Library 88/9, 89, 120, 123, 144, 155, 165, 166/7.

Introduction

Love, jealousy, revenge and despair – they are themes which everyone can understand. It may be hard to grasp the psychology of the mass murderer or the sex killer. But you do not need to be a monster to sympathise with the injured mistress in the bar-room saga of Frankie and Johnny:

> She shot her man
> 'Cos he was doin' her wrong.

This is a book of love stories in which someone feels themselves to be wronged – and someone pays the price. Often, the drama that unfolds will involve three people, figures caught in the eternal triangle which has wrecked loves and lives since the dawn of time.

In France and in certain other Latin countries, a special leniency is reserved for those charged with the *crime passionnel*. Broadly speaking, the term covers any crime due to lovers' jealousy or despair. If an outraged husband, for example, shoots his wife's lover he may secure a complete acquittal. The assailant is seen as defending the sanctity of his marriage, and the law is prepared to be flexible.

No such system operates in the Anglo-Saxon courts. The term 'crime of passion' is popularly used to describe any kind of offence rooted in the frenzies and frustrations of love. Jealousy, of course, remains the recurrent theme in real life as in folklore and literature. The 'green-eyed monster' lurks behind the majesty of Shakespeare's *Othello* as it does behind the honky-tonk chords of *Frankie and Johnny*.

A wealth of cases are described in the pages which follow: high romances, mysteries and horror stories – as well as some purely ludicrous episodes. What unites all the crimes is their passionate nature. Even the most coolly accomplished were conceived in the turmoil of hot blood.

Chapter
One

Hell hath
no fury

Playwright William Congreve is credited with the words, 'Hell hath no fury like a woman scorned.' Actually what the dramatist wrote was,

Heaven has no rage like love to hatred turned,
Nor Hell a fury like a woman scorned.

Either way, the truth is the same. And when a proud woman is rejected by husband or lover social status counts for little. Pauline Dubuisson was a medical student; Ruth Ellis a night club manageress; Yvonne Chevallier wife to a government minister. All succumbed to the same driving passion to destroy the man she had loved.

'I'll Kill Him!'

When 23-year-old Kittie Byron stabbed her lover to death on the steps of a London post office, the charge really had to be murder. And murder in 1902 was a hanging offence. It made no difference that Arthur Reginald Baker had behaved like a brute towards her; no difference that, when the flood of her fury was spent, she collapsed sobbing on his crumpled body, calling pitifully: 'Reggie . . . Dear Reggie . . . Let me kiss my Reggie . . .'

The crime was committed in broad daylight before a dozen witnesses. She had stabbed him twice: once through the back and once through the breast. The second blow was probably the one that killed him. He died almost instantly.

Yet everyone's sympathy was with the frail, dark-haired girl who had wielded the knife. The coroner's jury, for example, brought in a verdict of manslaughter. The officials were incredulous, and the coroner himself asked: 'Do you mean unlawful killing without malice?'

'Yes,' insisted the foreman, 'killing on the impulse of the moment. We do not believe she went there with the intention of killing him.'

In fact, all the evidence suggested that Kittie Byron went there with precisely that intention. And when she was brought for trial the following month, it was on a charge of murder.

For some months before the fatal episode, Kittie Byron had been living with Arthur Reginald Baker in rooms at 18 Duke Street, off Oxford Street, in the West End. Baker was a married man and a member of the Stock Exchange. But that did not prevent him from presenting himself and his mistress to the landlady as 'Mr and Mrs Baker'. He drank heavily, often knocked Kittie about, and on one occasion half strangled her. But Kittie was loyal. She never touched liquor herself, and tried to shield her lover from the consequences of his actions.

Events came to a head on the night of Friday 7 November 1902, when the landlady heard a furious row erupt in the bed-sitting room. She went up and entered; bed-clothes had been thrown all about and lay in chaos on the floor; to one corner was a hat which had been ripped into shreds. The landlady confronted the drunken Baker, but Kittie interceded. 'Oh, there's nothing the matter,' she said, 'We've been playing milliner.'

Not long after the landlady left the room, the quarrel broke out again. It went on all evening, and at 01.15 the householder went back again to try and stop it. She found Kittie in the corridor, shivering in her nightdress. She was plainly terrified – yet still she insisted that nothing was the matter.

The next morning the landlady gave the couple notice to leave the premises.

A weekend of calm followed, and on Monday morning Baker even took Kittie a cup of tea before leaving for the office. She kissed him goodbye – a domestic scene – nothing hinted at the coming drama. The date was 10 November 1902, the day of the fatal stabbing.

The whole sequence of events emerged clearly at the trial. Just before he left the house, Baker asked the landlady for a private word. He requested that they be allowed to stay in the house after all. The landlady, however, insisted that they must leave. It was then that Baker informed her that Kittie was not his wife. The girl was the cause of the trouble, he said. She was 'no class' and would leave tomorrow.

The conversation was overheard by a housemaid who immediately told Kittie that Baker was going to cast her aside. 'Will he?' fumed the enraged girl. 'I'll kill him before the day is out!' She made her own preparations for going out, and confessed to the landlady about the phoney marriage. 'Then why don't you leave him?' asked the landlady, who had assumed that only wedlock kept the couple together. 'I can't,' said Kittie, 'because I love him so.'

She went to a shop in Oxford Street and asked a cutler for a long, sharp knife. He showed her a large item with a sprung blade that fitted into the hasp. She seemed too slight a girl to handle it, and the cutler suggested alternatives. No, said Kittie, she had a strong grip, and she proved it by operating the spring action several times. Having bought the knife she slipped it into her muff and made her way to a post office in Lombard Street. The building stood in the heart of the City where Baker worked. It was Lord Mayor's Day. The crowds were out in the streets.

From the post office, Kittie sent Baker an express letter bearing the words: 'Dear Reg. Want you immediate importantly, Kittie.' But the messenger boy could not reach Baker at the Stock Exchange and returned to Lombard Street with the note. Kittie insisted that he go back again. The boy did so – and this time located Baker who returned with him to the post office.

Staff at the post office had noticed the girl's excited state. And they also noticed an absurdly trivial dispute which arose when Baker arrived. An extra charge of two pence had to be paid for the messenger boy's time. Baker flatly refused to hand the sum over; Kittie insisted that it be paid and offered her lover a florin. Somehow, the incident speaks volumes about the relative characters of the couple. Baker was still refusing to pay as he left the post office, with Kittie rushing after him. The staff noticed something flash in her hand as she made her exit.

She caught him on the steps. The two blows were swift, and bystanders noticed no blood. In fact, the several witnesses at first thought she was striking him with her muff. Baker may well have been dead before a workman grabbed Kittie's hand and the knife fell with a clatter to the pavement. The trance of her fury was shattered, and it was then that Kittie fell sobbing on her lover's body: 'Let me kiss my Reggie . . . Let me kiss my husband . . .'

Kittie Byron made two different statements to the police shortly after her arrest. In the first she said: 'I killed him wilfully, and he deserved it, and the sooner I am killed the better.' In the second: 'I bought the knife to hit him; I didn't know I was killing him.' At the trial which followed she only managed to whisper: 'Not Guilty' as her plea to the indictment.

She made a pitiable figure in the dock, a pale and delicate girl whose dark eyes wandered dazedly around the court. She wore a blue serge suit and a shirt whose white linen collar was high about her throat, fastened with a black tie. The court heard that her real name was Emma Byron, but it was not hard to see why she had earned the diminutive of 'Kittie'. Sir Travers Humphreys, then a junior brief for her defence, later recalled how she clung to the wardress who brought her into the dock: 'It seemed as if she would break down at the very outset.'

Some twenty witnesses were called by the prosecution, and Kittie did break down. It happened as a surgeon was indicating on his own body the position of her lover's stab wounds. A stifled wail was heard. All eyes turned to the dock where Kittie was racked with violent sobs.

The defence called no witnesses – not even Kittie herself. Her counsel was Henry ('Harry') Dickens, son of the great Victorian novelist, and a man who had inherited his father's genius for stirring the emotions. Dickens tried to make out a case for Kittie having intended to commit suicide rather than murder. It was an improbable thesis which ran contrary to the evidence. He was on safer ground in pointing to the plight and character of the injured girl, and in touching the hearts of the jurors.

The judge, in his summing-up, was candid about his own emotions: 'Gentlemen of the jury, if I had consulted my own feelings I should probably have stopped this case at the outset.' But he was equally candid in dismissing manslaughter as an appropriate verdict. The jury was out for ten minutes. They found her guilty of murder – but with a strong recommendation for mercy.

The form had to be observed. The black cap was brought forth, and the dread sentence was passed. Kittie, weakly professing herself innocent of wilful murder, was to hang by the neck until dead.

But she never did. Great waves of public sympathy had gone out to the frail and mistreated girl. A huge petition was quickly raised asking for a reprieve and no fewer than 15,000 signatures were obtained in a single morning. Three thousand signatures were raised from among the clerks at the Stock Exchange itself. In the event, the petition was never formally presented to the authorities, for the Home Secretary granted the reprieve before receiving the document.

Kittie Byron's sentence was commuted to penal servitude for life. In 1907, her sentence was reduced, and she was released the following year.

Death of a Minister

Pierre Chevallier's public career had been a story of brilliant success. He came from a family of well-to-do doctors and served as a medical officer during the early months of World War Two. As a result of his bravery in tending wounded soldiers under fire he was decorated. When the Germans occupied his native city of Orléans, Chevallier continued to practise medicine by day, but by night he headed the local Resistance. Before the Allies arrived to liberate the city, Pierre Chevallier had bravely led the attack which drove the Germans out.

Elected mayor of Orléans at the age of only 30, Chevallier threw himself into the task of postwar rebuilding. So masterfully did he manage the work that Orléans was officially cited as the best reconstructed city in France. Chevallier became parliamentary representative for Orléans. And on 11 August 1951, he won an even greater honour. Aged 41, he was given ministerial rank in the new government of René Pleven.

The following day, Pierre Chevallier returned from Paris to Orléans as Under Secretary of State for Technical Education. He was driven down in a big, black limousine decorated with the official tricolor cockade. He only really came for a change of clothes – there were ceremonies to attend. His wife Yvonne was waiting at their home, and told their younger son Mathieu to run and greet him with the words, *'Bonjour, Monsieur le Ministre'* (Good day, Minister).

The child ran to the doorway with his greeting. Chevallier was delighted with the reception, and tenderly hugged his son. There were, however, no joyous greetings for his wife.

Chevallier went upstairs to change clothes in the bedroom. Yvonne followed him up. There was a quarrel – and she shot him four times with a 7.65 mm Mab automatic.

Downstairs, little Mathieu heard the shots and started crying. Yvonne went down to comfort him and hand him for care to a maid. Then she returned to the bedroom. A fifth shot was heard – and a fifth bullet drilled into her husband's corpse.

He had been a minister for precisely one day. Soon, the whole of France was to learn that behind the glittering façade of Pierre Chevallier's life lay a story of failure – the failure of a marriage.

Pierre and Yvonne had married before the war. She was a nurse of peasant background who worshipped the dynamic young doctor. From the outset, Pierre's family considered the marriage a mistake, never really accepting it. And their judgement seemed to be confirmed as Pierre's fortunes rose. Yvonne lacked the social graces, becoming tongue-tied at dinners and receptions. When the smart talk started she would fall silent. A dull girl, his colleagues would say afterwards, a bit of a liability.

In fact, she loved her husband passionately, and none of her failings need have mattered if Pierre had returned her affection. But he did not. Bit by bit, Yvonne became distanced from her husband's career and concerns. The abyss opened when one of their two sons grew ill. The child's little bed was brought into the couple's bedroom while the sickness lasted. Pierre took to sleeping in his study. And when the boy recovered, Pierre continued to sleep in his own room. He never returned to the marriage bed.

The seed of suspicion was planted in Yvonne's mind. One day, searching through his pockets, she found a love letter to Pierre signed by someone called 'Jeanette'. She strongly suspected that it was written by a mutual friend, Jeanne Perreau, who was 15 years younger than herself. After a clumsy attempt to get a sample of her handwriting, Yvonne went round and accused her rival to her face. Jeanne denied that a liaison existed and back at home, Pierre told his wife to shut up and mind her own business.

But the suspicion did not die. Jeanne Perreau was the wife of a wealthy department store owner. She was a beautiful woman with luxuriant red hair and a very opulent figure. Above all, she was witty and sophisticated, shining at precisely those functions which for Yvonne were an ordeal. In June 1951, Pierre won his parliamentary seat and gave a lavish reception. His wife saw him there flirting openly with Jeanne Perreau. Yet when Yvonne herself tried to embrace her husband, he rebuffed her in front of everybody.

There was a terrible row that night. Yvonne demanded an explanation; she begged Pierre to return to their marriage bed. He replied cruelly that not only did he not want to make love to her – he did not even think himself capable of it. She had disgraced him at the reception: 'Can you really see yourself at the big banquets in Paris?' he taunted.

Pierre said that he wanted a divorce. Failing that she should take a lover. Yvonne was outraged and refused to countenance a separation. She loved him far too much for that.

Tensions were building up now to the point where something had to give. Yvonne had, for some time, been taking drugs: tranquillisers to make sleep possible, stimulants to nerve her for the day. She drank coffee in great quantities and smoked incessantly. And it was in this state of dangerous disorientation that she took the children off for a seaside holiday. From the coast she wrote a passionate letter to her husband saying that she would try to improve herself as a wife. Pierre did not reply. And when she came back, Yvonne took poison in an attempt to end her life.

Jeanne Perreau in the witness box

Yvonne Chevallier

She only just failed, and was desperately ill afterwards. Every attempt to get through to her husband met with cold scorn on his part. Yvonne followed Pierre to Paris and tried to see him at the Chamber of Deputies. She was told, through an official, that he was too busy. Then she ransacked his flat in the city, seeking evidence of his betrayal. She found it in the form of a railway timetable. He had ticked off the times for Châtelguyon trains – Jeanne Perreau was holidaying there.

Yvonne returned in a rage to Orléans and confronted the husband of her rival. M. Perreau at first tried to soothe her fears. But after a second visit he admitted that he knew Jeanne was having an affair with Pierre. Léon Perreau was not the least distressed about it either; he was one of those curious characters beloved in French farce – a *mari complaisant* or compliant husband who simply did not mind being cuckolded.

But Yvonne was no compliant wife. Pierre had found out about her trip to Paris and phoned her to call her a 'cow' and tell her to stop ruining his life. It was after this call, and Perreau's admission, that Yvonne went out and obtained a firearms licence.

There was no problem in getting the certificate; her husband was now an important political figure and she claimed he had dangerous enemies. Armed with the certificate, Yvonne went to a gun-shop where she asked for a weapon that was guaranteed to kill. They sold her the Mab automatic.

Killing was clearly in her mind – but killing whom? On 11 August Yvonne heard over the radio that Pierre had been appointed a minister. Immediately, she sent a warm telegram of congratulation. Then she contacted a nun who was a close friend and told her that she was going to commit suicide.

The nun, of course, advised her against the act. Pierre phoned later from Paris saying that he would be coming back the next day to pick up some clothes. He did not thank her for the telegram. Perhaps it was his curt and disdainful manner that mingled thoughts of murder with those of suicide.

She spent a terrible night. The next morning, Pierre's name was blazoned across every newspaper. Chevallier a Minister! – no mention, as customarily, of the loving wife. That must have rankled. Still, she mustered up enthusiasm to get little Mathieu to say his party piece – 'Bonjour, Monsieur le Ministre.'

Having kissed his son, Chevallier went upstairs with no word of kindness for his wife. He stripped to his trunks in the bedroom, and asked her to hand him clean linen. Yvonne demanded an explanation for his liaison with Jeanne. Chevallier replied with obscenities. He was going to marry Jeanne, he said, 'and you can remain in your own filth!' Amid the curses for his wife, he gloated over his appointment: 'I'm a minister!' he kept shouting.

Pierre remained unmoved when Yvonne fell sobbing to her knees and pleaded for a reconciliation. He called her worthless, he told her she stank, he piled insult upon insult. Finally, as she reached out pleading towards him, her hand brushed against his leg.

This was the catalyst. She had dared to *touch* the Under Secretary of State. Chevallier hurled a peculiarly foul-mouthed insult at his wife and made an especially obscene gesture.

Yvonne stiffened. She warned that if he went off with Jeanne she would kill herself. 'Go ahead,' he replied. 'It will be the first sensible thing you've done in your life.'

'I'm serious,' she cried, producing the automatic. 'I will kill myself.'

'Well, for God's sake kill yourself, but wait until I've gone.'

They were the last words Pierre Chevallier ever spoke. Yvonne came towards him firing as she walked: he was hit in leg, chin, chest and forehead. Having rushed downstairs to calm the crying Mathieu, she returned to the body in the bedroom. What happened next remains something of a mystery. By Yvonne's own account, she stooped over his body intending suicide. But thoughts of her children stayed her hand. As she rose from the corpse, the gun went off by accident and a fifth bullet lodged in his back.

France was outraged by the shooting. The war hero – the dynamic young mayor with his ministerial career just opening – had been cut down by what the

Pierre Chevallier

newspapers presented as a nagging wife. Feeling ran so high in Orléans itself that the trial was held in Rheims, far from the passions of the populace.

But when the case came to court, the mood changed. In part it was due to Yvonne and the tragic figure she made in the dock. Her face was a mask of suffering, the eyes dark and sunken from evident nights of anguish and remorse. Mechanically, she knotted and unknotted a handkerchief as the defence told of the humiliations she had endured. In contrast, the *soignée* elegance of Jeanne Perreau seemed almost an insult. Hissing was heard from the public benches as she gave evidence in the box. And Jeanne's husband, Léon Perreau, made a quite ridiculous impression as the *mari complaisant* in the case. It emerged that Jeanne had told him on the very first night that she had slept with Pierre. The affair had lasted 5 years, and throughout M. Perreau had been quite acquiescent. He had even been rather flattered to be cuckolded by the up-and-coming mayor. There were positive advantages too: Perreau's brother had been decorated with the Légion d'Honneur – on Chevallier's recommendation.

What a cosy arrangement for all concerned – except poor, suffering Yvonne. Public sympathy went out strongly to the deceived wife, and the prosecution sensed the climate of opinion. For example, the prisoner was not questioned about the mysterious fifth shot fired into the corpse. This could have been exploited at length as a possible act of malice and sacrilege. Nor did the prosecution make a ritual demand for the death penalty (as in the cases of Pauline Dubuisson and Léone Bouvier). It pressed instead for a short prison sentence, suggesting two years as an appropriate penalty.

The jury was out for less than an hour, one member asking for a point of clarification. The juror wanted to know precisely what was the obscene gesture that provoked Yvonne into reaching for the gun. The accused woman had broken into hysterical sobs when the question was asked during the trial; she had not been pressed at the time. Now, the authorities privately submitted an explicit description. It must have been thoroughly outrageous, for when the jury returned it acquitted Yvonne Chevallier of every charge against her. She left the court a free woman, cheered by a large crowd outside.

Although fully exonerated for her tragic action, Yvonne Chevallier selected a punishment for herself. A few months after the trial, she took herself and her two sons off to the benighted settlement at St Laurent du Maroni. This had been the site of one of France's notorious penal colonies in the mosquito swamps of French Guiana. The prison was closed, but a ramshackle community of natives and French settlers still lived there.

Banishing herself to that tropical hell, Yvonne Chevallier took up the post of a sister in charge of the maternity wing of the hospital. She was trained for the job. Yvonne had been a midwife before meeting Pierre and participating in his brilliant career.

Tess and the Wessex Hanging

She is the most moving of all Thomas Hardy's doomed heroines. Bright-eyed, peony-mouthed Tess of the d'Urbervilles is an innocent dairy maid seduced by a young man of means. Later, caught in a love triangle from which she sees no issue, Tess murders her seducer to liberate herself. Tried and condemned to death without reprieve she dies on the scaffold, a tragic sport of the gods.

Hardy drew on the country girls of his native Wessex when he painted her portrait; there was no one model for Tess. But a macabre event from his childhood provided the emotional inspiration for the novel, perhaps darkening the whole of his work. On 9 August 1856, young Thomas Hardy saw a woman hanged. Her name was Martha Brown and, like Tess, she was a victim of the eternal triangle.

Hardy was only 16 at the time. But the impression was to stay with him for the rest of his life. In 1925, when in his eighties, the novelist was to write of the execution: 'I remember what a fine figure she showed against the sky as she hung in the misty rain, and how the tight black silk gown set off her shape as she wheeled half-round and back.'

There is more than a trace of morbid sensuality in the passage; we can only guess what effect the experience may have had on the adolescent's awakening sexual impulses. The condemned woman's face had been hooded but the material, wet with rain, permitted her face to be seen quite clearly. This evidently haunted the novelist. He wrote: 'I saw – they had put a cloth over her face – how, as the cloth got wet, her features came through it. That was *extraordinary*.'

Tess, of course, has been made the subject of films, plays – and even an Italian opera by d'Erlanger. Martha Brown's story is not so well known. And yet it caused quite a sensation in its day.

Elizabeth Martha Brown was a handsome woman who lived at Birdsmoorgate, near Beaminster in Dorset. She was some 20 years older than her husband John Brown, a carrier by trade. He, it was whispered, had only married her for her money and he certainly had a roving eye. For one day in 1856, Martha caught him making love to another woman. Late that night the couple had a furious row at their home. John Brown struck his wife with his carrier's whip, and she responded by seizing an axe. The blow proved fatal.

In France, Martha Brown might have gone to trial confident of securing an acquittal. It was a classic domestic *crime passionnel*, in which sympathy for the outraged wife would surely have won leniency. But a sterner morality prevailed in Victorian Dorset. And the accused woman made matters very much worse by trying to conceal the crime. She claimed that her husband had been killed by a kick from his horse – a falsehood in which she persisted throughout her trial. It was only at the end that she confessed to having wielded the axe herself.

By then it was too late. She was condemned to death and despite immense public interest, the Home Secretary refused to grant a reprieve.

Thomas Hardy

THE WORLD'S GREATEST CRIMES OF PASSION

A crowd of some three or four thousand gathered at Dorchester Gaol to attend the hanging. Rain was falling, and a certain nervousness seems to have afflicted the officials. No woman had been hung there for some time, and the prison chaplain was too overcome with emotion to accompany Martha to the scaffold. A young clergyman was brought in to deputize (his name was Henry Moule and he was, as it happened, a friend of the Hardy family).

The public executioner, a man named Calcraft, was supposed to tie the condemned woman's dress around her so that it did not ride up to expose her as she dropped. Being out of practice, he forgot this item of procedure. Having made his way down to operate the trap, he had to climb the scaffold again.

Through all the grim preparations, Martha Brown remained calm and dignified. She had shaken hands firmly with the prison authorities before being led up the steps. And she waited in silence for the ordeal.

Young Thomas Hardy saw it all. He was apprenticed, at the time, to a Dorchester architect, and obtained a very close view of the gallows by climbing a tree close to the gaol's entrance. His second wife was to suggest that the episode tinged his life's work with bitterness and gloom. But Hardy's own references to it betray a ghoulish relish rather than melancholy. It was, no doubt, the same relish that had drawn the other thousands to the scene. In old age he professed to being ashamed of attending the hanging, 'my only excuse being that I was but a youth.'

Certainly the case fascinated him, and there is no question that the image of the condemned woman was with him as he planned his Tess. For in his personal scrapbook he kept a newspaper cutting in which a friend discussed the influence of the event on his most famous novel. Hardy pencilled in some corrections to minor points of detail (the text said that Martha had used a knife, for example). But he let the claims regarding Tess stand. And he also left the following:

> He never forgot the rustle of the thin black gown the woman was wearing as she was led forth by the warders. A penetrating rain was falling; the white cap was no sooner over the woman's head than it clung to her features, and the noose was put round the neck of what looked like a marble statue. Hardy looked at the scene with the strange illusion of its being unreal, and was brought to his complete senses when the drop fell with a thud and his companion on a lower branch of the tree fell fainting to the ground.

Hardy's boyhood companion was not alone in feeling the horror of the event. The execution provoked a leading article in the *Dorset County Chronicle*, which called for an end to the death penalty. And though it was over a hundred years before capital punishment was finally abolished in Britain, local sensitivities had clearly been aroused. For after the hanging of Martha Brown, there were no more public executions in Dorchester.

Delayed Action

Postwar France had no sympathy for collaborators. Most of the population had submitted to the German invaders, and resistance – at least until the last months of the war – was much more limited than is often supposed. Nevertheless, people who had actively assisted the Germans learned to tremble after the D-Day landings. They lived in terror of the midnight knock, of strangers at their door – of the fatal shots.

For girls who had gone out with German soldiers, a ritual humiliation was reserved. They had their heads shaved and were paraded through the streets to face the kicks, spittle and jeers of the populace. Pauline Dubuisson knew the ordeal; her head too had been shaved.

Her father was a successful engineer who lived in Dunkirk, scene of the famous beach evacuation. An admirer of Nietzsche's philosophy and of the authoritarian Nazi regime, he willingly undertook building contracts for the Germans. He brought Pauline up in a hard school. She was taught to think much and to feel little.

Pauline was only 13 when France fell, but soon she was flirting with enemy soldiers. At 17 she was mistress to a 55-year-old German colonel, and was listed by the Resistance as a collaborator. The price was paid after the Allied landings. Pauline was dragged into the main square and forced onto a stool while the men sheered off her long black hair.

Still, she had her whole life ahead of her. In 1946, the year after all hostilities ended, Pauline enrolled as a medical student at the University of Lille. Her first year report described her as intelligent, even brilliant at times, 'but she is not a steady worker. She is well balanced but haughty, provoking and a flirt. Her conduct is mediocre.'

It was at Lille that Pauline first met a handsome and athletic young student named Félix Bailly, who came from St Omer. They had a tempestuous three-year affair in which Pauline repeatedly cuckolded her lover, sleeping with other students and members of the faculty. Félix offered to marry her; it was Pauline who refused. She continued to behave promiscuously, even keeping a notebook in which she recorded details of her different lovers' performances. In the end, Félix decided to break with her. He left Lille and went to Paris to continue his medical course there.

What happened – or rather, what didn't happen – next, played a key part in the coming controversy. For some 18 months the couple saw nothing of each other. Félix settled down to his work as a diligent, well-liked student. And he also

23

became engaged to a beautiful fair-haired young woman named Monique Lombard. Back in Lille, meanwhile, Pauline was as promiscuous as ever. She even arranged a summer holiday in Germany where she resumed her friendship with the former German colonel. She made no attempt to contact Félix. Not until 1951.

Early in March of that year, a mutual friend who had been to Paris learned of Félix's marriage plans. Back in Lille Pauline heard all about the beautiful blonde and the happy future which beckoned Félix. She immediately went to Paris to meet her former lover, and try to rekindle his affections, but it didn't work. Something must have snapped then. On 10 March Pauline went back to Dunkirk to celebrate her birthday. Her father gave her 5,000 francs and with it, having acquired a fire-arms licence, she went out and bought a little .25 calibre automatic.

Pauline did not head straight for Paris. She first returned to Lille where she penned a note declaring her intention of killing both Félix and herself. The landlady had noticed the gun in her handbag, and after Pauline took the Paris train, she also discovered the threatening note. Realising the terrible danger Félix was in, the landlady telephoned Félix's father and sent a warning telegram to Félix himself.

It was less than a fortnight before his wedding was due. Félix recognised the peril, and on the night of 15 March he stayed away from his small apartment on the Left Bank, preferring to stop over at the flat of a friend, Georges Gaudel. The next night he did return to his apartment, but with Gaudel with him to act as a guardian. They were having breakfast together there on the morning of 17 March when a knock was heard at the door. It was Pauline.

She said that she wanted to see Félix alone; impossible, he replied, he had a friend with him. She persisted: 'I want to be alone with you, just for a moment . . .'

'Why alone?'

'Because I'm afraid of crying.'

Félix refused to admit her. But he did cautiously agree to a meeting in a public place, as long as Gaudel was present. They chose the Place Cambronne as a suitable site and arranged to meet there in three-quarters of an hour. Pauline left, and so in due course did Félix with Gaudel at his side.

However anguished Pauline may have been – with jealousy, despair or pure malice – there is no question that her brain now calculated with the utmost coolness and clarity. She never went to the Place Cambronne at all. Instead, she found a vantage point in a café opposite Félix's flat. There she sat and she waited, watching as the two men left, with a drink before her on the table.

Félix and Gaudel spent a nervous hour at the Place Cambronne, expecting Pauline at any moment. Eventually, though, Félix considered the danger over and decided to return to his flat. Gaudel, he said, could make his own arrangements for the day. But the companion was not so reassured. He insisted they phone another friend Bernard Mougeot to take over the role of guardian.

The call was made and Mougeot agreed to go to Félix's flat immediately. It seemed that they had covered every possible peril and Félix returned to the flat.

He was expecting Mougeot to be there already. But fate had determined otherwise. There was a transport strike in Paris that day, and the hurrying friend's taxi got stuck in a traffic jam. Pauline watched as her ex-lover returned alone to the apartment block. She paid for her coffee and followed him to the seventh floor where his flat was situated.

It is not certain how she gained admittance; probably, Félix heard a knock and assumed that Mougeot had arrived. What is beyond doubt is that Pauline shot her ex-lover three times. Any of the wounds could have killed him. The third bullet was apparently a cool *coup de grâce* delivered behind the right ear.

Pauline then tried to shoot herself too, but the gun jammed on the fourth bullet. Instead, she disconnected the pipe in the kitchen which led to the gas stove. Placing the free end in her mouth, she lay down and prepared for death.

It was some time before Bernard Mougeot arrived. He could smell the gas in the corridor and hurried in to find his friend weltering in blood on the living-room floor. Pauline, in the kitchen, was unconscious. Mougeot pulled the pipe from her mouth and summoned the fire brigade. They arrived quickly and managed to revive her with oxygen cylinders.

Pauline recovered in hospital. But the case was to claim another victim before it came to court. In Dunkirk, Pauline's father discovered what had happened. While the family discussed which lawyer to hire, he came to a decision of his own. Declaring the shame to be unendurable, he wrote a letter expressing grief and commiseration to Félix's parents. Then, having taken a dose of poison for good measure, he gassed himself in the kitchen. M. Dubuisson's will triumphed where Pauline's had failed. He was dead when they found him there.

It was many months before Pauline's trial came up in Paris. The date was set for 28 October 1952, but on that morning she was discovered unconscious in her cell, bleeding from her wrist. She had managed to open a vein with a needle and a splinter of glass. A suicide note, apparently written in the dark after her wrist was cut, expressed both regret for the crime and disdain for the coming trial: 'I think my family is accursed and myself also. I only hurt those whom I love most in the world. I have already lost over a litre of blood but I am still all right . . .'

Again revived, she was brought to trial a month later amid intense public interest. The *crime passionnel* is, of course, something of a French speciality. But the case of Pauline Dubuisson did not fit the classic pattern. The problem for the jurors and the fascinated public alike revolved around the timespan involved. Could jealous love really be quickened 18 months after the liaison was over? Or had Pauline acted purely out of malice: indifferent to Félix while she possessed him, wrathful when he sought happiness elsewhere?

The stigma of her wartime past inevitably weighed against her. She could scarcely be represented as an injured lover. If there was a woman in court to be pitied it was surely the beautiful Monique Lombard, bereaved fiancée of the murder victim. She appeared pitifully in the witness box, and the prosecutor at one point compared her innocent love with the malevolence of (pointing dramatically at Pauline) 'this bitch!'

The prosecution called for the death penalty, and pursued its case savagely. Even Pauline's suicide attempts were scorned. How convenient, it was insinuated, that the gun jammed before Pauline could shoot herself. Had she really tried to gas herself? Or did she turn the tap only when she heard the sound of someone arriving at the door? Remarkable, was it not, that she should have failed yet again when she cut her wrist. 'You are more efficient when it comes to murder', taunted the prosecutor.

The thrusts were vicious – and surely unfair. The murder weapon was found jammed on the fourth shot. Firemen testified that Pauline had second-degree asphyxiation when they arrived: she was foaming at the lips. And she had lost over a litre of blood when discovered in her cell.

But Pauline's character was such that things looked very black for her. Extracts from the notebook in which she described her lovers' performances were read out in court. The passages concerning Félix and her other lovers too were cold and acid in tone. In the dock she remained largely unmoved by others' grief – everyone noted the 'mask of pride' that she wore. To win an acquittal, the defence had to prove the case to be a *crime passionnel*. What did Pauline Dubuisson know of love?

Might she even go to the guillotine? No woman had been executed in France during peacetime since 1887. On that occasion, a writhing female victim had to be dragged under the blade by her hair. The episode was so sickening that the public executioner threatened to resign if any more women were brought before him. A convention had since developed, whereby even if a woman was sentenced to death, she would always be granted a reprieve.

If Pauline were found guilty of murder, would the convention hold? Perhaps there was a trace of doubt in the jury's mind, for they brought in a verdict of murder – but without premeditation. She was sentenced to penal servitude for life.

A curious verdict. Her behaviour for days before the shooting suggested that she had murder very much in mind. A curious sentence, too. For a more orthodox *crime passionnel* she might have expected much more lenient treatment.

Clearly this was a killing with an extenuating circumstance. It is hard to know how to define it, – unless you called it delayed-action love.

A Tale of Two Sisters

Chronic alcoholism is a deep-rooted problem in the French countryside. Wine is cheap and the hard routines of farming life can be monotonous. To escape them, many a working man daily stupefies his senses with the bottle. M. Bouvier of Saint-Macaire came from a long line of hereditary alcoholics. His special drink was not wine, as it happens, but a crude cider alcohol distilled in the region of western France where he lived. Bouvier used to get violently drunk and regularly threatened to murder his wife and two daughters. From an early age, the girls learned to help their mother with the almost nightly ordeal of strapping him down to the bed. Someone would then run for the doctor. The doctor would give him the injections that brought a fragile calm to the household.

This is the story of those two sisters. Georgette, the older one, plays only a peripheral role in the drama. Yet it was to be intensely significant in the life of Léone, the younger girl.

The village of Saint-Macaire lies near the town of Cholet in the Maine-et-Loire department. And at the local school, Georgette showed considerable intelligence. At the age of 18 she managed to escape the household by entering a convent at Angers. Forsaking the hell of her family life, she submitted to the pious disciplines of a nun's existence. And there, for a while, we must leave her.

Léone Bouvier, two years younger, cried for a week when her sister abandoned the household. She was alone now with the wreck of her father and a mother who had also taken to drinking. Léone was not bright; in fact, her school years had left her practically illiterate. The meagre salary she earned at a local shoe factory was absorbed by the family's needs. But her mother showed no gratitude. She mocked Léone for being worthless and dull-witted. And, rejected by all those closest to her, Léone looked for love elsewhere. She turned, in particular, to men.

She was not a pretty girl. Her eyes were wide-set, her nose was large and a ragged shank of dark hair fell across her low brow. A generous heart only made her an easier prey for the local lads.

Léone lost her virginity to a fellow factory worker at a hurried coupling in the corner of a field. She saw him the next day, laughing about the episode with his mates in the factory yard. Other sad encounters were to follow until she struck up with a decent-hearted young man in the Air Force. Fate never gave Léone a break, though; not long after they arranged to be married, the youth was killed in an accident.

It was in the bleak period following the incident that Léone met Emile Clenet, a 22-year-old garage mechanic from Nantes. Their first brief encounter was at a dance in Cholet, and they made a rendezvous for the following afternoon. Misfortune was Léone's constant companion, and while cycling to the meeting she had to stop to fix a puncture. By the time she arrived, he was gone.

Six months later, however, they met again at the Lent carnival in Cholet. 'You're six months late,' joked Emile. 'But never mind, we've found each other again.' They enjoyed all the fun of the fair together and afterwards, Emile took her to a hotel room. She had never been treated to clean sheets before. She learned to love him then.

The couple fell into a set pattern of meetings. To reverse the lyrics of the popular song, it was 'Only on a Sunday' for Emile and Léone. He was a hard worker and reserved only the seventh day for his pleasures. Every Sunday, Léone would cycle to a particular spot near Cholet, and Emile would pick her up on his motorbike. After picnicing and perhaps some evening dancing, they would retire to a cheap hotel.

There was talk of marriage, and Emile took her home to meet his parents, who rather liked their son's strange little girlfriend. It is hard to determine exactly what went wrong. Perhaps Emile never seriously intended marriage. Once, there was an accident with his motorbike and Léone took a knock on the head. She suffered headaches and bouts of depression after that.

Emile could be cruel, too. Once, snapped by a street photographer, the couple went to pick up the picture. Emile took one look and said he didn't want it. When Léone asked why, he said: 'Just look at that face and you'll understand.' She hurried off to cry alone. Since meeting Emile, Léone had been taking care of her appearance, indulging in all the feminine vanities. Words like those must have wounded deeply.

The real blow came when she found she was pregnant and Emile told her to get rid of the unborn child. She did so – but the headaches and depressions grew worse after that. Then, in January 1952, she lost her job. There was a furious row in her home that night: her mother raged at her and her drunken father tried to give her a thrashing. Léone fled the household. It took her all night to cycle the 30-odd miles to Nantes where Emile worked. But when she got there in the morning, Emile was annoyed. Their arrangement was only for Sundays, he said. It was a weekday. She must leave.

Utterly abandoned, Léone spent two weeks as an outcast in Nantes, wandering the cold, winter streets. A second attempt to see Emile resulted in another rebuff. He said he was too busy to see her for the next couple of Sundays. Her money ran out. She had nowhere to sleep. And though she was never very clear about what happened during that blank fortnight, it seems she slipped into prostitution.

During the days, Léone took to standing outside gun-shop windows, gazing dazedly in at the gleaming butts and barrels. Later, she was to say that she did not quite know why she did so; perhaps suicide had been in her mind. But she remembered one incident very clearly. As she stood there, shivering in the rain, a strange young man had appeared at her side. 'Don't', said the figure, 'He is too young. He has the right to live.' Then he disappeared.

Hallucination? Léone had been a victim all her life, and perhaps her conscious mind was moving towards thoughts of self-destruction. But perhaps, too, some last instinct to survive and strike outward was prompting from within. The impulse was to murder her lover. And to redress the balance, her conscience invented the phantasmagoric young man who seemed to know her thoughts.

Whatever the truth, that voice seems to have earned Emile a reprieve. For she did not yet buy a gun. Instead, physically and emotionally exhausted, she returned to her village. Nothing had changed there. On arrival, her father was in one of his frenzies. Mechanically, she helped her mother strap him to the bed.

She had come back from one hell to another, and only thoughts of Emile sustained her. 15 February 1952 was Léone's 23rd birthday. Would her lover remember? Last year he had bought her a bicycle lamp – the only present of her adult life. She summoned up her courage, took the last of her savings, and boarded the coach back to Nantes. Humbly and apologetically she approached him at the garage and asked if they could meet on Sunday at the usual place. He showed no sign of remembering her birthday. But – to her intense joy – he agreed to meet at the rendezvous.

When he came, he brought no birthday present. Emile made love brusquely that Sunday and he did not stay the night as usual. It was on the following day that Léone went into Nantes and sought out one of the gunshops. There she bought a .22 automatic. The pistol had recently been declared a 'sporting weapon'. Léone, who could barely sign her name, did not need a license.

She lived now only for their Sundays. Léone hung around in Nantes waiting for the next meeting, living from day to day in the dockside area by taking men into hotel bedrooms. When the grey haze of waiting hours was over she hastened

---

To Have And To Hold
On 27 August 1984, Mrs Jose Kubiczek returned to her home at Saint-Amand-les-Eaux. It was to be a final visit; she came only to take custody of her son. But it seems her husband could not face the future without her. The French police reported he had strangled his wife, then dressed her in a wedding gown. He was found lying beside her corpse on the conjugal bed.

to their rendezvous at Cholet. Emile was not there. She scoured the town and eventually found his motorbike parked outside a cinema. When the film was over she ran to meet him, but he brushed her off. He had flu, he said. He was going straight home. She must wait for the coming Lent carnival.

Fate, which had dogged Léone all her life, had reserved its completing irony for this meeting. It was at Cholet's Lent carnival that the couple had enjoyed their first night together two years earlier. It was at the Lent carnival too, with its hurdy-gurdy gaiety, that Léone Bouvier was to kill her lover.

Yet it started so well. Emile roared up on his motorbike at their rendezvous and she mounted pillion on the back just as in the old days. She kissed him as they rode into the town centre to mingle with the carnival crowds. They moved gaily among the stalls, the streamers and the balloons. Emile stopped by a shooting range to demonstrate his prowess. The weapon (fate again) was a .22 automatic. And above the staccato crackle of gunshot he told her he was leaving to work in North Africa. He was going, he said, for good.

'But what about me? We were going to get married . . .'

'So what?'

'You don't want to marry me any more, then?'

'*C'est la vie.*' Emile shrugged and mumbled platitudes, telling her she would find someone better than him. Léone was incredulous. She asked again. Again he said no, he would never marry her.

Emile drove her back to her bicycle, locked up at their rendezvous. There she implored him, 'Emile, you aren't going off and leaving me like this?'

Emile said nothing, but returned to his motorcycle and climbed on, preparing to leave. Léone took the gun from her handbag and slipped it under her coat. She came up behind him. 'Emile,' she whispered, 'kiss me for the last time . . .'

He did not respond. She put her left arm around his neck and pulled him tenderly towards her. Gently, she kissed his cheek. And as she did so she withdrew the pistol and placed the barrel-end against his neck. Then she pulled the trigger.

There was only one shot.

Afterwards she mounted her bicycle and fled, pedalling blindly to the only place she knew that offered sanctuary. It was to Angers that she cycled, to her sister's convent. She arrived there in distress, without explaining what had happened. Georgette gave her coffee and put her to bed – the poor, ruined child come like a ghost from her past.

The police came the following afternoon. Léone was arrested in the convent, but such are the procedures of French law that it was not until December 1953 that she was brought before the Assizes of Maine-et-Loire. French courts are traditionally flexible in the handling of a *crime passionnel*. Léone's misfortune was to face an unusually aggressive prosecutor and a hostile judge.

Judges play a more active role in the French courts than their English equivalents do. They may examine and cross-question a defendant at some length. And at Léone's trial in Angers, the judge showed himself entirely lacking in the subtlety associated with the French legal mind. What he had in abundance was the stubborn hypocrisy of the French provincial bourgeois.

He simply could not see that Léone's blighted childhood or her lover's callous rebuffs made one jot of difference to the case. Why did she not stay at her parents' hearth instead of wandering the dockside at Nantes? The answer should have been evident when Léone's father was brought to the witness box, sweating and shaking under the ordeal of a morning without a drink. The experts declared him an hereditary alcoholic. The mother, too, frankly admitted that they had all lived in mortal fear of his violence. But she explained that she'd done the best she could, adding the fateful reflection that her other daughter was a nun.

The judge pounced.

'You see!' he called, rounding on Léone, 'There was no need for you to go wrong. Why did you go wrong?' It is hard to exaggerate the part played by this circumstance. It seemed to nullify every mitigating factor of Léone's background. The writer Derrick Goodman has made the point eloquently: they did not come down hard on Léone because she had murdered her lover. It was because her sister was a nun.

The judge continued with his tirade, dwelling on the fact that Léone had killed Emile as she kissed him. This was a detail that seemed to him an incomprehensible outrage: '*atroce!*' he fumed, '*atroce!*'

Léone stood quietly in the dock, her head bowed low.

'Why did you kill him?' demanded the judge.

Tears were streaming down her cheeks as Léone raised her head.

'I loved him', she said simply.

The prosecution had called for the death penalty on the charge of premeditated murder. For reasons stated in the case of Pauline Dubuisson, there was no likelihood of Léone being executed. In fact, the defence had every right to expect a very lenient judgement. What was Léone's crime if not a *crime passionnel*? Middle-class ladies had walked scot-free in cases of this nature.

The jury was out for only a quarter of an hour. And it would seem that they arrived at the same formula as in the case of Pauline Dubuisson. They avoided the charge of premeditated murder, for that carried an automatic death penalty, and found her guilty of murder – but without premeditation.

The foreman complacently suggested that the prisoner be given the maximum penalty of penal servitude for life – a minimum of 20 years. The judge readily agreed. And so, with the afflictions of a simple mind and a warm heart, a horrific childhood and a succession of rejections, Léone Bouvier fell victim to the full weight of French law.

The Real Mrs Mainwaring

The town of Colditz in Upper Saxony is remembered today for its castle, built high above the River Mulde, which housed some of the most determined escapers of World War Two. But long before its masonry knew the silent excavations of the Allied POWs, that brooding silhouette had looked down on a drama of a very different kind.

It was to Colditz that, in the summer of 1871, there came an English gentleman named Mainwaring with a beautiful companion that everyone took to be his young wife. Mainwaring booked in at a well known hotel, and engaged a suite of apartments for his honeymoon. He even received letters there, postmarked from Ferrybridge in Yorkshire. All, it appears, went on as merry as a marriage bell until one day an Englishwoman, travelling incognito, arrived at the hotel, taking two rooms on the same floor as the loving couple.

Her name was Mrs Mainwaring.

For a day or two, the real Mrs Mainwaring bided her time, apparently maturing her plan for revenge. Then, one night, she crept stealthily along the passage leading to her husband's bedchamber. Entering, pistol in hand, she saw her husband and his partner together among the sheets. Without a second thought she levelled the gun and fired. The ball passed through Mr Mainwaring's head – he died almost instantly.

This classic Victorian drama of love and vengeance had a fittingly tragic outcome. The real Mrs Mainwaring, her 'fell purpose' accomplished, was duly arrested and taken to prison. However, she was found dead in her cell the next morning. According to *The Illustrated Police News* which reported the story, she had managed to conceal poison about her person and must have swallowed it soon after her incarceration. The doctors were unanimous in their opinion that she had been dead for several hours.

The Bigamists
Bigamy provides one way out of a love triangle. In one scandalous Victorian case, the Earl of Euston sought divorce from the Countess of Euston on the grounds that she had a husband living when she married. But it emerged at the trial that the husband in question had a wife living when he married her. The Earl was refused his divorce on the grounds that the Countess was free.

A Life for a Life

Early in July 1955, north country publican Albert Pierrepoint received official notice that he would be needed in London on the 13th. A small, tidy man, Pierrepoint made the appropriate arrangements for a journey he had made many times before. On the afternoon of 12 July he arrived at the gates of Holloway Prison in North London. Admitted by the authorities, he was given a cup of tea and then taken to the door of a cell where, through the peep-hole, he could see a pale young woman reading a Bible.

The officials supplied the statistics he needed to know: Height – 5 ft 2 inches; Weight – 103 lbs. Albert Pierrepoint, official hangman, studied her file and proceeded to the execution chamber where, using a sandbag for dummy, he tested the spring-loaded mechanism of the trap.

At 09.00 the following morning, 28-year-old Ruth Ellis entered the chamber to become the last woman hanged in Britain. She faced the noose with the same extraordinary calm as she had exhibited throughout her trial and her ordeal of waiting. Ruth Ellis asked neither for sympathy nor for mercy. From the condemned cell she had written, 'I say a life for a life.'

The hanging was efficiently accomplished. The post mortem noted the fractures to spine, thyroid and cartilage, but reported the air passages clear. She had not been strangled like so many before her: 'No engorgement . . . No asphyxial changes . . . Cause of Death: Injuries to the central nervous system consequent upon judicial hanging.'

Yet neither the prisoner's calm, Pierrepoint's expertise, nor any amount of paperwork could mask the essential horror of what had transpired. 1955 was the year when Rock'n'Roll hit Britain; the first year of commercial television. Yet at Holloway Prison, an Old Testament form of tribal retribution had been enacted upon Ruth Ellis. For days beforehand, friends, relatives, lawyers and MPs had been pressing desperately for a reprieve. On the eve of the execution, the crowds had already started to assemble outside the prison gates, equipped with Thermos flasks and sleeping bags, so as to be near as the macabre drama was played out. Among them was a vociferous minority chanting for the abolition of a penalty which seemed more barbarous than murder itself. The hanging of Ruth Ellis did not only shock because the condemned woman was young and blonde and attractive. It exposed an iron inflexibility in the British legal system. Even in 1955, there was hardly another country in the civilised world where a crime of passion was punishable on the scaffold.

Born Ruth Hornby at Rhyl in 1926, the condemned woman had led a chequered life. At 15 she had escaped from a difficult home background to start work as a waitress. In due course she found employment at a munitions factory and was already dyeing her hair with the peroxide that was to distinguish her in all the press photographs. Ruth was no shy maiden. With a slender, somewhat predatory sensuality she found it easy to acquire dancing partners among servicemen at the wartime clubs she began to frequent in London. In 1944 she had a child by a Canadian soldier, and no sooner had her figure returned than she took up a job as nude model in a Camera Club. In the years of postwar austerity, West End vice lords were already spinning their webs of sleazy excitement. Ruth became a club hostess and call girl. In 1950 she married George Ellis, an alcoholic dentist who frequented her low-life locales. The couple had a daughter but separated soon afterwards, and Ruth returned to the circuit. It was while working as manageress at the Little Club, a seedy upstairs drinking room in Knightsbridge, that she met David Blakely, the man she was to murder.

Blakely came from a very different background. Born in 1929, the son of a well-to-do Sheffield doctor, he was given a public school education at Shrewsbury, and throughout his brief life he retained his boyish good looks. Blakely remained immature in temperament too. For all his suave charm and his well-bred accent, he never held down a steady job. Feckless, emotionally vulnerable and prone to sulks, Blakely maintained abiding enthusiasms only for alcohol, for women and – above all – for racing cars. When he drank he became obstreperous, provoking fights he was too cowardly to see through. With his women he was a braggart and a largely unsuccessful lover. And his experiences on the motor circuits were hardly any happier.

Blakely raced at Silverstone and other well-known tracks, including Le Mans in France. But though he consorted at clubs and meetings with stars like Mike Hawthorne and Stirling Moss, victory almost always eluded him. Nor did racing offer him a career. His obsession for cars, as for drink and women, was financed chiefly by private money, including a £7,000 legacy from his father.

Blakely first met Ruth Ellis in 1953. The young racing driver was drunk and insulting on that occasion, and Ruth referred to him afterwards as a 'pompous ass', telling a friend, 'I hope never to see that little shit again.' But she did – with consequences disastrous to both.

Blakely took to frequenting the Little Club, where Ruth succumbed to his charm and expensive manners. David was 'class', and before long they were sleeping together at her flat above the premises. Ruth, at the outset, was clearly the dominant partner, confident and self-possessed while he was weak and ineffectual. Moreover, as Blakely frittered away more and more of his resources, he came to depend on her to subsidise his drinking.

After having a child of Blakely's aborted in December 1953, Ruth tried to cool

Ruth Ellis

the relationship by cultivating a more dependable lover, company director Desmond Cussen. At about the same time she lost her job at the Little Club, partly because of the time and money she had expended on David.

Ruth first moved into Cussen's apartment, and later to a flat at Egerton Gardens. Cussen loaned her the rent and was a frequent visitor there. But Ruth could not entirely break with her younger lover. She continued to sleep with Blakely, who eventually moved in with her at Egerton Gardens. It was a period of savage quarrels and recriminations between Ruth and David. He was intensely jealous, drank heavily, and sometimes beat Ruth so badly that she had to use make-up to camouflage the livid bruises on her limbs. She had a second abortion by him, and under the strain of the tempestuous relationship consulted a doctor who prescribed tranquillisers for her depression. Blakely, meanwhile, had invested what little capital he possessed in building a racing car. Predictably, the vehicle broke down in practice before its racing debut.

What bonded Ruth to her young lover? Love? Social ambition, or his periodic promises of marriage? Blakely had become a liability to Ruth, yet during this period of frenzied passion, the see-saw of emotional need began to tilt. Blakely had not lost his middle-class expectations, and to friends of his, a married couple called the Findlaters, he confided his despair and his own need to make a break with Ruth Ellis. Ruth had long suspected that David was having an affair with Mrs Findlater, and the more time he spent in the company of the married couple, the more her own jealousy quickened. Ruth could dish out violence as well as take it; once, it seems, she slashed Blakely in the back with a knife.

Things came to a head at Easter, 1955. On Good Friday, 8 April, Blakely confessed to the Findlaters that he was getting frightened of Ruth. They suggested he spend the weekend with them at their apartment in Tanza Road, Hampstead. Though he was due to meet Ruth at 19.30 that night, Blakely gratefully accepted.

For two hours, Ruth waited at Egerton Gardens for her lover to turn up. At 21.30 she phoned the Findlaters to find out if David was there. The au pair took the call and told her that neither Blakely nor the Findlaters were in the flat. An hour later, Ruth phoned again, and this time Anthony Findlater answered. Though he claimed to know nothing of her lover's whereabouts, Ruth did not believe him. Again and again that night she rang Tanza Road, and in the end Findlater simply hung up the receiver whenever her voice came on the line. At the trial it was learned that Blakely was indeed at Tanza Road – shaking with fear on the couch.

Frenzied with suspicion, Ruth had Desmond Cussen drive her round to Tanza Road. When she saw Blakely's green Vanguard parked outside the flat, she ran in fury to the front door and repeatedly rang the bell. No-one replied. Eventually, she vented her spleen on the Vanguard, thumping in its side

---

The Hangman's Verdict

For hanging Ruth Ellis, Albert Pierrepoint collected a fee of fifteen guineas (plus travelling expenses). He left Holloway practically besieged by a storming mob and needed police protection to get through. Pierrepoint returned to his pub, the Rose and Crown at Hoole, near Preston, and the wife who had never asked questions. And there he came to a decision: he would give up his macabre profession.

His had been an hereditary vocation, his father and uncle both having been listed as qualified executioners on the Home Office files. When the press learned of his resignation, it was rumoured that something exceptionally grim must have transpired in the death chamber. It had not – Ruth Ellis was 'the bravest woman I ever hanged' and there was 'nothing untoward'. Pierrepoint resigned because the furore caused him to examine his own conscience. Did hanging really deter murder? He concluded that it did not: 'Capital punishment, in my view, achieved nothing except revenge.'

---

windows which were held in place only by rubber strips. The glass did not break, but the noise brought Anthony Findlater to the door in his pajamas.

There was a furious scene in the street where Ruth kept demanding that Blakely come down, and Findlater denied that he was there. Already, the married couple had prudently phoned for the police. An inspector turned up and tried to calm the situation; after warning Ruth against breaching the peace he drove away.

Findlater slammed the door, leaving Ruth still fulminating in the street. Nor did she leave at once, but kept prowling around the Vanguard until a second police visit forced her from the scene. The long-suffering Desmond Cussen, who had waited and watched throughout the whole performance, drove her back to Egerton Gardens.

His role in the affair deserves a word of explanation. Cussen was infatuated with Ruth but, lacking David's youth and glamour, knew he must wait until the flame of her earlier love was extinguished. For that reason, it appears, he was prepared to acquiesce with Ruth in what became an ever more obsessive quest.

Ruth did not sleep that night. Early the next morning she took a taxi to Tanza Road and kept watch on the Findlaters' from a darkened doorway. At about 10.00 Findlater emerged, and beckoned Blakely out into the street. Having

David Blakely

examined the damaged car, the two men got in and drove off down the road.

Ruth's suspicions were confirmed – the Findlaters *were* shielding David from her. Armed with this certainty, she spent the next hours in attempts to track down her lover's movements. After lunch, she and Cussen took her ten-year-old son to the London Zoo, leaving him there with enough money for the afternoon. Then, with Cussen as chauffeur, she continued the hunt for her quarry.

Cussen drove her back to Hampstead where they located the now-repaired Vanguard outside the Magdala public house. After considerably more furtive reconnoitring, they returned to Ruth's flat, gave her son his supper and put him to bed. That night, Cussen again drove her to Tanza Road where the Findlaters were holding a small party. Listening from the street, Ruth could hear David's voice – and a woman giggling at his remarks. A new suspicion took root in Ruth's fevered mind. David was not pursuing an affair with Mrs Findlater – but with the couple's au pair! A trivial occurrence seemed to confirm this idea: at a certain point, the blinds went down in what Ruth took to be the girl's bedroom; and at the same time, she ceased to hear David's voice. The Findlaters, Ruth convinced herself, were using the au pair to prise her young lover away from her.

Cussen drove Ruth home at about 21.00, and she spent a second sleepless night, chain-smoking and nursing her mute fury. By the following evening, on Easter Sunday, she must have been practically unhinged. 'I was very upset', she acknowledged at her trial. 'I had a peculiar feeling I wanted to kill him.'

By her own account, Ruth Ellis made her way by taxi to Hampstead that evening. In her handbag she carried a heavy .38 Smith and Wesson revolver. Arriving at Tanza Road she saw no sign of the Vanguard, so she made her way on foot to the Magdala pub where she sighted David's car by the kerb. Peering through the windows of the hostelry, she could see David and a friend, Mayfair car salesman Clive Gunnell, drinking at the bar. In fact, the two men had only come to replenish stocks for an evening at Tanza Road. Having downed their drinks, they came out into the street carrying cigarettes and three quarts of light ale.

Neither noticed Ruth at first. With a quart of beer under his arm, David approached the Vanguard, fumbling in his pocket for the keys.

'David!' she called, but he did not seem to hear. Ruth approached, taking the revolver from her bag. 'David!' she called again, and this time he turned to see the blonde with the Smith and Wesson.

Immediately, he ran towards the back of the van. Two shots echoed in quick succession. Blakely was slammed against the side of the vehicle, then staggered towards his friend for cover.

'Clive!' he screamed.

'Get out of the way, Clive,' Ruth hissed in response. And as Blakely tried again to run for safety she fired a third shot that span him to the ground. Then, with every appearance of icy calm, Ruth Ellis came at her fallen lover and drilled two more bullets into his prone body. A sixth bullet ricocheted off the road to strike the thumb of a passing bank official's wife.

From the doorway of the pub, people were spilling out onto the street. An off-duty officer was among those present and he moved slowly towards her. 'Will you call the police?' Ruth asked softly as he took the gun. 'I *am* the police', he replied.

That, in bare outline, was the sequence of events that led Ruth Ellis to trial at the Old Bailey. In purely legal terms, it seemed a clear-cut case of wilful murder against which Ruth offered no substantial defence. She refused to ask for sympathy as a downtrodden mistress; in the dock she glossed over Blakely's beatings: 'He only used to hit me with his fists and hands, but I bruise very easily.' With all passion and anguish spent, Ruth Ellis *wanted* to die for the murder of her lover, and indulged in no tearful theatricals. To the disquiet of her lawyers, she even insisted on appearing in the dock with a full peroxide rinse. In the argot of the day she appeared the very archetype of a 'brassy tart'. Ruth's fate may have swung on that bottle of peroxide – with the chance injury to the bank official's wife's thumb.

In cross-examination, the prosecutor posed only one question:

'Mrs Ellis, when you fired that revolver at close range into the body of David Blakely, what did you intend to do?'

'It is obvious,' she replied with fateful simplicity, 'that when I shot him I intended to kill him.'

That, in effect, was that. The judge in summing up pointed out that jealousy was no defence under British law; the intention to kill was all-important. 'If, on the consideration of the whole evidence, you are satisfied that at the time she fired those shots she had the intention of killing or doing grievous bodily harm, then your duty is to find her guilty of wilful murder.'

Ruth herself had admitted her intention. The twelve members of the jury were out for only 23 minutes, and found the prisoner guilty of murder. Donning his black cap, the judge intoned the terrible words: 'The sentence of the Court upon you is that you be taken hence to a lawful prison, and thence to a place of execution, and that you there be hanged by the neck until you be dead . . .'

It all seemed so clear-cut. Yet, even under British law, it was not inevitable that Ruth Ellis should have hanged. Much about the case was never fully explored at the trial. Ruth's mental state, for example, was not discussed at any length: the effect of her second abortion, and the fact that she was taking tranquillisers on medical advice. The drugs, combined with alcohol she had consumed on the fateful day, may well have produced a state of serious psychological disturbance. Even on the given evidence, Blakely's violent provocations might have led the jury to recommend mercy. In the case of Kittie Byron (see page 10), such a recommendation had saved the prisoner from the gallows.

Then there was the question of the murder weapon. Ruth Ellis stated that she had been given the Smith and Wesson 'about three years ago by a man in a club whose name I don't remember.' Nobody believed this version of events even at the time. It was widely rumoured that Desmond Cussen had supplied the murder weapon, and also driven her to Hampstead on the fateful night. Interviewed in 1977, Cussen firmly repudiated the suggestions. The defence did not pursue the matter at the trial, since a hint of conspiracy to murder would have jeopardised the case for manslaughter, and the chance of a reprieve. Yet if someone did put the gun in Ruth's hand and drive her – befuddled with drink,

The notices of Ruth Ellis's execution are posted on the prison door

tranquillisers and lack of sleep – to the murder scene she would have been less easily presented as a cold-hearted blonde avenger.

During the last frenzied efforts to win Ruth a reprieve, this issue became electric. On the day before her execution, Ruth Ellis made a written statement to her solicitor Victor Mishcon:

> I, Ruth Ellis, have been advised by Mr Victor Mishcon to tell the whole truth in regard to the circumstances leading up to the killing of David Blakely and it is only with the greatest reluctance that I have decided to tell how it was that I got the gun with which I shot Blakely. I did not do so before because I felt that I was needlessly getting someone into possible trouble.
>
> I had been drinking Pernod (I think that is how it is spelt) in Cussen's flat and Cussen had been drinking too. This was about 8.30 p.m. We had been drinking for some time. I had been telling Cussen about Blakely's treatment of me. I was in a terribly depressed state. All I remember is that Cussen gave me a loaded gun . . . I was in such a dazed state that I cannot remember what was said. I rushed out as soon as he gave me the gun. He stayed in the flat.
>
> I had never seen the gun before. The only gun I had ever seen there was a small air pistol used as a game with a target.

Before signing the document, Ruth added:

> There's one more thing. You had better know the whole truth. I rushed back after a second or so and said 'Will you drive me to Hampstead?' He did so, and left me at the top of Tanza Road.

One view of this is that Ruth Ellis had no interest in saving her life at that stage, and was only persuaded to make her statement so that her ten-year-old son should know the truth. Desmond Cussen, however, in the 1977 interview, reiterated his claim to know nothing about the revolver, adding: 'She was a dreadful liar, you know.'

With only a few hours to spare, the statement was rushed by messenger to the Home Office. Scotland Yard was notified and Fleet Street buzzed with the news. Cussen, however, could not be found to comment on the statement and lacking a confession from him, the Home Secretary refused to consider the most urgent representations.

No reprieve was granted. Early in the morning of 13 July, Ruth Ellis wrote her last note to a friend from the condemned cell: 'The time is 7 o'clock a.m. – everyone (staff) is simply wonderful in Holloway. This is just to console my family with the thought that I did not change my way of thinking at the last moment. Or break my promise to David's mother.' That promise had been made in an earlier letter, in which Ruth had asked forgiveness and written, 'I shall die loving your son.'

And perhaps Ruth Ellis did die loving David Blakely. She spent her last hour in the death cell at prayer before a crucifix. Just before 09.00, the grim procession of officials entered and told her the time had come. They offered her a large measure of brandy which she gratefully accepted. Then, having thanked the authorities for their kindness, she walked steadily to the execution chamber where Albert Pierrepoint was waiting.

Chapter
Two

The Maddened Male

'Jealousy is cruel as the grave,' proclaims the biblical *Song of Solomon*. And since the dawn of time the malign spectre has haunted the precincts of love. Suspicion caused Dr Buck Ruxton to murder his blameless 'wife'; Elliot Bower to slay his best friend. At New York in 1906, a sensational drama of love and revenge was played out at Madison Garden's roof theatre. All were crimes committed by jealous husbands in the white heat of passion.

Yet a primitive belief attaches to the spectre of jealousy. By ancient tradition, when love is betrayed, vengeance is an honourable course. Two of Henry VIII's wives were found guilty of adultery and went to the block for high treason. Often, at lower levels of society, the maddened male may not see himself as a murderer at all – but as an executioner.

Murder on the Opening Night

It wasn't a very good show. Some of the biggest names in New York high society had turned up to see the new musical comedy opening on the roof garden of Madison Square Garden. *Mam'zelle Champagne* the entertainment was billed as, but its bubbles were flat and the fashionable socialites were yawning when the male lead got up to sing about love.

Then there was a gunshot; and another two shots. The orchestra stopped playing. And nobody yawned any more.

Harry Kendall Thaw, 34-year-old son of a Pittsburgh railroad magnate, was standing among the café-concert tables with a pistol smoking in his hand. Before him, Stanford White, the nation's most celebrated architect, was crumpled in his chair. Slowly he slid to the floor, blood spilling in crimson cataracts over his expensive shirt front. There were two bullet holes in his body. The third shot was lodged in his brain.

All around, people screamed and stampeded for the exits; vainly the manager called for the show to go on. The date was 25 June 1906, and the roof garden murder was to keep America reeling for months to come.

The public learned quickly that it was a love triangle killing. Thaw had publicly gunned down the seducer of his wife. 'I am glad I killed him. He ruined my wife', he had called on the fateful evening. But in this particular triangle were caught lurid shapes – of lust, sadism and madness – all refracted in the prism of big money.

The woman in the case was Evelyn Nesbit Thaw, the beautiful wife of the arrested gunman. Standards of prettiness change with the decades, but her beauty stands somehow outside time. The photographs show a pale, oval face, dark eyes, sensual mouth and lustrous curls. Frail and voluptuous, her features might have embodied the feminine mystique in a painting of any era.

In fact, Evelyn Nesbit had started out as an artist's model. But she soon moved on into the show world. At the age of 15 she was already appearing as a chorus girl in *Floradora*, a smash musical of the period. From the show one song is still well remembered: *Tell Me Pretty Maiden (Are There Any More at Home Like You?)* And from the high-kicking chorus line came another pretty maiden who appears in the pages of this book: Nan Patterson (see page 151).

Evelyn Nesbit had known the murdered architect long before she had known her husband. Stanford White was internationally respected for his building

Harry K Thaw dines in style behind bars

Stanford White

designs which included, ironically, Madison Square Garden itself. He was a large man with a florid complexion, moustachioed face and roué's lifestyle. On his first meeting with Evelyn he took her and another girl upstairs to a luxurious room in his apartment. It was equipped with a red velvet swing, and he gave the girls turns on it, pushing them right up to the ceiling where their feet reached a Japanese umbrella. But beyond his exotic décor and his playful games, White exhibited deeper passions. In his studio at the apartment, he soon had Evelyn posing for photographs in a silken kimono. On a later occasion, having dizzied her with champagne, he took her to a room whose walls and ceiling were covered with mirrors. There he seduced her while she was sleeping. She was still only 16 years old.

Evelyn went on to become one among several mistresses kept by the architect. He paid her weekly sums of money, brought her out into society and showed her off. Being married, to a very long-suffering wife, White could not offer the girl his hand. And that was one advantage which Harry K. Thaw had over the middle-aged architect.

Thaw met Evelyn Nesbit while she was going around with her seducer. And in the murder trial which was to come, his lawyers did what they could to suggest that Thaw had chivalrously redeemed the fallen showgirl. Certainly, Thaw was outraged by the story of the girl's initial seduction. He hated the architect, always referring to him as 'The Beast' and 'The Bastard'. But Thaw himself was no noble knight errant. Actually, he was a monster.

The spoiled playboy son of a millionaire family, Harry Thaw promised to marry Evelyn if she would run away with him to Europe. She accepted the offer, little knowing her admirer's sexual tastes. It was in the Tyrolean castle of Schloss Katzenstein that they were first revealed. One morning at breakfast in the rented castle, he stripped her of her bathrobe and left her naked except for her slippers. Producing a cowhide whip, he threw her onto the bed. 'I was powerless and attempted to scream,' the girl was to testify, 'but Thaw placed his fingers in my mouth and tried to choke me. He then, without any provocation, and without the slightest reason, began to inflict on me several severe and violent blows with the cowhide whip.'

She was in bed for three weeks afterwards, and other similar episodes were to occur before the marriage. It was one of Thaw's kinks, like the cocaine habit he had acquired. Other girls had received the same treatment at his hand.

Why did the chorus girl marry a man with such malevolent passions? Part of the answer must lie in the lure of the Thaw millions, amassed in railroads, coal and coke. There is evidence that some pressure was applied on Evelyn by her own family, and it is not hard to imagine their promptings: darling, your good looks won't last forever . . .

Stanford White could scarcely offer protection. In fact, he seems to have collaborated with her family in pressing for the marriage to go ahead. Whatever the reason, Evelyn Nesbit married Harry Thaw on 4 April 1905. It was a big society wedding in which the bride wore white despite the fact that the pair were known to have cohabited in New York already. The couple set up home in the Thaws' Pittsburgh mansion, and if the playboy's own family were none too happy about the marriage they made the best of it that they could.

It was Harry Thaw who became more and more unbalanced. He bought a pistol and was seen posing with it like a duellist in his bedroom. On 25 June, 1906, just over a year after his wedding, he took Evelyn to New York where they dined together at the Café Martin before going with friends to Madison Square Garden for the opening of *Mam'zelle Champagne*. Stanford White arrived later, and took a table on his own. The lacklustre performance had been going on for some time before Evelyn decided it was too dull to endure. The party rose, heading for the elevator. Evelyn in fact reached the lobby before noticing that her husband was not with the party.

Disarmed in the elevator moments after the shooting, Thaw was to explain to the District Attorney: 'I saw him sitting there, big, fat and healthy, and there Evelyn was, poor delicate little thing, all trembling and nervous.'

So spoke the sadist. The Thaw family was to spend hundreds of thousands of dollars not only on their son's legal defence, but on press campaigns to smear his victim. White, of course, presented an easy target for slander considering his roué's lifestyle. But Harry Thaw made no promising defendant either. His first trial for murder opened in January 1907 and did not end until some four months later. The jury eventually arrived at a split verdict. Seven declared Thaw guilty of first degree murder, but five held out for not guilty – by reason of insanity.

A year later, at a second trial, more was made of the issue of madness. Cases of mental disorder in the Thaw family were discussed; a brothel keeper described savage whippings that the defendant had administered to young girls. The jury on this occasion achieved a unanimous verdict. After 27 hours they voted Harry Thaw to be not guilty by reason of insanity.

Thaw was committed to the New York State Asylum for the Criminally Insane. And the story might have ended there but for the wealth and energy of his family who pressed continually for his release. Thaw did in fact taste freedom in 1913 – but not through any court decision. One morning in August he escaped the asylum, climbed into a waiting car and fled for sanctuary to Canada.

Much diplomatic pressure was exerted by the United States Government, and the fugitive was forced to return after only a month. He was jailed at Concord, New Hampshire, and eventually sent back to New York. Tirelessly, the Thaw family campaigned through their lawyers for his release. And in the end they won. In July 1915, as a result of yet another trial, Harry K. Thaw was declared both sane, and innocent of charges against him.

It was an extraordinary decision. Evelyn immediately divorced him and went off to live her own life. A free man, Harry Thaw responded to his good fortune only a few months later by kidnapping and cruelly horsewhipping a Kansas City youth who had incurred his displeasure. Again declared insane, he was again committed to an asylum. Again a court found him to be sane after all – and again, in 1924, he was released from custody.

Harry Thaw died of a coronary in Florida in February 1947. His case had made New York a Babel of gossip, loud rumour and frank accusation. But you do not have to be especially cynical to believe that, in the end, the most persuasive voice of all was the voice of money.

Harry and Evelyn Nesbit Thaw during a period of reconciliation

Suspicion

When Pauline Grandjean, a young dressmaker, became engaged to a man named Drouant she confessed a secret to her fiancé. The name she used, she said, was not her real one. There were good reasons for adopting the alias, but she was not prepared to divulge them.

Drouant accepted the arrangement, but he harboured his own suspicions. And when, one day in June 1905, he called unexpectedly at the girl's flat, those suspicions appeared fully confirmed. In her apartment was a postcard which bore the words: 'I shall come and see you this morning. You have my love in spite of all that has happened, and we will try and forget the past.'

His pulse quickening with jealous rage, Drouant concealed himself in the flat and awaited the arrival of the postcard's author. An hour or two later Pauline returned. She was followed almost immediately by a man who, on seeing her, fell into her arms.

Drouant sprang from his hiding place, forced the loving couple apart and plunged a knife deep into the man's back. The victim fell to the floor, his life ebbing with the blood that gushed from the wound.

'Murderer!' screamed the girl. 'You have killed my brother!'

It was a tragic episode which might have come straight from one of the stage melodramas of the period. The girl's brother had just served two years in prison and the pair had changed their names to avoid the stigma of his criminal record. He had written the card on the day of his release, intending to visit his sister briefly before going out to look for a job in Paris.

The victim was taken to hospital in his death throes. He refused to lay charges against his aggressor.

Chiller

An appalling crime of passion was reported from Paris in the Times in 1981. A Japanese student there shot his Dutch girlfriend dead because she refused to make love with him. Issei Sagawa, aged 32, then dismembered the body, putting parts in the refrigerator. These he subsequently ate.

The crime was discovered when the remainder of the body was found cut up and stuffed into two suitcases in the Bois de Boulogne. Mr Sagawa told police he had always wanted to eat a young woman.

Murder by our Paris Correspondent

How intrepid journalists are in detailing crimes of passion – how fearless in exposing lust and violence. These qualities were turned in on the profession by the great Morton-Bower scandal of 1852. The drama unfolded in Paris, and its male leads were both foreign correspondents.

Representing the *Morning Advertiser* was Mr Elliot Bower, aged forty and a bit of a wag. His friends knew him as a capital fellow much given to practical jokes. Once, for example, Bower crept up behind a blameless old gentleman who was studying the menu at an outside café table. The prankster suddenly grabbed him by the neck collar and the seat of his trousers and ran him along the boulevard. My, how they roared!

Representing the *Daily News* was Mr Saville Morton, elegant young man-about-town. Wealthy and much travelled, Morton was well known in the literary circles of the day. He was an intimate of Thackeray among other eminent writers, and became a foreign correspondent more for amusement than anything else. He did not need the money.

Both were Cambridge men who had been undergraduates together. And since they shared broadly the same liberal views, they worked closely together in Paris: swapping political gossip and sharing their insights into the latest intrigue. Morton was a bachelor, but Bower had married a Fanny Vickery in 1842. As chance would have it, Morton had known his friend's wife in London before the marriage. All seemed to conspire to cement the bonds of friendship, and the trio became boon companions who went to theatres and dined out constantly together. Sadly, it was not very long before the trio became a triangle.

Bower came to detect a threatening intimacy developing between his wife and his bachelor friend. At one stage there was a bitter quarrel, and Morton stopped visiting the Bowers' home in the rue de Sèze. The dispute was patched up, but it left an aura of mistrust which perhaps never entirely evaporated.

Elliot Bower, the jealous husband, was by no means irreproachable as far as the opposite sex was concerned. It must be remembered that the Paris of the day had a diamanté sparkle all of its own. This was the golden age of the *cocotte* and courtesan, of champagne and of *soupers intimes*. For the idling Englishman, the whole city glittered with temptation. And who could blame Mr Bower if, once in a while, he succumbed?

Mrs Bower could. The couple quarrelled frequently over Elliot's philandering ways. Some episodes sprang only from his prankster temperament: once, for example, he strolled up to a carriage in the Bois de Boulogne where a lady was seated in her carriage. Elliot thrust his hand through the window and squeezed her knee. As she gaped in astonishment, he made an elaborate bow and sped off in a waiting cab.

But there were more serious misdemeanours: candlelit suppers with *demimondaines* from which he came back late to the rue de Sèze. And things came to a head when Mrs Bower discovered that Elliot had been having an affair with an Englishwoman. Her name was Isabella Laurie, and Fanny found a letter from her husband's paramour, in which Isabella complained of having been seduced by Elliot and then cruelly cast aside.

Enraged, Mrs Bower turned to Saville Morton for comfort. Precisely what form that comfort took remains an issue in dispute. Certainly Mrs Bower wanted revenge against her husband, and was more than a little fond of Morton. The bachelor himself suggested a divorce and declared that he would marry her if she broke with her husband. Mrs Bower, however, demurred. It was not that she was unwilling, but the timing was awkward. The trouble was, she was expecting a baby.

It was in fact to be her fifth child. In due course, the baby was born with its mother still seething with rage. Two days after the event she had a message smuggled out via the concierge's wife: 'Go at once to Mr Morton, and tell him from me that the child is just like him.'

It all depends on how you interpret the case. Morton's reported reaction was, 'Goddam! Oh, what a nuisance.' This strongly implies that they had had an adulterous liaison which now threatened to be exposed. Buf if their love had never been consummated, it is possible to speculate that Morton thought the woman had become seriously unbalanced.

Whatever the truth, Morton kept a low profile *vis-à-vis* the Bowers for a fortnight after the birth. The issue was forced when Mrs Bower developed a fever and, tossing and turning in her delirium, kept calling out Morton's name. Despite her husband's objections, the bachelor was called for by the doctors to see if his presence would calm her. It did – and he stayed for several days and nights. The patient would only take medicine from Morton, who was put up in an adjoining room.

While the fever raged within her, Mrs Bower repeatedly insisted that her husband be kept away from her. Only once did she call him to her room. That was on the evening of 1 October 1852, and she took the opportunity to shriek imprecations against his infidelities. The tirade ended with the patient pointing to her sleeping child, and the words: 'Listen to me, you villain. That is not your child. Saville Morton, and not you, is its father. Oh, Queen of England, come to my help and rid me of this scoundrel!'

How was Queen Victoria to intercede? Bower thought that his wife had gone mad and remained dutifully at her bedside. But she persisted. She referred to a particular period when he was in London . . . she had spent a night then with Mr Morton.

Bower tensed. Suddenly, he rushed from the room and confronted Morton with the charge. Morton failed to reply, promptly making for the stairs instead. Bower grabbed a carving knife and hurried after him, brandishing the blade. With one lunge he gashed the bachelor with a wound that severed Morton's carotid artery. The blood spilled everywhere.

Panic-stricken servants had witnessed the whole affair, and it was Bower who told them to send for a doctor. In the confused comings and goings which followed the assault, he in fact showed remarkable composure. Bower did not wait for the police or the medical assistance to arrive. Instead, he changed clothes, grabbed a passport and made for the Gare du Nord. A train took him to Boulogne; a packet-boat to England and safety.

News crossed frontiers in 1852 that policemen seldom did. The Morton-Bower affair soon had newspaper readers enthralled on both sides of the Channel. But though Morton died as a result of his wounds, Bower remained at liberty. He strolled the London streets in perfect freedom without the need for disguise or alias. The French police did contact Scotland Yard, but they made no request for the fugitive's arrest. And lacking this formal requirement, the London police were in no position to act. Incredibly, Elliot Bower even gave his own account of the Morton-Bower case for the *Morning Advertiser*. It was a more accurate piece than many which had been published about the sensation, a unique exclusive, really: Murder by Our Special Correspondent, as it were.

What of Mrs Bower? She had been committed to a lunatic asylum shortly after the fateful event. But she did not take long to recover (there was doubt as to whether she needed treatment at all). And before long she too had returned to London. She did not meet Bower there though; Fanny would have nothing to do with her husband, and expressed complete indifference as to his fate.

What that fate was to be remained problematic. Though the French made no move to extradite the fugitive, they did set the official legal machinery in action. After police investigations, a *juge d'instruction* (examining magistrate) determined that the crime was not murder but homicide. This heartened Bower. And knowing French lenience towards jealous husbands in a *crime passionnel*, it also encouraged him to make a bold move. Of his own free will, Elliot Bower returned to France and surrendered himself to the authorities.

The Assize Court in Paris was packed on 28 December as the Englishman faced his accusers. Bower entered the dock dressed in sober black, and his general demeanour was widely admired by the women in the courtroom. Not, however, by the *Gazette des Tribunaux*, which noted that the accused was 'a man

THE WORLD'S GREATEST CRIMES OF PASSION

Springheeled Husband Pounced On Lovers

An irate husband flew into action on a homemade catapult when he saw his wife being cuddled by another man. He made a springboard out of a long plank and two car tyres and after a run launched himself into the air. He crashed head-first through the kitchen window of the house where his wife was being cuddled.

Mr Michael Garratt, prosecuting, told Dudley, Worcestershire, Crown Court that the husband landed in the sink and gently slid to the floor.

Graham Street, 21, of Rowley Regis, near Dudley, pleaded guilty to causing £1.49 damage to the window at the house on the Old Park Farm Estate at Dudley. He was put on probation for two years by Judge W.R. Davison and told not to 'indulge' in such 'amateur dramatics' again.

Mr John West, defending, said that the only person to get hurt was Street. He had no intention of interfering with his wife again.

Daily Telegraph

---

of between 35 and 40 years of age, blond, like most Englishmen, with luxuriant whiskers and an unfashionable moustache.'

The trial that followed in no way resembled the trials known to phlegmatic Anglo-Saxons. Take the supposedly neutral indictment, for example: this was one long torrent of abuse against the accused man, couched in terms of the most florid rhetoric. Describing, for example, Bower's philanderings it read: 'The villain flaunted his misconduct. And this in Paris! Oh, shame upon him!' Having luridly portrayed the assault on the unarmed Morton, it continued: 'What next? The murderer, blood on his hands and crime on his conscience, fled to England – to Perfidious Albion, where assassins are sheltered from outraged justice . . .'

All this before the prosecution began! Very little, it seemed, could be said for perfidious Englishmen with their unfashionable moustaches. The prosecution was an essay in defamation of character, in which foul innuendo, rank calumny and steamy prose jostled to take pride of place. Nobody disputed the fact that Bower had killed his rival. The main thrust of the prosecution's case was that the crime had been premeditated: Morton had been somehow enticed to the apartment in a cunning plot matured for some time beforehand. An absurd thesis, it is true, but it carried some weight when delivered with all the glowering malevolence that a Latin prosecutor can muster. Even Bower's voluntary surrender was scorned: a Frenchman would have done the honourable thing and given himself up on the spot. What did Bower do? He fled. Fled like an Englishman and now came brazenly back to cock a snook at the majesty of French law.

'I demand death for the murderer Bower!' roared the prosecutor at the end of his vehement declamation.

Even Bower, a cool enough customer, must have trembled inwardly as the dread words rang out. But help was at hand in the shape of a defence counsel equally armed with Gallic passion. He described the dastardly seduction of a previously chaste wife by a man thought to be a friend. He dwelled on the furtive liaison which developed, the passing of notes and so on. Bower's counsel had witnesses who confirmed that, on at least one occasion, Morton had spent a night with Mrs Bower when her husband was in London. And all the time the trusting and hard-working husband had been innocent of his betrayal!

The crime, declared the defence, was Morton's, not Bower's: 'What man among you, what husband and father worthy of the name would have acted otherwise? I tell you, gentlemen, the blow struck did him honour. The wife of his bosom had been seduced, her person possessed by another; and, as a result, adulterous offspring had been foisted upon him . . .'

The public in the court hissed and cheered at appropriate points. There was even one moment when, overcome by his own portrayal of the outraged husband's plight, the defence counsel actually broke down and wept piteously into a large handkerchief; the judge himself was so moved that the proceedings had to be halted for a while.

Then came the finale. The defence ended with a stirring appeal to those patriotic emotions which the prosecutor had tried to whip up.

'Remember that the accused has voluntarily surrendered to our courts, demanding justice at your hands. He has done well. French justice will not fail him. He will, by your verdict, go back to England and tell his countrymen there of the religious attention with which a French jury listens to the evidence, and that our French justice is everywhere the admiration of the world!'

Wild cheers! In no time at all, the jury declared for acquittal. The crowd roared its approval – strangers surged forward to wring Bower by the hand – the gendarmes even kissed him. It was as if the Englishman had been given the freedom of the city.

Bower did not, in fact, go back to England to celebrate French justice and French juries. On the contrary, Paris itself suited him very nicely. He lived there happily for the next 30 years, dying, aged 70, in 1884.

Wild Bill and his Women

In the old West, where female company was scarce, jealousy probably motivated more murders than cattle or bullion ever did. From bar-room brawls to main street showdowns the quarrels flared. Life was cheap, and many a legendary lawman owed notches on his gun not to zeal for the law – but to love of women.

Take Wild Bill Hickock, for example. The famed Union scout and Indian-fighter used to boast of a great Rock Creek shoot-out that began his crime-fighting career. The pistoleer claimed to have slain the ten-man McCanles gang single-handed: six bullets saw off Dave McCanles and five henchmen; he used a knife to cut down the other four villains. The West was well rid of the gang, said Hickock, for they were 'desperadoes, horse-thieves and murderers' to a man.

Wild Bill, of course, was one of the Wild West's great self-advertisers. Six foot two inches tall (wearing high-heeled shoes), with auburn curls that cascaded to his shoulders, the 'Prince of Pistoleers' made such an impressive figure that dude reporters from the East lapped up every word he said. In reality, James Butler Hickock was a drunk, a liar and a womanizer. As it happens, there was a McCanles episode – but it was not quite as Wild Bill told it.

In 1862, Hickock was working as a humble stable hand at the Rock Creek pony express station in Jefferson County, Nebraska. The manager there was a Mr Horace Wellman, and the stockkeeper a J.W. Brink. And in the offing, too, was a certain Sarah Shull (Kate Shell), something of a local belle.

Hickock stole the lady's affections from David C. McCanles, a landowner of the neighbourhood. And on 21 July 1862, the jealous McCanles rode out to the station threatening to 'clean up on the people' there. He was clearly intending a Wild-West style crime of passion, but had no cohort of desperadoes with him: just two neighbours and his 12-year-old son.

When the smoke cleared at Rock Creek that day, only the boy returned.

Years after the event, historical investigators succeeded in tracing the boy, Monroe McCanles. And he gave an account of the affair which reflected no credit on the legendary lawman. Monroe stated that when his father entered the station manager's house, Hickock shot him in the back with a rifle from a hidden position behind a curtain. Then Wild Bill turned the weapon on one of the neighbours, but only succeeded in wounding him; the man was beaten to death by Wellman who used a hoe. McCanles's second companion fled out into the scrub and was killed with a shotgun – Monroe could not say by whom.

So much for the solo slaying of ten desperadoes. Monroe's version of events

Wild Bill Hickock

was broadly confirmed in 1927, when investigators dug up court records from Nebraska. It appears that three men – Hickock, Wellman and Brink – were charged with the triple murder. The accused escaped punishment, however, on a plea of self-defence.

And did Wild Bill ride off into the sunset with the lovely Sarah Shull? Not a bit of it. He had a succession of paramours, and in 1865, his liaison with a certain Susanna Moore was to lead to the first Wild West showdown on record. A man named Dave Tutt took up with the lady and incurred the pistoleer's jealous wrath. A disputed card game provided Wild Bill with his pretext, and he challenged his rival to a gun duel in the public square at Springfield, Missouri.

The duel is an age-old means of settling a love-triangle quarrel: a kind of ritualised crime of passion. This one differed only from earlier gun duels in that the weapons were holstered. Tutt drew first, and missed. Before he had time to fire again, Hickock had put a bullet through his heart.

Off With Her Head!

Kings of the past possessed weapons of revenge unavailable to humbler citizens. A queen who took lovers threatened the royal succession. Adultery was treason, and two of Henry VIII's wives went to the block for the offence. The cases of Anne Boleyn and Catherine Howard were very different, but you could call each execution a judicial crime of passion.

Anne Boleyn was not, in conventional terms, an especially attractive woman. A contemporary described her as having a 'middling stature, swarthy complexion, long neck, wide mouth, bosom not much raised.' In fact, the observer declared, the Wiltshire girl had little to recommend her except for the king's appetite, 'and her eyes, which are black and beautiful and take great effect.'

Perhaps those dark eyes first drew Henry to her. Certainly, he wrote her some passionate love letters which have survived as evidence of real infatuation. Henry had his first marriage to Catherine of Aragon annulled in order to marry the English Anne. And though the first queen's failure to bear a male heir was a key reason for the divorce, Henry's love for Anne clearly strengthened his resolve.

When the pope refused to accept the divorce it sparked the immense upheaval of the English Reformation. And as for Henry and Anne, secretly married in January 1533, their union was not a success. The king's ardour soon cooled after the marriage and his eye started roving again. Anne bore him a daughter (the future Elizabeth I) instead of the son he desired. A second child miscarried and a third – a male heir – was dead at birth.

The stillborn child was delivered on 29 January 1536. And the unhappy event seems to have set the wheels of vengeance moving, for on 2 May, Anne Boleyn was sent to the Tower charged with adultery.

Four young courtiers were cited as her lovers: Sir Francis Weston, Henry Norris, William Brereton and Mark Smeaton. The most sensational charge, however, was that Anne had had carnal relations with her own brother, Lord Rochford; an accusation instigated by his spiteful wife. All except Smeaton protested their innocence, the latter confessing to guilt. All went to the block, Smeaton declaring on the scaffold that he 'deserved to die'.

Anne for her part persistently professed herself innocent. When she heard of Smeaton's last words she erupted with passion: 'Has he not cleared me of that public shame he has brought me to? Alas, I fear his soul suffers for it and that he is now punished for his false accusation.' She was tried and unanimously

King Henry VIII

Anne Boleyn

condemned by a court of 30 peers. The sentence carried with it an option for Henry – she could be either burnt alive or beheaded, according to the king's pleasure.

Henry, bountiful in her mercy, opted for beheading. He even had an especially sharp blade imported from the Continent for, as the queen observed with sad vanity: 'I have but a little neck.'

Anne went to the scaffold on 19 May, behaving with courage and dignity. It was said that she had never appeared more beautiful than on that fateful day. Still professing her innocence, she graciously declared that the king had done her many favours: first in making her a marchioness, second in making her a queen, third in sending her to heaven.

It is easy to imagine her a tragic victim of circumstance. Nevertheless, her own uncle presided over the court of peers which found her guilty. They saw evidence which was subsequently destroyed. And no-one, not even her own daughter Elizabeth, later tried to retrieve her reputation. Smeaton's confession, her friends' silence, the peers' unanimous judgement – all tend to suggest that she may well have been an unfaithful wife.

Still, callous statecraft clearly played its part in the affair. The king craved a male heir and did not mourn his second wife's passing. He was seen immediately after the execution wearing bright yellow garb with a feather in his cap. And the very next day he became betrothed to Jane Seymour, his third wife. She was to die not long after giving birth to the boy child he so desperately desired (the sickly Edward VI). The fourth wife, Anne of Cleves, lasted no time at all. Henry only married her to effect a German alliance, and found her so ugly on sight that he divorced her immediately. It was then that the ill-starred Catherine Howard came into his life.

Catherine was the orphaned daughter of a noble and gallant soldier, and was brought up in the household of her grandmother, Agnes, Duchess of Norfolk. The girl was pretty, young and vivacious and Henry, now 50, fell passionately in love with her. He called her his 'rose without a thorn,' and she seemed to come fresh with all the innocence of virginal maidenhood.

Unfortunately for all concerned, this was an illusion.

Catherine had committed many youthful indiscretions. And almost immediately after the wedding in July 1540, these came to the attention of the king's councillors. A former maidservant in the Duchess of Norfolk's household had confided to her brother Catherine's misconduct. The brother in turn approached Archbishop Cranmer. The queen, it appeared, had not been a virgin when she married, and the maidservant's story was as picturesque as it was disquieting:

'Marry, there is one Francis Dereham who was servant also in my Lady Norfolk's house which hath been in bed with her in his doublet and hose

Anne Boleyn being sentenced

between the sheets an hundred nights. And there hath been such puffing and blowing between them that once in the house a maid which lay in the house with her said to me she would lie no longer with her for she knew not what matrimony meant.'

Nor was it just Dereham who had dallied with the English rose. A man named Mannock 'knew a privy mark of her body.'

This was an awkward business. Cranmer himself had arranged the marriage and his reputation was at stake. He is said to have been 'marvellously perplexed' as to what to do about the report and called two other high officials of state who were equally troubled. Cranmer, they decided, really must inform the king, even if the story was just malicious gossip. The Archbishop agreed, but dared not face his sovereign in person. Instead he submitted a written report and waited for the storm to break.

Henry was outraged. He refused to believe it. He questioned Catherine about the allegations, and she was fierce in her denials. And though Henry desperately wanted to believe her, his obligations required that he secretly assemble a group of notables to investigate the allegations. Dereham and Mannock, the maidservant and her brother, were all tracked down and closely questioned. And when the various reports came back, the picture looked very dark for Catherine.

Henry Mannock, for example, turned out to be a musician who admitted that he 'commonly used to feel the secrets and other parts of her body.' Francis Dereham seemed once to have been betrothed to Catherine, and confessed that he had known her carnally 'many times both in his doublet and hose and in naked bed.' He also named three young ladies who had joined with them in the bedroom athletics. And he said that Thomas Culpepper, Catherine's own cousin, was another of her lovers.

Henry VIII – bold scourge of the pope and the monasteries – wept like a baby when he heard the news. For some time he was so overcome with emotion that words failed him entirely. He loved his English rose and still refused to credit the stories. But he was like a man trying to cross a muddy field in gumboots. With every step he took, the mire went on loading his feet.

As investigations proceeded, it became clear that practically the whole household of the Duchess of Norfolk had conspired to keep up a pretence of Catherine's chastity. Lady Jane Rochford (the spiteful wife of Anne Boleyn's executed brother) was reported to have encouraged Catherine's youthful frolics. She too was arrested and questioned – and was to go to the block in due course.

Bitterly galling all this must have been to the deceived monarch. But so far, the allegations all concerned Catherine's behaviour before the marriage. There was worse – much worse to come. Henry discovered that after the wedding,

Catherine had appointed the lusty Dereham to a post in her royal household. He had been writing some of the Queen's letters for her – they had been alone together in her bedchamber without the presence of servants or other members of the household.

Adulteress! The spell of the king's disbelief was broken and he had Catherine formally arrested. When questioned, she persisted in her denials until confronted with the haul of confessions from miscellaneous lovers and servants. Faced with their frank statements, she broke down and admitted her youthful unchastity to the Archbishop. She still maintained, however, that she had been faithful as a wife.

The queen's confession was enough to seal the fates of the leading men in the case. Culpepper, a man of noble birth, was beheaded. Dereham and Mannock, both lowlier paramours, were hanged and quartered. Assorted members of the Howard family and household were arrested on the charge of misprision of treason – that is to say, concealing their knowledge of an intention to deceive the king.

Poor, wretched Catherine was now charged with adultery. But still the anguished king and his distressed councillors were reluctant to act decisively. The Lord Chancellor, for example, asked the Lords for a delay in the trial proceedings. The queen, he said, must be given a chance to clear herself of the charge. The Lords willingly agreed to the proposal. But within a couple of days, the king's own Privy Councillors pressed for a speedy resolution. They did, however, add a clause which speaks volumes for Henry's miserable state of mind. The king, they declared, need not actually attend Parliament as it assessed the evidence; he need only sign the documents when judgement was passed. This unusual arrangement was suggested because the 'sorrowful story and wicked facts if repeated before him might renew his grief and endanger His Majesty's health.'

Henry agreed to the proposal, which must have been a great relief to the Lords. They would now be able to speak their minds freely without their impetuous sovereign glowering at them from behind his beard. As in the case of Anne Boleyn, the trial records were subsequently destroyed. But it appears that Catherine did confess to 'the great crime she had been guilty of against the most high God and a kind Prince and against the whole English nation.' She asked no mercy for herself, but only for the friends and relations who had been implicated with her.

Catherine Howard was beheaded on Tower Hill on 13 February 1542. We do not know how she faced her end. But we do know that the king took no more frisky nymphs to the altar. The following year he married the patient and motherly Catherine Parr – his 6th wife – who subsequently managed to outlive him.

The Headless Wife Case

It had all the ingredients of a Gothic horror story. They included the decomposing body of the beautiful wife – kisses delivered by her husband to the corpse – the severed head saved in remembrance. The story should have been set in some dark and sinister castle. But it wasn't. The drama unfolded in tranquil West Wycombe; it was a crime for the 1980s.

Michael Telling, 34, was a member of the vastly rich Vestey family behind the Dewhurst butchers' chain. His second cousin was Lord Vestey, multi-millionaire and polo-playing friend of royalty. In terms of material advantage, Telling enjoyed immense privileges. Being a beneficiary of the Vestey Trust, he received £1,200 a month pocket money – all his bills and credit card accounts were paid on top of that.

He could afford all the expensive toys he desired: fast cars, motorcycles, guns and stereo equipment. The Vestey millions paid for holidays all around the world. But they could not pay for the one thing that Telling needed. Money never did buy love.

He had had a miserable childhood. His father was an aggressive alcoholic who chased his pregnant mother brandishing swords. The mother herself was to testify that she had rejected her son. At an early age, Michael was packed off to boarding school and there, being a sickly boy, he was bullied mercilessly. When he reacted by stealing, starting fires and playing truant, he was beaten by the staff.

He became a problem child: emotionally disturbed and barely controllable in his actions. Twice expelled, he eventually went to a special school for maladjusted children, as well as becoming an inmate at a mental hospital. At home he was kept away from the family and raised by nannies and governesses. When only nine years old he was drinking sherry and smoking heavily. He kept carving knives in his room and once threatened his mother with a blade.

It was from this wrecked childhood that he entered adult life. In 1978, Michael Telling married his first wife, 18-year-old Alison, whom he had first met in Australia. The couple had a son, but the relationship was not to last. Telling was a 'coward who was unable to face his responsibilities,' she was to say. In 1980 he went to America to buy his latest toy, a Harley-Davidson motorcycle. While trying out his new machine at Sausalito near San Francisco, he pulled up at some traffic lights and fell into a conversation with a Mr and Mrs Zumsteg. They suggested that he meet their daughter, Monika.

Within three days of the encounter, he was sleeping with Monika. And shortly after his return to England, he informed his wife that he had found another woman. In 1981, a divorce was arranged. Less than a month later, Michael Telling married Monika Zumsteg.

Much was said at the trial about his bride. Monika was headlined in one paper as a 'SEX MAD GOLD-DIGGER', and she certainly lived her life in the fast lane. Monika drove a Pontiac Firebird and drank Benedictine and orange for breakfast. She used cocaine, heroin and marijuana. In her handbag she carried a gun and a vibrator.

The couple lived at opulent Lambourn House, West Wycombe in Buckinghamshire. Luxury items included a whirlpool bath on the lawn where Monika would frolic with naked party guests. Her husband used to sit on the sidelines, drinking. She said he was only good for money. On frequent occasions, she publicly belittled his sexual efforts, boasting to him of her own lovers both male and female.

When the marriage came to its gruesome end, neighbours were to confirm the stories. Richard Richardson, for example, was an odd-job man and a friend of the Tellings. He said that Monika told him she had no intention of making a life with her husband and that 'all she wanted was his money.' Once, she told Richardson that, 'I could f . . . any man, any woman better than any man can. I am AC/DC. Man or woman – I go with anybody.' She seemed to take a vindictive pleasure out of humiliating her husband. Richardson had been present on one occasion when Monika had ordered Telling to make coffee, shouting, 'Get off your f . . . arse, you mother-f . . . Make the coffee!' Telling begged her not to talk like that and affectionately ran kisses up her arm. On another occasion, the couple had a play fight in the kitchen. Monika took the opportunity to knee Telling in the groin. 'He went white, but said nothing.'

'He worshipped the ground she walked on,' said Richardson, 'but she showed no affection. She said she would only stay with him for two years to get money out of him.' Telling had to visit his son secretly because Monika disapproved, saying that the boy was horrible and she hated him.

Telling's first wife, Alison, told much the same story. Once, Monika had visited her home, bringing a bottle of gin and a cockatoo. She smoked cannabis, drank Drambuie and took four or five pills. She complained to Alison that Michael was no good in bed, saying she did not want a divorce until she'd got some of his money. Monika said that she was prepared to get herself pregnant and go back to America with the baby to get the cash.

Telling himself was to refer to countless humiliations. Once, he had seen her frolicking half naked with another woman on the living-room floor. Yet on their honeymoon night at the Hyde Park Hotel in London, she refused to have sex with her husband. In fact, she banned sex entirely with Telling for the last seven months of her life.

THE MADDENED MALE

Monika was doomed to become the Headless Wife. She never got a chance to defend herself against these allegations in court. But her father was to claim that the stories were outrageous: 'She was certainly not a saint, but she was nothing like she was painted. She was too flippant sometimes, like when she told a neighbour she was AC/DC. It's the kind of thing she would say for a laugh. Monika was a woman of great intelligence, kind and full of sensitivity.'

Whatever the truth, the relationship seems to have been founded on a disastrously flawed combination of personalities. She certainly liked fast living – he certainly needed love. And successive episodes illustrate how the marriage was heading for calamity. In 1982, Monika took up an Alcoholics Anonymous programme. Telling, meanwhile, underwent treatment in a psychiatric hospital. He was to claim that Monika tried to run him down with a car and attacked him with a whip. But he also admitted that he sometimes retaliated, and had attacked her on four occasions during their 17-month marriage.

The terrible climax came on 29 March 1983. By Telling's account, she was delivering a tirade in the living room, shouting that he ought to be sent to a mental hospital. The taunts finally shattered his eggshell personality. 'She came charging towards me. I thought she was going to attack me so I picked up the rifle and shot her.'

The weapon in question was a Marlin 30-30 hunting gun, and he shot her three times. She was hit in the throat and the chest. 'I kissed her then and said I was sorry. But I knew she was dead.'

If the case had ended there it would have been sensational enough. What happened next turned it into an almost unbelievable horror story. Telling left the body for two days where it was before carrying it into a bedroom: 'I went to look at her every day and kissed her often.' He also talked to the corpse as it lay on a camp bed. Eventually, he dragged the body to a summer house, a building half-converted into a sauna. And there it remained for five months.

Telling told his friends that Monika had left him to return to her native America. As 'protection' for himself, he installed an elaborate security system at his home, and even employed private detectives to find his wife.

During this period, as Monika's body lay decomposing at Lambourn House, Telling started to see a former friend called Mrs Lynda Blackstock. She spent three or four nights at his home, and he tried to woo her in his bedroom. But he could not make love successfully. 'He told me all about Monika', she was to say. 'He told me she was an alcoholic, a drug addict and a lesbian. Michael said she had gone back home to the U.S. – and he was glad.' At the trial, she was asked:

'There was not a hint that Monika lay dead in the very building you were visiting?'

Mrs Blackstock: 'Definitely not.'

Another recent girl friend, divorcée Mrs Susan Bright, also went to bed with

Telling after he had killed his wife. She slept with him several times and the couple went out for meals together. She said: 'He was very talkative, although he seemed very nervous . . . I asked him if he had heard from Monika at all and he said he thought she was in America.'

In September 1983, Telling hired a van and drove to Devon with the body. On Telegraph Hill outside Exeter he cut off Monika's head with an axe. He dumped the headless body there but could not bear to part with the head itself. Instead, he brought it home and hid it in the locked boot of his Mini in the garage. It was kept there wrapped in plastic.

Two days later, a Devon man stumbled on the headless body. Though badly decomposed by now, it still wore a distinctive Moroccan T-shirt. And although it had been decapitated, a chunk of hair and a few teeth were found at the site.

' The gruesome discovery made the national news, and Mrs Richardson's interest was alerted. She knew that Monika had a similar T-shirt, and was nonplussed when Telling confessed to her that he had killed his wife: 'She is in the sauna – it's stinking.'

Although Mrs Richardson did not believe him, she did eventually inform the police. At this stage, Monika was just one among many missing young women who vaguely fitted the description pieced together from the remains. But dental tests on the few teeth found revealed that the victim had suffered from a disorder of the gums. Monika, had recently undergone an operation for a gum infection.

Devon detectives went to the West Wycombe house and found the dead woman's skull in the Mini. Exactly a week after the body was discovered, Michael Telling was arrested.

He confessed the killing to the police. Asked why he had shot her he replied, 'There were 101 reasons. I can't really explain. She kept pushing me. I just snapped in the end. She was horrible in many ways.'

Horrible in many ways – the phrase might serve as an epitaph on the whole case. Asked why he had cut off her head, Telling replied, 'I did not want her identified because of my family. Even when she died I wanted her to be with me.'

The case was tried at Exeter Crown Court in June 1984. He pleaded not guilty to murder, but guilty to manslaughter by reason of diminished responsibility.

The press, of course, had a field day. 'MISTRESSES TELL OF SEX IN THE HOUSE OF HORROR' – 'SEX SESSIONS AS BODY LAY NEAR-BY', blared the headlines. The public learned that Telling had taken Mrs Bright out to a Chinese meal in High Wycombe just 24 hours after he had chopped off his wife's head.

If the press dwelled on the bizarre, macabre details, the courtroom wrangling revolved around Telling's state of mind. No-one denied that the defendant had killed his wife; he himself furnished most of the details. The question in dispute was whether he was responsible for his actions.

Michael and Monika Telling on their wedding day

The prosecution pressed for a verdict of murder. It dwelt on the 'amazing catalogue' of gruesome lengths to which Telling went to avoid detection. He had told a psychiatrist that the seed of the crime was planted four days before the event. On the evening before the killing, the time and method were, allegedly, decided. 'Despite his mental abnormality, this man determined to kill his wife. He could have prevented himself from doing so if he wished.'

Afterwards, to conceal the crime, he used his wife's Cashpoint card until the account was almost depleted, so giving the impression that she was still alive. He hired the private detectives. He made an 'elaborate pretence' of going on a camping trip when he travelled to Devon to dump the body. As for the head, the prosecution alleged, he did not take it home for remembrance – but to avoid identification of the corpse.

Set against all this apparent cunning was the testimony of psychiatrists, friends and relations. The defence stressed the defendant's maimed and disordered personality. Telling's grey-haired mother appeared in the witness box and described how as a boy he had witnessed violent arguments between herself and his alcoholic father. She told how he would run naked into the road in front of traffic; how he twice attempted suicide. She acknowledged that her son was a boy deprived of affection: 'Many of Michael's problems stem from his very lonely and unhappy childhood.'

Telling wept in the dock as his mother gave evidence, and he delayed the hearing by 15 minutes after passing a note to his lawyers asking for an adjournment. The note was strangely worded and misspelt: 'You get Mum away from this awful trial, or I will get up and let the bloody prosoqutor hear what I think off.'

He was visibly moved too when a former school companion entered the box 'out of a sense of guilt' after reading newspaper reports. The man, Bertram Lilley, described the vicious bullying that Telling had endured: before the boys would let him join in a game they made him roll in a patch of stinging nettles until he resembled 'one large blister'. Even then he could not play because he was too badly hurt.

Lilley's parents had lived in Africa at the time and he once spent a half-term at the Tellings. There was more love, he said, across the many miles to Africa 'than across the living room of that house.'

Telling was close to tears as the testimony was given. Otherwise he remained an enigma: slightly balding, dressed in Savile Row pinstripes and paying rapt attention to the trial. A psychiatrist described how Monika's sexual taunts and her ban on lovemaking would have been humiliating and distressing even to a normal man. But Telling was not normal; he did not know how to cope. His responsibility was 'substantially impaired' at the time of the killing.

The judge in summing up reminded the court that psychiatry is not an exact science. Ultimately, the jurors were as fit as anyone else to assess whether Telling was responsible for his actions. Yet they seem to have agreed with the psychiatrist. For after $2\frac{1}{2}$ hours deliberation, the jury found the defendant not guilty of murder but guilty of manslaughter on the grounds of diminished responsibility.

Gaoled for life, Michael Telling was to remain in custody until those responsible felt it 'safe and proper' to release him.

Edgar the Peaceful

'The reign of Edgar was somewhat uneventful,' muses the *Encylopaedia Britannica*. King of a united England (959–975), this Anglo Saxon monarch was noted mainly for his church reforms and known as 'Edgar the Peaceful' in consequence.

Yet his personal life did not lack excitements. Aged 17, the king sired a child by a nun at the convent of Wilton; she refused to marry him. Then Edgar took his first wife, and not long afterwards heard glowing reports about a beautiful Lady Elfrida, daughter of Devonshire's Earl Ordgar. To find out if the stories were true he sent his servant Athelwold to look her over as a prospective second wife. Athelwold went and found that Elfrida was all that had been rumoured. He fell in love with her and, instead of reassuring his monarch, sent a dispatch that the girl was stupid and ugly and he married her himself.

Athelwood took his new bride to his estate in Hampshire, and dared not present her at court. The king wondered why she never made her appearance, and so did Elfrida herself. Then came a fateful day when the king came to hunt in nearby forests. He sent word that he would spend the night at Athelwold's estate.

The courtier was in a quandary. He could not refuse his sovereign, and so ordered his wife to dress 'in fowle garments, and some evil favoured attire' so that her beauty would be hidden. Elfrida, however, refused to comply and decked herself out in all her finery. When the king saw her he was smitten with her loveliness. He took her husband hunting with him in a wood, 'not showing that he meant anie hurt, till at length he had got him within the thicke of the wood, where he suddenly stroke him through with his dart.'

Having murdered the deceitful courtier, Edgar the Peaceful married Elfrida. She bore him two sons (one of whom was Ethelred the Unready) and the couple presided together over the remainder of his tranquil reign.

Bunkum With a Capital B

The most infamous doctors in the annals of crime were generally cunning poisoners. Dr Ruxton's case was different. It is true that he used his medical knowledge to a gruesome degree in trying to cover up his atrocity. But all the facts indicate that the murder itself was an impulse killing accomplished in a state of high emotion. No science or stealth contributed to the initial act – his was a crime of passion.

He was born in Bombay as Bukhtyar Rustamji Ratanji Hakim and qualified in his native country. Moving to England, he was made a Bachelor of Medicine in London. After further studies at Edinburgh he took up a practice in Lancaster in 1930. It was at about that time that he changed his name by deed poll to that of Dr Buck Ruxton.

With him to London came Isabella Van Ess, a married woman from Edinburgh. Her husband divorced her when she followed the doctor down. And although Isabella never married Dr Ruxton she lived with him as his wife. She also bore him three children, and was known to everyone simply as Mrs Ruxton.

They lived with the children at No. 2 Dalton Square, Lancaster. The doctor was highly regarded in his profession and well liked by all of his patients. This was despite the fact that the doctor and his 'wife' had an intensely emotional relationship. The couple quarrelled incessantly and often came to blows. But they always made up afterwards. At the trial, patients were to remember how Mrs Ruxton would rush into her husband's surgery and urgently embrace him to achieve a reconciliation.

The rows, though, were more than mere tiffs. Ruxton commonly threatened his wife and once held a knife to her throat. On two separate occasions the police were called in, but Mrs Ruxton never pressed charges. On the whole, she seems to have given as good as she got. 'We were the kind of people who could not live with each other and could not live without each other', the doctor was to admit.

Once, Mrs Ruxton attempted suicide to try and escape from the bonds that tied them together. And in 1934 she fled to her sister in Edinburgh intending a final breach. Ruxton, however, followed her and persuaded her to come back to him and to their children.

The root of the problem appears to have been Ruxton's obsessive jealousy. Constantly he accused his wife of infidelity, complaining on one occasion that she behaved like a common prostitute. His morbid suspicions were entirely without foundation, but jealousy feeds on chance happening and trifling coincidence. Things came to a head in autumn 1935, when Ruxton persuaded himself that she was having an affair with a young town clerk named Robert Edmondson.

On 7 September, the Edmondson family drove up to Edinburgh. Their party included Robert, his sister and parents. And they agreed to take Mrs Ruxton up too for a visit to her native city.

Seething with suspicion, Ruxton abandoned his surgery and followed them in a hired car. He discovered that his wife was staying in the same hotel as the family, rather than with her sister as planned. It was for a perfectly innocent reason, but back in Lancaster, Ruxton was to rant for days at his wife about her supposed liaison.

On 14 September, the following weekend, Mrs Ruxton made another blameless excursion. Taking the doctor's Hillman, she drove to Blackpool as she did once every year to see the illuminations with her sisters. She left the resort at 23.30 that night, intending to go back the next day. But she never did return to Blackpool. In fact, having driven back to Dalton Square in the car, she never went anywhere again. Not in one piece, that is.

It is known that she reached home, because Ruxton was using the Hillman the next day and in the period that followed. It is known too that the doctor was in the house with his three children and the housemaid, Mary Rogerson. The children were all under five; Mary Rogerson was aged 20. But she could give no account of what transpired that night, for Mary Rogerson disappeared with Mrs Ruxton. The next time anyone but the doctor saw the two women they were barely identifiable: no more than dismembered chunks of bone, tissue and skin all wrapped up in bloodsoaked packages.

The story emerged at the trial. It has to be assumed that Ruxton was waiting in a mood of frenzied suspicion. There was yet another row which this time reached its climax in bloody murder. Ruxton killed his wife with a sharp-bladed instrument, and Mary Rogerson no doubt saw everything. She had to die too – and afterwards began the grisly business of destroying the evidence.

From what is known of Ruxton's character, anguish, remorse – and concern for his children – must have been coursing through his veins. But he set to work like a Trojan on the bodies of the two women and the welter of blood everywhere. Probably he worked all night while the children slept, and still there was much to be done.

One of the family's three charladies, Mrs Oxley, was due to arrive at 07.00 on Sunday morning. At 06.30, as she was preparing to leave her home, Dr Ruxton appeared on her doorstep. It was the astonished Mr Oxley who opened the door, with his wife standing not far behind him. Both heard what Ruxton said quite clearly: 'Tell Mrs Oxley not to trouble to come down this morning. Mrs Ruxton and Mary have gone away on a holiday to Edinburgh and I am taking the children to Morecambe. But tell her to come tomorrow.'

The 'murder ravine' where the bundles of human remains were found

At the trial, Ruxton was to deny that he had ever been to the Oxleys' house.

Returning home, Ruxton made the children's breakfast. He received the Sunday papers and milk, delivery women noting that he seemed to be shielding an injured hand. On a brief excursion in the Hillman he bought a full tank of petrol and two spare gallons besides.

Nursing his wounded hand, Ruxton was busy all Sunday. A woman patient turned up at Dalton Square with a child needing treatment. Ruxton postponed the appointment, saying that he was busy taking up carpets because decorators were due the next morning. At midday, he asked a neighbour to look after his children for the afternoon, saying that his wife had gone with Mary to Scotland and that he had cut his hand opening a tin of fruit at breakfast.

That afternoon he toiled undisturbed at the house until it was in a more or less presentable state. Then, at 16.30, he called on a friend and patient, Mrs Hampshire, to ask if she would help him get the house ready for the decorators. It was in a strange condition when she arrived. The carpets on stairs and landing had been taken up, and straw was scattered around. It even bristled out from under the two main bedroom doors – which were locked and remained so all evening.

In one room was a bloodstained suit; in the backyard were bloodstained carpets. Ruxton asked if she would be kind enough to clean the bath. It was filthy, with a grubby yellow stain extending high around the inside of the tub.

At the trial, Ruxton was to claim that the blood marks all derived from the severely gashed wound to his hand. But there was an awful lot of it about and, daunted by the size of the task, Mrs Hampshire asked if she could get her husband to help. Ruxton agreed, and the business of cleaning up went on until 21.30. As a reward for their labours, Ruxton offered the pair the stained suit and carpets, which they took with them when they left.

Presumably, the bodies were in the two locked bedrooms. No doubt the doctor was not idle that night. And he must have had nagging fears about the stained articles he had given the Hampshires, for first thing on Monday morning he went round to their house and asked for the suit back. He stood there, dishevelled and unshaven, explaining that he wanted to send it to the cleaner's. Mrs Hampshire insisted that she was quite happy to take it for cleaning herself. Ruxton then demanded that she take the name-tag from it, claiming that it would be improper for her husband to go around wearing a suit with another man's name in it. She duly cut it off. 'Burn it now', he demanded, and she tossed the tag onto her fire.

Afterwards, she looked at the suit and found the waistcoat so badly stained that she also put that on the flames. As for the carpets, she was to testify: 'The amount of blood on the third carpet was terrible. It was still damp where the blood was, and it had not been out in the rain. I laid the carpet in the backyard and threw about 20 or 30 buckets of water on it to try to wash the blood off, and the colour of the water that came off was like blood. I threw it on the line and left it to dry, and when it was washday I had another go at it with the yard brush and water, and still could not get the congealed blood off.'

In the week that followed, the doctor kept fires going night and day in his own backyard. He called in the decorators. And when the charladies complained of peculiar smells about the house he replied by spraying Eau de Cologne around.

To neighbours, Ruxton gave varied and inconsistent accounts about why Mrs Ruxton and Mary were away. To one he confided, sobbing and agitated, that the pair had gone to London, where his wife had eloped with another man. But Mary's parents, the Rogersons, were not easily convinced. Eventually, Ruxton told them that their daughter had been got pregnant and that this accounted for her going away. Mr Rogerson was undeterred. He threatened to ask the police to find his daughter.

At some stage (probably Thursday 19 September) Ruxton must have driven up to Scotland. For ten days later, exactly two weeks after the women vanished, the first grisly package was discovered.

A woman found it by a bridge near Moffat, off the Carlisle-Edinburgh road. She saw what seemed to be a human arm protruding from a wrapped bundle at the water's edge. Horrified, she called her brother who in turn summoned the police. The constable found four bundles: 'a blouse containing two upper arms and four pieces of flesh; a pillowslip enclosing two arm bones, two thigh bones, two lower leg bones, and nine pieces of flesh; part of a cotton sheet containing 17 pieces of flesh; and another piece of sheet containing the chest portion of a human trunk and the lower portions of two legs.'

More parcels were to turn up in due course. The police determined that pieces from two separate bodies had been jumbled up in the packages together. But certain distinguishing characteristics had been removed: some of the teeth, eyes and finger ends (presumably to prevent fingerprint identification). In fact, during the early investigation, the surgical removal of various organs made it impossible to discover the sex of the victims. The police began by announcing that they believed the bodies to be those of a man and a woman.

Reading this news in his daily paper seems to have given Ruxton some rare moments of good humour. In jovial mood, he told one of the charladies, 'So you see, Mrs Oxley, it is a man and a woman, it is not our two.' On another occasion: 'Thank goodness the other one in the Moffat case was a man and not a woman' – or people would be saying that he had murdered his wife and Mary.

But the police had already connected the Moffat bodies with the doctor's home town. One of the bundles had been wrapped in a copy of the *Sunday Graphic* dated 15 September (the murder morning). It happened to be a special edition sold only in Morecambe and Lancaster.

On 9 October, the Rogersons reported their daughter a missing person. On that day too, Ruxton asked Mrs Hampshire what she had done about the suit: 'Do something about it', he insisted. 'Get it out of the way. Burn it!' On 14 October, the doctor was taken into custody and questioned at length. In the small hours of the next day he was charged with Mary's murder. Cautioned, he protested, 'Most emphatically not, of course not. The furthest thing from my mind. What motive and why? What are you talking?' Some days later he was also charged with the murder of his wife, and it was on this indictment that he was to stand trial at the Manchester Assizes.

Precisely identifying the two bodies remained problematic for the authorities. The affair was to become something of a textbook case in medico-criminal history. A team of pathologists and anatomists fitted together their grim jigsaw of remains, proving that the age and size of the missing women roughly matched those of Bodies I and II. But key features had been removed. For example, Mrs Ruxton had prominent teeth and these had been withdrawn. Miss Rogerson had a squint – the eyes had been taken from their sockets. Nevertheless, it did prove possible to identify Mary's body by fingerprints. And Mrs Ruxton was identified when a photograph superimposed on Head II matched exactly.

It was proved that the doctor had been delivered the local edition of the *Sunday Graphic* for 15 September. Moreover, the linen sheet in which one bundle was wrapped was the partner of a single sheet left on Mrs Ruxton's bed.

The doctor made a miserable impression in the witness box. He vehemently denied the testimony of his charladies and his neighbours, claiming for example that he never visited the Oxleys; that he never asked Mrs Hampshire to burn the suit. His own account of his movements was deeply implausible and his manner both pitiable and arrogant. Sometimes he sobbed and became hysterical; sometimes he waxed bombastic. Once, taxed with murdering his wife and disposing of the witness, he replied, 'That is absolute bunkum with a capital B'.

A fit verdict on his own hopeless attempts to clear himself. Ruxton was found guilty, and when an appeal failed he was hanged at Strangeways Prison. The date was 12 May 1936. Soon afterwards, his own terse confession was published, a note penned at the time of his arrest:

> I killed Mrs Ruxton in a fit of temper because
> I thought she had been with a man. I was Mad at the time.
> Mary Rogerson was present at the time. I had to kill her.

It had been one of those cases that haunt the public imagination, and in the streets and playgrounds the children chanted their own summary in rhyme:

> Red stains on the carpet, red stains on the knife,
> For Doctor Buck Ruxton had murdered his wife.
> The maidservant saw it and threatened to tell,
> So Doctor Buck Ruxton he killed her as well.

Love Lives of the Medici Family

The great Medici family, merchants and bankers of Florence, are remembered both for their political eminence and their lavish patronage of the arts. Their love lives, however, left a very great deal to be desired. Take Cosimo I, Grand Duke of Tuscany (1519–74). He cruelly poisoned his faithless wife Eleanor of Toledo after having her lover done to death. It is said that Cosimo later rejoiced in the brutal double murder, boasting openly that 'killing the bull first and the cow after made the sacrifice all the more pleasing.'

Cosimo himself enjoyed the favours of his own daughter, the beautiful and intelligent Isabella. The artist Vasari once witnessed their incest while painting a ceiling at the Palazzo Vecchio. There was a dark moment afterwards when Cosimo suddenly remembered that the painter might be at work, and climbed the scaffolding dagger in hand. But Vasari prudently pretended to be asleep and so escaped assassination.

Isabella was married to the Duke of Bracciano. However, she enjoyed an illicit liaison with Troilus Orsini, one of her husband's bodyguards. When her lover got her pregnant he fled to France, but was tracked down there by Bracciano's men and murdered. Isabella sought protection with her loving father Cosimo, who sheltered both her and her illegitimate child. Bracciano did not dare to take his revenge on his wife immediately. Not long after Cosimo's death, however, Bracciano lured Isabella to his estate at Cerreto. There, on 16 July 1576, he strangled her.

Gothic Horror
Lord Bernage of Sivray, Chief Groom to France's Charles VIII in the 15th century, witnessed a lamentable sight while serving as ambassador in Germany. A noble lady there could be seen in the evenings drinking from a human skull.

It was the skull of her lover. The wretched woman was forced to sip from it by her vengeful husband who had murdered the miscreant.

Cosimo de' Medici

The Worm That Turned

The French have a useful expression to describe a certain sort of husband in a love-triangle quarrel. The term is *mari complaisant* (complaisant husband) and it refers to a man who is perfectly aware of his wife's adultery but meekly acquiesces in it. He is a stock figure of fun in French fiction and folklore, and recurs time and again in real-life cases.

One such was René de Villequier, an eminent nobleman in the court of Henri III. For some 15 years he tolerated the infidelities of his wife Françoise de la Marck. He knew all about the life she was leading, occasionally remonstrated with her, but also harnessed her appetites to serve his own political career.

Attending the court at Poitiers on the morning of 1 September 1577, de Villequier went into his wife's bedroom and after joining her between the sheets, joking and laughing with her, he gave her four or five thrusts with a dagger. He called one of his men to finish her off. Then, having stabbed a maidservant for good measure, he had his wife's body placed in a litter which was paraded before the king and his nobles.

Having taken the corpse back to his house for burial, de Villequier returned and put in an appearance at court. There he triumphed in his avenged honour. He declared that he would gladly have killed her lovers too, but since they formed a small army there might be difficulties.

Henri III records the scandal in his *Journal*, and censures both the killer and his victim. But of course, no action was taken against de Villequier. They have always been funny like that, the French.

All in the Family

When West German building firm owner Hans Appel married Renate Poeschke, each brought to the household a child by a previous marriage. Then Renate bore Hans a daughter – and the family expanded further when in 1973, Renate's brother Juergen moved in.

Hans made a shattering discovery one night as he was putting the children to bed. One of the infants confided that mummy and uncle Juergen had spent an afternoon in bed together – with no clothes on.

Incest possesses a power to shock as perhaps no other sexual transgression. Hans was appalled, but when he confronted the guilty couple neither replied with a firm denial. Instead, brother and sister quit the household and moved into the Sachsenhausen home of 21-year-old Dieter Poeschke. He was Renate's other brother, a garage mechanic and a married man.

The construction boss was still in love with his wife despite what he now suspected. While giving her presents to try and win her back, he also took to carrying a revolver. But he remained on good terms with Dieter Poeschke. On 7 January 1974, Appel accepted a lift in his brother-in-law's Mercedes which was going from Wiesbaden to Frankfurt.

As the car travelled along the road, Hans Appel unburdened himself of his problems. It seemed incredible, he said, but he suspected that Renate was having an affair with Juergen. Did Dieter believe such a thing?

'Of course,' replied the driver, 'Juergen and I both sleep with Renate all the time.'

Double incest! Appel was to say that something inside him snapped at that point. Witnesses saw the car swerve onto a pavement. Dieter rolled out and as he staggered to his feet, Appel shot him twice with the pistol. Then the outraged husband got out of the Mercedes and disappeared down the street.

It did not take the police long to discover the killer's identity. But the bizarre circumstances of this particular crime of passion provided strong mitigating factors. Tried in July 1974, Appel was sentenced to 21 months imprisonment. In fact, he never served any time at all, for the sentence was set aside on appeal.

As for Renate, she would not return to her husband but went on living with her brother Juergen.

Chapter
Three

Miscellaneous Mayhem

Not every crime of passion involves murder; many a lesser misdemeanour is rooted in thwarted love. The peace may be breached by a spring-heeled husband or calamitous kidnap attempt. More serious cases too may retain elements of grotesque comedy, as in the extraordinary affair of the Missing Mormon. Even murder itself may entertain – at a distance – through bizarre circumstances or consequences. Such at least was the case of Oxford's debt of dishonour, paid out over seven hundred years.

Everyone is a fool in love, and rampant passion does not only appall. It may amuse, intrigue – or frankly astonish – by exposing humanity's foibles.

The Missing Mormon

If a Mormon missionary were suspected of raping a beauty queen, the affair would provide ample material for sensational news treatment. But when, in 1977, a beauty queen was suspected of raping a Mormon missionary, the case had all the makings of a grand press block-buster. The newspapers went wild over the saga of Kirk Anderson and Joyce McKinney, devoting such an acreage of newsprint to it at one stage that the *Daily Mail* was constrained to advertise itself as 'The Paper *Without* Joyce McKinney'.

The story first broke in September 1977, with the disappearance and subsequent reappearance of American missionary Kirk Anderson. The *Sunday Times* noted on the 18th of that month:

> The Mormon missionary missing in Surrey turned up yesterday and said he had been kidnapped and held handcuffed and manacled for three days – it is believed on the orders of a wealthy, lovesick woman.
>
> Kirk Anderson, 21, was released unharmed near Victoria Station in London and telephoned Scotland Yard to say he was returning to his home at Milton Gardens, Epsom, by train. However, he boarded the wrong train and ended up at Sutton a few miles away, and had to call the police to pick him up.

That slip-up by the luckless missionary was a portent of stranger things to come. Anderson told the police of how he had long been persecuted by a 29-year-old former girlfriend named Joyce McKinney. They had had a brief affair in Salt Lake City, the Mormons' worldwide headquarters, and when he broke with her she had begun to harass him. The missionary alleged that windows at his home had been smashed, car tyres ripped up and a car he was driving in was rammed. He moved from Utah to California – the girl followed him. After continued harassment, the Mormon asked to be sent to Britain to avoid her. But she would not give up. Anderson kept on running: from East Grinstead, to Reading and finally to Epsom.

It was at Epsom, the Mormon claimed, that the kidnapping had occurred.

'This seems to have been a case of hell hath no fury like a woman scorned', said the detective who had headed the search for Anderson. At Orem, in Utah, Anderson's parents declared their relief on hearing that their son was safe. 'We don't know anything about this girl', said Mrs Anderson. 'I personally think he has been living very close to the Lord.'

Joyce McKinney was arrested some time later, with a male accomplice named Keith Joseph May, aged 24. They were charged with abducting

Anderson, and, on a second charge, accused of possessing an imitation .38 revolver with intent to commit an offence. It was made known that Joyce McKinney had entered Britain on a false passport. Yet the first press accounts gave the impression of a tearful ingénue. From the back of the prison van taking her to court, the girl protested her innocence, handing out messages written on pages of the Bible. One read: 'Please ask Christians to pray for me.'

It was at a preliminary hearing in November that the salacious details on the affair started to hit the headlines. The 'Sex-in-Chains' case swept all other issues from the front pages of the popular press.

Opening for the prosecution, Anderson's counsel described the couple's brief affair in Utah in 1975, and Joyce McKinney's subsequent persecutions. He alleged that on 14 September, the girl and her accomplice had forced Anderson into a car outside his church, using an imitation revolver and a bottle of chloroform. The car sped off to a cottage in Devon where it arrived some five hours later. Miss McKinney had then told her captive that she was not going to let him go until he agreed to marry her.

There was no doubt that sexual intercourse had taken place at the cottage. Nor was there any doubt that Anderson was tied to a bed while the act took place. The point at issue was that Anderson claimed to have been the victim of forced sex, while McKinney alleged that the shackles were merely instruments of bondage games.

In Anderson's version, Keith May had fastened him to the bed with chains and a leather strap. 'Joy told me if there was to be a ransom, the ransom would be that I would have to give her a baby.' Asked how female rape could have occurred, Anderson replied: 'She had oral sex'.

On the third night of his captivity, the missionary said, he was completely spread-eagled on the bed: 'When she came into the room there was a fire in the fireplace and she put some music on. She was wearing a négligée. She came to me as I lay on the bed. I said I would like to have my back rubbed. She proceeded to do that but I could tell she wanted to have intercourse again. I said I did not.' She left and returned with Keith May who used chains, ropes and padlocks to tie him down on his back to the four corners of the bed. She tore the pyjamas from his body and had her way with him.

Anderson firmly refuted the suggestion that the bondage equipment was for sex games. But the back rub? Wasn't that highly erotic, and bound to court temptation? Anderson was aggrieved: 'I do not look at a back rub like that. My mom gives me a pretty good back rub, but that does not mean that I want sex with her.'

During cross-questioning, Anderson alluded to a bizarre accessory of his own – an article of clothing unknown to the general public. This was the Mormons' sacred undergarment.

Above: McKinney outside Epsom Court; Right: Anderson leaving court

THE WORLD'S GREATEST CRIMES OF PASSION

Not only had Miss McKinney torn off his pyjamas; she had also violated a special one-piece undergarment which acted as a kind of male chastity belt. Anderson had since burnt the article. 'They are so sacred to me that anytime they are desecrated in any way the proper method to dispose of them is to burn them.'

Joyce McKinney's statements presented a very different version of events. Anderson had made love willingly, she said. They had indulged in oral sex and bondage games to sort out his sexual difficulties; he was lying, now, because he feared excommunication from the Mormon church.

'Mr Anderson lay willingly while I tied him up,' she said. 'If he had not, this little 120 lb girl could not have tied up a 250 lb, 6 ft 2 in man.' She was, in fact, terrified of Anderson's strength: 'His legs are as big round as my waist.' The missionary had revelled in the proceedings, and lay on the bed 'grinning like a monkey' and moving his hips with her.

McKinney invoked her own religious faith in her defence, claiming that back in Utah she had prayed for 'a very special boy' to come into her life. Anderson had 'teased me and kissed me until I was out of my mind.' In a much-quoted phrase, she declared: 'I loved Kirk so much I would have skiied down Mount Everest in the nude with a carnation up my nose.'

What was the public to make of it all? On the one hand, McKinney's protestations that 'this little girl' could not have tied down and ravished the hulking missionary carried some weight. But then, if Anderson was willing, what was Keith May's role in the affair? Her accomplice remained a somewhat shadowy figure. May's own counsel claimed that the Devon escapade was seen by his client as 'a rescue operation from the oppressive and tyrannical organisation' (the Mormon Church).

In all events, May and McKinney were granted bail prior to the trial proper, on condition that McKinney stayed indoors from 21.00 to 09.00 every night. On 13 March 1978, the conditions were eased so that the two defendants could go to the cinema in the evenings. The prosecution objected on the grounds that they might skip bail and flee the country. Nonsense, a spokesman for Miss McKinney insisted: 'She wants to remain in this country to clear her name.'

On 16 April, however, the world learned that the *Sex-in-Chains Girl* was missing. The police searched high and low – but to no avail.

What had happened was that, posing as a deaf mute, Joyce McKinney had fled to Canada. Safely across the Atlantic, having lost none of her old flair, she came out of hiding dressed as a nun.

The whole furore erupted again. Newspapers battled for exclusive interviews, and a legal war was waged between *Penthouse* (which claimed her own story) and the *Daily Express* (which published photographs and stories before the magazine reached the bookstalls). May 22 became Joyce McKinney Day as far as the popular press was concerned. The *Daily Mirror* managed to obtain a photograph of her in the nude. Lacking a comparable illustration, *The Sun* improvised by mocking up a montage of its own. Joyce McKinney's head was shown superimposed on the body of a naked woman skiing down snowy slopes – a carnation, of course, was shown protruding from a nostril.

'The gospel according to Mormon sex-in-chains girl Joyce McKinney is: Give a man what he wants,' blared the paper, and quoted the fugitive as saying, 'I'm a very old-fashioned girl. I believe that a man's home is his castle and that a husband should be pampered. All I wanted to do with Kirk was to satisfy and pleasure him. But he had deep inhibitions due to his upbringing. I wanted to get rid of those guilt feelings by doing sexually outrageous things to him in bed. I thought I had succeeded, but in the end the Mormon Church won.'

In reality, Joyce McKinney emerged as an all-American product. She was still remembered in North Carolina as a 'fine, fine girl', who had been a regular attender at Bible camp. As for being a beauty queen, the most that could be said was that she had once been elected Miss North Carolina High School. Her own account of her early affair with the missionary was described in true teen-magazine style. She had been out driving with a friend in her new Stingray convertible when the Mormon put his head through the window. 'I found myself gazing into the deepest pair of baby-blue eyes. He put Paul Newman to shame. My heart did flip-flops. I turned to my girlfriend and said: "Hey, get out – I'm in love"'. And of the affair which followed, Miss McKinney said: 'It was bombs, firecrackers, the Fourth of July every time he kissed me'.

Even her subsequent pursuit of the missionary seems to have been undertaken with a kind of blue-eyed innocence. According to a friend, she had visited skin-flicks and live sex acts in order to pick up tips on arousal. Then she placed an advertisement in an underground paper asking for 'a muscle man, a pilot and a preacher to help in a romantic adventure.' The proposed team was never assembled, but she managed to finance the trip to England with $15,000 paid to her by an insurance company for injuries received in a car crash.

Joyce McKinney's crime, if crime it was, had an ancient pedigree. She loved, not wisely, but too well. And after the last great orgy of confessions and interviews, the story died practically overnight. As far as the legal position was concerned, the fugitive forfeited her bail money, but proposals to extradite her for trial were abandoned.

For seven years, the case was almost forgotten. Then, in June 1984, newspapers announced, 'SEX-IN-CHAINS JOYCE IS AT IT AGAIN.' Incredibly, Joyce McKinney had hit the headlines for a new alleged harassment of Kirk Anderson. She was arrested in a car outside the ex-missionary's office at Salt Lake City, charged with disturbing the peace and giving false information to the police.

Anderson had married since the alleged kidnapping episode, and now worked for an airline company in Utah. It was the first time he had seen her in seven years. Anderson claimed that he had noticed Joyce shadowing him over the weekend and had stalked him to his office. He told police that he was very concerned she might be planning to snatch him again. A police spokesman said, 'When we arrested her we found a notebook detailing his every move. There were also pictures of Kirk and his wife Linda.'

A man was with Miss McKinney when the police swooped, but he was not arrested. Her lawyer, Jim Barber, said, 'She only wanted to see him for old times sake. She is writing a screenplay about her experiences and wanted to find out how the story ended.'

Appalling Assault by an Amazon

Absurd and terrible scenes were witnessed at the wedding of M. Augustin. The 45-year-old Parisian presented himself in 1871 to be married at the local mairie to a lovely young girl of 18. And the ceremony had just been concluded when the door of the hall burst open and a lady of gigantic stature stormed into the room and elbowed her way through the guests. Trailing behind her was a thin young lady of about 15 years old.

M. Augustin was a very little man.

'Wretch! Scoundrel!' cried the Amazon, addressing the diminutive groom. 'This is how you leave me in the lurch – I who have sighed during fifteen years for the day when I might call myself your wife!'

The groom turned as white as a sheet. The giantess grabbed him by the collar and jerked him up under her arm. Addressing the mayor in a voice like thunder, she boomed: 'Do I arrive too late?'

'The marriage is concluded', replied the official. 'Please put M. Augustin down.'

'Not without giving his deserts to the villain who leaves me with this girl.'

'No, no, that girl is not mine', piped the groom. This was a mistake.

'Repeat what you have said,' fumed the giantess, 'this child who is as like you as one pea is another – is she yours or not?'

M. Augustin made no reply. His persecutor then seized him by the nose and twisted it violently. Wedding guests tried to come to the man's aid, but the enraged woman now flailed him around like a battleaxe, forcing them back. In the furore which followed the mayor could be heard calling for the police, but the giantess at last relented.

'You need not give yourself the trouble. I will let go the rascal of my own accord.' Turning to the bride she said hoarsely: 'Here, my beauty, is your little bit of a man. I have not broken him. We have no further business here. Follow me, Baptistine.'

So saying she flung her victim at the foot of two policemen who just then appeared at the door. Then, muttering further terrible imprecations, she swept out with her daughter.

M. Augustin had fainted. But such was the awe of the wedding guests that nobody dared touch him until the last echo of heavy footsteps had died away in the distance. At last, they raised him to his feet and the assembly broke up in an atmosphere of silent gloom.

Debt Settled – 770 Years Later!

Student Slays His Mistress; a routine crime of passion, you might think. But sometimes the fascination of a case lies more in its aftermath than in the event itself. When one such murder occurred in mediaeval Oxford it helped to establish the world-famous university. And it led to a debt of dishonour paid, year in and year out, for more than seven centuries.

It all began in 1209, when a student at the newly founded university murdered his mistress, a woman of the town. The miscreant made a quick getaway. And the mayor and people responded in a rage by stringing up a couple of students in his place.

In compensation for the lynching, the papal legate ordered the town of Oxford to do penance, to feast the poorer students annually, and to excuse all scholars half of their rent annually for a space of ten years. Additionally, a yearly fine of 52 shillings was imposed on the townsfolk.

Few crimes of passion can have had more long-lived consequences. Payment began in 1214, the cash being deposited in a chest at St Mary's church. It amounted to a considerable sum which for a long time was about the only income the University possessed. The once-despised, starveling scholars became privileged people. They took to swaggering about the streets, and terrible Town and Gown riots resulted.

The fine itself continued to be paid annually for 770 years. The industrial revolution transformed the nation, the British Empire came and went, world wars were fought, men walked on the moon – and still the ancient blood money was paid *propter suspendium clericorum* (for the hanging of the clerks).

The Treasury had by now taken on the debt, calculated at £3.08 per annum. It was payable to the University Chest, and it was the duty of the Vice Chancellor to administer the sum for the relief of poor students. And this curious thread in the tapestry of history was not snapped until June 1984.

In that month, as part of an efficiency drive at the Treasury, a final payment was agreed on. The government presented the University with its last cheque – £33.08 as a once-for-all settlement of the account.

Mr William Hyde, secretary of the Chest, regretted the decision: 'We have not really any choice in the matter. They decided to buy it out. It's a pity from the nostalgic point of view to see the end of a 700-year payment of this nature.' But he agreed that no strong case could be made for perpetuating the debt of dishonour. Besides, he conceded, 'three pounds does not relieve a lot of poverty.'

Passionate Phantoms

A 17th century tombstone at Chagford church in Devon commemorates the death of Mary Whiddon. The unhappy girl was shot dead by a jealous lover, at the altar on her wedding day. A dramatic end to a love-triangle quarrel – but is it entirely ended? To this day, it is said, the ghost of the young bride haunts her home at Chagford. The building today is a guest house, and more than one visitor has been startled to see the wraith of a young woman in black smiling sadly from the doorway of what used to be Mary's room.

You don't have to believe in ghosts to appreciate how deeply memories of love tragedy have rooted themselves in the folklore of the nation. After the death of

Mrs Rattenbury (see page 163), her shrouded spectre was reported on several occasions to haunt the lonely scene of her end by the River Avon. The apparition was so often witnessed that in October 1935, the famous ghost-hunter Elliott O'Donnell spent a night's vigil in the misty watermeadow. An eerie experience – the investigator saw no phantom, but he did experience an overwhelming urge to drown himself in the river.

Longleat, the nation's most famous stately home, is reputedly haunted by a spectral Green Lady who frequents a certain corridor. She has been identified as Lady Louisa Cartaret, 18th century wife of the 2nd Viscount Weymouth. He killed her young lover in a furious fight fought out in the haunted corridor. Afterwards, so the story has always told, he buried the body in the cellar. Pure fairytale? Yet early in the 20th century, the cellar was excavated to lay pipes for central heating – and the skeleton of a man in 18th century riding boots was discovered under the flagstones.

The mostly widely reported spectral victim of love tragedy, though, is the ghost of Anne Boleyn. The ill-fated queen has been sighted at a number of old manors around the country, each claiming to be her birthplace. And nowhere does the apparition make a more spectacular appearance than at Blickling Hall in Norfolk. Every year on the anniversary of the queen's execution (19 May 1536) a spectral coach is said to convey Anne's ghost up to the door of the hall. The cortege arrives at midnight: the coachman is headless; the four horses are headless; Anne too is headless, of course, bearing the severed item upon her lap.

Chapter Four

Carefully laid plans

You might think that every crime of passion is committed on the impulse of the moment. Yet even in the classic cases, some premeditation may be involved in, for example, the purchase of a knife or gun. How long, after all, is a moment to an obsessed or injured lover: a split-second, an hour, a day? Sometimes, it seems, molten passion may be contained for longer still while the brain – soaring in some stratosphere of icy calm – maps out a scheme of vengeance.

The crimes in this section were all ones in which evidence of careful planning was brought before the courts. Sometimes that evidence was questionable, as in the tragedy of Edith Thompson. More often it was substantial enough. An Italian vet, a New Zealand justice minister and a French duke of noblest line are among the patient planners whose schemes ultimately went awry.

The Black Perambulator

The woman was found in a Hampstead street, lying on a heap of builders' rubbish. Moonlight played softly on her black jacket with its trimming of imitation Astrakhan. Her skull was crushed, and head itself had almost been severed from the body – it remained attached only by a sliver of skin and muscle.

The date was 24 October 1890, and rumours soon started to circulate. It was whispered that the murder was the work of Jack the Ripper, the phantasmal figure who had stalked the East End only two years earlier. Had the Ripper now returned to claim victims in North London?

A mile or so away was an abandoned perambulator whose cushions were soaked with blood. And the following day, detectives made another grim discovery. The corpse of an 18-month-old baby was recovered from waste ground in Finchley. It was not very long before the three gruesome finds were connected.

The murdered woman was found to have the initials P.H. embroidered on her underclothes. The fact was reported in a morning newspaper which caught the attention of a certain Clara Hogg, who lived in Kentish Town. She knew that her sister-in-law, Mrs Phoebe Hogg, had gone out on the afternoon of 24 October with her baby. She had not come back that night. The initials fitted the missing woman, and Clara went with a friend to the mortuary where the body had been taken. There, choking back her nausea, Clara recognised her sister-in-law as the grisly figure on the slab.

What puzzled the police was the behaviour of Clara's friend, a tall redheaded woman named Mary Pearcey. She insisted that the corpse was not Phoebe Hogg's; she became hysterical and tried to drag Clara away. It was, in fact, to visit Mary Pearcey that Phoebe Hogg had set out on the fateful afternoon. Yet the russet-haired Mary first denied the fact; then admitted that the visit had taken place.

Clearly, Mary Pearcey's role in the affair needed some investigation. And it did not take much probing for detectives to discover a familiar geometry in the mystery – the geometry of a love triangle.

Frank Hogg, husband of the murdered Phoebe, turned out to be a man with an eye for the ladies. A bearded and jovial furniture remover, he had lived with his wife at Prince of Wales Road, Kentish Town. But Frank also possessed the latchkey to Mary's home at Priory Road nearby. He was a regular visitor there, and had been since before his marriage.

Probing deeper, the police discovered that the marriage itself was a forced affair. While he was still a bachelor in 1888, Frank had been seeing both women. His true affection was for the strong-willed and vivacious Mary Pearcey. It was, however, the meeker Phoebe Styles who became pregnant by him. Although leading a double love-life, Frank was a regular church-goer who knew which course he ought to pursue. He wrestled for some time with his conscience, at one point proposing to abandon the whole mess by making a new life abroad. It was Mary Pearcey who told him not to emigrate, but to marry the pregnant Phoebe. The redhead wrote him passionate letters which expressed little jealousy of her rival: 'Oh, Frank! I should not like to think I was the cause of all your troubles, and yet you make me think so. What can I do? I love you with all my heart, and I will love her because she will belong to you.'

Again: 'Do not think of going away, for my heart will break if you do; don't go dear. I won't ask too much, only to see you for five minutes when you can get away; but if you go quite away, how do you think I can live? I would see you get married 50 times over – yes, I could bear that far better than parting with you for ever . . . you must not go away. My heart throbs with pain only to think about it.'

Mixed in with these protestations of love were phrases culled from the romantic novelettes which Mary read avidly. One has an especially ironic ring in retrospect: 'In this false world we do not always know who are our friends and who our enemies, and all need friends . . .'

In the end, Frank did marry Phoebe Styles, settling down with her, his mother and sister Clara at Prince of Wales Road. Phoebe seems to have known all about her husband's liaison with Mary, but raised no strong objections to it. Curiously, the two women were friends, and when Phoebe's second child miscarried, Mary even nursed her rival through the pain and trauma. As for the first baby, Mary doted on it, almost as if she shared in the motherhood of the infant in every way.

To this day, what triggered the bloody climax remains a mystery. The police did determine, though, that on the day before the fateful visit, Mary sent Phoebe a note: 'Dearest: come round this afternoon and bring our little darling, don't fail.' On that occasion, the blinds at Mary's house were seen to be drawn down as if in preparation. As it happened, Phoebe Hogg was unable to go round that day, but after receiving a second note she went to the house the following day.

Mary did admit to police that Phoebe arrived with the baby in the pram, but claimed it was only to borrow some money. Asked why she had first denied the visit, she replied improbably: 'I did not tell you before because Phoebe asked me not to let anybody know that she had been here.' Later, to a police matron, she was to hint that there had been an argument: 'As we were having tea Mrs Hogg made some remark which I did not like – one word brought up another. Perhaps I had better not say any more.'

The neighbours had heard screaming in Mary Pearcey's house at 16.00 – screaming, and the smashing of crockery.

The police produced a search warrant and examined the premises. They found that they had been recently cleaned, but not very thoroughly. Spatters of blood could be seen on the walls and ceiling; the poker had blood and hairs on it. In a dresser drawer was a carving knife, also stained with blood. A skirt, an apron, curtains, a rug – all bore tell-tale stains.

Mary Pearcey sat at a piano during the search, and tinkled out nursery rhymes. When asked why so many bloodstains were to be found about the place she continued to play at the keyboard, eerily chanting, 'Killing mice, killing mice, killing mice!'

Later, the police discovered that Mary was wearing two wedding rings; no ring had been found on the body of Phoebe Hogg.

Arrested and charged with murder, 24-year-old Mary Pearcey was tried at the Old Bailey in December 1890. Throughout the proceedings, the accused woman protested her innocence, but the circumstantial evidence against her was overwhelming. Some two hours after the cries were heard at her home, a neighbour had seen Mary Pearcey pushing the perambulator, draped with a black shawl, along Priory Road. Night had now fallen, and she was hunched over the vehicle as if hoping not to be recognised. The pram itself appeared heavily laden, with something strangely bulky crammed up towards the hood . . .

The extraordinary journey which followed covered a circuit of some six miles. The murdered woman was found at Crossfield Road, Hampstead, and the baby was abandoned off Finchley Road. There was no evidence of violence being done to the infant, but its clothing was stained with blood. The impression was that it may have been suffocated by the weight of the corpse above it. As for the perambulator, it was found abandoned in Hamilton Terrace, St John's Wood, its grim freight shed at last.

Frank Hogg admitted to the police that he had gone round to Priory Road late that night, and let himself in with his latchkey. When he found the place empty, he pencilled a brief note: 'Twenty past ten. Cannot stay.' Had he lingered, he might have encountered Mary Pearcey returning from her macabre excursion.

The jury took only an hour to consider its verdict and found Mary Eleanor Pearcey guilty of murder. Asked if she had anything to say why sentence of death should not be passed, she swiftly answered: 'Only that I am innocent of the charge.'

Now wretched and reviled, Frank Hogg refused to see his mistress in the condemned cell, a rebuff which Mary lamented: 'He might have made death easier to bear.' On 23 December 1890 she was led to the scaffold and she faced her end with great calm and composure. To the prison chaplain accompanying her, she observed enigmatically: 'The sentence is just; the evidence was false.'

A puzzling remark. And it is just one of the untidy strands left in the Pearcey case. Some have doubted whether Mary could have accomplished the crime alone: Phoebe had been clubbed senseless and had her head severed by a knife drawn across the throat several times. It was done with such force that it cut clean through the vertebrae. Then there was the business of cramming the corpse into the pram. This was a formidable task even granted the point made by F. Tennyson Jesse in her *Murder and Its Motives*: 'the matter was made easier by the fact that there was nothing to prevent the head being doubled right back.'

What provoked the maniacal assault? Was it premeditated, or sparked by that 'remark which I did not like'? And if the evidence was false, who had falsified it?

London in the 1890s was the city of yellow fog and gaslit streets known to readers of Sherlock Holmes stories. And for afficionados of great unsolved murder mysteries there is one tantalizing postscript piece which in no way fits the jigsaw.

It emerged at the trial that Mary Pearcey's true name was Mary Eleanor Wheeler. She had taken her surname from that of a carpenter, John Charles Pearcey, with whom she had once cohabited. He stated at the trial that they were never formally married, and that he had left Mary because of her roving eye. But some mysterious figure seems to have occupied a special place in her affections. For on the day of her execution, Mary instructed her solicitor to place the following advertisement in the Madrid newspapers: 'M.E.C.P. Last wish of M.E.W. Have not betrayed.'

There is little doubt that Mary Pearcey lured Phoebe Hogg to Priory Road and there killed the unfortunate woman. The motive seems clearly to have been rooted in jealous love. Who then was M.E.C.P.? And what was the secret they shared? The puzzle has prompted one fantastic solution: that Mary was a member of a nefarious secret society, and liquidated Phoebe when she found out about it. More prosaically, it has been suggested that Mary was secretly married as a teenager to a man whose name she did not want sullied at the trial. Finally, it is possible that the novelette-reading Mary simply invented a little enigma to lend romance to her appalling crime.

We simply do not know. But reading and re-reading the last cryptic message you cannot help believing that a fascinating dimension to the case of Mary Pearcey may have dropped into the void when the hangman's fatal trap was sprung.

A Crime That Rocked a Kingdom

It was an odd, odd business. The scandal that rocked France in 1847 helped to bring down a dynasty. It involved one of the noblest families in the nation, and no *crime passionnel* in French history has provoked more discussion. There is no question about the identity of the murderer in the Praslin affair, nor of the horrific savagery of the crime. Thick dossiers of letters and statements still survive in the Paris National Archives, along with trunkloads of material evidence: a silken bell pull, bloodstained clothing, bronze candlesticks and a hunting knife among other items. But despite all that has survived and all that has been written, mystery lingers about the case, elusive as the aroma of expensive tobacco and the musk of Old French roses. Underneath, it was an odd, odd business.

The young Théobald de Praslin married Fanny Sébastiani on 19 October 1824. He was only nineteen, she was two years younger, and they were very much in love at the time. The families on both sides being of immense wealth, the wedding was a glittering occasion. The young marquis was heir to the great Praslin dukedom, and his bride was an honorary goddaughter of Napoleon. Big interests blessed the marriage, which began rich in promise as an idyl of domestic happiness.

She bore him children – nine of them in less than fifteen years – perhaps too many in the light of what was to come. For under the strain of successive pregnancies and births, the Marquise lost her radiant looks. Her dark, romantic features – inherited from Corsican blood – thickened and became swart. She grew corpulent. And her temperament, once agreeably capricious, soured into a volatile and domineering nature.

Her husband, in contrast, was a passive, introverted man little given to displays of emotion. The more she nagged, ranted and threw tantrums the more he retreated into a shell of cold reserve. Fanny continued to love Théobald in her tempestuous fashion; but on his part, love turned slowly into detestation.

Before 1839, when their last child was born, the decline in their relationship had begun. Already he had taken to shunning her bedroom, and she was writing him letters of complaint. They were eloquent letters which sprang directly from the heart, but the themes were monotonously reiterated: she regretted her fits of temper, tried to patch up the latest quarrel, craved his pity for her uncontrollable emotions. 'I am no longer the mistress of my feeling', she wrote at one point. 'Something over which I have no control takes possession of me.'

The Marquis merely became more disdainful. And in 1840, things took a terrible turn for the worse when he required her to sign an extraordinary document. By the terms of this private agreement, Madame de Praslin was to give up her natural rights as a mother. The family's governess was to have sole charge of all that concerned the children: clothes, schooling, recreation and so on. Madame de Praslin was not even permitted to see them unless in the company of the governess.

It was, by any standards, an appalling document for a mother to sign, and historians have long puzzled over its implications. Madame de Praslin wrote privately about it, claiming that she had sacrificed all to try and regain her husband's affection. But there are hints that some specific incident or discovery lay behind her renunciation. Was it some violent outburst which had frightened the children and led her husband to think them unsafe in her presence? Or was it something darker than that?

A charge of somehow 'corrupting' the children seems to have been laid against Madame de Praslin. It is known that her own governess at one time had been a certain Madamoiselle Mendelssohn, suspected of lesbian relations with her pupils. Did the Marquis suspect his wife of the same proclivities? Had she interfered with her own children?

It is just one of the affair's lingering mysteries. The contract, the shunned bedroom – all this was in private. In public, the couple continued to appear amid the plush and chandeliers of the Court, to receive guests and dispense their hospitality. In June 1841, Théobald's father died and he became the fifth Duc de Choiseul-Praslin, inheriting not only some nine million francs but the magnificent château of Vaux-le-Vicomte.

This superb building survives as one of the great splendours of French Baroque style. With its domes and towers, fountains and tree-lined avenues, it was to provide the grandest backdrop imaginable for the drama which was to unfold.

To Vaux, with the new Duke and Duchess, came a new governess only recently hired. The orphaned and illegitimate daughter of a Bonapartist soldier, she had dragged herself out of a miserable childhood to serve with a noble English family. Fair-haired, green-eyed and socially accomplished, she came to the Praslins with the best possible credentials. In due course, the whole of France was to become fascinated by the Mademoiselle: her name was Henriette Deluzy.

Partisans of the Duchess were to paint her as a scheming adventuress who brought shame to a noble household. Others saw her as a decent girl placed in an intolerable position. History's verdict must draw a little from each portrait. Henriette Deluzy did not create the unhappy marriage – it was in a disastrous state when she arrived. Nor (this seems quite clear) did she and the Duke ever become lovers in the carnal sense. But the pretty young governess was both intelligent and ambitious. Coming from her own insecure background, the splendours of Vaux, the Praslin millions, all the ranks and privileges which went with them – these lures combined with the manifest unhappiness of the Duke must surely have excited her thoughts. After all, even decent girls may dream a little . . .

Praslin told her at the outset about the contract he had made with his wife. Though it struck her as strange, it also gave her unique powers in the household. Mademoiselle Deluzy accepted the position and was soon supervising all that concerned the children. Two of the daughters, Berthe and Louise, came quickly to adore her. The young instructress was bright, vivacious and thoroughly sane – in marked contrast to their unbalanced, faintly terrifying mother.

It was not long before the Duke, too, came to seek refuge from the chill of his marriage in the governess's warm little circle. He loved his children and he loved to see them happy. Temperamentally indolent as well as reticent, the Duke spent more and more time in their company.

The Duchess, of course, was reduced to paroxysms of rage. Mademoiselle Deluzy quickly became 'that woman', and night after night in her lonely bedchamber the Duchess wrote long impassioned letters to her husband. The governess, she fumed, was 'bold, familiar, dominating, thoughtless, inquisitive, gossipy, insolent and greedy.' She had split the family, and set daughters against their mother. One accusation repeatedly made is of especial significance in the light of what was to come. The Duchess claimed that the scheming governess was deliberately *making it appear* as if she was her husband's mistress. The Duchess, however, never at any stage seems to have suspected that her rival was actually sharing his bed.

Everybody else, though, came to believe that she was. Within a year or so of Mlle Deluzy's arrival the rumours were beginning to spread. In a Paris society that drank gossip like fine wine, the scandal began to ferment. In the summer of 1844 the Duchess publicly threatened suicide, creating such an embarrassing scene that the Duke decided that a break was called for. He took three of his daughters, with their governess, off on a long Mediterranean holiday. The Duchess remained at Vaux. And for the first time in print, there appeared in a Paris gossip column, a snippet concerning the Praslin ménage. The Duke, it was said, had gone off for a vacation with his mistress.

This delicious little item did not go unnoticed. The story circulated not only around the Paris boulevards, but reached the courts of Europe as well. Mademoiselle Deluzy would have to leave the household now, all the well-informed tattlers said. But she did not. To do so would only give credence to the rumours, and the Duke determined to remain aloof from such malicious gossip.

Shamed beyond endurance, the humiliated Duchess took to eating all her

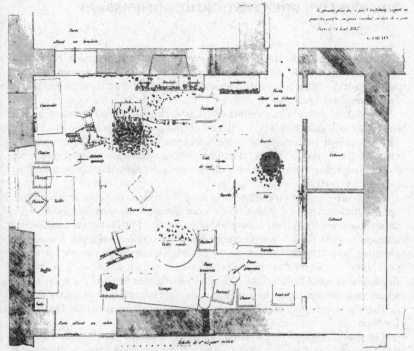

The bedroom of the Duchesse de Praslin

meals in the solitude of her bedchamber. She refused any contact with the governess and penned ever more eloquently hysterical letters to her husband.

The whole miserable business dragged on. In 1846, an unaccountable reconciliation appeared to occur, when the Duchess suddenly started making herself agreeable to the governess. It can only be explained as a change of tactics, though, for Madame de Praslin still fulminated in her letters to her husband about the 'little pair of green eyes behind your shoulder.' In reality, the mortified mother was maturing a plan for revenge.

She struck in June 1847. In that month, the Duke was suddenly but formally informed by his father-in-law that if the governess did not leave the household for good, his wife would sue for divorce and claim sole custody of the children.

The threat had terrible implications. The Duke himself clearly believed (for whatever reason) that his children were unsafe with their mother. Not only would he lose them to her, but the furore of the divorce would seriously affect his daughters' marriage prospects. The scandal would be immense, and what right-minded noble family would take on girls from this adulterous ménage? He could not doubt that Madame de Praslin would win her case – the scandal-mongering press had seen to that.

THE WORLD'S GREATEST CRIMES OF PASSION

Now the governess really did have to go. After a fierce but hopeless argument with his father-in-law, the Duke regretfully informed Mlle Deluzy that she should quit the household, with a generous life pension and a good reference for future employment.

She took it badly. Whatever private fancies she may have entertained about her future at Vaux, she certainly loved her charges; for six years the Praslin girls had comprised the only family she had ever known. That night she wept uncontrollably and swallowed laudanum in quantities that nearly took her life. But the next day she recovered, and in time she capitulated. She signed the annuity agreement.

And so the whole affair might have ended, but for the dark passions which the episode had engendered. The girls, for example, were unspeakably distressed by their separation from their beloved Mademoiselle. The Duke, meanwhile, was reduced to cold fury, a refrigerated rage which chilled even the triumphant Duchess. In a private memoir she wrote: 'He will never forgive me for what I have done . . . Every day the abyss between us will grow deeper. The more he thinks about what he has done, the more he will hate me and the more he will wreak vengeance on me. The future appalls me. I tremble when I think of it . . .'

There was not much of a future left, as it transpired, for either the Duke or the Duchess.

The discharged governess sought lodgings in Paris. But wherever she was accepted she would immediately find herself thrown back out onto the street. A certain Abbé Gallard was going the rounds, warning the owners off. Mlle Deluzy, said the cleric, was an immoral woman soon to be named in a divorce court. Also, he implied that she was pregnant. The Abbé Gallard was the Duchess's confessor.

Eventually, the embattled governess found a small room at the Pensionnat Lemaire, a school for young women in one of the seedier quarters of Paris. She was desperately unhappy and wrote pitiful letters to the Praslin girls imploring them not to forget her. They answered with equal *tendresse*: they had had terrible scenes with their mother, they wrote. Also: 'You are our real mother.'

On 26 July, Mlle Deluzy briefly met two of the Praslin children with their father in Paris. His face at that time seemed to have crumpled. And during the brief meeting he told the ex-governess something about the Duchess that quite appalled her.

We do not know what that something was.

It is another of the lingering mysteries. Among all the documents preserved in the National Archives, references to the dark secret seem to have been excised. From allusions that have survived it is known to have involved '*horrors*', 'secret carryings-on' and the Duchess's 'corruption of her sons'. Horace, the ten-year-old boy, had 'confessed infamies' to his father.

Some have interpreted these elusive references in the most literal way, suggesting that the Duchess had seduced at least one of her young sons. A more probable solution is proposed by Stanley Loomis in his authoritative study of the case, *A Crime of Passion* (1967). We know that after the governess had gone, the Duchess continued to threaten the divorce unless Mlle Deluzy actually left the country. That was what lay behind the persecutions of the Abbé Gallard. And it is possible that the Duchess had persuaded one or more of the boys to speak out against his father and the governess. He might even lie, pretending, for example, to have witnessed the couple in bed. Pure speculation, of course. What we do know is that the cold, reserved and rather weak-spirited Duke now plotted the murder of his wife.

All the pent rage inside him found expression in his plan of revenge. At the great Paris residence, the Hôtel Sébastiani, he began in the most comically inept way by removing the screws from his wife's bedposts. His idea was that the vast and weighty canopy above would collapse to crush or suffocate her. There is no doubt that he entertained this bizarre project, culled from the romantic fiction of the day. After the affair had reached its bloody climax, it was found that ceiling wax had been stuffed as camouflage into the holes where the screws had been.

Nor was this the Duke's sole preparation. At the Hôtel Sébastiani, he also used his trusty screwdriver to remove the bolt by which his wife could lock her door from his own connecting suite. If the canopy failed to kill the Duchess, he would then be guaranteed of access to finish the job. His plans made, the Duke gave orders that absolutely nobody should enter the Hôtel apartments until the next visit of his family to Paris.

That visit came on 17 August. While Madame de Praslin went straight to the Hôtel Sébastiani, the Duke and four of his children repaired first to the Pensionnat Lemaire for a tearful reunion with the discharged governess. During the brief call, the Duke promised that he would try and get letters of reference from the Duchess for Mademoiselle Deluzy.

Once back at the Hôtel, father and children retired to their various quarters. The lights were out by 23.30; all looked set for a peaceful night. It was at about 04.30 that a succession of blood-curdling, barely human shrieks ripped the dawn air over Paris.

The Duke, having perhaps waited hours for the canopy to collapse, had resorted to a furtive assault. He crept stealthily into his wife's bedroom, carrying with him a pistol and hunting knife. Bruises found on the corpse the following morning indicate that he clamped one hand firmly over her mouth as with the other he tried to cut her throat. But he only half-succeeded. With blood spurting from a gashed artery, Madame de Praslin woke and grabbed the double-edged blade, cutting her hand in the process. A big, strong woman, she managed to

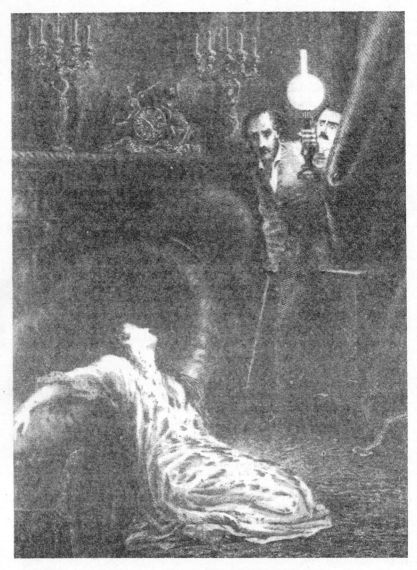

A contemporary print depicting the death of the Duchess

break free, to scream and to tug at the bell rope. A horrific fight and chase ensued, the Duchess staggering like a wounded animal around the room, steadying herself against the walls with her bleeding hand, frantic to escape her maniacal husband. Chairs and tables were knocked over; the bell rope was torn from its mounting. Later that morning, the copious bloodprints all around enabled the police to map the whole struggle with fine precision. It was on the sofa before the fireplace that the fifth Duke of Choiseul-Praslin finally cornered his wife. There, using a weighty brass candlestick taken from the mantlepiece, he clubbed her to the ground.

From the moment that the first terrible yelp had filled the Hôtel, servants had been trying to break into the suite. But all the doors were locked. Eventually, it was the Duke himself who admitted the staff. 'What has happened?' he asked them, feigning ignorance. The Duchess died moments later, and though the Duke tried to brazen it out by claiming that an intruder must have been responsible, his guilt was quickly established. When the head of the Sûreté Nationale first examined the appalling scene he remarked: 'This is not the work of a professional. It is the work of a gentleman.'

The Duke had had time to try and destroy the evidence, but in no satisfactory way. Smoke was seen pouring from the fireplace in his own bedroom, where he had burned bits of bloodstained clothing as well as a quantity of papers. The *robe de chambre* he was wearing was found to be damp with water applied to the red bloodmarks on the material. His hands were scratched and bitten, and the hunting knife was found concealed in his apartment.

Paris was in uproar. A crowd gathered immediately around the Hôtel, and called for the death of the murderer. For the indignant citizenry, the crime came to embody all the moral corruption with which the régime was tainted. The constitutional monarchy of Louis-Philippe was already reeling from a financial scandal in which two government ministers had been implicated. The next year the king was to be overthrown by revolution; and historians have identified the Praslin murder as being a key event which helped to trigger the insurrection.

In the public mind the issue was clear: the Duke had murdered his wife for love of an English-trained governess. And the fear was that because of his rank, the murderer would escape punishment. In reality, there was no likelihood that this would happen. The Duke was brought to trial before a Court of Peers who fully recognised the need to appease the public. In fact, the peers' greatest worry was that the Duke might commit suicide before sentence could be passed. 'What a mess!' the king was heard to exclaim as he signed the order summoning the court to convene. For the government, Count Molé wrote to a colleague: 'Impress upon the Chancellor Pasquier (head of the court) that it will be a public misfortune if this monster escapes by a voluntary death the fate which the law has reserved for him.'

In the event, however, the Duke did deprive the court of the satisfaction of dispensing its justice. While under close guard, he managed to swallow a dose of arsenic. It took him six days to die of the poison – six days of atrocious agony. He remained tight-lipped to the end, answering only evasively the questions put to him, and refusing to confess his guilt.

All the weight of public interest now fell on Mademoiselle Deluzy. She was kept in confinement for three months after the murder and subjected to the most exhaustive questioning. Had she been the Duke's mistress? Had she encouraged the crime? Throughout her ordeal, the ex-governess remained adamant in her denials. In the end she was released a free woman, but with an official proclamation hanging over her. The document acknowledged that there was no evidence to connect her with the crime. It did, however, charge her with having had a 'culpable liaison' with the Duke.

A now notorious woman, Mademoiselle Deluzy left France in 1849 to make a new life in America. Wearied by her trials but unbroken in spirit, she there married a young Presbyterian minister named Henry Field. The couple became leading lights in New York's church community, and though her past was known it was not held against her. Mrs Field died in 1875 at the age of 63. The obituaries barely mentioned the Praslin affair, but fêted her for her generous hospitality, her good works and her shining intellect. Before she died she had even written about France for her husband's religious periodical, *The Evangelist*. In her articles Mrs Field expressed her conviction that, whatever political upheavals might rock the country of her birth, one quality would guarantee the survival and well-being of France.

That quality was the strength which the nation derived from its happy family life.

The Chalkpit Conspiracy

At dusk on 30 November 1946, a man walking the North Downs near Woldingham in Surrey saw what looked like a heap of old clothes lying in a secluded chalkpit. Curiosity prompted him to look closer; and he found that the clothes were inhabited. Lying rigid in the trench was the body of a young man, trussed by a rope around his neck. A dirty piece of green cloth was entangled in the noose; the dead man's face was purple. When the experts first examined the body, it looked very much like a case of suicide. Yet there was no tree from which he might have suspended himself. And, though his clothes were smeared with chalk and mud, his shoes were spotlessly clean. Maybe the body had been carried there for disposal.

In the victim's pocket was an old wartime identity card which declared him to be John McMain Mudie, 35. Recently demobbed, he was found to have been working as a barman at the Reigate Hill Hotel some 12 miles from the chalkpit. A handsome young man, well liked by all who knew him, Mudie was nobody's idea of a killer or a killer's victim. He was too plain decent to be mixed up in murder.

Painstaking detective work led the police to uncover a conspiracy hatched in London. Three men in particular were implicated. One was Lawrence John Smith, a joiner; the second, John William Buckingham, who ran a car hire business. And the third was a very much more august figure: he was Thomas John Ley, 66, colossally fat, and a former Minister of Justice in New Zealand. He had been a noted spokesman there for Prohibition, and was known as 'Lemonade Ley' in consequence.

Evidence against them included statements from two gardeners who had seen a man loitering suspiciously at the chalkpit on the day before Mudie disappeared. The man had driven away in a car whose registration plate bore the number 101. Smith had, it transpired, hired a Ford Eight, FGP 101, for three days over the murder period.

Then there was the rag found entangled in the noose. It had been torn from a French polisher's cloth found at 5 Beaufort Gardens, Kensington, where Thomas Ley lived. A pickaxe, moreover, was found at the chalkpit where it seemed to have been used in partially filling in the trench. This too was traced back to 5 Beaufort Gardens; it had served there for mixing concrete.

Significant evidence, all of it – but it needed something stronger to support it. That came on 14 December, when Buckingham turned King's Evidence.

The story that unfolded was one in which hot-blooded jealousy and cold calculation had conspired to produce a quite senseless killing. The ex-justice minister had, it appeared, long been involved in an affair with a widow from Perth named Mrs Maggie Brook. They had come to London in 1930 and pursued their liaison quite openly. At one time it had been a sexual relationship, but Ley had been impotent for a decade. His love had endured beyond his capacity, however. The couple saw each other as regularly as ever.

Mrs Brook, 66, emerged at the trial as a kindly and sweet-natured lady – no storybook scarlet woman. Ley, in contrast, was a blusterer and a bully consumed by quite irrational jealousy. He had accused his partner of having affairs with three separate young men at the Wimbledon house where she lodged. And one of these was the blameless Jack Mudie.

Left: 5 Beaufort Gardens

Below: Mrs Maggie Brook covers her face to avoid the camera

Mudie had not exchanged more than a dozen words with Mrs Brook; their contact extended to no more than chance greetings on the stairs or in the lobby. Perhaps the ex-justice minister had observed some such exchange. In all events, his suspicions were aroused.

Jealousy worked on Thomas Ley, spreading like an infection until it inflamed his whole being. By late November in 1946, Ley was toxic with it.

He contacted Smith, the joiner, who had helped convert his Beaufort Gardens house into flats. Buckingham was introduced to him as a man who could 'keep his mouth shut'. Ley told the pair that he wanted to kidnap a blackmailer who was persecuting a lady of his acquaintance. The man should be brought back to his house, tied up and forced to sign a confession. Smith and Buckingham did not ask too many questions. Ley offered them money – 'more than a year's salary' for each of them.

The plot involved finding a way of getting Mudie peacefully into the house. Buckingham came up with the idea of using a woman. She should turn up at Mudie's bar with a chauffeur and limousine. Complimenting the proposed victim on his bar-tending skills, she would invite him back to her house to help out with a cocktail party of her own. One Lilian Bruce was hired for the role, with Buckingham's son to play chauffeur. Smith and Buckingham senior would follow in a second car, overtaking just before Beaufort Gardens, so that they could prepare a reception committee. Ley himself would be waiting there too – waiting for the delivery of his victim.

All went as planned on the evening of 28 November. Smith and Buckingham got into the house first through the front door. Mudie was ushered in by the back entrance. Mrs Bruce and her chauffeur then immediately disappeared, leaving the barman to his fate.

Nearly 40 years have passed since the Chalkpit Conspiracy was exposed. Yet even today, it is not known precisely what transpired at Beaufort Gardens. Buckingham claimed that once Mudie was tied up, his own role in the affair was over. Ley gave him £200 in one pound notes, and he left straight away with the payment. Smith, though, stayed some ten minutes longer . . . and it was Smith who, with Thomas Ley, was charged with murder at the Old Bailey.

Both denied the murder charge. Smith's statement roughly agreed with Buckingham's; he said that he too had left with Mudie trussed but fully conscious. But he gave no satisfactory reason for lingering that extra ten minutes. Moreover, there were details which suggested that he knew very well that Mudie would not leave the house alive.

They had used the French polisher's rag to gag him. A rug had been thrown over the victim's head while he was being tied up. Mudie had cried out: 'you're stifling me.' And either Smith or Buckingham had retorted: 'you are breathing your last.'

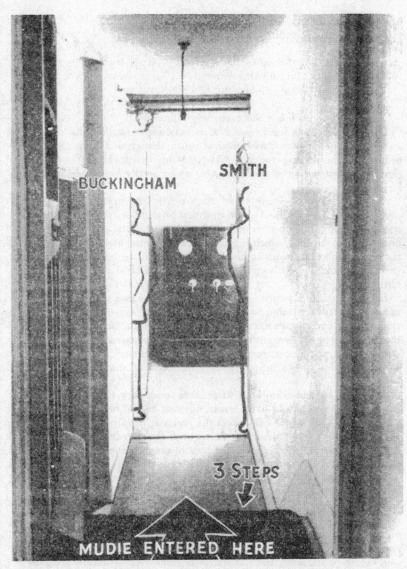

A picture reconstruction of how Mudie was lured to his death

The prosecutor taxed Smith on this point:

'He said, "you're stifling me"?'

'Yes.'

'And did you say the answer he got was, "you are breathing your last"?'

'That was only said in joking form.'

'Tremendously funny, do you think?'

'Well . . .'

'You appear to think it was extremely humorous.'

'No, not extremely humorous. No, it was done to frighten this man.'

Weighing much more heavily against Smith, though, was the fact that the car he hired had been seen at the chalkpit *before* Mudie disappeared. If he was at that time reconnoitring for a suitable grave, it can hardly have been for a living victim.

As for the precise mode of Mudie's death, the experts were in some disagreement. One inclined to the view that he had been subjected to a pretty heavy 'roughing-up'; another that all wounds were trivial apart from the rope-mark around the neck, which suggested that the victim had been suspended by the cord. Speculation along these lines might have been insignificant in themselves, but for the extraordinary testimony of a man named Robert Cruikshank.

He was brought forward by Ley's solicitors. And in a sensational development, he told the court that on the fatal night, he had been trying to burgle Ley's premises. He had found a man trussed up in a chair, and in panic had pulled at the rope. Had he accidentally killed the victim? Cruikshank, it transpired, had a police record, and his statements were widely disbelieved. Was he covering for Ley, hoping for a reward from him? It was doubtful that he was ever at the house.

As for Ley, he denied any knowledge of the conspiracy. He did not doubt that Mudie had been brought to his house, nor that he had been bound there and gagged with a rag which came from the premises. He simply brazened it out, offering no satisfactory alibi for the night of the murder. He blustered and rambled, apparently relying on the lack of direct evidence connecting him personally with the crime. The ex-justice minister had, after all, plotted his vengeance from afar. The jury could take the word of a former minister of state, or of two paltry London working men.

There is always a problem in long-distance plotting, though – the problem of the pay-off. Both Smith and Buckingham testified that Ley had paid them on the night £200 in one-pound notes. Ley's bank records showed that he had made two withdrawals of £250 and £300 shortly beforehand. And the withdrawals were in one-pound notes. Ley stated that the sums were for 'curtain furnishings'. Why not pay by cheque? His suppliers wanted cash, said the defendant. But he

John McMain Mudie

had receipts? No, Ley admitted, he had no receipt for either transaction.

The trial lasted for four days, but the jury took less than an hour to consider its verdict. When they came back into court, they declared both Ley and Smith guilty. Ley formally complained that the judge's summing-up had been biased, but a subsequent appeal failed. Both men were sentenced to be hanged.

The whole case had begun with a head in a noose – but it did not end in that way. Statements made during the trial had revealed a crazed, obsessive element in Ley's jealousy. And while awaiting execution, the ex-justice minister was examined by a Medical Board of Enquiry. It found him to be insane; not just given to jealousy but paranoid in the medical sense. Only three days before he was due to be hanged, a reprieve was granted and Ley was committed instead to Broadmoor.

That decision appeared to leave Smith alone to endure the ultimate penalty for murder. But, in a startling and controversial decision, he was also granted a reprieve. There was no question of the joiner being criminally insane; he had murdered strictly for cash. The Home Secretary's decision can only be explained in very human terms of fair play. Ley was clearly the moving force behind the murder, and Smith was only his instrument. To let the mastermind live and hang his subordinate would have been too dark an irony. The quality of mercy (however illogically applied) offered the only way out of the dilemma.

Lawrence John Smith had his sentence commuted to life imprisonment. And as for Ley, he did not enjoy a long period of grace. Fate dealt him the blow which the Home Secretary had withheld: he died at Broadmoor on 24 July 1947, succumbing to a haemorrhage of the brain.

'Oh, God, I am Not Guilty!'

Writer George Orwell set the scene. It is a peaceful Sunday afternoon in pre-war England. You have enjoyed the roast and the steam pudding, washed down with a cup of mahogany-brown tea. The fire is lit, you put your feet up on the sofa and reach for the Sunday newspapers. 'In these blissful circumstances, what is it that you want to read about? Naturally, about murder.'

For preference, the drama should be one of stealth and unfold against a background of intense respectability. Orwell cites a handful of classics in his *Decline of the English Murder*. There was the affair of Dr Palmer, for example, a Victorian physician who secretly poisoned 14 people. There was Crippen of course. And there was also the case of Thompson and Bywaters.

The domestic setting in suburban Ilford was perfect. Dark, driving passions lurked just beneath the surface. And Edith Thompson's sinister love letters seemed to prove that the crime was one of convenience, coolly arranged at a clandestine meeting beforehand.

And yet it wasn't like that. There were no carefully laid plans. And Edith Thompson's terrible cry rings as chill today as it did when the death sentence was passed upon her: 'I am not guilty; oh, God, I am not guilty!'

Percy and Edith Thompson had lived a largely uneventful life at their home in Ilford, Essex. He was a shipping clerk and she the book-keeper at a firm of wholesale milliners. Married in February 1915, both had their own careers, and the union produced no children. Still, all the neighbours agreed that they seemed a perfectly ordinary couple.

Young Frederick Bywaters came into their lives in the summer of 1921. He was one of a party of people who joined Percy and Edith for an August Bank Holiday on the Isle of Wight. There, he and Edith became mutually attracted, and after the holiday Bywaters lived for a while in the Thompsons' home as a lodger. But Percy grew suspicious: there was a row, and Bywaters quit the household.

Bywaters was only 19 at the time, and worked as a ship's writer on the P. & O. line. Eight years younger than the married woman, he was nonetheless of a strong and domineering temperament. He suggested a divorce, which Percy refused to grant, and the secret liaison continued for some time before the lovers managed to share a bed. Mostly, the affair was restricted to brief meetings in teashops and elsewhere. Because of his job on the S.S. *Morea*, Bywaters was only in England between voyages. And it was during the periods of separation that Edith wrote her fateful letters.

There was a mass of them. When the case came to trial, no fewer than 62 love letters were submitted by the prosecution. It was an extraordinary correspondence: passionate, sinister and utterly compelling.

Edith generally wrote to her lover as 'darlint' (a diminutive of 'darlingest'). And in the missives to her distant paramour she described how she was trying to get rid of her husband by putting poison or ground glass in his food ('big pieces too – not too powdered'). She returned to the theme on several occasions, complaining that her poisoning attempts had aroused Percy's suspicions: 'he puts great stress on the fact of the tea tasting bitter "as if something had been put in it," he says . . . when he was young (he) nearly suffocated by gas fumes. I wish

Frederick Bywaters is arrested at Ilford Station

we had not got electric light, it would be easy. I am going to try the glass again occasionally – when it is safe.'

Additionally, Edith sent her lover newspaper snippets concerning cases of death by poisoning. She hoped that the proposed crime would not affect their relationship: 'This thing that I am going to do for both of us will it ever – at all, make any difference between us, darlint? Do you understand what I mean? Will you ever think any the less of me?'

And she encouraged Bywaters to feel jealous. One passage in particular was to take on special significance: 'Yes, darlint, you are jealous of him – but I want you to be – he has the right by law to all that you have the right to by nature and love – yes, darlint, be jealous, so much so that you will do something desperate.'

All very damning on the surface. Yet the evidence suggests that Edith was playing mind-games: exciting herself with make-believe projects that many an unhappy wife may have entertained from time to time. Above all, she wanted to bond Bywaters to her. He was young, handsome and impetuous. By seeming willing to murder on his behalf, she hoped to secure his affections.

In September 1922, Bywaters returned from a voyage and the secret meetings resumed anew. On the afternoon of 3 October, the couple had a rendezvous in a London teashop. Afterwards, Edith went to the theatre with her husband. As they were walking home together from Ilford station along Belgrave Road, Bywaters sprang out from the shadows.

There was a brief quarrel. Bywaters pulled a knife and stabbed Thompson several times. A witness heard Edith scream: 'Oh, don't! Oh, don't!' The attacker fled back to the shadows as his victim fell, coughing blood, to the pavement.

Immediately, Edith ran for help, rushing until she met a group of people with the words: 'Oh, my God, will you help me, my husband is ill; he is bleeding.' A doctor was called for but arrived too late. Percy was dead, and Edith, now hysterical, sobbed: 'Why did you not come sooner and save him?'

Although Edith did not name the assailant, Bywaters soon fell under suspicion, was tracked down and arrested. Some of the love letters were found in his ship's locker; others were at his mother's home. Of course, they horribly implicated his mistress, and the pair went to trial at the Old Bailey together.

Home Life Of The Italians
Jealousy led a 42-year-old Italian to bite his wife's nose so hard that the wound needed 15 stitches.
    'Latins react differently from the British to domestic troubles', said Mr W.A. Ellis, at Prestatyn.
                              News of the World

THE WORLD'S GREATEST CRIMES OF PASSION

Frederick Edward Francis Bywaters was charged with murder, and Edith Jessie Thompson with incitement to the crime.

Thompson confessed to the killing, but claimed not to have intended murder. After he sprang from the darkness, the fatal quarrel allegedly ran as follows:

Bywaters: 'Why don't you get a divorce from your wife, you cad?'

Thompson: 'I've got her, I'll keep her, and I'll shoot you.'

Believing that Thompson was armed, Bywaters pulled a knife in fear of his life: 'I did not intend to kill him. I only meant to injure him. I gave him an opportunity of standing up to me as a man but he wouldn't.' Questioned about the love letters, he stated that it never entered his head that Edith had really tried to poison her husband: 'She had been reading books. She had a vivid way of declaring herself. She would read a book and imagine herself a character in the book.'

The prosecution alleged that the murder had been plotted in the teashop that afternoon. Bywaters repudiated the charge. But, given the mass of compromising material in the love letters, passion and premeditation seemed inextricably linked.

Edith's counsel had tried desperately to keep the damaging correspondence out of the courtroom as inadmissible evidence. The petition failed. The defence also failed in trying to persuade Edith herself to stay out of the witness box. She was not obliged to testify, and doing so only gave the prosecution a chance to cross-examine her about the letters. Edith, however, insisted on facing her accusers, and the damning passages were read out time and again in court.

And what of those sinister extracts? The selections read out in court were all passages chosen by the prosecution. In fact, only a very few refer directly to murder attempts. As in all love letters, the writer had obliquely mentioned all kinds of private secrets. The illicit lovers had considered many different ways out of their love tangle: divorce, elopement and even a suicide pact, for example. Murder was just one of the possibilities they toyed with, and many elusive references to a proposed 'drastic action' or similar were quite capable of a different interpretation.

Edith had penned thousands upon thousands of words, most of them just lover's 'gush'. It was only in the edited version that the correspondence appeared purely murderous. Some of the most apparently sinister passages clearly refer, in their context, to something the defence counsel dared not explain. This was an abortion which Edith was trying to arrange ('I am still willing to dare all and risk all if you are'). The defence obviously felt that it could not afford to be explicit. Enough stigma was attached to adultery; to throw in abortion would make Edith appear more infamous still.

The few direct references to murder attempts were Edith's calamitous fibs. She testified that she made them all up to try and bind Bywaters to her. If the

Bywaters at the inquest

prosecution was to be believed, Percy had been fed an almost daily diet of splintered glass and poison pellets. In fact, the pathologist stated that no trace of poison or of glass was found in Percy Thompson's body.

In effect, the evidence clearly indicates an impulse killing by Edith's lover. Bywaters had not specially armed himself for the encounter; the knife was one which he always kept in his coat pocket (seafarers, facing the hazards of foreign ports, commonly carry a blade). The witnesses' testimony agreed that the attack had dismayed and horrified Edith. She had cried: 'Oh, don't!', she had tried to summon help. 'Oh, God, why did he do it? I didn't want him to do it,' she had sobbed when she first learned that Bywaters had been arrested.

Yet it was as the scheming older woman that she was depicted. Contemporaries have described how, in the witness box, she seemed to exude a heady sexuality which turned the jury against her. The judge was strongly hostile to both prisoners in his summing up, and referred to Edith's 'wicked affection' for her lover. The jury took some two hours to consider its verdict:

> *Clerk of the Court*: Members of the jury, have you agreed upon your verdict?
> *Foreman of the Jury*: We have.
> *Clerk of the Court*: Do you find the prisoner, Frederick Edward Francis Bywaters, guilty or not guilty of the murder of Percy Thompson?
> *Foreman of the Jury*: Guilty, sir.
> *Clerk of the Court*: Do you find the prisoner, Edith Jessie Thompson, guilty or not guilty of the murder of Percy Thompson?
> *Foreman of the Jury*: Guilty.

Asked whether he had anything to say before sentence of death was passed, Bywaters answered: 'I say the verdict of the jury is wrong. Edith Thompson is not guilty. I am no murderer, I am not an assassin.' And when the dread penalty was announced, Edith cried out: '*I am not guilty; oh, God, I am not guilty!*'

An appeal failed. For Edith a petition signed by thousands was submitted to the Home Secretary, but no reprieve was granted. Edith's mother visited her in the condemned cell and asked: 'How could you write such letters?' The submissive mistress replied sadly: 'No one knows what kind of letters he was writing me.'

Bywaters himself protested Edith's innocence to the end. Calmly accepting his own fate he wrote: 'For her to be hanged as a criminal is too awful. She didn't commit the murder. I did. She never planned it. She never knew about it. She is innocent, absolutely innocent. I can't believe they will hang her.'

But they did. Thompson and Bywaters died within moments of each other on the morning of 9 January 1923. Frederick Bywaters faced his end bravely at Pentonville. At Holloway, Edith Thompson had to be carried to the scaffold; she was in a state of collapse as they fitted the noose around her.

The Deadly Apéritif

O n Friday 24 August 1973, a registered parcel arrived at the home of Tranquillo Allevi. His wife Renata took it in, as her husband was out at the time. She placed it on his desk, and when he returned, Tranquillo opened it up to find a bottle of apéritif. It was made by a well-known firm of Italian liquor manufacturers, and the accompanying letter invited him to become their local representative in a new sales campaign.

Allevi was a prosperous dairy farmer who lived near San Remo on the north Italian coast. Such invitations were not uncommon, and the 50-year-old dairyman took the bottle to his office where he put it in the fridge. It was a welcome gift, whether he took up the offer or not. Probably he forgot about it in his concern to get on with the day's business.

The bottle remained in the fridge that night and the whole of the following day. It was a Saturday – the day on which, by custom, he would take his wife to dine at the casino restaurant in San Remo. The evening passed pleasantly enough. Having driven Renata home after the meal, Allevi went on to his office to clear up some business. A salesman and another friend joined him there. The night was warm and the trio took off their jackets. Remembering the apéritif, Allevi went to the fridge and returned with the chilled appetizer.

He produced three glasses and poured out the drinks. Raising his glass in a toast, he tossed back its contents in one. The others only sipped – which was lucky for them. For, seconds later, Allevi crumpled to the floor. He was racked with spasms and gasping for breath.

Dismayed, his companions put down their glasses. One phoned the police who came quickly. The three men were rushed to hospital where the two friends were purged with emetics and recovered. Allevi, however, died.

Doctors were quick to diagnose death by poisoning. And in due course it was found that the apéritif contained enough strychnine to kill 500 men.

Who had tampered with the bottle? Enquiries at the manufacturers revealed that although they had sent out some samples with invitations, Allevi was not on their list. His letter followed their customary formula. But it had been typed on a plain sheet, not the company's headed notepaper. It was, moreover, unsigned.

Allevi had no special business rivals. He was generally well enough liked. And suspicion fell initially on Renata, Allevi's grieving wife. She was some 12 years younger than her husband. Enquiries revealed that she had several male admirers outside her marriage: her husband's bookkeeper; an Army officer; and a veterinary surgeon who had treated the dairy herds.

Renata, however, had been visibly distressed at the news of her husband's sudden death. She responded to questioning with every appearance of truthfulness. Far from trying to dissociate herself from the bottle, she herself informed police that she had taken it into the household. She also stated, unprompted, that it was her idea that the apéritif should be taken to the office and placed in the refrigerator to cool.

As investigation proceeded, the police checked up on the movements of her admirers on the fateful day when the parcel was posted. It had been sent from Milan, which seemed to let off two of the suspects. The bookkeeper could prove he had been in San Remo; the Army officer was on duty at the time. That left the veterinary surgeon, Dr Renzo Ferrari.

A suave professional man, Ferrari had been in Milan on the 23rd, renewing his veterinarian's license. Moreover, the police discovered that two days earlier he had bought six grammes of strychnine at a chemist's near his place of work. This was not in itself suspicious – the doctor often bought the substance there for treating sick cattle.

But there was stronger evidence against him. Checking up on typewriters he had access to, detectives discovered a machine at the town hall in Barengo. It appeared to match the typing on the poisonous invitation. Dr Ferrari was a local government officer. He used the town hall in his work.

Ferrari was charged with the murder, and the trial caused a sensation in Italy. This was no hot-blooded Latin-style *crime passionnel*. The defence counsel fiercely challenged the forensic evidence, and there were problems surrounding the precise motive. Ferrari had only recently become engaged to the daughter of a wealthy family. Why should he jeopardise his future? Ferrari claimed that his relationship with Renata was a purely sexual one. He said he was happy to break off the liaison when he met his fiancée.

Renata, dressed in widow's black, told a different story in the box. She testified that it was she who broke off the affair. It happened, she said, when her husband found out that she had been deceiving him. Ferrari refused to accept the breach. She had weakened at first, but then come to a final decision: 'I will not return to you.'

'We'll see,' the veterinarian had replied.

The poison, according to the prosecution, had been inserted by syringe through the cork of the intact bottle. And the final, damning evidence was supplied by a representative of the drinks firm. He stated that although no bottle had been sent from the company to Mr Allevi, one had been dispatched – with an invitation – to Dr Renzo Ferrari.

On 15 May 1974, a panel of judges found the accused guilty of murder with premeditation. The sentence amounted to some 30 years, including consecutive sentences for the attempted murder of Allevi's two drinking companions.

It should be remembered that almost anyone – including Renata – might have sampled the deadly apéritif. This, if anything ever was, was a case of bottled rage.

Otterburn?

Cowering in the lonely farmhouse on the Yorkshire moors, Dorothy Morton and her nurse-companion knew that something was wrong. It was past 3 o'clock in the morning and they were still fully dressed, waiting for Mr Morton's return. He should have been back hours ago from his trip to Oldham where he had gone to buy horses. The groom had been acting strangely all evening, and Mrs Morton had special cause for concern. Ernest Brown, the groom in question, had been her lover and was a violent man consumed with hatred for his employer. The two women heard creaking on the stairs. What was going on? Where was Dorothy's husband?

The creaking ceased. But at 03.30 the crackle of flames could be heard outside. Mrs Morton pulled back the curtain and saw that the garage was ablaze. Hurriedly, she rushed to the telephone to summon help, but as her fingers grasped the receiver no buzzing tone greeted her ears. The line was dead. Someone had cut the wire.

In stark terror, the two women fetched Mrs Morton's child and, with blankets under their arms, they fled from the house. The rest of the night they spent huddled under a hedge watching as the fire raged. In due course, the groom appeared on the scene and rushed to the house, calling, 'Mrs Morton! Mrs Morton!' Neither of the women called out in reply, but stayed in the shadows as he ran to release the startled horses. Some time later, the local fire brigade arrived to try and deal with the conflagration but it was daylight before the blaze was brought under control, and by that time quite a crowd had gathered. One person, though, who never arrived to view the damage was Mr Morton himself. The missing husband had been in the garage all the time – slumped in the passenger seat of the Chrysler saloon from which his charred remnant was eventually recovered.

The Moors' Garage Fire of 1933 came as the climax to a four-year drama. The dead man was Frederick Ellison Morton, prosperous managing director of a firm called Cattle Factors Ltd. His wife, Dorothy, was a beautiful woman with hazel eyes and fine, athletic build. She was especially fond of foxhunting, a pursuit which she enjoyed on the horses her husband kept. It seems that she was not averse to bedroom athletics either. And when in 1929, Ernest Brown was hired as a groom she found that they shared more than an interest in horses. The groom became Mrs Morton's lover, and a triangle took shape.

Ernest Brown was a personable man and a stylish dresser when not in his corduroys. He was by no means ill-educated either. But there was a streak of violence in his nature which soon came to disturb Mrs Morton. At the trial, she was to state that she learned to dislike him, only continuing the liaison through fear. Through threats, Brown forced his attentions on her and she rarely complied willingly.

The Mortons moved to Saxton Grange in the West Riding early in 1933. Mrs Morton had a 2-year-old child, and the nurse-companion, Ann Houseman, lived in. Ernest Brown was put up in quarters of his own – a little wooden cottage not far from the farmhouse. His servile status rankled and, in the jargon of the day, he had 'ideas above his station'. When, one day in June, he was asked to mow the lawns his fierce pride got the better of him. Ernest Brown threw up the job and quit the Morton household.

Mrs Morton's respite from her lover did not last long. Within days, Brown was back at the farm demanding reinstatement. As Mr Morton was away on a business trip, the groom insisted that his wife phone him. He stood over her as she made the call – with his hands about her neck, threatening to strangle her if she failed to persuade her husband.

Ernest Brown was reinstated – but not in his old post of groom. The man who had refused to mow the lawns was taken back only as an odd-job man. This was a bitter humiliation, and afterwards Brown seethed with hatred for Frederick Morton, a vindictive hatred in which jealousy and maimed pride jostled side by side. 'I will clout the little bugger one of these nights', he told a worker at the farm. On another occasion he threatened to ruin Morton's business: 'I can wreck this place and I shall do it.'

Brown nursed his resentment through the summer. And things were made worse when he learned that Dorothy Morton had taken another lover. This man was never identified at the trial, but Mrs Morton admitted his existence. The mystery man was referred to as the 'phantom lover', though his was an all-too fleshly reality.

On 5 September 1933, the tensions snapped. While Frederick Morton was buying horses in Oldham, Brown came into the farmhouse demanding to know what Mrs Morton had been doing that day. She admitted that she had gone bathing with 'Mr X' and this threw him into a fury. During the quarrel, Brown struck Dorothy Morton to the ground. And that evening began the sequence of events which culminated in a night of terror.

At 21.30, Dorothy and the nurse heard gunshot outside, and a hail of pellets rattled at the window. Soon after, they came upon Brown in the kitchen. He claimed to have been shooting at rats. At 21.45, there was a telephone call for Morton, which the nurse answered in the hall. She told the caller that her employer was not there but would soon be back, suggesting he call again at ten. Brown was loitering in the hall for no apparent reason and soon afterwards went into the kitchen to fetch a game knife. The caller did try to ring back at the appointed time – but he never got through. At some time before ten, the line had been cut.

Later, Brown appeared at the farmhouse again with a shotgun in his hand. He told the nurse that he wanted to see Dorothy, but the girl refused to let him meet her mistress alone. Eventually, Brown went away, leaving the two women frightened and anxious in the house.

At 23.30, Mrs Morton and the nurse thought that they heard a car coming. Assuming it was Frederick Morton, they went downstairs to wait for him. But he never turned up. Instead, when they opened the door, they found Brown again who told them, 'The boss has been in and gone out again.'

Gone out again? Brown's sinister prowlings had them seriously disquieted and when it became clear that he did not intend to leave they kept him talking about everyday matters. It was midnight before Brown finally left. There remained the long vigil until 03.30 when sounds of explosion announced the fire.

When help came to the scene of the conflagration, Brown told a bystander, 'By God! If the boss is in there, he will never be seen again.' And later he provided his own version of events for the police. The ex-groom said that Morton had indeed driven back that night, arriving at 23.30, in a drunken state (or 'clever side up'). Brown had left him racing the engine of the Chrysler in the garage where a second car was parked. The fire, he assumed, must have started through the Chrysler backfiring.

A plausible enough theory at first glance. But the police were to discover more sinister features in the case. There was the telephone wire, cut clean through with a knife. There was the emerging story of Brown's liaison with Dorothy. Above all, there was the grim mass of incinerated flesh which had been Frederick Morton.

Practically nothing remained of the managing director. When the gutted Chrysler was withdrawn from the debris, the victim's body could only be identified through two bunches of keys and a unique platinum diamond ring. Amid the charred remains, only one tiny scrap of scorched flesh still survived in recognisable condition. It was a portion from the stomach – and found to be peppered with shotgun pellets. From the concentration of wounds, forensic scientists determined that Morton had been shot at point blank range. He had not died drunk in an accidental fire – he had been murdered before the flames started. As the prosecutor noted when the case came to trial, 'If ever Fate played a murderer a dirty trick, it did so here. Had the wound been in the upper part, it would never have been discovered.'

Brown was the obvious suspect. To the end he protested his innocence, but the evidence against him was overwhelming. Apart from motive and opportunity, bloodstains were discovered on Brown's clothes and shotgun. The clinching detail was the game knife which the ex-groom had taken from the kitchen. From corresponding marks on blade and wire, it was determined that the knife had severed the cord.

The precise time of the murder could not be determined, but the prosecution contended that Brown probably shot his employer as early as 9.30, then concocted the story about 'shooting rats'. He had rained bullets at the window in case either of the two women had heard the sound of gunfire. As for the later sounds of a car arriving, it should be remembered that there were two vehicles in the garage.

The best the defence could do was to try and shift the blame, by implication, to the unnamed 'phantom lover'. The accused was asked, 'Is it your idea that some other lover of Mrs Morton's who disliked her husband shot him and set the place on fire?' Brown replied, 'It may well be.'

But it was a hopeless case. Ernest Brown was found guilty and hanged at Armley Prison, Leeds, on 6 February 1934. The only mystery surrounding the affair derived from the murderer's last words – but a big and tantalizing mystery it turned out to be. When masked and pinioned on the scaffold, Brown was asked by the chaplain if he wanted to make a confession. From beneath the hood, the condemned man's voice uttered three syllables: either 'Ought to burn' or 'Otterburn'.

Did he mean to imply that he ought to burn, as his former employer had burned? Or was he confessing to a sensational unsolved crime committed at Otterburn 100 miles away?

It had been an extraordinary incident – another 'blazing car murder'. In January 1931, 28-year-old Evelyn Foster had been found on a moor in a burning taxi belonging to her father's firm. In her agony, the dying girl described how she had picked up a fare near her Otterburn home. The man was heading for Ponteland, but during the journey he threatened and sexually assaulted her. She claimed he poured fluid over her from a bottle, and having set the vehicle ablaze launched it careering off onto the moor.

Evelyn Foster died of her injuries, the inquest reporting wilful murder. But it was suggested that the girl might have accidentally immolated herself while trying to burn the car for the insurance money. The police, in fact, issued a statement after the inquest, to the effect that no murderer had ever existed.

Were they doing her an injustice? And if so, was Ernest Brown the killer? Evelyn Foster described her assailant as a rather stylish dresser, and said that he had a slight Tyneside accent – details applying to Ernest Brown. The ex-groom was a man of violent temper, not above threatening his mistress to achieve forced intimacy. At the time of the Otterburn incident, he was still a groom in the Morton household, and his job involved travelling about the country to attend horse and cattle sales.

Was he a double murderer? We shall never know. Seconds after uttering his last three syllables Ernest Brown jerked into eternity.

Chapter Five

Was it murder?

A lovers' tryst is a private affair. But when two victims of flawed passion meet alone – and one of them is shot dead – it becomes an issue of public concern. Some of the most sensational courtroom dramas have followed love tragedies enacted behind closed doors.

Who pulled the trigger when Caesar Young was killed in a hansom cab with his chorus girl? Did Mrs Barney's pistol go off accidentally in the Knightsbridge Mews? And what was the intention of headmistress Mrs Harris when she drove to the fatal rendezvous with the world famous Scarsdale Diet doctor? Did she have suicide in mind? Or was it murder?

Death and the Diet Doctor

His book was a bestseller. When the case came to court it was found that eight out of the twelve women vetted for the jury had followed the Scarsdale Diet. A feeble joke went the rounds when the murder suspect was named: it was said that Mrs Harris had killed Dr Tarnower because she failed to lose weight as promised. And at the autopsy, a fascinating statistic was revealed. Dr Tarnower, 69, 'a moderately well-developed and well-nourished white male,' measured 70 inches tall and weighed 175 lbs. By his own diet plan, the millionaire physician was 15 lbs overweight!

Dr Herman Tarnower ('Hi' to his friends) lived in a fashionable section of New York's Westchester suburb. He helped to found a flourishing clinic at Scarsdale, and there used to recommend a diet programme for his overweight patients. Originally, the plan was no more than two pages long, but in 1979 the doctor published a greatly expanded version under the title of *The Complete Scarsdale Medical Diet*. 'Lose 20 lbs in 14 days', was the book's boast. Besides the initial Basic Plan there were Gourmet, International, Vegetarian and Money-saving variations. Millions followed the diet, and the doctor became world-famous.

Physically fit and active for his age, Tarnower had a taste for the good life. He enjoyed golf, fishing, travel to exotic places – and good eating, too, at the intimate dinner parties he gave at his Westchester home. A bachelor of long standing, Dr Tarnower also enjoyed women.

He had many casual affairs. But for some 14 years, the doctor had pursued a steady liaison with Mrs Jean Harris, headmistress of the highly respectable Madeira Girls' School in Virginia. It was a very 'adult relationship'. Mrs Harris was a divorcee whose own husband had died. She expressed no special jealousy about his philanderings. Nor did she ask for marriage; yet she was hostess at his dinners, the couple shared foreign holidays, and Mrs Harris helped to edit the famous book.

This civilised arrangement was jeopardised, however, when Lynne Tryforos entered the scene. She was the doctor's nurse-secretary at the clinic, an attractive young woman with whom Tarnower began to spend more and more time. In the year before the fatal event, for example, Dr Tarnower took two winter holidays: the first at Palm Beach with the headmistress; the second in Jamaica with the nurse.

Dr Herman Tarnower

THE WORLD'S GREATEST CRIMES OF PASSION

In March 1980, the time of the shooting, Mrs Harris was 56 and Lynne Tryforos only 37. The 'Swinging Diet Doc' as the press was to call him, was trying to jilt his long-standing mistress in favour of a replacement some 20 years younger. Nothing that emerged in the coming case could mask the essential callousness of the doctor's action. It was almost as if he were trading a life rather as he might have traded an old car – for a new model. Public sympathy was heavily in favour of Mrs Harris at the outset of the trial. And for feminists especially, she seemed to embody the whole plight of exploited womanhood.

The trial was one of the longest ever held in the history of New York State. And amid all the courtroom wranglings, some facts were beyond dispute. On Monday 10 March 1980, Mrs Harris drove the 500 miles from Virginia to New York in a blue Chrysler which belonged to the school. She arrived at around 23.00 on a stormy night and let herself into the house. With her she took a .32 calibre Harrington and Richardson revolver, bought some 18 months earlier. Five of its six chambers were loaded – five more rounds were on her person. She entered the doctor's bedroom while he slept, and in the period which followed several shots were fired. The doctor received four bullet wounds from which he died within the hour.

During the fracas, Tarnower's cook heard the buzzer from the bedroom sounding in the kitchen. She rushed and picked up the receiver, heard a shot and much shouting and screaming. The cook woke her husband and called the police as Mrs Harris left the house. A police officer in the neighbourhood drove to the scene and saw the blue Chrysler ahead. Mrs Harris did a U-turn in the road and went back to the house with the police car following behind.

'Hurry up, hurry up! He's been shot,' she said to the officer. Tarnower was crumpled on the bedroom floor when they arrived, his pajamas drenched in blood. He died in hospital.

The statements Mrs Harris made on the fateful night included: 'I've been through so much hell with him, I loved him very much, he slept with every woman he could find, and I had it.' She said she had come to the house with the intention of committing suicide. There had been a struggle with the gun, which went off several times. Asked who had control of the weapon and who did the shooting, she said: 'I don't know . . . I remember holding the gun and shooting him in the hand.'

Mrs Harris was brought to trial on a murder charge. The hearings began in October 1980, by which time the case was already a *cause célèbre*. And it was five weeks before the trial proper began with a full complement of jurors (8 women, 4 men) agreed on by both sides.

Mrs Harris pleaded not guilty, her counsel claiming, 'We don't want special sympathy because she is a woman, because of her age, because she is frail . . .' The defence asked for no mitigation on grounds of temporary insanity or diminished responsibility. Its case rested squarely on the contention that the defendant went to Westchester to take her own life, and the doctor died in a 'tragic accident'.

Formidable obstacles were ranged against this version of events. For example, if suicide was her intention, why did Mrs Harris take a loaded revolver – *and* carry spare rounds on her person? In fact, by a legal nicety, the prosecution was forbidden to mention that she had much more ammunition in the car.

Then there was the struggle itself. How come the doctor sustained four bullet wounds, and Mrs Harris none at all?

The defence marshalled plenty of evidence to show that Mrs Harris had been feeling suicidal. She had been taking drugs (prescribed by Dr Tarnower) to combat depression. She had recently been facing problems at her school. And she had left several farewell notes to friends and colleagues before the fateful night. One said: 'I wish to be immediately cremated and thrown away'. Another included the sad reflection, 'I was a person and no one ever knew.'

Briefly, her own account of events was that she arrived and found Tarnower in bed. 'Jesus,' he had said, 'it's the middle of the night,' and he told her to go away. She asked for a chance to talk for a little while, and he refused. Wandering into the bathroom, Mrs Harris saw a greenish-blue satin négligée (belonging to her rival). She went back into the bedroom and threw it to the floor. Returning to the bathroom she picked up a box of curlers and hurled them at the window. Tarnower came then to the bathroom and hit her across the face; her mouth was bruised when the police found her. She threw another box, and Tarnower hit her again.

Back in the bedroom she sat on the bed, saying 'Hit me again, Hi. Make it hard enough to kill.' Then, unzipping her bag, she took out the gun. 'Never mind,' she said, 'I'll do it myself.'

By her account, Mrs Harris raised the gun to her head, and as she squeezed the trigger he pushed it away. The shot exploded, Tarnower withdrew his hand and it was covered with blood. 'Jesus Christ,' he said. 'Look what you did.'

In a struggle that followed, Tarnower prised the gun off her, pressing the buzzer with his left hand. The gun lay briefly on the bed, Mrs Harris lunged for it and felt what she thought was the muzzle pressing into her abdomen. Again she pulled the trigger; there was a second explosion – and Tarnower fell back.

Now she held the gun to her head and pulled the trigger, but it only clicked. She tried again and a wild shot ricocheted somewhere. She put the gun to her head 'and I shot and I shot and I shot' but the gun just went on clicking. Back in the bathroom she banged the weapon repeatedly against the tub, trying to empty the chambers, planning to reload. In the end the gun just broke.

Tarnower was still conscious and she didn't realise he was dying as she ran out to find help. She was driving to a nearby phone booth when the police car

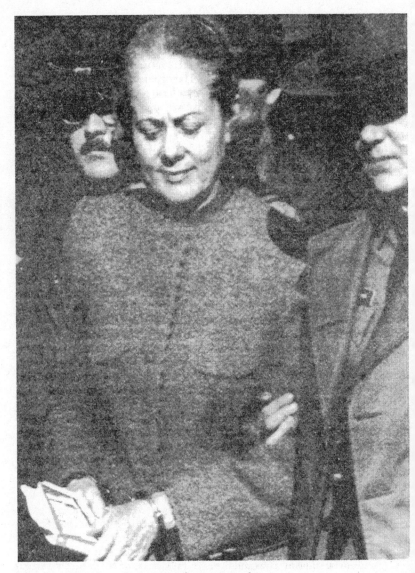

Mrs Jean Harris on her way to be sentenced

appeared with its flashing lights. Spotting it, she U-turned to lead it back to the house.

Incredibly complex ballistics evidence was heard at the trial, with abstruse talk about ricochet points, in-and-out gunshot wounds and so on. Additionally, it was shown that the police had behaved with some carelessness in handling the material evidence. Suffice to say that four bullet wounds were found in the doctor's body, and Mrs Harris could only remember three shots being fired. This tended to weigh against her. But it was easy to imagine that in the heat of the struggle, more shots might have been fired without murderous intent. Ultimately, the ballistics evidence was inconclusive.

It was in essence a psychological drama. Mrs Harris was something of an enigma even to partisans of her cause. Small, attractive and neatly turned out, she was very composed in the dock. She showed no apparent remorse for the death of her long-standing lover, and even handled the bloodstained sheets without visible emotion. Sometimes she was petulant with the prosecutor; constantly she could be seen forwarding notes to her own defence counsel. Hers was a sharp mind – she looked neither frail, aged nor abandoned. Nor did she look like a victim.

The defence stressed her suicidal weariness, claiming that no vengeful feelings had motivated her as she drove to Westchester that night. There was no hatred for Tarnower in her soul, only a mortal exhaustion. They had never quarrelled before, she quipped in the box, except over the correct use of the subjunctive. But one piece of evidence weighed massively against her version of events. It came to be known as the Scarsdale Letter.

This was a very long and very angry letter mailed by Mrs Harris on the very morning of the fateful day. It was sent to Tarnower by registered post and recovered from the mail. And the text was one long shriek of outrage against the wrongs she had endured.

Mrs Harris claimed in the letter that Tarnower had cut her out of his will in favour of Lynn Tryforos. She called her rival 'a vicious, adulterous psychotic', and a 'self-serving, ignorant slut.' The headmistress charged Lynne with ripping up dresses from her wardrobe at Tarnower's house. She suspected her of stealing her jewellery too, and of making anonymous phone calls.

The whole tone of the letter was ugly, betraying a violent intensity of emotions. Mrs Harris's central demand was that she be allowed to spend April 19th with Tarnower. This was an important occasion at which the doctor was to be honoured. Mrs Harris was determined to attend 'even if the slut comes – indeed, I don't care if she pops naked out of a cake with her tits frosted with chocolate!'

This from the headmistress of the Madeira Girls' School! The letter undermined all the character witnesses who had been brought from the school to the courtroom. But it did much more. It demonstrated unequivocally that jealousy and rage were burning in her soul. In the box the prosecutor had asked: 'Did you ever consider yourself publicly humiliated by the fact that Dr Tarnower was seeing Lynne Tryforos in public?' She had replied 'No'. Yet, in the letter, she had written: 'I have been publicly humiliated again and again and again . . .'

The defence had refused to plead for leniency on the grounds of diminished responsibility. They had decided to go for complete acquittal on the 'tragic accident' theory. And it now seemed with hindsight a downright mistake.

The prosecution described a phone call from the doctor on the fateful morning. 'Goddamit, Jean, stop bothering me', he had said. And this, it was alleged, was the triggering incident which caused her to take the revolver, the many rounds of ammunition, and head the blue Chrysler to Westchester. No doubt she did intend suicide. But she intended to kill the doctor first.

At the end of a trial lasting nearly a year, the jury delivered its verdict. And it agreed with the prosecution. On 24 February 1981, Mrs Harris was found guilty of the murder charge. She displayed no reaction, but two defence lawyers burst into tears when the result was announced. The verdict carried an automatic jail sentence of at least 15 years which was duly delivered by the judge. Standing upright in the dock, Mrs Harris replied with a lengthy statement beginning: 'I want to say that I did not murder Dr Herman Tarnower, that I loved him very much and I never wished him ill, and I am innocent as I stand here . . .'

She was sent to the Bedford Hills Correctional Facility in Westchester. In December 1981, *The Times* reported that Mrs Harris had abandoned the Scarsdale Diet and had gained 30 lb on prison food.

The Terrible Turk
Rejected by the girl he loved, Mr Darsun Yilmaz, a Turk from Damal, resorted to abduction. One night in August 1972 he crept stealthily into the girl's garden. Reaching her bedroom by means of a ladder he threw a blanket over her sleeping form. Then, with his moaning beloved cocooned over his shoulder, the Terrible Turk made his way down to his car and sped off into the night.

Great was his joy as he later wrestled with the blanket and strove to release the lovely contraband. Great was his chagrin when the cloth slipped away to reveal the girl's 91-year-old grandmother.

'There Has Been an Accident . . .'

They called them the Bright Young Things. In the 1920s, the gilded children of London society pursued gaiety with a special kind of frenzy. The horrors of World War One lay in the past; for the future few thoughts were spared. Instead privileged youth grasped feverishly for the here and now: drinking heavily, driving recklessly and making promiscuous love. They danced to jazz, they held fancy dress balls – life was a funfair of glittering silliness. And inevitably it happened that, once in a while, somebody fell off a roundabout.

Elvira Dolores Barney, 27, belonged to the lost generation. The daughter of Sir John and Lady Mullens, she was a conspicuous figure in society: slender, attractive and arrogant. A brief marriage to an older man had ended in quarrels and separation. With her own inheritance and a rich allowance from her parents, the young Mrs Barney returned to the circuit, looking for a good time – and a lover.

She found him in 24-year-old Michael Scott Stephen, one-time dress designer and all-purpose man-about-town. He was something of a gambler who also sponged off rich women. And when the couple set up home at 21 Williams Mews, Knightsbridge, it was Elvira Barney who paid the bills.

The house lay off Lowndes Square, and the couple scandalised the neighbours with their noisy parties. They had equally noisy quarrels too, and it was on the night of 31 May 1932 that one of these proved fatal.

Around midnight, Mrs Barney's doctor received a telephone call. The woman's voice at the other end of the line was near hysterical: 'For God's sake, doctor, come at once. There has been a terrible accident.' Arriving at the mews cottage, the doctor found Stephen lying dead in the upstairs bedroom. He had been shot at close range through the chest. Nearby was a .32 Smith and Wesson revolver, in which two of the chambers were empty.

'He can't be dead,' Mrs Barney was moaning. 'I love him so . . . Let me die, let me die. I will kill myself.'

That, then, was the tableau: Mrs Barney, her dead lover, and the gun. When the police arrived she was still in a state of distress. A detective asked her to accompany him to the station; she struck him, calling out: 'I'll teach you to put me in a cell, you foul swine.' Alternately tearful and imperious, Mrs Barney telephoned her parents, afterwards warning: 'Now you know who my mother is, you will be more careful of what you say.' But when her parents arrived she went quietly to the station. There she made the same statement that she had made to her doctor. It was a version of events from which she never departed.

She said that she and her lover had come back to the mews cottage, half drunk, from a party at the Café de Paris. Stephen declared that he was going to leave her, and she had threatened to kill herself if he did so. She took the gun from under a cushion where it had been hidden; he leaped at her to prevent the suicide. In the struggle which followed, Stephen grabbed the revolver which went off by accident and killed him.

Since Mrs Barney's was the only evidence then available, she was released from custody. Three days later, however, she was formally arrested. The police had been making enquiries in the neighbourhood.

No one could doubt the violent nature of Elvira Barney's romance. Three weeks before Stephen's death, for example, Mrs Hall, a resident, had seen him come to the mews cottage in the early hours of the morning. He was asking for money, but was told by Mrs Barney to go away. He did so, but came back later that night. He was repulsed again, and on that occasion Mrs Barney had looked out of her window, apparently naked, and shouted down, 'Laugh, baby, laugh for the last time!'

Then she had fired a revolver.

The same witness declared that on the fateful night there had been a loud argument in which Mrs Barney had cried out, 'I will shoot you!' before the gun was fired.

Brought to trial at the Old Bailey on a murder charge, Elvira Barney found some formidable forensic experts ranged against her. Sir Bernard Spilsbury, the eminent pathologist, testified that there were no smoke or scorch marks on the dead man's clothes or body. These were generally found when a victim was shot at point blank range. In fact, the angle of the bullet wound implied that Stephen had been shot from a distance of several feet. Moreover, the gunsmith Robert Churchill noted that the Smith and Wesson had a very heavy action – its pull amounting to 14 lbs. It was hard to see how it could have been fired by accident.

Finally, a mysterious bullet hole had been found in the bedroom wall, but no bullet had been recovered from it. If *two* shots had been fired, it made the case for an accident appear doubly improbable.

Defending Elvira Barney, however, was one of the most brilliant advocates of the day. His name was Sir Patrick Hastings, and although a specialist in civil actions he brought an outstanding legal mind to bear on the criminal case. Significantly, Mrs Hall who had first claimed to hear the words, 'I'll shoot *you*,' changed the words at the trial to 'I'll shoot.' This could well carry the implication that Mrs Barney was threatening suicide, not murder. Moreover Hastings had the same witness support the case for a suicide threat. Discussing the earlier shooting incident, Mrs Hall agreed that Stephen and Mrs Barney

Mrs Elvira Barney arriving at her parents' residence in Belgrave Square

Michael Scott Stephen

seemed very friendly on the morning after the 'Laugh, baby, laugh' episode.

'What conversation passed between you and the young man?' asked Hastings.

'I told him to clear off, as he was a perfect nuisance in the mews.'

'What did he reply?'

'He apologised and said he didn't want to leave Mrs Barney because he was afraid that she might kill herself.'

In fact, Hastings was to contend, the shot fired by Mrs Barney three weeks before Stephen died was not aimed after him in the mews. It was the shot which accounted for the mysterious bullet hole in the bedroom wall. Mrs Barney had fired the gun at random, hoping to persuade her lover that her suicide threats were genuine.

Spilsbury's apparently damning forensic evidence was dismissed as theorizing rather than hard fact. As for Robert Churchill's claim that the gun could not have gone off by accident, Hastings had a dramatic answer. Brandishing the revolver before the court, he pulled the trigger repeatedly at the ceiling. It was a gesture accomplished with the utmost panache (although Hastings is said to have later admitted that the effort made his finger sore).

Mrs Barney herself made a more than favourable impression. She spoke in low, dignified tones, her emotion evident but never overstated. She readily admitted that both her marriage and her affair had been unhappy. A tragic figure in the dock, she seemed more ill-fated than ill-intentioned. They had made love, she said, on the fateful night, but it had not been successful: 'He said that he was not pleased with the way things were going and he wanted to go away the next day and not see me at all. That made me very unhappy. He got up from the bed and dressed. I asked him not to leave me and said that if he did I should kill myself.'

'Did he say or do anything then?'

'He got up and took the revolver, saying, "Well, you don't do it with this!"'

There followed the struggle, and the shot.

In his final speech, Hastings meticulously reiterated the thrust of the defence's case. Only Mrs Barney could say what happened on the night of Stephen's death, and she had never departed from her story. In summing up, the judge paid tribute to the power of Sir Patrick's speech, but left the facts for the jury to interpret.

It was a case, *par excellence*, for a jury. The best experts available had given their testimony, the best legal minds had presided in court. But when all was said and done, the outcome had to revolve around a human assessment of the case. Did she do it, or didn't she?

After only one hour and 50 minutes, the jury declared that she didn't.

Elvira Barney's acquittal was greeted with cheers from a large crowd outside the court. A free woman, she went to France to escape the burden of publicity. But it seems that she had not been greatly chastened by the long courtroom ordeal. As chance would have it, Sir Patrick Hastings also crossed the Channel after the trial, for a holiday with his family. While driving from Boulogne he narrowly escaped death when a car coming from behind overtook him on the wrong side of the road. The driver of the car was Mrs Barney.

Socialite, beauty and subject of scandal, Elvira Barney never got a chance to outlive the label of Bright Young Thing. Four years after the trial she was found dead in a Paris hotel bedroom. She was 31 years old.

Sir Patrick Hastings

A Rifle at the Party

The pre-Christmas staff party at New Zealand's Dunedin General Hospital was held on 12 December 1954. Dr John William 'Bill' Saunders, 27-year-old medical officer, took Frances Kearney, a senior student at the hospital. Also present at the party was Dr Florence Whittingham, a house surgeon who had been Saunders' fiancée. She went alone to the party – alone, that is, except for a .303 rifle.

She arrived late. While the party was getting into its swing, Florence Whittingham stayed in her own apartment, writing to a friend a letter that she never in fact posted. Its sentiments were bitter and despondent: 'I can no longer cope and Bill makes things so miserable for me there seems little left. I have so much pain . . .'

She came after midnight, nursing her pain and her rifle. Groups of party-goers had by now crowded into the quarters of one of the hospital surgeons. Florence Whittingham found her former lover in the corridor; and suddenly, above the chatter and the chink of glasses in the living room, voices could be heard raised in anger outside. There was shouting and screaming – a shot detonated – and the guests rushed out into the corridor.

For a moment the scene was frozen, as in some nightmarish tableau. Dr Saunders was kneeling, blood-spattered, on the floor. Florence Whittingham stood before him and, as the wounded man swayed on his knees, she lent forward to embrace him. She was babbling hysterically: 'Bill, listen to me, Bill.' But the medical officer heard nothing as he slid dying from her arms. No-one called for a doctor – the apartment was crowded with medics. But all of their expertise counted for nothing in the case of Dr Saunders. He was dead before the stretcher arrived.

The case stunned New Zealand. Explosions of love and despair were not expected in the sober professional community of Dunedin, the South Island seaport founded by Scottish Presbyterians. And although clearly a crime of passion, the affair had its perplexing features too. A rifle is no natural choice of weapon for suicide. Did Dr Whittingham go to the party intending murder or, as she claimed, something else?

Dr Senga Florence Whittingham was 27 at the time; the same age as her former fiancé. And no-one could deny that she had cause for grievance in the events leading up to the tragedy. She had taken up the post of house surgeon at Dunedin early in 1953, and her duties involved working closely with Dr Saunders. Soon they formed a relationship which extended out of hours. As early as May 1953, the medical officer asked Florence to marry him and she was only too happy to accept. In June, the couple went to see Saunders' mother and announced their engagement. They hoped for an early wedding, for Florence was expecting a baby.

Mrs Saunders had her reservations. It had been a lightning romance, and both had their careers to think about. Mrs Saunders advised a period of reflection. They should not get married only for the baby's sake. If necessary, she declared, she would adopt it.

In the event, there was no quick wedding – indeed, no wedding at all. After that meeting with Mrs Saunders, the couple still went on seeing one another. But it seemed to Florence that Bill's ardour had cooled. She sensed that he no longer wanted the baby. When asked about his feelings, Bill denied that he was falling out of love, but he was evasive about the future.

That summer, Florence Whittingham procured an abortion. She knew immediately afterwards that a bond had been broken. Bill was clearly relieved, and in September, with no pressing reason for the marriage to go ahead, he broke off the engagement.

Florence was in despair. Even in the most supportive environment, an abortion may leave deep emotional scars. Had the child been truly 'unwanted' the loss might have been easier to bear. But this baby had been joyfully anticipated – by Florence, at least – as the fruit of love and in the promise of a shared future. She still loved Dr Saunders, still urgently wanted to marry him. But far from easing the relationship, her sacrifice had left her bereft of her lover too. For Dr Saunders, breaking the engagement recalled a more carefree way of living. Once again he became Dunedin's popular – and very eligible – bachelor medical officer.

It was when the bitter realisation of her double-loss dawned that Florence Whittingham bought the .303 rifle. She told a friend who once noticed the gun in her rooms that it was for her brother. In fact, Dr Whittingham had no brother. But if a sudden urge to violence provoked the purchase it seems to have faded away. She took no immediate action, enduring instead long months of waiting and of faint hope. Perhaps Saunders' love would quicken again?

It never did. Through all of 1954, Florence Whittingham was prey to black depression which eroded her vitality. She became a wraith in the corridors of the General Hospital, attending as capably as ever to her patients, but inwardly broken in spirit. Her health was affected and she underwent a major operation. To combat her loss of vitality, she began taking insulin, a drug normally prescribed for diabetics. It proved no cure, though, for lovesickness.

The affair was over, and no amount of pleading could bring Dr Saunders back. Yet she still saw him practically daily in the hospital, confident, ambitious and relishing his restored bachelorhood. What provoked the climax was a trivial enough event. Florence Whittingham learned that her ex-lover would be taking Miss Kearney to the staff party at Christmas. A sense of outrage seems to have seized Florence, for she phoned her rival and in a near-shriek declared, 'This is the mother of Bill Saunders' child speaking!' No doubt a pent flood of recrimination was at her lips, but she got no chance to release it. When Miss Kearney identified the caller's voice as Dr Whittingham's she prudently hung up.

Florence Whittingham was shut out now; shut out of her lover's life and his future. And it was in a mood of total frustration and despair that she had recourse to the rifle.

In the letter she wrote to her friend before taking the gun to the party, Dr Whittingham began: 'I should like you to be of special comfort to my mother and Bill's mother.' By implication, she was considering some kind of dramatic action if 'special comfort' would be required. But the rest of the text expressed, in broken paragraphs, only misery: 'I have had a year of hell . . . I love him but my pleadings are useless.' There was no specific threat.

After the sensational shooting at the party, she was to say quietly, 'It's the first time I've been at peace for a year.' And later: 'I loved him – I couldn't stop loving him. I wanted to frighten him. That's all. Just to frighten him.-I didn't mean to shoot him. Just frighten him. That's all.'

When a crime is committed in a state of high emotion, the word 'intention' becomes opaque. Dr Whittingham was brought to trial for wilful murder in February 1955, and the prosecution had a formidable case. The accused had, after all, taken a loaded rifle to the party. The letter she had written was shown in evidence. A ballistics expert, moreover, testified that the .303 could not easily be fired by chance.

In defence, Florence Whittingham's counsel contended that she had pointed the gun at Saunders only as a threatening gesture; the discharge was accidental. Obviously there was great sympathy for the accused when the story of her abortion and operation was made known. But assessing her precise intention at the moment of discharge called for careful consideration. At the end of the six-day trial, the jury deliberated over its verdict for more than seven hours. Returning to the crowded courtroom, the members found Dr Whittingham guilty of manslaughter, but added a strong recommendation to mercy on the grounds that the rifle was fired accidentally. She received a three-year sentence.

In retrospect, the case is as hard to assess as it was in the Supreme Court Building. But the verdict was a fair one. However the gun went off, its purpose at the party was not to destroy a life. It was brought to shock the victim into recognition of wronged love and misery endured. Behind the echo of gunshot, a voice was calling, 'Bill, listen to me, Bill. *Listen* to me.' It was the voice of love locked out.

'I am a Lady'

In March 1914, as war clouds gathered over Europe, a public scandal shook France to its roots. It was a shooting incident – an *affaire d'honneur* – which swept all other issues from the front pages. Even the assassination of the Archduke Franz Ferdinand at Sarajevo was given lesser prominence in the press. That obscure event in Bosnia was to usher in the holocaust of World War One but its significance was not at first grasped. France's Caillaux Affair, in contrast, was reported worldwide and followed with complete fascination.

It did not conform to the classic pattern of a crime of passion, but had all the elements associated with one. There were the tangled emotions of a love triangle, and shots fired by an outraged wife. The victim, though, was the newspaper editor who brought the affair to light.

Gaston Calmette, editor of *Le Figaro*, was the most influential journalist in France. For months he had used the power of his paper to direct a campaign against Henri Caillaux, Finance Minister. The attacks came daily in the form of lampoons as well as bitter textual denunciations. What provoked the editor's wrath was Caillaux's pacificism and – more serious – supposedly treasonable contacts with Germany.

Things came to a head when the editor resorted to personal smears. On the morning of 16 March 1914, *Le Figaro* published a compromising love letter from Caillaux on its front page. The letter was one of several written by the Minister during the period of his first marriage. They were addressed to Henriette, the society beauty who became his second wife. Caillaux's first wife had acquired some of the correspondence and had used it to obtain a hefty cash settlement after the divorce. The business was over, it was a private affair – but reflected no credit on the Minister.

It was the second Madame Caillaux who took action. When the letter was published Henriette could not find her husband, and so headed straight for a gunsmith. In the shop, having tested a Smith and Wesson, she judiciously opted for a Browning automatic. Then she went round to the offices of *Le Figaro* where she shot the editor dead with five bullets. As nervous staff sought to apprehend the killer, Madame Caillaux replied magisterially, 'Let me go. I am a lady. I am Madame Caillaux. I have my car waiting to take me to the police station.'

The Minister was forced to resign, and his wife was brought to trial at the Assize Court of the Seine in July 1914. She faced the charge of murder amid a national furore. Initially, at least, the dead man was presented as a patriot gunned down by a traitor's wife. The courtroom turned into a political theatre of war, in which charges and counter-charges were fired like mortar shells from the entrenched ranks of the rival counsels. In the end, the Caillauxs emerged the political victors, bringing evidence to show that Calmette himself had been involved in unpatriotic propaganda.

But what of the murder charge? Incredibly, Madame Caillaux declared herself innocent of the crime, on the grounds that the gun went off by accident. After the first chance shot, she contended, the rest of the bullets simply streamed out automatically. She gave evidence in the dock with a stately calm and with every appearance of truthfulness. The jury came to the unanimous verdict that Madame Caillaux was not guilty – and she walked from the court a free woman.

Two Cab Mysteries

When one of two lovers gets shot in a sealed cab, the event may be problematic for the law. Should the victim die, the case is likely to rest on the testimony of the survivor. The two stories that follow were different in outcome, yet they shared many features in common. Both shootings, for example, tragically concluded love affairs which were supposedly over already. Both also involved ladies of the stage and took place during the champagne years before the outbreak of World War One.

The first drama was played out in New York, 1904, where Mrs 'Caesar' Young had had enough. Everyone knew about her husband's affair with Nan Patterson, 22-year-old chorus girl from the hit musical *Floradora*. Mrs Young had thwarted one attempted elopement, and now booked passages for her husband and herself on a transatlantic steamer. Maybe a holiday in England would provide a chance of a reconciliation, in which memories of the chorus girl would fade from his mind.

Francis 'Caesar' Young, New York gambler and prominent man of the turf, agreed to the vacation. The passages were booked for 4 June 1904, but on the day before the ship was due to leave, Caesar Young spent a long time with Nan Patterson. The bonds that had united them could not easily be severed: he drank, they argued, and on the morning of the sailing he was again in Nan's company. The couple shared a hansom cab which led along Broadway to a theatreland sensation – and an amazing triple series of trials.

THE WORLD'S GREATEST CRIMES OF PASSION

Exactly what happened in the cab? One shot detonated in the vehicle and a passer-by heard Nan cry out, 'Look at me, Frank. Why did you do it?' First, the chorus girl told the driver to make for a nearby drugstore, then to hurry on to a hospital. But it was too late. When the cab doors were opened, Caesar Young was already dead, slumped in the lap of his mistress. His shirt was stained with blood from the bullet-wound in his chest, and the pistol was found in his coat pocket.

Nan Patterson was arrested and charged with murder. If a verdict of guilty was reached, she would go to the electric chair, a device used in New York from 1890, when it had been applied for the first time in the world.

Nan's case first came to court in November 1904, but a mistrial was announced before she could give evidence: one of the jurors had died. At trial two, held the following month, the jury could not agree on a verdict. At the third trial, held in April 1905, the jury was again unable to come to a majority decision.

Throughout her ordeal, Nan had fervently protested her innocence and public opinion was firmly on her side. Ten days after the last trial was concluded, the judge granted a motion that she be discharged. Outside the court, a delirious crowd cheered her to freedom, and in the playgrounds little children were heard to chant:

> Nan is free, Nan is free,
> She escaped the electric chair,
> Now she's out in the open air!

The second cab mystery occurred in the City of London, two years after Broadway's incident. At midnight on Saturday 28 September 1912, the driver of a taxi moving along Fenchurch Street heard three loud bangs behind him. Assuming his tyres had burst, the driver got out to examine the vehicle's wheels. A police constable on night duty also heard the reports and came up to find out what was going on. The tyres were firm and the driver opened the cab door to see if his two passengers were all right. Immediately, a woman toppled headlong out, moaning, 'Mind, cabby, he has a revolver. He has shot me. Drive me to a hospital.'

No sooner were the words uttered than two more deafening reports were heard. Inside the taxi, her companion had tried to shoot himself – blood was spattered all around. The driver rushed his cab with its freight of wounded fares to Guy's Hospital where the woman died within minutes of arrival from wounds to her head and chest. The man, though bleeding severely from head and hands, was saved from death. His name was Edward Hopwood, a failed company director. The dead woman was Florence Alice Silles, stage-name 'Flo Dudley', a music-hall comedienne.

Edward Hopwood was a short man – short of stature and short of funds.

Though married with children, he lived apart from his wife and was practically bankrupt when he first met Flo Dudley. The pair quickly became lovers and must have made a slightly improbable couple for she was statuesque and ample-bosomed, with the full-blown figure so admired in the period. Despite his dire financial straits and his matrimonial state, Hopwood proposed marriage to Florence. She was a widow at 34 and, having no idea that Edward had other commitments, readily accepted. Being a strict Catholic she insisted that they see a priest, to which her lover consented. She also brought Hopwood home to Ilford to meet the sister with whom she shared a house. He was introduced as her betrothed.

Florence's intended, though, seemed curiously evasive about naming the day. He offered a registry office wedding but even the would-be bigamist clearly baulked at the idea of a formal Catholic service. In August 1912, five months after the affair began, Florence would endure no further delay and broke the relationship off. She would have no more to do with the diminutive company director.

Edward grew jealous. He knew Florence was friendly with a man living in Southampton and desiring one last rendezvous, Hopwood resorted to subter-fuge. He went to Southampton and, using the other man's name, wired Florence to meet him for dinner at the Holbourn Restaurant for dinner on the night of 28 September.

It was the night of the fatal shooting. That Saturday morning, Hopwood bought an automatic revolver. In the afternoon, he made out his will and wrote a suicide note. At night he made his surprise appearance at the Holbourn Restaurant. Shortly before midnight, the couple hired a cab to go to Fenchurch Street Station. It was during the course of this short trip that the three shots rang out.

Edward Hopwood was tried for murder in December 1912. He refused legal aid, preferring instead to present his own case before the jury. Hopwood's contention was that he pulled out the gun intending suicide, but Florence grabbed him as he produced the revolver. The gun fired accidentally in one rapid burst of three shots.

The judge was by no means unsympathetic. But the prosecution brought forward a forensic scientist who testified that Florence's head wounds could not have been caused by chance. At one point during his final address to the jury, the accused was overcome with emotion and broke into a fit of sobbing. Eventually, when prompted by the judge to continue, Hopwood wept, 'I can say no more.'

There was no triple trial for Edward Hopwood. The jury found him guilty of wilful murder, and sentence of death was passed. Late in December, only three months after doctors at Guy's Hospital had saved Hopwood's life, the hangman took it back at Pentonville.

The Lost Flyer

On Saturday 15 April 1933, *The Times* reported:

> No news has been received of Captain Lancaster, who was flying from England to the Cape, since Wednesday. Our Algiers Correspondent reports that he left Reggan, an oasis in the Sahara, at half past six on the evening of that day for Gao, on the Niger. Sandstorms were causing bad visibility. A motor car was sent yesterday by the Trans-Saharan Company to search for him.

The celebrated airman had left England at 05.38 on the morning of 11 April, in an attempt to beat the record for a flight to the Cape. He had reached Oran at 21.00 that night and taken a brief rest there before setting out across the Sahara desert.

The following day he drifted off course because of heavy sandstorms. Nevertheless, he managed to reach Reggan where he rested for three hours, worn out. There was no moon, and a strong northwest wind was blowing. The local head of the Trans-Saharan Company told him it was madness to take off when he would not be able to see the day beacons on the main desert motor track. Lancaster did not even have lighting on his instrument board, for steering a compass course.

But Lancaster was determined to go. As for lighting, he said, he would manage with matches and a borrowed pocket torch. Witnesses saw him make a very bad take-off before vanishing into the evening sky. It was 18.30 on 12th April. He was not seen alive again.

Was he prompted to make the fatal flight by that reckless spirit shared by all the pioneer aviators? Or was something else on his mind, urging him to risk the treachery of the desert? Captain Lancaster had hit the headlines less than a year before, for something very different. At Miami in August 1932, he had been brought to trial on a charge of murder.

William Newton Lancaster had served in the RAF during World War One. He subsequently married and left the Air Force to make a name for himself as a long-distance flyer. The twenties was the decade of Lindbergh, Cobham and Kingsford Smith – men who opened up the world's air routes. Women, too, played their part in those pioneer years, and one of them was Australia's Mrs Keith 'Chubbie' Miller.

In 1927, Lancaster and Mrs Miller flew as partners in a record-breaking flight

Captain Lancaster and Mrs Miller set off on their record-breaking flight which covered the 13,000 miles from London to Australia. And although both were married they continued to fly as a team, becoming lovers on the ground as well as partners in the air. After their record-breaking flight to Australia, the couple did most of their flying in the United States, and it was there that their tragedy was enacted.

While Lancaster was in Mexico for a spell, Chubbie developed a liaison with American writer Charles Haden Clarke. The pair fell in love and wrote to Lancaster of their plans for marriage. Lancaster returned to Florida with a revolver and confronted the lovers at Mrs Miller's house. There followed a quarrel which ended when the three actors in the drama retired to their respective beds.

During that night, Chubbie was wakened by Lancaster who told her that Clarke had shot himself. The writer was slumped in his room with a pistol lying on the bed. Blood seeped from the head wound from which he later died. Lying by the dying man were typed suicide notes – written on Lancaster's machine.

The death occurred on 21 April 1932. On 2 August of that year, Captain W.N. Lancaster was brought to trial for murder. Much of the 16-day courtroom case revolved around the nature of the fatal wound. Forensic experts debated the possibilities of suicide and murder, while the character of the two men was discussed. According to Chubbie, Clarke had called Lancaster 'one of the finest men he knew.' The defence intended to support the case for suicide by bringing forward a doctor who, after post mortem examination, declared the dead man to be a drug addict. The doctor was sick at the time of the trial, and a motion for adjournment was denied. Nevertheless, after deliberating for six hours, the jury found Lancaster not guilty.

Chubbie had stood by the airman at his trial, but their relationship had inevitably suffered. Though both returned to England, Lancaster's record-breaking attempt of 1933 was a solo flight, made in the 100 h.p. *Southern Cross Minor* – a single-seater plane.

When the plane went missing over the Sahara, search parties were called out. But within ten days of the disappearance, the experts were acknowledging there was very little hope indeed of ever finding the missing aviator alive. In fact, the pilot was not to be found in any condition at all – until more than 29 years later.

In February 1962, a French desert patrol came upon the wreckage of Lancaster's Avro-Avian. The remains of the missing flyer were found beside the debris. His log-book contained entries for eight days after the crash – eight days awaiting death in the desert, in which he recorded his love for Chubbie Miller. Curiously enough, the last entry was made exactly one year to the day after Charles Haden Clarke's death.

What Kind of Murder?

It happened the wrong way round. When a husband comes home to find his wife with another man, it is the husband who traditionally resorts to violence. But the case of Melvyn and Lorraine Clark was rather different . . .

Melvyn Clark was an electronics engineer who lived with his wife and three children in a suburb of Boston. And beneath the surface of domestic content, there lurked illicit passions. When Melvyn was away from home, Lorraine used to attend wife-swapping parties. The partners were selected 'blind': men threw down keys, and the women picked them up without knowing whose bedroom they would be sharing.

Melvyn knew nothing of these frolics. On 10 April 1954, the engineer returned to his home unexpectedly to find Lorraine with another man. The interloper made his excuses and left. A quarrel broke out in the Clark household, during which Lorraine stabbed her husband with a darning needle. Then she shot him dead with two bullets from a revolver.

Afterwards, Lorraine trussed up her husband with wire and lugged his body into the car. She drove to a nearby river and, on the bridge, fixed weights to his legs and heaved him over the edge.

The body was discovered six weeks later, and during interrogation Lorraine confessed to the murder. But what kind of murder was it? Under United States law, first degree murder is deliberate and premeditated, designed to effect a death. Second degree murder is a killing in which deliberation and premeditation are missing. In Lorraine's case, the stab of the darning needle may well have been impulsive. But the two subsequent revolver shots . . .?

In a decision which aroused controversy, her plea of guilty to second degree murder was accepted, and she received a sentence of life imprisonment.

Chapter
Six

Whodunit?

A church minister and his choir singer mistress are gunned down in a lover's lane. A womanizing whist expert is shot dead in his locked home by an assailant who mysteriously vanishes. A romantic songwriter and her handyman lover make rival confessions to the same murder.

In these and other cases described, crimes of passion were proven or strongly suspected. The tormenting question for courts and public alike was one beloved of all crime aficionados: whodunit?

Reverend Babykins and His Gay Gipsy

On Saturday 16 September 1922, an adultery was exposed at a lover's lane in New Brunswick, New Jersey. The Reverend Edward Wheeler Hall, Rector of St John's Episcopal Church, was found lying under a crab apple-tree with Mrs Eleanor Mills, the sexton's wife. He was 41 and balding; she a petite 34-year-old. And the couple never got a chance to defend or explain their activities. For they were found dead – murdered at their rendezvous, their bodies scattered with their torn-up love letters.

The pastor's head had been pierced by a single bullet; a bloodsoaked Panama hat lay over his face. Eleanor Mills had been shot three times; her throat, moreover, had been slashed. And as for the love letters, they told in the clearest possible terms of the special relationship which had existed between the minister and the soprano who had sung in his choir.

The letters strewn all around had been written by Eleanor Mills. Scribbled in pencil, they bore witness to intense emotions: 'I know there are girls with more shapely bodies,' the sexton's wife had written, 'but I do not care what they have. I have the greatest of all blessings, the deep, true and eternal love of a noble man. My heart is his, my life is his, all I have is his, poor as my body is, scrawny as they say my skin may be, but I am his forever.'

Someone had emptied the minister's pockets, and his gold watch had been stolen. But mere theft could not have been the motive for the killing. Propped against the dead man's foot was one of his own visiting cards, as if advertising his identity. Whoever shot the lovers had also arranged their bodies side by side in a grotesque embrace. Special savagery had been reserved for Eleanor Mills; not only had her throat been slashed but her tongue and vocal cords had been cut out. With the confetti of love letters playing about the bodies, everything pointed to a crime of passion.

The police interviewed the dead clergyman's wife, Frances Hall. A plain, grey-haired woman nine years older than her husband, she professed complete ignorance of the liaison between her husband and his chorister. All she knew was that on the evening of Thursday 14th, her husband had received a phone call and left the house. He did not come back that night. And although it was a whole day and another night before the bodies were discovered, Mrs Hall at no stage called the police.

James Mills, husband of the dead woman, came up with a strikingly similar story. His wife had not come home on Thursday evening, but he too failed to call the police. When pressed, he said that he thought his wife might have been round at her sister's house. Like Frances Hall, he claimed to know nothing of the secret love affair.

There were many in the pastor's congregation who were not so blinkered. Rumours of the affair had been circulating in New Brunswick long before the murders took place. Perhaps one, or both, of the spouses did know of the liaison, and failed to call the police suspecting an elopement? Speculation along these lines led nowhere.

With the lack of concrete evidence, public interest in the case began to flag. But while a blameless suspect named Hayes was under investigation, a witness turned up – a colourful middle-aged Mrs Jane Gibson who came to be known as the Pig Woman.

Mrs Gibson kept pigs on a smallholding, and claimed to have seen the murder occur on the Thursday evening. Hearing noises that night, and suspecting thieves, she had mounted her mule and gone down the lane. Four figures were arguing under the crab apple-tree: two men and two women. One of these was a white-haired lady, and another a kinky-haired man. There were shouts of 'Don't, don't, don't.' Something glinted in the moonlight. Four shots rang out – and the Pig Woman fled the scene.

When questioned by the police, the Pig Woman identified Mrs Hall as the white-haired woman, and her brother Willie Stevens as the kinky-haired man.

Could the testimony be believed? The case came alive again, and the new evidence coincided with the publication of a batch of letters between Eleanor Mills and the late minister. They were all that a sensation-seeking public could have wished.

To the pastor, for example, Mrs Mills had written: 'I am on my knees, darling, looking up at my noble man, worshipping, adoring . . . I want you – your arms to hold me and hold me close if only to forget this pain for a minute. Dearest, give me some words of comfort.'

In reply, the clergyman had penned a note arranging a tryst for the following day: 'My dearest, my treasure, my anchor, my rock – oh, how I did want to fly off with you this afternoon – I wanted to get away to dreamland – heaven-land – everything seemed so sordid, earthy, commonplace . . . Dearest – love me hard, hard – harder than ever, for your Babykins is longing for his mother.'

Earthbound in New Brunswick, the clandestine lovers had allowed their fancies to roam in an illicit paradise where truth, nobility and wonder, crystal eyes and crushing embraces, were all yearned for with equal intensity. Eleanor was the pastor's 'gay gipsy' and, 'when my arrow enters your haven I am transported to ecstasy,' wrote the stalwart.

And where had this new correspondence come from? The cache of letters was sold to the press for $500 by James Mills. The transaction of course cast considerable doubt on the sexton's claim to know nothing of his wife's affair.

A grand jury was convened in November to assess the case. But the inquiry led to no indictment. For four years the case was as if frozen, neither formally closed nor under active investigation. What broke the ice was a bombshell lobbed from within the late pastor's household.

Louise Geist, who had served the Halls as a maid, got involved in a lawsuit for marriage annulment. Her husband claimed that Louise had been bribed to keep silent before the grand jury: she had in fact accompanied Mrs Hall and her two brothers to the scene of the crime and been a witness to – or a participant in – the vile deeds.

Back to the front pages came the Crab Apple-tree murder. Back to the limelight came James Mills, the Pig Woman and the rest. And into the dock went the clergyman's wife, with her brothers Willie and Henry Stevens.

The trial was held at Somerville, New Jersey, in November 1926. And it seemed at last that the solution was clear. But was it? Actually, Louise Geist repudiated her husband's claims, still insisting she knew nothing of the murder. The Pig Woman was readier than ever to point the finger at Mrs Hall and her brothers, but the hog-farming witness was now dying of cancer. She had to be brought into court on a stretcher, and her aged mother confounded everyone by constantly interrupting: 'She's a liar, a liar, a liar! That's what she is, and what she's always been.'

James Mills, meanwhile, was fiercely cross-questioned and now candidly admitted that he had known all about the affair between his wife and the clergyman. He had read the love letters and, it seemed, had quarrelled bitterly with his wife about the liaison.

Maybe Mills did it? Maybe the Pig Woman did it! (This suggestion was actually made by the defence counsel.)

At the end of the long, confused trial the jury retired for five hours. When they returned, it was with a verdict of not guilty.

Mrs Hall and her brothers were discharged, the pastor's widow becoming a recluse and dying in 1942. The whole affair had scandalised America, and remains one of crime's great unsolved mysteries. One plausible theory has been put forward by William Kunstler in his *The Minister and the Choir Singer* (1964). He suggests that the Ku Klux Klan engineered the double murder as retribution for the couple's violation of Bible teaching on adultery. Certainly, the disposition of the bodies and the mutilation of the errant choir singer suggest ritual elements in the crime. But the theory remains pure conjecture. All that can be said with certainty of the affair is that the love between Edward Hall and Eleanor Mills was true love lived in a morass of deception. And that the lovers paid a terrible price for their idyll in heaven-land.

Whose Hand On the Mallet?

In a conventional whodunit you might expect to find a host of different suspects. But the Rattenbury case of 1935 had a very limited cast. There was Mrs Alma Rattenbury, 38, a writer of popular songs. There was her lover, George Stoner, a chauffeur-handyman barely 18 years of age. And there was 67-year-old Francis Rattenbury, the brutally murdered husband.

The distinguished architect was found battered to death in his favourite armchair. His hair was matted with blood, and there were bloodstains too on the carpet. Rattenbury had been clubbed with a mallet by three heavy blows struck from behind. The question which tormented the public concerned who had wielded the weapon.

Mrs Rattenbury? Her lover? Or had the pair connived at the murder together?

When Alma married Francis Rattenbury in 1925, some comment was made about the disparity between their ages. She was an attractive young woman of great musical talent who had been awarded the *Croix de Guerre* for her services as a nurse in World War One. He in contrast was already middle-aged, a solitary and rather morose man. Rattenbury had, however, won fame and fortune for his architectural designs (his parliament buildings at Victoria B.C. still stand). Alma had no money to speak of.

Yet for ten years their union was happy enough. Not long after the wedding, the couple retired to the Villa Madeira, a pleasant residence in the quietness of Bournemouth. Alma had a son by a previous marriage who came to visit them at holiday time. Rattenbury too had had children by his first wife. And now Alma bore the architect a new son named John. On the whole, the Rattenburys' was an affectionate ménage, in which such tensions as existed hinted little at the coming tragedy.

'Ratz', as his wife called him, was still prone to his fits of melancholy. Sometimes in the evenings he drank rather too much whisky; sometimes he talked morbidly of suicide. But Alma usually restored his spirits, and to occupy her days she took to writing popular songs. She won considerable success in this field, under the name of 'Lozanne'. Her music was published, broadcast and recorded, the most popular of her discs being *Dark-Haired Marie*:

Are you waiting in your garden
By the deep wide azure sea?

Are you waiting for your loveship,
Dark-Haired Marie?

I shall come to claim you someday,
In my arms at last you'll be,
I shall kiss your lips and love you,
Dark-Haired Marie.

The lyrics, like many of Alma's, evoke a troubled and sensual yearning which is not hard to understand. After the birth of their son John, she and her husband no longer slept together: they had their own separate bedrooms. Rattenbury told her she could 'lead her own life', and perhaps there were many evenings when the Dark-Haired Marie of the Villa Madeira dreamed of the loveship that would come to claim her. It arrived in the form of George Percy Stoner, hired as a chauffeur in September 1934.

He gave his age as 22; in reality he was not yet 18. The affable, good-looking son of a local bricklayer, Stoner was soon driving Alma to the London shops, theatres and cinemas. By the end of November, she and Stoner were lovers, and the young man had moved in to the Villa. It was not a big house. His room was just across the landing from hers.

They quarrelled sometimes. Stoner was an inexperienced young man who clearly felt the need to assert his masculinity before the woman who was old enough to be his mother. He told her to give up drinking cocktails, for example, as they were bad for her. Alma agreed. He used to carry a knife with him and on one occasion threatened to kill her; on another he expressed the urge to take his own life. Perhaps the older woman derived some dark excitement from these adolescent theatricals. But she knew her responsibilities. When he confessed his real age, Mrs Rattenbury tried unsuccessfully to break off the relationship. And when Stoner hinted to her that he was taking drugs, she became worried for her children. Alma confessed the whole affair to the family doctor, and asked him to warn the youth off drug-taking, which Dr O'Donnell duly did.

The affair continued into the spring of 1935. In March 1935, the couple took rooms at a Kensington hotel, posing as brother and sister. They went on a shopping spree in which Mrs Rattenbury bought for her lover a suit, shirts, shoes and silk pyjamas. She even bought him a ring which, humiliatingly, he then presented to her as a token of his love. It was on the day after their return to Bournemouth that the tragedy occurred.

On Sunday 24 March, 'Ratz' was in one of his moods. At teatime he read aloud passages from a novel in which the hero contemplates suicide. Alma only managed to brighten his spirits by suggesting that they take a trip to Bridport the next day, and stay there that night. Rattenbury had a friend and business

Mrs Rattenbury accompanied by her doctor

THE WORLD'S GREATEST CRIMES OF PASSION

Right: the rear of the Villa Madeira in Bournemouth

Below: the constable called to the scene of the suicide takes Mrs Rattenbury's umbrella and handbag to the court

colleague at Bridport, called Mr Jenks. The architect was worried at the time about raising finances for a block of flats. Jenks could help him out in this respect.

The Bridport trip was duly arranged, and the couple played cards that night. At exactly 21.30, Alma went up to bed while her husband returned to his armchair and his novel. Ironically, the book was found folded the next day at a passage where the hero meditates on the problems faced by elderly men who marry younger women . . .

Around 22.15 the home help, Irene Riggs, came back to the Villa Madeira after visiting her parents. She heard a strange, heavy breathing coming from somewhere in the house, but after a brief investigation thought no more of it. Her employer was not in his bedroom; no doubt he had dozed off downstairs. Upstairs, she met Stoner on the landing. He was wearing pyjamas and said he was checking to see that the lights were out. Irene Riggs then went to bed, and was briefly joined in her room by Mrs Rattenbury who often dropped in last thing at night to chat about the day's events. Alma seemed in good spirits, and was looking forward to the proposed trip to Bridport.

Alma then left, and Irene Riggs was just dozing off when she heard someone rushing downstairs. Alma's voice shrieked, 'Irene!' and the servant followed quickly down to the drawing room. The lights were on, and there in his chair sat her employer, his head a wreck of blood. Mrs Rattenbury was desperately trying to bring him round, cramming his false teeth into his mouth so that he could speak to them. Her first words to Irene were 'Someone has hurt Ratz! Telephone the doctor!'

In the panic which followed, Alma started drinking whisky continuously. The pair tried to bathe and bandage the victim. Mrs Rattenbury was specially worried that her little son John would come down and be frightened by the blood. The doctor arrived at 23.15 and a surgeon was called for. Later, an ambulance arrived at the Villa, but the victim was to die in the operating theatre without ever regaining consciousness.

By the time the police arrived at 02.00 Alma had consumed a lot of whisky. She was chattering, now, in hysterical fashion: she played records and danced and even tried to kiss a policeman. Out of the wild staccato of her utterances, several key phrases were recorded: 'I know who did it! I did it with a mallet! It is hidden . . . Ratz has lived too long. No, my lover did it. I will give you £10. No, I won't bribe you.'

Informed at about 03.30 that her husband's condition was critical, she said: 'I will tell you in the morning where the mallet is. I shall make a better job of it next time. I made a proper muddle of it. I thought I was strong enough.'

The doctor gave her an injection of morphia and put her to bed. She came round at one point and said: 'I know who did it – his son . . . but he is not here.' Lastly, when she appeared much calmer, she made a written statement:

About 9 p.m. on Sunday, 24th March 1935, I was playing cards with my husband when he dared me to kill him, as he wanted to die. I picked up the mallet. He then said: 'You have not guts enough to do it.' I then hit him with the mallet. I hid the mallet outside the house. I would have shot him if I'd had a gun.

When Mrs Rattenbury was being escorted from the house the next morning, she was met by Stoner who was heard to say: 'You have got yourself into this mess by talking too much.'

Stoner himself had been questioned by police during the night and claimed that the first he knew of the murder was when he heard Mrs Rattenbury shouting for help from the drawing room. Three days later, however, he made a confession: 'Do you know Mrs Rattenbury had nothing to do with the affair? When I did the job I believed he was asleep. I hit him, and then came upstairs and told Mrs Rattenbury. She rushed down then . . .'

What were people to believe? Each suspect had confessed to the murder, each claiming to be the sole person responsible. Which of them did it? Or had they collaborated in the assault and were now trying to shield each other?

The case was picked up by the national press which made the most of its sensational aspects. BOY CHAUFFEUR'S ORDEAL – STONER TOOK COCAINE – VORTEX OF ILLICIT LOVE – PYJAMAS AT 60/- A PAIR! screamed the headlines. And at the outset popular opinion was set firmly against Mrs Rattenbury. Alma was more than twice her lover's age, and seen both as adulteress and seducer. Stoner had been a perfectly normal, decent boy before he fell into her clutches. Perhaps the youth was only behaving chivalrously in confessing belatedly to his own guilt.

The trial was held at the Old Bailey, and the two accused were to be tried individually, but in the same court. This created problems in itself, since statements made in one case could not necessarily be used as evidence in the other. Further confusion was caused by the fact that both Mrs Rattenbury and her lover ended up by pleading not guilty. But for the public, the ultimate puzzle was provided by the fact that Stoner never entered the witness box. This could be interpreted in one of two ways. Either his counsel considered that his appearance would damage his own case or the boy was nobly refusing to say anything in the box which might incriminate Mrs Rattenbury.

It was, in fact, a trial of either/ors. But one certainty did emerge. The police had found the murder weapon, with blood and hairs on it, hidden behind a trellis in the garden. It was Stoner who had obtained the mallet – he had borrowed it from the home of his grandparents at 20.00 on the fateful evening.

Unlike Stoner, Alma did enter the witness box, and she made an impressive figure. She spoke in a low, clear voice which gave every appearance of truthfulness. Moreover, she was perfectly frank about her adultery.

She said that shortly after she phoned Mr Jenks to arrange the Bridport trip, Stoner had approached her in a jealous rage and cornered her in the dining room. He was emphatic that she should not go to Bridport with her husband. He threatened to kill her if she did. He claimed to have seen her making love to her husband that very afternoon in her bedroom.

Alma denied his claim, and tried to soothe all his fears about Bridport. She thought she had succeeded in calming her lover, but he left the house not long afterwards. The timing implied that it was about then that Stoner went off to fetch the mallet.

That night, having said goodnight to her husband and had her chat with Irene, Alma retired to her bedroom. Stoner joined her soon afterwards in his pyjamas, looking 'a little queer'. She asked what the matter was, and after much prompting he explained. 'He told me that I was not going to Bridport the next day as he had hurt Ratz. It did not penetrate my head what he did say to me at all until I heard Ratz groan, and then my brain became alive and I jumped out of bed . . .'

Downstairs with Irene she tried to revive her wounded husband. She also started drinking whisky 'to block out the picture'. The last thing she remembered was putting a white towel round her husband's head, and the episode with the false teeth. She had trodden on them with her bare feet. They had made her hysterical.

All that followed was a blank to her. The records, the dancing, the babbling, the bribe and the flirting with policemen – all were erased from her mind. She only 'came to' about midday the following morning.

Mrs Rattenbury's statements coincided closely with Irene's. In truth, there was precious little evidence against her apart from her own hysterical and contradictory confessions. Her temporary amnesia was curious, true. But it was not hard to see how the shock of the discovery, the whisky and the morphia might have combined to 'blank her mind'.

As the trial progressed, things pointed more and more to the guilt of the jealous young chauffeur. In fact, his defence counsel was reduced to trying to limit the damage by elaborating on his cocaine addiction. This, it was implied (but never stated) might account for an unreasoned attack for which a verdict of manslaughter might be appropriate. Unfortunately for the youth who stood silent in the dock, serious doubts were raised as to whether he even knew what cocaine looked like. Interviewed by a medical officer at Brixton, Stoner had been asked to describe the drug's appearance. He replied that it was brown with black flecks in it. Cocaine, of course, is a white powder.

The jury took little more than an hour to consider their verdict. They found Alma Victoria Rattenbury not guilty; and they found George Percy Stoner guilty.

Mrs Rattenbury faltered forward, calling weakly 'Oh . . . oh, no,' and was ushered hurriedly from the dock. Stoner was left standing manfully before the judge, a lone figure bravely containing his emotion. The black cloth was brought out. Asked if he had anything to say before sentence was passed, Stoner answered 'Nothing at all, sir.' They were the only words he spoke during the trial.

Often, the acquittal of a woman on a hanging offence has been greeted with cheers by the crowd. But they booed Mrs Rattenbury as she was hurried away in a taxi. Cruel words had been spoken about her in court; the judge himself had severely censured her conduct. Freedom would be no easy burden to bear. Above all, there was her young lover, waiting in the death cell – how could she endure the day when the trap door would be sprung?

On Tuesday 4 June, three days after her acquittal, Alma Rattenbury took a train on the London-Bournemouth line. But she did not reach the Villa Madeira. Instead, she alighted at Christchurch and wandered the backwaters of the River Avon. By a railway bridge (from which Stoner had once felt the impulse to hurl himself to his death), Mrs Rattenbury sat down in the grass and pencilled a few notes on the backs of envelopes taken from her handbag. 'One must be bold to do a thing like this. It is beautiful here, and I am alone. Thank God for peace at last . . .'

A farmworker nearby saw her walk into the lily-strewn water, a blade glinting in her hand. She gazed fixedly as she walked. He rushed towards her, but when he got there it was too late.

At the post mortem it was found that she had plunged the knife no fewer than six times into her chest. Three wounds had pierced her heart, one of them so severe that she must have worked the blade backwards and forwards before she withdrew it. Alma Rattenbury was dead before the water claimed her and carried her drifting from the bank.

Relief From Tension

You should not expect great depths of cunning from the passionate criminal. When a 78-year-old Florida man discovered that his wife was having an affair he resorted to violence. One day, while the woman was in bed with her paramour, the irate husband lobbed a petrol bomb through the window. Then he fled the scene.

It did not take the police long to nail their suspect. The unfortunate husband suffered acutely from constipation. The bottle he hurled had originally contained a well-known brand of prune juice.

George Stoner, at the death cell in Pentonville, collapsed sobbing when he heard the news. A petition for his reprieve was already being gathered, to which thousands put their names. And four days after Alma's death, his lawyers lodged a formal appeal.

For the first time, Stoner submitted his own version of the events. He was entirely innocent of any part in the murder, he said. He had fetched the mallet for perfectly ordinary reasons and left it in the coal shed. When he made his way into Mrs Rattenbury's room that night, she appeared terrified. When a groan was heard from the drawing room, she leapt out of bed and rushed downstairs . . .

This was a remarkable twist to the tale. Was Mrs Rattenbury guilty after all? In the event, the judges decided that there was no case for an appeal, nor would they accept Stoner's new statement. It appeared no more than a cynical strategy to start making claims now that he would not make while his mistress was alive.

Stoner did not, however, hang. On the day after the appeal was turned down the Home Secretary granted a reprieve, and his death sentence was commuted to penal servitude for life.

Does an element of mystery still linger about the affair? If Stoner was guilty, what was it about the trip to Bridport that provoked his murderous wrath? An exhaustive study of the case (*Tragedy in Three Voices*, 1980) points to a piece of information which only came to light over forty years after the events. A friend of Alma's stated in a 1978 interview that she had asked Mrs Rattenbury in Holloway what had made Stoner so unusually angry. Alma replied that the chauffeur had overheard her conversation with her husband about the proposed business trip. 'Ratz', it appeared, had suggested to her that she use her charm on the Bridport man so that financial arrangements for the flats would go through smoothly. She might even have an affair with him if necessary.

This, by implication, was too much for the jealous lover. He could tolerate Alma's affectionate companionship with her elderly husband. But to countenance his beloved being used in this way was quite impossible.

It is a theory which fits the known facts. Stoner has commonly been represented in crime writing rather as Mrs Rattenbury's counsel portrayed him – as a youth whose love turned him into a 'Frankenstein's monster' with passions his mistress could not control. But that view misses the essential decency of the boy which everyone noted at the time. It was his decency which was outraged by the Bridport proposal, as much as his jealousy was aroused.

George Percy Stoner served only seven years in penal servitude. Released with good conduct during World War Two, he took part in the D-Day landings and after the war settled down to a respectable married life. Alma was buried at a Bournemouth cemetary in June 1935. Her shroud, wreaths and draperies were in pink, her favourite colour; she always had a horror of white.

The Kenya Scandal

It was January 1941. The Blitz had been raging over London for some six months, and in the sands of North Africa the see-saw struggle for Italy's desert colonies had begun. Kenya was then a British territory, and a mustering point for Allied forces planning the push on Mussolini's Ethiopia. At Nairobi, the Military Secretary was Josslyn Hay, Earl of Erroll and hereditary High Constable of Scotland.

During his brief career as an administrator, the 39-year-old Hay proved brilliant at his job. And his achievements came as something of a surprise to the settler community. For the Earl was chiefly notorious as a member of the Happy Valley Set, a permissive and pleasure-seeking section of the local white aristocracy.

Its centre was the Wanjohi river, cutting a declivity among the beautiful White Highlands of Kenya. One bastion of luxury was the exclusive Muthaiga Country Club, laid out with ballroom, golf course, squash courts and croquet lawns like something plucked from the landscape of the Home Counties. Cocaine circulated among the elite, and alcohol was consumed in great quantities: pink gins, sundowners, champagne and whiskey among the favourite tipples. By night, a mood of drunken licentiousness prevailed, and the denizens played roaring hooligan games.

Another centre of the Set was a large mansion called Clouds, the home of Lady Idina Gordon. The weekend house parties held there were notorious for their shameless excesses. Wives and partners were regularly swapped in the guest bedrooms. Josslyn Hay had flourished in this setting. He had been Lady Idina's third husband, and a predator in the jungle of luxury.

Dismissed from Eton and named as a 'very bad blackguard' by the judge in an English divorce court, Hay was a specialist in seduction. For quarry he preferred the wives and girlfriends of his aristocratic companions; his motto was 'to hell with husbands'. And when, in the early hours of 24 January 1941, he was found shot through the head on the floor of his Buick, no-one dwelled long on the possibility of a political murder. Predictably, the prime suspect was a husband: specifically, 57-year-old Sir Henry 'Jock' Delves Broughton.

The trial caused a sensation at the time. It was the scandal of Africa and followed with relish throughout the English-speaking world. The case came, no doubt, as a relief for a public weary with stories of bombings and evacuations. But it also provoked intense outrage, exposing an extravagant and dissolute way of life lived outside the cauldron of the war. The case continued to fascinate long after the fighting was over, and the question 'Who Killed Lord Erroll?' provided one of the world's classic unsolved mysteries.

Sir Henry Delves Broughton was a devotee of horse-racing and a member of a great English landowning family. In November 1940, he had married the glamorous Diana Caldwell, a blue-eyed ash-blonde who was young enough to be his daughter. Sir Henry was recently divorced from his first wife, and acknowledged the difficulties his new marriage might face by entering an extraordinary contract with Diana. Six weeks before the wedding, he agreed with her that if she fell for a younger man and wanted a divorce he would not stand in her way. Moreover, he agreed to provide her with £5,000 annually for at least seven years after a divorce.

The couple never shared a bedroom. And the contract implied no confidence in the durability of their relationship. But even Sir Henry cannot have anticipated how quickly his marriage was to come into jeopardy.

A week after the wedding, the Broughtons emigrated to Kenya. And on 30 November, at the Muthaiga Club, Diana met Lord Erroll for the first time. They fell for each other immediately. Diana later recalled that on the very first moment they found each other alone, Erroll said: 'Well, who's going to tell Jock? You or I?'

Erroll himself was free at the time: his first marriage to Idina Gordon had ended in divorce; his second wife, also a Countess, had died of drink and drugs in 1939. And he wasted no time in establishing his new liaison; but no-one told 'Jock' – not yet.

Soon, Broughton, Diana and Erroll were dining regularly together at the Club. The two men got on well together, for Broughton, like Erroll, was an Old Etonian. At his trial, the injured husband was to call his wife's lover 'one of the most amusing men I have ever met'. Broughton added that, 'if you can make a great friend in two months, then Joss Erroll I should describe as a great friend.'

It was not long before the passion shared by Diana and the Earl became conspicuous. At a party at the Club on 22 December, they could be seen dancing together locked in embrace. In the first week in January they shared a weekend alone together at the house of a discreet friend. And if Broughton had not guessed by now what was going on, there were alert eyes and ears all around. On Monday 6 January he found an anonymous note in the pigeon-hole at the Club. It read:

> You seemed like a cat on hot bricks at the club last night. What about
> the eternal triangle? What are you going to do about it?

What was he going to do about it? Broughton made light of the note with Diana, but the problem would not go away. At a party the following week, Broughton sat watching his wife dance with her lover. Lady Delamere, a mutual friend, said, 'Do you know that Joss is wildly in love with Diana?' By his own

Lord and Lady Erroll

admission, Broughton became rather distrait: 'It confirmed my worst suspicions.' He did not try to break up the liaison, but he did talk over the situation subsequently with Diana: 'I think you are going out rather too much with Joss.'

This meek reprimand was ignored; the affair continued and Broughton took to drinking more heavily than usual. Seeking advice from a friend, he was told that he should ask Erroll if he was really in love with Diana. 'If he says no, tell him to buzz off. If they are in love with each other, cut your losses. Pack your boxes and get off back to England.'

The pressure was mounting. Not long after this conversation, Broughton received a second anonymous note:

Do you know that your wife and Lord Erroll have been
staying alone at the Carberrys' house at Nyeri together?

On that same afternoon, 18th January, Diana broke the ice and said she was in love with Erroll. The Broughtons had been married barely two months.

Broughton tried to stall. He had been planning a 3-month trip to Ceylon and suggested that she should come with him to see how her feelings were affected. He also saw Erroll, proposing that Diana should accompany him on the Ceylon trip, and that Erroll might leave Kenya for a while.

Erroll, of course, was an old hand at dealing with injured husbands. He said he could not possibly go away – after all, 'there was a *war* on.'

The situation had reached an impasse. That night, Broughton went home alone while Diana and Erroll dined out with friends at the Muthaiga Club. She came back wearing a new set of pearls – a gift to her from her lover.

The following sequence of events had immense importance in the coming trial. The next day, Diana declared that she could not remain in her husband's house under the circumstances, and went off with a friend to stay at Erroll's. On 21 January, while she was away, Broughton reported a burglary to the police. He said that two revolvers, a cigarette case and a small sum of money had been stolen from his living room.

Also on the 21st, Broughton and Erroll both saw their lawyers about a divorce. On the surface at least, Sir Henry appeared ready to capitulate, for he wrote to a friend, 'They say they are in love with each other and mean to get married. It is a hopeless position and I'm going to cut my losses. I think I'll go to Ceylon. There's nothing for me to live in Kenya for.' He also received a third anonymous note:

There's no fool like an old fool. What are
you going to do about it?

The 23rd January was a fateful day for all of the parties concerned. The three principals in the drama lunched with a fourth friend, Mrs Carberry, at the Muthaiga Club. Erroll told a colleague, 'Jock could not have been nicer. He has agreed to go away. As a matter of fact, he has been so nice it smells bad.'

There was a celebration dinner at the Club that night. And there, Broughton astonished everyone by proposing a toast to the lovers: 'I wish them every happiness,' he said. 'and may their union be blessed with an heir. To Diana and Joss.'

Erroll took Diana dancing that night, having agreed to bring her back by 03.00. Broughton was driven home at about 02.00, apparently tired and somewhat drunk. June Carberry helped him upstairs, and they said goodnight before she retired to her room.

Erroll's Buick turned up some 15 minutes later. There was laughter in the hall, the car door was heard slamming, and Diana came upstairs.

Around 03.00 that morning, two African labourers saw the Buick off the main Nairobi-Ngong road. It had travelled only $2\frac{1}{2}$ miles from the Broughtons' home, and though its lights were blazing the vehicle had plunged steeply into a pit off the wrong side of the road, 150 yards ahead of an intersection. Crouching under the dashboard was the body of Lord Erroll. His hands were clasped in front of his head. When police examined the corpse, it was found that he had been shot thr ugh the head at point-blank range with a .32 calibre revolver.

Much about the circumstances was perplexing. For example, the car had armslings which, it was known, had been in place on the day before the murder. These had been removed – wrenched off or unscrewed – and lay on the floor of the car. The position of the fatal wound suggested that Erroll had been shot either by someone sitting on the seat beside him, or through the open window from the running board. Had the murderer flagged Erroll down on the road, or been in the car with him all the time? And how did the body of a full-grown man get to be crowded down into the footwell? Had it slipped there as the car lurched – or been crammed under the wheel on purpose?

Precisely *how* the murder was accomplished remains a complete mystery to this day. But it did not take the police long to establish a prime suspect. Enquiries quickly revealed that Sir Henry had both the motive and the opportunity. The fact of murder was hushed up for 24 hours, and the Broughtons were first led to believe that Erroll had broken his neck in a motor accident. When the police arrived to take statements that morning, Diana was hysterical and not pressed for questioning. Broughton's immediate reaction was to ask 'Is he all right? Is he all right?'

Before noon, Broughton drove into Nairobi. He said that Diana wanted a handkerchief placed on the dead man's body: 'My wife was very much in love with Lord Erroll,' he explained. He seemed very nervous as he made the request, and was not permitted to enter the mortuary. A policeman, however, took the handkerchief and performed the office.

Returning home just after midday, Broughton immediately made a big bonfire in the rubbish pit in the grounds. He ordered his head boy to bring petrol for the blaze; it was a curious act under the circumstances. Broughton explained it at the trial by saying that he just liked making bonfires, and always had, ever since childhood. The charred remains of a golf stocking were all that were retrieved from the site. That stocking, however, was bloodstained – with the blood of his victim? The police began to assemble their case.

Erroll's funeral was held on 25 January. Broughton arrived late, and dropped a letter from his wife onto the coffin of the Earl. Ever watchful, the police had the scrap of paper exhumed. It turned out to be a simple love-note. On one side, Diana had written 'I love you desperately', and on the back Erroll had replied, 'and I love you forever.'

When the fact of murder was publicly announced, Diana loudly accused her husband of the crime. Broughton made no reply. But on 10 March, when her husband was arrested, her mood softened. It was Diana who went to Johannesburg to hire the most brilliant advocate in Africa. His name was H.H. Morris, K.C., and he specialised in winning difficult murder cases.

The prosecution had its motive. And it had much more besides. There was the business of the burglary, for example. One of the guns 'stolen' on that occasion had been a .32 calibre weapon. Broughton had done some target practice with it when he first arrived in Kenya. And, searching the informal practice ground, the police found four .32 calibre bullets which, it was alleged, exactly matched two discovered at the scene of the crime. The murder weapon, in other words, was Broughton's own gun – and the 'burglary' had been a pure invention.

To confirm its thesis, the prosecution went on to point out that all six bullets had been fired with an old-fashioned 'black powder' propellant. This had been unobtainable in Kenya for more than 25 years. A ballistics expert testified that the chances of two people using black powder bullets were remote in the extreme.

Could the elderly Broughton have made it to and from the murder point in the time available to him? According to Mrs Carberry, he knocked on the door of her room at about 03.30 to ask 'if she needed anything'. This, according to the prosecution, was 'a most peculiar thing to do.' But it made sense as an attempt to establish an alibi. Imagine the scenario: Broughton slips out of the house when the couple return. Then he furtively enters the car – or runs to the road junction – and murders his rival out of earshot. Hastening back to his home, he knocks on Mrs Carberry's door solely to give the impression that he never left the house.

There was the mysterious bonfire, and the bloodstained golf stocking – all suggesting a carefully premeditated plot and a subsequent cover-up. Presumably, the planning began with the fake theft of the revolvers and included the magnanimous champagne toast at the Club. Of course, it implied a considerable deviousness on the part of the murderer. But this was an era when Agatha Christie was all the rage: the case against Sir Henry looked formidable.

Sir Henry and Lady Broughton and Colonel Sam Ashton leaving for Africa

Yet from the outset of the trial, the defence counsel, Harry Morris, had made it known that he had something up his sleeve. It was something simple, he said, 'so simple that I almost mistrust it.' But he would not divulge what that secret was – not even to the defendant.

The bombshell burst during cross-examination on the ballistics evidence. The experts had testified that all six bullets came from the same .32 calibre revolver, with five grooves and a right-hand twist. Morris asked innocently whether these were features of Colt revolvers. No, came the reply, all Colts had six grooves and a twist to the left. So the murder bullets could not have been fired from a Colt? The expert agreed that they could not.

Now Morris played his trump. He let it be known that Broughton's two stolen revolvers were registered as Colts – the firearms certificates confirmed it. Erroll, then, could not have been shot with one of the stolen guns!

For a *coup de grâce*, Morris pointed out that the murder weapon had not been recovered. And its barrel was needed to positively identify the practice bullets Broughton had fired with the two found at the scene of the crime. He pressed the ballistics expert: 'The claim that all six bullets were fired from the same weapon cannot be proved. Is that not so, Mr Harwich?'

'It is.'

Suddenly, the prosecution's case against Sir Henry began to look terribly shaky. The 'black powder' issue became practically irrelevant. And with nothing to connect Broughton in any way with the murder weapon, what did remain as hard evidence against him? The motive? Yet even before his marriage Sir Henry had indicated by the contract that he was the least possessive of husbands. He made a dignified and impressive figure in the witness box: a little forgetful it is true on some points of detail (he did not recall knocking on Mrs Carberry's door, for example). But he was quite candid about being cuckolded. Once, for example, he had invited Erroll to stay the night in full knowledge of his wife's adultery: 'She could ask whom she liked. I should not have tried to stop her in any event. I see no point in it. We met every day at the club and I cannot see it makes any difference if a man comes to stay the night. It would be extremely bad strategy. In my experience of life, if you try and stop a woman doing anything she wants to do it all the more. With a young wife the only thing to do is keep her amused.'

As to the famous toast to Diana and Joss, was that sincere on his part? 'Certainly it was. The whole party was very happy and everybody on their top form. I was resigned to losing my wife and I cut my loss.'

Broughton was masterful during his three days of cross-examination. He came across as a bluff old racing man who had known when he was beaten. Could the deviousness implied by the prosecution really be imputed to him? Harry Morris did not think so, for he returned to Johannesburg without even bothering to wait for the verdict. When it came, on 1 July 1941, Broughton was found not guilty, and he walked from the court a free man.

Did he really do it? And if not, who did? Rumour was rife in Kenya's white community. There were other injured husbands to consider; there was talk of hired native assassins. Then there were the women of the Happy Valley Set: those who plumped for a female killer tended to opt for the chic, exquisite and faintly mad Alice de Janzé, a one-time lover of Erroll's. She was no stranger to firearms – she had once shot herself and an earlier lover on the platform of the Paris Gare du Nord; both had survived and she was acquitted of attempted murder on the grounds of *crime passionnel*. In Kenya at the time of the Erroll murder, Alice visited the Earl in the mortuary where she placed the branch of a tree on his body. According to a friend, she also kissed his body saying 'Now you're mine forever.' Later that year she committed suicide in a flower-filled room asking (in true Happy Valley style) that a cocktail party be held over her grave.

In truth, however, she was just one among Kenya's élite whose name was linked with the affair. There were so many loose ends: who, for example, had written the anonymous letters to Broughton?

The Happy Valley Set never survived the scandal, and Broughton never recovered from the stigma of the trial. He did take Diana on the long-projected trip to Ceylon, but there suffered a back injury which partially paralysed him. On 5 December 1942, he died in Liverpool having taken massive overdoses of Medinal. He left two suicide notes referring to the strain of the trial and the pain of his recent injury. He did not, in the text, declare himself guilty of murder, however.

Forty years after the events described, the case continued to fascinate and torment. Through painstaking research and interviews with survivors, reporter James Fox produced a brilliant study of the Erroll affair (*White Mischief*, Jonathan Cape, 1982). The book arrives at a firmly implied conclusion about the murderer's identity. It would be invidious to betray the last pages of this account of a real-life Whodunit. But it is fair to comment that Sir Henry Delves Broughton's background included some shady episodes. Suspicions of devious insurance fraud and blackmail attach to the memory of the reasonable old cove who walked free from the Kenya courtroom.

Saved by a Judge's Blunder

It probably qualifies as the World's Easiest Murder Mystery. Everyone knew who killed Rose Pender in the early hours of 21 August 1911. The suspect's name, his motive and his murder weapon were clearly established at the trial. But because of a judicial blunder, the murderer walked free from the Court of Criminal Appeal. Officially, the case remains open.

It was a seedy affair, peopled with wretched and depraved characters from the London underworld. Thieves, pimps and prostitutes filed into the witness box to give evidence at the Old Bailey. At the outset, no-one could have imagined that the case would become an historic one, marking a watershed in British legal history.

THE WORLD'S GREATEST CRIMES OF PASSION

Charles Ellsome, who described himself as a labourer, was brought to the dock in September 1911, for the murder of Rose Pender, his mistress. She was a prostitute, 19 years of age, and Ellsome had lived on her immoral earnings. And when she eventually left him for an Italian boy, Ellsome publicly threatened vengeance.

A few days before the fateful night, Ellsome borrowed a shilling from a friend and with it bought a long-bladed chef's knife. He told the same friend, 'I am going to do that Italian in for taking Rosie away.' In the small hours of the 21st, a man on his way to work in Clerkenwell heard a girl's voice crying, 'Don't, Charles! Don't!' Later, a milkman found Rose's dead body in the street, bloodstained with multiple stab wounds.

Police enquiries quickly revealed Ellsome to be the prime suspect. Prostitute friends of the victim confirmed that for some time her ex-lover had been threatening to do Rosie in. To one witness he had even confided, 'A fortune-teller told me the gallows were in my cards, and that she was the girl I should swing for.'

On the 22nd Ellsome was tracked down and arrested. He gave his name as 'Brown' to police, but he said, 'It's me you want.' And a thief named Fletcher supplied damning evidence by describing how, shortly after the body was found, Ellsome had come to his house in a breathless condition and confessed the murder to him.

The case came to trial at Court No. 1 at the Old Bailey. The curious procession of miscreants was brought into the box to give evidence. And Mr Justice Avory, a usually meticulous judge, presided over all. In fairness to him it should be said that he had endured a very heavy week. The court agenda was crowded, and only that morning he had summed up at the end of a wife-murderer's trial. The Ellsome case came up after lunch – it lasted only for one extended afternoon session.

Formidable evidence was heard against the accused, the chief prosecution witness being the thief, Jack Fletcher. He lived with two ladies of the streets, and testified that when Ellsome arrived at his house on the murder night, he announced, 'I have killed her stone dead.'

Fletcher asked who he had killed, and Ellsome replied, 'Rosie, my missus. I killed her stone dead, Jack. She drove me to it.'

Ellsome had then produced the knife and showed it to his friend. He said he had met the girl by chance in the street and explained exactly how things happened: 'I asked her to come back to me, but she said she liked her Italian boy best. Then I lost my temper, pulled out the knife, showed it to her and said, 'I'll kill you first.' She said, 'Here you are then; I don't care' – and bared her breasts. I plunged the knife in. She cried, 'Don't, Charlie, don't,' and I knew I had done the damage, so I stabbed her eight or nine times afterwards.'

Fletcher's two women had been in the house at the time, and they corroborated his account. When interviewed by the police, Fletcher himself had made further statements, filling in additional details but in no way departing from his original story.

For the defence, it was a hopeless case. The accused had no alibi, and the best that the defence counsel could do was to try and cast aspersions on the character of the various witnesses. Fletcher, in particular, came in for a grilling, and emerged as a rather flash character. It was learned that he carried a police whistle in his pocket (it came in handy when danger threatened in some of his low-life locales). And it was clear that he knew the courtroom ropes. At one point the defence counsel asked:

'You are very nicely dressed; where did you get the clothes from?'

'Singing outside theatres.'

'May I suggest that it was by thieving?'

'This is a case of murder, and not felony, and I refuse to answer.'

'I must ask you, however?'

'Well, then, I thieve for my living and am proud of it.'

The judge began his summing up in the most impeccable way. He started by explaining that if the character of a witness was questionable, then corroboration was of vital importance. Then he made his blunder. He suggested that there was no discrepancy between the thief's first statement to police and his evidence in the witness box.

This was perfectly true. But the first statement (which had been produced at the police court trial) had never been put in evidence at the Old Bailey. Technically, it was quite improper to direct the jury that Fletcher's evidence was corroborated by his first statement. The jury had not seen the document in question.

Did the jury even notice the slip? It took them less than an hour to bring in their verdict of guilty. Asked if the prisoner had anything to say, Ellsome replied:

'No, sir. I have only one Judge.'

Mr Justice Avory brought out the black cap, and Ellsome was sentenced to

---

Peculiar Passion

New York – A man who allegedly broke into a house twice to tickle the feet of two sleeping sisters has been arrested and charged with burglary. 'He just likes women's feet,' a detective said. 'Some people like other parts of the female body, and he just likes feet.'

The Times

death. But he never went to the gallows. His defence counsel, A.S. Carr, was quick to pounce on the judge's error. It had come like a gift from the gods, and while his client awaited the end in the condemned cell, Carr took the case to the Court of Criminal Appeal.

This was a newly founded institution, set up in 1907 after considerable public pressure. Behind it lay a humane concern for victims of miscarried justice. The court might allow an appeal if it considered that the verdict of a jury was unreasonable, or could not be supported by the evidence – or that the judgement should be set aside on a point of law.

Until the Ellsome affair, no appeal in a murder case had succeeded. But on the issue in hand, Mr Justice Darling ruled that there was really no option. Indisputably, the Old Bailey judge had misdirected the jury by introducing a statement which was not in evidence. Darling regretted that the Court had no power to order a new trial. He declared that the Court could not express any view as to whether Ellsome was guilty or not. But he quashed the conviction – and Ellsome walked out of the Appeal Court a free man.

There was a tremendous irony in the ruling. The Court had been established to protect the innocent; a guilty man was acquitted on the first successful appeal. In the event, the Court survived as a valued institution – but it was 20 years before another convicted murderer was to make a successful appeal.

Death in the House of Cards

There are 52 cards in a deck. And when the famous bridge and whist expert Joseph Elwell was found murdered at his New York home, the police quickly came up with a list of suspects. Elwell had so many mistresses that he had to keep records of their names and addresses. In his desk was found a card index containing a host of entries, with pet names and telephone numbers. In all, 53 women were recorded. You could call it a full deck of suspects – and perhaps the extra card was the maverick Joker that brought his outstanding career to an end.

Joseph B. Elwell had started his working life as a Brooklyn hardware salesman. But from adolescence onwards, he had excelled at card-playing. Bridge and whist were his favoured games, and in his early twenties he was already winning big stakes at the fashionable New York gambling clubs. It was not long before he gave up selling hardware to teach bridge to wealthy socialites. And he also wrote two authoritative books about the game. *Elwell on Bridge* and *Elwell's Advanced Bridge* were classics in their day.

He married in 1904, and had a son the following year. With his winnings, his royalties and his tutoring fees he was soon able to set up home in Manhattan. By 1916, when Elwell separated from his wife, he was already a wealthy man. For his estranged spouse he set aside $2,400 a year, as well as paying all his son's expenses. The sums involved were trifling. From his book sales alone, Elwell was said to be receiving some $10,000 per annum, and this was a fraction of his total income.

Bridge is more of a science than a game – it is no diversion for reckless gamblers. Elwell invested his earnings wisely. Apart from following up financial tips offered by his wealthy pupils, he diversified into horse-racing. Not by betting, of course: Elwell set up the Beach Racing Stable, supplied from a Kentucky stud farm where he owned some two score thoroughbreds. His partner in the enterprise was William H. Pendleton, a prominent man of the turf.

By 1920, the year of his murder, Elwell had a yacht, an art collection and three separate cottage retreats. In New York, he lived in a three-storey house in West Seventieth Street. Apart from his own bachelor suite, there was a special guest boudoir for female visitors. This was luxuriously furnished, and the ladies came in exotic succession: wealthy wives, fashionable divorcées, glamorous show girls, titled women and many others. His appetite is attested by his card index file – and by other material found in the house. The police discovered dozens of love letters, photographs, and even a kind of pension list recording sums paid monthly to discarded mistresses.

On the evening of 10 June 1920, Elwell went to dine at the Ritz-Carlton Club. His female escort on that occasion was Viola Kraus, a woman divorced that very day. Her sister, Mrs Lewisohn, was present with her husband Walter Lewisohn, a businessman connected with the show world.

By a curious coincidence, the foursome ran into Viola's ex-husband at the Club. His name was Victor von Schlegell, and he was dining with a young lady singer. There seems to have been no rancour between the recently divorced couple, and all laughed heartily over the encounter. They were to laugh again later that night. For Elwell's party went on to the New Amsterdam Theatre where *Midnight Frolics* was playing. Who should be sitting at an almost adjacent table but von Schlegell and his young singer? Victor quipped at the time, 'I can't keep away from Vi even if the judge said today that we needn't be together again.'

The evening's entertainment ended at 02.00. The Lewisohns offered Elwell a lift home in their taxi, but the card-player claimed it was too crowded. He had also had a slight tiff with Viola, which may account for the refusal. Instead, he stopped a cab for himself and was driven home alone. The driver was to testify that, having received a tip from him, he saw Elwell enter the door of his house at 02.30.

Elwell employed three people as domestic staff: a valet, a chauffeur and a housekeeper. But none of them lived on the premises. To find out what happened behind the locked doors that night, the police were to consult telephone company records.

Shortly after his arrival, Viola phoned him, perhaps to patch up the quarrel. As a card-player, Elwell was something of a night-hawk and does not seem to have slept much afterwards. At 04.39 he rang his racing colleague, Pendleton, but received no reply and put the phone down after 5 minutes. At 06.09, Elwell telephoned a Long Island number. Whom he called is still not known to this day.

Dawn light broke over New York and the milkman deposited his bottles at the house. At 07.10 the postman delivered the mail. Elwell was still alive at that time. For when the housekeeper arrived at 08.10, she found her employer sitting in his pajamas in a living-room armchair. The morning mail was on the floor before him, an open letter was in his lap. And exactly between his eyes was the hole left by a .45 calibre bullet.

Blood from the wound stained carpet and pajamas, spattering the wall behind the chair. Elwell was still breathing, though unconscious – he died in hospital some two hours later.

The case was perfectly baffling. The two side-doors into the house were firmly locked, and the housekeeper had found the front door locked too. All the windows were fastened from the inside, except Elwell's own inaccessible window on the third floor. Murder by an intruding burglar appeared to be deeply improbable. There was no sign of a break-in, no sign of a struggle. Assorted items of jewellery as well as $400 in notes lay untouched about the house. Besides, what self-respecting burglar would still be on the premises so late into the morning?

The front door lock had recently been changed. Only Elwell and the housekeeper, Mrs Larsen, possessed keys. Everything pointed to the conclusion that the victim himself had admitted someone into the house. And the circumstantial detail suggested that, if the murderer was a woman, he must have known her very intimately.

The bridge expert was a vain man. Aged 45, he customarily wore a plate of false teeth to fill the gaps in his smile. He was balding, too, and wore a toupé (he had 40 of them in all). When Elwell was found barefoot and dying in his pajamas, he was wearing neither wig nor denture. Those accessories were found neatly placed on the dresser. It was unlikely he would have invited a lady in, unless on sufficiently intimate terms to have seen him like that before.

Elwell was shot between 07.10 (when the post arrived) and 08.10 (when the housekeeper found him dying). Medical experts further determined that he had been hit at least 45 minutes before Mrs Larsen arrived. That meant that the shot had been fired between 07.10 and 07.25. But of course, it was possible that the killer had been with Elwell in the house for hours beforehand – especially if the murderer was a bedroom companion.

Had he entertained a woman that night? It seemed unlikely, for his own bed appeared to have been only lightly lain upon. The cover was turned back and the pillow slightly dented, as if he had relaxed there on the sultry June night. The pillow beside his was undented; and in the guest boudoir, the bed was perfectly made. A pink silk kimono was, however, found hanging in the wardrobe. Given the number of his mistresses, the possibility of a female killer could not be entirely discounted.

Of course, the bewildering variety of his bedmates all had their attendant lovers, husbands or relations. Ballistic evidence did tend to suggest a male murderer. Elwell had been shot with a heavy .45 calibre army automatic pistol; hardly an obvious choice of weapon for a woman. The U.S. service cartridge was found, and the shot was a clean one fired from some 3–4 feet. Close range, certainly – but not point blank. The gun, moreover, seemed to have been fired from the hip, or from a crouching position. The bullet had followed an upward trajectory, entering the forehead, exiting an inch higher at the back and going on upwards to smash against the wall. By a macabre chance it had then ricocheted back to land quite neatly on the side table right by the victim's elbow.

The murderer had disturbed nothing, left no fingerprint. The only remaining clue was one cigarette stub (of a brand other than Elwell used) found on the living-room mantelpiece.

Hazily, the picture suggested a brief visit, probably made after the mail arrived. Elwell admitted the murderer and was so unconcerned in his or her presence that he went on riffling through his letters. He had permitted the gun to be drawn and the murderer to approach within little more than a yard before firing.

It might, of course, have been a business associate. But Elwell had no special rivals: his racing-stable partner was among those questioned and he was fully exonerated. For the police, however, the bridge expert's love life opened up a Pandora's Box of possibilities. All 53 women named in the card index were investigated and closely questioned, along with others, men and women, discovered through the letters. Husbands, lovers and relations were also explored – everyone appeared to have an alibi. One by one the suspects were ticked off – the valet, the chauffeur, the housekeeper's husband, a Polish countess, an Egyptian princess . . . the list of possibilities appeared endless.

THE WORLD'S GREATEST CRIMES OF PASSION

Names that featured repeatedly in the press stories included three prominent suspects:

Mrs Elwell The estranged wife had learned some time before the murder that her husband had struck her out of his will. But she had a cast-iron alibi. Moreover, she stood to lose by Elwell's death, for her son's expenses and the $2,400 a year would be cut off.

Viola Kraus She had been with Elwell on the murder night, they had quarrelled and she had phoned him at his home. It was also established that she was the owner of the pink silk kimono in the boudoir. However, the Lewisohns testified that she was with them at their home overnight and through the murder period.

Victor von Schlegell Did Viola's husband, so recently divorced, still feel possessive about her? Victor had breakfasted with his young singer on the following morning, but went out early to pick up his car from a garage. He arrived there at 08.00, and might *just* have had time to kill Elwell before arriving at the garage. However, nothing indicates that he had any jealous feelings about Viola (he married his singer in due course).

No solution was ever found. But in the realm of pure speculation it is interesting to consider the enigma of 'Annie'.

One of the letters found in Elwell's desk had been sent by a 16-year-old Kentucky girl. She signed herself simply 'Annie' and complained to Elwell that she was going to get 'into trouble'. She begged him to 'do the right thing' by her.

Sidney Sutherland, a writer of the 1920s, toyed with the idea that her father, or brother, may have come to New York to persuade Elwell to 'do the right thing', and plugged him between the eyes when he refused. It is as plausible a theory as any: you can imagine Annie's seduction on one of Elwell's trips to the stud farm. You can picture the straight-shootin' Kentucky man with his old service pistol. He arrives by dawn light and puts his proposition fair and square to the rich northern city slicker. Toothless and balding in his expensive pajamas, Elwell brushes him off and returns petulantly to his armchair and his mail. One shot (it has to be from the hip) sees off the card player. The avenger nonchalantly stubs out his cigarette and goes back to Kentucky, never speaking of the episode again.

Plausible – but pure hypothesis. The fact is that the Elwell murder remains a complete and utter mystery; and every theory is as insubstantial as a house of cards.

'Are You Going to Sleep All Day?'

At 14.30 in the afternoon of Sunday 24 October 1943, the nanny at Patricia Lonergan's apartment knocked at the door of her mistress's bedroom. 'Young woman,' she cried, 'are you going to sleep all day?'

There was no reply. The heiress had returned from a late-night party in the small hours of the morning, and the nanny took the 18-month-old baby out. She did not return with the child until 7 in the evening when she tried the door again. It was still locked, and still there was no reply. Disturbed now by the ominous silence, the nanny sent for help. The door could not be broken down – it had to be removed bodily from its frame. And when the helpers finally attained the bedroom they discovered a grim tableau.

The nude body of the 22-year-old heiress was sprawled out across her wide bed, overlooked by its bronzed figures of Winged Victory. Blood had seeped from her head wounds through the sheets and blankets, down through the mattress and on to the floor where it formed a large dark stain. Mrs Patricia Burton Lonergan, heiress to a seven million dollar brewing fortune, would not be awakening that evening or ever again. She was dead: strangled and bludgeoned, police were to establish, by the pair of antique onyx-inlaid brass candlesticks that lay discarded on the floor.

The assailant had evidently fled via a second, automatically sprung door. It did not look like the work of a thief, for there was cash and jewellery in the suite as well as the victim's mink jacket neatly folded at the foot of the bed. But the struggle had been a violent one in which the heiress had scratched her attacker: traces of scraped skin were found under her manicured fingernails. In due course, the police were to establish that the time of death was about 09.00. Patricia Lonergan had been a corpse all day.

In the investigation which followed, police brought in her escort of the night before. He was Mario Gabelline, a 40-year-old Italian man-about-town. He stated that he had brought the heiress back to her apartment at 06.15 in the morning, but had left her in the lobby and returned immediately to his waiting cab. The taxi-driver was traced and confirmed his story. Gabelline was held on bail as a material witness, but he made an unlikely suspect.

More suspicion attached to Wayne Lonergan, 27-year-old former husband of the victim. He had been separated from the heiress only two months before the murder and had gone to live in Canada. Having no private means, he enlisted as a serviceman in the Royal Canadian Air Force. Though he lived in Toronto, it was discovered that Lonergan had been in New York on the weekend of the murder, staying in a friend's apartment.

Some curious facts were discovered about Wayne Lonergan's movements. On the Saturday evening he had gone to his ex-wife's apartment. He found that she was out, but was admitted by staff and played with his child for a while. That night he had taken an attractive blonde on a tour of New York night clubs before leaving her at her home at 03.00. Then (so it seemed) he retired to the friend's apartment where he wakened at about 10.30. He had called loudly for coffee and scrambled eggs, and phoned to make a lunch date with the blonde. When he turned up for the meal, he was not wearing his blue serviceman's uniform as he had done before. Instead, he was wearing a grey suit that ill-fitted his 6 ft 2 in frame. An explanation for his garb was discovered in the friend's apartment, in the form of a hastily written note:

> John: Thank you so much for the use of your flat. Due to a slight case of
> mistaken trust, I lost my uniform and so borrowed a jacket and trousers
> from you. I shall return these on my arrival in Toronto.
>
> Yours,
>
> Wayne.

PS – I will call and tell you about it.

Another discovery was made at the apartment too: in the drawer of the owner's desk was the plate of scrambled eggs that he had ordered for his Sunday breakfast.

Apprehended in Toronto, Lonergan appeared not to know what fate had befallen his ex-wife. He explained the business of the missing uniform by saying that after taking the blonde home early on the fateful Sunday morning, he had gone for a short stroll and met a US soldier waiting for a bus. They fell into conversation and Lonergan offered to put him up. On waking, he discovered not only his uniform but also some money gone. The soldier's name, he said was Murray Worcester and he was stationed somewhere on the East Coast. As for the enigmatic scrambled eggs, he had ordered them for the dog that his friend kept in the apartment. When the dog failed to show up, Lonergan hid the eggs not wanting to appear wasteful.

When first approached in Toronto, Lonergan had scratch marks on his chin. He claimed that he had recently cut himself shaving. To detectives who regarded him as the prime suspect, there came baffling confirmation: not only the blonde, but other witnesses too had seen him during the course of the Sunday. They were emphatic in declaring that his chin at the time was unmarked.

Nor had Lonergan appeared in any way to be in an excitable state. In fact, prior to the lunch, he had gone round to his ex-wife's apartment taking with him a 3 ft toy elephant for his son. He arrived some time after eleven, and receiving no answer left the toy with the note: 'For Master Billy Lonergan.'

The case aroused intense interest in the press. Patricia Lonergan, the beautiful socialite, had been immensely rich, living on an annual income of $25,000. Lonergan, in contrast, had lived a chequered life and had been a tie salesman on Madison Avenue when first introduced to the heiress. The couple had eloped to marry in Las Vegas in July 1941, and when Patricia bore a child it seems that she wanted to settle down. Lonergan, though, had enjoyed the life of luxurious irresponsibility. Only two months before the murder, the couple had separated and Mrs Lonergan had cut him out of her will.

While the newspapers speculated about the murder and its motives, Lonergan was persuaded to return to New York where he faced a severe grilling by detectives. At one stage he was confronted with a tall thin man that he said he had never seen before in his life. The man was Mr Maurice Worcester, a former US soldier, traced through searches of army records. The police were to claim that Lonergan had simply plucked the man's name out of thin air in seeking to explain the theft of the missing uniform. It was purely by chance that a real Maurice Worcester existed – and hardly surprising that Lonergan failed to recognise him.

After 84 hours of questioning, Lonergan made a confession which was leaked to the press. He said that he had slipped out of his friend's apartment on the murder morning, and arrived at Patricia's apartment shortly before 09.00. She was in bed and they quarrelled over Lonergan's intention to have lunch with the blonde. In a jealous rage, Patricia shoved him from her, shouting, 'Stay out of here, don't ever come back. You will never see the baby again!'

This, in Lonergan's version, provoked his fatal assault. Afterwards, at his friend's apartment, he rang for breakfast but found that he could not eat and so hid the plate of scrambled eggs, not wanting to arouse suspicion. He packed his bloodstained uniform in a duffel bag and dropped it, weighted with a dumbell, into the East River.

As for the scratch marks missing from his chin at the lunch date, police found a simple explanation. A powder compact containing Max Factor Suntan No. 2 was discovered in the friend's apartment. It was contended that Lonergan had bought this at a drugstore shortly after fleeing the scene of the crime. Careful application of the heavy cream was all that was needed to camouflage evidence of the fight.

Wayne Lonergan was indicted for first degree murder, and after a mistrial in February 1944, was tried again in March. Effectively, through the leaked confession, the press had found him guilty already. But some irregularities emerged in the courtroom.

Lonergan pleaded not guilty. His defence contended that he had been offered the lower plea of second degree murder if he would confess. In fact, the confession was not signed or authenticated by him. It was never shown that Lonergan had visited the apartment at the time of the murder, nor that he had handled the onyx candlesticks. Above all, he had no motive for deliberately killing his ex-wife. He was not jealous of her Italian escort, nor did he stand to gain financially by her death. The prosecution's case left room for reasonable doubt: a panic-stricken intruder might have been responsible.

In the event, the jury was out for more than 9 hours, and returned with a verdict of guilty to murder in the second degree (murder without premeditation). On 17 April 1944, the prisoner was sentenced to 35 years to life imprisonment.

Wayne Lonergan served 22 years in Sing Sing, and was paroled in 1965.